THE ARDEN SHAKESPEARE

THIRD SERIES

General Editors: Richard Proudfoot, Ann Thompson,
David Scott Kastan and H.R. Woudhuysen

TWELFTH NIGHT,
OR
WHAT YOU WILL

THE ARDEN SHAKESPEARE

ALL'S WELL THAT ENDS WELL	edited by G.K. Hunter*
ANTONY AND CLEOPATRA	edited by John Wilders
AS YOU LIKE IT	edited by Juliet Dusinberre
THE COMEDY OF ERRORS	edited by R.A. Foakes*
CORIOLANUS	edited by Philip Brockbank*
CYMBELINE	edited by J.M. Nosworthy*
DOUBLE FALSEHOOD	edited by Brean Hammond
HAMLET	edited by Ann Thompson and Neil Taylor
JULIUS CAESAR	edited by David Daniell
KING HENRY IV Part 1	edited by David Scott Kastan
KING HENRY IV Part 2	edited by A.R. Humphreys*
KING HENRY V	edited by T.W. Craik
KING HENRY VI Part 1	edited by Edward Burns
KING HENRY VI Part 2	edited by Ronald Knowles
KING HENRY VI Part 3	edited by John D. Cox and Eric Rasmussen
KING HENRY VIII	edited by Gordon McMullan
KING JOHN	edited by E.A.J. Honigmann*
KING LEAR	edited by R.A. Foakes
KING RICHARD II	edited by Charles Forker
KING RICHARD III	edited by James R. Siemon
LOVE'S LABOUR'S LOST	edited by H.R. Woudhuysen
MACBETH	edited by Kenneth Muir*
MEASURE FOR MEASURE	edited by J.W. Lever*
THE MERCHANT OF VENICE	edited by John Drakakis
THE MERRY WIVES OF WINDSOR	edited by Giorgio Melchiori
A MIDSUMMER NIGHT'S DREAM	edited by Harold F. Brooks*
MUCH ADO ABOUT NOTHING	edited by Claire McEachern
OTHELLO	edited by E.A.J. Honigmann
PERICLES	edited by Suzanne Gossett
SHAKESPEARE'S POEMS	edited by Katherine Duncan-Jones and H.R. Woudhuysen
ROMEO AND JULIET	edited by Brian Gibbons*
SHAKESPEARE'S SONNETS	edited by Katherine Duncan-Jones
THE TAMING OF THE SHREW	edited by Barbara Hodgdon
THE TEMPEST	edited by Virginia Mason Vaughan and Alden T. Vaughan
TIMON OF ATHENS	edited by Anthony B. Dawson and Gretchen E. Minton
TITUS ANDRONICUS	edited by Jonathan Bate
TROILUS AND CRESSIDA	edited by David Bevington
TWELFTH NIGHT	edited by Keir Elam
THE TWO GENTLEMEN OF VERONA	edited by William C. Carroll
THE TWO NOBLE KINSMEN	edited by Lois Potter
THE WINTER'S TALE	edited by John Pitcher

* Second series

THE ARDEN SHAKESPEARE

TWELFTH NIGHT, OR WHAT YOU WILL

Edited by
KEIR ELAM

Bloomsbury Arden Shakespeare
An imprint of Bloomsbury Publishing Plc

BLOOMSBURY
LONDON • NEW DELHI • NEW YORK • SYDNEY

Bloomsbury Arden Shakespeare
An imprint of Bloomsbury Publishing Plc

Imprint previously known as Arden Shakespeare

50 Bedford Square
London
WC1B 3DP
UK

1385 Broadway
New York
NY 10018
USA

www.bloomsbury.com

**BLOOMSBURY, THE ARDEN SHAKESPEARE and
the Diana logo are trademarks of Bloomsbury Publishing Plc**

This edition of *Twelfth Night* by Keir Elam,
first published 2008 by Arden Shakespeare
Reprinted by Bloomsbury Arden Shakespeare 2009, 2010, 2011 (twice),
2012, 2013 (three times), 2014 (three times)

The general editors of the Arden Shakespeare have been
W. J. Craig and R. H. Case (first series 1899–1944)
Una Ellis-Fermor, Harold F. Brooks, Harold Jenkins and
Brian Morris (second series 1946–82)
Present general editors (third series)
Richard Proudfoot, Ann Thompson, David Scott Kastan
and H. R. Woudhuysen

British Library Cataloguing-in-Publication Data
A catalogue record for this book is available from the British Library.

ISBN: HB: 978-1-9034-3698-1
PB: 978-1-9034-3699-8
ePDF: 978-1-4081-4346-9
ePUB: 978-1-4081-4347-6

Library of Congress Cataloging-in-Publication Data
A catalog record for this book is available from the Library of Congress.

Series: The Arden Shakespeare Third Series

Printed and bound in India

The Editor

Keir Elam is Professor of English Literature at the University of Bologna, where he is Head of the Department of Modern Languages. His publications include *Semiotics of Theatre and Drama* and *Shakespeare's Universe of Discourse: Language-Games in the Comedies.* He is general editor of the BUR Shakespeare (Rizzoli, Milan). With Lilla Maria Crisafulli he has edited *Women's Romantic Theatre and Drama: History, Agency, Performativity* (Ashgate, forthcoming).

For Alice and Viola

CONTENTS

List of illustrations   ix

General editor's preface   xiii

Preface   xviii

Introduction   1
  Ay, that's the theme: topics in Twelfth Night   1
   Endings and beginnings   1
   Or what you will: the pleasures and trials of
     spectatorship   3
   We three: the interpretation compulsion   10
   Around Twelfth Night   17
   A very opal: the play of perspective   24
   'Tis my picture: deciphering visual images   32
   Changeable taffeta: materials and materiality   39
   In what chapter of his bosom?: reading the body   50
    Sicken and so die: disease, contagion and death   55
    As an eunuch: castration, civility and
     intertextuality   57
   This is Illyria, lady: space and place   68
   The whirligig of time: levels of temporality   77
   Words are very rascals: language and discourse   78
  Make a good show on't: Twelfth Night *in*
  performance   87
   If this were played upon a stage: performances
    virtual and actual   87

Contents

First Night   93

Later Nights: adaptations and rearrangements   96

*Our shows are more than will: Victorian special
     effects and modernist experiments*   100

Seasonal Nights   106

Illyrian variations   110

The mettle of your sex: gender and homoeroticism   111

Show you the picture: Twelfth Night *on film*   117

Are you a comedian?: players and parts   122

Art any more than a steward?: Malvolio   123

Your drunken cousin: Sir Toby   130

*An ass-head and a coxcomb and a knave:
     Sir Andrew*   132

An allowed fool: Feste   134

A noble duke: Orsino   137

Here comes the Countess: Olivia   138

I am not that I play: Viola   142

TWELFTH NIGHT, OR WHAT YOU WILL   155

Appendix 1: The text and editorial procedures   355

Appendix 2: Casting   380

Appendix 3: Music   383

Abbreviations and references   395

Abbreviations used in notes   395

Works by and partly by Shakespeare   396

Editions of Shakespeare collated   397

Other works cited   400

Index   417

LIST OF
ILLUSTRATIONS

1 Contents page from Charles I's autograph copy of the
   Second Folio (by permission of the British Library, shelf
   mark LB.31.c.11071)   5

2 'We Three' (1): 'We Three Loggerheads', portraying the
   jesters Derry and Archie Armstrong (by permission of the
   Shakespeare Birthplace Trust)   12

3 'We Three' (2): The sign of the We Three Loggerheads Inn,
   Mold, Wales (Graham Cattherall Photography, North Wales)   13

4 William Dudley's set for Peter Gill's 1974 RSC production
   (photograph by Morris Newcombe)   31

5 'Philautia' ('self-love': see 1.5.86), from Andrea Alciato,
   Book of Emblems (1531) (by permission of the British
   Library, shelf mark YC.1996.a.4649)   33

6 'Patience on a monument' (2.4.114), from Cesare Ripa's
   Iconologia (1593) (by permission of the British Library,
   shelf mark X.950/18949)   35

7 Arion and the dolphin: Bernardo Buontalenti's set design
   for an intermezzo celebrating the 1589 wedding between
   Ferdinando de' Medici and Christina of Lorraine at the
   Pitti Palace in Florence (by permission of the British
   Library, shelf mark YC.1996.b.7280)   36

8 'Such a one I was this present' (1.5.227): Salomon Mesdach's
   portrait of Adriana van Nesse, with the inscription 'Aetatis
   suae, 19, Anno 1611' (at the age of 19, in the year 1611) (by
   permission of the Rijksmuseum, Amsterdam, Photo RMN)   37

9 'Is't not well done?' (1.5.228): Olivia unveiling, by Edmund
   Blair Leighton, 1888 (by permission of the Folger
   Shakespeare Library, shelf mark ART Flat a24)   38

10 'Viola' by Johann Heinrich Füssli, c. 1777 (by permission
    of the British Library, shelf mark LB.31.b.18329)   39

11 Buttery-bar (1.3.68) (by permission of the British Library,
    shelf mark 11762.f)   41

12 The bed of Ware (3.2.45) (by permission of the British
    Library, shelf mark 11762.f)   42

13 Parish top (1.3.40) (by permission of the British Library,
    shelf mark 11762.f)   43

14 Sheriff's posts (1.5.144) (by permission of the British
    Library, shelf mark 11762.f)   44

15 Cross-gartering, from Abraham de Bruyn, *Omnium pene
    Europae, Asiae, Aphricae atque Americae gentium habitus.
    Habits de diverses nations . . .* (Antwerp, 1581) (by
    permission of the British Library, shelf mark 810.k.2(1))   48

16 Ginevra disguised as Cesare, from Curzio Gonzaga's
    Gli inganni (1592) (courtesy of the Biblioteca Nazionale
    in Florence)   62

17 The caper or 'back-trick' (1.3.118), from Thoinot Arbeau,
    Orchésographie (1589) (by permission of the British Library,
    shelf mark 1551/534)   65

18 'The new map with the augmentation of the Indies'
    (3.2.75–6), from Edward Wright's *Map of the World*, 1600
    (by permission of the British Library, shelf mark ST 461/59)   74

19 'Mutual joinder of your hands' (5.1.153): the handfasting
    ceremony, from George Wither, *A Collection of Emblems*
    (1635) (by permission of the British Library, shelf mark
    YC.1990.b.6473)   76

20 Norman Wilkinson's futurist set for Harley Granville-
    Barker's 1912 production (by permission of the British
    Library, shelf mark YC.2002.b.3057)   104

21 Orson Welles's storybook set for his 1932 production (by
    permission of the British Library, shelf mark X.981/
    21434, and courtesy of Hortense and Roger Hill)   106

22 Malvolio (Anthony Sher) and Olivia (Deborah Findlay) in
    Bill Alexander's 1987 RSC production (photograph by
    Alena Melichor)   109

23 Malvolio in the doghouse: Philip Voss (Malvolio) and Stephen
    Boxer (Feste) in Adrian Noble's 1997 RSC production
    (photograph by Mark Douet)   114

24 'One face, one voice, one habit and two persons' (5.1.212):
    Eddie Redmayne (Viola) and Rhys Meredith (Sebastian)
    in Tim Carroll's 2002 Middle Temple production (by
    permission of Shakespeare's Globe theatre, photograph
    by Jonathan Root)   116

25 Laurence Olivier as Sir Toby in Tyrone Guthrie's 1937
    Old Vic production (Angus McBean photograph,
    © The Harvard Theatre Collection, Houghton Library)   131

26 'He cannot by the duello avoid it' (3.4.301–2): Francis
    Wheatley's painting of the 1771 production, with Elizabeth
    Younge as Viola, James Dodd as Sir Andrew, James Love as
    Sir Toby and Francis Waldron as Fabian (© Manchester Art
    Gallery)   133

27 Mrs Abington as Olivia in 1771 (by permission of the
    British Library, shelf mark 11770.g.3(16))   140

28 The opening scene in the First Folio text (by permission of
    the Folger Shakespeare Library, sig. Y2r/page 255,
    STC 22273, fo. 1 no. 05)   357

29 A passage from page 267 (sig. Z2^r) of the First Folio
    (3.3.18–37), showing the preferred spellings of Compositor
    B: 'do', 'go', 'heere' and 'deere' (by permission of the
    British Library)   360

30 A comparison between the First Folio text of *Twelfth Night*
    and the open letter to the York Herald, Ralph Brooke, which
    the printer William Jaggard added to Vincent's *Discovery of
    Errors*. The two works were set contemporaneously, and the
    final paragraph of the letter contains several types distributed
    from *Twelfth Night*. Shown here are two passages from

page 267 (sig. Z2^r) of the Folio (3.3.18–21, 3.4.69–76) – each containing two of the types in question – and the final paragraph of Jaggard's letter in which all four types reappear. From Peter W.M. Blayney, *The First Folio of Shakespeare* (Washington: Folger Library Publications, 1991, by permission of the Folger Shakespeare Library (Z8811.B62))   363

31 'Viol-de-gamboys' (1.3.23–4), from Christopher Simpson, *The Division-Viol, or The Art of Playing Extempore upon a Ground* (1667) (by permission of the British Library, shelf mark X.0431.109(20))   384

GENERAL EDITORS' PREFACE

The earliest volume in the first Arden series, Edward Dowden's *Hamlet*, was published in 1899. Since then the Arden Shakespeare has been widely acknowledged as the pre-eminent Shakespeare edition, valued by scholars, students, actors and 'the great variety of readers' alike for its clearly presented and reliable texts, its full annotation and its richly informative introductions.

In the third Arden series we seek to maintain these well-established qualities and general characteristics, preserving our predecessors' commitment to presenting the play as it has been shaped in history. Each volume necessarily has its own particular emphasis which reflects the unique possibilities and problems posed by the work in question, and the series as a whole seeks to maintain the highest standards of scholarship, combined with attractive and accessible presentation.

Newly edited from the original Quarto and Folio editions, texts are presented in fully modernized form, with a textual apparatus that records all substantial divergences from those early printings. The notes and introductions focus on the conditions and possibilities of meaning that editors, critics and performers (on stage and screen) have discovered in the play. While building upon the rich history of scholarly activity that has long shaped our understanding of Shakespeare's works, this third series of the Arden Shakespeare is enlivened by a new generation's encounter with Shakespeare.

THE TEXT

On each page of the play itself, readers will find a passage of text supported by commentary and textual notes. Act and scene divisions (seldom present in the early editions and often the product of eighteenth-century or later scholarship) have been retained for ease of reference, but have been given less prominence than in previous series. Editorial indications of location of the action have been removed to the textual notes of commentary.

In the text itself, unfamiliar typographic conventions have been avoided in order to minimize obstacles to the reader. Elided forms in the early texts are spelt out in full in vese lines wherever they indicate a usual late twentieth-century pronunciation that requires no special indication and wherever they occur in prose (except where they indicate non-standard pronunciation). In verse speeches, marks of elision are retained where they are necessary guides to the scansion and pronunciation of the line. Final -ed in past tense and participial forms of verbs is always printed as -ed, without accent, never as -'d, but wherever the required pronunciation diverges from modern usage a note in the commentary draws attention to the fact. Where the final -ed should be given syllabic value contrary to modern usage, e.g.

> Doth Silvia know that I am banished?
> (*TGV 3.1.214*)

the note will take the form

> **214 banished** banished

Conventional lineation of divided verse lines shared by two or more speakers has been reconsidered and sometimes rearranged. Except for the familiar *Exit* and *Exeunt*, Latin forms in stage directions and speech prefixes have been translated into English and the original Latin forms recorded in the textual notes.

COMMENTARY AND TEXTUAL NOTES

Notes in the commentary, for which a major source will be the *Oxford English Dictionary*, offer glossarial and other explication of verbal difficulties; they may also include discussion of points of interpretation and, in relevant cases, substantial extracts from Shakespeare's source material. Editors will not usually offer glossarial notes for words adequately defined in the latest edition of *The Concise Oxford Dictionary* or *Merriam-Webster's Collegiate Dictionary*, but in cases of doubt they will include notes. Attention, however, will be drawn to places where more than one likely interpretation can be proposed and to significant verbal and syntactic complexity. Notes preceded by * discuss editorial emendations or variant readings from the early edition(s) on which the text is based.

Headnotes to acts or scenes discuss, where appropriate, questions of scene location, Shakespeare's handling of his source materials, and major difficulties of staging. The list of roles (so headed to emphasize the play's status as a text for performance) is also considered in the commentary notes. These may include comment on plausible patterns of casting with the resources of an Elizabethan or Jacobean acting company and also on any variation in the description of roles in their speech prefixes in the early editions.

The textual notes are designed to let readers know when the edited text diverges from the early edition(s) or manuscript sources on which it is based. Wherever this happens the note will record the rejected reading of the early edition(s), in original spelling, and the source of the reading adopted in this edition. Other forms from the early edition(s) recorded in these notes will include some spellings of particular interest or significance and original forms of translated stage directions. Where two or more early editions are involved, for instance with *Othello*, the notes also record all important differences between them. The textual notes take a form that has been in use since the nineteenth century. This comprises, first: line reference, reading adopted in the text and closing square bracket; then: abbreviated reference, in italic, to the earliest edition to adopt the accepted reading, italic semicolon and noteworthy alternative reading(s), each with abbreviated italic reference to its source.

Conventions used in these textual notes include the following. The solidus / is used, in notes quoting verse or discussing verse lining, to indicate line endings. Distinctive spellings of the basic text (Q or F) follow the square bracket without indication of source and are enclosed in italic brackets. Names enclosed in italic brackets indicate originators of conjectural emendations when these did not originate in an edition of the text, or when the named edition records a conjecture not accepted into its text. Stage directions (SDs) are referred to by the number of the line within or immediately after which they are placed. Line numbers with a decimal point relate to centred SDs not falling within a verse line and to SDs more than one line long, with the number after the point indicating the line within the SD: e.g. 78.4 refers to the fourth line of the SD following line 78. Lines of SDs at the start of a scene are numbered 0.1, 0.2, etc. Where only a line number precedes a square bracket, e.g. 128], the note relates to the whole line; where SD is added to the number, it relates to the whole of a SD within or immediately following the line. Speech prefixes (SPs) follow similar conventions, 203 SP] referring to the speaker's name for line 203. Where a SP reference takes the form e.g. 38+SP, it relates to all subsequent speeches assigned to that speaker in the scene in question.

Where, as with *King Henry V,* one of the early editions is a so–called 'bad quarto' (that is, at text either heavily adapted, or reconstructed from memory, or both), the divergences from the present edition are too great to be recorded in full in the notes. In these cases the editions will include a reduced photographic facsimile of the 'bad quarto' in an appendix.

INTRODUCTION

Both the introduction and the commentary are designed to present the plays as texts for performance, and make appropriate reference to stage, film and television versions, as well as introducing the reader to the range of critical approaches to the plays. They discuss the history of the reception of the texts within the theatre and scholarship and beyond, investigating the interdependency of the literary text and the surrounding 'cultural text' both at the time of the original production of Shakespeare's works and during their long and rich afterlife.

PREFACE

Editing a play, like staging a play, is a collaborative enterprise. This edition is the result of the efforts not of the volume editor alone but of many members of the Arden Shakespeare team, some of whom left while others joined and still others stayed on the scene, as work on the play was caught up in the whirligig of time. Three of the general editors of the Arden Shakespeare played a substantial role during the production of this volume. Richard Proudfoot lent me his formidable knowledge and wisdom, on textual and other matters. David Kastan's acute critical judgement, expressed with his inimitable wit, was illuminating, particularly in the shaping of the Introduction. Ann Thompson offered me unsparingly her expertise, intelligence and friendship at every stage of the editing, from its conception onwards, and my gratitude to her is boundless.

Other members of the Arden team have also played a significant role. Jessica Hodge greatly encouraged me during and after her time as publisher. Her successor Margaret Bartley has been an exceptionally positive and supportive publisher, with unusual gifts of diplomacy; to her a special thank-you. I also owe a real debt of gratitude to Linden Stafford, the best copy-editor one could hope for: sharp, insightful, with a genuine understanding of language, grammar and style (Shakespeare's and even the editor's); among other things, I will always cherish her passionate and persuasive defence of the parenthetical comma. An earlier copy-editor, Nicola Bennett, went well beyond the call of duty in her searching questions and thoughtful suggestions, putting at my disposal her learning and her keen sense of dramaturgy. The edition also benefited from the tireless researches, especially in the visual field, of Philippa Gallagher and Charlotte Loveridge.

Thanks to Alissa Chappell for taking care of the edition in its final stages. I also wish to thank Jane Armstrong for her kindness when she was a leading player in the Arden team. To my fellow Arden editor Jonathan Bate my thanks for his early encouragement to join the team.

The collaborative effort extended beyond Arden, however. Of the many friends and colleagues from whose help and support I have benefited, I wish in particular to thank the following: Alessandro Serpieri for the many fruitful interchanges and collaborations on Shakespeare and company over the years; William Dodd for keeping me on my toes regarding new critical discourses; Nora Crook for intriguing leads regarding Mary Shelley and Illyrian same-sex marriages; Steve Sohmer for enlightenment on dates and calendars; George Walton Williams for stimulating suggestions on prosody and lineation; Tom Craik, my predecessor as editor of the Arden *Twelfth Night*, for his helpful advice in the early stages of the editing; Paola Pugliatti for her leads on beggars and vagrants; Fernando Cioni, our man at the Folger, for information on editions and sources; Fabio Liberto for timely bibliographical assistance with Plato. Liz Schafer brought her great knowledge of the field to her reading of the performance history sections of the introduction and commentary. I wish to thank especially our two leading scholars of Shakespeare's grammar: Jonathan Hope allowed me to see a draft of his book and commented helpfully on my own linguistic discourse, as did Norman Blake, who, with unparalleled generosity, corresponded with me over a long period of time about text, punctuation, discourse markers, meaning and spelling, opening up new interpretative vistas.

The following friends gave me the opportunity to explore different aspects of *Twelfth Night* by inviting me to give lectures or seminars on the play and by engaging me afterwards in thought-provoking discussion: William Carroll and James Siemon at Boston University and the Harvard Shakespeare seminar; Virginia Vaughan at Clark; Gary Taylor at Alabama; Gary Kelly at Edmonton; Michele Marrapodi at Palermo; Rosa Maria Colombo at Roma la Sapienza; Debs Callan at the Globe theatre, where I was a Sam Wanamaker fellow; Lynette Hunter and Ann Thompson at Gresham College, London; and Gail Kern Paster and Carol Neely at the 'Mediterranean Bodies' panel of the World Shakespeare Conference in Valencia. Other friends helped equally by inviting me to contribute articles or chapters on the play: Gail Kern Paster in *Shakespeare Quarterly*; Stanley Wells in *Shakespeare Survey*; Terry Hawkes in *Alternative Shakespeares 2*.

I have also had the good fortune to be able to discuss *Twelfth Night* with directors and actors involved in staging it. Tim Carroll, director of the celebrated Middle Temple production of 2002, generously shared information and illumination on his and the company's work. Paul Chahidi, an extraordinary Maria in the same production, volunteered enlightening insight into his character's infertility. Declan Donnellan, great director of *Twelfth Night* and countless other plays, shared his brilliant views on the comedy, Shakespeare and the world at large in various venues: in Taormina, in Pisa and, most memorably, over tea at the Middle Temple, of which he is a member.

Like every editor of a Shakespeare play, I am indebted to my distinguished predecessors, whose work has been an invaluable point of reference for my own, especially to the editors of the Oxford edition, Stanley Wells and Roger Warren; of the Arden second series edition, Tom Craik and Jim Lothian; and of the Penguin edition, Molly Mahood.

Last but certainly most, I wish to thank Lilla Maria Crisafulli for her tireless and loving support both moral and material, especially during the times when I was lost in the dark room of the editing process; to her I can no other answer make but thanks, and thanks, and ever thanks.

INTRODUCTION

'AY, THAT'S THE THEME': TOPICS IN *TWELFTH NIGHT*

Endings and beginnings

A play, like a cat, has several lives. It has a pre-theatrical life as an authorial manuscript, being read and perhaps modified by producers, actors and others. It later becomes a performance script, undergoing rehearsal and possible further revision. It then comes fully to life onstage, in the interplay between actors and audience. The performance takes on its own life, and may be described, debated and reviewed in other private or published texts. Each subsequent staging of the play is a new beginning, producing new responses. If the text of the play is printed or otherwise circulated, it may also enjoy various kinds of afterlife: revivals, successive printings or editions, adaptations, film versions, quotation in other works, critical analyses, even paintings of given scenes, etc. This introduction will give an account of some of the many lives of Shakespeare's *Twelfth Night, or What You Will* – the multiple factors that make up its rich textual, theatrical, critical and cultural history.

Twelfth Night continues to maintain its long-established place as one of the most popular and admired of Shakespeare's plays. The reasons for the enduring fortune of the comedy have to do with both production and reception. It is a play that demonstrably works onstage, even in relatively modest performances, a fact that secures its stable position in both professional and amateur repertories. There is probably no other Shakespeare comedy, moreover,

1

that gives so many actors the chance to shine, and indeed the play's stage history suggests that the star performance may come not from Malvolio or Viola but from Feste, Sir Toby, Sir Andrew or even Maria (see p. 122). As a text for performance, *Twelfth Night* is also an open challenge to the director to come up with a strong reading. For example, the interpretation of 'Twelfth Night' and 'Illyria' – not only as seasonal and geographical settings but also as dominant symbolic time and space – creates an all-important frame for the understanding of the overall action. Over time this challenge has provoked actor-managers and directors – from Beerbohm Tree to Granville-Barker, and from John Barton to Sam Mendes – to produce some of their most innovative and characteristic work. As for reception, *Twelfth Night* has enjoyed, at least from the eighteenth century onwards, approval from audiences and critical judges alike, and is often considered Shakespeare's finest and maturest comedy. It has attracted over the decades an unusual degree of interpretative attention, and in recent years has returned to the centre of critical debate, thanks especially to its dramatization of currently fashionable issues such as gender and sexuality.

It is not, however, an easy play to place within the development of Shakespearean comedy. It is by no means the last of its kind – being followed by *Measure for Measure*, *All's Well That Ends Well* and other comedies – but it does in various ways represent a point of arrival within the genre. It is the last of the so-called 'romantic' comedies (see Frye). It is the last and arguably the most successful of the four cross-dressing comedies (after *The Two Gentlemen of Verona*, *The Merchant of Venice* and *As You Like It*). It is one of the last of the Elizabethan comedies, composed at the close of Elizabeth's reign and reflecting the anxieties and uncertainties of its historical moment. It has been seen as the last of Shakespeare's so-called 'happy comedies' (Wilson), or indeed as the dramatist's 'farewell to comedy' (Quiller-Couch, xi). Alternatively, it can be seen as a first. It is probably Shakespeare's first seventeenth-century comedy, and is in many ways a beginning-of-century play, inaugurating a new poetics: some commentators have seen it as the first of the 'dark comedies', foreshadowing with its representations of actual and feared deaths the later development of tragicomedy. As a result, *Twelfth Night* is an elusive play, as the history of its theatrical and critical reception suggests. It might be useful to turn our attention to that history.

Or what you will: the pleasures and trials of spectatorship

Let us begin at the end. The concluding line of *Twelfth Night* is an implicit appeal to the audience for indulgent applause: 'And we'll strive to please you every day,' promises the clown Feste at the close of his epilogue song. The applause usually arrives, because, however conventional Feste's appeal to the audience may appear, the comedy has in fact received (with a few exceptions) a largely enthusiastic theatrical and critical response – if not 'every day' then certainly over the centuries. The *Twelfth Night* story is on the whole a prolonged success story, and the play's audiences have performed a prominent and active part in the narrative. Indeed, the earliest news that we have of the comedy foregrounds the reactions of a series of conspicuous spectators in the form of personal responses in private diaries.

Twelfth Night is unique among Shakespeare's plays in having received a contemporary review, after a performance by the Lord Chamberlain's Men. The diary of John Manningham, fourth-year law student at the Middle Temple (one of the Inns of Court, or law colleges, in London), has the following entry for 2 February (Candlemas) 1602:

FEBR. 1601.[1]
2. At our feast wee had a play called ~~Mid~~ 'Twelve night, or what you will'; much like the commedy of errores, or Menechmi in Plautus, but most like and neere to that in Italian called Inganni.

1 The year 1601 in the old Julian calendar corresponds to 1602 in the reformed Gregorian calendar introduced in 1582 but not adopted in England until 1752. In Shakespeare's day the New Year began on 25 March.

A good practise in it to make the steward beleeve his
Lady widowe was in Love with him, by counterfayting
a letter, as from his Lady, in generall termes, telling
him what shee liked best in him, and prescribing his
gesture in smiling, his apparraile, &c., and then when
he came to practise, making him beleeve they tooke him
to be mad.

(Manningham, 48)

Manningham was in many ways an ideal spectator: young and well
educated, he brought to the performance an impressive array of
precise literary and theatrical knowledge, enabling him to place
the comedy culturally. He knew Shakespeare's earlier comedies,
as is suggested by his crossing out of 'Mid' – presumably because
he had started to write 'Midsummer night's dream' – and the
comparison of 'Twelve night' with 'the commedy of errores',
which had also been performed at an Inn of Court, Gray's Inn, in
1594. He was also able to compare the play with the Latin source
of *The Comedy of Errors*, Plautus's *Menaechmi*, and to identify
as the most similar comedy, and thus as another possible source,
the *Inganni*, one of the Italian versions of the story. There is one
revealing inaccuracy in the account: Manningham mistakenly
describes Malvolio's 'Lady' as a widow, an error that may derive
from seeing Olivia in the performance dressed in black in mourning for the death of her brother (rather than from his knowledge
of Shakespeare's main English source, Riche's story of 'Apolonius
and Silla', where the Olivia figure is indeed a widow).

The benevolent tone of Manningham's account of the play, and
the particular praise he reserves for the 'good practise in it' of the
gulling of the steward, set the tone and the terms for later spectators, who regularly place Malvolio at the centre of their responses.
The second mention of the comedy is also a diary entry, again for
2 February and again centred on Malvolio. In 1623 the Master
of the Revels, Sir Henry Herbert, records in his diary that 'At
Candlemas Malvolio was acted at Court by the King's Servants'

(Winter, 13); on this occasion the most prominent spectator was King James I, who presumably commissioned the performance (the second at his court following an earlier representation given on 6 April 1618). Herbert's reference to a comedy entitled 'Malvolio' may indicate an adaptation or may instead suggest that the court audience, like Manningham, was best pleased with the duping of the steward. This preference is implicitly confirmed by James's successor as the play's most privileged spectator and reader: King Charles I wrote marginal notes to the list of contents in his copy of the 1632 Second Folio indicating the leading – or perhaps his favourite – characters; against the title *Twelfe Night, or what you will*, he wrote 'Malvolio' (Fig. 1). Eight years later

122 .... *Loves Labour's lost.*

Pyramus & Thisby. 148 .. *Midsommers nights Dreame.*

163 .. *The Merchant of Venice.*

Rosalinde . 185 ... *As you like it.*

208 .. *The taming of the Shrew.*

Mr James 230 *All's well that ends well.*

Malvolio 255 .. *Twelfe night, or what you will.*

277 .. *The Winters Tale.*

Histories.

1 . *The life and death of K. Iohn.*

23 *The life & death of K R. the 2.*

46 *The life and death of K. H. 4.*

74 *The second part of K. H. the 4.*

1 Contents page from Charles I's autograph copy of the Second Folio

the royal approval of this character was extended into collective audience enthusiasm in the laudatory poem by Leonard Digges appended to the edition of Shakespeare's *Poems* published in 1640, shortly before the closure of the theatres, which reports how 'The Cockpit Galleries, Boxes, all are full / To heare Malvolio that crosse garter'd Gull'.

The *Twelfth Night* story was resumed immediately after the Restoration, and again coincides in large part with the history of its reception, in the guise of three entries in the most celebrated and most 'private' of English diaries. When the comedy was revived for the first time by William Davenant's Company at the Duke of York's on 11 September 1661 the monarch, in this case King Charles II, was again present; we have no news of the king's reaction, but we do have the unsentimental testimony of another conspicuous spectator, the diarist Samuel Pepys, who gave the play its first bad review, although his response seems to have little to do with the actual performance or with the comedy's merits: 'observed at the Opera a new play, "Twelfth Night" was acted there, and the King there; so I, against my own mind and resolution, could not forbear to go in, which did make the play seem a burthen to me, and I took no pleasure at all in it.' Despite this disappointing non–event, Pepys went back for more; the diary entry for 'Twelfth Day' (6 January) 1663 registers a more perfunctory impatience with the comedy, although not with the performance: 'after dinner to the Duke's house, and there saw "Twelfth Night" acted well, though it be but a silly play, and not related at all to the name or day.' Six years later, none the less, he was back for a third attempt; on 20 January 1669, his judgement is still more severe: 'thence to the Duke of York's house, and saw "Twelfth Night", as it is now revived; but, I think, one of the weakest plays that ever I saw on the stage.'

Although the company's prompter, John Downes, defends Davenant's production in his *Roscius Anglicanus*, alleging that it 'had mighty success by its well performance' (Winter, 15), Pepys's judgement was evidently shared by other spectators at the time, probably because the predominant neo–classical taste of the period found the comedy wanting and indeed downright 'silly'. As a result, it disappeared from the London stage repertory – with the exception of an unsuccessful 1703 adaptation (see pp. 96–7) – for over seventy years, until 'rediscovered' by Charles Macklin in 1741. From the middle of the eighteenth century onwards, instead, its theatrical and critical reception has been a more or less uninterrupted success. The most authoritative critical responses of the eighteenth and nineteenth centuries restore Manningham's benevolence, and his emphasis on the pleasurable comic appeal of *Twelfth Night*, especially in performance. 'This play is in the graver part elegant and easy, and in some of the lighter scenes exquisitely humorous,' declared Dr Johnson in 1765. Four decades later William Hazlitt concurred, and attempted to define audience response to the comic action: 'This is justly considered as one of the most delightful of Shakespear's comedies. It is full of sweetness and pleasantry. . . It makes us laugh at the follies of mankind, not despise them.' (Hazlitt, 1.221). The Victorian editor Halliwell in 1853 likewise saw the play as a great comic vehicle, going so far as to elect *Twelfth Night* 'the chief monument of the author's genius for Comedy, and the most perfect composition of the kind in the English or any other language'.

In the case of *Twelfth Night*, the spectator plays the part of co–protagonist. This role is inscribed in the text, beginning with Shakespeare's gesture, in the play's second title, of leaving the responsibility to the audience: the 'you' in *What you will* is addressed directly to us spectators and readers, and can be interpreted either self-referentially as 'find your own title' (compare Olivia's use of the same expression towards Malvolio at 1.5.105, in the sense of 'do whatever you think fit'), or more amply as 'make of the play what you wish'. The comedy goes on to invite an unusual degree of audience complicity with the main action, first in Viola's disguise plot, then in the 'good practice' of the duping of Malvolio, encouraging us to join the company of the plotters hidden in the box tree or sneering in the dark room.

In electing the spectator as co-protagonist of the events, the comedy also interrogates the ethics and psychology of audience participation, obliging us to be acutely and sometimes uncomfortably aware of our own part. Commentators have frequently noted how a shift in spectator sympathies occurs at some point during the tormenting of Malvolio, as a result of a perception of excess in his punishment. Ralph Berry identifies the cross-gartering scene (3.4) as the moment in which the play 'begins to insinuate unease into the audience's consciousness . . . The joke has been taken too far, and we know it' (Berry, 111). In many performances, however, it is the 'dark room' scene (4.2), with its literal imprisoning of the 'mad' steward, that causes the audience to reconsider its complicity in the events and to change its allegiances. In either case, the result, as Mark Van Doren observed in 1939, is that 'Modern audiences have bestowed more sympathy upon Malvolio than Shakespeare perhaps intended, so that the balance is now not what it was. It can scarcely be overthrown, however, whatever changes the whirligig of time brings in' (Van Doren; quoted in Everyman, 211).

The audience's uneasy sense of being caught up in pleasures of a dubious kind is reflected in the unflattering image of spectatorship that the play itself offers, again with reference to the maltreatment of the steward. The recurrent trope used by the plotters in the letter scene (2.5) is that of blood sports: woodcock-trapping (82), trout-tickling (19–20), badger-hunting (102) and above all bear-baiting, the species of violent spectacle that Shakespeare's audience could enjoy at the arenas close to the Globe theatre. When Fabian justifies his unexpected participation in the scene by recalling Malvolio's puritanical disapproval of this sport – 'You know he brought me out o'favour with my lady about a bear-baiting here' (where the adverb 'here' suggests a physically contiguous arena, if not the Globe stage itself) – Sir Toby promises him an appropriate form of retribution, a kind of sporting justice: 'To anger him, we'll have the bear again, and we will fool him black and blue' (2.5.6–9). The play takes on the force of a potentially bloody revenge comedy. The implications of this trope for the audience are not altogether complimentary: if Malvolio is a bear fooled black and blue, his tormentors, us included, are by the same token aggressive hounds. The culmination of this derogatory mirroring of the lookers-on is Malvolio's parting curse in the finale: 'I'll be revenged on the whole pack of you!' (5.1.371), in which the term 'pack' identifies his tormentors precisely as sanguinary dogs and in which the second person pronoun addressed to the assembled company onstage may be extended – as with the 'you' in the play's second title – to the assembled company in the audience.

The pleasures of spectatorship of *Twelfth Night*, therefore, are not quite the straightforward delights, all 'sweetness and pleasantry', applauded by Hazlitt. Nor is the audience's laughter necessarily the benevolent amusement at human foibles detected by the Romantic critic. There seem to be obscurer transactions at play. Not by chance, the comedy's twentieth-century critical history coincides to a considerable degree with reflections precisely on the role of the audience, in the endeavour to define better what is going on in the interaction between stage and auditorium. Thus John Draper's *The 'Twelfth Night' of Shakespeare's Audience* (1950) tries to reconstruct the cultural perspective of the Elizabethan audience, arguing that spectators at the time would have been particularly interested in the play's darker social themes and struggles, such as class relationships. From a more formal perspective, in 1960 Bertrand Evans argues that the dramatist contrives to give the spectator a perceptual advantage over the dramatis personae, not only in the Malvolio scenes but in the twins plot, thereby complicating our response to events: 'The emotional conflict which rises from this unlaughable treatment of a laughable situation' (B. Evans, 128).

Later inquiries deepen and darken the picture. Ralph Berry's 1981 essay, '*Twelfth Night*: the experience of the audience', examines the 'moral responsibility' that the spectator is obliged to assume, and comes to the sobering conclusion that 'the ultimate effect of *Twelfth Night* is to make the audience ashamed of itself' (Berry, 119). Less severe is Stephen Booth's '*Twelfth Night*: I.I: the audience as Malvolio', which identifies the primary delights of spectatorship as intellectual or cognitive: 'I submit that much of our joy in *Twelfth Night* drives from triumphant mental experiences like our modest but godlike achievement in comprehending scene i.' (Booth, '*Twelfth*', 167). Stephen Greenblatt, in his well-known essay 'Fiction and Friction', discerns pleasures of a less cerebral kind, arguing that the 'heat' generated by verbal and corporeal play in the comedy translates into a non–cathartic and decidedly erotic charge for the spectator, especially in his or her post–theatrical experience: 'Shakespeare invested his comedies with a powerful sexual commotion, a collective excitation, an imaginative heat that the plots' promise will be realized offstage, in the marriage beds toward which they gesture' (Greenblatt, 89).

We three: the interpretation compulsion

Watching *Twelfth Night* may be ethically disturbing, intellectually invigorating or erotically arousing, but it is also potentially perilous. In one of his better jokes, Feste offers the audience an implicit warning, a 'caveat spectator'; arriving on the scene in 2.3, in which Sir Toby Belch and Sir Andrew Aguecheek have already begun their serious carousing, the clown opens with a riddle:

SIR ANDREW Here comes the fool, i'faith.

FESTE How now, my hearts? Did you never see the picture of 'we three'?

SIR TOBY Welcome, ass. Now let's have a catch.

(2.3.14–17)

Feste's enigma alludes to a popular painting or inn sign which represented two asses or loggerheads and bore the caption 'We Three' (see Figs 2 and 3), a puzzling tag that inevitably prompted its reader to pose the fatal question: 'Who is the third ass?' To which the reply, of course, was: whoever poses the question. Sir Toby gets the point, identifying Feste as the third member of a company of fools ('Welcome, ass'). His interpretation may not be complete, however. Deciphering the riddle involves a paradox: as Elizabeth Freund observes, 'the interpreter is obliged to take a position both inside the frame and outside it . . . Without conceding asshood, the reader cannot unriddle the picture; but if he fails to read the picture, he is palpably an ass' (Freund, 476). By describing the picture, the clown seems to place himself inside it as participant but outside it as onlooker, leaving the deciphering, or asshood, to others. And not only to Sir Toby: the implication seems to be that the third loggerhead is the audience – us – witnessing and trying to make sense of the joke. Even if Stephen Booth optimistically assures us that 'Audiences of *Twelfth Night* do not, and therefore should not, feel like fools looking at fools, or jackasses looking at jackasses' (Booth, '*Twelfth*', 167), there can be little doubt that Feste's gaze goes out beyond the bounds of the stage.

Feste is the best guide we have to the play's underlying themes, and his visual-verbal riddle is emblematic from various points of view. It is one of a series of enigmas within what is in many ways one of Shakespeare's most enigmatic plays. It foregrounds the spectator not only as interpreter but also as object of inquiry. It makes explicit a question that runs throughout the play: who is the true fool (or, indeed, are we all fools)? And it warns us of the danger of making fools of ourselves through interpretation, including the interpretation of *Twelfth Night* itself, even as, like much else in the play, it irresistibly invites an interpretative response. Among the desires aroused by *Twelfth Night*, perhaps the strongest is cognitive desire, the yearning to know and to understand. A comedy that insistently presents itself as a 'mystery' play, it provokes the temptation – to paraphrase Orsino – to unclasp the book of its secret soul.

One of the play's 'structural' mysteries, a major cause of audience – and especially critical – puzzlement, is its large number of loose ends, whereby plots, events or performances are announced and then abandoned. As William Dodd puts it, 'There is hardly

11

2   'We Three' (1): 'We Three Loggerheads', portraying the jesters Derry and Archie Armstrong

3   'We Three' (2): The sign of the We Three Loggerheads Inn, Mold, Wales

one initial project which isn't either forgotten or shelved by the characters involved in the tangled love plot, or eased from the centre of the stage by the playwright himself' (Dodd, 147). The most notorious of these 'forgotten' projects is Viola's plan, declared in her first scene, to present herself at Orsino's court 'as an eunuch' (1.2.53). No further (explicit) mention is made of the idea and, when at 2.4.23–6 Viola-as-Cesario alludes obliquely to her love for Orsino, Coleridge is led to affirm: 'And yet Viola was to have been presented to Orsino as a eunuch. Either she forgot this, or Viola had altered her plan' (Coleridge, 1.96). In reality the 'disappearance' of the castrato theme is only apparent (see p. 57–62), but it certainly leaves a 'blank' (2.4.110) at the centre of the main action. In the same announcement, Viola also leads us to expect future musical performances at the duke's court: 'for I can sing / And speak to him in many sorts of music' (1.2.54–5); she fails to perform, and all the singing is left to Feste.

The clown is involved in another of the mysteriously shelved projects. When in 2.3 Maria announces her scheme for the gulling of Malvolio, she includes Feste as participant spectator, telling Sir Toby and Sir Andrew, 'I will plant you two – and let the fool make a third – where he shall find the letter' (2.3.168–9). In the event, however, it is Fabian, introduced for the first time in the scene, who makes the third spectator in the letter episode (2.5), rather than the clown. These loose ends or false starts have been interpreted as signs of authorial revision or as changes dictated by casting problems, but they undoubtedly leave question marks in the text, although whether audiences are really troubled by the missing links, or indeed whether they even notice them, is another matter.

Feste is also the main source of the comedy's more discursive enigmas, riddles and puzzles. His citing, for example, of invented Latin authorities – 'For what says Quinapalus? "Better a witty fool than a foolish wit"' (1.5.33–4) – invites us to search for the deformed 'originals' (Quintilian[us]? Apuleius?; see 33n.). Likewise his 'fooling', reported by the drunken (and not very reliable) Sir Andrew, with its 'Pigrogromitus', 'Vapians' and 'Queubus' (2.3.22–3), has sent commentators into a flurry of hermeneutic inquiry: Furness sees 'Pigrogromitus' as a corruption of 'Tetragrammaton'; Hotson discerns Platonic cosmology in Queubus/Cubus, etc. (see commentary). The clown is the chief exponent of another enigmatic mode that pervades the comedy and that likewise keeps us guessing, namely what John Kerrigan calls 'ontological riddling' (Kerrigan, 109), which consists in pseudo–philosophical affirmations of a tautological kind – 'That that is is'; 'for what is "that" but "that" and "is" but "is"?' (4.2.14–16) – or of a logically self-contradictory variety: 'Nothing that is so is so' (4.1.8). The same riddling mode seems to infect Viola–as–Cesario in her cryptic signals to Olivia, to Orsino or to the audience: 'I am not that I play' (1.5.179); 'I am the man' (2.2.25); 'What I am and what I would are as secret as maidenhead' (1.5.209–10).

Twelfth Night repeatedly professes its own secrecy. As Kerrigan suggests, '*Twelfth Night* pushes one's perception of Renaissance secrecy beyond the usual categories', to include, among other modes of occultation, 'the circulation of secrets as gossip' (Kerrigan, 90). Thus Viola's 'secret as maidenhead', like Orsino's 'secret soul' (1.4.14) or the captain's pledge of silence ('your mute I'll be', 1.2.59), evoke the idea of hidden herme-neutic gems, occult meanings to be uncovered in interpretative treasure hunts. Correspondingly, much of the play's action is taken up with the attempt to decipher impenetrable texts (in the form of letters), bodies (notably Viola's), hearts (Orsino's, Olivia's, Cesario's) and events (such as the shipwreck and its consequences). It is a play 'about' interpretation, as well as a play that has received more than its share of interpretations. The culminating expression of this interpretative compulsion, the desire to disclose illuminating secret meanings, is of course Malvolio's catastrophic attempt to decode 'Olivia's' billet-doux with its notorious conundrums: '*M.O.A.I. doth sway my life.*' . . . what should that alphabetical position portend?' (2.5.106–17). This 'fustian riddle', as Fabian calls it, is a perfect semantic trap for Malvolio, playing on his fatal narcissism. His interpretation is circular; he starts out from the will to 'make that resemble some-thing in me' and ends up finding precisely his own resemblance: '"M." Malvolio. "M" – why, that begins my name!' (2.5.123–4). By discovering his name reflected in the scrambled letters – with perhaps more difficulty than is warranted by the simple enigma itself – the steward elects himself as the object not of Olivia's but of his own interpretative desire, thereby making an ass, or 'a rare turkey–cock', of himself (2.5.28).

Despite the unenviable fate of the steward, and despite the unflattering image of interpretation that the episode presents, the fustian riddle has proved an equally fatal attraction to the comedy's spectators and commentators, who, affected by a sort of mimetic syndrome, are tempted to 'become' Malvolio (Booth) in the endeavour to unscramble the letters. Over the years interpretative speculation on the riddle has reached improbable heights of ingenuity. Hotson (166), for example, sees the letters as the initials of the four elements: Mare (sea), Orbis (earth), Aer (air) and Ignis (fire) – although, as Craik points out (Ard², 68), the first two elements should surely be Aqua and Terra. L.S. Cox in 1962 read them as an anagram of 'I am O[livia]' – although they might equally well be taken as a clue to the dubious authorship of the letter: M(aria or) O(livia) A(m) I? Some readings have been based on early modern theories of language. Thus Elam (*Shakespeare's*, 159–64) sees Malvolio's hermeneutic labours as a parody of the earnest anagrammatic endeavours of Renaissance magi to discover the sacred Tetragrammaton, the secret four-letter name of God (in this case Malvolio himself; compare 'Pigrogromitus' above). Peter J. Smith in 1998 also finds a key in the Renaissance conception of meaning as being inherent to language rather than merely conventional, and suggests that the letters, embodying their referent directly in its initials, allude to Sir John Harington's Ovidian parody *The Metamorphosis of Ajax* (*Metamorphosis Of A Iax*), which was at the time the object of scandal; since Harington's 'ajax' plays on 'a jakes', slang for lavatory, the 'inherent meaning' or referent of the acrostic becomes 'toilet' (hence, presumably, the allusion to Olivia urinating in a further letter-riddle: 'thus makes she her great P's', 2.5.87)

There are other insidious enigmas to interpret (or, more wisely, to resist) in the letter, and especially, as it were, in the letters of the letter. On picking up the billet–doux, Malvolio first notices the handwriting, which he attributes to Olivia:

MALVOLIO [*Takes up letter.*] By my life, this is my lady's
    hand. These be her very c's, her u's and her t's . . .
SIR ANDREW Her c's, her u's and her t's. Why that?

                            (2.5.85–9)

Sir Andrew's ingenuous demand for an explanation – he is the only one present not to get the joke – may reflect today the puzzlement of modern audiences, for whom the word 'cut' has lost its Elizabethan slang meaning, having in the meantime gained a letter ('cunt'). But, like Malvolio's own will to knowledge, Aguecheek's desire to understand has also infected critical commentators. Indeed, in recent years c, u and t have attracted even more attention than M.O.A.I. Most of these contemporary readings are surgical or anatomical, from Jonathan Goldberg's association of the letters with the symbolic gelding of the boy actor (Goldberg, 217), to Dympna Callaghan's somewhat analogous discerning of a 'feminized, ridiculed, castrated' Malvolio (Callaghan, 'All', 436; on the theme of castration, see pp. 57–62), to Gail Kern Paster's tracing of a trajectory in Malvolio's voyeuristic desire 'from the genital to the excretory' (Paster, 33). The episode may also point to Malvolio's ambition for social mobility: the idea of watching Olivia pee is not so much an erotic fantasy as a dream of social equality, since only her husband, the 'count' (a title achieved with the addition of another letter: see 2.5.32) has the right to do so. Leah Scragg, instead, offers a socio–historical decoding, suspecting an allusion to the 'cutpurse', the breed of thieves that exercised their skills in the midst of Shakespeare's audience (Scragg, 15–16).

Around Twelfth Night

The impelling need to interpret the play has not been limited to cracking the codes of such local puzzles. There has been a more general interpretative anxiety about what is really going on in

Illyria (itself an enigmatic venue). The main symptom of such anxiety has been the frequently expressed urge to decipher the comedy's main title, despite Pepys's peremptory sentence that it is 'not related at all to the name or day'. A title that is not directly descriptive of the main action (unlike, say, *The Taming of the Shrew*), of the main characters (*The Two Gentlemen of Verona*), of place (*The Merchant of Venice*), of dominant atmosphere (*A Midsummer Night's Dream*) or even overall moral (*Measure for Measure*, *All's Well That Ends Well*), becomes inevitably a happy hermeneutic hunting ground. The meanings given to 'Twelfth Night' tend to reflect the prevailing cultural concerns of the time. Interpretative emphasis has thus shifted over the decades from an early concern with topical and biographical issues, such as the occasion of the 'original' Twelfth Night – the date of the supposed first performance, together with the related identity of Elizabethan personages supposedly alluded to in the dialogue (Hotson; see pp. 93–4) – to a more socio–cultural interest in Twelfth Night as synonym of carnivalesque revelry.

The association of the play with carnival was first suggested in 1867 by the French critic E. Montegut, who observed that 'the title recalls one of those festivals which were most dear to our forebears', in which, as in carnival, 'it was the world turned upside down, a rational hierarchy topsy-turvy, authority created by chance, and the more grotesque the surprise, the merrier the festival' (*SC*, 1.554). This line of interpretation was taken up by Enid Welsford in her 1935 study of the fool: 'Shakespeare transforms into poetry the quintessence of the Saturnalia . . . Illyria is a country permeated with the spirit of the Feast of Fools, where identities are confused, 'uncivil rule' applauded, cakes and ale successfully defended, and no harm done' (Welsford, 572). Such readings culminate in C.L. Barber's seminal 1959 volume, which affirms that '*Twelfth Night* deals with the sort of folly which the title points to, the folly of misrule' (Barber, 248) – that is, the revels associated in early modern England with the last day of the Christmas season, and in particular with the election of a 'Festus' or 'Lord of Misrule' to preside over the maskings, interludes, music, song and other forms of merrymaking. The appointment of a winter festive mock king on 6 January had pagan roots, evoking the anarchic spirit of the ancient Saturnalia or Kalendae (S. Billington; Horner).

Twelfth Night owes a good deal to this saturnalian tradition, most apparently in the scenes of revelry echoing the feasting and especially the communal drinking (traditionally from the wassail bowl) associated with 6 January celebrations. The affinities may run deeper, however. One of the central events of the celebrations was disguising or mumming, later transformed into the court masque, which survived as a Twelfth Night event until the fall of the monarchy in 1642 (see Hutton, *Stations*, 11–22). In this sense, Viola disguised – at the court of Orsino – may be as much a participant in the rites as the noisy revellers. It is also possible to detect in the comedy's frequent acts of donation – Olivia's ring and miniature for Cesario, the repeated tips for Feste, etc. – an allusion to the Twelfth Day custom of bearing gifts (deriving from the presents of the three magi for the infant Christ). The question of which character, if any, represents what the historian John Stow termed the 'master of merry disports' remains an open one. Feste is nominally and professionally closest to the role of Festus (from which his name may derive), but it is Sir Toby who seems to preside over the scenes of 'disports' or misrule. Perhaps we should not exclude the candidacy of Maria, author of the comic revenge plot against Malvolio, especially since there had been a well-known historical winter queen in the person of Mary Fleming, who reigned on Twelfth Day in 1563 (Hutton, *Stations*, 106–7). It may be that misrule in the comedy has a collective master-mistress.

The saturnalian reading of title and play gains force from the oppositional presence of a 'Puritan' steward. Protestant fundamentalists reserved special bile for Christmas misrule as a mode of spectacle, at which, in the words of the Protestant hack Philip Stubbes (whose attitude resembles Malvolio's disdain towards the revellers), 'the foolish people they look, they stare, they laugh, they fleer . . . to see these godly pageants solemnized in this sort' (Barber, 28). The post-Reformation censorship of revelry seems to be re-enacted in Malvolio's interruption of the festivities in 2.3: 'Have you no wit, manners nor honesty but to gabble like tinkers at this time of night? Do ye make an alehouse of my lady's house?' (86–8). Sir Toby's riposte – 'Dost thou think because thou art virtuous there shall be no more cakes and ale?' (2.3.112–13) – may have particular resonance, beyond the generic defence of the right to party. Stubbes directed a violent diatribe against 'Church-ales'. As for 'cakes', the medieval European Twelfth Night cake had been imported into England late in Elizabeth's reign by way of a ritual electoral system, namely the baking of a coin in a cake and awarding the title of 'bean king' (a variant of Festus) to the man who found it in his slice (Hutton, *Rise*, 110). This practice likewise met with disapproval from the nonconformists.

If the censorship of Twelfth Night revelry had historical resonances for Shakespeare's audience in general, the struggle between festivity and sobriety, or misrule and order, may have had specific piquancy for John Manningham and other members of the Middle Temple audience in 1602. Election of a Lord of Misrule had been expressly banned at the Inns of Court since 1580. There had, however, been notorious transgressions against the ban and exemplary punishments, such as the temporary suspension of Richard Martin and others from the Inns of Court for 'making outcries, forcibly breaking open chambers in the night, [and] levying money as the Lord of Misrule's rent' (Hopwood, 1.308). At the same time, the comedy may have recalled for its audience recent and authorized Twelfth Night events at the Middle Temple such as the entertainment of 1597–9, the *Prince d'Amour*, which satirized the folly of lovers (S. Billington, 36). The Middle Temple lawyer Anthony Arlidge goes so far as to argue that *Twelfth Night* was written expressly as a Temple entertainment (see p. 95).

The ideological implications of the saturnalian reading may not be as simple or as neutral as they seem, however. If the comedy is taken to re-enact the century-long struggle between the old 'Merry England', with its vestiges of Christianized pagan ritual, and the reformation of English customs and manners, then the punishment of the 'Puritan' Malvolio looks like revenge comedy of a particular historical and cultural kind. The play's comic plot becomes the expression of nostalgia for a pre-Reformation world, part of a late Elizabethan phenomenon that the social historian Ronald Hutton describes as 'a sentimental reaction in favour of old-style popular merry-making among writers and their patrons' (Hutton, *Rise*, 152).

From a broader – and arguably less conservative – anthropological perspective, the play's festivities and confusions may be seen as part of the movement towards social and individual renewal. This is the 'natural perspective' proposed by Northrop Frye, who detects in *Twelfth Night* and other romantic comedies a tripartite movement from an 'anticomic society' which is 'opposed to the comic drive' (Frye, 73: Orsino's melancholy, Olivia's bereavement, and so on), through a 'second period of confusion and sexual licence' (76: Viola's disguise, the revels), towards the final phase of 'the discovery of identity' (78), which coincides with the renewing force of spring. Here 'Twelfth Night' becomes a seasonal – and specifically 'solstitial' – indicator (121), associated initially with winter and death but looking forward to the later festivities anticipated by Fabian: 'More matter for a May morning' (3.4.138).

Twelfth Night, however, was not exclusively or even primarily the occasion for carnivalesque anarchy or solstitial feasting. It was above all a significant date in the church calendar, the Epiphany, feast of the revelation of Christ. Various commentators have traced the presence of specifically Christian themes. Thus Barbara Lewalski elects Viola and Sebastian as comic types of the incarnate Christ, in the guise of two miraculously delivered outside agents who will help to cure the inhabitants of Illyria. Somewhat analogously, Hassel (77–93) classifies the comedy as part of a specific performance genre, one of a number of early modern epiphany plays (together with Lily's *Campaspe* and *Midas*,

Fletcher's *The Faithful Shepherdess*, and so on). He also argues for the pervasiveness of epiphanic topics, notably that of revelation itself, best expressed in the double recognition (Viola–Sebastian) of the comedy's denouement.

The Epiphany is not the only church festival associated with *Twelfth Night* and its reception history. The two earliest performances mentioned in diaries are dated 2 February, at Candlemas, feast of the purification of Mary. This was a festival of enlightenment, traditionally associated with the bearing of candles in a procession (a tradition again suppressed after the Reformation). Some commentators have seen the comedy's emphasis on the light–dark opposition – and especially the 'purification' of Malvolio in the dark room – as an exploration of the message of the church festival (with the implication that Manningham's Middle Temple performance may have been the first, thereby rendering the play's title deceptive: see Hassel, 94–8). Wishing to stretch what is already an arguable point, the agency of Maria – or 'Marian', as Sir Toby calls her at 2.3.13 – might be linked to the exquisitely Marian devotions of the feast (notably in the form of the 'purifying' of Malvolio).

With regard to the comedy's more explicit religious themes, a long-debated issue has been how seriously – especially in the context of nostalgia for pre-Reformation customs – we are to take Malvolio's supposed Puritanism. Joseph Hunter was the first commentator, in 1845, to see Malvolio as a 'grand attack' on Puritanism, part of 'a systematic design of holding [it] up to ridicule' (397); some later critics have concurred, although in 1884 William Archer objected that 'he is not a Puritan but a Philistine' (Archer, 277). The internal evidence concerning the steward's radical Protestant allegiances is contradictory. Maria first makes the accusation – 'Marry, sir, sometimes he is a kind of Puritan' (2.3.136), provoking in Sir Andrew the impulse to 'beat him like a dog' (137) – and then withdraws it a few lines later (142–3) by denying the steward any ideological coherence: 'The devil a Puritan that he is, or anything constantly but a time-pleaser'. The suspicion remains in the air, however, re-emerging later in Sir Andrew's odd – and uncharacteristically well-informed – allusion to a specific sect of Protestant radicals: 'I had as lief be a Brownist as a politician' (3.2.30).

Some critics have uncovered in the play not merely an opposition between festivity and censorship but what Richard Wilson terms a 'dialectic between Carnival and Lent, Catholic and Protestant, or secrecy and disclosure' (R. Wilson, 251). Wilson finds support in the comedy for his thesis that Shakespeare was a 'secret' Catholic, noting, for example, the presence of pre-Reformation habits such as swearing 'by Saint Anne, and ginger' (*TN* 2.3.114; R. Wilson, 150). Whether or not one subscribes to Wilson's claim that 'Shakespeare's Illyria maps the religious politics of Elizabethan London' (279) – or to such specific historical decodings as Sir Topas being a parodic version of the Jesuit Henry Garnet, or his 'Master Parson' (4.2.15) being an allusion to the Jesuit priest Robert Parsons – it is true that the comedy seems at certain points to evoke the pre-Reformation church calendar, through what Steve Sohmer terms 'calendrical markers' (Sohmer, 199). These include not only Feste's swearing by St Anne but, perhaps more significantly, the number of characters bearing the names of saints, especially of early saints associated with winter feast days, as if by seasonal association with the Epiphany. Thus the play has its Sebastian, named after the saint condemned to death by the emperor Diocletian ('an Illyrian': Sohmer, 206) around AD 288 in Rome, whose feast day is 20 January; its Fabian, from St Fabianus, who died in 250, again in Rome, and who shares the same feast day as Sebastian; its Valentine, from the legendary martyr and patron saint of lovers, who likewise died in Rome in the third century (feast day 14 February); an Antonio, perhaps from Antonios, religious hermit and one of the founders of monasticism, who died in 356 (feast day 17 January); not to mention Andrew, named after one of the Twelve Apostles and the patron saint of Scotland (feast day 30 November), whose name, ironically for the character who bears it, means 'manly' in Greek.

The overall message of these modes of interrogating the text may be that *Twelfth Night* is a play that promises an epiphany – a secret or encoded transcendental signified waiting to be revealed – but strategically withholds it. Hence the search for a semantic key to open up the comedy's supposed mysteries. The danger is the one indicated by Feste and underlined by Montaigne in Florio's 1603 translation, namely over-interpretation: 'There's more adoe to enterprete interpretations, than to interpret things . . . We doe but enter-glose [inter-gloss] ourselves' (Montaigne, 602). But the risk of interpreting interpretations – a risk doubtless incurred in this edition – is one that the comedy itself challenges us to run, and it cannot and should not put an end to speculative herme-neutic readings. Inevitably, and rightly, spectators, critics and even editors continue to find in the play what they will.

A very opal: the play of perspective

In another of his illuminating – or indeed epiphanic – observations, Feste makes fun of the violent mood-changes of Duke Orsino: 'the tailor make thy doublet of changeable taffeta, for thy mind is a very opal' (2.4.73–5). The clown's double metaphor incisively targets Orsino's changeable humours under the pressure of desire: the contrasting tones of the warp and woof of taffeta (shot silk) produce, like the opal stone, an iridescent effect of colour change when viewed from different angles. At the same time, the clown's opalescent image is a powerful trope for the comedy as a whole, demonstrating once again that Feste is the most astute commenta-tor on the play of which he is part. It points to the central question of the arbitrariness of desire and the tyranny of the passions (see pp. 54–5). It introduces the important issue of materiality – of the fabrics, cloths and clothing, jewels and other prestigious objects that make up an important part of the comedy's own texture (see pp. 42–7). But also, and more crucially, it figures what is perhaps the most intriguing characteristic of *Twelfth Night* as a dramatic construct, namely – to coin an oxymoron – its constant mutabil-ity under the play of alternative perspectives. Such perspectival iridescence is doubtless one of the main reasons for the multiple interpretations to which the comedy has been subjected, but it is at the same time a vital dramatic principle.

The play of perspective involves in the first instance inter-personal relations between the various characters in the comedy, relations constructed on a series of parallels between the different characters' situations and traits in a prismatic process of multiple mirroring. Such parallels are strongly implied by the extraordinary number of anagrammatic names within the List of Roles, suggesting that the borders between one role and the next are uncertain and unstable, their identities overlapping. 'Viola' and 'Olivia' are virtual anagrams, and this in turn reflects a complex network of parallels and reciprocal identifications between the two female co-protagonists: they have in common a dead father, a 'dead' brother (and hence an initial state of bereavement) and unrequited love (a characteristic they both share with Orsino), as well as such qualities as sexual attractiveness (and attractedness), independence, wit, eloquence, playfulness and a particular partiality towards Feste's fooling. Not by chance is Viola at the outset attracted to the countess through resemblance or identification – 'O that I served that lady' (1.2.38) – just as later Olivia is attracted to her own 'reflection' in Viola-as-Cesario.

The game of the anagrammatic name suggests likewise a negatively specular relationship between the two women and Malvolio, whose own name contains both of theirs but at the same time opposes them through the pejorative combining form 'mal': if he has in common with them a form of frustrated 'desire', he is their negative image on all other fronts, resisting, for example, all forms of playfulness, especially Feste's fooling.

The comedy is characterized by other modes of parallelism and doubling between characters, notably between Feste and others. The clown and Cesario both act as go-betweens, moving between the courts of Olivia and Orsino. Feste, moreover, takes over Viola-as-Cesario's announced role as court singer, while, as we have seen, Feste's part as spectator in the letter scene is taken over by Fabian, appearing from nowhere. In his professional role as truth-sayer, Feste becomes a specular figure, a deforming mirror in which the duke and the countess can see themselves, should they wish to do so. His ventriloquism permits him to double as himself and as 'Sir Topas' in the dark room scene. 'Sir Topas' is another specular figure: his name is in part a deformation of Sir Toby, whose vengeful role in the punishing of Malvolio he takes over, while also acting as a glass reflecting the 'madness' of the imprisoned steward.

The theme of the double finds its fullest expression, of course, in the relationship between Viola and Sebastian. *Twelfth Night* is Shakespeare's second play with twins, his first and only play with opposite-sex twins. If his earlier 'twin' comedy, *Comedy of Errors*, exploited physical similarity almost exclusively for purposes of farce, *Twelfth Night* makes much more of the intersubjective psychological potential of the device. Viola's first thoughts in the play are dedicated to her twin, suggesting the priority of bereavement as a motivating force for her decision to cross-dress. Indeed, one of the primary aims of her disguise must be to keep her 'dead' brother alive, by way of a sort of talismanic magic. As Cesario, she ceases merely to resemble Sebastian, in order to 'become' him; she is not merely his twin but his *doppelgänger*. This process of identification is rendered explicit in one of the comedy's extraordinary moments of psychological awareness; Viola-as-Cesario, on hearing Antonio name her brother, confesses to having created and embodied his literal mirror-image: 'He named Sebastian. I my brother know / Yet living in my glass . . . / For him I imitate' (3.4.376–80). It is her ability to 'imitate' Sebastian's dress and behaviour that explains in part Viola's success in taking on a male role; it also explains the surprising ease with which Sebastian in turn substitutes Cesario in Olivia's affections: he is taking his 'rightful' place, usurped until now by Viola. Cesario is a point of converging identity between Viola and Sebastian.

The doubling of Viola and Sebastian as Cesario is at the centre of the play's criss-cross weave of intersecting desires and interconnecting plots, wreaking havoc among the other characters: Viola-as-Cesario desires Orsino and is desired by Olivia; Olivia in turn is supposedly desired by Orsino, courted at a distance by Sir Andrew and more directly by Malvolio; Sebastian takes the place of his twin Viola-as-Cesario as object of Olivia's desire, which he reciprocates, while Orsino's desire is redirected towards Viola-as-Cesario, and so on. Viola-as-Cesario is a 'blank' (2.4.110), a space into which others project their desires and their own identity anxieties. The result is what the German Romantic critic, August Schlegel, termed 'ideal follies', whereby Cesario is merely the agent rather than the cause of arbitrary and self-deceiving desire, which resides fully in the mind of the beholder: 'the proud Olivia is entangled by the modest and intriguing messenger of the duke, in which she is far from suspecting a disguised rival, and at last, by a second deception, takes the brother for a sister' (Schlegel, 2.175; see also Burwick, 172–3).

The comedy's most slippery conceptual terrain is the definition of gender identity. As Northrop Frye comments, 'In *Twelfth Night* the discovery of sexual identity is combined with the identical-twin theme: Orsino and Olivia are languishing in melancholy until out of the sea comes an ambiguous figure "that can sing both high and low", who eventually becomes male to Olivia and female to Orsino' (Frye, 83). Viola-as-Cesario represents not so much an androgen, half male and half female, as an indeterminate middle ground where the genders of the boy actor playing the role, the female character and the male (or 'eunuch') disguise are superimposed: 'What I am and what I would are as secret as maidenhead' (1.5.209–10), she announces cryptically, alluding to the sexuality that she disguises (as Cesario), that she feigns (as actor) and that she protects (as the virginal Viola).

Viola's cross-dressing and thereby doubling as her own twin have, in Catherine Belsey's words, the effect of disrupting sexual difference: 'Of all Shakespeare's comedies', she affirms, 'it is perhaps *Twelfth Night* which takes the most remarkable risks with the identity of its central figure' (Belsey, 185). She goes on to ask who is speaking in Viola-as-Cesario's dialogue with Orsino in 2.4: 'The answer is neither Viola nor Cesario, but a speaker who at this moment occupies a place which is not precisely masculine or feminine, where the notion of identity itself is disrupted to display a difference within subjectivity, and the singularity which resides in *this* difference' (187). Marjorie Garber goes further, claiming that Viola's cross-dressing 'offers a challenge to easy notions of binarity, putting into question the categories of "female" and "male" whether they are considered essential or constructed, biological or cultural' (Garber, 17). Indeed, Viola's transvestism questions all categorial distinctions and oppositions, creating 'a space of possibility structuring and confounding culture: the disruptive element that intervenes, not just as a category crisis of male and female, but the crisis of category itself' (17). Thus Malvolio's description of Cesario as an unclassifiable liminal figure suggests a category crisis with regard not only to gender but to age: 'Not yet old enough for a man, nor young enough for a boy . . . 'Tis with him in standing water between boy and man' (1.5.152–5).

As a result of these shared problems of perspective, a central cognitive and thematic role in the comedy comes to be played by perception. Observers are led by events to doubt the perceptual and sensorial data they receive, giving rise to a widespread instability regarding the reading of the world of the play. Since the effects of disguise and 'doubling' are mainly optical – and since, in any case, the theatre operates in a primarily visual dimension – the major emphasis throughout is on ocular perception. There are a great number of self-dramatizing or self-doubting references by the play's various perceivers to 'mine eyes', beginning with Orsino's rhapsodic 'O, when mine eyes did see Olivia first', in the opening scene (1.1.18). Olivia herself confesses that Cesario's qualities 'creep in at mine eyes' (1.5.290), and admits her consequent 'fear to find / Mine eye too great a flatterer for my mind' (301–2). The destabilizing impact of the gaze is confirmed by the object of her adoring perception, Cesario, who recounts how 'methought her eyes had lost her tongue' (2.2.20), while Cesario's double, Sebastian, surprised by Olivia's amorous effusions, is led to doubt the reliability of his own perceptual data: 'I am ready to distrust mine eyes' (4.3.13).

This visual discourse reaches its climax in the final scene, with the simultaneous presence of both twins on stage, an event described in terms of optical illusion: 'One face, one voice, one habit and two persons: / A natural perspective, that is and is not' (5.1.212–13). Orsino is alluding to one of the instruments used to create optical 'special effects' (including those employed on the baroque stage, for example in Italy): either anamorphic mirrors or lenses that created distorted or multiple images, or, on the contrary, a perspective glass, namely a tube with faceted lens making multiple images appear as one. There are two complementary conceits involved here: the anamorphic doubling of Cesario into two identical selves, or alternatively the reduction of two separate objects or identities to a single, albeit repeated, image. The choice between the two is a question, precisely, of perspective.

A further variation on the specular and perspectival theme is the issue of self-mirroring, and hence of narcissism. In her celebrated defence of Feste and his verbal fooling in response to Malvolio's severe critique, Olivia puts her steward in his place with a devastating diagnosis of his major vice: 'O, you are sick of self-love, Malvolio' (1.5.86). In the early modern period 'self-love' was primarily a moral malaise consisting in an excess of *amour propre* or self-esteem, but the term could take on a stronger and more literal meaning, namely affective or even erotic self-infatuation. It is the pathology of which the poet accuses the Fair Youth in Sonnet 1 ('But thou, contracted to thine own bright eyes, / Feed'st thy light's flame with self-substantial fuel') and himself in Sonnet 62 ('Sin of self-love possesseth all mine eye / And all my soul, and all my every part'). That Malvolio's self-preoccupation may go beyond the realm of esteem and into the sphere of full-blown narcissism is suggested by other observers. In a play much concerned, as we have seen, with mirror-images, it is significant that he is caught *in flagrante* by Maria in an admiring rapport with his own reflection: 'He has been yonder i'the sun practising behaviour to his own shadow this half-hour' (2.5.14–15). Maria's anatomy of his inability to resist himself and her use of this trait as a trap against him are pitiless: 'the best persuaded of himself, so crammed, as he thinks, with excellencies that it is his grounds of faith that all that look on him love him, and on that vice in him will my revenge find notable cause to work' (2.3.144–8). Malvolio is, in Fabian's words, 'a rare turkey-cock' – by antonomasia a foolishly self-loving beast – who 'jets under his advanced plumes' (2.5.28–9).

If the sin of self-love is a psychopathology in the comedy, it risks becoming an epidemic, as Peter Gill's 1974 RSC production of the play suggested, with its outsize portrait of Narcissus dominating the set (see Fig. 4). D.J. Palmer ('Echo') has shown that Narcissus is the play's governing Ovidian deity (on the play's debt to Ovid, see also Carroll, *Met.*, 80–102, and Bate, 144–51). Other characters are valid potential targets for Olivia's awesome put-down, including, perhaps, Olivia herself, who is not only hermetically self-enclosed in the opening act but becomes infatuated with what is in effect a mirror-image, in the form of the disguised Viola. The leading candidate, however, is without doubt Olivia's supposed admirer, the self-advertising and self-dramatizing Orsino. The duke's (and the play's) opening rhetorical performance is a virtual confession of auto-erotic fixation. Not by chance his effusions on the spirit of love that 'falls into abatement and low price' (1.1.13) recall the complaint of Ovid's Narcissus that 'my plenty makes me poore' (Ovid, *Met.*, 3.587, 38^r; see Palmer, 'Echo', 73). Apparently rhapsodizing on his unrequited passion for Olivia, Orsino ends up declaring – by way of an allusion to another myth, that of Acteon, torn to pieces by Diana's hounds – the real object of his desire, namely himself: 'And my desires, like fell and cruel hounds, / E'er since pursue me' (1.1.21–2). In the same scene he imagines himself, in a fantasy of political and sexual imperialism, as absolute monarch of Olivia's body and soul (and, presumably, fortune) on the Malvolio-like grounds of his erotic irresistibility: 'These sovereign thrones, are all supplied, and filled

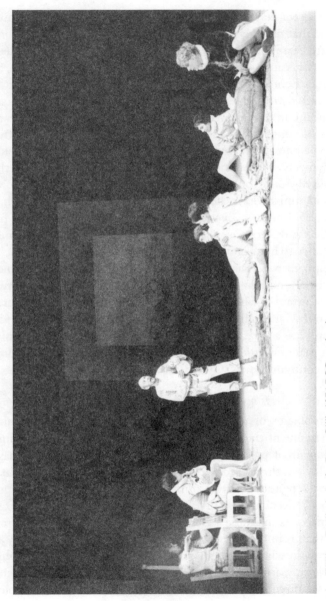

4   William Dudley's set for Peter Gill's 1974 RSC production

/ Her sweet perfections with one self king!' (1.1.37–8). It might be said that the only characters to save themselves from the condition are Feste and Viola; as Jonathan Bate observes, 'Viola redeems the play because she proves to be selfless, not selfish, in love. She becomes Echo instead of Narcissus' (Bate, 148).

Narcissistic self-concern is one of the forms taken by self-deception in the comedy, and is thus a mode of moral and social blindness. It is also one of the prime causes and effects of foolishness: Malvolio, Orsino and even Olivia make fools of themselves in failing to perceive the illusory nature of their supposed desire, only nominally directed outside of themselves. Each is punished for the 'sin' of self-love: Malvolio through the letter exposing his *amour propre*; Orsino through Olivia's fully justified indifference; Olivia herself through Cesario's caustic resistance to her advances, whereby, in René Girard's words, 'the triumphant narcissism of a woman is overturned by the indifference of another woman in masculine disguise' (p. 106). What is less certain is whether these punishments represent a therapy – even if Maria calls the letter for Malvolio a 'physic' (2.3.155) – and still less a cure, for the pathology, despite Girard's optimistic claim that '*Twelfth Night* suggests the reversibility of all narcissistic configurations' (Girard, 110).

'Tis my picture: deciphering visual images

The problems of perspective and interpretation are particularly acute in one of the comedy's most recurrent visual fields, namely the domain of pictures, paintings and other iconographic images. Feste's 'We three' scene – which is presented as, and actually quotes, a 'picture' – is part of the comedy's insistent concern with forms of visual and graphic representation, including, for example, maps, as in Maria's gibe about Malvolio's face having 'more lines than is in the new map' at 3.2.74–5 (see p. 73). The play also abounds in what we might term optical allusions to Renaissance iconology, particularly emblems, i.e. 'enigmatic' images which (like 'We three') are interpreted through a verbal caption. Emblems were a popular and widely circulating art form, and as such readily recognizable by Shakespeare's audience; they were a model of powerful interaction between word and image, and thus had close affinities with the stage. Several of Shakespeare's Ovidian allusions were illustrated and interpreted in the most prestigious Renaissance emblem book, Andrea Alciato's highly influential *Emblemata* of 1531: Actaeon (Emblem 52), Arion (Emblem 90), Narcissus (Emblem 69, labelled 'Philautia', self-love: see Fig. 5), and so on. The strategic evocation of emblems is most evident in another explicitly pictorial moment in the comedy, Cesario's

5 'Philautia' ('self-love': see 1.5.86), from Andrea Alciato, *Book of Emblems* (1531)

description of his 'sister': 'She sat like Patience on a monument, / Smiling at grief' (2.4.113–14). Cesario appears to be referring to a relatively 'high' public art – an allegorical figure on a memorial or funerary monument – but is probably alluding instead to an emblem from Cesare Ripa's *Iconologia* (1593), which represents Patience as a woman sitting on a stone and bearing a yoke on her shoulders, her feet placed on thorns (see Fig. 6). Cesario takes up Ripa's 'pazienza', but reinterprets it as a sign not of feminine submission but of heroic self-denial, possibly leading to death (hence the funeral monument).

The emblem game may involve a moment of explicitly theatrical iconography. The captain's Ovidian description of Arion on the dolphin's back (1.2.14), was a favourite topic not only of the emblem books but of painted scenery, especially in opera, since Arion was a symbol of the magical and redemptive powers of music. He presided, for example, over the operatic spectacles celebrating the 1589 wedding between Ferdinando de' Medici and Christina of Lorraine at the Pitti Palace in Florence (Fig. 7 shows Buontalenti's set design, where Arion is in the bottom right-hand corner).The allusion may thus be cryptically self-celebratory on the part of one of Shakespeare's most musical plays.

Twelfth Night's most self-conscious iconographic moment involves Olivia's highly theatrical self-revelation to Cesario; playfully but seductively unveiling, she figures the gesture as a sort of vernissage: 'But we will draw the curtain and show you the picture. [*Unveils.*] Look you, sir, such a one I was this present. Is't not well done?' (1.5.226–8). Drawing the curtain has theatrical connotations – evoking, perhaps, the fabric covering the stage doors of the Elizabethan stage – but Olivia's primary reference is to the dust cover protecting a painting. This is something of a standing joke in the comedy, as in Sir Toby's feigned admiration for Sir Andrew's dancing talents: 'Wherefore have these gifts a curtain before 'em? Are they like to take dust, like Mistress Mall's picture?' (1.3.120–2). Like Feste, Olivia figures herself

PATIENZA.

6 'Patience on a monument' (2.4.114), from Cesare Ripa's *Iconologia* (1593)

overtly as a painting, but here the reference is to a 'high' artistic form – portraiture – which had a somewhat ambiguous status, being a more or less public art representing, at the same time, the private subjectivity of the sitter. Hence the power of Olivia's gesture in revealing or publicizing herself at the moment of greatest intimacy, her private bereavement.

7   Arion and the dolphin: Bernardo Buontalenti's set design for an intermezzo celebrating the 1589 wedding between Ferdinando de' Medici and Christina of Lorraine at the Pitti Palace in Florence

8 'Such a one I was this present' (1.5.227): Salomon Mesdach's portrait of
Adriana Van Nesse, with the inscription 'Aetatis suae, 19, Anno 1611' (at the
age of 19, in the year 1611)

Olivia goes on to interpret her own portrait: 'such a one I was
this present', namely, this is what I looked like at the time
the portrait was painted (i.e. this very instant). Here she is
rather cryptically evoking the inscription frequently found on
Renaissance portraits, *aetatis suae* (of her or his age: see Fig. 8),

playing on her double presence as painter and subject of her self-portrait, whereby the time of composing and the time of looking at the picture coincide. There is a certain poignancy to Olivia's speaking and breathing picture, since she is exhibiting precisely the fact that, unlike her mourned brother, she is still alive. She plays on such intimacy later, when she presents Cesario with a literal portrait (''tis my picture', 3.4.203), a miniature set in jewels so that her represented body in the picture can be in close contact with Cesario's 'real' body.

The pictorial qualities of *Twelfth Night* have not gone unnoticed by painters, who have often represented the very 'picture' scenes in question: Olivia's unveiling (Edmund Blair Leighton's painting, Fig. 9) and Viola's monument (Johann Heinrich Füssli's watercolour panels, Fig. 10).

9   'Is't not well done?' (1.5.228): Olivia unveiling, by Edmund Blair Leighton, 1888)

Changeable taffeta: materials and materiality

Orsino's emblematic 'doublet of changeable taffeta' (2.4.74) can be taken literally as part of the comedy's obsessive discourse of materials and material goods. Indeed, although it is traditionally seen as a romantic, even somewhat ethereal comedy, *Twelfth*

10 'Viola' by Johann Heinrich Füssli, *c.* 1777

Night is in many ways the most material of Shakespeare's plays, uniquely concerned with cloth and clothing, dress and dressing, precious and common objects, architecture, furniture, receptacles, tools, and all the practical and physical aspects – or what Olivia calls 'every particle and utensil' (1.5.238) – of everyday life.

Since the action takes place between two households, both indoors and outdoors, there is much concern with domestic architecture, particularly with reference to Olivia's house and estate: from her 'orchard' or garden (3.2.6, 3.4.218) with its gates (1.5.95, 113, 122, 192, 260), 'garden door' (3.1.90), walls and walks (2.5.14), to its interior spaces: the chamber that she waters daily with her tears (1.1.28), the room where Malvolio is enclosed (4.2: the 'dark room' scene) and especially the kitchen (2.3: the 'kitchen' scene). Even erotic fantasies are worked out in terms of domestic structures, as in Maria's joke about bringing Sir Andrew's hand to the buttery-bar or pantry (her breasts, 1.3.68; see Fig. 11). Malvolio's social and sexual reverie, instead, is figured in terms of status furniture: he dreams of lounging in a canopied chair of state (2.5.42) and of getting up from his day-bed, where the sleeping Olivia lies (2.5.45–6). In a more satirical furniture fantasy, Sir Toby imagines Sir Andrew's sheet (of writing paper) fitting the enormous and legendary bed of Ware (3.2.45; see Fig. 12), with a possible allusion to the sexual union with Olivia that Aguecheek, like Malvolio, will never enjoy.

Household implements abound. Within the confines of Olivia's kitchen, Sir Toby's favourite activity introduces a world of drinking receptacles, from his 'unfilled can' or empty tankard (2.3.6) to his 'stoup' of wine (2.3.13). Being the most earthly of the play's characters, his speech is littered with material tropes: he imagines Sir Andrew's hair being curled by tongs (1.3.93–6) and – in another grotesque sexual fantasy – being spun off by a 'housewife' or hussy with a distaff between her legs (1.3.98–100). Elsewhere, the trunk in which, presumably, Viola's maiden weeds are kept (5.1.251) has its own stage history (see 1.2.0.1n.) and reappears in

11 Buttery-bar (1.3.68)

Antonio's metaphor of Sebastian's 'false' virtues as 'empty trunks'
(3.4.367).

Other everyday objects fill the play's discursive spaces. In
a comedy in which letters play such a prominent part, there
is a natural concern with writing materials: sheets of paper,
'gall' (ink coloured with oak–gall dye: 3.2.46), the 'goose-pen'
or goose-feather quill (alluding to Sir Andrew's goose-like
cowardice: 3.2.47). The comedy's interest in play is reflected in

41

[*The Bed of Ware*

12 The bed of Ware (3.2.45)

allusions to games and their material parts, from the 'cherry-pit', involving the rolling of cherry stones into a small hole (with probable sexual double entendre: 3.4.113), to the 'philosophers' table' with its double board ('*Primo*, *secundo*, *tertio*', 5.1.33). Such domestic material consciousness extends outwards to familiar community games and objects: the parish whipping-top used as a warming-up exercise (1.3.40; see Fig. 13); the painted 'sheriff's post' on which proclamations were affixed (1.5.144; see Fig. 14), and so on.

The comedy's materiality is best expressed, however, in its intense preoccupation with cloth and clothes. As in no other Shakespeare play, material – the textile, weave and colour of fabric – determines not only distinctions between characters and their

[*Parish Top.*]

13 Parish top (1.3.40)

respective social status but events themselves, as Malvolio discovers to his cost. As Oscar Wilde observes, 'Even small details of dress, such as the colour of a major-domo's stockings, . . . become in Shakespeare's hands points of actual dramatic importance, and by some of them the action of the play in question is conditioned absolutely' (Wilde, 173). There is in consequence a widespread concern with fabrics and textiles, both literal and metaphorical: from the plain, straight and unworked flax of Sir Andrew's hair,

14 Sheriff's posts (1.5.144)

waiting to be broken and spun by spinsters (1.3.98–100), to more sophisticated worked fabrics such as the transparent cypress crepe that 'hides', or fails to hide, Olivia's heart (3.1.119–20), to luxurious cloths like taffeta, damask silk (2.4.112) and velvet (2.5.45).

The comedy's discourse of fabric echoes the language of the sumptuary laws in force in Elizabethan England, designed to prevent excessive luxury and expenditure and especially to regulate dress codes according to social class, with the additional purpose of stemming the increasing affectation and effeminacy of English male fashions. The 1574 sumptuary statute decrees, among other vetoes, that 'None shall wear in his apparel . . . Velvet in gowns, coats, or other uttermost garments . . . except men of the degrees above mentioned, barons' sons, knights and gentlemen.' Thus Malvolio's fantasy of social promotion in which he fancies himself luxuriously garbed in a 'branched velvet gown' (2.5.44–5) represents an imaginary sumptuary transgression, taking him into the forbidden material realms of the gentry.

One of the most exclusive and frequently mentioned materials in the sumptuary laws is silk – together with satin, taffeta or damask – presumably because its glossy sheen bespoke both luxury and dubious masculinity: 'None shall wear satin, damask, silk, camlet, or taffeta . . . except the degrees and persons above mentioned' (*Proclamation*). Here Feste's taffeta metaphor may take on other resonances: Duke Orsino is the play's one male authorized to wear luxury fabrics (and in many productions he is portrayed as showily decked out in silk). The clown's allusion to his silken doublet may, however, imply excess and effeminacy, of dress as of mind, his 'changeable' moods being a traditionally 'feminine' trait. There may in addition be theatrical implications involved. One of the complaints of Protestant reformers against the theatre was the players' wearing of the costumes of their betters, since the companies received clothing from their noble patrons, including silk and velvet gowns. Feste's phrase 'changeable taffeta' (2.4.74) appears twice in the diary of the theatrical impresario Philip Henslowe. From this viewpoint, Orsino is just a dressed-up player like the rest.

The language of cloth also conditions the comedy's discourse of gender. The Elizabethan 'None shall wear' refrain, applied to the ladies, specifies 'any velvet, tufted taffeta, satin . . . except wives of barons, knights of the order, or councillors' ladies, and gentlewomen of the privy chamber and bed chamber, and the maids of honor' (*Proclamation*). In her semi-autobiographical 'Patience on a monument' story in 2.4, Viola-as-Cesario tells Orsino how the young girl 'let concealment . . . Feed on her damask cheek' (2.4.111–12). This material metaphor can be interpreted as an allusion to Viola's 'real' sex, by way of reference to her own silk-like feminine skin, or to her 'real' social class as a member of the damask-wearing gentry. In any case Orsino, as usual, fails to get the point.

It is not surprising that a comedy whose action is dominated by different forms of 'transgressive' dressing-up – Viola's cross-dressing, Malvolio's cross-gartering and yellow hose, Feste's disguising as a priest – is also the Shakespearean play most obsessively preoccupied with dress and with dressing at large. References to modes of dress are legion: to the clown and his 'gaskins' (wide breeches) and their 'points' (laces) in Maria's joke (1.5.21–3); to Antonio and his remembered 'sea-cap' (3.4.327); to Malvolio and his fashion accessories: his pocket watch (2.5.57) and imaginary 'rich jewel' (2.5.58). Even the manly Sebastian is clothes-conscious, apologizing for being 'grossly clad' (as, presumably, is Viola-as-Cesario). It is thanks above all to clothing that Viola is able to imitate and so 'save' her brother: 'he went / Still in this fashion, colour, ornament' (3.4.378–9).

Clothing serves as a means of self-concealment, not only in Viola's 'eunuch' disguise but also in the veil that Olivia uses to hide her face from Cesario (1.5.161) or the transparent 'cypress' silk that she says hides, or fails to hide, her heart, as opposed to a more opaque 'bosom' (the part of the dress covering the breast, 3.1.119). Clothing is a sign of status or professional role, as in Malvolio's steward's garb and chain of office, or Feste's motley. Such livery becomes, however, intimately linked to personal identity. Malvolio in yellow becomes another, a 'madman'. And despite the clown's claim that his costume is merely exterior – '*cucullus non facit monachum*: that's as much to say as I wear not motley in my brain' (1.5.51–3) – it is instead the expression of his whole way of being and of doing in the play, so much so that when he changes identity in acting the role of Sir Topas he changes his attire, despite the total darkness: as Maria points out, 'Thou mightst have done this without thy beard and gown. He sees thee not' (4.2.63–4). But the priest's garb is necessary to the role, and without it Feste cannot do the voices.

Alternatively, clothing is seen – albeit self-deceptively – as a powerful means to social advancement, not only by Malvolio but, for example, by his 'rival' for Olivia's hand, Sir Andrew Aguecheek.

Sir Andrew – an *arriviste* in social drag, a 'carpet' knight who has purchased his knighthood on the titles market (3.4.230) – is an aspiring dandy, displaying false confidence that his leg 'does indifferent well in a flame-coloured stock' (1.3.129–30) and that this will help him to a place in Olivia's house, if not her heart. There is bad news for him and his yellow 'stock', as well as for the steward and his, in Maria's revelation that yellow is 'a colour she [Olivia] abhors' (2.5.193). Onstage Aguecheek often wears yellow, and on Maria's line the other characters look at him tellingly: the destiny he shares with Malvolio – as excluded other – is signalled by their fashion choices.

Dress, therefore, determines personal identity and personal destiny in the play. As Jones and Stallybrass (18) observe, '*Twelfth Night* presents perhaps the most radical vision of the centrality of clothes to the fashioning of a person.' This is nowhere truer, of course, than in the case of Malvolio, who is fooled not only into betraying his personal integrity by dressing up showily against all his puritanical principles, but also into revealing his fatal ignorance of the codes that govern the world he aspires to be part of. Not only does he completely mistake his target by dressing in the yellow that Olivia abhors and by appearing 'cross-gartered – a fashion she detests' (2.5.194), but his chosen form of 'transvestism' is itself a joke, at least for Shakespeare's early audiences. The cross-gartering fashion (see Fig. 15) was tangentially derived from the order of the garter, and thus may appeal to Malvolio's dreams of social promotion, but, as Marie Channing Linthicum pointed out in 1936, by 1600 cross-garters 'were worn chiefly by old men, Puritans, pedants, footmen, and rustic bridegrooms' (Linthicum, 264). This is implicitly confirmed by Maria: 'Most villainously [cross-gartered], like a pedant that keeps a school i'th' church' (3.2.71–2). The joke is thus that Malvolio, aspiring to gentrification and to prestigious marriage, succeeds instead in associating himself with the lower classes from which he desperately wants to distance himself.

Equitis Germani domesticus vestitus.

15 Cross-gartering, from Abraham de Bruyn, *Omnium pene Europæ, Asiæ, Aphricæ atque Americæ gentium habitus. Habits de diverses nations . . .* (Antwerp, 1581)

Malvolio's mode of 'cross-dressing' – or of would-be cross-class-dressing – is in some ways a negative image of Viola's: it is as disastrous as hers is all too successful, and, while the steward mistakenly believes he is dressing up socially, she has to dress down (her blood being, as she puts it, 'Above my fortunes': 1.5.270). Viola's own transvestism, the comedy's central violation of dress codes, has been the subject of much recent critical debate, particularly with regard to the degree of 'transgressiveness' involved in the figure of the doubly cross-dressed boy actor (dressed as girl dressed as boy). Lisa Jardine believes that in performance the play, in arousing homoerotic passion, went some way towards justifying the accusations of anti-theatrical reformists such as John Rainolds, who attacks plays 'not [only] for making young men come forth in whore's attire, like the lewd woman in the Proverbs; but for teaching them to counterfeit her actions' (Jardine, *Daughters*, 9–36). Laura Levine suggests that it brought to the surface deep-seated fears regarding the stability of gender distinctions and thus of the self (Levine, 10–25). A different point of view is maintained by Kathleen McLuskie,[1] who argues that transvestism was a conventional aspect of the Elizabethan stage that did not challenge gender roles; Jean Howard likewise contests the transgressive force of Viola's cross-dressing: 'Despite her masculine attire and the confusion it causes in Illyria, Viola's is a properly feminine subjectivity; and this fact countervails the threat posed by her clothes and removes any possibility that she might permanently aspire to masculine privilege and prerogatives' (Howard, 432). For Howard it is Olivia, with her social and financial independence, who represents 'the real threat to the hierarchical gender system in this text, Viola being but an *apparent* threat' (432).

It is true that what Viola calls 'this my masculine usurped attire' (5.1.246) paradoxically allows her to express her female identity, and indeed the comedy explores feminine subjectivity

---

1   Kathleen McLuskie, 'The act, the role, the actor: boy actresses on the Elizabethan stage', *New Theatre Quarterly*, 13 (1987), 120–30

like no earlier dramatic text. Unlike Shakespeare's previous cross-dressed heroines, Viola confesses her discomfort at two points in the play, first when she perceives the effects of her cross-dressed persona on Olivia – 'Disguise, I see thou art a wickedness . . .' (2.2.26ff) – and later in her crisis in the face of the 'phallic' role of sword-wielding duellist, when her confessional aside – 'A little thing would make me tell them how much I lack of a man' (3.4.295–6) – alludes to her 'lack' of manly physical attributes and character. At the same time, to see Viola's disguise as merely a parenthesis that in the end confirms the sexual and gender status quo is misleading. Not only does Viola-as-Cesario arouse bilateral homoerotic passions, in Olivia (since she is a woman) and in Orsino (since she is his male servant), but the play signally, and uniquely, fails to restore the social order of gender differentiation, in that Cesario never gets round to putting on the 'maiden weeds' of which Viola divests herself at the beginning, and remains 'boy' to Orsino till the end (5.1.263); as Phyllis Rackin notes, 'the boy actor cannot put on Viola's clothes, and the play ends on an equivocal note' (Rackin, 127).

The issue of homoeroticism in the comedy concerns equally the bond between Antonio and Sebastian. Their mutual devotion can in part be situated, as some earlier critics argued, within the tradition of friendship literature, in which male bonding often took on quasi-romantic connotations. But the explicit eroticism of Antonio's language – 'I do adore thee so', 2.1.43; 'My desire, / More sharp than filed steel' (3.3.4–5), etc. – goes quite beyond the bounds of such literary conventions. Censored in nineteenth-century stage productions (see p. 98), Antonio's homoeroticism is an open secret in contemporary performances, which have the two friends kissing or even found in bed together (see p. 112).

In what chapter of his bosom?: reading the body

As the clothing and cross-dressing issues suggest, the interpretation compulsion in *Twelfth Night* centres above all on the body, which is subjected to constant scrutiny and anatomy. Indeed, perhaps the major activity in the play is the reading or misreading of the body, turning it into a kind of text. This can be seen at its most literal in Malvolio's self-deceptive deciphering of Olivia's false epistle, which posits her body as a set of alphabetical signifiers (her c's and u's and t's: see p. 17). It also emerges in what we might call the 'blazon' game that Viola and Olivia play with each other and off each other. This game is a literary variation on surgical anatomy, in which the beloved body is as it were dissected into her constituent parts, each of which is then praised hyperbolically (see Sawday). The blazon is very much a male poetic genre, which the supposed 'ladies' have appropriated. Olivia plays the game, for example, in praising Cesario's 'gentle' or gentlemanly qualities: 'Thy tongue, thy face, thy limbs, actions and spirit / Do give thee fivefold blazon,' she exclaims ecstatically at the end of their first encounter (1.5.284–5). And even if her reading is mistaken on the gender plane it is actually quite correct on the social plane, since she rightly interprets Viola's behaviour as a 'blazon' – or armorial sign – of her high-class origins, despite Cesario's servant status. The game also enters into their dialogue itself when Viola launches into her speech in praise of Olivia – ''Tis beauty truly blent, whose red and white . . .' (1.5.231–5)– and Olivia interrupts her with another parody of the anatomical blazon, which she transforms into a catalogue or shopping list: 'as, item, two lips, indifferent red; item, two grey eyes, with lids to them; item, one neck, one chin and so forth' (1.5.238–40).

This idea of the body as text reaches its climax in the same scene with reference to the body of Orsino. Olivia asks Cesario to come to the point of his mission as Orsino's go–between:

OLIVIA Now, sir, what is your text?

VIOLA Most sweet lady –

OLIVIA A comfortable doctrine, and much may be said of
it. Where lies your text?

VIOLA In Orsino's bosom.

OLIVIA In his bosom? In what chapter of his bosom?

(1.5.214–19)

Olivia justifiably questions Orsino's sincerity here, implying that the duke's 'bosom' or heart is an empty text. Olivia claims to be able to 'read' Orsino without hearing the speech, because the enamoured discourse of his languishing body is *déjà vu* or *déjà lu*, full of romantic clichés. Her joke is blasphemous in that what she is actually parodying is a sermon taking as its 'text' (or theme) a passage from the Scriptures. Orsino is not any old text but a sacred text, holy writ.

Immediately afterwards in the same dialogue Olivia and Cesario shift textual genre when the body in question becomes Olivia herself as supposed object of Orsino's desire:

VIOLA . . . Lady, you are the cruell'st she alive
    If you will lead these graces to the grave
    And leave the world no copy.
OLIVIA O sir, I will not be so hard-hearted. I will give
    out diverse schedules of my beauty. It shall be
    inventoried, and every particle and utensil labelled to
    my will: as, item, two lips, indifferent red; item, two
    grey eyes, with lids to them; item, one neck, one chin
    and so forth.

(1.5.233–40)

The textual joke here is on 'copy'. Viola is using a printing metaphor – a copy is literally a printed transcript – for 'child', which Olivia refuses to create by marrying Orsino. There is also a self-ironic allusion here to Cesario himself as a copy or simulacrum, as fake male and as stand-in for Orsino (copy of a copy). Olivia's 'schedules' instead puns on the legal meaning 'copyhold' or transcript of possessions, thereby transforming her into a legal document: she is not holy writ like Orsino but a judicial writ.

The comedy's intensive reading of the body extends to its interior physiological workings and their effect on character, what we might term the psychosomatics of behaviour. The framework available for the exploration of the bodily bases of psychology was the Greek physician Galen's theory of the humours, i.e. psychological dispositions deriving from the dominance of one or other of the internal organs. The first act dedicates particular attention to the dispositions of the moody Orsino, whose position enables him to exercise what Malvolio admiringly terms 'the humour of state', the autocratic temperament befitting the great (2.5.49), as in his rapid mood changes in the opening scene, reflected in Cesario's speculation that Valentine may 'fear his [Orsino's] humour', 1.4.5. Orsino aims to exercise his power by commanding the organs and humours of Olivia: her heart – which, within the Galenic system is, as Cesario puts it, 'the seat / Where love is throned' (2.4.21–2) – and her liver, the seat of passion, and as such the dominant organ within the play's humoural discourse. Rejected by Olivia and her liver, Orsino resentfully decrees that woman's love is 'No motion of the liver, but the palate' (2.4.98). Fabian rightly predicts of Malvolio that the letter 'wins him, liver and all' (2.5.94), and disingenuously assures the lily-livered Sir Andrew that Olivia's indifference towards him is designed 'to put fire in your heart and brimstone in your liver' (3.2.19).

Still in the hepatic realm, the comedy offers a veritable anatomy of the most fashionable of humours, melancholy, caused by an excess of black bile secreted by the liver, but which in the play more often than not turns out to be a behavioural pose. Olivia's initial *malinconia* is justified by her grief, but is impossibly hyperbolic in its effects, especially in her decision to live in seclusion for seven years. The authenticity of her melancholic disposition is immediately placed in doubt by the rapidity with which she abandons it on meeting Cesario, who in turn alludes to the 'green and yellow melancholy' of his 'sister' (2.4.113). Meanwhile, Orsino's pose as melancholic lover ('my woes', 1.4.26) is mocked by Feste: 'Now the melancholy god protect thee' (2.4.73). Malvolio likewise affects 'sadness' as part of his 'Puritan' severity: 'He is sad and civil,' says Olivia approvingly in her melancholy mode, 'And suits well for a servant with my fortunes.' (3.4.5–6). Although Fabian imagines the steward being 'boiled to death with melancholy' (paradoxically, it being the coldest of humours; 2.5.3), his suppos-edly sad humour is as short-lived as Olivia's grief; upbraided by his mistress for his lover's smile, he reneges his former 'blackness' (the colour of melancholy-provoking bile): 'Not black in my mind, though yellow in my legs' (3.4.25–6). In the end, however, he is lit-erally plunged back into melancholy blackness in the dark room.

The liver, organ of passion, works overtime in *Twelfth Night*. The comedy discloses a wide-ranging discourse of what Thomas Wright termed *The Passions of the Mind* (1601); like the humours, from which they derived, the passions were a fashionable object of inquiry and theorization at the beginning of the seventeenth century. The term 'passion' appears eight times in the play together with a range of synonyms: fire, fervour, will, motion, etc. The prevailing notion in the comedy is of the passion as a mode of affliction or 'perturbation': 'Methought', claims Orsino after Feste's song, 'it did relieve my passion much' (2.4.4). Such is the passionate force of the 'motion of the liver', as Orsino calls it (2.4.98), that it threatens to overwhelm reason. The opposition between passion and reason (or between 'wit' and 'will': 1.5.30) becomes a topos in the comedy. Olivia declares herself intellec-tually disarmed before the force of her desire for Cesario ('Nor wit nor reason can my passion hide', 3.1.150), thereby losing all control over her behaviour and her discourse, as Cesario testifies: 'methought her eyes had lost her tongue, / For she did speak in starts, distractedly' (2.2.20–1). Olivia's speaking in 'starts' con-firms the disruptive effects of the passions, according to theorists such as Thomas Wright, in producing inarticulacy (compare Shakespeare's *Richard III* on the mimesis of powerful emotion: 'Murder thy breath in middle of a word? / Then again begin, and stop again': *R3* 3.5.2–3).

Olivia's broken speech raises the issue of the representation of the passions in the comedy. The problem, as with melancholy, is one of authenticity, namely the correspondence between the external expression of emotion and the actual inner experience of the subject. The supposedly love-stricken Orsino, unlike Olivia, never loses control over his own eloquence, and indeed delegates the manifestation of his perturbed mind to Cesario: 'O then unfold the passion of my love' (1.4.24). Thus Viola-as-Cesario, obliged to dissimulate her own feelings towards Orsino, is called upon to simulate those of her employer, which she does with excessive emphasis, thereby casting doubt on the sincerity of her source. Olivia is justifiably unimpressed by this performance ('Are you a comedian?') but, invited to reciprocate Orsino's passions ('And let your fervour like my master's be', 1.5.279), she does so, but towards Cesario himself. The result is a passion triangle in which Viola's 'true' feelings (for Orsino) are expressed through her acting out of Orsino's more dubious feelings (towards Olivia) and are reciprocated by Olivia's 'authentic' passion (towards Cesario).

Sicken and so die: disease, contagion and death

The body in *Twelfth Night* is not always an edifying text; it sometimes resembles an epidemiological treatise. The play is replete with references to illness and infection. Sir Andrew's surname, like his gaunt appearance, is a 'symptom' of sickness (*ague*), boding ill for his future; his dull brain and deficient humours have been further debilitated by an excess of roast beef (1.3.82–4), while Sir Toby, in imagining him between the legs of a housewife spinning off his hair, may be wishing him, among other things, a dose of venereal disease, causing his yellow hair to fall out (1.3.98–100). The urine of the 'distempered' Malvolio, meanwhile, is to be analysed for signs of illness (3.4.99). The language of disease becomes general currency for interpersonal relations in the play, above all through the metaphor of contagion: Sebastian warns Antonio that 'the malignancy of my fate might perhaps distemper [i.e. infect] yours' (2.1.4–5); Malvolio has 'taken the infection' of Maria's plot (3.4.125), which in turn might 'take air and taint' or become infected (127–8); the carousing Feste has a 'contagious breath': an infectious singing voice and at the same time a sweet but potentially deadly respiration, 'dulcet in contagion' (2.3.53–5).

Feste's infectious breath reminds us that the most fearful of spectres for Shakespeare's audience, and the most recurrently evoked malaise in the play, was the bubonic plague: the joke on the clown's dulcet contagiousness alludes to the early modern belief that the epidemic was transmitted by means of respiration, making not only singing and carousing but all forms of human intercourse potentially perilous. In this context an idiomatic expression such as Sir Toby's 'What a plague . . .' takes on possible added significance, especially when referring to the death of Olivia's brother – 'What a plague means my niece to take the death of her brother thus?' (1.3.1–2) – just as Olivia's 'Even so quickly may one catch the plague?' (1.5.287) is both a conventional metaphor for falling in love and a stark affirmation of medical fact.

It has not gone unnoticed that this 'happy comedy' is much preoccupied – among other unhappy topics – with death. Frederick Furnivall, for example, noted the 'shadow of death and distress across the sunshine' (*SC*, 1.537), while W.H. Auden observed that in the comedy 'darkness verges on thoughts of death' (*SC*, 1.521–2). The greatest concentration of such deathliness is in the play's triply mortal opening: in the first scene Orsino, musing on both existential and erotic dying, is told by Valentine that Olivia is bewailing 'A brother's dead love' (1.1.30); in the second scene, Viola likewise mourns her lost brother, and the captain mentions not only the death of Olivia's brother but also the earlier demise of her father; the third scene begins with Sir Toby complaining at Olivia's excessive mourning for her brother. This heavy dose of mortality – and specifically of male mortality – is in part the play's version of the 'anticomic' opening typical of Shakespearean comedy (Frye, 73). The shadowy presence of death, however, extends beyond the first act. In the final scene Cesario's proof of his 'true' identity is his knowledge that the twins' father 'died that day when Viola from her birth / Had numbered thirteen years' (5.1.240–1). Elsewhere this presence is marked by recurrent allusion: by Maria's prediction that Sir Andrew 'would quickly have the gift of a grave' (1.3.30–1); by Feste's death-wish song requested by

Orsino (in 'Come away, come away death', 2.4.51ff.); by the supposed threat of the 'intercepter' attending Cesario in his 'mortal arbitrement' with Sir Andrew at 3.4.255; by the priest's measuring of time as movement 'toward my grave' at 5.1.158, and so on. To be male in this comedy is to be in danger of one's life.

Against this insistence on masculine frailty is a powerful lobby on behalf of the affirmation of life; the play's most explicit spokesman against the deadly dictates of the reality principle is Sir Toby, whose opening words are a veritable manifesto on behalf of unrestrained vitality: 'I am sure care's an enemy to life' (1.3.2). He goes on to develop this position in his outraged refusal to 'confine' himself (1.3.9), namely (among other senses) to be shut up in a coffin. The life principle is represented above all, however, by the play's female characters. Viola 'saves' her brother from his putative death by becoming him, just as she saves Orsino from the deadly self-infatuation of the opening scene. Olivia – who likewise contributes to saving Sebastian – is elected as a totem against the plague itself: 'O, when mine eyes did see Olivia first', exclaims Orsino, 'Methought she purged the air of pestilence', thus comparing her to the nosegays or perfumes worn by Shakespeare's contemporaries to ward off the disease (1.1.18–19).

As an eunuch: castration, civility and intertextuality

Still in the domain of the body – and specifically of the mutilated rather than diseased body – the comedy's most conspicuous 'forgotten' project, namely Viola's design to present herself 'as an eunuch' (1.2.53) at the court of Orsino, is often interpreted as the result of Shakespeare's change of plan, or as a sign of mere forgetfulness: 'no further reference', we are told, 'is made to this part of [Viola's] plan' (Ard[2], 10). Viola's second scene, 1.4, is usually taken to indicate her immediate abandoning of her 'eunuch' role, since Orsino addresses her as 'good youth' (15) and 'Dear lad' (29), just as he later calls her 'boy' (2.4.15, etc.), and treats her as a young male servant (although he is hardly likely in any case to address her as 'Dear eunuch').

It is true that no further explicit reference is made to Viola's supposed disguise as castrato, and it is possible to read her single direct allusion in purely metaphorical terms. Her cross-dressing can be seen, for example, as a form of social self-castration, since in becoming a servant she is obliged to deny the 'gentle' blood that Olivia detects in her (1.5.281–5). Alternatively, it might be taken as a mode of sexual self-denial. Stephen Orgel – noting that 'Cesario', the chosen name for Viola, derives from *Caesarius*, 'belonging to Caesar', but also suggests the participle *caesus*, 'cut', and thus castration (Orgel, 53) – observes that 'Viola as eunuch, then, both closes down options for herself and implies possibilities for others – possibilities that were . . . illicit' (56); that is, her denial of her own sexuality proves attractive to both sexes (Orsino and Olivia).

In this respect, the affinities between *Twelfth Night* and the most important Renaissance treatise on civilized behaviour – Castiglione's *Il cortegiano* (*The Book of the Courtier*, 1528) – are instructive. Cesario's celebrated 'Patience on a monument' speech (2.4.110–18), which tells the story of his 'sister', pining perhaps fatally from unspoken love, strikingly resembles Cesare Gonzaga's story in *Il cortegiano* of tragic self-sacrifice by a young woman. In love with a lord who had been forced to marry another, she similarly pined from unexpressed desire until she 'through longe passion verie feint, at the three yeeres ende, died' (Castiglione, Gg3ᵛ). Gonzaga tells the story as an example of extreme sexual self-restraint, of the kind exercised by Castiglione's female protagonist, the Countess Elisabetta Gonzaga, who, married to the impotent Duke Guidobaldo, lived 'xv yeeres in companye with her husbande, like a widowe' (Hh3ʳ). Viola-as-Cesario's story is of course autobiographical, describing Viola's own predicament – not 'like a widow' but 'as an eunuch' – of not being able, because of her false gender and her false social class, to tell her love.

Viola's disguise is in this sense a *mise-en-scène* of 'civilized' female decorum, and is not by chance a response to Orsino's misogynistic speech in which he claims that women are biologically and morally inferior because 'they lack retention' (2.4.96) – in the two senses that they lack the capacity for real love and that they lack sexual self-control – since they are dominated by mere animal 'appetite' (97). The duke's tirade again resembles the speech of Gonzaga's interlocutor in *Il cortegiano*, Gaspare Pallavicino, who argues that women are 'unperfect creatures, and consequently of lesse worthinesse than men', that they are incontinent (i.e. promiscuous) and that they are indeed mistakes of nature, mere males *manqués*: 'when a woman is borne, it is a slacknesse or default of nature' (Castiglione, 199–200). At stake here are two opposing versions of female 'castration': Pallavicino's (and Orsino's) vision of woman as an incomplete and uncivilized man, and Gonzaga's (and Viola's) opposing vision of women's capacity for self-castrating virtue. Thus Viola-as-Cesario's enigmatic 'A blank, my lord', in response to Orsino's enquiry into the girl's fate ('And what's her history?': 2.4.109–10), is precisely a confession of her 'castrated' state, deprived as she is of her identity, her social status and her sexuality, just as her admission in the duel scene that 'A little thing would make me tell them how much I lack of a man' (3.4.295–6) discloses the absence of the male 'weapon' that would enable her to combat.

It may be, then, that Viola's eunuch plan does indeed receive 'further reference', even if the reference is somewhat oblique. In another dialogue with his servant, Orsino seems to come close to questioning his messenger's gender; referring, in the first instance, to Cesario's voice, he affirms 'Thy small pipe / Is as the maiden's organ, shrill and sound, / And all is semblative a woman's part' (1.4.32–4). It is hard not to read 'small pipe' as a punning allusion to Cesario's (undeveloped) 'organ' – which in reality is a 'maiden's' organ or 'woman's part' – while the characterization of his voice as 'shrill and sound' alludes at once to its unbroken highness and to its strength. What the duke seems to evoke here is the figure of the castrato singer much in vogue in early seventeenth-century Europe, notably in operas such as Iacopo Peri's *Euridice*, first performed in Florence in 1600 (in the presence, among others, of Duke Orsini of Bracciano, who shortly thereafter set out for the court of Elizabeth I; see p. 93). This may give added meaning to Viola's claim 'for I can sing' (1.2.54), even if her singing is purely discursive: Viola-as-Cesario's vocal performance, with its eloquence and charm, has the same captivating effect as the *evirato* sopranos' voices on the musical stage.

The eunuch trope may not be limited to Viola, since there are strong hints in the play that the same curtailed condition is shared by others. The financial emasculation of Sir Andrew Aguecheek is figured in a series of insinuations regarding his impotence and infertility, from Maria's 'dry jest' and 'now I let go your hand I am barren' (1.3.74, 77), to Sir Toby's description of Sir Andrew's lank hair (which resembles that of Chaucer's eunuch-like Pardoner) in feminine and detumescent terms: 'it hangs like flax on a distaff' (1.3.98). Sir Andrew confirms these innuendoes in his reluctance to use his masculine weapon in the duel with the equally unarmed Cesario (3.4). As for Malvolio, the clues to his 'castrate' status are more cryptic, like the letter in which they are hidden. As John Astington has pointed out, the 'some are born great' passage in the false billet-doux from Olivia (2.5.141–3) is modelled on Christ's discourse on marriage to his disciples: 'For there are some Eunuches, which were so borne from their mothers wombe: and there are some Eunuches, which were made Eunuches of men: and there be Eunuches, which haue made themselues Eunuches for the Kingdome of heauens sake' (Matthew, 19.12, in the King James version). The implicit suggestion is that Malvolio himself belongs to this category, and indeed his public humiliation can be read as 'a displaced gelding' (Astington, 26).

Viola's plan to play the part of an 'unmanned' man has a venerable dramatic genealogy. It signalled, at least to Shakespeare's more learned spectators, the play's debt to the Latin prototype of cross-dressing drama, namely Terence's *Eunuchus* ('The Eunuch'), whose male protagonist, Cherea, disguises himself precisely 'as an eunuch' in order to gain access to the slave girl Pamphila, whom he proceeds, ironically, to rape. Several of the

Italian comedies of cross-dressing and identity confusion, which serve as analogues if not as sources of *Twelfth Night*, draw on the castration theme, as in *Gli inganni* ('Deceptions'), the 1592 version of the 'Twelfth Night' story by the Mantuan nobleman and poet Curzio Gonzaga, in which Leandro falls in love with two twins, one the real Lucrezia, the other her cross-dressed brother, while Lucrezia in turn falls in love with Cesare, who is 'himself' a cross-dressed girl, namely Ginevra (the 'Viola' figure: see Fig. 16). Ginevra-as-Cesare is nearly found out by the maid Filippa, who perceives him/her – in a scene somewhat analogous to *Twelfth Night*'s 'small pipe' exchange – as being either a eunuch or a hermaphrodite:

CESARE (Ginevra) Maybe you thought I was a woman?

FILIPPA Look, Cesare, if I didn't believe you to be a girl, I judged at least from your behaviour that you were double-sexed [*facesti del doppio*], or that you were a meunuch [*megnuco*].

CESARE A eunuch? Ha, ha, you were really crazy, don't you think so now?

FILIPPA I don't know what to think; if you let me touch it with my hand [*se me 'l farai toccar con mano*] I'll know I'm not talking nonsense.

(Gonzaga, 21)

In Barnaby Riche's prose romance 'Of Apollonius and Silla' (1581) – probably the play's most immediate source – the cross-dressed Silla-as-Silvio, accused of getting Julina pregnant, reflects on her lack of the necessary 'implements' for such an act: 'was not this a foule oversight of Julia, that would so precisely sweare so greate an othe that she was gotten with childe by one that was altogether unfurnishte with implements for suche a tourne' (Riche, 361). Silvio's 'unfurnishte' gender status is revealed in a striptease in which he/she 'shewed Julia his breastes and pretie teates' convincing Julia that her lover (whose virility, i.e. that of Silla's twin,

16   Ginevra disguised as Cesare, from Curzio Gonzaga's *Gli inganni* (1592)

she has already verified) is a hermaphrodite (359; for an extended treatment of the castration theme, see Elam, 'Fertile').

As its all-revealing denouement suggests, Riche's romance is a good deal more brutal than Shakespeare's treatment of the same narrative material. Compare, for example, the respective roles of the sea captain in each work: in Riche he endeavours unsuccessfully to rape Silla, while in *Twelfth Night* he offers Viola moral and material aid. There are similarly striking differences between Shakespeare's play and the 'prototype' of the *Twelfth Night* story, *Gl'ingannati* ('The Deceived'), first produced by the Accademia degli Intronati, Siena, in 1533. The Sienese comedy is full of verve, and its female roles, Lelia (Viola) and Isabella (Olivia) have something of the wit and personality of their Shakespearean equivalents (although they were played by women). Indeed, *Gl'ingannati* seems to offer an early version of the rapport between the female protagonist and the audience, as well as a psychological exploration of female subjectivity, notably in Lelia's confession of the difficulty of maintaining her cross-dressed role, apparently analogous to Viola's 'Disguise, I see thou art a wickedness' speech (2.2.27ff.):

'Oh, how I would deserve it [*come mi starebbe bene*] if one of these young rakes took me by force and, dragging me into some house, tried to find out whether I am male or female! That would teach me to go outdoors at this hour . . . Oh what a cruel destiny is mine!' (Intronati, 104). Lelia's reverie of having her real gender 'verified' through rape is in fact far closer to a male erotic fantasy than to feminine introspection. The eroticism of *Gl'ingannati* is cruder and more physical than Shakespeare's: thus the seduction scene between the passionate Isabella and the reluctant Lelia (2.6, roughly equivalent to *TN* 3.1) reaches its climax, in all senses, in the prolonged, passionate kiss between the two girls, accompanied by the obscene comments of two voyeuristic servants, in a *mise-en-scène* of the erotic male gaze.

In addition to the castration theme, *Twelfth Night* inherits from its Italian antecedents – probably through the mediation of Riche's romance – many of its central narrative topics: its combination of the separated twins theme with that of the cross-dressed heroine; its dramatization of intersecting and cross-gender desire; its emphasis on modes of deception (*inganni*) and especially of self-deception, and so on. Whatever its debts to earlier versions of the story, however, *Twelfth Night* seems to enact a 'civilizing' and 'discursivizing' of the often violent sexual and social intercourse of its predecessors. Indeed, from this point of view, the comedy might be said to be more 'Italian' than its Italian models, closer to the courtly ideal of 'civil conversation' as the interplay of ironical and persuasive wit. The affinity of the play's discourse with the conversational and ideological texture of *Il cortegiano* is in many ways more direct than that of *Gl'ingannati* and its offspring. This can be seen in the respective social settings of the plays: the Intronati comedy is set in a bourgeois world of avid *mercanti* (Lelia's merchant father Virginio has promised her in marriage to another old merchant Gherardo), where financial interest is the primary social value. *Gl'ingannati*, moreover, has a precise geographical and historical setting, namely Rome immediately after the traumatic Sack of 1527, whereby the often brutal interpersonal relationships reflect the violence of the political moment. Nothing could be further removed from the Illyrian courts of Orsino and Olivia, dominated by verbal *cortesia*. Not by chance *Twelfth Night* owes a discursive and behavioural debt to Italian courtesy books, not only Castiglione – possibly alluded to at 1.3.41, if we accept Thomas's emendation of *Castiliano vulgo* to 'Castiglione voglio' – but also Stefano Guazzo's influential *Civile conversazione* (*The Civil Conversation*, translated 1586), which Shakespeare sometimes seems to quote or paraphrase, as at 4.1.50 and 4.2.8 (see commentary).

In its more farcical scenes, *Twelfth Night* dramatizes the effects of importing the Italian discourse of civility into Illyrian (or English) culture. In particular, Sir Andrew has difficulty in adapting his behaviour to the polite body languages of dancing and fencing. In 1.3 Sir Toby dazzles his gull with his knowledge of dances, especially the livelier and more sophisticated variety: the courtly coranto or running dance (124), the lively French cinquepace, deformed to 'sink-apace' (125), as well as its English equivalent, the galliard (115); Sir Andrew cannot resist boasting, in reply, of his ability in the 'back-trick', i.e. the *ricacciata* or backward caper that he is obliged to show off (118; see Fig. 17), usually with disastrous consequences in performance.

Worse, and potentially fatal, things happen when the discourse turns to fencing. The aborted duel between Sir Andrew and Cesario in 3.4 evokes and parodies another popular treatise designed to 'civilize' physical combat, the 1595 fencing manual by the immigrant Italian Vincentio Saviolo, which aims to teach the English how to behave, in Sir Toby's phrase 'by the duello' (3.4.301), that is by the Italian rules of duelling. The proper procedure for initiating the duello, according to Saviolo's guide, is by 'giving the lie', challenging the opponent on an unjust accusation. Saviolo, warning of the danger of 'foolish lyes', gives a comic example of how not to challenge 'as he who will giue the lye ere the other speake, saying: if they saye that I am not an honest man, thou lyest in thy throate' (Saviolo, 353). This is a perfect

CAPRIOLE.

Capriol.

17 The caper or 'back-trick' (1.3.118), from Thoinot Arbeau, *Orchésographie* (1589) (see List of Ills)

description of the behaviour of Aguecheek, whose altogether unjustified challenge reads, 'But thou liest in thy throat; that is not the matter I challenge thee for' (3.4.151–2). Sir Toby's stylistic advice to Sir Andrew on the writing of the challenge also looks like a parody of Saviolo, who recommends 'the greatest brevity that may be possible, framing the quarrell with certaine, proper, and simple woordes'. Belch's version is more brutal – 'Go, write it in a martial hand, be curst and brief' – but he adds the self-contradictory recommendation, 'It is no matter how witty, so it be eloquent and full of invention' (3.2.41–2), an open invitation to indulge in witless prolixity, as Sir Andrew proceeds to do (see 3.4.143–65). As for actual fencing technique, Sir Toby sadistically overturns Saviolo's rules, warning his crony to avoid responding to his opponent's 'stuck', or *stoccata*, since 'on the answer, he pays you' (3.4.270–1); Saviolo advises the exact opposite, exhorting the fencer to defend himself against the stuck: 'break the stoccata with his left hand, and answer him again with the other' (Saviolo, 17).

There may be a further echo of Saviolo in Sir Toby's description of Cesario as a 'firago', i.e. virago, defined by Florio as 'a manlie or mankynde woman': this description comes close to unmasking Viola, but at the same time recalls Saviolo's praise for various man-like woman combatants, from the Amazons to Joan of Arc, and especially for cross-dressed female warriors such as the 'Portingall gentlewoman that for religions sake about 4. yeeres now past, lefte of the apparell of her sexe' (Saviolo, 484). Viola's own behaviour fails conspicuously to match these heroic models, but Sebastian replaces her in time to justify Sir Toby's description.

Sir Andrew's incompetence in alien bodily arts is matched by his difficulties with foreign languages: despite Sir Toby's claim that his crony 'speaks three or four languages word for word without book' (1.3.24–5), he fails to understand simple French – 'What is 'pourquoi'?' (1.3.89), although he does manage a French greeting at 3.1.69 – and admits, 'I would I had bestowed that time in the tongues that I have in fencing' (1.3.89–91; time ill-bestowed, as we have seen). Not surprisingly, the most evident lexical and cultural presence in the play is Italian, with its particular cultural kudos; Sir Toby, for example, uses Italian as a mode of mystification in promising Sir Andrew to call on him 'at the cubiculo' (i.e. his chamber, with a possible pun on 'culo', arse: 3.2.50). Shakespeare probably derived this term, like 'intercepter' (*intercettore*) (3.4.217) and others, from John Florio's Italian–English dictionary. The following list (taken from Florio, *World*) shows some of the lemmas and definitions that may have influenced the comedy.

Coranta, Corranta, *a kinde of French-dance.*

Cubiculo, *a chamber.*

Culo, *the arse, taile, fundament or bum.*

Duello, *a single combat, a fight between two.*

Festa, *a feast, a holyday a banquet, ioy, pleasure, solace, a shew.*

Intercettore, *a preuenter, a forestaller, an encrocher, an interceptor.*

Maléuolo, *malitious, maleuolent, spitefull, that oweth ill will, that beareth a grudge, enuious.*

Maleuolére, *to hate, to lothe, to detest, to wish euill vnto,*
   to grudge.
Maluoluto, *hated, lothed, grudged at.*
Orsino, *a young beare whelpe.*
Stoccata, *a foyne, a thrust, a stoccado giuen in fence.*
Vióla, *a flower called a Violet. Also an instrument called*
   a Violl or Violine.
Vióla di gamba, *a viol de gamba.*
Virago, *a woman of stout and manlie courage, a manlie or*
   mankinde woman.

With regard to its intertextual debts, however, the comedy's
strongest affinities are probably with Shakespeare's own earlier
cross-dressing comedies, *Two Gentlemen*, *Merchant of Venice* and
As You Like It. It revisits many of the earlier plays' themes and
topoi: a hostile (or 'anticomic') situation facing the female protagonist, and her consequent decision to cross-dress; bisexual desire
resulting from gender ambiguity (in *As You Like It* Rosalind is
courted by both Orlando and Phebe); the presence of a truth-
telling clown (Touchstone); a finale bringing about the revelation
of identities and the announcement or enactment of double
weddings, etc. *Twelfth Night*, nevertheless, differs from its predecessors in several important ways. The inclusion of a different-sex
twin multiplies the gender confusion exponentially and introduces
a new psychological motivation for Viola's transvestism: unlike the
earlier heroines, Viola neither cross-dresses for love nor is already
in love when she decides to change gender; she disguises from
material necessity and in order to keep her brother 'alive'. Her proposed 'eunuch' disguise is unprecedented: Julia in *Two Gentlemen*
dresses as a 'well-reputed page' (*TGV* 2.7.43); Portia in *Merchant
of Venice* as a 'young doctor' of law (*MV* 4.1.151), Rosalind as a
youth in a 'swashing and martial outside' (*AYL* 1.3.114). Viola
is the only cross-dressed Shakespearean heroine to experience
difficulty in sustaining her male performance. Rosalind – apart
from her reported fainting at the sight of Orlando's blood – plays

her double gender role with great verve and absolute confidence, while Portia defeats Shylock with supreme dialectical skill. Viola, instead, confesses both her consternation at the effects of her disguise and her inability to handle her phallic weapon. Shakespeare exploits her predicament for some of the most profound moments of feminine introspection in the canon.

Unlike those of the earlier comedies, moreover, the play's denouement fails conspicuously to tie up the loose threads of its various plots. Viola, unlike her predecessors Julia, Portia and Rosalind, remains cross-dressed until the end, with the result that the nuptial celebrations are postponed until she reappears – some time in the post-dramatic future – in her 'maiden's weeds' (5.1.251). The comedy's outsiders, meanwhile, either leave unreconciled (Malvolio) or are left unassimilated (Sir Andrew, Antonio).

Twelfth Night also entertains significant intertextual relations with other Shakespearean plays, not all of them comedies. There are particular narrative and discursive affinities with a near-contemporary tragedy, *Hamlet*, with which it shares dead fathers, a presumed madman, a duel scene (Hamlet 'gives the lie' to Laertes), letters read aloud, and a number of verbal or conceptual constructions (see 2.1.29n., 3.1.41n., 4.2.22n.).

This is Illyria, lady: space and place

Unlike most of its possible dramatic sources or intertexts, *Twelfth Night* distributes its action between two domestic spaces, the twin aristocratic courts of Orsino and Olivia. The cultural model for such courts in the Renaissance was undoubtedly Italian (Castiglione, Guazzo), although by the beginning of the seventeenth century they had spread throughout Europe and England itself, so that the domestic interiors and exteriors of the play are without predetermined national identity. In the first two acts the location alternates between these two poles: 1.1, 1.4 and 2.4 are set in Orsino's court, 1.3, 1.5, 2.3 and 2.5 in Olivia's. The action shifts increasingly, however, towards Olivia's and away from Orsino's court, which is altogether absent from the last three acts. This is significant in terms of the 'power' relations within the comedy, which see a growing predominance of Olivia, not only through her economic independence and her sense of initiative but also because she is at the centre of the play's network of interpersonal exchanges: she is at once object of desire for Orsino, Aguecheek and Malvolio and subject of desire for Cesario/Sebastian, in addition to being the employer of Feste and Maria (and perhaps Fabian) and the long-suffering 'hostess' of Sir Toby and Sir Andrew. Orsino's court is a centrifugal space from which characters (notably Cesario) set out; Olivia's court is a centripetal space which attracts all the play's characters and action; in the end even Orsino comes to Olivia's domain, thereby acknowledging the effective shift in power.

Olivia's court is further articulated into two spatial areas, internal and external. The internal space is the area of domestic intimacy into which only the immediate members of the household (and hangers-on like Sir Andrew) are admitted. The outdoor space is a venue for receiving outsiders – Cesario, Sebastian, Orsino – but becomes also a more or less undifferentiated location for all the later events, from courtship to duels to arrests. The opposition between outside and inside is significant in Olivia's exercise of power and of desire: in 4.3 she invites Cesario/Sebastian into one of the indoor spaces, the chantry, for the pre-marital contract, but not into her 'house' proper (presumably until they are married); Orsino is kept strategically outside, as Olivia herself underlines in promise of future hospitality, again, presumably, when she is fully married: 'Here at my house, and at my proper cost' (5.1.313). Because of its open and inclusive quality, Olivia's outdoor space is the play's primary venue (six scenes) – 1.5, 3.1, 3.4, 4.1, 4.3 and 5.1 – whereas the more exclusive internal area has four scenes: 1.3, 2.3, 3.2 and 4.2.

Within the action and dialogue, Olivia's indoor 'house' is further divided into more specific venues of transgression and of punishment: a convivial space for carousing in 1.3 and 2.3, traditionally represented onstage as the kitchen, and a claustrophobic space for Malvolio's imprisonment in 4.2, referred to as the 'dark room'. The outdoor space in Olivia's court is alluded to alternatively as 'orchard' and 'garden' (the two terms were synonyms). There is a suggestion that this area also has its subdivisions: Olivia's command, 'Let the garden door be shut', at 3.1.90 implies that her conversation with Cesario takes place in a walled garden or *hortus conclusus* – fashionable in the Renaissance as a space for private exchange – whereas more public scenes, especially 5.1, seem to take place in a more open territory.

Beyond the two main poles of the action, there are other locations that act as transitional spaces between the two courts or between scenes or events: the seashore in 1.2 and perhaps in 2.1; the unspecified location (often indicated as the 'street') of the encounters between Sebastian and Antonio; the place (again the 'street'?) where Malvolio catches up with Cesario on his way to Orsino's house in 2.2. There is, however, nothing fixed about these spatial differences, which are often simply functional to the dialogue. Locations are never specified in Folio stage directions and rarely referred to directly in the play. The open and fluid acting area of the Elizabethan stage did not pose many problems of setting, so that the venue could remain unspecified; the problem arose for later directors (and editors). The fluidity of the represented spaces is suggested by certain inconsistencies within the dialogue, as in 3.4: Sir Toby refers to the venue as the 'orchard' (218), whereas later Antonio recalls his 'private brabble' with the officers in the same scene as taking place 'Here in the streets' (5.1.60).

The play's economy of space feeds into its poetics of place. Viola's opening question on finding herself stranded on the shore – 'What country, friends, is this?' – is one that spectators, directors and critics often pose. The play itself does not do much to answer it, especially since the captain's response – 'This is Illyria, lady' – only raises further questions. Even for Shakespeare's early audiences, 'Illyria' probably did not ring distinct geographical bells. Leah Marcus suggests that 'Illyria was scarcely familiar territory, more significant, perhaps, for its evocation of like-sounding exotics – Elysium, delirium – than for concrete geopolitics' (Marcus, 161). The name therefore discouraged the audience from linking the setting with any contemporary geographical or geopolitical reality.

Historically, Illyria was an ancient region of the Balkan peninsula, designating roughly the Adriatic coast north of central Albania and west of the Dinaric Alps. The region was inhabited from the tenth century BC by the Illyrians, an Indo-European people who later became notorious for acts of piracy against Roman shipping. After a series of wars with Rome, it was defeated in 168 BC and established as the Roman province of Illyricum. Occupied by the Slavs from the sixth century, its name eventually changed to Albania. In Shakespeare's time the name Illyria could still be used to refer to part of the Adriatic coast – roughly Dalmatia – at the time under the dominion of the Venetian republic. It was thus historically a hybrid land, geographically Mediterranean, ethnically Slav but politically 'Italian'.

There are few traces in the comedy of this heritage, with the possible exception of the Italian names, perhaps suggesting the contemporary Venetian connection (although the historical Duke Orsini was actually a Roman aristocrat). Antonio's warning to Sebastian that the terrain is 'Rough and unhospitable' (3.3.11) may allude obliquely to the traditionally warlike character of the Illyrians and especially to their notoriety for piracy (compare *2H6* 4.1.108, 'Bargulus, the strong Illyrian pirate'). The latter association is more directly invoked by Orsino when he addresses his former enemy Antonio as 'Notable pirate, thou salt-water thief' (5.1.65), with reference to a somewhat obscure episode of naval hostility not mentioned elsewhere and rarely developed in performance (with the exception of Trevor Nunn's film; see p. 119). Other possible hints of Mediterranean culture are still more tenuous. Viola's decision to disguise herself as a eunuch

(1.2.53) may suggest a southern Mediterranean world, more Turkish than Dalmatian – as indeed does the captain's reply that he will be her 'mute', as in an eastern harem, subject to the harsh laws enforcing the secrecy of the sultan's inner conclave: 'When my tongue blabs then let mine eyes not see' (60).

In many ways, however, the play's principal place–name is more mythical than geopolitical, and its best–known associations were intertextual rather than international: in Ovid's *Metamorphoses*, Cadmus and his wife, like Viola, are shipwrecked 'Upon the c[o]ast of Illirie' (Ovid, *Met.*, 4.701). Likewise the birthplace of the twins, 'Messaline', probably owes more to Plautus's *Menaechmi* than to the historical Massilia (Marseille). Back on the beach, Viola punningly associates the place–name with that of another ideal space: 'And what should I do in Illyria? / My brother he is in Elysium' (1.2.2–3). Illyria is a utopia, a no–place that could be any place. As such, it serves Shakespeare as an alibi, an 'elsewhere' not fully identifiable with any well–defined territory. This in turn allows audiences and directors to project their own mental sets onto the space

With respect to Shakespeare's England, Illyria was certainly, if somewhat vaguely, 'eastern'. As Constance C. Relihan notes, however, the dramatist goes out of his way to dilute the orientalism of its main source, Barnaby Riche's story 'Apollonius and Silla' set in Constantinople and Cyprus. Relihan attributes this erasure of the east to Shakespeare's design to explore his main themes of (English) gender and sexuality, without the interference of the 'Turkish' cultural stereotypes of the source. Still, the play recuperates a degree of exoticism – albeit from a strictly western viewpoint – through reference to travel abroad. The comedy's two allusions to the Sophy (or Shah) of Persia – Fabian's 'pension of thousands' (2.5.174–5) and Sir Toby's 'fencer to the Sophy' (3.4.272) – evoke an oriental world of hyperbolic abundance and fearful prowess, or at least imply the English perception of that world. Both references are inspired by the 1599 eastern voyage of Sir Anthony Shirley and his brothers, whose exploits, including the receipt of lavish gifts, had been recently recounted in two pamphlets: an exoticism knowingly filtered through the eyes of western explorers and narrated, with the necessary exaggerations, for English readers hungry for accounts of 'New World' wonders.

Similarly, Maria's conceit of Malvolio's face having 'more lines than is in the new map with the augmentation of the Indies' (3.2.74–6) alludes to strictly western, and more specifically English, representations of the east: in her case, to Edward Wright's 1600 map of the East Indies (Fig. 18), 'augmented' because of its inclusion for the first time of the island of Nova Zembla, a novelty made possible by the disastrous 1596–7 expedition of the Dutch explorer Willem Barentsz, which came to a premature end in the icefields off the island. Barentsz's unhappy expedition gets a second mention, in Fabian's elaborately figurative warning to Malvolio, 'you are now sailed into the north of my lady's opinion, where you will hang like an icicle on a Dutchman's beard' (3.2.24–6), a warning that it is safer and wiser to stay at home (as well as in one's social place) rather than wander into uncharted regions.

The re-importing of eastern colour into a largely deorientalized setting may be related to the issue of sexuality, since the 'east' – notably Turkey – was generically associated with prohibited sexual practices and especially with homoeroticism; as Relihan puts it, 'The play's authorization of male homosexual desire is linked directly to its delicate negotiation between eastern cultures and English values' (Relihan, 91). With reference to same-sex relationships there is a possible final intriguing note to the play's Balkan affiliations. As P. Näcke pointed out in 1908, and as John Boswell has more extensively demonstrated in 1994, in 'Illyria' and particularly in Albania the Catholic and Orthodox churches sanctioned for a period of over a thousand years a ceremony that permitted the lifelong union of same-sex couples. This ceremony, the *adelphopoiia* rite, is described by Mary Shelley as 'the oaths of friendship which it is usual for the Illyrian warriors to take one

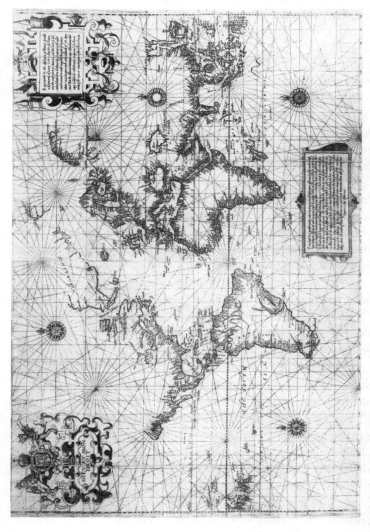

18 'The new map with the augmentation of the Indies' (3.2.75-6), from Edward Wright's *Map of the World*,1600

with the other. Two men thus united are called *Pobratimi*, or half-brothers; they often sacrifice their lives for each other' (Shelley, 73; the text of the ceremony was first published by Jacques Goar in 1647). It is possible that the practice was known to Shakespeare and his contemporaries, as it was to Byron and his. This may cast an oblique light on the unions in *Twelfth Night*: Antonio's passionate attachment to Sebastian, the bond between Orsino and his 'boy', or the 'handfasting' ceremony (see Fig. 19) which supposedly takes place between two women (Olivia and the cross-dressed Viola) but which on the Elizabethan stage was performed by two men.

From many points of view, however, Illyria resembles nothing more than Shakespeare's England. Despite its Italianate names, the comedy presents a gallery of recognizable English social types, from the tankard-wielding knight to the 'Puritan' steward to the professional motley-clad clown or fool (or indeed his alter ego, the ignorant country parson Sir Topas). It also presents evocations of English folklore, such as Sir Toby's comical allusion to the bed of Ware 'in England' (3.2.45), reminding us that we are supposedly abroad. More specifically, there are indications that events are located in the English capital. One of the play's running jokes is a series of allusions, some of them quite overt, to contemporary London. The most explicit of these are Antonio's references in 3.3, where he gives Sebastian money to go sightseeing in what the latter calls 'this city' (24). Antonio's dubious tourist agency advice is to visit 'the south suburbs' (39), the notorious 'liberties' south of the Thames, known not only for their theatres but also, according to a 1596 Privy Council order, for 'stables, ins, alehowses, tavernes, garden howses converted to dwellings, ordinaries, dicying howses, bowling allies and brothell howses' (Browner, 35; see also Mullaney, 20–55). It looks as though Antonio is financing the *ingénu* Sebastian to discover a world of questionable new pleasures. He also has ideas for accommodation: 'at the Elephant, / Is best to lodge'; this continues the joke, since the Elephant Inn on Bankside,

19 'Mutual joinder of your hands' (5.1.153): the handfasting ceremony, from
George Wither, *A Collection of Emblems* (1635)

doubtless well known to Shakespeare's audience, was infamous
precisely as one of the 'brothell howses' condemned by the Privy
Council (Ungerer, 103).

There may be a further, more occult, reference to a London
tavern in Feste's 'nonsense' during the nocturnal revels of 2.3: 'the
Myrmidons are no bottle-ale houses,' he affirms (2.3.26–7), with
a probable punning allusion to the Mermaid Inn in Cheapside,
in the City (on the other side of the river from the Elephant). In
the same scene Aguecheek's 'I sent thee sixpence for thy leman'
(23–4) would have evoked for the audience another East London

location, Leman Street, just as the clown's evocation of 'the bells of Saint Bennet' (5.1.35) probably refers to the church of St Bennet Hithe in Paul's Wharf, close to the Mermaid.

In order to get from the City to the south bank with its play-houses and brothels, Londoners crossed the Thames by London Bridge or by boat-taxis; Viola-as-Cesario alludes to this southward and westward river crossing in an exchange with Olivia: 'OLIVIA There lies your way, due west. / VIOLA Then westward ho!' (3.1.132). 'Westward ho!' was precisely the cry of passengers hailing wherrymen to take them across the river: Cesario is ready to set out in the same direction as Sebastian on his sightseeing tour.

The whirligig of time: levels of temporality

Not surprisingly, in a comedy declaredly dedicated to a seasonal occasion, there is a good deal of concern with the passage of time. This is sometimes perceived with anxiety, as in Olivia's 'The clock upbraids me with the waste of time' (3.1.128) and the First Officer's 'The time goes by. Away!' (3.4.361). The play is correspondingly full of references to clocks and watches (2.5.57, 3.1.128, etc.: see Potter, 17) and has its maniacal timekeepers, such as the priest who measures every moment of his mortality: 'Since when, my watch hath told me, toward my grave / I have travelled but two hours' (5.1.158–9). Time, however – and in particular the slow time of personal and social maturation – is also the medium of redemption. Viola twice entrusts her fate to its long-term workings: 'What else may hap to time I will commit' (1.2.57); 'O time, thou must untangle this, not I' (2.2.40). Time is also the object of ideological strife: the play opposes the reality principle of Malvolio's sense of temporal decorum ('to gabble like tinkers at this time of night', 2.3.86–7) to the pleasure principle of Sir Toby's investment in timelessness ('We did keep time, sir, in our catches', 2.3.91).

What this suggests is that there are different perceptions and different levels of time at work in *Twelfth Night*. These differences find expression in the play's notorious 'double' time scheme, whereby on the one hand Valentine congratulates Viola-as-Cesario on becoming the duke's favourite in 'but three days' (1.4.3), while on the other Antonio informs Orsino that he has known Cesario/Sebastian 'for three months', and the duke confirms that 'Three months this youth hath tended upon me' (5.1.95). Such discrepancies do not trouble audiences, and the temporal allusions need not be taken too seriously or too literally, especially as 'three' seems to be the conventional measure of time in the play – Malvolio fantasizes having been married 'three months' to Olivia (2.5.41); the captain calculates the distance of Orsino's court 'Not three hours' travel' from the shore (1.2.21), etc. None the less they do mark differences in the rhythm of events between, on the one hand, the relatively slow development of the overall narrative frame and, on the other, the hectic comings and goings onstage, conducted at a more rapid pace. In the end, these different rhythms converge in the real time of the performance, which alternates episodes of busy stage traffic (3.4, 5.1) with more static scenes of leisurely exchange (1.5, 2.3): 'golden time convents', as Orsino puts it (5.1.375).

Words are very rascals: language and discourse

Everything in a play text is filtered through language, the most important weapon in the dramatist's armoury. In *Twelfth Night* language is both a richly varied expressive means and a significant object of dramatic and comic reflection. The most evident, but not always unproblematic, aspect of the play's linguistic make-up is its division into verse and prose. Malvolio's 'Soft, here follows prose' (2.5.138–9) signals an awareness of the strategic importance of prose and verse distribution within the dialogic economy of the play. In general, verse and prose indicate 'high' and 'low' language respectively, but this distinction is by no means rigid. Verse seems to be set up as the play's 'default' mode in the two opening scenes; Orsino invariably speaks in verse, as does Olivia in her formal moments, and Viola and Sebastian in their more dramatic or 'romantic' scenes. Normally those addressing Orsino adopt his own verse mode – as a sign of decorous respect – with the exception of Feste, licensed to speak prose with everyone. Viola and Sebastian speak verse on their mutual rediscovery (5.1). Verse is also the vehicle of thought in soliloquies.

Prose, the medium of idiomatic realism, is invariably spoken in the 'low' scenes involving Sir Toby and his cronies; it is spoken by Feste (with the exception of his songs) and by Malvolio, as well as by Olivia in informal scenes, for example when she is fooling with Feste, conversing with Sir Toby and, sometimes, with Maria. The verse–prose distinction is not always coherent: Sebastian and Antonio speak prose in their first scene (2.1) and verse in their second (3.3). Other scenes are 'mixed', signalling differences in class and linguistic register: in the dialogues between Olivia and Maria, for example, the former usually speaks verse, the latter prose.

Verse is the medium of Shakespeare's lexical inventiveness. Apart from Feste's playful nonce-words ('impeticos thy gratility', etc.) Shakespeare's apparent neologisms appear especially in verse scenes of particular lyricism, such as 1.4, or dramatic intensity, such as 5.1: for example, 'unprofited' (1.4.22), 'rubious' (1.4.32) and 'semblative' (1.4.34); 'triplex' (5.1.34), 'baubling' (5.1.50), 'unauspicious' (5.1.109), 'joinder' (5.1.153), 'interchangement' (5.1.155) and 'grizzle' (5.1.161). These coinages, a sign of Shakespeare's linguistic creativity in his poetry, contrast with the simpler and more familiar language of the prose, with its mimesis of colloquial conversational discourse. The prose passages make abundant use of 'everyday' idioms, for example so-called discourse markers, namely 'small words and phrases which add emotional tone and colour to what is being said' (Blake, *Grammar*, 290), and which have little direct referential meaning; the master of these typically spoken forms is Sir Toby, with his 'why's, 'what's, 'come come's, 'tut's, 'how now's, 'go to's, 'I say's, and the rest (on the punctuating of discourse markers, see Appendix 1).

Other small but significant words that mark the social and interpersonal dimension of the play's discourse, especially in the prose scenes, are personal pronouns, and in particular the so-called pronouns of power – 'you' and 'thou' – that indicate the degree of familiarity, formality or relative dominance between two speakers. These terms are an important aspect of comedy's representation of social and class relationships. Again it is Sir Toby who displays the greatest degree of skill and self-awareness in deploying these potentially lethal pronominal weapons. He strategically adopts familiar 'thou' with Sir Andrew, while the latter uses a more formal 'you' in their exchanges; such familiarity might be interpreted merely as a sign of equality or of friendly informality, were it not for his advice to his gull to 'thou' Cesario in his letter of challenge, as a sign of contempt (3.2.42–3); this suggests that Sir Toby's own 'thou'-ing of Aguecheek is likewise a calculated put-down. He uses equally dismissive 'thou's towards Malvolio, and even the strategic omission of the pronoun serves to underline the point in his ineffably disdainful 'Art [thou] any more than a steward?' (2.3.112).

The strategic and self-aware deployment of 'thou' and 'you' is part of the play's broader rhetoric of social and class interaction. *Twelfth Night* is perhaps Shakespeare's most class-conscious play, and at its centre is the irresistible drive towards upward social mobility that characterized early seventeenth-century England. The movement towards 'the degree of my betters' (1.3.113) involves all characters who are not already of the gentry, with the exception of Feste, for whom social promotion would entail loss of role and identity. The distribution of social prizes is ironical: those who ardently aspire to gentrification, such as Malvolio and Sir Andrew, fail miserably to achieve it, whereas those on whom it is most generously bestowed, Viola and Sebastian, do not actually desire it. Only Maria manages to pull off the social mobility she tacitly seeks.

The chief domain of *Twelfth Night*'s discursive exploration of social class is the relationship between master/mistress and servant. The comedy presents a veritable catalogue of kinds of domestic staff, including a steward, a 'servingman', a chambermaid and a jester, as well as unspecified servants and attendants. It is, moreover, the only Shakespeare play in which servants (Viola, Malvolio, Maria, Feste, perhaps Fabian) are leading characters, not on behalf of their betters (as with the ingenious servants of the classical tradition, for example in *Comedy of Errors* or *Two Gentlemen of Verona*) but in their own right. Accordingly, it is replete with allusions to service, beginning with Viola's double reference in her first scene, adumbrating her go-between role between two noble houses and two noble rivals for her services: 'O that I served that lady' (1.2.38); 'I'll serve this duke' (1.2.52). Events in the play cause the verb 'serve' to take on the double meaning of 'be a servant to' and 'be romantically devoted to', since both its main and its secondary plots are based on superiors becoming 'servants' (enamoured) of their servants: Olivia and Orsino are both enamoured of Cesario; Olivia is supposedly infatuated with Malvolio (who is 'limed' by the idea of becoming master of the countess – '*She that would alter services with thee*' (2.5.153–4; note the intimate '*thee*'); Sir Toby dotes on and eventually marries Maria (on service and love in the comedy, see Schalkwyk). This overlapping of the domestic and romantic service reaches its climax with Viola-as-Cesario's 'Your servant's servant is your servant, madam' (3.1.100: i.e. Viola, devoted to Orsino, in turn enamoured of Olivia, is at the disposition of the countess as the servant Cesario).

The social rhetoric of *Twelfth Night* is centred precisely on the figure of Viola-as-Cesario, who adopts different discursive strategies, respectively, towards the duke and the countess, even if with both she/he is involved in an asymmetrical relationship (servant–master and messenger–noblewoman respectively), clearly marked by the you–thou dialectic. Cesario respectfully 'you's the duke throughout, even after the latter's proposal of marriage, while the duke 'thou's his servant from the outset. The servant also adopts a systematic strategy of politeness towards his master, both in the observation of conventional deferential forms acknowledging the difference in rank and power between them ('On your attendance, my lord', 'Sure, my noble lord') and in his explicit willingness to subordinate his will to his master's, most notably in his readiness to die in obedience to the duke's violent whim in the final scene ('And I most jocund, apt and willingly / To do you rest a thousand deaths would die', 5.1.128–9; on politeness strategies in Shakespeare, see Magnusson, *Dialogue*, 17–57). Viola-as-Cesario's extreme politeness towards the duke, her/his constant anxiety to be 'very worth his service' (1.2.56), is of course motivated primarily not by social constraints but by interest, since her/his desire 'to serve this noble count' plays on the twin senses of 'serve', the professional and the amorous. Cesario's hyperbolic sense of service at once masks and expresses Viola's love.

Cesario's strategy with Olivia is quite different. While Olivia alternates uneasily between 'you' and 'thou' in their second meeting (3.1), Cesario, as Orsino's reluctant go-between, always duly 'you's his social superior and appears to adopt appropriately deferential modes of address: 'My duty, madam, and most humble service' (3.1.93), etc. In practice, though, he undermines his superficially polite mode through parodic exaggeration – 'Most radiant, exquisite and unmatchable beauty' (1.5.165) – and by blatantly casting doubt on the very identity and social status of the interlocutor: 'The honourable lady of the house, which is she?' (163). This conflict between apparent politeness and actual effrontery is not lost on the countess, who complains, 'Sure you have some hideous matter to deliver when the courtesy of it is so fearful' (201–2). In a play which, as David Schalkwyk observes, 'is as much a study of service and master–servant relations as it is a comedy of romantic love' (Schalkwyk, 86), it is not surprising that politeness should become an overt issue. Viola-as-Cesario's 'fearful' courtesy, or discourtesy, again expresses her/his own interests: Cesario's transgressive flouting of the rules of politeness expresses Viola's desire to sabotage the love mission on the duke's behalf. The irony, of course, is that in practice it only acts to increase the countess's desire – for the servant.

The comedy's social rhetoric is intertwined with its figurative rhetoric. The use of rhetorical figures in the play is selective and strategic, serving specific purposes within given scenes or dialogues. The most rhetorically dense scenes are those in verse, where a figurative flourish may serve to set a 'high' or dramatic tone; here rhetoric becomes a mode of performance, notably in Orsino's self-dramatizing exhibitions, as in the overwrought similes ('like the sweet south', 1.1.5ff.) and elaborately extended metaphors or allegories ('O, when mine eyes', 18ff.) with which he presents his credentials in the opening scene. Rhetorical figures play particular dramatic or comic roles precisely when, as in Orsino's opening performance, they are strategically overdone. This is the case with one of the comedy's most characteristic tropes, the figure of excess *par excellence*, namely hyperbole, which Puttenham baptizes 'the Ouer reacher' and defines as 'when we speake . . . beyond the limites of credit' (Puttenham, 159). Hyperbole, usually in the form of exaggerated metaphor or simile, is at times used in earnest, as in the exchanges of intensely polite and possibly homoerotic compliments between Antonio and Sebastian, 'If you will not murder me for my love, let me be your servant' (2.1.32–3), varied ironically by Maria with reference to Malvolio, 'I have dogged him like his murderer' (3.2.72); or in Olivia's emphatic expressions of amorous effusion towards Cesario: 'I had rather hear you to solicit that / Than music from the spheres' (3.1.107–8). More often than not, however, the hyperbolic mode in the play is pushed towards the verge of parody, as in Cesario's over-emphatic courtesies towards the (hyperbolic) Olivia, designed to make Orsino's courtship look shoddy and to make fun of the countess's own attitude: 'Most radiant, exquisite and unmatchable beauty' (1.5.165). In general, hyperbole becomes so much part of the comedy's linguistic and behavioural texture that Feste, disguised as Sir Topas, attributes the devil's supposed tormenting of Malvolio to it: 'Out, hyperbolical fiend' (4.2.25).

In the same 'dark room' scene, Feste proves himself master of another recurrent figure in the play, namely paradox; indeed it is Sir Topas's disorienting paradoxes, rather than the devil's hyperboles, that torment Malvolio: 'Why,' he says of the dark room, 'it hath bay-windows transparent as barricadoes, and the clerestories toward the south-north are as lustrous as ebony' (4.2.36–8). Being a figure of logical self-contradiction, paradox is one of the main weapons in Feste's armoury as 'artificial' or philosophical fool, allowing him to overturn the conventional wisdom or false politeness of his interlocutors: 'the better for my foes, and the worse for my friends,' he responds to Orsino's 'friendly' but condescending 'How dost thou, my good fellow?' (5.1.9–11). Elsewhere, paradox is the direct verbal expression of stage situations that are in themselves straining with logical self-contradiction, such as the possible simultaneous death and survival of Sebastian, which prompts Viola-as-Cesario to produce the paradoxical conceit, 'Tempests are kind, and salt waves fresh in love' (3.4.381). It is likewise the internal and psychological tensions within the narrative that give rise to a related figure of logical contradiction, oxymoron. Viola-as-Cesario's nautical paradox in the last scene is echoed in her oxymoronic 'happy wreck' (5.1.262), while she also uses oxymoron to express the increasing difficulties of her disguise role after Olivia has fallen in love with her, characterizing it (and her/himself) as the 'proper false' (where 'proper' means both handsome and true; 2.2.29). The dangers inherent in the disguise are similarly condensed in Antonio's 'beauteous evil', used of the treacherous Cesario/Sebastian (3.4.366). Champion of the oxymoron as a mode of ironic put-down, instead, is Sir Toby, while its inevitable victim is Sir Andrew: Toby addresses him as 'dear venom', making fun of his momentary anger (3.2.2), and goes on to mock his 'dormouse valour' as a fighter (3.2.18).

A particularly significant role in this comedy of twins and doubles is played appropriately by syntactic figures of splitting and doubling. Ploce, which Puttenham nicknames 'the doubler' (Puttenham, 168), is a device involving the repetition of a word separated by one or more other words, whereby the meaning of the repeated term changes (or 'doubles'); not by chance it is the figure that Viola and the captain resort to with reference to the former's 'lost' twin, who may or may not have died: 'Perchance [i.e. perhaps] he is not drowned,' suggests Viola hopefully; 'It is perchance that you yourself were saved,' replies the captain, changing the meaning of the word to a less optimistic 'by chance'; 'And so perchance may he be,' she insists (1.2.4–6). A more ironic but perhaps more sinister use of the same device is Maria's reply to Sir Toby's claim that Sir Andrew is blessed with 'the good gifts of nature': she splits the 'gifts' in question into 'the gift [i.e. talent] of a coward' that he possesses and 'the gift [i.e. present] of a grave' that awaits him.

Another prominent splitting or doubling figure in the play is hendiadys, significantly rebaptized by Puttenham as 'the figure of Twynnes', since through it 'ye will seeme to make two of one not thereunto constrained' (Puttenham, 147). It consists in the use of two nouns connected by a conjunction in place of a noun and qualifier: 'that miracle and queen of gems', instead of 'miraculous queen', in Orsino's effusion on Olivia's beauty (2.4.85). Like ploce, this figure of twins is adopted precisely by one of the twins, Sebastian, in a metaphor recalling the storm that separated them: his allusion to Olivia's unexpected passion for him as 'this accident and flood of fortune' (in place of 'accidental flood'; 4.3.11). The opposite process also arises in the comedy, namely a form of ellipsis that we might call hendiadys in reverse; here a phrase comprising two nouns linked by a conjunction is transformed into noun and qualifier: 'I could not with such estimable wonder overfar believe that' (instead of 'esteem and wonder') says Sebastian, with reference to his similarity to Viola (2.1.25–6). These two figures not only mirror each other but mimic the optical mirroring between the twins themselves: the final scene presents the two possibilities of a doubled image (a kind of visual hendiadys) or of two separate images contracted into one (hendiadys in reverse).

The language and metalanguage of the play are marked by a degree of rhetorical self-awareness, often playful or ironical (as in Feste's 'hyperbolical'). In encouraging Sir Andrew to write his challenge, Sir Toby invokes two of the five parts of rhetoric: 'It is no matter how witty, so it be eloquent and full of invention'

(3.2.41–2); the double allusion is to *inventio*, the finding of arguments (for the challenge) and *elocutio*, style. The joke, of course,
is that the letter observes neither, proving sublimely witless rather
than 'witty'. Sir Andrew none the less endeavours to show off rhetorical knowledge in his disastrous exchange with Maria. Bemused
by her semantic acrobatics and suspecting hidden meanings, he is
prompted to ask, 'Wherefore, sweetheart? What's your metaphor?'
(1.3.69–70). This gives Maria another chance to hint at his impotence ('It's dry, sir'), thereby provoking another semantic crisis:
'SIR ANDREW But what's your jest? / MARIA A dry jest, sir' (73–4).
Maria's 'dry jest' may be another rhetorical allusion: the 'drye
mock' was Puttenham's term for irony (Puttenham, 157), of the
kind Maria adopts against her hapless interlocutor.

   Such linguistic self-awareness is part of a broader metalanguage
running through the play regarding the very nature of the linguistic sign. The comedy's chief interrogator of the sign is Feste, who
repeatedly expresses a radical scepticism concerning the reliability
of language as a means of representing the truth: 'words are grown
so false I am loath to prove reason with them' (3.1.23–4). Feste's
distrust is posited on the arbitrariness of the sign, whereby the relationship between signifier and signified is merely conventional and
thus unstable, open to continuous change and easy manipulation:
'A sentence is but a cheverel glove to a good wit: how quickly the
wrong side may be turned outward' (3.1.11–13). Such scepticism
towards the sign is close to – and may echo – that of Montaigne:
'There is both the name, and the thing . . . the name, is neither
part of the thing nor of substance: it is a stranger-piece ioyned to
the thing' (Montaigne, 359). The clown's specific accusation, made
playfully but at the same time in earnest, is that the arbitrariness
of the sign renders it promiscuous, since it is always open to new
semantic relationships, especially in the hands or on the tongue of
an able word-player: 'They that dally nicely with words may quickly
make them wanton' (3.1.14–15). The paradox of this position, of
course, is that it is precisely Feste's professional task to exploit the
semantic wantonness of words in order to produce the punning and

fooling of which he is master: as he admits, 'I am indeed not her fool, but her corrupter of words' (3.1.34–5).

In his encounter with Sebastian, Feste hints at a more radical critique of our pretence to knowledge, affirming drastically that 'Nothing that is so is so' (4.1.8). This suggests a 'Platonic' diffidence not only towards language but to all modes of representation and thus towards all forms of supposed knowledge. The events of the play – in which all visual as well as verbal data are overturned and all representations turn out to be deceptive – go some way to validating his claim, although, lest we take his ontological negation ('Nothing . . . so') too seriously, he states the exact opposite in Sir Topas's parody of logical analysis, namely, 'That that is is' (4.2.14–15: see commentary). This shifting between negation and affirmation feeds into the comedy's dialectic between semiotic scepticism and faith. Feste's critique of the sign runs counter to other moments in the play that affirm emphatically the magical potentialities of verbal and visual representations, from Sebastian's 'wonder that enwraps me thus' before the words and actions of Olivia to the latter's 'Most wonderful!' and Fabian's 'Which I have wondered at', faced with the spectacle of the finale (5.1.221, 352). The last scene brings about a reconciliation between Feste's negation ('Nothing that is so is so') and affirmation ('That that is is') in the duke's 'that is and is not' (213). In *Twelfth Night* the sign is at once itself and its own opposite.

MAKE A GOOD SHOW ON'T: *TWELFTH NIGHT* IN PERFORMANCE

If this were played upon a stage: performances virtual and actual

Twelfth Night is a play unusually aware of its destiny as a script for performance. At several points in the comedy Shakespeare toys with awareness of the *mise-en-scène* in progress: the most explicit of these moments is Fabian's affirmation, in the full flow of the cross-gartering episode, that 'If this were played upon a stage now, I could condemn it as an improbable fiction' (3.4.123–4). This is an 'authenticating' device (Burns), since it presupposes that the scene is *not* being played but is really happening 'now' and here. At the same time it raises a laugh from the real audience, amused by the irony of Fabian's apparent lack of knowledge of where he is (but also by the suspicion that really he does know).

The comedy is replete with the language of performance, hinting at a secret consciousness of what is taking place – or that *it* is taking place – onstage. Viola's début as Cesario, for example, introduces an insistent theatrical vocabulary that goes beyond the simple playing of a disguise role. To Olivia's question 'Are you a comedian?' (1.5.177) – dangerously close to theatrical as well as dramatic truth – Cesario responds, still more dangerously, 'I am not that I play' (179). What gives this metatheatrical language its piquancy is its gendered quality. When Cesario claims that he has taken pains to 'con' his speech, he is not only using actor's parlance but is hinting at the gender complications at work, since 'con' is (French) slang for the female genitals, which Viola conceals and the boy actor feigns to possess. Similarly when, later in the scene, Cesario praises Olivia's charms, but with the proviso 'if God did all' (229), he is alluding in part to the cosmetic transformation of male player into aristocratic female beauty.

Such self-consciousness is linked to a peculiar characteristic of *Twelfth Night*, namely its unusually detailed scripting or inscribing of a virtual performance. Because of its close attention to modes of dress and other forms of behaviour, the play is unusually 'coercive' in specifying the details of what transpires onstage: Malvolio, for example, must have some form of yellow hose and gartering for the joke to work in 3.4, just as Olivia must cover her face in 1.5. There is likewise a strict correspondence between text and performance in the verbal indication of minimal physical actions at the moment they occur onstage, or a moment before or after they occur, from Sir Andrew's capering, to Maria's playing with his hand, to her dropping of the letter, to the men hiding in the box-tree to the innumerable takings of hands and exchanges of objects (Olivia giving a ring and miniature to Viola or a pearl to Sebastian, Orsino and others giving money to Feste, and so on). The text's minimalist implied 'stage directions' in the dialogue even include precise modes of movement such as Sir Toby's 'halting' gait when drunk and injured (5.1.187).

This does not mean, of course, that *Twelfth Night* must always be performed in more or less the same way. What it entails, rather, is an extraordinary interaction between the character's 'virtual' body, appearance and movement and his or her actual representation onstage through the real body of the actor. One of the means of creating this relationship is deictic reference (e.g. through demonstrative pronouns) to the actor's gestures or to props, as in Sebastian's astonished 'This is the air, that is the glorious sun; / This pearl she gave me' (4.3.1–2), which implies an accompanying gesture taking us from the general environment to the particular object in his hand. Such a relationship is one of the causes of intense audience involvement, since the spectator often has the heady impression of witnessing in real time a series of micro-performances planned and commented on by the characters themselves.

A particularly important discursive role in the comedy is played by doors, virtual and (in performance) actual. As Lois Potter notes, '*Twelfth Night* is unusual in the amount of attention that is paid to the business of getting in and out of these doors' (Potter, 25). The two doors of the Middle Temple screen and the two (or possibly three) of the Globe stage become the locus not only of the play's busy onstage traffic but of references, gestures and jokes within the dialogue. Attention to doors is created in part by the difficulty of entering Olivia's household, underlined in Orsino's exhortation to Cesario, 'Be not denied access, stand at her doors' (1.4.16), and in Cesario's obedient obstinacy, 'he says he'll stand at your door like a sheriff's post' (1.5.143–4). Olivia herself later orders, 'Let the garden door be shut' (3.1.90). Olivia's door is varied in the gate to her garden (still represented in performance by a stage door): 'there is at the gate a young gentleman,' Maria informs Olivia (1.5.95). 'What is he at the gate, cousin?' the latter asks anxiously (112–13). The puns on gait/gate (1.4.15, 3.1.81) further foreground the difficulty of entry. The comedy's business with doors includes the split-second timing of simultaneous entrances and exits: Cesario and Malvolio entering at separate doors at 2.2.0.1–2, Sir Toby and his cronies exiting at one door as Sebastian enters at the other at 5.1.204, and so on. Such simultaneity may be exploited in performance for comic effect: for example, the interrupted exits of Orsino and Cesario at 5.1.138ff., both frozen by Olivia's 'husband' (see p. 115), or Malvolio's often exaggerated calling to Maria at the door at 1.5.159–60.

Such onstage comings and goings bring us to the actual business of the play's staging. *Twelfth Night* is fairly long, comprising 2,580 lines (compared, for example, to the 2,299 of *Two Gentlemen* or the 2,222 of *Midsummer Night's Dream*; *As You Like It* is longer at 2,797).[1] It does not, however, make excessive demands in terms of staging or scenery. There is no evident use of balconies or discovery spaces. The only significant item of stage furniture is the box-tree in 2.5, which might be an actual plant or merely a screen or other symbolic representation (in the original staging a property carried or pushed on and off the stage through a door) or may have been purely imaginary: Bernard Beckerman observes that 'the box tree is not really required. No further mention is made of it' (Beckerman, 196). A means of setting apart Malvolio's dark room is needed in 4.2: in modern productions, this requirement can be met by lighting, whereas on the Elizabethan stage the likeliest solution was the trap (as sometimes also in modern productions).

Otherwise, the action can unfold rapidly on a relatively empty stage. As Granville-Barker notes, 'There is much to show that the play was designed for performance upon a bare platform stage

1   These statistics refer to the through-numbering of lines in Charlton Hinman's edition of the First Folio.

without traverses, inner rooms and the like. It has the virtues of this method, swiftness and cleanness of writing and simple direct-ness of arrangement even where the plot is least simple' (Barker, 'Preface', 562). The play is therefore straightforward in its staging demands, although paradoxically it is perhaps the very simplicity of its 'virtual' staging that has provoked some directors and stage-managers to devise elaborate sets: the representation of Orsino's court and Olivia's garden and kitchen, for example, exercised designers' imagination in the nineteenth and twentieth centuries (see pp. 100–1).

Other specific physical requirements are likewise minimalist. Only minor props are called for: letters, tankards, swords, purses, coins, rings, jewels (including a 'miniature'), in addition to Feste's pipe and tabor, although certain extra props, such as trunks and pipes, have become part of the play's stage history. The action and dialogue contain some specification of costume: Viola's male disguise (presumably identical to Sebastian's costume); Feste's motley or some variation of it; his gown and beard as Sir Topas; Malvolio's stockings and garters and chain of office; Olivia's mourning dress and in particular her veil; possibly Sir Andrew's coloured 'stock'. Here too, as with props, certain staging conven-tions unwarranted by the text have grown up, such as Malvolio's nightshirt (see p. 128).

Certain physical features of the players are also implied, such as Sir Andrew's hair hanging, according to Sir Toby (1.3.98), like flax, and traditionally represented as long, straight and yel-low; Sir Toby's other joking reference to him as 'tall' at 1.3.18 is sometimes taken literally, as is his final insult – 'a thin-faced knave' – at 5.1.203; this combination, together with Sir Andrew's own sickly surname, has produced an endless line of lanky and skinny Aguecheeks. Sir Andrew's appearance contrasts strategically, of course, with the corpulence of his exploiter, Sir Toby, implied in the latter's general behaviour and in his specific refusal to 'con-fine' himself at 1.3.9. Feste's claim at 4.2.6 to be 'not tall enough' to play a priest has also been interpreted perhaps over-literally in some productions, as has the analogous smallness of Maria implied in Cesario's sarcastic allusion to Olivia's 'giant' (1.5.199) and in Sir Toby's affectionate epithet 'wren' (3.2.63). But the greatest 'physical' challenge facing actors and producers is how to achieve a convincing likeness between the twins: a challenge that has more often been failed than met.

One of the issues involved in staging *Twelfth Night* is the choice of rhythm. Some directors have seen the play as divided into roughly two halves: a relatively slow and 'romantic' first half, and a more frenetic and comic second half (see M. Billington, xvii). In reality the play is constructed according to a principle of alternation: the languorous opening scene is followed by the more urgent and dramatic 'shipwreck' scene of 1.2, which in turn gives way to the more static domestic comedy of 1.3, and so on. It is true that from the letter scene (2.5) on there is a crescendo of farce, involving not only the gulling of Malvolio but the simultaneous 'duel' and Sebastian's unwitting involvement in both the fighting and the romance; but the interweaving of rhythms and moods better characterizes the play than any binary splitting into 'romantic' and 'comic' halves.

Problems may arise with the staging of the long and busy final scene, which gathers together all the comedy's various narrative threads and brings onstage most of the main characters. The scene is so full that Granville-Barker, one of the play's most innovative directors, was led to complain: 'From any cause, we certainly have a scandalously ill-arranged and ill-written last scene, the despair of any stage manager' (Barker, 'Preface', 563). The difficulty lies not only in stage-managing the scene's endless series of entries and exits and its various *coups de théâtre* – culminating in the 'natural perspective' of the identical twins, notoriously difficult to stage credibly – but in keeping the audience's attention, in the midst of the comings and goings, focused on the twists and turns of the dramatic narrative.

The success of *Twelfth Night* onstage is in part demonstrated by the sheer number and frequency of productions. The list of

120 productions at the end of this Introduction gives a necessarily selective and incomplete summary of the play's performance history from 1602 to 2004. Each production has been assigned a number (in parentheses) which will be referred to in the subsequent discussion.

First Night

As we have seen (p. 3), the first known staging of *Twelfth Night* bears the date 2 February 1602. If the play's title refers, as is often supposed, to the occasion of its first performance, it was presumably staged on 6 January of the same year, or possibly the year before (an even earlier date is improbable, since Manningham would presumably have known about the comedy). The question of the play's theatrical début clearly influences the issue of the date of composition: a first performance early in January implies composition late in the preceding year (i.e. in 1600 or 1601).

The first plausible hypothesis regarding the comedy's début was advanced by the nineteenth-century German critic Gregor Sarrazin, who linked the play to the presence at Queen Elizabeth's court of Don Virginio Orsini, Duke of Bracciano, on 6 January 1601. Shakespeare, according to Sarrazin, conceived his Duke Orsino as a homage to Duke Orsini in a performance commissioned for the latter's visit. This Italian connection, later taken by J.W. Draper and then elaborated into a full historical narrative by Leslie Hotson in *The First Night of Twelfth Night*, is supported by contemporary documents such as a memorandum of the Lord Chamberlain, Lord Hunsdon (patron of Shakespeare's company), referring to the choice, on the occasion of the Queen's 1601 Twelfth Night festivities, of a play 'that shalbe furnished with rich apparel, have great variety and change of Musicke and daunces, and of a Subiect that may be most pleasing to her Maiestie' (Hotson, 15). It is almost certain that the Lord Chamberlain's Men, Shakespeare's company, performed the chosen play; that it was a comedy is demonstrated by a letter sent by Duke Orsini to his wife, the Duchess Flavia, on 18 January, in which he informs her that 'a comedy was performed, mixed with music and dances', adding, disappointingly, 'but I will save this as well [like other details] to tell you about it in person'[1] (230).

Hotson's 'discovery' has been treated with condescension by later commentators, who have almost unanimously dismissed it. There are, however, a number of striking coincidences, at the least: the presence of Duke Orsini (not Orsino, as Hotson rebaptizes him); the performance of a Twelfth Night comedy by Shakespeare's company; the plausibility of 1601 as a date for first performance, and so on. Some of the arguments against the hypothesis are rather weak. The fact that news of the visit by Orsini – who was passing through London on his way home to Italy after accompanying Maria de' Medici to her wedding in France – arrived only on 25 December, leaving insufficient time to write and rehearse the play (Cam[2]), does not exclude the possibility that the duke's name in the comedy was simply changed to Orsino for the occasion. Likewise the fact that there is music but no dancing in the play – in contradiction with both quoted documents (Ard[2]) – means little, since dances could well have been added, for example in the play's finale (as in the 2002 Middle Temple performance). More serious is the objection that the lovesick Orsino is a dubious compliment to the (married) Italian guest, and thus probably not 'most pleasing to her Maiestie' (see Cam[2]). It might also be added that Orsini fails to note in his letter the extraordinary fact that his namesake is the comedy's male lead (unless he saved this too for his oral account to his wife).

If the Orsino–Orsini hypothesis is, in the end, more suggestive than persuasive, this does not mean that there is no connection at all. It is possible, for example, that Shakespeare, present as an actor at the Whitehall banquet, remembered Duke Orsini when he wrote his comedy, perhaps later in the same year or early in the next. This brings us to the second hypothesis, advanced by John

---

1   My translation of 'si rappresentò una commedia mescolata con musica e balli, e questa ancora mi riserbo a dire in voce'.

Dover Wilson, namely that the first night was Manningham's night, 2 February 1602. Wilson's belief that the play was written for an Inn of Court audience is based largely on his claim that 'the prose scenes are full of legal jests' (Cam[1], 95; Fabian is sometimes played as a law student: see Potter, 34). Wilson's idea has been revived more recently by the Middle Temple barrister Anthony Arlidge, who suggests that the play was written not only for lawyers but with specific Middle Temple lawyers in mind. Like Dover Wilson, Arlidge adduces by way of internal evidence the comedy's supposed plethora of legal references and 'inn jokes', but also presents external evidence for Shakespeare's Inn connections. The most direct link is the dramatist's (somewhat distant) relative Thomas Greene, a student at the Inn at the time of the performance who later – in addition to becoming treasurer of Middle Temple – lived with the Shakespeares in Stratford, where he became town clerk. Shakespeare's close friend Thomas Russell was also a Middle Templar (Duncan-Jones, 138). Arlidge also reads the play's two allusions to the Shirley brothers' expedition to Persia in 1599 (2.5.175 and 3.4.272: see pp. 72–3) as compliments to the brothers' (again distant) relative John Shurley, treasurer of the Temple in 1602. These connections, however, hardly make up a crushing case for the defence of the Middle Temple theory regarding the play's début.

Twelfth Night, moreover, is not in any obvious way a lawyer's play. It is indeed, like other Shakespearean plays, rich in legal allusions, but when the law is invoked in *Twelfth Night* it is more often than not in the context of legal transgressions, in keeping with the carnivalesque anarchy or 'misrule' that governs much of the comedy (see pp. 18–21). For example, Sir Andrew Aguecheek, in his anger against his supposed rival Cesario, appeals to the contemporary English – officially Illyrian – law on battery, only with a view to overturning it completely: 'I'll have an action of battery against him if there be any law in Illyria. Though I struck him first, yet it's no matter for that' (4.1.33–5). Fabian eggs on Sir Andrew in his altogether unjustified challenge, still supposedly in the name of Illyrian law: 'A good note, that keeps you from the blow of the law' (3.4.148–9; see also 159–60). Rather than a play for lawyers, it often looks like a play that suspends the law.

Manningham himself provides no evidence for or against the Middle Temple first night theory. Certainly, a début on 2 February would have rendered the play's title irrelevant, or at best ironic (it should be something like 'Candlemas'). If the title is indeed referential, the likeliest date of first performance is presumably 6 January 1602, which would have meant that the comedy was still fresh less than a month later at the Candlemas performance, which would thereby become 'second' night. Since there is no record of a Temple performance for that date, it must have been staged elsewhere, probably in another private hall, and may have been commissioned for the festive occasion.

There are, in summary, four possible first nights for *Twelfth Night*: at Whitehall on 6 January 1601; at the Middle Temple on 2 February 1602; at the public theatre – the Globe – rather than a private venue, presumably some time in 1601; or on 6 January 1602 in some other private performance space, prior to its appearance at the Middle Temple, and then on the public stage. This last hypothesis is probably the most plausible, but in the lack of new evidence the jury is likely to be out for a long time to come.

Later Nights: adaptations and rearrangements

As for the second performance for which we have a 'review', the precise contents of the 'silly play' that Samuel Pepys repeatedly and disapprovingly saw in the 1660s (see p. 6) is uncertain: the *Twelfth Night* performed at the Duke of York's may well have been an adaptation by Shakespeare's supposed 'natural son', William D'Avenant. What is certain is that the following production we have precise news of was indeed a radical adaptation, namely William Burnaby's *Love Betray'd: or, the Agreable* [*sic*] *Disapoinment* [*sic*] of 1703 (no. 7), which merges Malvolio and Aguecheek into a single character, Taquilet, who is fooled by Drances (Sir Toby) into believing that Villaretta (Olivia) loves him, while the tangled identity problems are solved through the agency of an invented character, Laura, who had served Cesario in France. The adaptation aroused little interest and survived only for a few nights.

The later performance history of *Twelfth Night* demonstrates that it invited, if not adaptation, at least restless rearrangement, especially on the nineteenth-century stage. The innumerable changes made by producers to the Folio's sequencing of episodes suggest that the structure of the play (in some ways akin to the traditional *commedia dell'arte* scenario, where the order of episodes was likewise highly variable) is modular rather than linear. The three main plots – Viola's, Sebastian's and Malvolio's – intersect and alternate with situations involving parallelism and simultaneity, rather than following a strict narrative order. There are relatively few logical cause-and-effect constraints on the sequencing: the delay in Sebastian's first appearance (2.1), for example, is dictated by dramaturgic rather than chronological motives (i.e. the creation of uncertainty regarding his destiny); the scene in turn delays the presumably simultaneous meeting between Cesario and Malvolio in 2.2, which is logically a continuation of 1.5.

The presiding scene structure is the duologue, namely one-to-one exchanges of a more or less intimate kind, and it is precisely the duologic scenes, especially those involving the twins (1.2, 2.1, 2.2, 3.3, etc.), that were most frequently moved in nineteenth-century productions. Elizabeth Inchbald's 1808 edition – closely related to Kemble's Drury Lane stagings – switches 1.1 and 1.2 and then runs 2.1 into 2.2 without a break. The inversion of the two opening scenes, which became common theatrical practice (see Osborne), was provoked partly by theatrical architecture: the proscenium-arch stage made it more economical to get the seaside scene out of the way in order to concentrate on the alternation between the two houses of Orsino and Olivia. But it was also dictated by a sense of the dramaturgic potency of beginning a play with a tempest rather than a disquisition, and by the opportunity of immediately foregrounding Viola's agency. The transposition of the opening scenes continues today, as in Branagh's 1987 production (no. 102) and Nunn's 1996 film (no. 109). Later acting editions (Oxberry, Cumberland, Lacy, etc.) extend Kemble's gesture by similarly moving the 'twin' duologue scene with the first appearance of Sebastian (2.1) to the end of 2.2. In the Folio text the scene acts as a parenthetic episode, interrupting the narrative sequence that begins with Olivia's sending of her ring to Cesario via Malvolio (1.5) and ends with Cesario's receiving it (2.2). Sebastian's unexpected appearance complicates matters, tying a further knot in the plot; the move turns it, instead, into an 'untying' scene, simplifying matters after Viola's lament, 'It is too hard a knot for me t'untie' (2.2.41).

Kemble's own acting edition also rearranged other scenes: the Malvolio episode in 2.2 (1–16) becomes a separate scene, 1.6, placed after Cesario's interview with Olivia; Antonio's and Sebastian's second meeting, 3.3, is moved forward to follow the gulling of Malvolio (2.5), thus preceding Olivia's declaration of love (3.1) and Sir Andrew's plan for a duel (3.2). Karen Greif suggests that Kemble 'realigned the scene order so that each act comprised a defined block of action, usually with strong opening and closing scenes that centred attention on Viola or Malvolio, the two leads' (Greif, 62). The changes, however, are often modes of censorship, especially on moralistic (sexual) grounds (Osborne, 81–92). Throughout the nineteenth century the two scenes between Antonio and Sebastian were continually cut or moved around, a sign of the embarrassment they caused producers, who systematically omitted Antonio's more ardent effusions in 2.1 and eliminated the parallels between Antonio's declaration of love and those of Viola and Olivia. Equally subject to censorship were Sebastian's 'excessive' thanks to his friend at 3.3.13–16, together with his underlining of Olivia's passion for another woman ('maid and man', 5.1.255–9). Kemble, followed by others, also transforms Viola's 'eunuch' (1.2.53) into the more conventional 'page'.

The scene transposition was varied at the end of the century by Daly, whose 1894 production (no. 37) reduced the play to four acts, cutting around 600 lines (Malvolio appeared only in the dark room scene). It began with 2.1 (Sebastian and Antonio), to which 1.2 was tacked on, while 1.1 (now 1.2) was fused with 1.4 (Cesario as go-between) so as not to change the elaborate set of Orsino's palace. Daly likewise fused 1.3 and 1.5 with 2.2 (Malvolio and the ring; Odell, 406). In the same year, Henry Irving (no. 36) combined 1.1 and 1.4, thereby anticipating Viola's presence at the duke's court; this change was repeated in Nunn's film (no. 109), which has Viola-as-Cesario present as the duke's silent pianist. Beerbohm Tree (no. 41) condensed the comedy into a 'well-made' three-act play whose interminable second scene on Olivia's terrace brought together seven separate Folio scenes in rearranged order (1.2, 1.3, 2.1, part of 3.3, 1.4, 1.5 and 2.2).

Perhaps because of its intense concern with music, the comedy has often been subject to musical adaptation. In 1820 Frederick Reynolds produced a controversial version (no. 23), described by Leigh Hunt in *The Examiner* as being 'interspersed with songs, glees and duetts, taken from the German and English masters' (quoted in Odell, 137). Reynolds drew on a wide range of composers, and imported into *Twelfth Night* extraneous Shakespearean songs and sonnets, together with the masque of Juno and Ceres from *The Tempest*. John Genest complained that 'this was Shakspeare's play degraded to an Opera – it was a wretched piece of business' (Genest, 9.99). Analogously, Augustin Daly's highly successful 1894 adaptation (no. 37), which ran for 111 performances, added a violent opening storm and a moonlit rose garden where Orsino serenaded Olivia in Act 3. Other musical embellishments included 'Come unto these yellow sands', from *The Tempest*, sung by fishermen and peasants before the two shipwreck scenes (1.2 and 2.1), while another group of musicians intoned 'Who is Olivia?' to Schubert's setting of 'Who is Sylvia?' (*TGV*) at the end of Act 3.

A number of modern musicals have taken on this most music-centred of Shakespeare's comedies (in addition to a ballet choreographed in 1943 by Andrée Howard to music by Edvard

Grieg (no. 65)). Hal Hester and Danny Apolinair's 1968 rock musical *Your Own Thing* (no. 86) is set in the city of Manhattan Island, Illyria, where Orson is a theatrical agent and Olivia the operator of a discotheque, while Viola and Sebastian, both rock singers, have lost all their music in a shipwreck. Cheryl L. West's 1997 *Play On!* (no. 111) is instead a jazz version, set to music by Duke Ellington. In 1940s Harlem, Vy, a talented young woman from Mississippi, is determined to succeed as a songwriter. The clown Jester dresses her as a man and introduces her to the great bandleader Duke. Vy-Man, as she's now called, falls in love with Duke, but the latter pines for the singer Lady Liv. Peter Mills's well-received 2002 musical *Illyria*, directed by Cara Reichel (no. 117), is more operetta-like; maintaining characters' names and following Shakespeare's plot fairly faithfully, it incorporates parts of his dialogue into the lyrics (the livelier songs including Feste's 'Silly Little Syllogisms', Sir Toby's drunken 'Cakes and Ale' and Sebastian's 'The Lady Must Be Mad'). Slapstick vaudeville numbers were performed below stairs, while Ames Adamson's farcically snobbish Malvolio expressed himself in Gilbert and Sullivan doggerel.

Our shows are more than will:
Victorian special effects and modernist experiments

The nineteenth century culminated in productions dominated by stage designers. In 1884 Henry Irving (no. 36) cut most of the music and songs and concentrated on the spectacular scenery of designer Hawes Craven, who provided a giddy succession of sixteen different lavish sets, including a palace for Olivia by a palm-lined blue sea. Herbert Beerbohm Tree's 1901 revival (no. 41) was governed by the set designers Hawes Craven (again) and Joseph Harker. Craven created a hyper-realistic Italianate garden for Olivia, in which the shipwrecked Viola was washed up directly in 1.2; it was based on a picture in *Country Life*, and provoked 'an "Oh!" of surprise and delight' from spectators (*The Sketch*). Dominated by a long grass-covered flight of stairs (down which

Malvolio fell spectacularly), it boasted three box-trees, a marble fountain, a bridge, a griffon-adorned stone bench, green lawns and countless colourful flowers under a hazy painted sky (this was the first in a series of optimistic summer productions), and no fewer than six entrances, put to conspicuous use in the letter scene.

The first reaction against such scenographic excesses came from Germany. In 1881 the Royal Theatre of Saxe-Meiningen, under the direction of Duke George II, visited Drury Lane with a production (no. 34) which restored the (translated) text and offered a simple set and Elizabethan costumes, achieving notable results 'by the excellence of ensemble playing alone' (Koller, 85). Modern directorial readings of the comedy are usually taken to begin, instead, with William Poel, whose productions were again a response to Victorian overindulgence. In order to start afresh, Poel and his Elizabethan Stage Society attempted a return to 'early modern' simplicity, and chose an emblematic theatrical space for the enterprise, namely the Middle Temple Hall, where on 2 February 1897 – 295 years after Manningham's 'first night' – they performed the play before the Prince of Wales (no. 39). The Temple production, advertised as being 'after the manner of the sixteenth century', used a mixed-sex cast (no boy actors) and created a curious architectural hybrid in the use of the hall: instead of employing the 'original' empty performance space, Poel endeavoured paradoxically to achieve sixteenth-century 'authenticity' by erecting within it a mini-Swan theatre inspired by the famous de Witt sketch, consisting of a raised platform with a roof supported by carved columns, and complete with gallery (Speaight, *Poel*, 110). There was no scenery and the only furnishing comprised a table and chair, while the costumes were modelled on those of the Elizabethan court. Renaissance music was played on sixteenth-century Italian instruments (a virginal and lute) and a bass and treble viol. Poel was probably influenced by nineteenth-century musical versions of the play in casting the roles with an ear to the operatic vocal qualities of the actors. The resulting performance, at times inaudible, was dismissed by William Archer as 'staged (more or less) after the manner of the sixteenth century and acted after the manner of the Nineteenth Century Amateur' (quoted in Speaight, *Poel*, 135). Two later productions returned to the primal scene of the Middle Temple Hall. On 2 February 1951 (a year early, because of a misinterpretation of Manningham's diary entry), Donald Wolfit produced a 350th anniversary staging (no. 72), dominated by his hyperbolically pompous Malvolio. On 25 January 2002 (eight days early, but performances continued throughout February) the Globe Theatre Company celebrated the 400th anniversary with a highly successful revival (no. 114).

Poel helped create a fashion for performances in the 'Elizabethan' manner. Ben Greet in his 1904 New York production (no. 43) employed a pseudo–Middle-Temple stage, with raised platform, boxed and panelled set and timbered ceiling. The early years of the century also witnessed the desire for a return to Shakespeare's text after the manipulations of the preceding hundred years. In 1914, also in New York, Margaret Anglin courageously used the unedited Folio text, even if this created some difficulties for the audience (no. 47).

It is in the context of a concerted break with the Victorian tradition that there arose the first modernist staging – and the most influential twentieth–century presentation. Harley Granville-Barker's legendary 1912 Savoy production (no. 46) was described by the poet John Masefield as 'much the most beautiful thing I have ever seen done on the stage' (quoted in Styan, 91), a judgement shared by many commentators. Barker, like Poel and Greet, aimed to achieve simplicity and rapidity of performance through continuous staging, with minimal breaks in the action, on a relatively uncluttered stage, while the text, left virtually uncut, was delivered at a fast pace and with a light 'musical' touch; the *Daily Telegraph* praised 'the long multiplex cadences, the sweet melody, the bewitching variety of Shakespearean rhythm'. Unlike his predecessors, however, Barker went far beyond 'archaeo–logical' reconstruction in his endeavour to invent what he called 'a new hieroglyphic language of scenery' (Styan, 91). Norman Wilkinson's extraordinary non–realist set (see Fig. 20) gave Orsino a palace made up of 'twisted barley–sugar pillars in pink' (Trewin, 55) against a Cubist backdrop of pink and green triangles. Olivia had a formal garden with pale green 'Noah's ark' trees, perhaps in parody of Hawes Craven, while the box–trees in the letter scene were represented by two 'Futurist space needles' (Kennedy, 75–6). Wilkinson's costumes were likewise of bright primitivist colours, notably Orsino's 'decadent' pink, set off against Olivia's severe black.

Two years later another ground–breaking 'avant–garde' staging, much admired by Barker, took place at the Théâtre du Vieux-Colombier in Paris. Jacques Copeau's 1914 version (no. 48), like Barker's, 'immediately became one of those rare productions that assume almost mythical proportions' (Kennedy, 81). Copeau (who also played Malvolio) and his designer, Louis Jouvet (who doubled as Sir Andrew), used an empty forestage with a pink drop, cutting off the rest of the space for Orsino's palace, while Olivia's palace was figured by a single locale comprising a cube, a one–step platform, a central recess, and two artificial shrubs; a yellow drop marked a space for exterior scenes, and the entire set was framed by white curtains. Copeau used groupings to create a series of stunning tableaux marked by harmoniously choreographed movement and speech.

In the 1920s and 1930s the Old Vic became the London 'home' of *Twelfth Night*. Robert Atkins's rather conventional productions (nos 50, 55) were an annual event for many years and employed many of the great names of the London stage. The Vic witnessed two rather more adventurous productions by Tyrone Guthrie; the first, his fast–moving 1933 staging (no. 57), again attempted to recapture something of the openness and fluidity of Elizabethan performance; Wells Coates's austere set, comprising 'two curving staircases [and] two formidable pillars' was 'a scene of the utmost severity, massive, stony, bare . . . not a sprig of nature anywhere, even in a pot, and one dreams in vain of the yew–hedge through

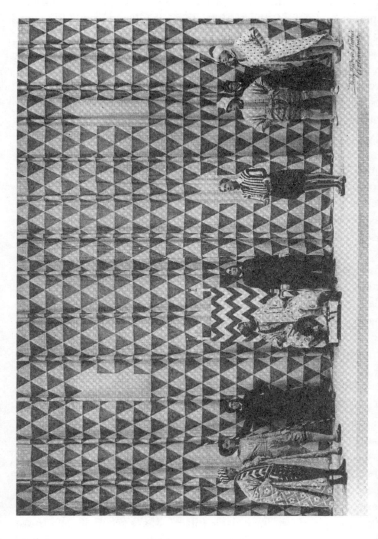

20 Norman Wilkinson's futurist set for Harley Granville-Barker's 1912 production

which the knights were wont to whisper' (*Times*). On this naked stage Guthrie achieved strikingly beautiful groupings. His 1937 staging (no. 58), likewise 'played in a nimble and quick-spirited style', was decidedly downbeat in mood, dominated by the awareness of mortality: 'And over all there hangs, like the shadow cast by a sundial, the knowledge that youth's a stuff will not endure'; even the revels were played against 'an ominous background of darkness' figuring 'the shadow of death' (Stephen Williams, *Evening Standard*). Still at the Vic, Harcourt Williams in 1932 (no. 54) introduced what was to become a recurrent feature in later productions, namely a seventeenth-century setting with Caroline costumes. The production boasted an urban set of the same period, 'with a permanent section of red brick wall, steps, and a verandah that gives something of the flavour of a Dutch picture' (J.G.B., *Evening News*).

In the same year a seventeen-year-old American student directed a highly ingenious staging at the Chicago Drama Festival (no. 56). Orson Welles's all-male Todd Troupers performance, originally produced for his school, won first prize at the festival. It featured a twelve-foot-high 'storybook' set (see Fig. 21), in vivid expressionistic colours, representing a volume whose pages turned with each new scene, symbolizing how dramatic life sprang from the text (Berg & Erskine, 396, France, 38). Welles, who played Malvolio, devised for the production a narrative prologue ('Once upon a time, long, long ago, there was a storm at sea . . .'; compare the prologue to Nunn's 1996 film: see p. 118) and a dialogue between Shakespeare and Burbage. In this, Burbage complains at the size of his part: 'What is offered me, me, Richard Burbage, at the zenith of my own personal career? The Duke! The Duke! In a play about twins!' (Mercury, 8–9). A short 16 mm film version was shot in 1933, while Welles's adapted text was published in his *Everybody's Shakespeare* series a year later.

Some of the more innovative productions before and after the Second World War were the work of women directors. In 1939 Irene Hentschel became the first woman to direct at the

21   Orson Welles's storybook set for his 1932 production

Stratford Shakespeare Festival (no. 62), and her production, according to one irate reviewer, 'shrieks at the conventions, flouts all the traditions' (*Birmingham Mail*, quoted in Schafer, 216). Particularly irksome to traditionalists was the farcical staging of many scenes. This was, moreover, one of the first Stratford productions to choose a modern historical setting, or rather a strategically changeable period style. Hentschel brought in a team of women designers, known appropriately as 'Motley', to create inconsistent costumes: a Dickensian Malvolio, a Regency Orsino, an Edwardian Sir Toby, and so on. An equally controversial event was Joan Littlewood's Theatre Workshop opening production at the legendary Theatre Royal, Stratford East (London), on 2 February 1953 (no. 74), which, with its ensemble Brechtian acting techniques, set out to involve its audience, who showed their feelings enthusiastically, some of them throwing pennies and toffees at the stage (Goorney, 99).

Seasonal Nights

One can divide many of the stagings of the last fifty years or so into two main directorial camps: 'Twelfth Night' productions and 'Illyrian' productions. The former have a primarily temporal and specifically seasonal emphasis, the latter a more spatial – and especially 'exotic' – take on the play.

Seasonal 'Twelfth Night' productions were effectively inaugurated by Peter Hall's highly successful 1958 staging (no. 81), with its 'mistily russet autumnal sense' (Trewin, 238). The evocative sets by Lila de Nobili (designer for Luchino Visconti at La Scala in Milan) included a gauzy Adriatic coastline complete with cloud-topped towers, which gave way to an English garden, suggesting the mixed geographical allegiances of the comedy. The Caroline historical setting (recalling Harcourt Williams's 1932 staging) underlined the ideological conflict at the heart of the play, pitching a Puritan Malvolio against the others, all in cavalier costumes. Hall's aim was also to deconstruct the binary festivity/melancholy opposition by injecting melancholy into the comic scenes and comedy into the 'serious' ones (see Speaight, *Shakespeare*, 278)

Hall's production created a fashion for seasonal interpretations of the comedy that went on to dominate performances, especially in Stratford, for the next three decades. One of the most celebrated modern versions, John Barton's 1969 RSC staging (no. 87), was also decidedly autumnal in mood (although also brilliantly comic). It was visually dominated by Christopher Morley's set, a 'box tapering in false perspective to a small opening upstage which opens to reveal a garden or a shipwreck' (B.A. Young, *Financial Times*), recalling the illusory 'natural perspectives' of the Renaissance, but at the same time evoking 'a skeletal Riviera of sun-streaked reed lattices, wicker garden furniture and parasols' (Ronald Bryden, *Observer*). Much use was made of the perspective-framed entrance of characters, notably Malvolio 'practising behaviour to his own shadow' (2.5.15) as he moved towards the audience. Barton placed great emphasis on the theme of madness, which infected all the characters in different ways, and put Feste at the perceptual centre of the play, so that events were seen largely from his disenchanted perspective.

Ten years later, still at the RSC, Terry Hands (no. 95) gave a Northrop Frye-like reading of the comedy as a life-renewing seasonal passage from snow-laden and frosty-branched midwinter to daffodilly spring. John Caird, again at Stratford in 1983 (no. 98), took Illyria back to autumn in a version that presented the play unambiguously as a dark comedy; Robin Don's set, inspired by Giorgione's *La Tempesta*, figured a bare rocky promontory accompanied by the sound of the surge of the sea, and dominated by a great gnarled autumnal tree that conditioned the entire performance, not least the movements of the actors. This was very much an 'outdoor' production, as was, four years later, Bill Alexander's summertime RSC staging (no. 100) – returning to the sunny solstitial tradition created by Tree in 1901 (no. 41) – in which Kit Surrey's set of lath and plaster against a blue cyclorama figured a sun-drenched white-walled Greek island (see Fig. 22), its main locale being an open square (in the letter scene the plotters overlooked Malvolio from the windows of surrounding buildings). Alexander took the steward's madness literally, representing him – in Anthony Sher's hyperbolic performance (see p. 126) – as a passion-crazed fanatic in Greek orthodox garb.

In the same year (1987), away from Stratford, Kenneth Branagh's Renaissance Theatre Company touring production (no. 102) was, by contrast, staged at the winter solstice, in keeping with its primarily subdued and at times funereal atmosphere: 'He has taken the title literally and his Edwardian Illyria is locked in the grip of an icy winter,' observed Charles Spencer (*Daily Telegraph*). Bunnie Christy's main set was a snow-covered cemetery littered with 'balustrades, broken masonry, scattered statuary, ivy-twined gates, bare trees' (Martin Hoyle, *Financial Times*). Branagh also made the increasingly popular choice of a Victorian-to-Edwardian Christmas setting, with decorated tree and all. The production was strong on interpersonal mirroring: not only Viola and Sebastian but Orsino and Olivia resembled each other both physically and behaviourally in an intriguing game of multiple reflection. Even more overtly Christmassy, and betraying no fear

22 Malvolio (Anthony Sher) and Olivia (Deborah Findlay) in Bill Alexander's 1987 RSC production

of bad taste, was Ian Judge's 1994 RSC version (no. 107) with its traditional Christmas-card set by John Gunter, featuring a row of snow-roofed, half-timbered Stratford houses against which the characters posed in conventional Elizabethan costumes. Judge affirmed the pure Englishness, indeed Stratfordness, of the play and its setting: 'When I look through the hedges of New Place, or sit in the gardens of Hall's Croft,' he told his cast, 'I understand Illyria' (quoted in Holland, 191). Victorian 'Englishness' had also marked Griff Rhys Jones's 'maritime' production for the RSC in 1991 (no. 104), in which Terence Hillyer's Orsino, in a fancy-dress admiral's uniform and surrounded by a court of naval officers, appeared on a huge ship-deck designed by Ultz out of Gilbert and Sullivan's *HMS Pinafore* (Holland, 83).

Illyrian variations

Because of its 'festive' qualities, *Twelfth Night* has often been used to inaugurate or reopen theatres (see nos 28, 53, 66, 73 and 74). Hugh Hunt's 1950 production (no. 69) reopened the Old Vic, the play's traditional home, and also started off a long line of 'Illyrian' productions, emphasizing the geographical and cultural rather than solstitial setting, and thereby removing the revels from their traditional English habitat. Hunt chose an Italianate picture set portraying 'a small island off the Dalmatian coast' (Hugh Hunt, 1954; in *SC*, 26.233), inhabited by fake *commedia dell'arte* clowns tumbling and striking endless poses, together with a chorus of skipping, clapping and dancing urchins. Despite the local colouring, however, the overall effect was drab post-war British. A more convincing attempt to break with the standard Elizabethan-to-Edwardian English mode was Clifford Williams's athletic, farcical and essential *commedia*-style rendering for the RSC in 1966 (no. 84), decidedly more vigorous and less sentimental than Hunt's picturesque Neapolitanism.

Further away in both fictional and real space, a more radical break with geopolitical tradition was made by Ariane Mnouchkine at the 1982 Avignon Festival (no. 97), in a reading influenced by

Asian theatre and 'adapting an Indian look but not an Indian performance style' (Kennedy, 237). Orientalism, especially Indian culture, has been a recurrent feature of some of the more challenging stagings over the past two decades or so. Michael Kahn's acclaimed 1989 Folger Shakespeare production in Washington (no. 103) had a post-colonial emphasis, being set on an 'eastern' island, somewhere between India, Sri Lanka and Cambodia, at the time of British occupation. Designer Derek McLane drew on a mixture of eastern architectural styles in a set dominated by thousands of movable bamboo slats through which seeped the light of the surrounding jungle. Kahn used the eastern setting to suggest parallels between the rigid social order of Illyria and the regime imposed by the colonialists. Peter Webster's romantic raja Orsino and Kelly McGillis's sexy Viola, splendidly metamorphosing from damp négligé to colonial khaki, clashed with Yusef Bulos's somewhat Chaplinesque Asian clown.

More recently, Stephen Beresford's 2004 Albery production (no. 120) was not generically Asian but unmistakably Indian. The transposition of Illyrian events to modern-day India was posited on a powerful analogy between the early modern class hierarchy and the Indian caste system, above all in the relationship between householders and their servants. Modern India with its maharajas and soothsayers is a workable cultural translation of Renaissance society with its dukes and truth-telling fools, and this interpretation was largely convincing. The production opened spectacularly with a monsoon lashing down on shuttered houses in Jonathan Fensom's set, which was tilted at an angle so as to suggest a world emotionally out of joint. The all-Indian cast (speaking with undisguised Indian accents) included the Bollywood star Neha Dubey and the television celebrity Kulvinder Ghir.

The mettle of your sex: gender and homoeroticism

One of the most important developments in recent productions – parallel to the analogous development within critical studies – has been an increased emphasis on the questions of sexuality and gender dramatized in the comedy. One of the earliest stagings to place the themes of androgyny and sexual ambiguity at the centre of the performance was Peter Gill's 1974 RSC production (no. 93), dedicated primarily to the 'erotic metamorphoses' of the central characters (Irving Wardle, *The Times*), notably Orsino, who, caught 'hugging Cesario to his breast with rapturous abandon' (Michael Billington, *Guardian*), underwent a somewhat dubious conversion to heterosexuality. The overall theme of erotic self-infatuation was emblematically represented by William Dudley's plain box set dominated by the sketch of 'an ambisextrous [*sic*] Narcissus figure gazing into a pool' (Billington, *Guardian*: see Fig. 4).

Lindsay Posner's 2001 RSC version (no. 113) similarly, if less systematically, focused on the play of cross-gender desires, at the centre of which was positioned Cesario, who was alternately kissed vigorously by Olivia and fondled lovingly by Orsino. The production's homoerotic *coup de théâtre*, however, was the discovery of Sebastian and Antonio getting dressed on an unmade double bed on the beach in 2.1 (presumably the bed was washed ashore from the wreck, perhaps with the lovers in it). Even more provocative was Cheek by Jowl's 1986 touring production, directed by Declan Donnellan (no. 99), in which Orsino was caught wholeheartedly petting Cesario, while an unmistakably gay Antonio struck up a liaison with Feste at the end of the dramatic proceedings. Equally controversial in this staging was the mixed-accent crassness of many characters, including a saxophone-playing Maria with a Brooklyn twang and an Aguecheek performed as 'a tumescent jack-rabbit from the boondocks of Middle America' (Michael Ratcliffe, *Observer*).

Adrian Noble's highly inventive, and no less controversial, 1997 RSC staging (no. 110) also began, as one critic put it, 'on a distinctly gay note – with Orsino surrounded by an intimate clutch of young courtiers in crushed velvet suits' (Nicholas de Jongh, *Evening Standard*). Noble's main interests, however, lay in the shifting modes of behaviour and styles of performance to which the play's 'opalescent' mutability lends itself. Like Irene Hentschel's experimental 1939 version (no. 62), Noble's presented shifting periods of costume: Aguecheek sported a 1920s blazer, the women 1940s New Look dresses, and so on. A late-twentieth-century pop-art set, designed by Anthony Ward, featured a lurid sky-blue electric arch and a bright-green cartoon hedge which doubled as topiary in the letter scene. Each scene offered a different stage scenario: in 1.2 Viola was discovered in a hospital bed with intravenous drip, while the captain had his arm in a sling; 1.3 was set in a music hall; in 1.4 Orsino and his court emerged semi-naked from showers; 2.3, the kitchen scene, was dominated by a huge refrigerator full of bottles. The most audacious scene was undoubtedly 4.2, which placed Malvolio literally in the doghouse, a garish pink kennel labelled 'Sowter' (see 2.5.121), through the roof of which Feste fed the steward dog-meal and urine (see Fig. 23).

The most striking and most widely publicized aspect of Tim Carroll's 2002 anniversary production at the Middle Temple (no. 114) was its 'Elizabethan'-style all-male cast. This turned out to be far more than an attention-seeking publicity device. The female parts were performed by adult males, some of them very young (Eddie Redmayne's Viola), others decidedly more mature (Mark Rylance's Olivia and Paul Chahidi's Maria), all of whom achieved a convincing degree of femininity without resorting to falsetto voices or camp gesture. One of the real advantages of this generalized cross-dressing was that it allowed the audience to accept quite happily what often seem improbable fictions, beginning with the mistaken identity between the twins: when Rhys Meredith's Sebastian made his first appearance, his likeness to Eddie Redmayne's Viola/Cesario (see Fig. 24) was so perfect as to send spectators looking at their cast lists, and there were several later moments of justified uncertainty as to which of the two had come on. It also allowed sexual and gender implications to emerge clearly without heavy underlining: Olivia's uncontrollable attraction towards the boy-actor's Viola or

23 Malvolio in the doghouse: Philip Voss (Malvolio) and Stephen Boxer (Feste) in Adrian Noble's 1997 RSC production

passionate kissing of Sebastian were at once innocent, comic and erotically charged. In addition, it made sense of what might have seemed rather forced comedy in the last scene, such as Orsino's kneeling before the wrong twin at 'Boy, thou hast said to me a thousand times' (5.1.263; the 'boy' becomes disturbingly real), or his preparing to go off with Sebastian on 'Your master quits you' (315). Above all, the twins' same-sex likeness produced a genuinely spectacular denouement at their reunion, making the *trompe l'œil* illusion of Shakespeare's 'natural perspective' a moment of true optical magic, and turning Olivia's breathless 'Most wonderful!', at the sight of her doubled lover (221), into a sublime delirium of desire.

Unlike Poel's 1897 Temple performance, there were no mini-Swan theatres in this revival; indeed, one of the main challenges facing the company was to invent staging solutions within a restricted and difficult acting area. Carroll's production was a quest not so much for 'authenticity' as for vitality. Much use was made of the full length of the hall through the invention of a third exit (actually the fire exit) at the opposite end from the screen with its two classical doors, allowing greater liberty of movement, and at the same time imposing a rapid pace on exits, entrances and stage movements in order to counteract the inevitable slowness in negotiating the long vertical axis of the hall. As in Poel's version, Elizabethan musical settings were played on early modern instruments. Carroll's production – probably like the Lord Chamberlain's Men's – later transferred to the Globe, whose stage is notoriously deep; but much of the verticality, as well as the rapidity, of the original staging was saved by exploiting its equally great width, with the action spread out along and across the entire platform. The knowing use of the theatre's plethora of doors (three, plus two curtained openings, making a dizzying total of five, a number that might have astonished Shakespeare's company) allowed rapid simultaneous entrances and exits, and business being conducted at two or more doors at the same time. This gave rise to moments of brilliant physical comedy, as in the final scene when Orsino and Cesario, on the point of exiting together, stop in their tracks and stare at each other, frozen, when Olivia pronounces the fateful word 'husband' (5.1.139).

The second main anniversary performance in 2002, Sam Mendes' otherwise acclaimed Donmar production (no. 116), was

24 'One face, one voice, one habit and two persons' (5.1.212): Eddie Redmayne (Viola) and Rhys Meredith (Sebastian) in Tim Carroll's 2002 Middle Temple production

accused of insensitivity towards the topic of sexuality and gender (suggesting that critics and audiences now expect this issue to be central). Mendes' decidedly heterosexual and overtly Chekhovian reading (the play doubled with his *Uncle Vanya*) placed at the theatrical and iconographic centre of the play, in the award-winning set again designed by Anthony Ward, the theme of the projection of desire, by means of a large gilt picture frame in which the image of a given character's object of affection appeared whenever spoken of: thus Olivia materialized both in 1.1, veiled, during Orsino's speech on love, and in the letter scene, where she turned her back on Malvolio during his reverie. More literally Chekhovian was Declan Donnellan's highly comic 2003 Russian-language International Chekhov Festival production (no. 118), in which 'The vodka-swilling, below-stairs antics' were 'reminiscent of the late-night drinking scenes from Chekhov's *Uncle Vanya*' (Helen Meany, *Irish Times*).

Show you the picture: Twelfth Night *on film*

Twelfth Night offers film directors a variety of outdoor and indoor settings, a fast-moving plot and a number of potential star roles. The first film version of the play – and one of the earliest Shakespeare films ever – is Charles Kent's silent ten-minute Vitagraph production of 1910 (no. 45), with Kent himself as Malvolio and Florence Turner as Viola. Kent creates what was to become a cinematic convention by opening with a narrative 'prologue', here in the 'primitive' form of a caption ('Viola separated from her twin brother Sebastian by a shipwreck'; compare Nunn). The film owes a good deal to nineteenth-century stage productions, especially Tree's 1901 version, whose scenery is recalled in the film's garden set, with its fountain and long flight of steps; and some of its stage business is included, such as Malvolio's placing of the ring on the end of his wand in 2.2. As in various Victorian productions, Viola's arrival on shore (with her brother's trunk) is followed immediately by the rescue of Sebastian. Malvolio becomes a purely comic character, with the omission of the dark room scene, while Antonio is virtually absent. The film's denouement hints at the theme of androgyny by showing a 'feminized' Sebastian, adorned like Viola in long curls and tunic, re-embracing his identical sister.

In the opening of Yakov Fried's Russian-language Lenfilm version of 1955 (no. 78), Sebastian's survival is again shown immediately after Viola's. Combinatory filming (Osborne, 111) allowes Klara Luchko to appear as both twins in the same scene

(5.1), a cinematic possibility exploited in later video versions (see nos 91 and 101). Illyria was 'Russianized', with Feste singing Russian popular songs, while Fried develops the theme of visual and pictorial perception by employing several shots 'quoting' Renaissance art, and by offering 'a first view by Viola of "the coast of Illyria" that looked like a Symbolist painting' (Hattaway, 87).

Ron Wertheim's 1972 film of *Twelfth Night* by *Playboy* Productions (no. 91) – a mixture of sexual-revolution exuberance and soft-porn kitsch – has Orsino as an ageing rock star, while Antonio becomes the black Antonia (thereby eliminating any hint of homosexuality), and Feste, played by Wertheim, the gardener and chauffeur to Olivia, widow of a movie mogul. Nikki Gentile, like Klara Luchko, plays both twins. The film's denouement resolves all gender ambiguities by having Gentile's Viola reveal all, Playmate-fashion (thereby provoking a closing orgy).

Trevor Nunn's ambitious 1996 feature film (no. 109) is notable above all for its long opening sequence dedicated to a realistic account of a *Tempest*-like shipwreck, preceded by an off-screen voice declaiming a bad pseudo-Shakespearean blank-verse prologue: 'Once, upon Twelfth Night – or what you will – / Aboard a ship bound home to Messaline, / The festive company' (evidently this Shakespeare has read his C.L. Barber). The maritime sequence continues with an on-board Victorian party in which the twins, identically disguised in harem-like yashmaks leaving only their eyes visible, perform 'O mistress mine' (2.3.38–43) as a music hall duet; when they reach line 40, 'That can sing both high and low', one voice is indeed high, while the other is baritone: the question is whose voice is which. The piano-playing twin proceeds to pull the yashmak from the concertina-playing sibling's face, revealing a moustache; the other twin in turn peels away the piano player's moustache, whereby the latter is 'fully confirmed as a girl' (Nunn, 4). The climax, as the piano player reaches out, apparently to peel off the other twin's moustache – thereby multiplying the gender confusion exponentially – is interrupted by the storm. All the while Antonio gazes intently from the shadows, 'concentrating on the concertina player' (i.e. Sebastian; Nunn, 3; see Chillington Rutter, 248–50).

This episode elaborately and teasingly anticipates the themes of androgyny and cross-dressing, which are briefly taken up in a later sequence showing Viola's transformation into Cesario, in which she cuts her hair, binds her chest, pads her crotch, attaches a blond moustache (again) and tries out masculine walks. Otherwise, however, the film fails to explore gender issues much further, and indeed it is curious, given these preliminaries, including their masquerade orientalism, that Nunn should have censored Viola's 'eunuch' allusion (as well as the captain's mediation), with awkward and ungrammatical results: 'I shall present me [*sic*] as a boy to him' (Nunn, 12). The film's most original emphasis, instead, is on a background military conflict between Illyria and Messaline, the twins' place of birth, pre-announced in the prologue ('For Messaline with this country is at war') and represented in *Hamlet*-like preparations for war; this makes sense, among other things, of Antonio's and Orsino's past naval skirmishes, referred to at 3.3.26–8 and 5.1.47–72.

Twelfth Night is a point of intertextual reference in another commercially successful end-of-century film, John Madden's *Shakespeare in Love* (1998), written by Marc Norman and Tom Stoppard. Among a myriad of other Shakespearean allusions, the film involves a 'contamination' between *Romeo and Juliet* – which Joseph Fiennes's young Shakespeare is seen writing and rehearsing – and *Twelfth Night*, a version of which he 'lives' by falling in love with Viola de Lesseps (Gwyneth Paltrow), cross-dressed as a male actor. After the triumphant performance of *Romeo and Juliet* – in which Paltrow, like the Cushman sisters combined (no. 26), ends up playing Juliet instead of Romeo – and before Viola leaves for America as Lady Wessex, Judi Dench's Queen Elizabeth commissions a new comedy: 'And tell Master Shakespeare, something more cheerful next time, for Twelfth Night.' The voiceover's closing lines resemble the prologue of Nunn's film in narrating the opening storm of *Twelfth Night*: 'WILLIAM SHAKESPEARE: "My story starts at sea . . . a perilous voyage to an unknown land . . . a shipwreck . . . It will be a love story . . . for she will be my heroine for all time. And her name . . . Viola."'

Twelfth Night has often been seen as a play particularly suited to the television screen, perhaps because of its 'intimacy' and its domestic interiors, although the results have not always confirmed such suitability. The first television production of the comedy, the 1937 BBC transmission (no. 59), starred Greer Garson as Viola. Two years later the BBC returned to the play in another 'first night', namely the first broadcast of a Shakespeare play (and the second of any stage play) from a theatre, confirming the comedy's vocation as inaugurating event. The programme failed to please the *Times* critic, who complained that the camera's distance made the actors appear too small: 'The impression given was one of extreme restlessness. Viola was now a tiny figure scarcely distinguishable from half-a-dozen others equally diminutive . . . The result was to falsify the fluid grace of the production.' *Twelfth Night* provided the occasion for another 'first' in 1949, the first live stage play broadcast by a major American studio, the NBC (no. 68); the text was much reduced to conform with the studio's timing demands, causing Jack Gould to describe the event as 'A procession of episodes rather than a piece of integrated theatre' (quoted in Rothwell & Henkin, 303).

Later television productions have mostly not been much better received. Harold Clayton's 1950 BBC version, starring Geoffrey Dunn as Malvolio (no. 70), was decidedly melancholic in tone, and was criticized for its lack of comedy. Caspar Wrede's BBC production six years later, with Dilys Hamlett as Viola (no. 79), failed to impress, as did David Greene's stagy 1957 NBC production (no. 80), complete with painted theatrical backcloths, in which Maurice Evans reproduced his 1940 Malvolio (see no. 64), playing him again with a false nose and a strong cockney accent (see p. 126); Sir Toby corrected his pronunciation of 'slough' at 2.5.34, with a glance at Olivier's stage performance two years earlier (no. 77). The most memorable episode was the dark room scene, in which Evans was surrounded by a multitude of mocking masks; at the end of the play the platform from which Malvolio launched his parting curse exploded, to the joy of the assembled company (Rothwell & Melzer, 305).

Somewhat more successful was the 1970 ATV broadcast (no. 88), produced by John Dexter and directed by John Sichel, starring Ralph Richardson as Sir Toby (the role in which he had triumphed in the early thirties: nos 53 and 54), Alec Guinness as Malvolio and Joan Plowright as both twins. This is a distinctly 'televisual' version, full of strategic close-ups (not to mention fadeouts for commercial breaks). As in other video versions, the opening has been reworked, with 1.2 'containing' 1.1, while Sebastian's first and second scenes (2.1 and 3.3) are collapsed into one (see Osborne, 112). John Gorrie's rather dull 1980 production for the BBC Shakespeare series (no. 96) respects the scene order of the Folio text, but is otherwise distinguished only by Alec McCowen's supercilious and somewhat effeminate Malvolio and Trevor Peacock's 'lumbering and loveable mutt' of a Feste (Carr, 5). Perhaps the most convincing of all the television versions is Paul Kafno's rendering of Kenneth Branagh's 1987 Riverside Studios staging (no. 102) for Thames Television, which captures all the stage production's wintry-cemetery and subdued-colour melancholy. Of considerable interest also is Tim Supple's 2003 Channel 4 television film (no. 119), in which Parminder Nagra's Viola and Ronny Jhutti's Sebastian are represented as asylum seekers who have been driven from their native land by a military coup (a 'political' allusion recalling Nunn's film) and washed up in an Illyria that closely resembles contemporary multicultural London, where Feste is a rock star shades of the 1968 musical (no. 86) and the 1972 *Playboy* film (no. 91). The production's many cuts included the 'eunuch' reference, while its additions, as in Nunn's film, included the scene of Viola cross-dressing.

Are you a comedian?: players and parts

Twelfth Night has always been a vehicle for star performers but, unlike those in most plays, the star roles vary. As one would expect, stage productions down the centuries have frequently been memorable for their Malvolios (from Charles Macklin to Richard Bensley, and from Laurence Olivier to Donald Sinden), but equally so for their Violas (Peg Woffington, Dorothy Jordan, Ellen Terry, Suzanne Bing) and their Sir Tobys (Thomas Betterton, John Palmer, Cedric Hardwicke). Historical testimony shows, more surprisingly, that the star performance may occasionally be Sir Andrew, as with James Dodd in the late eighteenth century. Feste has dominated some stagings (especially in recent times, from Emrys James to Mark Hadfield), and Olivia has taken the honours in others (Frances Abington, Geraldine McEwan), while there have even been productions where the star, or at least the co-protagonist, has arguably been Maria (Paul Chahidi). Orsino, despite being the 'romantic' hero, has rarely dominated stage Illyrias, although Alan Howard came close in 1966. It is rare for all the roles to be performed at the same level of skill, but the existence of such a gallery of parts guarantees that at least some scenes will work: an off-day for Belch gives Feste his chance of glory.

One of the features of the performance history of *Twelfth Night* is the way in which actors move across parts, confirming the specularity and interchangeability of the dramatis personae. A notable eighteenth-century case in point is Richard Yates, who started life in the play as Feste in Macklin's 1746 revival (no. 10) and then moved on to become a celebrated Malvolio in 1763 (no. 11). John Palmer was promoted from Sebastian to Sir Toby in 1776 (no. 13); Lily Brayton moved from Viola in 1901 (no. 41) to Olivia a year later; Andrew Leigh from Fabian to Sir Andrew in 1920 (no. 50) to director in 1940 (no. 63); Leon Quartermaine from Sir Andrew in 1912 (no. 46) to Malvolio in 1933 (no. 57); John Laurie from Feste in 1932 (no. 55) to Malvolio in 1939 (no. 62); Laurence Olivier from Belch in 1937 (no. 58) to Malvolio in

1955 (no. 77); Alec Guinness from Sir Andrew in 1937 (no. 58) to director in 1948 (no. 67) to Malvolio in 1970 (no. 88); Judi Dench from Maria in 1958 (no. 81) to Viola in 1969 (no. 87); Emrys James from Feste in 1969 (no. 87) to Malvolio in 1983 (no. 98), and so on. Such role-shifting is not just a matter of career promotion or ageing, but suggests something of the psychological and performative overlapping of the roles, and a characteristic may become a strategic part of a given production: Sybil Thorndike, for example, alternated the roles of Viola and Olivia in the 1916 Old Vic production (no. 49).

The play's performance history has inevitably featured twins or siblings in the parts of Viola and Sebastian: Dorothy Jordan and her brother George Bland (who were more or less of the same height and of similar appearance) in 1790 (no. 18), Mrs Henry Siddons and her brother William Murray in 1815 (no. 22), the Cushman sisters in 1846 (no. 26). In one production, Robert Atkins's 1927 Old Vic version (no. 52), the cast was virtually composed of a single family, the Forbes-Robertson dynasty, perhaps suggesting the almost incestuous quality of relationships in the play. An alternative solution has been for the same actress to play both twins: Madame Meyer Bourke in 1851 (no. 29), Kate Terry in 1865 (no. 32), Jessica Tandy in 1937 (no. 58). Such doubling is decidedly easier in film, a medium that invites optical illusion: Klara Luchko in Yakov Fried's 1955 film (no. 78), Ingrid Adree in the 1962 West German TV production (no. 83), Joan Plowright in the 1970 ATV production (no. 88), and Gillian Jones in Neil Armfield's 1987 film (no. 101) all doubled as the twins.

Individual actors in single parts, however, have naturally dominated the stage history of *Twelfth Night*. Some of the outstanding performances of the play's major roles merit closer attention.

Art any more than a steward?: Malvolio

There is little doubt that in early performances the play's protagonist was the steward. We do not know which actor John Manningham saw and appreciated in 1602: possible candidates are Joseph Taylor and John Shancke. In later seventeenth-century performances Malvolio may have lost his primacy to Sir Toby, but he emphatically reclaimed his place at centre stage in the first significant eighteenth-century production. After the longest interruption in the play's performance history, the great Irish actor Charles Macklin appeared as the steward at Drury Lane in 1741 (no. 8), the same year as his celebrated Shylock (another outsider). Along with Garrick, Macklin was the most revolutionary performer of his age, introducing a naturalistic style of acting; he was famous for the severity of his stage presence, and he gave Malvolio an air of pompous authority.

One of the productions of *Twelfth Night* that have left the strongest traces in theatre history is Robert Bensley's 1785 staging at Drury Lane (no. 16), in which Bensley played Malvolio opposite Dorothy Jordan's celebrated Viola, the gigantic John Palmer's Sir Toby and James Dodd's Sir Andrew. Charles Lamb (not an altogether reliable witness[1]) recalls, thirty years later, Bensley's great dignity and the Hispanic style he lent the part: '[He] threw over the part an air of Spanish loftiness. He looked, spake, and moved like an old Castilian. He was starch, spruce, opinionated, but his superstructure of pride seemed bottomed upon a sense of worth' (C. Lamb, 189). Bensley, a former soldier, first adopted, according to Lamb, a self-important martial gait (although James Boaden recalled that 'his stage walk reminded you of the "one, two, three, hop" of the dancing master': quoted in Winter, 23); then, after reading the letter, 'The man seemed to tread upon air, to taste manna, to walk with his head in the clouds, to mate Hyperion' (C. Lamb, 190).

Under Bensley's influence, 'dignity' became the key word in interpretations of the part. John Liston in 1811 (no. 21) was similarly noteworthy, according to the diarist Henry Crabb Robinson, for his 'inimitable gravity' as well as his 'incomparable smiles, in the Cross-gartered scene' (Winter, 27). Bensley's 'Spanish

1   See Sylvan Barnet, 'Charles Lamb and the tragic Malvolio', *SQ*, 33 (1954), 177–88.

loftiness' likewise became a recurrent topos in later performances. Samuel Phelps in 1848 (no. 27) performed the role as a slow-moving and self-adoring Golden Age *señor*, all grandeur and pride: 'Walled up in his own temple of flesh, he is his own adorer,' observed Henry Morley (139). Henry Irving, in 1884 (no. 36), presented a Quixote-like figure, tall and gaunt, with a pompous walk, wielding his prominent staff of office: 'He looked like some great Spanish hidalgo, a painting of Velasquez',' recalled a later Malvolio, Frank Benson (quoted in Saintsbury & Palmer, 245). Irving's humourless interpretation was much criticized, although Edward Aveling claimed that 'The gradual growth of the great idea in his mind that Olivia loved him was shown as I believe none other could show it' (Salgādo, 116). The 'Spanish' mode survived until relatively recent times: Michael Hordern in 1954 (no. 76) appeared 'dried up, emaciated, elongated . . . like one of those tortured figures in an El Greco' (Harold Hobson, *Sunday Times*).

Not all Malvolios have been aspiring Hispanic grandees, however. Another tradition, beginning at the turn of the century, represented him as a grotesque fantastic entirely lacking in dignity. Following the unpopular austerity of Irving's performance, Beerbohm Tree's altogether more farcical and emphatically over-the-top 1901 interpretation (no. 41) was much better received; his steward was an 'intolerably condescending blue-eyed peacock with a red twirl of beard and a quizzing-glass' (Trewin, 18), and accompanied by four smaller Malvolios who aped his dress and behaviour (as George Bernard Shaw reports, approvingly). Tree gave rise to a line of maniacal Malvolios that has survived into the present. Donald Sinden's universally acclaimed 1969 performance (no. 87), 'a portly soul struggling to get out of an absurdly spindly body' (Hilary Spurling, *Spectator*), had the merit of 'leaving the right bitterness in the mouth when the play's flight from realism might have seemed too precipitate' (Speaight, *Shakespeare*, 439). The grotesque-fantastic tradition continued with John Woodvine's 1979 steward (no. 95), adorned with ringlets and, in the cross-garter scene, an entire yellow body stocking with bulging codpiece.

Another modern Malvolio, Emrys James, a memorable Feste in 1969 (no. 87), performed the role in 1983 (no. 98) as a 'strutting velvet uniformed grotesque' (Irving Wardle, *Times*) and 'a finger-wagging tyrant' (Michael Billington, *Guardian*).

A relatively recent development in the 'grotesque' school of acting has been to transform the maniacal into the psychopathic, making Malvolio literally mad. Alexander's 1987 RSC production (no. 100) was dominated by what one critic called 'Sher madness' (Sheridan Morley, *Punch*), namely Anthony Sher's highly popular but controversial interpretation of the part as 'a mad holy man on the run, a corseted hysteric with gobstopper eyes' (Michael Ratcliffe, *Observer*). Sher's Malvolio, afflicted by an authentic erotic *furor* towards Olivia, became genuinely mad, and was last seen 'still essaying cross-gartered high kicks as if his wits have finally turned' (Michael Billington, *Guardian*). Less overacted, but still disturbingly unhinged, was Richard Briers's steward in the same year (no. 102), 'a frock-coated, wildly ambitious fanatic' (Billington, *Guardian*), with a 'fussy air of primly affronted fastidiousness' (Martin Hoyle, *Financial Times*). Equally fastidious and neurotically driven was Simon Russell Beale's award-winning corpulent 2002 Malvolio (no. 116), who looked as if 'he must have emerged from the womb with that self-important beard and punctilious moustache', while his gait was 'an effeminately officious cross between a march and a scamper' and his tone of voice 'a prissily sibilant sneer' (Paul Taylor, *Independent*).

One of the more interesting lines of interpretation of the role has been in terms of class, whereby the real ambition of Malvolio – of visibly or audibly humble extraction – becomes social promotion rather than erotic satisfaction. In Margaret Webster's 1940 New York production (no. 64) Maurice Evans played him as a 'downstairs' English butler with a distinct cockney accent. The main trait betraying the origins of Laurence Olivier's 1955 steward (no. 77) was 'a rather tortured lisp, as of an aspiring barrow-boy earnestly improving his English at night-school' (Eric Keown, *Punch*). Olivier had comical difficulty in pronouncing the more recherché words in the letter. In 1966 (no. 84) Ian Holm – who physically resembled the Droeshout portrait of Shakespeare (another social climber) – exhibited a 'mongrel' accent composed of 'eccentric gentility and a basis of raw bullying cockney' (*Times*), in representing the steward as an officious and disciplinarian sergeant-major obsessed with his rank.

A variation of the lower-class (usually London cockney) colouring of the character has been a regional, predominantly Welsh, characterization. In 1974 (no. 93) Nicol Williamson's 'immensely tall, bad-tempered, nasal Welshman, stiff-jointed and intolerably haughty' (John Barber, *Daily Telegraph*), made his Welshness a synonym of Puritanism. Another Welsh Malvolio, Desmond Barrit in 1994 (no. 107), used the accent as added colouring for his already farcical music-hall steward, 'a lugubrious man-mountain . . . massively pirouetting in yellow' (Benedict Nightingale, *Times*). A more functional brand of geographical difference marked Paul Bhattacharjee's 2004 Indian Malvolio (no. 120), a bossy white-suited valet with impeccable 'English' manners who is transformed in the cross-gartering scene though his 'extravagant make-up and ghastly, glassy smiles' (Charles Spencer, *Daily Telegraph*).

Being a comedy concerned with the forms, eccentricities and aberrations of behaviour and dress, *Twelfth Night* lends itself to the actor's skill in inventing or varying comic stage business. This is particularly the case with Malvolio: certain lazzi (comic gestures, more or less absurd effects with costume and props, business involving scenery, etc.) introduced by earlier Malvolios have become established over the centuries as conventions, to be transmitted, repeated or modified by their successors. Actors playing him often find themselves, willy-nilly, 'quoting' earlier performances, thereby setting up a kind of intertextual or inter-actorial relationship with their predecessors. Knowledgeable audiences, moreover, have come to expect comic business at certain points in the play, and may even begin to titter in expectation.

The primary source of much traditional stage business was Bensley (no. 16), some of whose lazzi are still present in modern performances. As Boaden notes, Bensley embellished one of the play's great comic moments, Malvolio's cross-gartered entry in 3.4, by introducing a cross-stage movement that mimicked the garters themselves: 'the sliding zig-zag advance and retreat of his figure fixed the attention to his stockings and garters' (Winter, 23). Ever since, the scene has produced funny walks or other forms of conspicuous behaviour: Olivier (no. 77), for example, waved from behind a yew tree, before disappearing suddenly (Brown, 257). Bensley also introduced the convention in the letter scene – an endless opportunity for comic invention – of 'filling in' the pause after 'play with my . . .' at 2.5.57; Lamb describes 'with what ineffable carelessness would he twirl his gold chain; what a dream it was!' (C. Lamb, 190). This has been taken up and varied by almost every actor since: recent examples include Desmond Barrit (no. 107) toying with his genitals and then ordering laughing spectators to leave, and Guy Henry's hand dangling uncertainly in front of his pelvic region (no. 113).

Another potentially grotesque entrance is the steward's inter-rupting of the kitchen scene at 2.3.84.1. A venerable convention has him come on in his night-shirt; this is usually attributed to another great source of stage business, Beerbohm Tree (no. 41), but actually dates from Kemble's 1811 production (no. 21), whose promptbook specifies that Malvolio enters 'in a Gown and Cap, with a Light'; the idea is still alive today, as at the Middle Temple in 2002 (no. 114). Donald Sinden (no. 87) pompously wore his chain of office over his night-shirt (Potter, 65). Malvolio often sports a night-cap as well, or alternatively – in early twentieth-century productions – curling papers, as if he had been interrupted in the midst of his toilette (Sprague & Trewin, 84). That tradition was parodied by Mendes' 2002 production (no. 116), which had Malvolio in a hairnet. Posner in 2001 (no. 113) had the steward enter in a red dressing-gown and red shoes. Among Beerbohm Tree's contributions to *Twelfth Night*'s performance history is the often repeated business in 2.2 of placing the ring on the tip of the wand and dropping it at Cesario's feet; this was 'quoted' in Kent's 1910 film (no. 45), as well as in later performances.

The letter scene provides a third entrance (at 2.5.20.1) traditionally exploited for slapstick farce. Tree famously had, in the words of Shaw, 'a magnificent flight of stairs on the stage; and when he was descending it majestically, he slipped and fell with a crash sitting . . . Tree, without betraying the smallest discomfiture, raised his eyeglass and surveyed the landscape as if he had sat down on purpose' (Shaw, 249). Tree's show-stopping entry has often been repeated, or otherwise transformed into more sober variations: Emrys James (no. 98), for example, came onstage like Ophelia, bearing a basket of flowers, 'knighting' himself with one of the sprigs before dusting the tree stump and sitting down to read the epistle.

The innumerable micro–episodes making up the letter scene, in which Malvolio is betrayed into 'practising behaviour' on stage, have all given rise to long-lasting lazzi. In many productions Malvolio touches the seal at 'soft' (2.5.91), to discover that the wax is indeed soft; Sher (no. 100) rubbed his chest, repeating the word three times. The steward's pronunciation difficulties with 'M.O.A.I.' (119, 136) and '*slough*' (145), first exploited by Olivier (Pennington, 17), have become common comic stock: Nicol Williamson (no. 93) 'tortures the MOAI conundrum into experimental Welsh words' (Irving Wardle, *Times*), while Desmond Barrit (no. 107) produced a cat–like 'mee–ow'. The letter's invitation '*still smile*' (2.5.171) often prompts Malvolio to practise his smile, as in the case of Mark Hadfield (no. 113); Olivier (no. 77), 'after several wry attempts to smile into a mirror, achieves a satisfied asinine grin' (*Times*, quoted in Brown, 247).

The supreme moment in Malvolio's reading, however – which audiences anticipate with glee – is his reaction to the imperative '*revolve*' (2.5.140). The standard joke is for the steward to misinterpret the verb as 'turn around', which is often what actors do: for example, Emrys James (no. 98) and Philip Voss (no. 110). Fuller Mellish in 1914 (no. 47) 'span round on his heel';

Donald Sinden (no. 87) and John Woodvine (no. 95) turned the letter round; Sher (no. 100) revolved his upper body, and so on. Recently actors have played on spectators' expectations: Barrit (no. 107) looked at the audience, then shook his head; Oliver Cotton in 2002 (no. 114) gazed wonderingly at the expectant spectators and did nothing.

Your drunken cousin: Sir Toby

If the earliest seventeenth-century performances belonged to Malvolio, the star role in the three stagings witnessed by Pepys (nos 4–6) was another: the Duke of York company's male lead, the great Thomas Betterton – usually associated with tragic protagonists such as Hamlet and Macbeth – played Sir Toby. This may be less surprising than it appears, since Belch is the play's longest, if not 'biggest' part (see Appendix 2), and is full of opportunities for both verbal and physical comedy. The Toby seen by Manningham sixty years earlier may have been Thomas Pope – who probably played Buffone in Jonson's *Every Man out of His Humour* – although another candidate is John Heminge, one of the two 'editors' of the Folio and possibly the original Falstaff. Later Belches have often incarnated just such a Falstaffian quality, disenchanted of wit and conspicuous of girth: for example, the great Ralph Richardson in 1931 (no. 53) and 1970 (no. 88), George Devine in 1938 (no. 60) and Bill Fraser, who in 1969 (no. 87) knowingly played Sir Toby as an ageing and somewhat melancholy Sir John. In 1937 (no. 58) a transformed Laurence Olivier – 'a trifle too much bubukled and whelked and knobbed' (*Sunday Times*: see Fig. 25) – was likewise 'a rustic Falstaff whose stupid drunken jollity has its own wretched pathos' (Stephen Williams, *Evening Standard*). Olivier's Falstaffian Belch was malicious and dangerous: '[he] delightedly over-played Sir Toby like a veteran Skye terrier, ears pricked for mischief' (Trewin, 164).

The huge John Palmer, nicknamed 'plausible Jack', in 1776 (no. 13) and 1785 (no. 16), was the most notable Belch of the eighteenth century. One of the most brilliant all-round actors of

25 Laurence Olivier as Sir Toby in Tyrone Guthrie's 1937 Old Vic production

his day, he was instead one of the tallest Tobys in stage history;
William Dunlap describes his strategic use of his length: 'Palmer's
gigantic limbs outstretched seemed to indicate the enjoyment of
the physical superiority which nature had given him, even while
debasing it by the lowest of vices' (quoted in Winter, 25).

The kind of comedy produced by the role has varied widely,
from the farcical – with emphasis on the corporeal and the alcoholic, as with Barry Stanton in 2001 (no. 113), who at 1.5.116,

instead of belching, threw up in front of Olivia – to the aristocratic, as in the 1931 (no. 53) performance of Ralph Richardson's 'ripe, rich and yellow Sir Toby' (W.A. Darlington, *Daily Telegraph*), 'a courtly Sir Toby whose quality was never lost in his cups' (*Times*); and of Cedric Hardwicke's elegant and ironic Belch, undisputed star of Alec Guinness's 1948 production (no. 67): 'Sir Toby was the man in this Illyria . . . Keeping a glazed dignity he led Andrew with drily casual care and a smile that oozed at the corners of his mouth' (Trewin, 211).

An ass-head and a coxcomb and a knave: Sir Andrew

Even Sir Toby's gull has had his day. The importance given in Davenant's Restoration productions to the play's more farcical scenes is confirmed by the presence of the celebrated Henry Harris (Romeo to Betterton's Mercutio) as Sir Andrew (no. 4). The 1771 Drury Lane production (no. 12) was memorable above all for James Dodd's Aguecheek. Lamb vividly re-evokes Dodd's sublime slow-wittedness – what Boaden termed his 'native imbecility' (Winter, 25) – in the later 1785 production (no. 16) in which Dodd reappeared as Aguecheek: 'You could see the first dawn of an idea stealing slowly over his counte-nance, climbing up little by little, with a painful process, till it cleared up at last to the fulness of a twilight conception – its highest meridian' (C. Lamb, 190–1). The 1771 production inspired a noteworthy portrait by Francis Wheatley of the duel scene (Fig. 26), which captures Dodd's frightened gesture of drawing his sword, 'encouraged' by James Love's Sir Toby; Dodd's expression is mirrored in the equally reluctant leaning pose of Elizabeth Younge's Viola. The costumes are also of interest: including his lank flaxen hair, Dodd's Sir Andrew is emphatically decked out in the colour Olivia detests, cowardly yellow, with the exception of his 'thin legs in scarlet stockings' (Dunlop, quoted in Sprague, 6); while Cesario's pink and blue 'changeable taffeta' suit, plumed turban and red slippers sug-gest, in addition to effeminacy, an exotic 'Illyrian' or Middle

Eastern flavour (a Turkish eunuch?). A later specialist in slow-wittedness in 1850 (no. 28) was Robert Keeley, who, 'in the expression of semi-idiocy or rustic wonderment . . . had few equals' (Joseph Knight, *DNB*).

Modern Sir Andrews have often accentuated the pathos of the role, best expressed in Aguecheek's most memorable line, 'I was adored once too' (2.3.176). Michael Redgrave in 1938 (no. 60), described by James Agate as 'a giddy, witty maypole', was for W.A. Darlington 'a likeable lunatic' suffering from 'a kind of moonstruck pathos' (*Daily Telegraph*). Richard Johnson in 1958 (no. 81), looking with his long flaxen wig like 'a lachrymose spaniel', played him as a 'paranoid manic-depressive, strongly reminiscent at times of Lucky in *Waiting for Godot*' (*Observer*, 27 April 1958; quoted in Brown, 218). Barrie Ingham represented

26 'He cannot by the duello avoid it' (3.4.301-2): Francis Wheatley's painting of the 1771 production, with Elizabeth Younge as Viola, James Dodd as Sir Andrew, James Love as Sir Toby and Francis Waldron as Fabian

him in 1966 (no. 84) as a hapless and ageing Scottish clown with bagpipes, ever searching for coins in his sporran (and yet capable of a spectacular back-leap), while David Bradley's lugubrious and insecure Sir Andrew behaved in 1987 (no. 100) 'like some irritable newt, muttering all his remarks as though he would rather have snatched them back before releasing them to the sure mockery of the world' (Michael Ratcliffe, *Observer*).

An allowed fool: Feste

The one almost certain presence in the Chamberlain's Men's performance was Robert Armin in the part of the clown, since Armin had joined the company before it left the Curtain and transferred to the Globe in 1599, the year in which his predecessor Will Kemp left (see Wiles, 145). Armin, who had probably already played Touchstone in *As You Like It* and would go on to play the Fool in *King Lear*, was known as a good singer – an essential aspect of the role – and, being also a gifted ventriloquist, specialized in multiple roles (a quality put to good use in 4.2). His intellectual agility and inventiveness are attested to by his work as a comic dramatist in his own right. There is little doubt that Armin lent the role great stage presence, a caustic comic acumen and a beauty of musical performance.

There may be more or less direct traces in the text of Armin's presence in the first production of the play. Olivia's reprimand of the clown's truancy at 1.5.38, after his unauthorized absence at the court of Orsino – 'you grow dishonest' – probably alludes to Armin's 'promiscuity' as comic performer: like Feste on his first entrance in 1.5, Armin first arrived on the Globe stage, and in the company of the Lord Chamberlain's Men, from service for another lord, Lord Chandos, with whose theatrical company he toured the country in 1595–7 and performed at another theatre, the Curtain. Armin alternated – again like Feste – between rival venues, probably continuing, even after joining Shakespeare's company, to appear at the Curtain, as well as in less formal performance spaces such as halls and taverns. Likewise, the clown's doubling of roles as Feste and Sir Topas the curate in 4.2 reflects Armin's well-known ability as a ventriloquist, as in his playing of both the clown Tutch and the fool John i' the Hospital in performances of his own comedy, *The History of the Two Maids of More-clacke*. In the same scene Armin's notorious dwarfishness is directly evoked in Feste's feigned reluctance to play Sir Topas on the grounds that 'I am not tall enough to become the function well' (4.2.6–7). Viola's homage to the clown's art at 3.1.58–64 ('This fellow is wise enough to play the fool . . .') is probably intended as a direct compliment to Armin and may indeed echo his own pamphlet *Quips upon Questions*, published in 1600 ('A merry man is often thought unwise', Armin, *Quips*, sig. C1^r; see Mahood), just as Sir Toby's less flattering description of Feste as a 'sot' at 1.5.117 and at 5.1.193 may allude to Armin's pamphlet *Fool upon Fool or, Six Sorts of Sots*, likewise published in 1600.

The most significant trace of the shadow cast by Armin over the play, however, is Feste's abundant singing, one of the actor's main trademarks as a performer. Feste's 'replacement' of Viola as the play's resident singer has been explained precisely with reference to Armin's presence in the company. Since Armin appears to have been a counter-tenor, moreover, his high-pitched voice was an appropriate substitute for the unbroken voice of the boy actor (see Feste's reference to a lover-singer 'That can sing both high and low': 2.3.40). The clown's songs may constitute the comedy's most direct debt to Armin as contributing author: it is at least possible that the words of the final song ('When that I was and a little tiny boy, / With hey, ho, the wind and the rain') are by Armin himself, the more so since an adapted version of Feste's song – 'He that has and a little tiny wit, / With heigh-ho, the wind and the rain' – is sung in *King Lear* (3.2.73–7) by the Fool, likewise played by Armin.

The next Feste we know of is Cave Underhill in the 1660s Duke of York's performances (nos 4–6); Underhill, awkward and ill proportioned, was praised by Colley Cibber for his gift of wooden comic fixity: 'He looked as if it were not in human passions to alter a feature of him' (Winter, 17). Richard Suett produced a similarly celebrated verbal–corporeal performance in 1785 (no. 16): 'a loose and shambling gait, a slippery tongue . . . in words, light as air, venturing truths deep as the centre' (Oxberry, *Dramatic*, 3.226).

Later, the role was marginalized and subject to drastic cuts – already apparent in Bell's 1774 acting edition – and began to regain its original importance only at the beginning of the twentieth century, especially in Beerbohm Tree's 1901 production (no. 41) in which Courtice Pounds's Feste, a presiding and defining presence, was according to Max Beerbohm 'as constant and as indispensable as punctuation' (Greif, 63). This overturning of the eighteenth- and nineteenth-century marginality of the clown, making his the central viewpoint on events (Greif), has been repeated several times since, notably in Barton's 1969 staging (no. 87), in which Emrys James's highly praised clown set the sardonic tone for the whole performance. Equal importance was given to Geoffrey Hutchings's 1979 Feste (no. 95), onstage throughout. Ben Kingsley's clown, in Trevor Nunn's 1996 film (no. 109), likewise provides a defining perspective; as Katherine Eggert observes, 'The film even insinuates that Feste has engineered or at least foreseen the main plot' (Eggert, 84), since at the end of the film Feste returns to Viola a necklace she discarded during her cross-dressing as Cesario.

Another tendency in modern productions has been to make the clown older and more embittered than in the traditional image of the part. Granville-Barker (who restored all Feste's songs) affirmed that he is 'not a young man', and in his staging (no. 46) C. Hayden Coffin, a veteran musical comedy performer then aged fifty, represented him as mature and melancholy. Twenty years later, in Tyrone Guthrie's first production (no. 57), Morland Graham's clown had become a white-haired old man; while in the RSC's 1960 revival (no. 81) Max Adrian's celebrated performance also presented him as elderly and sardonic.

The caustic potential of the role has on occasion turned into raging anger. In conflict with the highly decadent court in Gill's 1974 production (no. 93), Ron Pember's Feste became a Malvolio-like Puritan, described by one critic as 'another life-hater infiltrating the hedonists like a member of Angry Brigade at a coming-out ball . . . angrily banging his drum and baring his teeth on "Come away, death"' (J.W. Lambert, *Sunday Times*). Even more enraged was Anton Lesser's decidedly misanthropic clown in 1987 (no. 102), 'a faintly gypsy-like hobo with a carpet bag, whose smouldering anger and contempt reach a natural climax with the furious baiting of the imprisoned Malvolio' (Martin Hoyle, *Financial Times*).

Feste's ventriloquism, born with Armin, has re-emerged in recent performances. Mark Hadfield's memorable clown in Posner's 2001 RSC production (no. 113), 'a born loner used to corrupting words to grub a living' (Michael Billington, *Guardian*), adopted different voices, shifting from his normal classless southern English to mock-Jewish for the 'Quinapalus' nonsense in 1.5, to homiletic pomposity as Sir Topas. The vocal range was part of his music-hall conception of the role: tiny, sporting a Charlie Chaplin suit and Buster Keaton flat hat and string tie, he moved in a gangling Max Wall fashion and delivered his final song in cabaret style. In Nunn's film (no. 109) the Feste played by the half-Indian actor Ben Kingsley breaks twice into 'mimicry of a colonial-Indian native soldier' (Eggert): first in the 'nonsense' regarding 'Malvolio's nose' (2.3.25), thereby associating the steward with an 'exotic' outsider; and later at 'ginger shall be hot' (114), where the accent perhaps suggests Indian food. Equal 'post-colonial' vocal versatility was put on show by Kulvinder Ghir in 2004 (no. 120), a chameleon-like Indian song-and-dance street artist: 'Now he's a tranny, now he's an untouchable' (Alistair Macaulay, *Financial Times*).

A noble duke: Orsino

Despite being the comedy's 'official' male lead, and ruler of Illyria to boot, Orsino has rarely wielded power onstage. Hotson speculates that the 'original' Orsino may have been Augustine Phillips, but there is no evidence for this. Later dukes tended to fall into a limited range of stereotypes, the most recurrent being the sincerely passionate Petrarchan lover, despite the text's hints at the instability of his desire and the suspicious staginess of his effusions in the opening scene. This characterization prevailed especially in the nineteenth century and occasionally appears today, as in Mark Strong's 2002 performance (no. 116). In the later twentieth century the standard duke became instead a languidly self-indulgent and at times decadent figure, and the play's incipit (Orsino's big scene) served to dramatize his effete sensualism by discovering him in self-pitying prostration, as in the case of the recumbent 'lotus-eating Duke' (Ronald Bryden, *Observer*) in 1969 (no. 87), or Toby Stephens's 'young militarily-dressed man [lying] full-length on a chaise, his left hand covering his eyes, his right arm cradled in a sling' in Nunn's film (Nunn, 13). This tradition found its most extreme expression in Peter Gill's 1974 production (no. 93), in which John Price's Orsino was discovered 'lolling languidly on cushions or homosexually [*sic*] fumbling his page' (John Barber, *Daily Telegraph*; see Fig. 4).

Attempts have been made to overcome this cliché of horizontal preciosity, for example by underlining Orsino's verbal – and potentially physical – violence in 5.1. In 1966 (no. 84) Alan Howard's energetic, angular and anti-romantic duke, like a Petruccio in the wrong play, 'enters the first scene at a run and conducts his campaign against Olivia's affections more in a military than romantic spirit' (*Times*), while Terence Maynard's muscular, shaven-headed and emphatically vertical black Orsino cut a vigorously macho figure in 2002 (no. 114), despite his fancy satin tunic, his lace collar and cuffs and his pearl earring.

Here comes the countess: Olivia

Traditionally conceived as a gracefully mature figure, perhaps because she is a countess – even though the text hardly justifies this, and though her behaviour is anything but aristocratically sedate – the role of Olivia has undergone an evolution over the last century. Little is known of the first 'female' Olivia, Ann Gibbs (the future Mrs Thomas Shadwell) in the 1660s. Later actresses tended to play the role relatively late in their careers: in 1741 (no. 8) 35-year-old Kitty Clive, the liveliest comedienne and best comic singer of her age (she was given an air to music by Thomas Arne), played opposite 26-year-old Peg Woffington's Viola. The former street singer Frances Abington (see Fig. 27), queen of the 'grand coquettes' (Edward Dutton Cook, *DNB*), lent wit and elegance to the part in 1771 (no. 12), at the age of thirty-four, and was likewise given a 'French air' to sing; Charlotte Rusport praised her 'incomparable modulation', claiming that 'her articulation is so exact, that every syllable she utters is conveyed distinctly and even harmoniously' (quoted in *Biographical Dictionary*). Mrs Charles Kemble, née Marie-Thérèse de Camp, known for her French charm, first played the role in 1811 (no. 21), aged thirty-seven, and was described by Leigh Hunt as possessing 'a beautiful figure, fine large dark eyes, and elevated features, fuller of spirit than softness, but still capable of expressing great tenderness' (Hunt, *Autobiography*). The tall and powerful Violet Vanbrugh was also thirty-seven when she appeared in Daly's production in 1894 (no. 37).

The 41-year-old Russian former ballerina, Lydia Lopokova, Lady Keynes, did not break with the 'mature' tradition in Tyrone Guthrie's 1933 production (no. 57), but she was one of the first to depart from the 'graceful countess' commonplace, playing the part with skittish impulsiveness (and with a strong Russian accent), thereby incurring the disapprobation of Virginia Woolf, who found her insufficiently stately, detached and immutable: 'Madame Lopokova loves everybody. She is always changing. Her hands, her face, her feet, the whole of her body, are always quivering in sympathy with the moment' (Woolf, 209). Lesley Brook in Irene Hentschel's 1939 staging (no. 62) similarly disturbed the critics by playing her not as 'the stately and mature lady we are used to but a charming little wilful heiress scarcely out of

Olivia by M.ʳˢ Abington

Look you, Sir, such a one I wear.

Act I. Scene 9.

Publish'd by J. Harrison, Jan.ʸ 1779.

27   Mrs Abington as Olivia in 1771

the school-room' (*Daily Telegraph and Morning Post*, quoted by Schafer, 217). In 1947 (no. 66) the traditional age politics were reversed: 19-year-old Daphne Slater contrasted with Beatrix Lehmann's 44-year-old Viola and was 'less the Madonna and grand lady than the impulsive and warm-hearted girl' (*Guardian*). In 1958 (no. 81) Geraldine McEwan, in her mid-twenties, presented Olivia analogously as 'a squeaking flibbertigibbet' (Trewin, 238), 'a pouting, giggling, squealing *poseuse*' (M. Billington, xvii); visibly attracted to Cesario, she threw herself on her knees before him on 'Nor wit nor reason can my passion hide' (3.1.150). In a similar vein, Estelle Kohler, in her early twenties, played her in 1966 (no. 84) as 'a vain and coquettish girl recently released from male protection' (*Times*). Neha Dubey's beautiful Indian aristocrat (2004; no. 120) first appeared deceptively dressed in a solemn black sari, but rapidly metamorphosed into a frivolous young girl sporting a series of colourful, eye-catching saris as a sign of her transformation.

Recent Olivias have given free expression to their sexual impulses: Kate Nicholls in 1979 (no. 95) 'flirtatiously rub[bed] up against Malvolio' and then physically assaulted the disguised Viola, 'leaping at her, cuddling her and pursuing her pell-mell through the garden' (Benedict Nightingale, *New Statesman*); Caroline Langrishe in 1987 (no. 102) was more aristocratic but made it clear that 'she could not wait to get her hands on Orsino's boy-emissary' (M. Billington, xxx). Equally passionate was Mark Rylance – aged forty-two, and male to boot – in the 2002 Middle Temple production (no. 114). His Olivia was in total control of household and stage power; more than a countess, Rylance looked like a perennially embalmed Elizabeth I, complete with white facial mask and coronet, sliding across the stage as if on royal rollers, and delivering his lines with an intriguing mixture of artfulness and ingenuousness. In the Globe revival, Rylance played the part for its comic value, producing moments of outright slapstick under the effect of passion: his Olivia threw a basket at Sir Andrew and a prayer book at Malvolio, wielded an enormous halberd, lost a shoe, had trouble taking off her ring, fainted, fell, screamed and repeatedly stuttered, giving new meaning to Cesario's claim that she 'did speak in starts'. Rylance's Olivia was rivalled in stage presence and comic force by Paul Chahidi's Maria, whose 'flustering and matron-like control is splendidly camp yet convincing' (Lisa Whitbread, *Stage*). If Olivia was a queen (Elizabeth), Chahidi's Maria was 'an actress playing an old queen who plays an old girl ripe for a bit of fun – the actress, in this case, being Edith Evans' (Rhoda Koenig, *Independent*); Evans played the role of Viola in 1932 (no. 54).

I am not that I play: Viola

The play's female protagonist, as we have seen (p. 50), unconventionally underlines her difficulties in acting her disguise role (see 2.2.27–41, 3.4.295–6, etc.), thereby ironically foregrounding the acting of her part by a cross-dressed male actor. In many ways this paradox, written into the text, has conditioned the performances of women (and occasionally men) actors: the degree of their success in reconciling the transition from Viola to Cesario has been one of the benchmarks for critical judgements of their performances.

The first actress to play Viola may have been Mrs Davenport in the 1660s Duke's Theatre productions (nos 4–6). The first certain name that has come down to us is that of Hannah Pritchard, who played opposite Macklin in 1741 (no. 8): a considerable tragic actress, she brought a degree of *gravitas* to the part, unlike her celebrated successor in the 1746 revival (no. 10), the notoriously sensuous Peg Woffington, a popular specialist in breeches roles (male characters *en travestie*) who attracted audiences at least in part by showing off her feminine graces, notably her breeched legs; Woffington's beauty and *savoir-faire* compensated for her 'unpleasant squeaking pipe' of a voice (Tate Wilkinson, quoted in *Biographical Dictionary*). Woffington was probably the first in a long series of unmistakably female Violas whose femininity showed through to greatest effect precisely in the cross-dressed scenes. Similarly, in 1783 (no. 15), Mary Robinson's striking figure was 'seen to great advantage in the masculine dress' (Joseph Knight, *DNB*), captivating, among others, the future George IV, who became her lover. In 1820 (no. 23) Maria Tree was likewise unmistakably female: 'To our taste, indeed, we confess she never looked *so* feminine, as when

142

habited in the costume of the other sex . . . Then her figure was beautifully formed; and her "masculine usurped attire" . . . displayed it to peculiar advantage' (Oxberry, *Dramatic*, 1.205–6); in 1836 (no. 25) her sister Ellen Tree similarly 'puts not off the woman with her attire, but becomes yet more womanly' (*Athenaeum*). Adelaide Neilson's 1877 performance (no. 33) again emphasized delicate femininity, above all as Cesario: she was 'incarnate April sunshine, – an embodiment of exquisitely bright and tender womanhood' (Winter, 42). In 1955 (no. 77) Vivien Leigh's somewhat cold and detached performance worked better in the Cesario scenes, where her beauty was more intriguing: 'As a boy Miss Leigh is charming, as Viola herself curiously unromantic' (Eric Keown, *Punch*).

One of the 'tricks' of actresses wishing to signal their womanliness in the disguise scenes has been to caricature the masculinity of Cesario: a famous example is Ellen Terry (no. 36), who managed to be wittily feminine, even though she had her arm in a sling and had to perform sitting down, playing the part with 'grace, sweetness, and delicate touches of pathos' (Aveling, 117), in spite of, or partly thanks to, her 'charming and laughing assumption of a mannish walk' (*Saturday Review*).

There have been rather fewer attempts to bestow on the Cesario scenes a genuine and non-parodic mimesis of masculinity. Madame Meyer Bourke (1851; no. 29), playing both twins, achieved a form of gender-crossing ventriloquism, prompting the diarist Henry Crabb Robinson to note that 'when personating [Sebastian], she gave a manliness to her voice and step which would have almost deceived us as to her identity' (Robinson, 2.327). Charlotte Cushman, opposite her sister Susan's Olivia in 1846 (no. 26), cut a fine masculine figure in her knee-length skirt and velvet jacket, with a sash and dagger at her waist.[1] Viola Allen likewise attempted a fully fledged male impersonation in 1904

---

1   Joseph Leach, *Bright Particular Star: The Life and Times of Charlotte Cushman* (New Haven, Conn., 1970), 177.

(no. 42; Winter, 80–1), while in 1947 (no. 66) the 44-year-old Beatrix Lehmann was 'every inch a man' (*Guardian*).

More challenging, but also more difficult to bring off successfully, is a 'middle ground' in which the poles of masculine and feminine are suspended in an indeterminate gender identity. Judi Dench in 1969 (no. 87) went some way in this direction by being attractively ambiguous, 'a dashing cavalier in green velvet, all swagger and girlish trepidation' (Colin Frame, *Evening News*). A more radical attempt at sustained androgyny was made by Jane Lapotaire in Peter Gill's 1974 gender-confusing production (no. 93), although she was criticized for it, for example by Irving Wardle of the *Times*, who complained of her being 'a blank screen on to which others project their fantasies'; this, however, is in many ways precisely what Viola-as-Cesario is: 'blank' (2.4.110). One of the successes of the all–male 2002 Globe theatre revival (no. 114) was the effortless co–existence of biological boyishness and non–camp feminine seductiveness in Michael Brown's 'lovely, willowy Viola' (Kate Kellaway, *Observer*).

A recurrent trait of successful Violas has been their vocal and especially musical quality, as if to justify the character's claim to be able to speak 'in many sorts of music' (1.2.55). Hannah Pritchard's voice (no. 8) was 'deliciously musical' (Winter, 18). In the performance of the great Dora Jordan in 1785 (no. 16) Sir Joshua Reynolds praised 'the music of her melancholy' and 'the music of her laugh' (quoted in Winter, 22), while according to Leigh Hunt, 'Mrs Jordan seems to speak with her soul; her voice, piquant with melody, delights the ear with a peculiar and exquisite fulness' (Hunt, *Criticism*, 163), and for Hazlitt '[her] voice is a cordial to the heart, because it came from it, rich, full, like the luscious juice of the ripe grape; to hear whose laugh was to drink nectar' (quoted in *Biographical Dictionary*). John Hoppner's celebrated portrait of Mrs Jordan (*c.* 1790, Iveagh Bequest) in her Cesario disguise – a hussar costume and hat, with bright red hatband, necktie and belt – in the open against a backdrop of pillars and stormy sky, captures the pathos for which her vocally enchanting performance was known.

Still on a musical note, in Ellen Tree's 1836 performance (no. 25) 'Not a tone of voice but touches the heart' (*Athenaeum*). G.B. Shaw praised 'the true Shakespearian music' of Ada Rehan's performance in Daly's (highly musical) 1894 production (no. 37); Lily Brayton's Viola in Tree's 1901 revival (no. 41) was marked by her 'passionate and satin-voiced' delivery (Trewin, 19), while Julia Marlowe (1905; no. 44) was praised for her 'melodious, sympathetic voice' (Winter, 90). In 1950 (no. 69) Peggy Ashcroft quite dominated Hugh Hunt's staging, not least in the silent music of her rapt stillness in 2.4.

In one memorable interpretation, exquisite musicality was orchestrated with choreographic movement in a richly meaningful dialogue: according to Granville-Barker, Suzanne Bing in Copeau's 1914 version (no. 48) 'spoke very beautifully; she moved with grace. But the movements did not exist apart from their meaning, and every sentence came out conceived as a whole, as a thought and a feeling' (*Observer*; quoted in Speaight, *Shakespeare*, 189). Suzanne Bing is one of the earliest Violas to take full command of the stage. The last century saw an increasing shift – onstage as in critical discourse – away from Malvolio (or Sir Toby) towards Viola as the dramatic and theatrical centre of the play, a shift confirmed in the powerful performances of Peggy Ashcroft, Judi Dench, Jane Lapotaire and – more controversially – Vanessa Redgrave, who played her in 1972 (no. 89) as 'a scrambling, shouting, gawky adolescent' (Michael Billington, *Guardian*). It is quite likely that this centrality of Viola-as-Cesario – more than justified by the text of the comedy – will continue in future.

Performance history: 120 productions of *Twelfth Night*[1]

(1)	**1602** (2 Feb.) Middle Temple; Lord Chamberlain's Men
(2)	**1618** (6 Apr.) King's Men at court (as *Twelfth Night*)
(3)	**1623** (2 Feb.) King's Men at court (as *Malvolio*)
(4)	**1661** (11 Sept.) Duke's; AA: Henry Harris; Fe: Cave Underhill; Mal: Thomas Lovell; To: Thomas Betterton; Ol: Ann Gibbs
(5)	**1663** (6 Jan.) Duke's; probably same cast as 1661
(6)	**1669** (20 Jan.) Duke's; possibly same cast as 1661
(7)	**1703** (Mar.) Lincoln's Inn Fields; William Burnaby's adaptation *Love Betrayed*
(8)	**1741** (15 Jan.) DL; AA: Henry Woodward; Mal: Charles Macklin; Ol: Kitty Clive; Vio: Hannah Pritchard
(9)	**1742** (6 Jan.) Smock Alley, Dublin
(10)	**1746** (15 Apr.) DL; Fe: Richard Yates; Mal: Charles Macklin; Ol: Kitty Clive; Vio: Peg Woffington
(11)	**1763** (19 Oct.) DL; Mal: Richard Yates; Vio: Miss Plym
(12)	**1771** (10 Dec.) DL; AA: James Dodd; Mal: Thomas King; Ol: Frances Abington; Vio: Elizabeth Younge
(13)	**1776** (10 Sept.) DL; AA: James Dodd; Mal: Robert Bensley; To: John Palmer
(14)	**1777** (17 Mar.) CG; AA: John Quick; To: John Dunstall; Vio: Mrs Barry Spranger
(15)	**1783** (7 May) CG; Mal: John Henderson; Vio: Mary Robinson
(16)	**1785** (11 Nov.) DL; AA: James Dodd; Fe: Richard Suett; Mal: Robert Bensley; To: John Palmer; Vio: Dorothy Jordan
(17)	**1789** (19 Mar.) DL; Mal: John Philip Kemble

---

1 The abbreviations adopted in this table are as follows: DL: Drury Lane; CG: Covent Garden; SW: Sadler's Wells; Hay: Haymarket; OV: Old Vic; dir: director; des: designer; prod: producer; AA: Sir Andrew; Fe: Feste; Mal: Malvolio; Mar: Maria; Ol: Olivia; Ors: Orsino; Seb: Sebastian; To: Sir Toby; Vio: Viola.

(18) **1790** (10 Feb.) DL; Seb. George Bland; Vio: Dorothy Jordan (his sister)

(19) **1794** (3 Feb.) The Theatre, Boston (first recorded American performance); Mal: Snelling Powell

(20) **1804** (11 June) Park theatre, NY; Mal: John G. Martin

(21) **1811** (5 Jan.) CG; revised J.P. Kemble; Mal: John Liston; Ol: Mrs Charles Kemble

(22) **1815** Theatre Royal, Edinburgh; Seb: William Murray; Vio: Mrs Henry Siddons (his sister)

(23) **1820** (8 Nov.) CG; prod: Frederick Reynolds; AA: John Liston; Mal: William Farren; Vio: Maria Tree

(24) **1824** (10 Aug.) Chatham Garden theatre, NY; Mal: Henry Wallack

(25) **1836** (31 Aug.) Hay; Mal: William Farren; Vio: Ellen Tree

(26) **1846** (25 June) Hay; Ol: Susan Cushman; Vio: Charlotte Cushman

(27) **1848** (26 Jan.) SW; Mal: Samuel Phelps

(28) **1850** (28 Sept.) Princess's (opening prod.); prod: Charles Kean; AA: Robert Keeley; Fe: John Pritt Harley; Vio: Ellen Tree

(29) **1851** (16 June) Court Theatre, Dresden; Vio/Seb: Meyer Bourke

(30) **1852** (29 Mar.) Chambers Street, NY; To: William Evans Burton

(31) **1856** (24 Mar.) Wallack's Lyceum, NY; dir: James Wallack; Mal: John Brougham

(32) **1865** (7 June) Olympic; Vio/Seb: Kate Terry

(33) **1877** (7 May) Fifth Avenue theatre, NY; dir: Augustin Daly; Vio: Adelaide Neilson

(34) **1881** (31 May) DL; *Was Ihr Wollt*, Royal Theatre of Saxe-Meiningen; dir: Duke George II; Fe: Herr Teller; Vio: Fräulein Werner

(35) **1881** (31 Oct.) Fifth Avenue theatre, NY; adapted Charles Webb; AA: Stuart Robson; To: William H. Crane

(36) **1884** (8 July) Lyceum; des: Hawes Craven; prod: Henry Irving; Mal: Irving; Vio: Ellen Terry

(37) **1894** (8 Jan.) Daly's theatre; dir: Augustin Daly; Ol: Violet Vanbrugh; Vio: Ada Rehan

(38) **1895** (21 June) Burlington Hall (Elizabethan Stage Society: first prod.); dir: William Poel

(39) **1897** (10 Feb.) Middle Temple (Elizabethan Stage Society); dir: William Poel

(40) **1900** (23 Mar.) Lyceum; Mal: Frank Benson; Ol: Lily Brayton; Vio: Constance Benson

(41) **1901** (5 Feb.) Her Majesty's; dir: Herbert Beerbohm Tree; des: Hawes Craven & Joseph Harker; Fe: Courtice Pounds; Mal: Tree; Ol: Maud Jeffries; Vio: Lily Brayton

(42) **1904** (8 Feb.) Knickerbocker theatre, NY; dir: Charles Frohman; Vio: Viola Allen

(43) **1904** (22 Feb.) Knickerbocker; dir: Ben Greet; Mal: Greet; Vio: Edith Wynne Matthison

(44) **1905** (16 Oct.) Knickerbocker; dir: E.H. Sothern; Mal: E.H. Sothern; Vio: Julia Marlowe

(45) **1910** (3 Feb.) Silent film (Vitagraph); dir: Charles Kent; scenario: Eugene Mullin; Mal: Charles Kent; Vio: Florence Turner

(46) **1912** (15 Nov.) Savoy; dir: Harley Granville Barker; costume and des: Norman Wilkinson; AA: Leon Quartermaine; Fe: Hayden Coffin; Mal: Henry Ainley; Vio: Lillah McCarthy

(47) **1914** (25 Mar.) Hudson theatre, NY; dir: Margaret Anglin; Mal: Fuller Mellish; Vio: Margaret Anglin

(48) **1914** (15 May) Théâtre du Vieux-Colombier; Paris; dir: Jacques Copeau; des: Louis Jouvet; costume: Duncan Grant; AA: Louis Jouvet; Mal: Jacques Copeau; Vio: Suzanne Bing

(49) **1916** (3 Jan.) OV; dir: Ben Greet; Mal: Ben Greet; To: Robert Atkins; Ol:/Vio: Sybil Thorndike (alternating); Vio: Viola Tree

(50) **1920** (15 Nov.) OV; dir: Robert Atkins; AA: Andrew Leigh

(51) **1923** (28 May) BBC radio; AA: Nigel Playfair; Mal: Herbert Waring

(52) **1927** (17 May) St James's; dir: Robert Atkins; Ol: Maxine Forbes-Robertson; Priest: Johnson Forbes-Robertson; Vio: Jean Forbes-Robertson

(53) **1931** (6 Jan.) SW (reopening prod.); Mal: John Gielgud; To: Ralph Richardson

(54) **1932** (29 Mar.) OV/SW; dir: Harcourt Williams; Mal: Robert Speaight; To: Ralph Richardson; Vio: Edith Evans

(55) **1932** (24 May) New Theatre; dir: Robert Atkins; Fe: John Laurie; Vio: Jean Forbes-Robertson

(56) **1932** Chicago Drama Festival; dir: Orson Welles; Mal: Orson Welles (film version 1933)

(57) **1933** (18 Sept.) OV; dir: Tyrone Guthrie; des: Wells Coates; Fe: Morland Graham; Mal: Leon Quartermaine; Ol: Lydia Lopokova

(58) **1937** (23 Feb.) OV; dir: Tyrone Guthrie; AA: Alec Guinness; To: Laurence Olivier; Vio:/Seb: Jessica Tandy

(59) **1937** (14 May) BBC TV; Ol: Dorothy Black; Vio: Greer Garson

(60) **1938** (1 Dec.) Phoenix; dir: Michel Saint-Denis; AA: Michael Redgrave; To: George Devine; Vio: Peggy Ashcroft (broadcast BBC TV, 2 Jan. 1939)

(61) **1938** (30 Aug.) CBS radio; dir: Orson Welles

(62) **1939** (13 Apr.) Stratford; dir: Irene Hentschel; des: Motley; AA: Alec Clunes; Mal: John Laurie; Ol: Lesley Brook

(63) **1940** (15 Feb.) Kingsway; dir: Andrew Leigh and Donald Wolfit; Mal: Donald Wolfit; Vio: Rosalinde Fuller

(64) **1940** (19 Nov.) St James Theater, NY; dir: Margaret Webster; Mal: Maurice Evans; Vio: Helen Hayes

(65) **1943** (29 June) Lyric (ballet version); music: Edvard Grieg; choreog: Andrée Howard

(66) **1947** (23 Apr.) Stratford (first post-war prod.); dir: Jack Hylton; AA: Paul Scofield; Mal: Walter Hudd; Ol: Daphne Slater; Vio: Beatrix Lehmann

(67) **1948** (21 Sept.) New (OV prod.); dir: Alec Guinness; Mal: Mark Dignam; Seb: Donald Sinden; To: Cedric Hardwicke

(68) **1949** (20 Feb.) NBC TV: live broadcast from Philco Playhouse; dir: Fred Coe; Mal: John Carradine; Vio: Marsha Hunt

(69) **1950** (14 Nov.) OV (reopening); dir: Hugh Hunt; Mal: Michael Horden; Ors: Alec Clunes; Vio: Peggy Ashcroft

(70) **1950** (6 Jan.) BBC TV; dir: Harold Clayton; Mal: Geoffrey Dunn; Ol: Patricia Kneale; Vio: Barbara Lott

(71) **1950** Floridiana, Naples; dir: Orazio Costa; Mal: Salvo Randone; Vio: Anna Proclemer

(72) **1951** (2 Feb.) Middle Temple; dir: Donald Wolfit

(73) **1951** (25 Aug.) Palazzo Grassi (Venice; opening prod.); dir: Giorgio Strehler; Mal: Gianni Santuccio

(74) **1953** (2 Feb.) Theatre Royal, Stratford East, London (opening prod.); dir: Joan Littlewood; AA: Harry H. Corbett; Ors: Gerry Raffles

(75) **1954** Teatro di Via Manoni (Milan); dir: Renato Castellani; Mal: Memo Benassi; To: Glauco Mauri

(76) **1954** (6 Jan.) OV; dir: Denis Carey; Fe: Paul Daneman; Mal: Michael Hordern; Ors: John Neville; To: Richard Burton; Vio: Claire Bloom

(77) **1955** (12 Apr.) Stratford; dir: John Gielgud; Mal: Laurence Olivier; Ol: Maxine Audley; Vio: Vivien Leigh

(78) **1956** Soviet film *Dvenadtsataia noch*; dir: Yakov Fried; Mal: M. Yanshin; Ol: Anna Larionova; Vio:/Seb: Klara Luchko

(79) **1957** (10 Mar.) BBC TV; dir: Caspar Wrede; Mal: John Moffatt; Ors: Robert Hardy; Vio: Dilys Hamlett

(80) **1957** (12 Dec.) NBC TV; dir: David Greene; AA: Max Adrian; Mal: Maurice Evans; Vio: Rosemary Harris

(81) **1958** (22 Apr.) Stratford; dir: Peter Hall; des: Lila de Nobili; AA: Richard Johnson; Ol: Geraldine McEwan; Vio: Dorothy Tutin (revived 1960; Fe: Max Adrian; Mal: Eric Porter)

(82) **1962** (18 Feb.) Royal Court; dir: George Devine; Fe: Albert Finney; Mal: Nicol Williamson; Vio: Lynn Redgrave (prod. without décor)

(83) **1962** West German TV (*Was Ihr Wollt*); dir: Franz Peter Wirth; Vio/Seb: Ingrid Adree

(84) **1966** (16 June) RSC; dir: Clifford Williams; AA: Barrie Ingham; Mal: Ian Holm; Ol: Estelle Kohler; Ors: Alan Howard; Vio: Diana Rigg

(85) **1967** Swedish TV; *Trettondagsafton*; dir: Hans Dahlin; Vio: Bibi Andersson

(86) **1968** (13 Jan.) Orpheum, NY; *Your Own Thing* (musical) by Hal Hester and Danny Apolinair; book by Donald Driver

(87) **1969** (21 Aug.) RSC; dir: John Barton; Fe: Emrys James; Mal: Donald Sinden; To: Bill Fraser; Vio: Judi Dench

(88) **1970** (13 July) ATV; dir: John Sichel; prod: John Dexter; Fe: Tommy Steele; Mal: Alec Guinness; To: Ralph Richardson; Vio:/Seb: Joan Plowright

(89) **1972** (16 May) Shaw theatre; dir: Michael Blakewell; Vio: Vanessa Redgrave

(90) **1972** (19 Apr.) Landestheater, Salzburg (*Was Ihr Wollt*); dir: Otto Schenk; Ors: Klaus Maria Brandauer; Vio: Christine Ostermayer (TV version ORF TV, Austria, 2 Sept. 1973)

(91) **1972** Film (*Playboy* Productions); dir: Ron Wertheim; Fe: Wertheim; Vio:/Seb: Nikki Gentile

(92) **1974** (14 May) BBC TV; dir: David Giles, prod: Cedric Messina; Mal: Charles Gray; Vio: Janet Suzman

(93) **1974** (22 Aug.) RSC; dir: Peter Gill; des: William Dudley; Fe: Ron Pember; Mal: Nicol Williamson; Vio: Jane Lapotaire

(94) **1975** (10 June) Stratford, Ontario: dir: David Jones; Mal: Brian Bedford; Vio: Kathleen Widdoes

(95) **1979** (12 June) RSC; dir: Terry Hands; des: John Napier; Fe: Geoffrey Hutchings; Mal: John Woodvine, Ol: Kate Nicholls; Vio: Cherie Lunghi

(96) **1980** (27 Feb.) BBC TV; dir: John Gorrie; prod: Cedric Messina; Fe: Trevor Peacock; Mal: Alec McCowen; Vio: Felicity Kendall

(97) **1982** (10 July) Palais des Papes, Festival d'Avignon (Théâtre du Soleil); dir: Ariane Mnouchkine

(98) **1983** (20 Apr.) RSC; dir: John Caird; Mal: Emrys James; Vio: Zoë Wanamaker

(99) **1986** Cheek by Jowl touring prod.; dir: Declan Donnellan; des: Nick Ormerod

(100) **1987** (7 July) RSC; dir: Bill Alexander; des: Kit Surrey; AA: David Bradley; Mal: Anthony Sher

(101) **1987** Film (Australia); dir: Neil Armfield; AA: Geoffrey Rush; To: John Wood; Vio:/Seb: Gillian Jones

(102) **1987** (3 Dec.) Riverside Studios (Renaissance Theatre Company); dir: Kenneth Branagh; des: Bunnie Christy; music: Pat Doyle and Paul McCartney; Fe: Anton Lesser; Mal: Richard Briers; Ol: Caroline Langrishe (Thames Television version, 13 Dec. 1988; dir: Paul Kafno)

(103) **1989** (29 Sept.) Shakespeare theatre, Washington, DC; dir: Michael Kahn; des: Derek McLane; Fe: Yusef Bulos; Ors: Peter Webster; Vio: Kelly McGillis

(104) **1991** (6 Apr.) RSC; dir: Griff Rhys Jones; des: Ultz; Mal: Freddie Jones; Ors: Terence Hillyer

(105) **1992** (16 June) Théâtre National de Chaillot (Paris); dir: Jérôme Savary

(106) **1992** *Animated Twelfth Night*, adapted Leon Garfield; dir: Mariya Muat

(107) **1994** (25 May) RSC; dir: Ian Judge; des: John Gunter; Mal: Desmond Barrit

(108) **1995** Deutsches Nationaltheater, Weimar; dir: Katja Paryla; Mal: Bernd Lange; Vio: Cornelia Sikora

(109) **1996** Film; dir: Trevor Nunn; Fe: Ben Kingsley; Mal: Nigel Hawthorne; Ol: Helen Bonham-Carter

(110) **1997** (19 Nov.) RSC; dir: Adrian Noble; des: Anthony Ward; Fe: Stephen Boxer; Mal: Philip Voss

(111) **1997** (20 Mar.) Brooks Atkinson theatre, NY; *Play On!* (musical) by Cheryl L. West; dir: Gary Halvorson; music Duke Ellington; Lady Liv: Tonya Pinkins; Vy: Cheryl Freeman

(112) **1998** (16 July) Lincoln Center, NY; dir: Nicholas Hytner; des: Bob Crowley; Vio: Helen Hunt (broadcast by PBS TV)

(113) **2001** (13 Apr.) RSC; dir: Lindsay Posner; Fe: Mark Hadfield; Mal: Guy Henry; To: Barry Stanton; Vio: Zoë Waites

(114) **2002** (25 Jan.) Middle Temple (Globe Theatre Company); dir: Tim Carroll; Mal: Oliver Cotton; Mar: Paul Chahidi; Ol: Mark Rylance; Ors: Terence Maynard; Vio: Eddie Redmayne (revived Globe theatre, 11 May)

(115) **2002** (21 July) Delacorte, NY; dir: Brian Kluick; Vio: Julia Stiles

(116) **2002** (5 Sept.) Donmar Warehouse; dir: Sam Mendes; Fe: Anthony O'Donnell; Mal: Simon Russell Beale; Ors: Mark Strong; Vio: Emily Watson

(117) **2002** (12 Apr.) Hudson Guild Theater, NY (Prospect Theatre Company); *Illyria* (musical) by Peter Mills; dir: Cara Reichel; Mal: Ames Adamson

(118) **2003** (May) International Chekhov Festival, Moscow (in Russian); dir: Declan Donnellan; des: Nick Ormerod; (revived Olympia, Dublin, Oct. 2004; Vio: Andrei Kuzicher; Ol: Alexei Dadonor; Mal: Dmitri Shcherbina, and Barbican, London, June 2006)

(119) **2003** Film (Channel 4 TV); dir: Tim Supple; Mal: Michael Maloney; To: David Troughton; Vio: Parminder Nagra

(120) **2004** (2 Sept.) Albery; dir: Stephen Beresford; Fe: Kulvinder Ghir; Mal: Paul Bhattacharjee; Ol: Neha Dubey

TWELFTH NIGHT,
OR
WHAT YOU WILL

LIST OF ROLES

VIOLA	*a shipwrecked lady, later disguised as Cesario*	
CAPTAIN	*of the wrecked ship, who befriends Viola*	
SEBASTIAN	*Viola's twin brother, also shipwrecked*	
ANTONIO	*a sea-captain, who befriends Sebastian*	
ORSINO	*Duke of Illyria*	5
CURIO	*gentlemen attending on Orsino*	
VALENTINE		
Two OFFICERS		
OLIVIA	*a countess*	
MARIA	*Olivia's waiting-gentlewoman*	10
SIR TOBY Belch	*Olivia's kinsman*	
SIR ANDREW Aguecheek	*companion to Sir Toby*	
MALVOLIO	*Olivia's steward*	
FESTE	*clown, Olivia's jester*	
FABIAN	*a member of Olivia's household*	15
PRIEST		
SERVANT	*in Olivia's household*	

Musicians, Lords, Sailors, Attendants

Twelfth Night, or What You Will

LIST OF ROLES The list of characters' names, not present in F, first appears in the Douai MS, while the first printed version is included by Rowe. Rowe's list respects traditional gender and class hierarchy, giving male names first and opening with the duke; Viola's name appears next to last.

1 VIOLA The play's female lead is Shakespeare's fourth cross-dressed heroine – after Jiulia (*TGV*), Portia (*MV*) and Rosalind (*AYL*). Her name is possibly inspired by 'Violetta', the cross-dressed protagonist of Emanuel Forde's romance *Parismus*. In F her first entry SD (TLN 461; 1.5.162.1) has *Enter Violenta* (see Appendix 1). 'Viola', in addition to being a musical instrument, is Italian for 'violet'. The musical connotations of her name are taken up in Sir Toby's 'viol-de-gamboys' (1.3.23–4), while its floral associations are alluded to in Orsino's opening speech ('bank of violets', 1.1.6). The name as such, however, is not mentioned in the dialogue until 5.1.240, where the metre seems to call for the pronunciation ['vaɪələ] (accent on the first syllable). The name of Viola's disguise role, Cesario – deriving from Latin *Caesarius*, 'belonging to Caesar' – may recall Cesare, adopted name of the heroine Ginevra in another version of the story, Curzio Gonzaga's play *Gli inganni* (1592).

3 SEBASTIAN Viola's twin is named after a famous third-century Christian saint (see p. 23), popularized by Renaissance painters, who generally depict him as a beautiful youth pierced by arrows. It may be its association with death that suggested the name (since Sebastian is presumed drowned).

4 ANTONIO another saint's name (see p. 23), common in Shakespeare. It occurs, for example, in *TGV*, *MA* and *Tem*. The homoerotic emphasis of Antonio's attitude towards Sebastian recalls another Antonio, the friend and benefactor of Bassanio in *MV* (see Pequigney). Antonio has a somewhat enigmatic military past, having been involved in naval action against Orsino,

who addresses him as 'Notable pirate' (5.1.65). In F the name appears as '*Antonio*' in the entry SD and dialogue in his first scene (2.1), but as '*Anthonio*' in his second scene (3.3) and last scene (5.1), while his third (3.4) has '*Antonio*' in the entry SD and '*Anthonio*' in the dialogue.

5 ORSINO The name of the play's male protagonist (meaning literally 'little bear' in Italian) probably alludes to the Orsini, one of the most ancient and distinguished families of the Roman nobility. At 1.2.22–3 the Captain describes Orsino as being 'A noble duke / In nature, as in name', and Viola has heard her father name him (25). There may be a more specific allusion to Shakespeare's contemporary Virginio Orsini (1572–1615), second Duke of Bracciano. Son of Paolo Giordano Orsini, the notorious first Duke, and of Isabella de' Medici, daughter of the Grand Duke of Tuscany, Virginio had an eventful childhood: in 1576, when he was four, his father probably strangled the duchess in a fit of jealous rage, and later had her lover assassinated. Having fled to Rome, the duke in turn became the lover of Vittoria Accoramboni, wife of Francesco Peretti (nephew of Pope Sisto V); Orsini appears to have had Peretti assassinated in 1583. The couple married shortly before being assassinated themselves in separate incidents in 1585, the year in which Virginio (then aged 13) succeeded to the Duchy of Bracciano. These events inspired Webster's *The White Devil* (1612), in which Virginio becomes 'Giovanni'. Despite the unusual circumstances of his infancy, Orsini became a respected and respectable figure. In 1601 he was sent as envoy to England by his uncle Ferdinand de' Medici; at the court of Elizabeth he witnessed a play, probably performed by Shakespeare's company. It is possible that the character is named after him following this visit: see p. 94. Shakespeare's Orsino is referred to as both duke and count; Duke Virginio

157

Orsini was also Count of Anguillara.

6 CURIO probably named after Gaius Scribonius Curio, a Roman tribune and ally of Julius Caesar (he is mentioned in Plutarch's *Life of Julius Caesar*, source of *JC*). Curio's is the first name pronounced in the play, at 1.1.16.

7 VALENTINE This, the name of the patron saint of lovers, had become common in romantic comedy: see, for example, *TG*. 'Valentine' is associated with 'Orson' in the French romance *Valentine and Orson* – a story of separated twins – translated into English around 1550, and of a lost anonymous play of the same title, entered in the Stationer's Register on 23 May 1595. Unlike Curio, Valentine is never named in the dialogue.

9 OLIVIA Like 'Viola', 'Olivia' may derive from Forde's *Parismus*, which has a character of the same name. Being a countess, Olivia is inferior in rank to Orsino, as Sir Toby underlines: 'She'll none o'th' count. She'll not match above her degree' (1.3.105–6).

10 MARIA This is the form of the name that appears in all SDs in F, while in the dialogue it alternates with the English equivalent '*Mary*' (four occurrences each, plus a solitary diminutive '*Marian*', TLN 712; 2.3.13); SPs in *F* are abbreviated to *Mar.*, which would allow either version. In textual and stage history the Italian form has always prevailed, partly because there are other Italian names in the play. It is usually given, however, the anglicized pronunciation [mə'raɪə], rhyming with fire, rather than Italian [ma'ri:a]. Sir Toby describes her as 'My niece's chambermaid' (1.3.49), but the term indicated a more elevated rank than it does today: *OED* (giving this example) glosses as 'lady's maid'.

11 SIR TOBY Belch Toby is a typical English name, diminutive of the biblical Tobias (the holy man protagonist of the eponymous Old Testament book, whose name in Hebrew means 'God is good'). Unlike Sir Andrew's, his knighthood is apparently hereditary rather than acquired (see 3.4.229–30).

The precise degree of Sir Toby's kinship with Olivia is uncertain (see note to 1.3.1, 4), as is his age: Aguecheek's gaffe at 1.3.114, referring to him as an 'old man', need not be taken literally, and he is often played as a relatively young man. His surname speaks, as it were, for itself as a sign of his gastronomic and alcoholic excesses; it is literalized at 1.5.116.

12 SIR ANDREW Aguecheek Andrew is the patron saint of Scotland (see p. 23), and Aguecheek is sometimes played as a Scotsman. 'Ague' (pronounced as two syllables) was a generic term in Early Modern English for a fever or fit of shaking; 'cheek' probably has both its modern meanings: facial part (cf. 'Agueface', 1.3.42) and buttock. Sir Andrew's composite surname thus suggests leanness (cf. *JC* 2.2.113: 'that same ague which hath made you lean'), paleness and cowardice (cf. *Cor* 1.4.37–8: 'faces pale / With flight and agued fear'). It may also imply, more literally, a sickly disposition: see Maria's 'he would quickly have the gift of a grave', 1.3.30–1. This is indeed the way Sir Andrew is often portrayed in performance: thin, sickly and highly strung. His nominal cowardice, meanwhile, is confirmed in the 'duelling' episode in 3.4. His fellow knight Sir Toby hints at 3.4.229–30 that Sir Andrew has purchased his title.

13 MALVOLIO In Italian *malvoglio* means literally 'I dislike': the opposite to Benvolio, name of Romeo's cousin in *RJ*. It may have been suggested by the expression 'mala voglia' (ill will), which occurs several times in Bandello's prose version of the 'twelfth night' story (cf. also Florio, *World*, 'Maleuolo, *malitious*', p. 212). He is in turn disliked by others ('Malvoluto, *hated*': Florio, *World*). The morpheme *mal*, moreover, is synonymous with evil or sickness, and indeed Olivia accuses him of being 'sick of self-love' (1.5.86; see p. 29).

14 FESTE The clown's personal name – Italian for 'revels': cf. Florio's 'Festa, *a feast, a holyday*' (Florio, *World*; see

p. 212) – is mentioned only once in the dialogue in F, and never in SDs or SPs, where he is always indicated as *Clo(wne)*, while the other characters usually refer to him as *fool*. The name may be a casual afterthought on Shakespeare's part, chosen to suggest his role in the revelries within Olivia's household, or perhaps because in Elizabethan pronunciation it rhymed with 'jester' (in the jingle 'Feste the jester', 2.4.11). In 4.2 Feste dresses up as a priest and assumes the name Sir Topas. In literary and theatrical history, this is the name not of a priest but of a knight: first, the protagonist in Chaucer's burlesque romance *The Tale of Sir Thopas* in *The Canterbury Tales* (Chaucer, *Works*, 164–6), and then a braggart knight, Sir Tophas, in Lyly, *Endimion*; both characters act out what is in some ways a false role, like Feste's in 4.2. (On the knight–priest relationship, cf. Cesario's contrasting of 'Sir Priest' and 'Sir Knight' at 3.4.265.) The name, as well as the clerical disguise, may allude to the 'exorcizing' of Malvolio, since according to Scot the topaz stone had therapeutic effects in the treatment of madness: 'a topase healeth the lunatic person of his passion of lunacie' (Scot, 294; see also Burton, 2.4.1.4, 441). The name can also be seen as a deformation of 'Sir Toby', for whom Feste is as it were a representative in this episode (see Sir Toby's 'To him, Sir Topas', 4.2.17). At the same time, the changeable colouring of the gemstone, with its yellow, white or green prismatic crystals, makes it appropriate to Feste's change of dress and identity in this scene (compare his 'very opal' metaphor for Orsino's mind at 2.4.75), while also alluding, perhaps, to the yellow and green of his fool's motley. The spelling *Topas* (rather than 'Topaz') in F may also indicate a pun on top-ass, suggesting that Malvolio is to be made a fool of (by a fool).

15 FABIAN another saint's name (see p. 23). It may have been partly suggested to Shakespeare by 'Fabio', the pseudonym of the cross-dressed Lelia in *Intronati*. A somewhat enigmatic figure, Fabian appears suddenly as a replacement for Feste in the gulling plot in 2.5. He is often played as a servant or member of Olivia's household, or alternatively as a law student, since he refers twice to the law in 3.4 (but also with reference to the play's early performance at the Middle Temple: Shakespeare may have 'brought on' a member of the Inn at the last moment).

TWELFTH NIGHT,
OR WHAT YOU WILL

1.1 *[Music.] Enter* ORSINO, Duke of Illyria, CURIO *and*
other Lords.

ORSINO

> If music be the food of love, play on,
> Give me excess of it, that surfeiting

TITLE *F's 'Twelfe' is a variant spelling of 'twelfth' (*OED* twelfth *a.* 1a)
but may also reflect, in pronunciation,
the loss of 't' before 'n' and 'd' (see
Kökeritz, 320). The comedy's second
title, *What You Will*, is a proverbial
catchphrase, not always benevolent
(Dent, W280.5): cf. 1.5.105, where
Olivia uses it to express her impatience towards Orsino's courtship.
John Marston's comedy *What You
Will* was probably performed slightly
earlier than *TN*.

1.1 The opening scene – often performed as the second scene because of
its supposed lack of theatricality (see
p. 97) – introduces the important
themes of love, death and the powers
of music, and presents Orsino in his
role as poetic lover. Coleridge observes
of Shakespeare's opening scenes that
they may 'strike at once the key-note,
give the predominant spirit of the play,
as in the *Twelfth Night*' (Coleridge,
1.38); this is not altogether true, since
this scene is in reality quite unlike much
of the rest of the comedy in its intense
lyricism. Rowe locates this scene in '*The
Palace*', which Capell further specifies
as '*A Room in the Duke's Palace*'. The
action shifts in the first act between
Orsino's palace and Olivia's house, and

then (apart from a brief excursion in
3.3) settles in the latter.

0.1 *Music* F has no SD in this scene
regarding the use of music, but *Enough,
no more* (7) suggests that music is playing at the opening of the play. The
music might have been provided by a
single musician on stage, or by a group,
perhaps situated in the gallery.

Illyria On the historical and symbolic
implications of the play's setting, see
pp. 70–2.

0.2 *Lords* The size of Orsino's entourage
is unclear and varies in productions.

1 SP *See List of Roles, 5n.

1 **music** It is not by chance that this is
the comedy's opening noun. *TN* is one
of Shakespeare's most musical plays,
and music takes on an important metaphorical as well as literal significance,
as a means of expression and persuasion and as a medium for change. See
Appendix 3. Cf. *AC* 2.5.1–2, 'music,
moody food / Of us that trade in
love'.

2 **excess** one of the comedy's key semantic categories (varied in *surfeiting*):
cf. e.g. 1.3.7–13, 36–40; 1.5.116–17;
2.3.85–90.

it refers back to *music* but also to *food
of love*, which Orsino desires in great
quantities

TITLE] *(*Twelfe Night, Or what you will*),* Rowe   **1.1**] *(Actus Primus, Scaena Prima.)*   0.1 *Music*]
Smock Alley; Musick attending. / Capell *after Lords 0.2*   1 SP] *Mahood; Duke.* F

The appetite may sicken and so die.
That strain again, it had a dying fall.
O, it came o'er my ear like the sweet south   5
That breathes upon a bank of violets,
Stealing and giving odour. Enough, no more,
'Tis not so sweet now as it was before.   [*Music ceases.*]
O spirit of love, how quick and fresh art thou
That, notwithstanding thy capacity   10

2–3   Orsino's conceit is to free himself of desire (*appetite*) by an over-
abundance causing nausea (*sicken*),
i.e. by having too much of a good
thing, with the added optimistic aspi-
ration to achieve freedom through
sexual release (*die* = end and climax
sexually). Shakespeare is possibly
mixing and varying the proverbs
'Too much honey cloys the stom-
ach' (Dent, H560) and 'Every surfeit
foreruns a fast' (Dent, S1011).

4   **strain . . . fall** refers to a musical
cadence (*OED* fall *n.*[1] 10, first occurrence), while continuing the pun on *die*
– i.e. the *strain* (= melody and sexual
effort) ends with a diminuendo.

5   *****south** Pope's emendation meaning
'south wind' (see *OED* south B 5a),
which bears both sound and odour
(disproving Furness's prediction that
'Hunter [1870] will prove to be the last
editor to adopt Pope's change'). F's
'sound' (as a synonym for *strain*) makes
5 tautological. Cf. Fenner, *Song*, 'com
O South, / And on my garden blowe'
(sig. C2ʳ). On the wind–breath conceit, cf. Sidney, *Arcadia*, 2: 'her breath
is more sweete than a gentle South-
west wind, which comes creeping ouer
flowrie fieldes and shadowed waters in
the extreme heate of sommer.'

6   **violets** a possible 'hidden' and pro-
phetic allusion to Viola, whose name
is the original (Latin) form of the

flower (see List of Roles, 1n., and cf.
1.3.23–4n.); cf. Lydgate's 'Sweetest
viola, that never shall fade' (Lydgate,
300).

7   **Stealing . . . odour** i.e. the wind takes
the perfume from the flowers and distributes it. Cf. *Son* 99.1–3, where the
'forward violet' itself, according to the
speaking 'I', is the 'Sweet thief' (of his
'love's breath'). A sharp sensory shift
from hearing to olfaction.

9–14   *****O . . . minute** F's punctuation
renders Orsino's baroque conceit syn-
tactically ambiguous, especially with
regard to the subject of *Receiveth* (11):
the full stop after *sea* makes the subject
the *spirit of love* which, despite (*notwithstanding*) its small size (*capacity*),
receives or contains as much as the
sea. Adams defends this reading. Rowe
emended F's stop after *sea* to a comma,
making *thy capacity* the subject of
Receiveth and therefore equal to that
of the *sea*. This simplifies the paradox
of Orsino's conceit – that, despite
the limitless *capacity* of the *spirit of
love*, it rapidly devalues whatever it
devours. Orsino thus justifies his own
capriciousness.

9   **quick** sharp, lively (*OED* 18c)
       fresh hungry (*OED* 11b)

10   **That** in that (Blake, *Grammar*,
5.3.2.1d)
       capacity ability to receive or contain
(*OED* 1a)

5 south] *Pope;* sound *F;* Wind *Rowe;* south-wind *Keightley*   8 SD] *Collier³; after* 7 *Capell*
9–10 thou / That,] *this edn;* thou, / That *F*

Receiveth as the sea, naught enters there
Of what validity and pitch soe'er
But falls into abatement and low price
Even in a minute. So full of shapes is fancy
That it alone is high fantastical.   15

CURIO

Will you go hunt, my lord?

ORSINO   What, Curio?

CURIO   The hart.

ORSINO

Why so I do, the noblest that I have.
O, when mine eyes did see Olivia first
Methought she purged the air of pestilence;
That instant was I turned into a hart,   20

---

11 **Receiveth . . . sea** can swallow unlimited quantities: proverbial (Dent, S181: 'The sea is never full'). Orsino returns to the idea of the sea-like capaciousness of his love at 2.4.100–1.
there the sea; love's capacity

12 **what . . . soe'er** whatever (split by the interpolation of other words – a form of tmesis); cf. *TNK* 4.3.6.
validity value
pitch height, and thus status: a term from falcony (*OED n.² * 18a); cf. *R3* 3.7.187, 'Seduc'd the pitch and height of his degree'.

13 **falls . . . price** i.e. depreciates; *abatement* = diminution (*OED n.¹ * 2a, giving this example)

14–15 **So . . . fantastical** an allusion to Plato's doctrine of the divine creative frenzy (*Ion*, 533e–534a; Plato, 1.103–17, 107–8) that inspires 'The lunatic, the lover, and the poet', who 'Are of imagination all compact' (*MND* 5.1.7–8). 'The Platonicks', says Puttenham of the poetic variety, 'call it furor' (Puttenham, 1). On the erotic 'furor' or *frenzy*, cf. Olivia at 5.1.277 (see n.); see also 1.5.248n., 2.2.21n., 3.4.14–15n. Cf. *LLL*

2.756–9, 'As love is . . . Full of strange shapes, of habits and of forms'.

14 **shapes** imaginary forms
fancy love (Onions, 2)

15 **alone** exclusively
high fantastical imaginative in the highest degree (*OED high adv.* 10b, giving this example)

16–17 The pun on *hart* (stag) and 'heart' is an Elizabethan commonplace. Orsino hunts his own heart, a suggestion of narcissism confirmed at 20–2.

19 **she . . . pestilence** Orsino compares Olivia to one of the air sweeteners used to cleanse the atmosphere, in times of visitation by the plague: 'It is good also', advises Lodge in his *Treatise of the Plague*, 'to weare sweet savors and perfumes about us . . . for such an odour . . . altereth the pestilence of the ayre'(Lodge, sigs C4ʳ–C4ᵛ). Cf. 1.3.1n. and 1.5.287n.

20–2 Orsino's allegory alludes to the story of Actaeon, who – having seen Diana naked – was transformed by her into a stag and then hunted to death by his own *hounds* (Ovid, *Met.*, 3.205–304, fols 33ᵛ–34ʳ; on Diana,

---

11 sea,] *Rowe³*; Sea. *F*   naught] *(*Nought*)*, *Kittredge*   16 SP1] *(Cu.)*, *Inchbald*

And my desires, like fell and cruel hounds,
E'er since pursue me.

Enter VALENTINE.

How now, what news from her?

VALENTINE

So please my lord, I might not be admitted,
But from her handmaid do return this answer:
The element itself till seven years' heat   25
Shall not behold her face at ample view,
But like a cloistress she will veiled walk
And water once a day her chamber round
With eye-offending brine – all this to season
A brother's dead love, which she would keep fresh   30
And lasting in her sad remembrance.

ORSINO

O, she that hath a heart of that fine frame

---

see also 1.4.31n.). Ironically, Orsino,
refused by Diana–Olivia, ends up
hunting, or desiring, himself, suggesting the malady of 'self-love' of which
Olivia accuses Malvolio at 1.5.86 (see
pp. 29–32). For the conceit of the
self-consuming heart, cf. the opening
line of the first sonnet in Petrarch's
Canzoniere, '*quei sospiri ond'io nudriva
il core*', 'those sighs on which I fed my
heart' (ed.'s translation).
21 **fell** fierce
23 **might not** could not; *might* is here the
preterite of 'may', in the sense of 'was
[not] permitted' (Blake, *Grammar*,
4.3.7.9a).
25–9 **The . . . brine** Olivia's behaviour
is a catalogue of the symptoms of
female bereavement; cf. Burton on the
melancholy typical of maids, nuns and
widows: 'They are apt to loath, dislike,
disdain, be weary of every object . . .
apt to weep, and tremble' (Burton,

203). Cf. *KL* 4.6.191–3.
25 **element** air – as one of the *four elements* (see 2.3.9n.), i.e. earth, water, air
and fire. Cf. also 1.5.267.
   till . . . heat for seven summers; *heat*
is a metonymy, effect for cause
26 **ample** full
27 **cloistress** cloistered or enclosed nun
(*OED*, sole occurrence)
27–9 **walk . . . round** i.e. walk around her
room weeping
   veiled veilèd
29 **eye-offending brine** salt water (tears)
hurting her eyes
   season embalm (in *brine*; *OED v.* 3,
giving this example)
30 **brother's dead love** love for her dead
brother and that brother's love for
her, which she has lost (anastrophe or
inverted word order)
31 **remembrance** memory (pronounced
as four syllables)
32 **of . . . frame** so finely made

22 SD] *Dyce; after 22 F*   23 SP] *(Val.), Cam¹*   25 years' heat] years hence *Rowe³*

To pay this debt of love but to a brother,
How will she love when the rich golden shaft
Hath killed the flock of all affections else   35
That live in her – when liver, brain and heart,
These sovereign thrones, are all supplied, and filled
Her sweet perfections with one self king!
Away before me to sweet beds of flowers: 39
Love-thoughts lie rich when canopied with bowers.   *Exeunt.*

1.2   *Enter* VIOLA, *a* Captain *and Sailors.*

VIOLA
What country, friends, is this?
CAPTAIN   This is Illyria, lady.

---

34 **golden shaft** In Ovid, *Met.*, 1.565–8, fol. 8ᵛ, Cupid's armoury includes a gold-tipped arrow that provokes love.

35 **all affections else** i.e. all other feelings of love (except those for Orsino)

36–7 **liver . . . thrones** According to early modern (essentially Galenic) humour theory, the liver is the seat (*throne*) of passion, the brain that of thought and the heart that of sentiment.

37 **supplied** occupied; cf. *Cor.* 3.3.34–5, 'Keep . . . the chairs of justice / Supplied with worthy men.'

38 **perfections** pronounced as four syllables
one self king one and the same king, namely Orsino (who thereby confirms his high opinion of his own *self*)

1.2 For the theatrical tradition making this the play's opening scene, see p. 97. A brief but intense scene of dramatic exposition, it narrates the storm, establishes the geographical setting and introduces us both to Viola – who conceives her cross-dressing

strategy – and (verbally) to her brother, Sebastian. Capell gives as location '*The Sea-coast*', representations of which have varied widely onstage; in Beerbohm Tree's 1901 production, Viola was washed ashore directly on the 'Terrace of Olivia's House' (Tree).

0.1 *Sailors* non-speaking extras, referred to by Viola at 4, their costumes providing a visual clue to the scene's location; often omitted in performance. In some productions (mainly nineteenth century), however, they have been brought on as stage hands to carry a trunk containing Viola's possessions (in Posner's 2001 production a golden trunk was dragged on by the captain himself). This stage tradition may have been prompted by the reference at 5.1.251 to Viola leaving her *maiden weeds* with the captain, but presumably these are the clothes she comes to shore in before she is provided with *man's attire* (see 1.4.0.1–2n.).

---

37 These] Three *Warburton*   38 perfections] perfection *Capell*   self] self same *F2*   **1.2**] *(Scena Secunda.)*   0.1 Sailors] Sailors, *carrying a Trunk. / Kemble*   1 SP1] *(Vio.), Inchbald*

VIOLA

And what should I do in Illyria?

My brother he is in Elysium.

Perchance he is not drowned. What think you, sailors?

CAPTAIN

It is perchance that you yourself were saved.   5

VIOLA

O my poor brother! And so perchance may he be.

CAPTAIN

True, madam, and to comfort you with chance,

Assure yourself, after our ship did split,

When you and those poor number saved with you

Hung on our driving boat, I saw your brother,   10

Most provident in peril, bind himself –

Courage and hope both teaching him the practice –

To a strong mast that lived upon the sea,

Where, like Arion on the dolphin's back,

---

3 **Elysium** in Greek mythology, the state or abode of the blessed after death: hence, in this context, heaven. Viola plays on the assonance with *Illyria* (rhetorical figure: paronomasia).

4, 5, 6 **Perchance** Viola first uses the adverb in the sense of 'perhaps', willing her brother alive against the odds. The captain's benevolent quibble plays on the etymological meaning of the word, i.e. by chance or fortune, which Viola then optimistically echoes.

7 **chance** The captain continues to play on the multiple meanings of the word: here, possibility (that her brother has survived).

8 **split** break up, because of a storm (*OED v.* 9); cf. *Tem* 1.1.62, 'We split, we split, we split!'

9 **those poor number** The use of a plural demonstrative adjective (*those*) with a singular noun of multitude (*number*) is relatively rare (*OED* II 2c, giving this example).

10 **driving** driven by the wind (*OED ppla.* 2, first occurrence)
boat small open boat (presumably of the kind often pulled by large ships to use as tenders); cf. *CE* 1.1.76–7, 'The sailors sought for safety of our boat, / And left the ship, then sinking-ripe, to us.'

11 **provident** prudent, resourceful; literally, making provision for the future (*OED* 1)

12 **practice** method

13 **lived** remained afloat (a nautical term); cf. Ralegh, 'we . . . brought the Galley as neere as we could, but she had as much adoe to liue as could be' (Ralegh, 89).

14 ***Arion** stressed on second syllable **Arion . . . back** semi-legendary Greek poet and musician who, in order to escape being robbed and murdered by sailors, sang, accompanied by his lyre, to charm a dolphin that carried him safely ashore to the island of Corinth (Ovid, *Fasti*, 2.79–118): illustration of

14 Arion] *Pope; Orion F*

I saw him hold acquaintance with the waves　　　　15
So long as I could see.

VIOLA　　　　　　　　　　For saying so, there's gold.
Mine own escape unfoldeth to my hope –
Whereto thy speech serves for authority –
The like of him. Knowst thou this country?

CAPTAIN
Ay, madam, well, for I was bred and born　　　　20
Not three hours' travel from this very place.

VIOLA
Who governs here?

CAPTAIN　　　　　　　　A noble duke
In nature as in name.

VIOLA　　　　　　　　What is his name?

CAPTAIN
Orsino.

VIOLA
Orsino: I have heard my father name him.　　　　25

the importance and redemptive powers of music in the comedy. Ashore, Arion was helped by his friend Periander, as Sebastian will be by Antonio (2.1). A spectacular water pageant before Elizabeth I at Kenilworth Castle, near Stratford, was reported in 1575, in which '*Arion* that excellent & famous musicien' appeared 'ryding aloft upon his olld friend the Dolphin, (that from hed to tayl was a four & twenty foot long)'; Arion sang 'a delectable ditty of a song' (Laneham, 42–3).

15 **hold acquaintance with** ride, surf

17–19 **Mine . . . him** My own escape leads me to hope – encouraged by your testimony – that he too has escaped.

17 **unfoldeth** makes plain (*OED v.*¹, giving this example)

18 **authority** testimony

19 slightly irregular, possibly explained by a medial pause before *Knowst*,

reflecting Viola's change of subject, or by trisyllabic pronunciation of *country* ('countery'), known as anaptyxis (Kökeritz, 292; cf. F's 'Countrey')

22–3 **noble . . . in name** 'Orsino' is noble both because the Orsini were a noble Italian family and because in Italian the word means 'little bear', considered a noble beast (and represented as such in the Orsini family stem). See List of Roles, 5n. Viola's comment at 25 confirms that the name was well known.

25 **my father** a recurrent point of thematic contact between Viola and her brother; the latter, named after him, speaks of 'My father . . . Sebastian of Messaline' at 2.1.16. Viola mentions both father and brother at 2.4.107, 120–1 and, finally, at 5.1.228–41, where knowledge of the year of their father's death is decisive confirmation of the twins' respective identities.

19 country] (Countrey), *Rowe*　20 Ay] (I)　21 travel] (trauaile)　22–3 A . . . name.] *this edn; one line* F

He was a bachelor then.

CAPTAIN

And so is now, or was so very late,

For but a month ago I went from hence,

And then 'twas fresh in murmur – as you know

What great ones do the less will prattle of –   30

That he did seek the love of fair Olivia.

VIOLA

What's she?

CAPTAIN

A virtuous maid, the daughter of a count

That died some twelvemonth since, then leaving her

In the protection of his son, her brother,   35

Who shortly also died, for whose dear love,

They say, she hath abjured the company

And sight of men.

26–7 **a bachelor . . . late** Spedding (cited in Furness) notes that 'if [Orsino] were still a bachelor there would be no female court; therefore no fit place for [Viola]': hence the necessity for her disguise.

27 **late** lately (*OED adv.* 4a)

29 **'twas . . . murmur** there was a new rumour (see *OED* murmur *n.* 3, giving this example)

32 **What's she?** Of what condition and rank is she? (Blake, *Grammar*, 3.2.2.4); 'what' could also mean 'who', permitting comic misunderstanding between the two. Cf. 1.2.50; 1.3.48–9 and n.; 1.5.112–24 and n., 206, 209 and n.; 3.4.228, 310.

33–6 **A . . . died** continues the emphasis on male mortality

34 **some twelvemonth since** about a year ago; for *since* as adverb ('ago'), cf. Blake, *Grammar*, 5.1.3.3 (giving this example).

36 **dear** great (an intensifier); cf. 1.4.25.

37–8 ***company / And sight** Hanmer's inversion of the two nouns in F saves the metre and gives the sentence a stronger climactic structure.

38–41 ***I . . . is** i.e. I might serve that lady and my true identity might not be presented in public (*OED* deliver $v.^1$ 8c, giving this example) until the time is ripe. The syntax is somewhat complex: 'What my estate is' is a redundant object, which qualifies the main object *I* (38), in a passive construction (see Blake, *Grammar*, 3.3.2.1h). Cf. 50 and 1.5.242. Main verb *delivered* (39) and the object *What . . . is* (41); are separated and qualified by the adverbial clause *Till . . . mellow* (40), as indicated by the emended punctuation, which makes *mellow* an adjective, whereas in F it seems to be a transitive verb. Cf. Olivia's equivalent desire 'To keep in darkness what occasion now / Reveals before 'tis ripe' (5.1.149–50).

37 hath] had *F3*   37–8 company / And sight] *Hanmer;* sight / And company *F*

VIOLA   O that I served that lady,
And might not be delivered to the world –
Till I had made mine own occasion mellow –   40
What my estate is.
CAPTAIN   That were hard to compass,
Because she will admit no kind of suit,
No, not the duke's.
VIOLA

There is a fair behaviour in thee, captain,
And though that nature with a beauteous wall   45
Doth oft close in pollution, yet of thee
I will believe thou hast a mind that suits
With this thy fair and outward character.
I pray thee – and I'll pay thee bounteously –
Conceal me what I am, and be my aid   50
For such disguise as haply shall become
The form of my intent. I'll serve this duke.
Thou shalt present me as an eunuch to him.

40 Cf. *LLL* 4.2.72, 'upon the mellowing of occasion'.
41 **estate** true identity and social status
   compass achieve (*OED v.*[1] 11, giving this example)
42 **admit** allow (*OED v.* 2a, giving this example)
   suit supplication, courtship
43 **not** not even
46 **close in** enclose (*OED* 17a)
   pollution (moral) uncleanness or contamination, alluding to the biblical parable of the whited sepulchres 'which indeed appear beautiful outward, but within full of . . . all filth-iness' (Matthew, 23.27). Cf. 1.3.120n.
47–8 proverbial (Dent, F1)
48 **character** 'The face or features as betokening moral qualities; personal appearance' (*OED n.* 10, giving this example)
49 *pray thee F's 'prethee' may be a compositorial substitution: 'Compositor B regularly imposed his preferred form "prethee", a sophistication that would obscure the symmetry of "pray thee" / "pay thee"' (*TxC*, 421).
50 Cf. 1.2.38–41n.
51–2 **haply . . . intent** will perhaps be apt to represent my purpose
51 **become** be fitting to
52 **I'll . . . duke** Johnson observes that 'Viola is an excellent schemer, never at a loss; if she cannot serve the lady, she will serve the duke.' Cf. 26–7n.
53 **eunuch** On the implications of Viola's 'eunuch' disguise, see pp. 57–61.

40 mellow –] *Mahood*; mellow *F*   49 pray thee] *Oxf;* prethee *F;* prithee *Ard*[2]   53 eunuch] page *Inchbald*; boy *Nunn*

It may be worth thy pains, for I can sing
And speak to him in many sorts of music,   55
That will allow me very worth his service.
What else may hap to time I will commit;
Only shape thou thy silence to my wit.

CAPTAIN

Be you his eunuch, and your mute I'll be.
When my tongue blabs then let mine eyes not see.   60

VIOLA

I thank thee. Lead me on.   *Exeunt.*

1.3   *Enter* SIR TOBY [Belch] *and* MARIA.

SIR TOBY   What a plague means my niece to take the death

54 **I can sing** one of the play's loose ends,
since Viola gives us no demonstration of
her musical talents. All singing is del-
egated to Feste or his drunken companions. Shakespeare may have changed his
mind, because the voice of the boy actor
playing Viola had broken, or because the
clown Robert Armin, a famously gifted
singer, was available to play Feste.

55 **speak . . . music** Viola's choice of verb
has two possible, and complementary,
implications: that she will use music as
a mode of persuasive discourse, or that
she will use speech as a charmingly
musical means of expression (the second
comes closer to describing later events);
many sorts may indicate either different
types of song (or speech), or instrumental as well as vocal performance.

56 **allow me** show me to be
   worth worthy of

57 I will entrust my fortunes to the workings of time; cf. 2.2.40–1, where Viola
appeals directly to *time* to *untangle* the
knot that her disguise has created.
   hap chance to happen
   commit entrust (*OED* 1)

58 **wit** ingenuity

59 **mute** dumb guard. The captain devel-

ops Viola's idea at 53, since eunuchs
traditionally had mutes as subordi-
nates in eastern courts.

60 **let . . . see** In Turkish harems the
guards were supposed to watch over
but not look (and still less tell), on pain
of being blinded.

1.3 This scene represents virtually a third
'opening' to the play, introducing
not only a new environment (Olivia's
household) but also a distinct mood,
that of the frenetic revelry presided
over by Sir Toby.

1–2 Sir Toby's life-affirming attitude
shifts the emphasis away from the
preoccupation with death in the preceding scenes – the possible drowning
of Viola's brother and Olivia's loss of
her brother and father.

1 **What a plague** an idiomatic imprecation, frequent in Shakespeare (cf.
1.5.116, 3.4.276), but in this context
of multiple (male) deaths it may take
on a particular force. Sir Toby makes
the play's most resolute stand against
death and in favour of the pleasure
principle.

1, 4 **niece, cousin** On these kin words,
see List of Roles, 11n.

59 eunuch] page *Inchbald*   **1.3**] *(Scaena Tertia.)*   0.1 Belch] *Malone*   1 SP] *(Sir To.), Cam¹*

of her brother thus? I am sure care's an enemy to life.

MARIA   By my troth, Sir Toby, you must come in earlier
o'nights. Your cousin, my lady, takes great exceptions
to your ill hours.   5

SIR TOBY   Why, let her except, before excepted.

MARIA   Ay, but you must confine yourself within the
modest limits of order.

SIR TOBY   Confine? I'll confine myself no finer than I
am. These clothes are good enough to drink in, and   10
so be these boots too; an they be not, let them hang
themselves in their own straps.

MARIA   That quaffing and drinking will undo you. I heard
my lady talk of it yesterday, and of a foolish knight that
you brought in one night here to be her wooer.   15

SIR TOBY   Who, Sir Andrew Aguecheek?

MARIA   Ay, he.

SIR TOBY   He's as tall a man as any's in Illyria.

MARIA   What's that to th' purpose?

SIR TOBY   Why, he has three thousand ducats a year.   20

---

2   **care's . . . life** proverbial (Dent, C84).
Sir Toby's concern for Olivia's state
of mind is 'not altogether unselfish'
(Furness): he is afraid that it will
restrict his own revels.

3   **By my troth** by my faith: a mild oath
or discourse marker

4   **o'nights** of nights: at night

6   **let . . . excepted** let her object before
being objected to (by me). Sir Toby
is quibbling on the legal expression
exceptis excipiendis (excepting those
things that are to be excepted), as
if defending himself in court (*OED*
except *v*. 2, giving this example).

8   **modest . . . order** bounds of moderate behaviour

9   **confine** dress up; slim down. Sir Toby
puns on Maria's sense of 'restrict your
behaviour' in 7.

11, 59, 61, 86   **an** if

11–12   **hang . . . straps** a variation on the
proverbial expression 'He may go hang
himself in his own garters' (Dent, G42)

13   **quaffing** drinking deep

14   **foolish** an epithet frequently applied
to Sir Andrew (as he says at 2.5.79,
'many do call me fool'): cf. also 22, 28
and 62–4 and 2.3.82n.

18   **tall** valiant (Onions, 3)

19   Maria responds to *tall* (18) as if its
only meaning were 'of great height'.

20   **three thousand ducats** A ducat was
a gold coin (originally a silver Italian
coin) worth approximately nine shillings
(*OED* 1a). Sir Toby thus estimates Sir
Andrew's fortune at 27,000 shillings or
£1,350 per annum, but this sum is something of a Shakespearean convention (cf.
MV 1.3.1 and see Elze, 157).

---

3 SP] *(Mar.)*, *Inchbald*__4 o'nights] *(*a nights*)*, *Capell*__18 any's] any *Douai MS*, *Pope*__20, 82 has]
*(*ha's*)*, *F3*

MARIA Ay, but he'll have but a year in all these ducats.
   He's a very fool and a prodigal.

SIR TOBY Fie that you'll say so! He plays o'th' viol-de-
   gamboys, and speaks three or four languages word
   for word without book and hath all the good gifts of   25
   nature.

MARIA He hath indeed, almost natural, for, besides that
   he's a fool, he's a great quarreller, and, but that he
   hath the gift of a coward to allay the gust he hath in
   quarrelling, 'tis thought among the prudent he would   30
   quickly have the gift of a grave.

SIR TOBY By this hand they are scoundrels and substractors
   that say so of him. Who are they?

21 **he'll . . . ducats** i.e. he'll lose all his
money within a year (precisely Sir
Toby's intent: cf. 2.3.177–8n.); *in* = 'to
enjoy'

22 **very** true
   prodigal spendthrift (either noun, a
   prodigal; or adjective, a *prodigal* fool).
   For Sir Toby this is Sir Andrew's chief
   merit.

23 **Fie** Shame on you

23–4 **viol-de-gamboys** a playful corruption of 'viola da gamba' (Italian:
'leg viol'), a bowed, stringed musical
instrument, possibly one of those
played in the 'music room' during the
performance of *TN*, as in Carroll's
2002 Middle Temple production.
Florio's gloss – 'because men hold
it betweene or upon their legges'
(Florio, *New World*, 602) – perhaps
hints at a sexual allusion likewise
present in Sir Toby's deformation
gam*boys*; cf. 99–100n. There is also
another possible 'secret' reference to
Viola, anticipating the duel in 3.4 (cf.
1.1.6n.).

24 **speaks . . . languages** an ironic
claim belied by Andrew's ignorance of
French at 89 and by his own confes-

sion (89–92) that he has not studied
the *tongues*

25 **without book** by heart (*OED* book
n.15, giving this example); proverbial idiom (Dent, B532). Officially it
is a compliment, but it implies that
Sir Andrew has never actually opened
a book, or that he has learned foreign
expressions parrot-fashion.

27 **almost natural** quibble: nearly natural; all most natural, i.e. half-witted
(Onions, 4)

28 **fool** a *natural* one, as opposed to an
allowed professional one such as Feste
(see 1.5.90n.)
   quarreller wrangler; duellist (looking
   forward to Sir Andrew's challenge to
   Viola in 3.4). Maria's epithet, together
   with *coward* (29), portrays Aguecheek
   as a kind of *miles gloriosus*, the cowardly braggart of classical comedy.
   but that were it not for the fact that

29, 31 **gift** The repetition (rhetorical
figure: ploce) plays on two meanings:
talent and present.

29 **gust . . . in** taste or relish for

32 **substractors** a (drunken?) deformation of 'detractors' (*OED*, sole occurrence)

27 indeed, almost] indeed all, most *Furness*

MARIA   They that add, moreover, he's drunk nightly in
your company.   35

SIR TOBY   With drinking healths to my niece. I'll drink
to her as long as there is a passage in my throat and
drink in Illyria. He's a coward and a coistrel that will
not drink to my niece till his brains turn o'th' toe, like
a parish top.   40

Enter SIR ANDREW [Aguecheek].

What, wench, *Castiliano vulgo*, for here comes Sir
Andrew Agueface.

SIR ANDREW   Sir Toby Belch! How now, Sir Toby Belch?

SIR TOBY   Sweet Sir Andrew.

SIR ANDREW [*to Maria*]   Bless you, fair shrew.   45

---

38 **coistrel** knave, base fellow. Shakespeare
may have picked up the insult from
Riche's *Farewell*, 'to haue her Chastitie
assailed, by suche a simple coisterell'
(sig. D2ʳ).

39 **brains . . . toe** head spins; 'turn o'th'
toe' (*o'th'* = on the) seems to have been
used with reference to whipping, as in
Nashe, *Traveller*: 'he for his trecherie
was turnd on the toe' (sig. C4ʳ).

39–40 **like . . . top** proverbial (Dent,
P57); in Shakespeare's day a large vil-
lage whipping-top was frequently kept
for use in cold weather as a warming-
up exercise (see Fig. 13).

41 ***Castiliano vulgo** The F text may
be corrupt here: the meaning of Sir
Toby's phrase is obscure, and there
is even disagreement as to which
language he is using. Accepting F's
wording, Mahood takes *Castiliano* as
a synonym for 'devil', since Castiliano
is the name assumed by a devil in
Grim, the Collier of Croydon (written
c. 1600 or earlier, though only printed
in 1662); she takes *vulgo* (Latin for

'in the common tongue') as having
the force of a Latin or Italian verb
meaning roughly 'I talk of'. Sir Toby
thus varies the proverbial phrase 'talk
of the devil', appropriately enough, as
Sir Andrew is entering as he speaks.
However, 'castilian' was a variant form
of 'castellan', one living in or belonging
to a castle (*OED n.*¹). It is perhaps
more likely, therefore, that *Castiliano* is
equivalent to the proverbial expression
'lad of the castle', a merry term for
a reveller or carouser (Dent, C124.1;
cf. *1H4* 1.2.46). Sir Toby is thus
characterizing Sir Andrew as a fellow
drinking companion using a current
colloquial term: 'What, wench, a lad
of the castle, as they say.' Cf. Marlowe,
Jew, sig. H4ʳ, 'Hey *Riuo Castiliano*, a
man's a man.'

45 **shrew** Presumably Sir Andrew intends
this as a compliment, meaning 'shrew-
mouse', a term of endearment (cf.
mouse 1.5.59); the colloquial sense of
the word, however, was a bad-tempered
woman or scold (as in the title of *TS*).

40.1] *this edn; after 42 F*   Aguecheek] *Malone*   41 *Castiliano vulgo*] *Castiliano volto / Hanmer;
Castiglione voglio (Thomas)*   43 SP] *(And.), Cam*¹   45 SD] *Oxf*

MARIA   And you too, sir.

SIR TOBY   Accost, Sir Andrew, accost.

SIR ANDREW   What's that?

SIR TOBY   My niece's chambermaid.

SIR ANDREW   Good Mistress Accost, I desire better   50
acquaintance.

MARIA   My name is Mary, sir.

SIR ANDREW   Good Mistress Mary Accost.

SIR TOBY   You mistake, knight. 'Accost' is front her, board
her, woo her, assail her.   55

SIR ANDREW   By my troth I would not undertake her in
this company. Is that the meaning of 'accost'?

MARIA   Fare you well, gentlemen.

SIR TOBY   An thou let part so, Sir Andrew, would thou
mightst never draw sword again.   60

SIR ANDREW   An you part so, mistress, I would I might
never draw sword again. Fair lady, do you think you
have fools in hand?

---

47 **accost** engage with, assail (*OED v.*6), as Sir Toby defines it at 54–5; originally a naval term meaning 'go alongside' (*OED v.* 3; cf. *board*, 54). As Mahood notes, great play is made with the verb 'accostare' in *Intronati*.

49 Sir Toby pretends to understand 48 as 'Who's that [woman]?' or 'Accost whom?' Cf. 1.2.32n.
chambermaid not in the sense of a woman who cleans bedrooms, but in the socially more elevated (and now obsolete) sense of lady's maid (*OED* 2).

52 **Mary** See List of Roles, 10n.

54–6 **Accost . . . undertake** Sir Toby's definitions of *accost* can be interpreted discursively as 'amorously address' or physically as 'have sex with'. Sir Andrew responds to the second sense.

56 **undertake** take in hand (*OED v.* 5c), in two senses: deal with and have sexual relations with; the second mean-

ing is taken up in the puns on *hand*, 64–77.

56–7 **in this company** in the presence of Sir Toby himself (and the audience: the actor may indicate the spectators, as in Carroll's 2002 Middle Temple production)

59 **An . . . so** i.e. if you let her go without having accosted her

60, 62 **never draw sword** i.e. cease to be a sword-carrying gentleman. Sir Andrew's parroting of the phrase (cf. 25n.) leads him unwittingly to suggest a desire to be impotent (or emasculated). The drawing of swords as a sign of masculinity reappears in 3.4, where both Sir Andrew and Viola are reluctant to unsheathe their weapons. Sebastian has no such problems in 4.1.

62–3 **do . . . hand** 'do you think I am a fool' (*have in hand* = deal with)

---

50 SP] *F2 (An.); Ma. F*   Accost] *Rowe;* accost *F*   53 Mary Accost] *Rowe³;* Mary, accost *F*
59 let part] let her part *F3*

MARIA   Sir, I have not you by th' hand.

SIR ANDREW   Marry, but you shall have, and here's my   65
hand.

MARIA [*Takes his hand*.]   Now, sir, thought is free. I pray
you, bring your hand to th' buttery-bar, and let it drink.
[*Brings his hand to her breast*.]

SIR ANDREW   Wherefore, sweetheart? What's your
metaphor?   70

MARIA   It's dry, sir.

SIR ANDREW   Why, I think so. I am not such an ass but I

64 Maria pretends to take *in hand* literally, and by doing so implies that Sir
Andrew is indeed a fool (perhaps also
insinuating his impotence).

67 **thought is free** 'if you say so'; a
proverbial expression (Dent, T244), in
answer to the question 'Do you think I
am a fool?' (see 62–3), and prompted
by Sir Andrew's unwitting admission
and demonstration of his folly in giving Maria his hand. Cf. Lyly, *England*
(fol. 30ʳ), 'why then quoth be, doest
thou thinke me a foole, thought is free
my Lorde quoth she, I will not take
you at your word.'

68 **bring . . . bar** A *buttery* is a room
where liquor and provisions are stored:
cf. *TS* Induction 1.101–2, 'take them
to the buttery, / And give them friendly welcome every one.' The room has
a hatch, the ledge of which is the *buttery-bar*, over which drinks and food
are served (*OED*, giving this example;
see Fig. 11). Maria is still toying with
sexual innuendo, presumably inviting Sir Andrew to touch her breasts
(where milk or butter is stored), and
in some productions the actress helps
him do so.

69–73 **What's . . . dry** Sir Andrew
takes Maria's metaphorical *dry* (see
71n.) as a literal reference to his
hand, thus revealing his ignorance
of what a *metaphor* really is. Cf. *AW*

5.2.10–13, where the word 'meta-
phor' itself is literalized: '*Parolles*
You need not stop your nose, sir,
I spoke but by a metaphor. *Clown*
Indeed, sir . . . if your metaphor
stink I will stop my nose.'

71 Maria characterizes her *metaphor*
of the *buttery-bar* (68) as *dry*, that
is witty or ironic (see 74n.), but
she also metaphorically rejects Sir
Andrew's inept advances by saying that the *bar* is *dry* ('there's no
drink there for you'). Paul Chahidi,
who played Maria in Carroll's 2002
Middle Temple production, pointed
out privately that this may be an
ironical allusion to the male actor,
whose breast would indeed be *dry*
(i.e. without milk).

72–3 **I am . . . dry** An allusion to the
proverb 'Fools have wit enough to
keep themselves out of the rain' (Dent,
F537), with an unintentional quibble
on masturbation. Johnson proclaims
his bafflement: 'What is the jest of *dry
hand*, I know not any better than Sir
Andrew.' The 'jest' probably includes
a further reference to Sir Andrew's
lack of virility: *dry* was a synonym for
'castrated', as in Isaiah, 56.3, 'neither
let the eunuch say, Behold I am a dry
tree' (see Rubinstein, 83); *dry* hand was
correspondingly a sign of impotence, a
moist hand proverbially signifying the

67 SD] *Kemble*   68 SD] *this edn*

can keep my hand dry. But what's your jest?

MARIA A dry jest, sir.

SIR ANDREW Are you full of them?   75

MARIA Ay, sir, I have them at my fingers' ends. [*Lets go of his hand.*] Marry, now I let go your hand I am barren. *Exit.*

SIR TOBY O knight, thou lack'st a cup of canary. When did I see thee so put down?

SIR ANDREW Never in your life, I think, unless you see   80
canary put me down. Methinks sometimes I have no more wit than a Christian or an ordinary man has; but I am a great eater of beef, and I believe that does harm to my wit.

SIR TOBY No question.   85

SIR ANDREW An I thought that, I'd forswear it. I'll ride home tomorrow, Sir Toby.

SIR TOBY *Pourquoi*, my dear knight?

SIR ANDREW What is 'pourquoi'? Do, or not do? I would

---

opposite (see Tilley, H86, 'A moist hand argues an amorous'; and cf. *Oth* 3.4.36–8, 'This hand is moist, my lady . . . This argues fruitfulness').

74 **dry jest** arid joke; Maria may also be referring to her own ironical or sarcastic mode of speech: Puttenham (157) rebaptizes irony as 'the drye mock'.

76 **at . . . ends** always ready (proverbial: Dent, F245)

77 **now . . . barren** i.e. I am empty of jests now I have let go of the butt of them; *barren* also because of Sir Andrew's ineffective *hand* (a further insinuation of impotence). The actress often lets go of the hand in question at this point, immediately prior to her exit. As at 71, there may be an allusion to the male actor, who by definition cannot bear children.

78, 81 **canary** a light sweet wine from the Canary Islands (*OED n.* 2, giving this example)

79 **put down** i.e. defeated in repartee; cf. 1.5.80.

81 **put me down** knock me out (as when drunk)

82 **a Christian** an average human being, as distinct from a beast (*OED* 5a); cf. *TGV*, 3.1.267–8, 'She hath more qualities then a water-spaniel, which is much in a bare Christian.'

83–4 **eater . . . wit** According to popular 'medical' lore, beef was supposed to dull the brain; cf. Boorde, *Dyetary*, sig. H3ʳ, warning that 'olde beef . . . doth ingender melancolye and leprouse humoures'; also *H5* 3.7.150–1, 'And then give [the foolish English] great meals of beef'.

86 **An** if

89 **'pourquoi' . . . do?** suggests a sexual allusion (*OED* doing 1b = copulation) and confirms Sir Andrew's ignorance of foreign languages (hence the adoption here of roman for the French,

---

76 Ay] *(I)*   76–7 SD] *Kemble subst.; after 77 Cam¹ Collier*   89 'pourquoi'] *(purquoy), Cam*   77 SD] *(Exit Maria)*   88 Pourquoi] *(Pur-quoy),*

I had bestowed that time in the tongues that I have in   90
fencing, dancing and bear-baiting. O, had I but followed
the arts.

SIR TOBY   Then hadst thou had an excellent head of hair.

SIR ANDREW   Why, would that have mended my hair?

SIR TOBY   Past question, for thou seest it will not curl by   95
nature.

SIR ANDREW   But it becomes me well enough, does't not?

SIR TOBY   Excellent, it hangs like flax on a distaff, and I
hope to see a housewife take thee between her legs and
spin it off.   100

rather than F's italic; cf. 24n.). He
suspects *pourquoi* is a verb equivalent
to *accost* (47). Perhaps he hears, or
repeats, something like 'poke her'.

90 **tongues** languages

91 **fencing** a fashionable pastime among
the gentry (to which Sir Andrew
aspires) as well as a professional skill
of actors; Sir Andrew's claim to have
studied it is belied by his evident
inability to duel in 3.4, 4.1 and 5.1.
dancing Sir Andrew's claim to be an
expert dancer is also highly dubious:
his demonstration of his dancing skills
usually suggests otherwise in performance (see 136n.).

93–100 These references to Sir Andrew's
hair have given rise to a lasting stage
tradition that represents him with long
and straight yellow locks (see Fig. 26).

93 Sir Toby pretends to understand *tongues*
(90) as 'tongs' (for curling hair), pronounced the same way (Kökeritz, 45).

94 **mended** amended, improved

95–6 **curl by nature** Playing on Sir
Andrew's *tongues* (= tongs; 90), and
arts (92), Sir Toby maliciously suggests that Sir Andrew's appearance
could be improved by the 'art' of a
hairdresser.

98 **hangs like flax** Long thin strands of
flax fibre were used to produce linen, and
were characteristically of a soft yellow

colour; 'flaxen hair' was idiomatic (*OED*
flaxen *a.* 2b). Sir Toby's description of
Sir Andrew echoes Chaucer's portrait of
the effeminate Pardoner in the General
Prologue to the *Canterbury Tales*, 675–6:
'This Pardoner hadde heer as yellow as
wex, / But smothe it heeng as dooth
a strike of flex' (Chaucer, *Works*, 23):
another hint at impotence perhaps (*hangs*
implies detumescence). In Dekker's
Blurt, flaxen-haired men are said to be,
like Sir Andrew, 'Chicken-heartes (and
yet great quarrellers)' (Dekker, *Blurt*,
sig. C4ʳ).

distaff forked rod on which fibre
was wound for spinning (a symbol of
female labour, and thus of femininity).
In Sir Andrew's case, it is an ambiguous
image, representing both the phallus
(with pun on 'staff') and effeminacy.

99 **housewife** pronounced 'hussif'
('huswife' in F); meaning either a
woman who keeps house or a hussy or
prostitute (Onions)

99–100 **take . . . off** puns on *take thee* (as
a *distaff*; sexually) and *spin it off* (spin
your hair off the *distaff*; bring to a
sexual climax). Underlying the bawdy
joke is the comic implication that Sir
Toby hopes to see Sir Andrew bald.

99 **between her legs** recalls Sir Toby's
earlier equivocal reference to the viola
da gamba (see 23–4n.).

93 Then] *fondles him.* Then *Cam¹*   hair.] hair. *curls Andrew's hair with his whip* / *Tree*   95 curl by]
Theobald; coole my *F*   97 me] *F2;* we *F*   does't] *(*dost*), Rowe*   99 housewife] *(*huswife*)*

SIR ANDREW Faith, I'll home tomorrow, Sir Toby. Your
niece will not be seen or, if she be, it's four to one she'll
none of me. The count himself here hard by woos
her.

SIR TOBY She'll none o'th' count. She'll not match above   105
her degree, neither in estate, years nor wit – I have
heard her swear't. Tut, there's life in't, man.

SIR ANDREW I'll stay a month longer. I am a fellow o'th'
strangest mind i'th' world. I delight in masques and
revels sometimes altogether.   110

SIR TOBY Art thou good at these kickshawses, knight?

SIR ANDREW As any man in Illyria whatsoever he be,
under the degree of my betters; and yet I will not
compare with an old man.

SIR TOBY What is thy excellence in a galliard, knight?   115

102–3 **she'll . . . me** she'll have nothing
to do with me

103 **hard by** close

105–6 **She'll . . . degree** confirms the
indeterminacy of Orsino's rank (see
List of Roles, 5n.): if he is a *count* he
is not above the *Countess Olivia* (2.2.1,
5.1.93) in *degree*.

107 **Tut** expression of impatience
there's life in't there's still hope (proverbial: Dent, L265; cf. L269, 'While
there's life there's hope'

109–10 **masques and revels** The
masque, in which dancing played a
prominent role, arrived in England
from continental Europe during the
sixteenth century, and became a court
entertainment for Elizabeth I under
the control of the Master of the
Revels. Perhaps Sir Andrew fancies
himself at court.

110 **altogether** all together: at one and
the same time (*OED* 2)

111 **kickshaws** dainty trifles (from
French *quelque chose* (*OED* 2, giving
this example)); originally a fancy dish,
as in *2H4* 5.1.27–8, 'A joint of mutton,

and any pretty little tiny kickshaws'
(cf. 117n.). In this context of dance
discourse, there is probably a pun on
'kicks', and Williams, 1128, suggests
a sexual innuendo, as in Fletcher's
The Elder Brother, where Brisac tells
the maid Lilly, 'And th'hast another
Kickshaw, I must taste it' (Fletcher,
4.4.53–4, sig. H2ᵛ).

112–13 **As . . . betters** i.e. as good as
anyone except my social superiors: a
characteristically redundant claim

113–14 **I . . . compare** I am not to be
compared

114 **an old man** failed attempt at a
compliment: Sir Andrew presumably
intends 'old hand' or expert (*OED* old
a. 5), with reference to Sir Toby, but
ends up committing a *faux pas* regarding the latter's age. On the age of Sir
Toby, see List of Roles, 11n.

115 **thy excellence** aspect in which you
excel (*OED* 2, giving this example)
galliard a quick and lively court dance
in triple time consisting of five steps,
with a *caper* or leap before the fifth
(*OED n.*¹ B 2, giving this example);

111 kickshawses] *(*kicke-chawses*), Cam;* kick-shaws *F4*

SIR ANDREW Faith, I can cut a caper.

SIR TOBY And I can cut the mutton to't.

SIR ANDREW And I think I have the back-trick simply as
strong as any man in Illyria. [*Dances.*]

SIR TOBY Wherefore are these things hid? Wherefore   120
have these gifts a curtain before 'em? Are they like
to take dust, like Mistress Mall's picture? Why dost
thou not go to church in a galliard and come home in
a coranto? My very walk should be a jig. I would not
so much as make water but in a sink-apace. What dost   125

otherwise known as 'cinquepace' (see
125n.), although Riche (sig. A3ʳ) considers this a less sophisticated form
of *galliard*: 'Our Galliardes . . . are
so full of trickes and turnes, that he
whiche hath no more but the plaine
Sinquepace, is no better accoumpted
of then a very bungler'. Elizabeth I is
said to have practised galliards as her
morning exercise.

116 **cut a caper** dance or leap in a fantastic (literally, goat-like) way (see Fig.
17). In some productions, the actor
comically demonstrates the jump here,
as at 136 SD.

117 **mutton** a quibble on Sir Andrew's
caper, in the sense of the pickled bud
used to make a sauce for mutton; *mutton* was also slang for 'prostitute' (*OED*
4). Cf. 'The old lecher hath gotton
holy mutton to him a Nunne my Lord'
(Greene, *Friar*, H3ʳ).

118 **back-trick** presumably a backward
caper in a *galliard* (*OED*, giving this
example); perhaps an unconscious
reference to sexual intercourse, from
behind

120 **Wherefore . . . hid?** ironical allusion
to the biblical parable of the talents kept
hidden beneath a bushel (Matthew,
25.14–30; cf. 1.2.46n. on *pollution* and
1.5.14n.). Cf. Primaudaye, 'hide not
this talent, but teach it others, and
giue thy selfe an example unto them of

well doing, and of profiting euery one'
(Primaudaye, 374).

121 **curtain** used to protect a picture from
dust and from fading; cf. 1.5.226.

122 **Mistress Mall** This looks like a
topical allusion; if so, the most likely candidate is Mary Fitton (*Mall*
is a diminutive of 'Mary'), one of
Elizabeth I's maids of honour, who fell
into disgrace when she bore a child to
the Earl of Pembroke in 1601 (Hotson,
103–6). Alternatively, Sir Toby may
simply be referring to Maria.

124 **coranto** courtly 'running' dance in
2/4 time (Italian, from French '*cour-
ante*'), characterized by a running or
gliding step, as distinguished from
leaping; cf. *HV* 3.5.32–3, 'They bid us
to the English dancing-schools / And
teach lavoltas high and swift corantos.'
jig an improvised northern folk dance
performed with rapid footwork and
a rigid torso; in Shakespeare's day it
became fashionable at the court of
Elizabeth I and as a stage dance.

125 **sink-apace** cinquepace (French, literally 'five steps'): another term for the
galliard (see 115n.). Sir Toby's *make
water* suggests a pun on 'sink', i.e.
cesspool or sewer (*OED* sink *n.¹* 1a–b).
The pun is varied in *MA* 2.1.69–70,
'and with his bad legs falls into the
cinque-pace faster and faster, till he
sink into his grave'.

119 SD] *Collier³ subst.* 124 coranto] *(Carranto), Rowe* 125 sink-apace] *(Sinke-a-pace), Mahood;*
cinque-pace *Hanmer*

thou mean? Is it a world to hide virtues in? I did think
by the excellent constitution of thy leg it was formed
under the star of a galliard.

SIR ANDREW Ay, 'tis strong, and it does indifferent well
in a flame-coloured stock. Shall we set about some   130
revels?

SIR TOBY What shall we do else? Were we not born under
Taurus?

SIR ANDREW Taurus? That's sides and heart.

SIR TOBY No, sir, it is legs and thighs – let me see   135
thee caper. [*Sir Andrew capers.*] Ha, higher! Ha, ha,
excellent.   *Exeunt.*

1.4   *Enter* VALENTINE, *and* VIOLA *in man's
attire* [*as Cesario*].

127 **constitution** composition, forma-
tion (*OED* 4a, giving this example)
127–8 **formed . . . galliard** made to
dance (ironical)
129 **indifferent well** well enough
130 **in . . . stock** On this line in Posner's
2001 RSC production, Sir Andrew
raised his trouser legs to show off his
(dun-coloured) stockings, anticipating
Malvolio in 3.4.
***flame-coloured** F's 'dam'd' (damned)
is dubious – since nowhere else in the
play does Sir Andrew swear so strongly
– and is an odd qualifier for 'coloured
stock': a colour word seems more likely. Rowe[3]'s emendation is rejected by
Collier[2] in favour of 'dun', and Wilson
(114) concurs ('dam'd' being a likelier
compositorial misreading of 'dunne'
or donne'), but 'dun-coloured' is weak
(i.e. colourless): unless this is the point
of the joke. Oxf's 'divers-coloured' is
interesting in that it suggests a fool's
attire, but is somewhat improbable as a
misreading. Everett's 'lemon-coloured'
has the attraction of anticipating the

yellow stockings that Olivia hates and
that Malvolio will wear, but then so
does Rowe[3]'s emendation, adopted
here.
132–5 **born . . . thighs** The signs of the
Zodiac were thought to govern different parts of the body. Taurus governed
neck and throat, the body parts dearest
to drinkers. Sir Andrew gets his signs
and organs mixed up. Sir Toby's further
misattribution deliberately prompts Sir
Andrew into a *caper* (116).
136 SD Sir Andrew shows off the dancing
skills he has boasted of, usually with
disastrous results in performance, making Sir Toby's praise (*excellent*, 137)
ironic. In Posner's 2001 RSC production, Sir Andrew failed to move until
Sir Toby tried to 'impale' his feet with
his walking stick, forcing him to skip.
1.4 Here Viola appears for the first time
disguised as Cesario in the duke's court,
and has already had time ('but three
days', 3) to gain Orsino's favour and to
fall in love with him, complicating her
task as go-between on his behalf.

130 flame-coloured] *Rowe[3]*; dam'd colour'd *F*; damask-coloured *Knight*; dun-coloured *Collier[2]*;
lemon-coloured *Everett*; divers-coloured *Oxf*   stock] stocken *F3*; stocking *Pope*   set] *Rowe[3]*; sit
F   134 That's] *F3*; That *F*   136 SD] *Oxf*; Capers awkwardly *Douai MS; Sir Andrew dances again /
Collier[3]*   1.4] *(Scena Quarta.)*

VALENTINE   If the duke continue these favours towards
you, Cesario, you are like to be much advanced. He
hath known you but three days, and already you are no
stranger.

VIOLA   You either fear his humour or my negligence that   5
you call in question the continuance of his love. Is he
inconstant, sir, in his favours?

VALENTINE   No, believe me.

Enter ORSINO, CURIO *and Attendants.*

VIOLA   I thank you. Here comes the count.

ORSINO
Who saw Cesario, ho?   10

VIOLA   On your attendance, my lord; here.

ORSINO [*to Valentine, Curio and Attendants*]
Stand you awhile aloof. [*to Viola*] Cesario,
Thou knowst no less but all: I have unclasped
To thee the book even of my secret soul.

0.1–2 *in man's attire* presumably an out-
fit identical to that of Sebastian, to
permit the subsequent confusions

2   **Cesario** This is the first name that
the audience hears with reference
to Viola, who is not named in the
dialogue by her real name until the
final scene (5.1.240). Her adopted
name, equally Italian, may derive
from 'Cesare', the assumed name of
the cross-dressed heroine in Curzio
Gonzaga's comedy *Gli inganni*, the
version of the 'Twelfth Night' story
which comes closest – in both time
and tone – to Shakespeare's.
advanced promoted (*OED ppla.* 3)

3   **three days** Temporal references in
the comedy are neither precise nor
consistent: contrast *three months* at
5.1.90 and 95. Here the emphasis is

on the rapidity with which Cesario
has entered into Orsino's favour. On
the play's multiple time scheme, see
pp. 77–8.

5   **humour** disposition or temperament
(*OED* 4), with the implication of
capriciousness
that in that

6   **continuance** permanence (*OED* 6,
giving this example)

8.1   *Attendants* Cf. 1.1.0.2n.

11   **On your attendance** at your service
here i.e. I am here, ready (*OED adv.*
1b)

13–14   **unclasped . . . book** alludes to the
often elaborate clasps that fastened
the covers of valuable books, especially
bibles; the first of a number of references to Orsino's body and mind as a
book (cf. 1.5.219)

0.2 *as Cesario*] Munro *subst.*   8.1 ORSINO] *Munro; Duke* F   12 SD1] *this edn*   SD2] *Mahood*

Therefore, good youth, address thy gait unto her,   15
Be not denied access, stand at her doors
And tell them there thy fixed foot shall grow
Till thou have audience.

VIOLA   Sure, my noble lord,
If she be so abandoned to her sorrow
As it is spoke, she never will admit me.   20

ORSINO
Be clamorous and leap all civil bounds
Rather than make unprofited return.

VIOLA
Say I do speak with her, my lord, what then?

ORSINO
O then unfold the passion of my love,
Surprise her with discourse of my dear faith.   25
It shall become thee well to act my woes.
She will attend it better in thy youth
Than in a nuncio's of more grave aspect.

VIOLA
I think not so, my lord.

---

15 **address thy gait** direct your steps
(*OED* address *v.* 5, giving this example)
16 **access** accèss
17 **fixed** fixèd
   grow take root
19 **abandoned** totally given up (*OED v.*
4, giving this example)
21 **civil bounds** limits of courtesy; cf.
1.5.202n., 4.2.33n. On the issue of
courtesy, see pp. 58–64.
22 **make unprofited return** come back
empty-handed; *unprofited* is the first
occurrence in *OED ppla.*
25 **Surprise** capture by force (a military expression; *OED v.* 2b). Cf. *Tit*
1.1.288, 'Treason, my lord – Lavinia is
surprised.'

discourse discòurse
dear Cf. 1.2.36n.
28 *****nuncio's** messenger's; the genitive
form may be due to the fact that *a
nuncio's . . . aspect* is intended to be a
parallel with *thy youth* (27): since *thy*
is a possessive (genitive), Shakespeare
turned the parallel noun into a possessive, thereby producing a double genitive (*-s*, *of*), possible in Early Modern
English (NB; cf. Hope, 1.1.4d).
more grave graver. Shakespeare often
uses *more* with monosyllabic adjectives in comparative forms (Blake,
Grammar, 3.2.3.4, giving this example): cf. *more smooth* (32), and 3.1.145,
3.3.5, 3.4.3 and 4.2.47.
aspect aspèct

15 gait] *(gate), Capell*   28 nuncio's] *F4* (Nuncio's*); Nuntio's *F*; Nuntius *(TxC)*

ORSINO   Dear lad, believe it,
For they shall yet belie thy happy years   30
That say thou art a man. Diana's lip
Is not more smooth and rubious. Thy small pipe
Is as the maiden's organ, shrill and sound,
And all is semblative a woman's part.
I know thy constellation is right apt   35
For this affair.
[*to Valentine, Curio and Attendants*]
                    Some four or five attend him –
All, if you will – for I myself am best
When least in company. [*to Viola*] Prosper well in this
And thou shalt live as freely as thy lord,
To call his fortunes thine.
VIOLA   I'll do my best   40
To woo your lady. [*aside*] Yet a barful strife:

---

30 **belie . . . years** misrepresent your
youthful age
31 **thou . . . man** Orsino unwittingly
points out the ambiguity of Cesario's
gender while apparently alluding to
his age. The following passage plays
on Viola's position as a boy (actor)
disguised as a girl (Viola) disguised as
a boy (Cesario) or *eunuch* (1.2.53).
31 **Diana's lip** Diana, already alluded
to by Orsino at 1.1.20–2 (see n.) with
reference to Olivia, was the Roman
moon-goddess, patroness of hunting,
fertility and virginity (her *lip* having
never been kissed by man). Cesario's
face becomes the epitome of feminine
beauty.
32 **more smooth** smoother; cf. 28n.
rubious ruby-coloured (*OED n.*[1], first
occurrence)
small pipe high treble voice (*OED*
pipe *n.*[1] 2a, giving this example); also
alluding to the sex of the boy actor
who played Viola (cf. Partridge, 160),

or to her disguise as a *eunuch* (1.2.53);
cf. *Cor* 3.2.113–14, 'a pipe / Small as
an eunuch'.
33 **organ** voice (*OED n.*[1] 5b, giving this
example); female genitals (cf. 32 n.)
shrill and sound high-pitched and
unbroken; cf. *LLL* 5.2.415, 'sound,
sans crack or flaw'.
34 **semblative** resembling (Onions;
OED, first occurrence)
woman's part woman's appearance;
female dramatic role; female sex
35 **constellation** disposition or character,
as determined by the influence of the
stars (*OED* 1b, giving this example)
39–40 **live . . . thine** live as independ-
ently as your lord, using his fortune
as he does: an 'unknowing' glance
towards the end of the comedy
41 **a barful strife** i.e. an internal struggle full of bars or impediments
(because against her natural inclination); *OED* gives this as sole occurrence of *barful*.

---

33 shrill and] shrill in *Dyce*[2]   36 SD] *this edn*   38 SD] *Oxf*   41 SD] *Capell subst.*

Whoe'er I woo, myself would be his wife.   *Exeunt.*

1.5   *Enter* MARIA *and* FESTE.

MARIA Nay, either tell me where thou hast been or I will
    not open my lips so wide as a bristle may enter in way
    of thy excuse. My lady will hang thee for thy absence.

FESTE Let her hang me. He that is well hanged in this
    world needs to fear no colours.   5

MARIA Make that good.

FESTE He shall see none to fear.

MARIA A good lenten answer. I can tell thee where that
    saying was born of 'I fear no colours'.

FESTE Where, good Mistress Mary?   10

MARIA In the wars, and that may you be bold to say in
    your foolery.

FESTE Well, God give them wisdom that have it; and

---

42 There is a probable pun on *would* and wooed, pronounced in the same way (Kökeritz, 155–6).

1.5 This long scene is dominated by the highly ironic duologue in which the disguised Viola, pleading on behalf of Orsino, succeeds instead in winning Olivia's love for herself. Rowe suggests '*Olivia's House*' as the location.

0.1 FESTE This name is mentioned only once in the dialogue, at 2.4.11, and never in stage directions or speech headings in *F*, where Feste is always indicated as *Clown*; see List of Roles, 14n.

1–3 Maria upbraids Feste, Olivia's jester, for his truancy at the court of Orsino, stressing the clown's role as a link between the two houses, a function shared by Viola.

1–2 **I . . . enter** I will keep my mouth firmly closed

2 **bristle** hair (literally, hog hair)
  in by

4–5 **He . . . colours** i.e. a hanged man need

fear no foes (since he cannot see them: cf. 7); *fear no colours* is proverbial (Dent, C520), the 'colours' being originally those of a regimental flag (*OED* colour *n.*[1] 7a; also 7d, giving this example). In the context of hanging, there is probably a pun on colours/collars (Kökeritz, 99). A sexual quibble may also be present, *well hanged* = 'well hung' (Hotson, 168): a well-endowed man need fear nobody or, possibly, need not fear blushing from embarrassment (*OED* colour *n.*[1] 3b); Cotgrave glosses French *couillatris* as 'well hanged (between the legs)'.

6 **Make that good** prove that

8 **lenten** weak, dismal (literally, pertaining to Lent, the season of fasting: *OED* 2, giving this example).

8–9 **where . . . born** the origin

11 **In the wars** of military origin; in trouble, as Feste is with Olivia for his truancy

13 **God . . . it** a paradox: *have* in place of 'lack'

1.5] *(Scena Quinta.)*   0.1 FESTE] *Munro; Clowne F*   4 SP] *Munro; Clo. F*   8 lenten] *(lenton)*

those that are fools, let them use their talents.

MARIA Yet you will be hanged for being so long absent.   15
Or to be turned away – is not that as good as a hanging
to you?

FESTE Many a good hanging prevents a bad marriage; and
for turning away let summer bear it out.

MARIA You are resolute then?   20

FESTE Not so neither, but I am resolved on two points.

MARIA That if one break the other will hold; or if both
break your gaskins fall.

FESTE Apt in good faith, very apt. Well, go thy way. If Sir
Toby would leave drinking, thou wert as witty a piece   25
of Eve's flesh as any in Illyria.

MARIA Peace, you rogue, no more o'that.

Enter Lady OLIVIA *with* MALVOLIO
[*and Attendants*].

---

14 **let . . . talents** another ironical allusion to the parable of the talents (cf. 1.3.120n.): let all make the most of what they have. There may be a pun here on 'talons' (cf. *LLL* 4.2.65–6), i.e. let those who have no wisdom use their claws.

16 **turned away** dismissed (from Olivia's employment)

18 **Many . . . marriage** proverbial (Tilley, H130, 'Better be half hanged than ill wed'); *good hanging* also retains here its slang sense of virility (cf. 4–5n.), i.e. a generous sexual endowment improves married life.

19 **for turning away** as for dismissal
bear it out make it (i.e. dismissal) bearable, by means of good weather

20 **resolute** determined

21 **resolved** determined: a synonym of *resolute* (20), which Feste pretends to contradict (*Not so neither*).
points matters, particulars (*OED n.*[1] 5a)

22–3 Maria puns on *points* (21) as the tagged laces attaching breeches to a doublet; cf. *1H4* 2.4.207–8, 'Their points [= swords] being broken – / Down fell their hose.'

23 **gaskins** wide breeches

24–6 **If . . . Illyria** This looks forward to the comedy's finale (5.1.356–8), in which we learn that Maria has married Sir Toby.

25–6 **as . . . flesh** as clever a woman. Feste compresses Maria's two potential attractions: her intelligence (*witty*) and her body. Cf. *MA* 4.2.83–4, where Dogberry comically considers himself 'as pretty a piece of flesh as any is in Messina'.

24 apt] apt . . . *she turns to go Cam*[1]   27.1–2] *this edn; after* 29 F   27.2] *Capell subst.*

Here comes my lady; make your excuse wisely you were
best.   [*Exit.*]

FESTE   Wit, an't be thy will, put me into good fooling!   30
Those wits that think they have thee do very oft prove
fools, and I that am sure I lack thee may pass for a wise
man. For what says Quinapalus? 'Better a witty fool
than a foolish wit.' [*to Olivia*] God bless thee, lady.

OLIVIA   Take the fool away.   35

FESTE   Do you not hear, fellows? Take away the lady.

OLIVIA   Go to, you're a dry fool, I'll no more of you.
Besides, you grow dishonest.

FESTE   Two faults, madonna, that drink and good counsel
will amend: for give the dry fool drink, then is the fool   40

28 **wisely** ingeniously (*OED* 3, giving
this example)
28–9 **you were best** you were best
advised to
30 **Wit . . . fooling** i.e. Wit, don't desert
me now. Feste is turning the proverbial
opposition of *Wit* (= intelligence) and
will (= desire) on its head, by suggesting that *Wit* has *will*.
an't if it
31–2 **Those . . . fools** Feste alludes to a
proverb of biblical origin: 'make the
fool answer to his foolishness, lest he
be wise in his own conceit' (Proverbs,
26.5; cf. Dent, C582).
33 **Quinapalus** an invented Latin
authority, probably inspired – given
the context of rhetorical and logical
discussion (cf. *syllogism*, 46) – by
Quintilian(us), author of the *Institutio
Oratoria*, a book much studied in
Elizabethan schools and universities.
This allusion may be 'contaminated'
by another Latin *auctoritas*, Apuleius,
author of *The Golden Ass*, and by the
name of the Roman coin *quinarius* or
quinary, worth five bronze 'asses' and
bearing the type of the victoriate, whose
'weight standard had come from Illyria'
(*Britannica*, 16.535). Shakespeare seems

to be imitating Rabelais's pseudo-
pedantic way with invented *auctoritates*.
In any case, as Mahood observes, 'this
no longer gets a laugh.'
33–4 **Better . . . wit** a variation of the
biblical proverb alluded to at 31–2
(see n.).
35–7 **Take . . . you** Olivia's contemptuous
dismissal of Feste seems to confirm
Maria's prediction regarding her anger
at his long absence (3, 15). These lines,
however, are often performed in a playful fashion, an interpretation justified by
Olivia's jesting with the clown at 55–70
and by her defence of fooling at 89–90.
37 **Go to** come, come: an expression of
disapproval (*OED* go v. 93b)
dry dull, i.e. barren of jests (as at
1.3.69–70)
38 **dishonest** unreliable (because of his
truancy)
39, 133 **madonna** my lady (*OED* 1a: from
Italian *mia donna*); used by Shakespeare
only for Feste in *TN*. Feste's use of an
Italian form of address may help to
define Olivia's Mediterranean background. The modern meaning 'Virgin
Mary' entered into the language later.
40–1 **give . . . dry** punning on *dry* (37)
as 'thirsty'

29 SD] *Pope*   34, 212 SDs] *Oxf*   35 SP] (*Ol.*), *Cam¹*   37 you're] (*y'are*)

not dry; bid the dishonest man mend himself – if he
mend, he is no longer dishonest, if he cannot, let the
botcher mend him. Anything that's mended is but
patched: virtue that transgresses is but patched with
sin, and sin that amends is but patched with virtue. If   45
that this simple syllogism will serve, so; if it will not,
what remedy? As there is no true cuckold but calamity,
so beauty's a flower. – The lady bade take away the fool,
therefore I say again, take her away.

OLIVIA   Sir, I bade them take away you.   50

FESTE   Misprision in the highest degree! Lady, *cucullus
non facit monachum* – that's as much to say as I wear not

41, 42 **mend** reform (*OED v.* 1b, giving
this example)

43 **botcher** mender of clothes
mend repair; Feste develops the pun
on *mend* with *patched* at 44.

44 **patched** 'implying a hasty, clumsy,
imperfect, or temporary manner'
of repair (*OED* patch *v.* 2, giving
this example); falsely equated by
Feste with *mended* (43). The point is
that a patch is merely a superficial
overlay, hence equally applicable to
sin patching *virtue* (which can hardly
be seen as repairing) and vice versa.
Malone proposes a further allusion
to the patchwork or parti-coloured
costume of the fool.

44–5 **virtue . . . virtue** Having reduced
virtue and sin to the patches on a
garment, Feste sophistically maintains,
in his own defence, the superficiality
and relativity of transgression and
amendment.

45–6 **If that** if (an older form)

46 **syllogism** an argument comprising
three propositions (see 43–5). Feste's
syllogism parodies logical reasoning
in a self-mocking attempt to raise the
tone of his defence.

47 **what remedy** it can't be helped
(rhetorical question); extending the

quibble on *mend* (41–3) and *amends*
(45)

no true . . . calamity Only one 'wed-
ded to calamity' (*RJ* 3.3.3) is really
faithless, i.e. it is inevitable that Olivia
will abandon her mourning in favour
of life and love.

48 **beauty's a flower** i.e. it will fade; the
classic 'seize the day' topos, Horace's
'*carpe diem*' (Horace, *Odes*, 1.11.8). Ard[1]
quotes *Summer's Last Will and Testament*
(1600), 1588–9: 'Beauty is but a flowre, /
Which wrinckles will deuoure.'

51 **Misprision** misunderstanding (*OED
n.*[1] 3); wrongful arrest (*OED n.*[1] 2)

51–2 *cucullus . . . monachum* the hood
does not make the monk; proverbial
(Dent, H586). Feste alludes to his
fool's attire (see *motley*, 53), and in
particular to his cap (possibly also
looking forward to his disguise in
4.2). The same tag appears in Latin
in *MM* 5.1.261 and in English in *H8*
3.1.23.

52 **as . . . say** as much as to say (a common Early Modern variant); cf. *2H6*
4.2.16.

52–3 **I . . . brain** i.e. I am a fool only
by profession, not by nature (contrast
Maria's gibe on Sir Andrew as a 'natural' fool at 1.3.27–8).

motley in my brain. Good madonna, give me leave to
prove you a fool.

OLIVIA   Can you do it?   55

FESTE   Dexteriously, good madonna.

OLIVIA   Make your proof.

FESTE   I must catechize you for it, madonna. Good my
mouse of virtue, answer me.

OLIVIA   Well, sir, for want of other idleness I'll bide your   60
proof.

FESTE   Good madonna, why mourn'st thou?

OLIVIA   Good fool, for my brother's death.

FESTE   I think his soul is in hell, madonna.

OLIVIA   I know his soul is in heaven, fool.   65

FESTE   The more fool, madonna, to mourn for your
brother's soul being in heaven. – Take away the fool,
gentlemen.

OLIVIA   What think you of this fool, Malvolio, doth he not
mend?   70

MALVOLIO   Yes, and shall do till the pangs of death shake

---

53 **motley** the fool's parti-coloured
costume
56 **Dexteriously** dextrously, cleverly (an
Early Modern variant)
57 Demonstrate it (continuing the
pseudological discourse).
58 **catechize** interrogate systematically,
as in a catechism; cf. *Oth* 3.4.16–17,
'I will catechize the world for him,
that is, make questions, and by them
answer.' Feste proceeds to conduct
a mock-religious interrogation of
Olivia, perhaps to provoke the upright
Malvolio (Oxf[1]).
58–9 **Good . . . virtue** my good virtuous
little one. Feste inverts the noun phrase
(determiner *my* and modifier *good*), by
analogy with expressions like 'Good
my lord' (Blake, *Grammar*, 3.3.5a).
This may suggest mock deference on

the clown's part, since Blake suggests
that such inversion often signals a
submissive attitude on the part of the
speaker to the person spoken to. *Mouse*
is a term of endearment for a woman
(*OED* 3a): cf. *Ham* 3.4.181.
60 **idleness** pastime
bide wait for; endure
67 *soul being F's punctuation ('soule,
being') has Olivia mourn her brother's
soul, despite the fact that he is in
heaven; Rowe, adopted here, makes her
mourn the very fact that his soul is in
heaven, taking up her statement in 65.
70 **mend** improve (his fooling); cf. 41n.,
42n., 43n.
71–2 **Yes . . . him** Malvolio interprets *mend*
(70) as 'improve in his folly', and sar-
donically reinforces this by adding that
Feste's folly will increase until he dies.

56 Dexteriously] Dexterously *F4*   66 fool] fool you *F3*   67 soul being] *Rowe;* soule, being *F*   71
SP] *(Mal.), Cam[1]*

him. Infirmity, that decays the wise, doth ever make the
better fool.

FESTE   God send you, sir, a speedy infirmity, for the better
increasing your folly. Sir Toby will be sworn that I am   75
no fox, but he will not pass his word for twopence that
you are no fool.

OLIVIA   How say you to that, Malvolio?

MALVOLIO   I marvel your ladyship takes delight in such a
barren rascal. I saw him put down the other day with an   80
ordinary fool that has no more brain than a stone.
Look you now, he's out of his guard already. Unless
you laugh and minister occasion to him, he is gagged.
I protest I take these wise men that crow so at these set
kind of fools no better than the fools' zanies.   85

72–3 **Infirmity . . . fool** i.e. disease or
old age (*OED* infirmity 2, giving this
example) favours fools by reducing
wisdom and increasing foolishness

74 **infirmity** illness

76 **no fox** not clever or crafty (in antithesis with *no fool*, 77). Feste adopts
elaborate and quasi-formal balanced
clauses (rhetorical figure: isocolon) in
making the point that, even if he is the
official fool, it is Malvolio who should
fear the *infirmity* of true foolishness.
pass pledge (*OED v.* 48a, giving this
example)

80 **barren** lacking in wit; possibly sterile.
Cf. 1.3.77.
put down . . . with defeated . . . by (in
verbal combat); cf. 1.3.79.
with by (*OED prep.* 40a)

81 **ordinary . . . stone** proverbial phrase
(Dent, W550: 'He has no more wit
than a stone'), probably with a barely
disguised allusion to the well-known
Elizabethan jester John Stone, referred
to in Jonson's *Volpone* as a 'taverne-
foole' (2.1; Jonson, *Works*, 465). If this
is so, *ordinary* takes on, as noun, the

added meaning 'tavern', i.e. where the
fool performs (*OED n.* 14b).

82 **out of his guard** defenceless, off his
guard (*OED* guard *n.* 5c, first occurrence)

83 **minister occasion** provide an opportunity
gagged speechless (*OED v.*[1], giving
this example)

84 **crow** laugh loudly; cf. *AYL* 2.7.30.

84–5 **these . . . fools** The demonstrative
adjective *these* agrees, here and elsewhere
in Shakespeare, with the main noun
(*fools*) rather than the determiner *kind* as
in present-day English (Blake, *Grammar*,
6.1.2.3, giving this example).
set contrived, unspontaneous

85 **zanies** stooges, attendants; derives from
the Italian *commedia dell'arte* figure of
the *zanni* (literally, Giovanni), assist-
ant to the clown, and in its English
form came to mean secondary figure or
poor imitator, as in *LLL* 5.2.463, 'Some
carry-tale, some please-man, some slight
zany'. This is rightly taken by Olivia as
a discourteous stab at her for laughing
uncritically at the 'barren' fool.

---

81 brain] brains *F4*   84 wise men] (Wisemen*)*, *F3*

189

OLIVIA   O, you are sick of self-love, Malvolio, and taste
    with a distempered appetite. To be generous, guiltless
    and of free disposition is to take those things for bird-
    bolts that you deem cannon bullets. There is no slander
    in an allowed fool though he do nothing but rail;   90
    nor no railing in a known discreet man though he do
    nothing but reprove.
FESTE   Now Mercury endue thee with leasing, for thou
    speak'st well of fools.

Enter MARIA.

MARIA   Madam, there is at the gate a young gentleman   95
    much desires to speak with you.
OLIVIA   From the Count Orsino, is it?
MARIA   I know not, madam. 'Tis a fair young man, and
    well attended.
OLIVIA   Who of my people hold him in delay?   100
MARIA   Sir Toby, madam, your kinsman.

---

86 **sick of self-love** Olivia's *sick* (taken up in *distempered*, 87) suggests that she is accusing Malvolio of something more than an excess of *amour propre* or proud self-centredness, namely morbid self-infatuation or narcissism; cf. *Son* 62.1, 'Sin of self-love possesseth all mine eye.'

87 **distempered** sick

88 **free** magnanimous (Onions, 1)

88–9 **bird-bolts** blunt-headed arrows used for shooting birds (*OED*, giving this example), and as such relatively harmless

89–90 **There . . . rail** Olivia's defence of fooling is less exuberant than Jaques's encomium to the 'motley fool' in *AYL* 2.7.12–43, but it is still noteworthy in a comedy so much concerned with different kinds of 'folly'.

89 **no slander** an allusion to the proverb 'His tongue is no slander' (Dent, T389)

90 **allowed** licensed, permitted by authority to jest without restraint (*OED ppla.* 2, giving this example)
    rail use abusive language; jest (*OED v.*[4] 2a)

91 **no railing . . . man** no abuse in someone known to be judicious. This appears to be an attempt by Olivia to mitigate her criticism of Malvolio, although the question remains whether he is *discreet* or *distempered*.

93–4 **Now . . . fools** May Mercury (the god of deception) teach you to lie, since you speak well of fools, i.e. truthfully.

93 **endue** endow
    leasing telling lies (*OED v.*[2])

99 **well attended** with several attendants; cf. 1.4.36.

100 **Who** Which
    hold . . . delay detains him

OLIVIA   Fetch him off, I pray you, he speaks nothing but
    madman. Fie on him.   [*Exit Maria.*]
    Go you, Malvolio. If it be a suit from the count, I am
    sick, or not at home. What you will to dismiss it.   105
                                                  Exit Malvolio.
    Now you see, sir, how your fooling grows old and
    people dislike it.
FESTE   Thou hast spoke for us, madonna, as if thy eldest
    son should be a fool,

Enter SIR TOBY.

    whose skull Jove cram with brains, for here comes one   110
    of thy kin has a most weak pia mater.
OLIVIA   By mine honour, half drunk. [*to Sir Toby*] What is
    he at the gate, cousin?

102 **Fetch him off** bring him (Sir Toby)
    away; a hunting term, implying that
    Sir Toby may be savaging the *fair
    young man* (98)
103 **madman** madman's talk, with
    reference to Sir Toby's drunken state
    (confirmed on his arrival, 116 ff.)
103 SD *Maria does not exit in F,
    although she comes on again at 160.1;
    Olivia's order to *fetch off* Sir Toby
    (102) is surely addressed to her rath-
    er than to Malvolio, who is sent off
    immediately afterwards to take care of
    the visitor.
105 **What you will** do whatever you
    think fit (proverbial, echoing the play's
    second title; cf. Dent, W280.5)
106 **old** stale
110 **Jove** Mahood claims that 'Here and
    elsewhere this is almost certainly a
    substitution for "God" in the play's
    original text', as a result of the 1606
    Act prohibiting profane oaths. Since,
    however, there are 16 occurrences of
    God, as opposed to 9 of *Jove*, this

hypothesis is unconvincing. Feste jocularly invokes a pagan deity, as at 93
and 3.1.43. Cf. 2.5.95, 168 and n., 172;
3.4.72, 79; 4.2.11 and n.
*for . . . one F's punctuation confus-
ingly suggests that Olivia's theoretical
eldest son and Sir Toby are one and the
same. Malone, adopted by most editors, does not resolve the confusion.
Rowe[3], by eliminating the pronoun
'he', allows for an easier associative
transition from Olivia's unborn child
to her present *kin*.
111 **pia mater** brain: literally 'meek
mother', the delicate innermost
membrane enclosing the brain
112–24 **What . . . devil** Olivia's *What*
(112, 123) means 'who' and 'what
kind of man'; Sir Toby interprets
it first as 'what rank', hence *gentleman* (114), and then as 'what sort
of thing', hence *devil* (124). At 206
Olivia gets to ask the *gentleman*
himself (see 206–11 and 209n.). Cf.
1.2.32n.

103, 213 SDs] *Capell*   109.1] *this edn; opp.* comes *110 F; after 111 Rowe[3]*   110 for . . . one] *Rowe[3];*
for heere he comes. Enter Sir Toby. / One *F;* for here he comes, one *Malone;* or – here he comes – one
Cam   112 SD] *this edn*

SIR TOBY   A gentleman.

OLIVIA   A gentleman? What gentleman?   115

SIR TOBY   'Tis a gentleman here. [*Belches.*] A plague
   o'these pickle herring! [*to Feste*] How now, sot?

FESTE   Good Sir Toby.

OLIVIA   Cousin, cousin, how have you come so early by
   this lethargy?   120

SIR TOBY   Lechery? I defy lechery. There's one at the
   gate.

OLIVIA   Ay, marry, what is he?

SIR TOBY   Let him be the devil an he will, I care not. Give   124
   me faith, say I. Well, it's all one.   *Exit.*

OLIVIA   What's a drunken man like, fool?

FESTE   Like a drowned man, a fool and a madman: one

116, 116 SD *Capell's suggestion that *here* stands for an SD indicating a belch seems improbable (it presumably means 'here at your gate'), but clearly a burp is called for at this point and is not otherwise indicated in F. Sir Toby acts out his surname. In Posner's 2001 RSC production he threw up over the carpet.

116–17 **A plague o'** Cf. 1.3.1n.

117 **pickle herring** i.e. pickled herring, the immediate cause, together with the accompanying wine, of Belch's belching. In *Palladis Tamia*, Francis Meres recalls the tragicomic death of one of Shakespeare's fellow playwrights from the same cause: '*Robert Greene* died of a surfet taken at Pickeld Herrings, & Rhenish wine, as witnesseth *Thomas Nash*, who was at the fatall banquet' (Meres, fol. 286ᵛ). The Pickle Herring was a type of clown in the *Englischen Comedien und Tragedien . . . samt dem Pickelhering* ('English comedies and tragedies . . . with Pickle Herring') and the musical *Pickelherings-spiele* ('Pickle Herring plays') performed in early seventeenth-century Germany (*OED*).

sot fool or drunkard (or perhaps, as an insult, drunken fool); Robert Armin, who probably played Feste, was the author of the pamphlet *Foole upon Foole or, Six Sortes of Sottes* (1600). See pp. 34–5.

119 **come . . . by** become possessed . . . by (*OED* come 40b, giving this example)

121 **Lechery** Sir Toby mishears *lethargy* (120), thereby exchanging one vice for another.
   one someone

124 **an** if

124–5 **Give me faith** I'm on the side of *faith* (not the *devil*); may allude playfully to the Protestant doctrine whereby man is justified by grace through faith, as opposed to works; cf. 3.2.67n.

125 **it's all one** it makes no difference; cf. 5.1.192, 366–7, 400.

127–9 **one . . . drowns him** one glass too many, warming him above his normal bodily temperature, makes him a fool, two glasses drive him mad, three overwhelm him (another allusion to drowning; cf. 1.2.4)

---

116 SD] *Theobald*   117 SD] *Mahood; Clown laughs Cam¹*

draught above heat makes him a fool, the second mads
him and a third drowns him.

OLIVIA   Go thou and seek the crowner, and let him sit   130
o'my coz, for he's in the third degree of drink – he's
drowned. Go look after him.

FESTE   He is but mad yet, madonna, and the fool shall
look to the madman.   *[Exit.]*

Enter MALVOLIO.

MALVOLIO   Madam, yon young fellow swears he will   135
speak with you. I told him you were sick. He takes on
him to understand so much, and therefore comes to
speak with you. I told him you were asleep. He seems to
have a foreknowledge of that too, and therefore comes
to speak with you. What is to be said to him, lady? He's   140
fortified against any denial.

OLIVIA   Tell him he shall not speak with me.

MALVOLIO   Has been told so, and he says he'll stand at
your door like a sheriff's post and be the supporter to a
bench, but he'll speak with you.   145

OLIVIA   What kind o'man is he?

MALVOLIO   Why, of mankind.

128–9 **mads him** makes him mad; cf. *R2*
5.5.61, 'This music mads me!'

130 **crowner** coroner

130–1 **sit . . . coz** hold an inquest on
my cousin (i.e. relative; see List of
Roles, 11n.). Cf. the second clown on
the drowned Ophelia, 'The crowner
hath sat on her and finds it Christian
burial', *Ham* 5.1.4–5.

131 **in . . . degree** at the third (and last)
stage (*OED phr.*, first occurrence)

133–4 This anticipates the 'dark room'
scene in 4.2, where the disguised Feste
will *look to* the 'mad' Malvolio.

134 **look to** look after

137, 139 **and therefore** for which reason

143 ***Has** Omission of personal pronouns (here 'he') was available in Early
Modern English (Blake, *Grammar*,
3.3.2.1f); cf. 5.1.171, 192 and 281.
and yet

144 **sheriff's post** Two painted posts – on
which proclamations were affixed – were
set up at the sheriff's or mayor's door
(*OED*; see Fig. 14); thus they (literally)
stand for the epitome of firmness.

147 **of mankind** i.e a human being;
Malvolio gives a non-answer

130 crowner] Coroner *Rowe*   134 SD] *Rowe*   135 yon] *(yond)*   143 Has] *(Ha's), Dyce;* He has
Douai MS, Pope; 'Has *Dyce²;* He's *Mahood*

OLIVIA What manner of man?

MALVOLIO Of very ill manner: he'll speak with you, will
you or no.   150

OLIVIA Of what personage and years is he?

MALVOLIO Not yet old enough for a man, nor young
enough for a boy, as a squash is before 'tis a peascod,
or a codling when 'tis almost an apple. 'Tis with him in
standing water between boy and man. He is very well   155
favoured, and he speaks very shrewishly. One would
think his mother's milk were scarce out of him.

OLIVIA Let him approach. Call in my gentlewoman.

MALVOLIO [*Goes to door.*] Gentlewoman, my lady   159
calls.   *Exit.*

Enter MARIA.

OLIVIA

Give me my veil; come throw it o'er my face.

148, 149 **manner** kind, temper (respectively)

149–50 **will . . . no** equivalent to modern
'willy-nilly'; cf. 'Would I or not', 295.

151 **personage** appearance

153 **squash** unripe peapod
peascod synonym of *squash*; Kökeritz,
133, detects a pun on 'codpiece'.

154 **codling** unripe apple (*OED* 1a, giving
this example); slang for scrotum and/or
testicles (cf. *Witch of Edmonton*, 20, 2.1,
'Has she a minde to codlings already?';
and *AYL* 2.4.49–50, where Touchstone
gives 'two cods' from a 'peascod' to his
beloved). The irony is that the *codling*
Cesario has no codlings.

154–5 **in . . . man** at the turn of the
tide, midway between childhood and
adulthood; recalls Golding's description of Narcissus, 'he seemde to stande
betweene the state of man and Lad, /
The hearts of divers trim yong men

his beautie gan to move, / And many
a Ladie fresh and faire was taken
in his love' (Ovid, *Met.*, 3.438–40).
The effect of Narcissus' beauty on
both sexes resembles the havoc that
Cesario's androgynous appeal is about
to wreak.

155 **standing** still, i.e. not ebbing or
flowing (*OED* 7a, giving this example)

155–6 **well-favoured** good-looking

156 **shrewishly** sharply (*OED* 2b, giving
this example); with a shrill (shrew-
like) voice

157 **his mother's . . . him** proverbial
(Dent, M1204)

161 **Give . . . veil** In theory, since she is
in mourning, Olivia should be wear-
ing her veil continuously in public; in
practice – since she has to be visible
to the audience – she puts it on only
in this episode to hide her face from
Cesario. Cf. 1.1.27.

149 manner] manners *F3*   159 SD] *Cam¹*   161 veil;] veil: *Puts Olivia's veil on – then her own. /
Powell MS*

We'll once more hear Orsino's embassy.

Enter VIOLA [*as Cesario*].

VIOLA   The honourable lady of the house, which is she?
OLIVIA   Speak to me, I shall answer for her. Your will?
VIOLA   Most radiant, exquisite and unmatchable beauty   165
  – I pray you, tell me if this be the lady of the house,
  for I never saw her. I would be loath to cast away my
  speech, for, besides that it is excellently well penned, I
  have taken great pains to con it. Good beauties, let me
  sustain no scorn: I am very comptible, even to the least   170
  sinister usage.
OLIVIA   Whence came you, sir?

162.1 *VIOLA F's 'Violenta'* is presumably a compositor's error. The page,
sig. Y3ᵛ, on which it appears, was
the first page of the play to be set
in type; Compositor B would therefore not yet have been familiar with
the name '*Viola*'. Turner, 130, suggests that he may have expanded an
abbreviated manuscript form '*Vio.*' in
the SD to '*Violenta*', having last met
this name in F when he set sig. X1ᵛ
in *AW* (though he had set all of *KJ*
and some of *R2* in the interim). See
Appendix 1.

163 **which is she?** Probably ironical,
since Olivia should be recognizable
from her veil, although some productions have made Viola's confusion
genuine by having Maria and other
attendants wear veils as well.

165 **Most . . . beauty** The beginning
of Viola's speech, *excellently well
penned* (168), is a conventionally complimentary performance delivered in
an appropriately 'high' tone. In Sam
Mendes's 2002 production, Viola had
a written speech that she began to

read here – unnecessarily, since she
has 'taken great pains to con it' (169;
cf. n.).

167–79 **I would . . . play** This passage is full of theatrical jargon (*speech,
con, studied, part, comedian, play*), as
Viola plays the role assigned to her
by Orsino.

167 **cast away** throw away, waste

168 **excellently well penned** superla-
tively well written

169 **con** learn by heart (*OED v.*[1], 3, giving this example). Viola underlines the
studied staginess of her performance.
Williams, 289, discerns a sexual pun
on French '*con*', which Cotgrave glosses as 'A woman's &c.'; cf. the French
princess in *H5* 3.4.47–8, 'De foot, *et* de
coun? *O Seigneur Dieu, ils sont les mots
de son mauvais*' ('O Lord God, they are
words of evil sound').
  sustain be subjected to (*OED* 9a,
giving this example)

170 **comptible** sensitive (*OED* countable
a. 1c, sole occurrence)

170–1 **least sinister usage** slightest
discourtesy

162.1 VIOLA] *F2; Violenta F   as Cesario*] *Cam¹*   164 will?] *Rann;* will. *F*   165–6 beauty –] *Rowe;*
beautie. *F*

VIOLA   I can say little more than I have studied, and that
question's out of my part. Good gentle one, give me
modest assurance if you be the lady of the house, that I   175
may proceed in my speech.

OLIVIA   Are you a comedian?

VIOLA   No, my profound heart. And yet – by the very
fangs of malice, I swear – I am not that I play. Are you
the lady of the house?   180

OLIVIA   If I do not usurp myself, I am.

VIOLA   Most certain if you are she you do usurp yourself,
for what is yours to bestow is not yours to reserve. But
this is from my commission. I will on with my speech
in your praise, and then show you the heart of my   185
message.

OLIVIA   Come to what is important in't – I forgive you
the praise.

---

173 **I can . . . more** Viola refuses to
answer Olivia's question about her
background and thus identity.
than . . . studied than what I have
learnt by heart, i.e. my role
174 **out . . . part** not written in my
speech
gentle one lady; *gentle* often signified
social status.
175 **modest** moderate, just enough
177 **comedian** professional actor (*OED*
1a, first occurrence); an example of the
sinister usage feared by Viola at 171 (see
170–1n.), i.e. an impatient (though
appropriate) riposte to Viola's insistence on confining herself to her *part*
178 **No . . . heart** absolutely not (*my
profound heart* is an intensifier rather
than a direct address to Olivia). This
emphatic denial reminds the audience
of the gender complexity of Viola's
role: as a woman she could not be an
actor.
179 **fangs of malice** an oath, deriving

from the biblical association of evil
with the serpent
I am . . . play i.e. I am not equated
solely with the part of Orsino's emis-
sary; I am not what I seem: the first
of several hints by Viola that she is
assuming a disguise
181, 182 **usurp** Olivia playfully means
'supplant' (*OED* 6, giving this example); Viola shifts the sense to an accu-
satory 'assume improper authority
over'.
183 **what . . . reserve** i.e. as 'lady of the
house' you shouldn't be concealing
yourself by wearing a veil (hence, also,
withholding yourself improperly from
marriage); *reserve* = withhold
184 **from my commission** outside my
commissioned speech (synonymous
with 'out of my part', 174); for *from*
as 'outside', cf. Blake, *Grammar*, 5.4.2
(giving this example). Cf. 224n.
on continue
187 **I forgive you** I can do without

175 I] *only as catchword on sig. Y3^v in F*   179 fangs] *(phangs), Rowe^3*; Pangs *Rowe*

VIOLA Alas, I took great pains to study it, and 'tis
poetical.   190

OLIVIA It is the more like to be feigned, I pray you keep
it in. I heard you were saucy at my gates, and allowed
your approach rather to wonder at you than to hear
you. If you be not mad, be gone. If you have reason, be
brief. 'Tis not that time of moon with me to make one   195
in so skipping a dialogue.

MARIA Will you hoist sail, sir? Here lies your way.

VIOLA No, good swabber, I am to hull here a little longer.
– Some mollification for your giant, sweet lady. Tell me
your mind, I am a messenger.   200

190–1 **poetical . . . feigned** a playful
allusion to Renaissance theories of
poetry (and of artistic representation
in general, especially drama) as a lie, a
doctrine derived from Plato (*Republic*,
376d–383c; Plato, 2.1–499, 220–9)
and adopted by the Puritans in their
attack on literature and the stage; cf.
Touchstone's 'the truest poetry is the
most feigning', *AYL* 3.3.18–19.

192–3 **allowed . . . approach** let you
come in

194–5 **If you be . . . brief** i.e. either have
the courtesy to leave or get on with
the message. F's 'not mad' has often
been unnecessarily emended (see t.n.)
because it is synonymous with 'If you
have reason' rather than antithetical
to it.

195 **'Tis . . . me** I'm not in the mood; I'm
not *mad* myself. Changes in the moon
were thought to influence the human
mind, hence its association with madness (i.e. 'lunacy').

195 **to make one** to participate

196 **skipping** mad (Johnson); incoherent

197 **hoist sail** go away

Here . . . way proverbial (Dent, D556:
'Here is the door and there lies your
way')

198 **swabber** deckhand; a gibe at Maria's
rank, taking up her own nautical language in 197

hull stay at anchor with furled sails;
cf. *R3* 4.4.438–9, 'And there they hull,
expecting but the aid / Of Buckingham
to welcome them ashore.'

199 **Some . . . giant** Please pacify your
protector. In the romance tradition giants acted as guards for ladies
(Johnson), but there is probably also an
ironical reference here to the diminutive size of the boy actor playing Maria
(cf. 2.5.11, 3.2.63).

199–200 **Tell . . . messenger** Many
editors, following Hanmer, emend F
by attributing 'Tell me your mind'
to Olivia as an impatient imperative,
'get on with it'; Viola's 'I am a messenger' becomes a defensive response
('I'm only a go-between'). F, however, makes sense in the context of
Viola's irritation both with Olivia's
indirectness at 194–5 (see n.) and
with Maria's presumptuousness, i.e.
as a messenger, I only take orders
from the lady of the house (to whom
my message is addressed), so you tell
me if you want to hear my message
or not.

194 not mad] mad *Rann (Mason)*; but mad *(Staunton)*   197 way.] way. *she opens the door to thrust her
out Cam¹*   199 Tell] OLIVIA Tell *Hanmer*   200 I] VIOLA I *Hanmer*

OLIVIA Sure you have some hideous matter to deliver
       when the courtesy of it is so fearful. Speak your office.
VIOLA It alone concerns your ear. I bring no overture of
       war, no taxation of homage. I hold the olive in my hand:
       my words are as full of peace as matter.   205
OLIVIA Yet you began rudely. What are you? What would
       you?
VIOLA The rudeness that hath appeared in me have I
       learned from my entertainment. What I am and what
       I would are as secret as maidenhead: to your ears,   210
       divinity; to any other's, profanation.
OLIVIA [*to Maria and Attendants*] Give us the place alone,
       we will hear this divinity.   [*Exeunt Maria and Attendants.*]
       Now sir, what is your text?
VIOLA Most sweet lady –   215
OLIVIA A comfortable doctrine, and much may be said of
       it. Where lies your text?

---

202 **courtesy** preliminary ceremonies; an
    important theme word in the play (cf.
    4.2.33)
    fearful frightening: referring to
    Viola's bluntness, and perhaps to her
    obstinacy at the gate (cf. 206n.)
    Speak your office deliver your
    message
203 **alone** only
    overture declaration (*OED* 2)
204 **taxation of homage** demand for
    payment of dues
    olive olive branch, as a symbol of
    peace (punning on *Olivia*)
205 **my . . . matter** all the contents of
    my message are peaceful
206 **rudely** discourteously: probably refer-
    ring to Viola's behaviour at the gate
    What Cf. 112–24n.
209 **entertainment** reception (by
    Malvolio and Sir Toby at the gate)
209–11 **What . . . profanation** i.e. my
    role as messenger and my personal

identity are so confidential and intimate
that they are strictly for your ears only
209 **What** refers primarily to Viola's
    function as intimate go-between, but
    inevitably hints at the question of her
    true identity ('who') and gender ('of
    what sex'). Cf. 1.2.32n.
211, 213 **divinity** religious discourse;
    introduces a dense passage of pseudo-
    religious terms
214 **text** passage from the Scriptures
    used as the subject of a sermon (*OED*
    n.[1] 4a)
215 **Most sweet lady** – often declaimed
    in production as the beginning of
    Viola's prepared speech (or *text*),
    nipped in the rhetorical bud
216 **comfortable** bringing religious
    comfort; cf. *RJ* 5.3.148, 'O comfort-
    able Friar'.
    doctrine lesson. Olivia ironically takes
    Most sweet lady as a statement of the
    subject matter or *text* (in answer to 214).

204 olive] *(*Olyffe*), Rowe* 206–7] *Pope; F lines* you? / you? / 211 other's] *Rann; others
F 212–14] *Pope; F lines* alone, / text? / 215 lady –] *Theobald;* Ladie. *F*

VIOLA   In Orsino's bosom.

OLIVIA   In his bosom? In what chapter of his bosom?

VIOLA   To answer by the method, in the first of his heart.   220

OLIVIA   O, I have read it, it is heresy. Have you no more
to say?

VIOLA   Good madam, let me see your face.

OLIVIA   Have you any commission from your lord to
negotiate with my face? You are now out of your text.   225
But we will draw the curtain and show you the picture.
[*Unveils.*] Look you, sir, such a one I was this present.
Is't not well done?

VIOLA   Excellently done, if God did all.

OLIVIA   'Tis in grain, sir, 'twill endure wind and weather.   230

VIOLA

   'Tis beauty truly blent, whose red and white

---

218 possibly a playful echo of the biblical expression 'in Abraham's bosom'
(Luke, 16.22), i.e. heaven, a blessed
abode
219 Cf. 1.4.13–14n.
   chapter as of the biblical *text* to be
quoted
220 **by the method** in the same style
   the first the first chapter
221 **heresy** i.e. contrary to the *doctrine*
(216) of Olivia's own thoughts and
desires
224 **commission** authorization (recalling *my commission*, 184). In connection
with the verb *negotiate* (225), there is
probably a more specifically financial
meaning here, i.e. 'authority given to
act as agent . . . for another in the conduct of business or trade' (*OED* 10).
225 **negotiate** do business; cf. *MA*
2.1.163–4, 'Let every eye negotiate for
itself, / And trust no agent.'
   out . . . text straying from your stated
theme
226 Olivia reveals her face as if taking the dust cover off a portrait; cf.
1.3.120–2.

227 **such . . . present** this is what I looked
like today. Portraits usually bore the
date of composition and the age of
the sitter (Cam²); see Fig. 8. In this
case the date of the live portrait is *this
present*, the usual form for 'today' when
dating letters (*present* is an adjectival
noun, stressed on the first syllable). The
unveiling ceremony is pronounced by
Olivia with mock solemnity.
229 **if . . . all** if it is all natural, i.e.
unaided by cosmetics. The actor playing Olivia was made up.
230 **in grain** ingrained: indelible (*OED*
grain *n.*[1] 10c, giving this example)
231–5 Viola suddenly changes tone
and turns to verse, paying Olivia a
Petrarchan compliment typical of love
poetry, as in *Son* 20.1 (addressed to
the fair youth), 'A woman's face with
nature's own hand painted'.
231 **truly blent** naturally blended.
Nature and not art has mixed the
colours of Olivia's complexion harmoniously (*OED* blend *v.*[2] 4a, giving
this example); this atones for the irony
of 229.

227 SD] *Craig; after* 228 *Rowe; after* curtain 226 *Capell*

Nature's own sweet and cunning hand laid on.
Lady, you are the cruell'st she alive
If you will lead these graces to the grave
And leave the world no copy.   235

OLIVIA   O sir, I will not be so hard-hearted. I will give out
diverse schedules of my beauty. It shall be inventoried,
and every particle and utensil labelled to my will, as,
item, two lips, indifferent red; item, two grey eyes, with
lids to them; item, one neck, one chin and so forth.   240
Were you sent hither to praise me?

VIOLA

I see you what you are, you are too proud;
But if you were the devil you are fair.
My lord and master loves you. O, such love
Could be but recompensed, though you were crowned   245

---

232 **cunning** skilful
    laid on painted
233 **she** woman; pronoun used as a full
    noun (Hope, 1.3.2j, giving this exam-
    ple)
234 **graces** beauties, with a possi-
    ble allusion to the three Graces of
    Greek mythology, givers of charm and
    beauty
235 **copy** child; cf. *Son* 11.14, 'Thou
    shouldst print more, not let that copy
    die.'
236–7 ²**I . . . beauty** Olivia proposes
    circulation of a written catalogue of
    her *graces* (234) as the form of *copy* she
    will *leave* (235).
237 **divers schedules** various lists; *sched-
    ule* is a bureaucratic term referring to
    'any tabular or classified statement'
    (*OED n.* 2, giving this example). Olivia
    proceeds to give an inventory of her
    parts, by way of a parody of the 'bla-
    zon' or complimentary anatomizing
    of the woman's body (cf. 281–5 and
    285n.).
    inventoried listed

238 **particle** atom of my body (literally,
    minute quantity of matter)
    utensil 'part of the human frame
    serving a special purpose' (*OED* 3a,
    first occurrence; originally domestic
    vessel or implement)
    labelled . . . will itemized according
    to my wishes; itemized in a codicil
    affixed to my last will and testament
    (punning on Viola's *leave*, 235)
    will desire; testament
239, 240 **item** literally 'likewise' (Latin),
    used to introduce each new article in a
    list (*OED adv.* A, giving this example)
239 **indifferent** fairly (adverb)
240 **lids** eyelids, with a probable pun on
    the lids of pots (see 238n. on *utensil*)
241 **praise** commend; appraise, make a
    valuation of (*item* by *item*)
242–3 'alluding to Lucifer's beauty in
    heaven, and his fall through pride'
    (Ard²); cf. also Dent, L572: 'As proud
    as Lucifer'.
245 **Could . . . recompensed** would
    receive no more than its due reward (if
    you accepted it) (Ard²)

237 schedules] *(scedules), Rowe*

The nonpareil of beauty.

OLIVIA   How does he love me?

VIOLA

With adoration's fertile tears,
With groans that thunder love, with sighs of fire.

OLIVIA

Your lord does know my mind: I cannot love him.
Yet I suppose him virtuous, know him noble,   250
Of great estate, of fresh and stainless youth,
In voices well divulged, free, learn'd and valiant,
And in dimension and the shape of nature
A gracious person; but yet I cannot love him.
He might have took his answer long ago.   255

VIOLA

If I did love you in my master's flame,
With such a suffering, such a deadly life,
In your denial I would find no sense,
I would not understand it.

OLIVIA   Why, what would you?

VIOLA

Make me a willow cabin at your gate   260

246 **nonpareil** queen (literally, unequalled representative)
247 ***adoration's** Rann's emendation has the advantage of creating three parallel phrases beginning *With*, without resorting to the more radical emendation offered by Pope.
fertile abundant (*OED* 3, giving this example)
248 **thunder** violently manifest
fire passion; a variation on the theme of the amorous furor (see 1.1.14–15n.)
251 **estate** rank; wealth
252 **In . . . divulged** well spoken of; this probably stands alone (as in F), but may govern the adjectives that follow, i.e. 'well spoken of as being'
252 Cf. 1.2.38–41n.

253 **dimension** proportions (*OED* 4, giving this example)
shape of nature natural form
254 **gracious** elegant, attractive
255 **took** taken
256 **in . . . flame** with Orsino's passion
257 **deadly** death-like; cf. *KL* 5.3.288, 'All's cheerless, dark and deadly.'
260 **willow cabin** 'temporary shelter' (*OED* cabin 1a, giving this example), made out of willow branches. In Barton's 1969 RSC production the stage was dominated by a willow-cabin set, anything but temporary (see pp. 107). The willow was the emblem of sorrowful love: cf. *MA* 2.1.172, 199–200, and Desdemona's 'willow' song at *Oth* 4.3.39–56.

247 adoration's] *Rann;* adorations, *F*   fertile] with fertile *Pope*   257 suffering] *(suffring)*

201

And call upon my soul within the house;
Write loyal cantons of contemnèd love
And sing them loud even in the dead of night;
Hallow your name to the reverberate hills
And make the babbling gossip of the air   265
Cry out 'Olivia!' O, you should not rest
Between the elements of air and earth
But you should pity me.

OLIVIA   You might do much.
What is your parentage?

VIOLA
Above my fortunes, yet my state is well: 270
I am a gentleman.

OLIVIA   Get you to your lord.
I cannot love him; let him send no more,
Unless perchance you come to me again
To tell me how he takes it. Fare you well.
I thank you for your pains.   [*Offers money.*]
                        Spend this for me.   275

---

261 **call . . . soul** supplicate my beloved
    (i.e. Olivia)
262 **loyal cantons** songs pledging loy-
    alty (*cantons* is a variant of 'cantos';
    cf. *OED* canton *n.*² and loyal *a*. 3, both
    giving this example)
    contemned contemnèd: despised
264 **Hallow** holla, shout; with a pun on
    hallow in the sense of 'bless' (Kökeritz,
    111); cf. *2H4* 1.2.188–9.
    reverberate reverberating, echoing
    (*OED ppla.*, giving this example)
265 **babbling . . . air** echo, alluding
    both materially to the sound of the
    shouted name being repeated by the
    hills and mythopoetically to Echo,
    the mountain nymph who, in Ovid,
    fades away for love of Narcissus and

becomes mere voice; cf. 'A babling
Nymph that *Echo* hight' (Ovid, *Met.*,
3.443, fol. 36ʳ; see Bate, 148). Cf. also
Viola's story of her pining *sister* at
2.4.110–21; *babbling* is itself echoed
at 3.4.352..
267 **elements . . . earth** Cf. 1.1.25n.
268 **But** unless
270 I am better born than my present
    circumstances (*fortunes*) indicate; *state*
    = rank by birth
271 **gentleman** of gentle birth, i.e. not
    of noble rank but entitled to a coat
    of arms (see 285n.) and to bear arms.
    The definition is virtual in respect
    of Viola's gender but applies fully to
    Sebastian, whom Olivia will address as
    gentle friend at 4.1.50.

264 Hallow] Hollaw *F2;* Hollow *F3;* Holla *Malone;* Halloo *Collier*   270 fortunes] fortune *Craig*
275 SD] *Collier³*

VIOLA

> I am no fee'd post, lady; keep your purse.
> My master, not myself, lacks recompense.
> Love make his heart of flint that you shall love,
> And let your fervour like my master's be   279
> Placed in contempt. Farewell, fair cruelty.   *Exit.*

OLIVIA

> 'What is your parentage?'
> 'Above my fortunes, yet my state is well:
> I am a gentleman.' I'll be sworn thou art –
> Thy tongue, thy face, thy limbs, actions and spirit
> Do give thee fivefold blazon. Not too fast, soft, soft –   285
> Unless the master were the man. How now?
> Even so quickly may one catch the plague?
> Methinks I feel this youth's perfections
> With an invisible and subtle stealth
> To creep in at mine eyes. Well, let it be.   290
> What ho, Malvolio.

276 **fee'd post** hired messenger (*OED* feed *ppla.* 2, giving this example)

278 Not ... plague May Cupid (*Love*) make him that you love have a heart as hard as stone. This recalls the allusion to Cupid's *golden shaft* at 1.1.34: his other arrow was lead-tipped and caused aversion.
that refers back to the possessive *his* rather than the noun *heart* (Hope, 1.4.2f, giving this example)

279 **fervour** passion; cf. 1.1.14–15n.

285 **blazon** coat of arms (here *fivefold*, i.e. having five decorative elements, as listed in 284), which it was the privilege of a *gentleman* (271) to bear (*OED* 2, giving this example); in Cesario's case, it is his own bearing that declares his gentle birth. The term also designated a sixteenth-century poetic mode, 'the detailed enumeration of the parts of the woman's body' (Norbrook, 43; see also Sawday): unwittingly, Olivia has in fact just anatomized Viola's body (284). Cf. 236–40 and 237n.; also *Son* 106.5–6.

285–7 **Not ... plague** Olivia's incoherence under the effect of passion here bears out Viola's recollection at 2.2.21 of her speaking *in starts*, even if Viola has already left the stage and does not actually witness Olivia's soliloquy.
soft slowly; cf. 2.5.91, 118, 138.

286 **Unless ... man** i.e. unless the servant Cesario took the place of Orsino; or unless he was actually the *master*, Orsino himself, in disguise

287 **catch the plague** be infected by love; a further metaphorical allusion to the literal and ever-present danger of the plague in the period (*Even so quickly* indeed). Cf. 1.1.19n.

288 **perfections** pronounced as a four-syllable word

289 imperceptibly and insidiously

290 **at mine eyes** Cf. Dent, L501: 'Love comes by looking in at the eyes.'

276 fee'd post] *(*feede poast*)*, *Rowe*

Enter MALVOLIO.

MALVOLIO   Here, madam, at your service.
OLIVIA
Run after that same peevish messenger
The county's man. He left this ring behind him,
Would I or not. Tell him I'll none of it.   295
Desire him not to flatter with his lord,
Nor hold him up with hopes: I am not for him.
If that the youth will come this way tomorrow,
I'll give him reasons for't. Hie thee, Malvolio.   299
MALVOLIO   Madam, I will.   *Exit.*
OLIVIA
I do I know not what, and fear to find
Mine eye too great a flatterer for my mind.
Fate, show thy force, ourselves we do not owe.
What is decreed must be – and be this so.   [*Exit.*]

2.1   *Enter* ANTONIO *and* SEBASTIAN.

---

294 *county's* count's, a common Elizabethan form (from French *conté* or Italian *conte*); cf. *RJ* 4.2.45, 'County Paris'. Capell's emendation restores the metre.
295 **Would . . . not** whether I wanted it or not: cf. 149–50n.
296 **flatter with** fill with false hope (*OED v.*[1] 7a, giving this example)
297 **hold him up** sustain him; delude him
299 **Hie thee** hurry
302 my eye has deceived my mind (into loving Orsino's messenger)
303–4 **Fate . . . so** proverbial: what must be must be (Dent, M1331). Cf. *Faustus*: 'What doctrine call you this, *Che sera, sera* / What will be, shall be?' (Marlowe, *Faustus*, 1.1, A3[r]).

303 **owe** own
2.1 This duologue, in which the audience learns of the survival of Sebastian, befriended by Antonio, parallels 1.2, where the shipwrecked Viola is helped by the captain. Such structural mirroring underlines the bond between the separated twins, even if this scene, unlike 1.2, is in prose. The dialogue explores male friendship in terms that can be read as the language of romantic attachment and desire. Rowe indicates the location as '*The Street*', while Capell suggests '*The Sea-coast*', underscoring the parallel with 1.2. (Kemble specifies '*The Sea-coast. The same as Scene 1 – Act 1*', i.e. 1.2.)

---

294 county's] *Capell;* Countes *F;* Counts *F2;* count his *Keightley*   304 SD] *Rowe; Finis, Actus primus. F*   **2.1**] *(Actus Secundus, Scaena prima.)*

ANTONIO Will you stay no longer, nor will you not that I
    go with you?

SEBASTIAN By your patience, no. My stars shine darkly
    over me, the malignancy of my fate might perhaps
    distemper yours. Therefore I shall crave of you your   5
    leave that I may bear my evils alone. It were a bad
    recompense for your love to lay any of them on you.

ANTONIO Let me yet know of you whither you are
    bound.

SEBASTIAN No, sooth, sir. My determinate voyage is mere   10
    extravagancy. But I perceive in you so excellent a touch
    of modesty that you will not extort from me what I am
    willing to keep in, therefore it charges me in manners
    the rather to express myself. You must know of me
    then, Antonio, my name is Sebastian, which I called   15
    Roderigo. My father was that Sebastian of Messaline

---

1 **nor . . . I** or do you not wish me to;
    probably a double negative construc-
    tion ('nor . . . not'), common in Early
    Modern English (Hope, 2.1.9, Blake,
    Grammar, 6.2.3.3), although *nor* is
    often used for 'and', as may be the case
    here (Blake, *Grammar*, 6.2.3.1)
3 **By your patience** by your leave
    darkly ominously (*OED adv.* 3, giving
    this example); an allusion to the ship-
    wreck
4 **malignancy** evil influence: an astro-
    logical term (see *stars*, 3)
5 **distemper** infect: another astrological
    term
5–6 **I shall . . . may** I beg you to let me.
    Throughout the exchange the two men
    employ the language of chivalric cour-
    tesy (see 32n.)
6 **evils** misfortunes
8 **of** from
10 **sooth** in truth
10–11 **My . . . extravagancy** my only
    travel plan is to wander aimlessly

10 **determinate** intended (*OED a.* 4,
    giving this example)
11 **extravagancy** wandering (*OED* 1,
    first occurrence); cf. *Oth* 1.1.134, 'an
    extravagant and wheeling stranger' (of
    Othello).
12 **modesty** courtesy, self-control
12–13 **I am willing** I wish
13 **it charges me** I am obliged
    in manners from good manners
14 **express** reveal
15–16 **which . . . Roderigo** Sebastian's
    reference to his earlier disguise remains
    unexplained; it may be simply a means
    of motivating his self-revelation to
    Antonio, and thus to the audience,
    and/or a way of 'filling' the time since
    the shipwreck.
16 **Messaline** perhaps from Massilia, the
    Latin name for Marseille; Mahood
    notes that in the *Menaechmi* (a play
    about twins, and the main source of
    Shakespeare's *CE*) Plautus mentions
    the inhabitants of Marseille and Illyria

1 SP] *(Ant.), Cam¹*   3 SP] *(Seb.), Cam¹*   16 Roderigo] *(Rodorigo)*   Messaline] *Metelin / Hanmer*

whom I know you have heard of. He left behind him
myself and a sister, both born in an hour. If the heavens
had been pleased, would we had so ended. But you, sir,
altered that, for some hour before you took me from the   20
breach of the sea was my sister drowned.

ANTONIO Alas the day!

SEBASTIAN A lady, sir, though it was said she much
resembled me, was yet of many accounted beautiful.
But though I could not with such estimable wonder   25
over-far believe that, yet thus far I will boldly publish
her: she bore a mind that envy could not but call fair.
She is drowned already, sir, with salt water, though I
seem to drown her remembrance again with more.

ANTONIO Pardon me, sir, your bad entertainment.   30

---

together, 'Massiliensis, Hilurios'
(Plautus, 2.1.235, sig. B2ᵛ), translat-
ed by Warner as '*Massylia, Ilyria*'.
The name also humorously recalls
Messalina, notoriously licentious and
corrupt wife of the Roman emperor
Claudius.

17 **heard of** echoes Viola's 'I have heard
my father name him [Orsino]' at 1.2.25.
Famous absent fathers are something
of a Shakespearean topos: cf., for
example, the pedant's 'I have heard of
him [Vincentio]' in *TS* 4.2.97.

18–21 **a sister . . . drowned** Sebastian's
sorrow for his 'drowned' sister parallels Viola's concern for her lost brother
at 1.2.3–4.

18 **in an hour** within one hour of each
other (as twins); the article *an* here has
the force of 'one' or 'the same' (Hope,
1.1.2a, giving this example).

19 **would . . . ended** I wish we could have
died together

20 **some hour** shortly

21 **breach** breaking of waves, surf (*OED*
n. 2, first occurrence)

25–6 **But . . . that** although I cannot
give too much credit to that (i.e. that
she was beautiful); Sebastian continues his somewhat awkward attempt
to praise Viola without praising himself.

25 **estimable wonder** esteem and
wonder (rhetorical figure: a form of
'hendiadys in reverse'; see p. 85)

26 **over-far** to too great an extent
publish speak of

27 **that . . . fair** that envy itself could not
deny was beautiful; *envy* is a personification here, as at 5.1.54.

29 **more** more salt water (i.e. tears).
Cf. Laertes on his drowned sister,
'Too much of water hast thou, poor
Ophelia, / And therefore I forbid my
tears', *Ham* 4.7.183–4.

30 **your bad entertainment** the inad-
equate hospitality you have received
from me

18 an] one *F3*

SEBASTIAN   O good Antonio, forgive me your trouble.

ANTONIO   If you will not murder me for my love, let me
   be your servant.

SEBASTIAN   If you will not undo what you have done, that
   is kill him whom you have recovered, desire it not. Fare   35
   ye well at once. My bosom is full of kindness, and I am
   yet so near the manners of my mother that upon the
   least occasion more mine eyes will tell tales of me. I am
   bound to the Count Orsino's court. Farewell.   *Exit.*

ANTONIO

   The gentleness of all the gods go with thee.   40
   I have many enemies in Orsino's court,
   Else would I very shortly see thee there.
   But come what may I do adore thee so
   That danger shall seem sport, and I will go.   *Exit.*

2.2   *Enter* VIOLA *[as Cesario] and* MALVOLIO
                    at separate doors.

31 **your trouble** the trouble I have caused
you (possessive adjective *your* in objective sense: Blake, *Grammar*, 3.3.4.5b,
giving this example)

32 **If . . . love** if you do not want me to
die of a broken heart in losing you.
Both Antonio here and Sebastian at
34–5 use the hyperbolic language of
courtly love to express their mutual
affection.

35 **recovered** restored to life

36 **kindness** tenderness

37 **yet** still
manners . . . mother womanish
readiness to weep; cf. *H5* 4.6.31–2,
'And all my mother came into my eyes
/ And gave me up to tears.'

38 **occasion more** further occasion
tell . . . me betray my feelings (with
tears)

40 **gentleness** favour

41 **enemies . . . court** The somewhat
mysterious enmity between Antonio
and Orsino is referred to at greater
length – but still enigmatically – at
5.1.56–72, and leads to Antonio's
arrest at 3.4.324–5.

43 **adore thee so** the climax of Antonio's
rhetoric of 'religious' worship for
Sebastian

2.2 This brief duologue is the sequel to
1.5, with Malvolio obediently but contemptuously 'returning' Olivia's ring,
thereby giving Viola the opportunity
for her first soliloquy, in which she
reflects on the difficulties of her cross-
dressed role. Capell locates the scene
in '*A Street*'.

0.2 **at separate doors** Their more or less
simultaneous entry suggests that
Malvolio has been searching for
Cesario since their separate exits in

41 many] made *F3*   **2.2**] *(Scaena Secunda.)*   0.1 *as Cesario*] *Munro subst.*   0.2 *separate*] *this edn;*
seuerall F

MALVOLIO Were not you e'en now with the Countess
    Olivia?

VIOLA Even now, sir; on a moderate pace I have since
    arrived but hither.

MALVOLIO She returns this ring to you, sir. [*Shows ring.*]   5
    You might have saved me my pains to have taken it
    away yourself. She adds, moreover, that you should put
    your lord into a desperate assurance she will none of
    him. And one thing more: that you be never so hardy
    to come again in his affairs, unless it be to report your   10
    lord's taking of this. [*Offers ring.*] Receive it so.

VIOLA She took the ring of me, I'll none of it.

MALVOLIO Come, sir, you peevishly threw it to her, and
    her will is it should be so returned. [*Throws down ring.*]

1.5 and has at last caught up with him.
In many productions Malvolio rushes
onstage, while Cesario walks on at *a
moderate pace* (3); in others, Cesario
comes on first as Sebastian is exiting,
so that for a moment the two twins are
simultaneously onstage, without seeing each other.

1 **e'en** (even) just

3 **Even now** Viola's repetition stresses
the recentness of her encounter with
Olivia in 1.5: barely a moment ago (as
the audience can testify).
    on at (Blake, *Grammar*, 5.4.2)
    since i.e. since I was with Olivia

4 **but hither** this far

6 **to have taken** by taking

7–8 **put . . . assurance** make your lord
hopelessly certain

8–9 **will . . . him** will have nothing to
do with him

9 **hardy** foolhardy, bold (*OED a*. 2); not
used elsewhere by Shakespeare in this
sense

10 **in his affairs** on his business

11 **taking of this** i.e. this message (not
this ring)

Receive it so Take the ring on these
conditions. There is a potentially confusing play of deictic terms here (11,
this = message; 12, *it* = ring), so much
so that Collier glosses the phrase as
'understand it so', still referring to the
message. Onstage Malvolio's gesture of
offering the ring resolves any ambiguity.
On deictics in the comedy, see p. 89.

12 **She . . . me** Dyce[2] is surely mistaken
in emending F's 'the ring' to 'no ring'
(see t.n.). Cesario goes along with
Olivia's invented story (her supposed
returning of Orsino's ring), presumably out of politeness and surprised
curiosity.
    of me from me

13–14 **you . . . returned** Malvolio,
recalling Olivia's earlier reference to
a *peevish messenger* who 'left this ring
behind him' (1.5.293–4), elaborates
the invented episode even further as a
pretext for throwing the ring contemptuously to the ground.

14 **so** in the same way (as you gave it to her);
or, in the following way (see 14 SD):
another ambiguous deictic (see 11n.)

5 SD] *this edn*   11 SD] *Cam¹*   12 the ring] no ring *Dyce² (Malone*   14 SD] *Douai MS, Kemble*

208

   If it be worth stooping for, there it lies, in your eye; if   15
   not, be it his that finds it.   *Exit.*

VIOLA [*Picks up ring.*]

   I left no ring with her. What means this lady?
   Fortune forbid my outside have not charmed her.
   She made good view of me, indeed so much
   That methought her eyes had lost her tongue,   20
   For she did speak in starts, distractedly.
   She loves me sure. The cunning of her passion
   Invites me in this churlish messenger.
   None of my lord's ring? Why, he sent her none.

14 SD The actor can make comic business out of throwing down the ring;
traditionally, Malvolios let it slide
down the steward's wand, so as not to
have to stoop (Brown, 232).

15 **in your eye** in your sight. In Posner's
2001 RSC production Guy Henry's
Malvolio pointed first to Cesario's eye,
then to the ground where he had
thrown the ring.

17–41 As in her other soliloquies and
long asides (see 3.1.58–66; 3.4.370–3,
376–81), Viola speaks in verse, as distinct from the prose she uses in her
exchange with Malvolio (unless 12 is
taken as verse).

18 **forbid . . . not** a double negative,
common in Early Modern English: cf.
2.1.1n.
   outside appearance; cf. *AYL* 1.3.117,
'We'll have a swashing and a martial
outside.'
   charmed enchanted (cf. *the last
enchantment*, 3.1.110, referring back to
this scene)

20 The proposed emendations (see t.n.)
suppose a missing monosyllable after
That; F2's 'sure' is perhaps suggested
by 22. The line as it stands, however,
creates no real difficulty for the actor.

her eyes . . . tongue her ogling
me had made her lose the power of
speech

21 **in starts** in broken phrases (*OED*
start *n.*[2] 4e, first occurrence). Broken
speech was considered a sign of passion, and indeed 'start' meant a fit of
passion (*OED n.*[2] 4d); cf. *1H4* 3.2.125,
'the start of spleen'. In *MND* Theseus
defends emotional speakers who 'Make
periods in the midst of sentences'
(*MND* 5.1.96; on the passions, see
p. 54). Olivia actually speaks *in starts*
only after Cesario's exit, in her confused and self-interrupting soliloquy
at 1.5.281–90 (see 1.5.285–7n.).
   distractedly madly (*OED*, giving this
example). Olivia, like other characters
in this play, is affected by the amorous
furor; cf. 1.1.14–15, 5.1.277 and notes.

22 **cunning** artfulness

23 **Invites** entices, tries to attract (*OED v.*
1d)
   in by means of

24 **None . . . ring** Viola seems to be
quoting not from Malvolio's message
('she will none of him', 8–9) but from
Olivia's discourse to Malvolio in 1.5
('I'll none of it', 295), despite the fact
that she was not present.

17 SD] *Oxf*   20 That methought] That sure me thought *F2;* That, as methought *Dyce*[2]*;* That
straight methought *Oxf (RP)*

I am the man. If it be so, as 'tis,   25
Poor lady, she were better love a dream.
Disguise, I see thou art a wickedness,
Wherein the pregnant enemy does much.
How easy is it for the proper false
In women's waxen hearts to set their forms.   30
Alas, our frailty is the cause, not we,
For such as we are made of, such we be.
How will this fadge? My master loves her dearly,
And I, poor monster, fond as much on him,

25 **I . . . man** i.e. that she loves; cf. *AYL* 3.3.2–3, 'And how Audrey, am I the man yet?' This line can be played for laughs; G.H. Lewes disapproved of the way Ellen Tree did so in 1850: 'The look with which she said "I am the man" was perfect; but that little saucy tip of her head, with the playful swagger which followed it, though they "brought down the house", appeared to us to betray a forgetfulness of [the character of] Viola' (Brown, 233).

26 **Poor lady** In Hall's 1958 Stratford production, Dorothy Tutin's Viola pronounced these words in a mischievous drawl, raising a big laugh (M. Billington, xviii).
she were better she had better, i.e. it would be better for her to (Blake, *Grammar*, 3.3.2.1b, giving this example)

27–8 Viola's apostrophe to her disguise is the only instance in Shakespeare where the heroine questions the moral validity of her cross-dressing. Her allusion to the devil in 28 implicitly compares her transvestism to Satan's disguising himself as a serpent in Genesis. For an apparently analogous passage in *Gl'ingannati* (Intronati), see pp. 62–3.

28 **pregnant enemy** the devil, or, as Johnson puts it, 'the dexterous fiend, or enemy of mankind'; *pregnant* here means 'ready', 'receptive' (*OED a.²* 3d):

an almost exclusively Shakespearean usage; cf. 3.1.87.

29 **proper false** handsome but deceitful (men): oxymoron. In Viola's case male beauty is literally *false*.

30 to imprint their appearance on women's receptive hearts (like the image impressed in wax by a seal). The 'women are wax' conceit is recurrent in Shakespeare: cf. *MND* 1.1.49–51, *MM* 2.4.128–9, *Luc* 1240–6 (AT).

31–2 *The emendations adopted here (see t.n.) make the overall sense become 'Alas, it is not our [i.e. women's] fault but that of our weakness, because being made of weak flesh we are weak ourselves' – with an evident allusion to the biblical expression 'the flesh is weak' (Matthew, 26.41). Viola's *we* marks a shift from the position of deceptive false man to that of member of the deceived and suffering female sex: she is at once cause and effect.

33 **fadge** turn out

34 **monster** i.e. because she is a hybrid or androgynous creature, half *man* (36) and half *woman* (38). Cf. William Harrison's complaint against his cross-dressed compatriots: 'Thus it is now come to passe, that women are become men, and men transformed into monsters' (W. Harrison, 172).
fond dote (verb: *OED v.* 2, giving this example)

29 proper false] proper-false *Malone*   31 our] *F2;* O *F*   32 made of,] *Rann (Tyrwhitt);* made, if *F;* made, ev'n *Hanmer*

And she, mistaken, seems to dote on me.   35
What will become of this? As I am man,
My state is desperate for my master's love;
As I am woman, now alas the day,
What thriftless sighs shall poor Olivia breathe?
O time, thou must untangle this, not I.   40
It is too hard a knot for me t'untie.   [*Exit.*]

2.3   *Enter* SIR TOBY *and* SIR ANDREW.

SIR TOBY   Approach, Sir Andrew. Not to be abed after
    midnight is to be up betimes, and *diluculo surgere*, thou
    knowst.

35 **mistaken** under a misapprehension,
i.e. that I am a man (*OED* 3, giving this
example)
36 **become** be the outcome (*OED* 4, giving this example)
36, 38 **As** in so far as (Blake, *Grammar*,
5.3.2.2)
36 **man** i.e. as Cesario; also alludes to the
gender of the Elizabethan actor
37 **state** condition
desperate hopeless (cf. 8)
for . . . love on account of my love
for my master: *master's* is an objective
genitive (Blake, *Grammar*, 3.3.1.1b)
39 **thriftless** unprofitable (*OED* 2, giving
this example)
41 **knot** probably a reference to the intri-
cate Gordian knot of Greek legend
– tied by King Gordius of Phrygia
(cf. 3.1.50n.) and virtually impossible
to undo – that Alexander the Great
cut through with his sword. Cf. *Cym*
2.2.34, 'As slippery as the Gordian
knot was hard'. There may also be an
allusion here to the maidenhead, as in
Per 4.2.135, 'Untied I still my virgin
knot will keep' (see Carroll, 'Virgin').
2.3 This scene of revelry, parallel to 1.3, is
interrupted by the 'Puritan' Malvolio,
who presents himself as the play's
chief upholder of rule and order. The

steward's reproaches set off Maria's
plan for revenge. The scene was traditionally set in the kitchen (and sometimes still is, as in Rhys Jones's 1991
RSC production), and thus became
known as 'the kitchen scene'. In 1958,
instead, Peter Hall placed it in Olivia's
garden, even though this setting was
incompatible with Maria's threat to
have Malvolio 'turn you [Sir Toby] out
of doors' at 73.
1 **Approach** perhaps suggesting that
Sir Andrew is reluctant to join him
onstage
2 **betimes** early in the morning
diluculo surgere part of the Latin
proverb '*Diluculo surgere, saluberrimum
est*', quoted in Lily's *Grammar* (sig.
C4^r). Lily's gloss – 'To aryse betyme
in the morning is the most whole-
some thing in the worlde' – is echoed
(*betimes*) by Sir Toby, who ironically
turns the proverb into a justification
for not going to bed. Since Lily's
Grammar was used in all Elizabethan
schools, Sir Andrew's puzzled response
at 4 suggests his lack of education. F
spells '*Deliculo*', perhaps indicating Sir
Toby's drunken pronunciation. There
may also be a pun on Italian *culo*, back-
side (cf. *cubiculo*, 3.2.50 and n.).

41 SD] *Rowe*   2.3] (*Scoena Tertia.*)   0.1 ANDREW] Andrew discovered *smoking* / *Powell MS;*
ANDREW *discovered, drinking and smoking* / *Lacy*   2 *diluculo*] *F2 (Diliculo); Deliculo F*

211

SIR ANDREW   Nay, by my troth I know not; but I know to
be up late is to be up late.   5

SIR TOBY   A false conclusion. I hate it as an unfilled can.
To be up after midnight and to go to bed then is early, so
that to go to bed after midnight is to go to bed betimes.
Does not our life consist of the four elements?

SIR ANDREW   Faith, so they say, but I think it rather   10
consists of eating and drinking.

SIR TOBY   Thou'rt a scholar; let us therefore eat and
drink. [*Calls.*] Marian, I say, a stoup of wine.

Enter FESTE.

SIR ANDREW   Here comes the fool, i'faith.

FESTE   How now, my hearts? Did you never see the   15
picture of 'we three'?

SIR TOBY   Welcome, ass. Now let's have a catch.

SIR ANDREW   By my troth the fool has an excellent breast.

6   **unfilled can** empty tankard
9   **four elements** fire, air, water and earth
(see 1.1.25n.). In ancient and medieval science the four elements were
believed to exist in every substance and
to combine within the human body to
form the four humours: choler, blood,
phlegm and melancholy. Sir Toby may
be implicitly asserting here his own
sanguine humour against Sir Andrew's
tendency towards melancholy.
13   Sir Toby's call for wine here is frustrated, since it is Feste who comes
on, not Maria. He repeats the request
at 117, but Malvolio intervenes to
reprimand Maria. It may be that Sir
Toby's *can* remains comically *unfilled*
(6) throughout the scene, although
in most productions the wine flows
freely.
   Marian diminutive of 'Maria'
   stoup large tankard

15–16   **picture . . . 'we three'** alludes
to a painting or inn sign representing
two asses or loggerheads; the caption
'we three' implicated the spectator –
here presumably Feste himself – as
the third ass or loggerhead (i.e. fool:
see pp. 10–11 and Figs 2 and 3). In
Carroll's 2002 Middle Temple production, Peter Hamilton Dyer's Feste held
up a dead rabbit on either side of his
face; in Posner's 2001 RSC production, instead, Mark Hadfield's clown
brayed like an ass.
17   **catch** round, i.e. a humorous part-
song in which one voice 'catches' or
follows on immediately from another;
cf. 'like a singing catch, some are
beginning when others are ending'
(Cornwallis, sig. Ff1').
18   **breast** singing voice (*OED n.* 6, giving this example; rhetorical figure:
metonymy)

9 life] *Rowe³;* liues *F*   12, 116 Thou'rt] *(*Th'art*)*   13 SD] *Cam¹ subst.*   Marian] *Maria / Pope*
13.1 FESTE] *Munro; Clowne F*

I had rather than forty shillings I had such a leg, and
so sweet a breath to sing, as the fool has. In sooth, thou   20
wast in very gracious fooling last night, when thou
spok'st of Pigrogromitus, of the Vapians passing the
equinoctial of Queubus. 'Twas very good, i'faith. I sent
thee sixpence for thy leman. Hadst it?
FESTE   I did impeticos thy gratility – for Malvolio's nose   25

---

19 **forty shillings** two pounds, a considerable sum in Shakespeare's day. Here
and at 24 (*sixpence*) Sir Andrew counts
in English currency, while Sir Toby
refers to continental *ducats* at 1.3.20
(see n.).
leg i.e. for dancing (rhetorical figure:
metonymy)

21 **gracious** pleasing

22–3 **Pigrogromitus . . . Queubus** Sir
Andrew's recollection of the clown's
apparently nonsensical fooling may
be drunkenly distorted. The general
theme seems to concern the heavenly
bodies, with possible religious overtones. Furness sees *Pigrogromitus* as a
deformation of Tetragrammaton (the
ineffable four-letter name for God).
Alternatively, it might be the name
of an imaginary constellation, formed
from *pigro* and *gomito* (Italian for 'lazy'
and 'elbow'), with a probable play also
on plain English 'pig'. *The Vapians*
may recall 'Vesper', the evening star
(or plural 'vespers', i.e. evensong),
perhaps contaminated by 'vapours'
(exhalations damaging to health). The
equinoctial is presumably the celes-
tial equator (*OED n.* 1), although
Hotson suggests that 'the Equinoctial
or Equator of Cubus . . . in Plato's
cosmology, is the Earth' (Hotson, 157),
with *Queubus* being a corruption of
Plato's 'Cubus'. Alternatively it may
be a deformation of 'quibble' (or of its
Latin origin, *quibus*), i.e. the very kind
of verbal play Sir Andrew is quoting.

It might be noted that in Dutch *kwibus*
means 'fool'.

24 **sixpence** in Shakespeare's day a silver
coin of some value: it cost sixpence to
sit in the galleries of the public theatres such as the Globe (compared to
one penny to stand in the yard).
leman sweetheart. In this meaning
the word was something of a 'poetic'
archaism, and thus incongruous in
the present context; cf. Spenser, *FQ*,
3.8.40, 'To be his Leman and his Lady
trew' (*FQ*, 165). It became instead
synonymous with 'whore', as in Nashe,
'Lemmans this yeere shal be plenty,
insomuch that many shall use them
to bedward' (Nashe, *Prognostication*,
A4ᵛ), with a pun on 'lemon', which
may also be present here (cf. Kökeritz,
123; Williams, 799–800). In any
case, no further reference is made to
Feste's supposed girlfriend (but cf.
4.2.71–9n.). As Leman Street is a road
in East London (AT), this may also be
one of several 'hidden' allusions to the
capital (cf. 3.3.39n.).
Hadst it? Did you receive it?

25 **impeticos** pocket (verb): nonce-word
compounded from the verb 'impocket'
and the noun 'petticoat', i.e. the long
coat that fools usually wore, with a possible echo of 'impetigo', an unpleasant
pustular skin disease. In other words,
Feste put the sixpence for his sweetheart straight into the pocket of his
own motley coat.
gratility a deformation of 'gratuity'

---

16 'we three'] *Cam;* we three *F*   24 leman] *Theobald;* Lemon *F*   25 impeticos] impeticoat *Steevens*
(Johnson)   gratility] gratuity *Steevens²*

is no whipstock, my lady has a white hand and the
Myrmidons are no bottle-ale houses.

SIR ANDREW   Excellent! Why, this is the best fooling,
when all is done. Now a song.

SIR TOBY [*to Feste*]   Come on, there is sixpence for you.   30
Let's have a song.

SIR ANDREW [*to Feste*]   There's a testril of me too. If one
knight give a –

FESTE   Would you have a love-song, or a song of good
life?   35

25–7 **for . . . houses** Feste's obscure
explanation of why he impeticosed Sir
Andrew's gratility (*for* = because) has
usually been taken as pure nonsense.
Aguecheek's *best fooling* (28) may suggest, instead, that there is an overall meaning, namely that the clown
needs money, and neither Malvolio nor
Olivia gives him any.

26 **whipstock** whip handle (*OED* 1a),
possibly implying that the mean and
puritanical Malvolio is not easily
manipulated into giving money (NB);
or, whipping-post (*OED* 2), perhaps
implying again that money is not going
to be easily beaten out of him
  my lady i.e. Olivia, not Feste's *leman*
  white hand a sign of her nobility;
also, perhaps, an indication that she
is not going to sully herself by giving
filthy lucre to Feste (NB)

27 **Myrmidons** in Homer's *Iliad*, the
followers of Achilles at the siege of
Troy (the 'mangled Myrmidons'
of Shakespeare's *TC* 5.5.33). The
term also had the slang sense of
'unscrupulously faithful' followers or
hirelings (*OED* 3), the likely meaning
here, presumably alluding to Feste
himself as faithful servant of the *lady*
Olivia. The comparison with *bottle-ale
houses* (27) suggests that Feste may
also be punning on 'Mermaid Inn',
the famous London tavern where

Shakespeare supposedly drank with
Ben Jonson.
  bottle-ale houses low-class taverns;
cf. *2H4* 2.4.123, 'you bottle-ale rascal'
(of Pistol). Feste is implying that he
has expensive tastes in drink, hence
his need for another *gratility* from his
companions.

30 **there is sixpence** In Carroll's 2002
Middle Temple production, Ian Talbot's
Sir Toby got Angus Wright's Sir Andrew
to give Feste the tip on his behalf.

32 **testril** sixpence: a corruption of 'test-
er', slang word for this coin (*OED*,
first occurrence). As usual, Sir Andrew
imitates Sir Toby's gesture.

33 *****give a –** In F the suspended indefinite article ends a justified line of
type, and it is possible that the compositor unwittingly omitted the rest
of the sentence in the following line.
It is unlikely that Sir Andrew simply
comes to a halt. F2 adds a hyphen,
probably intended as a dash indicating
an interruption. If this is taken as an
incomplete line of dialogue, one would
expect it to continue with further reference to a sixpence or testril. It may
be, rather, that Aguecheek is beginning
a song, rapidly quashed by Feste.

34–5 **song . . . life** drinking song. Sir
Andrew at 37 seems to understand
instead a 'song about virtuous living',
which does not appeal to him.

30, 32 SDs] *Oxf*   33 a –] *F2; a F*

SIR TOBY   A love-song, a love-song.

SIR ANDREW   Ay, ay. I care not for good life.

FESTE (*Sings.*)

>   O mistress mine, where are you roaming?
>   O stay and hear, your true love's coming,
>   That can sing both high and low.   40
>   Trip no further, pretty sweeting;
>   Journeys end in lovers meeting,
>   Every wise man's son doth know.

SIR ANDREW   Excellent good, i'faith.

SIR TOBY   Good, good.   45

FESTE [*Sings.*]

>   What is love? 'Tis not hereafter,
>   Present mirth hath present laughter.
>   What's to come is still unsure.
>   In delay there lies no plenty,
>   Then come kiss me, sweet and twenty.   50
>   Youth's a stuff will not endure.

SIR ANDREW   A mellifluous voice, as I am true knight.

38–43 **O . . . know** It is not certain that the words of Feste's song, like his other songs, are by Shakespeare, and it is not known whether the music was that of the instrumental version by Thomas Morley published in 1599; see Appendix 3.

40 **high and low** i.e. in either pitch or volume. Cf. Viola's claim, 'I can sing . . . many sorts of music' (1.2.54n., 55n.); Feste appears to take her place as versatile singer.

41 **Trip** Go
sweeting sweetheart, darling

43 **Every . . . son** every fool; an ironic allusion to the proverb 'A wise man often has foolish children' (Dent, M421)

46–51 For the words and music of this song, see Appendix 3.

48 **still** always

49 **plenty** profit

50 **sweet and twenty** not a literal reference to the beloved's age but a conventional term of endearment; cf. 'his little wanton wagtails: his sweet and twenties . . . as hee himselfe used commonly to call them' (Brewer, sig. C4ᵛ).

51 **stuff** material

52 **mellifluous** sweetly flowing. In *Palladis Tamia* Francis Meres praises the 'mellifluous & hony-tongued *Shakespeare*' (Meres, fol. 281ᵛ): could this be a self-ironical echo?
am true knight The indefinite article ('a') is often omitted by Shakespeare when the noun acts as a complement (here, of the verb *am*: see Blake, *Grammar*, 3.3.4.3d, giving this example).

---

38 SP] *Munro; not in F; Clo. / Capell*   SD] *(Clowne sings.)*   46 SD] *Cam¹*   52 true] a true *Douai MS, Rowe*

SIR TOBY   A contagious breath.

SIR ANDREW   Very sweet and contagious, i'faith.

SIR TOBY   To hear by the nose it is dulcet in contagion!   55
But shall we make the welkin dance indeed? Shall we
rouse the night-owl in a catch that will draw three souls
out of one weaver? Shall we do that?

SIR ANDREW   An you love me, let's do't. I am dog at a
catch.   60

FESTE   By'r Lady, sir, and some dogs will catch well.

SIR ANDREW   Most certain. Let our catch be 'Thou
knave'.

FESTE   'Hold thy peace, thou knave', knight? I shall be
constrained in't to call thee knave, knight.   65

SIR ANDREW   'Tis not the first time I have constrained

---

53 **contagious breath** catching voice.
Less poetically, the phrase also implies
halitosis (*contagious* = 'foul', *OED* 5c),
making contradictory nonsense of Sir
Andrew's *sweet and contagious* at 54.
There may also be a further reference here to the plague, which was
popularly thought to be transmitted
through the breath (cf. 1.1.19n.).

55 **To . . . contagion** to judge by hearing and smell, Feste's breath is sweet,
because it carries his contagiously
sweet voice; alternatively, it is catching
only in the sense that it spreads foul-
ness. There is a possible allusion to
venereal contagion, particularly syphi-
lis, which could cause the erosion of
the nose.
dulcet sweet (especially of sounds, but
here extended to smell)

56 **welkin** sky

57 **three souls** a reference to the ancient
theory that living beings were made up
of three souls or principles (the vital,
the sensitive and the rational)

58 **weaver** This may playfully suggest
that the *three souls* (57) are 'woven'
together. Weavers had specifically musi-

cal associations, being reputed to sing as
they worked – especially psalms, since
many of them were Puritans: cf. *1H4*
2.4.126–7, 'I would I were a weaver; I
could sing psalms, or anything.'

59 **An** if
dog at good at (proverbial catchphrase:
Dent, D506); cf. Launce talking to his
dog Crab in *TGV* 4.4.12–13, 'to be, as
it were, a dog at all things'.

61 **By'r lady** by Our Lady (the Virgin
Mary): an oath
some . . . well i.e. some dogs will
catch a ball or prey well; cf. *MA*
5.2.11–12, 'Thy wit is as quick as the
greyhound's mouth, it catches.'

62–4 **Let . . . 'Thou knave'** The round
they are about to sing has them
comically repeat the phrases *hold thy
peace*, telling each other to shut up
(cf. Feste's comment at 69), and *thou
knave*, insulting each other.

65 **constrained** compelled

66–7 **'Tis . . . knave** Sir Andrew may
simply be trying to say that he has
often sung this round, but he succeeds
in implying that he is a quarrelsome
knave (cf. 1.3.28).

59 dog] a dog *F3*   64 knight?] *Capell;* knight. *F*

one to call me knave. Begin, fool. It begins 'Hold thy
peace'.

FESTE   I shall never begin if I hold my peace.   69

SIR ANDREW   Good, i'faith. Come, begin.   *They sing the catch.*

Enter MARIA.

MARIA   What a caterwauling do you keep here! If my lady
have not called up her steward Malvolio and bid him
turn you out of doors, never trust me.

SIR TOBY   My lady's a Cathayan, we are politicians,
Malvolio's a Peg-o'-Ramsey and [*singing*] 'Three merry   75

---

69 **hold my peace** Feste pretends to
mistake the opening words of the
song for the command 'keep quiet'.
Rubinstein, 189, suggests a pun on
piece, Elizabethan slang for 'penis'.

70 SD For the music to the round 'Hold
thy peace', see Appendix 3.

71 **caterwauling** a shrill howling or wail-
ing noise made by cats before mating
or fighting

74–6 **My . . . 'Three . . . we'** Sir Toby
adopts Feste's mode of drunken and
apparently nonsensical free association
(cf. 25–7).

74 **Cathayan** literally, a person from
Cathay, the ancient Mongolian name
for China, but which Shakespeare's
contemporaries believed to be a
separate geographical entity (Billings).
Sir Toby appears to use the word in a
derogatory sense. Steevens glosses
'thief' or 'sharper', a supposed
quality of the Chinese (cf. *OED*'s 'a
man of Cathay or China . . . a thief,
scoundrel, blackguard', giving this
example). It is unlikely, however, that
Sir Toby would call Olivia a thief. In
MW – the only other Shakespearean
occurrence – Page's 'I will not believe
such a Cataian' (2.1.126) implies the
meaning 'liar', possibly deriving from

the mendacious accounts of Cathay
by Mandeville and other travellers
(Billings). The association with *lady*
may recall Ariosto's *Orlando furioso*,
where Angelica is described as 'the
Ladie faire, / That of Cataya was
undoubted haire [= heir]' (Ariosto,
147), especially since Angelica is
described as being 'Full of deceit'
in Boiardo's *Orlando innamorato*
(Boiardo, sig. B4ʳ). Toby may be
implying, more blandly, that Olivia
exaggerates, and so her bark is worse
than her bite. The first syllable of
the word (pronounced 'cat') probably
plays on *caterwauling* (71).

politicians deceitful schemers. The
word invariably has a derogatory
meaning in Shakespeare, connoting
self-serving 'Machiavellian' devious-
ness: cf. Hotspur's 'this vile politician
Bolingbroke . . . this king of smiles'
(*1H4* 1.3.238–43). There is thus a
semantic link between *Cathayan* and
politician, two kinds of liar. Cf. 2.5.157,
3.2.30.

75 **Peg-o'-Ramsey** There are two ballads to tunes of this title. The first,
'A Merry Jest of John Tomson and
Jakaman his Wife . . . to the Tune
of Peg of Ramsay', entered into the

---

70 SD] *(Catch sung)*   74 Cathayan] *(Catayan), Oxf*   75 o'-Ramsey] *Oxf;* a-ramsie *F*   75–111
SDs] *Cam¹*

217

men be we'. Am not I consanguineous? Am I not of her
blood? Tilly-vally, lady! [*Sings.*] 'There dwelt a man in
Babylon, lady, lady.'

FESTE   Beshrew me, the knight's in admirable fooling.

SIR ANDREW   Ay, he does well enough if he be disposed,   80
and so do I too. He does it with a better grace, but I do
it more natural.

SIR TOBY [*Sings.*]
        O'the twelfth day of December –

MARIA   For the love o'God, peace.

Stationers' Register in 1586, narrates
the story of a jealous wife who ends up
wearing – intriguingly, with reference
to this play – 'the yellow hose' (i.e. the
trousers), prompting the man's doleful refrain, 'Give me my yellow Hose
againe' (cf. 2.5.149, 162, 166, 193;
3.2.68–9; 3.4.15.1, 45–7; 5.1.332). The
second ballad, 'Bonny Peggy Ramsey',
first published in Playford, 5.139–40,
is a bawdy tale of a lusty lass who, in
order to make her water-mill work in
times of drought, 'Up she pull'd her
Petticoats and piss'd into the Dam' (cf.
2.5.86n.; see Ungerer, 98–9). In this
case, Malvolio is implicitly compared
to another 'loose woman', like *Jezebel*
(cf. 2.5.38n.).

76 **consanguineous** related by blood (to
Olivia: cf. *of her blood*, 76–7; *OED* 1,
first occurrence)

77 **Tilly-vally**: nonsense (equivalent to
'fiddlesticks!': *OED*, giving this example); cf. *2H4* 2.4.82.
   lady probably addressed scornfully
to Maria, rather than being – as many
editors assume – a mocking echo of
Maria's *my lady* at 71, alluding to
Olivia

77–8 **'There . . . lady.'** The opening
line and refrain of the popular ballad

'Constant Susan', which tells the story
of Susanna and the Elders from the
Apocrypha: another tale of a supposedly 'loose' woman (cf. 75n., 2.5.38n.),
wrongly accused of unchasteness
by the Elders. Wilson (Cam[1]) argues
that Sir Toby implies a parallel with
Maria and the men in this scene. The
same song is quoted by Sir Hugh
Evans in Q1 of *MW*. For the music,
see Appendix 3.

79 **Beshrew me** curse me: a mild imprecation (discourse marker)

82 **natural** spontaneously. Sir Andrew
unwittingly confesses his stupidity,
since *natural* as noun meant 'idiot': cf.
1.3.27n.

83 The opening line of another song,
possibly the ballad on the battle of
Musselburgh Field, begins 'On the
tenth day of December' in Child,
3.378–9, but in a 1665 version it
begins as here (Kittredge). Sir Toby
may, however, be drunkenly misquot-
ing 'The Twelve Days of Christmas',
which – appropriately enough in this
play – traditionally begins with 'On
the twelfth day of Christmas', i.e. on
Twelfth Night. Many modern productions of the play adopt the music for
the latter song.

77 Tilly-vally, lady!] *Oxf[1]*; tilly vally. Ladie, *F*; tilly vally. Lady! *F2*   83 O'] *Cam[1] (Walker)*; O
F   December –] *Theobald*; *December. F*   84.1 MALVOLIO] Malvolio *in nightgown (with lighted candle.)*
/ *Powell MS*

Enter MALVOLIO.

MALVOLIO   My masters, are you mad or what are you?   85
Have you no wit, manners nor honesty but to gabble like
tinkers at this time of night? Do ye make an alehouse of
my lady's house that ye squeak out your coziers' catches
without any mitigation or remorse of voice? Is there no
respect of place, persons nor time in you?   90

SIR TOBY   We did keep time, sir, in our catches. Sneck
up!

MALVOLIO   Sir Toby, I must be round with you. My lady
bade me tell you that though she harbours you as her
kinsman she's nothing allied to your disorders. If you   95
can separate yourself and your misdemeanours, you
are welcome to the house; if not, an it would please
you to take leave of her, she is very willing to bid you
farewell.

SIR TOBY [*Sings.*]
Farewell, dear heart, since I must needs be gone.   100

---

86 **wit** intelligence
honesty decency (*OED* 2)
86–7 **gabble like tinkers** proverbial
phrase; itinerant tinkers were held
in low repute as a species of noisy
vagrant; cf. similar expressions such as
'drunk as a tinker' (equally appropriate
to this scene; *OED* tinker *n.* 1a); *gabble*
= chatter
88 **squeak out** sing in a squeaky voice
(*OED* squeak *v.* 3a, giving this example)
coziers' catches cobblers' songs.
Cobblers enjoyed much the same
unenviable reputation as tinkers (cf.
86–7n.).
89 **without . . . voice** without any lower-
ing or interruption of your loud singing (*OED* mitigation 1, *OED* remorse
3c, both giving this example)
91–2   **Sneck up!** Go hang (yourself)!
(*OED* snick *v.*[1] b, giving this exam-

ple). Cf. John Taylor the Water-Poet's
Praise of Hempseed: '*Snickup*, which is
in English Gallow-grasse' (J. Taylor,
66).
93 **round** plain, possibly with an unwitting musical pun on Sir Toby's *catches*
(91)
94 **harbours** lodges
95 **nothing allied** in no way favourable
disorders irregular behaviour (*OED*
disorder *n.* 2b, giving this example)
97 **an** if
100–10 an adapted version of the first two
stanzas of a ballad published in Jones
(sigs D4[v]–E1[r]). The original stanzas,
together with Jones's music, are given
in Appendix 3. The men conflate the
two stanzas into one and change the
words so as to turn the song into a
comic dialogue, in which the protagonist becomes Sir Toby (*I*) rather than
the parting beloved (*you*).

97 an] (*and*)

MARIA   Nay, good Sir Toby.

FESTE [*Sings.*]

    His eyes do show his days are almost done.

MALVOLIO   Is't even so?

SIR TOBY [*Sings.*]

    But I will never die.

FESTE [*Sings.*]

    Sir Toby, there you lie.   105

MALVOLIO   This is much credit to you.

SIR TOBY [*Sings.*]

    Shall I bid him go?

FESTE [*Sings.*]

    What an if you do?

SIR TOBY [*Sings.*]

    Shall I bid him go, and spare not?

FESTE [*Sings.*]

    O no, no, no, no, you dare not.   110

SIR TOBY [*to Feste*]   Out o'tune, sir – ye lie. [*to Malvolio*]
    Art any more than a steward? Dost thou think because
    thou art virtuous there shall be no more cakes and ale?

---

103 **Is't even so** i.e. is this how you
respond to my warning

105 **there you lie** in this you are lying.
In the 1789 Drury Lane production,
Sir Toby was made to fall drunkenly
on *never die* (104) and Feste delivered
the line standing over him, thereby
equivocating on the meaning of *lie* (see
t.n.). In Posner's 2001 RSC production Mark Hadfield's Feste directed
you lie towards Malvolio.

106 **you** this is presumably plural,
addressed to all present

111 **Out o'tune** wrong: a response to
Feste's sung accusation *you dare not*

112 **Art . . . steward** Sir Toby rapidly
changes target, putting Malvolio in
his place, as if in anticipation of the

latter's dream of social promotion
(2.5.21–69). The omission of the
subject pronoun *thou* is quite frequent in Shakespeare, especially in
questions (Blake, *Grammar*, 6.3.1.2,
giving this example), but here it
accentuates the use of the second
person singular verb form (*Art*), so
as to underline that Sir Toby is
addressing an inferior.

113 **cakes and ale** the food and drink
traditionally associated with church
festivities such as saint's days and
holy days (like Twelfth Night), and
as such particularly unpalatable to
ceremony-hating 'Puritans' like
Malvolio (cf. 130–2). In his *Anatomy
of Abuses* the Puritan Philip Stubbes

---

104 die.] die. *Falls down singing / Harrison;* die. *Falls / Powell MS*   105 lie.] lie! *standing over him /
Powell MS*   111 tune] time *Theobald*

FESTE   Yes, by Saint Anne, and ginger shall be hot i'th'
mouth too.   115

SIR TOBY   Thou'rt i'th' right. [*to Malvolio*] Go, sir, rub
your chain with crumbs. – A stoup of wine, Maria.

MALVOLIO   Mistress Mary, if you prized my lady's favour
at anything more than contempt, you would not give
means for this uncivil rule. She shall know of it,   120
by this hand.   *Exit.*

MARIA   Go shake your ears.

SIR ANDREW   'Twere as good a deed as to drink when

attacks 'Church-ales' which result in
'swilling and gulling, night and daye,
till [the parishioners] bee as drunke
as Rattes and as blockishe as beastes'
(Stubbes, sig. 95ʳ). The phrase
cakes and ale – following this play
– has become proverbial for 'a good
time'.

114 **Saint Anne** the mother of the
Virgin Mary: a common oath, perhaps intended here – because it is of
Catholic origin – as a provocation to
the 'Puritan' Malvolio
ginger used to spice ale and cultivated
for its supposed aphrodisiac powers.
'Ginger heateth and drieth in the third
degree . . . prouoking Venerie', affirms
Gerard, 55; cf. *WT* 4.3.43.

115 Ard² and some other editions have
Feste exit on this line, on the grounds
that he takes no further part in the
scene, and that Maria's 'and let the
fool make a third' (168–90) implies
his absence. The clown's exit at this
point, however, is unmotivated, and
Maria's phrase could equally well be
addressed to the other two in Feste's
presence. What to make of his silence
is partly a matter of directorial choice:
in Hall's 1958 Stratford production he
fell asleep.

116–17 **Go . . . crumbs** go and clean your
chain of office (as steward): another
reminder of Malvolio's lowly status.
On this method of cleaning the chain,
cf. 'the chippings of the Buttry fly after
him, / To scowre his gold Chaine'
(Webster, *Malfi*, 3.2, sig. G2ᵛ).

118 **Mistress Mary** Malvolio is calling
Maria to order, reminding her of her
role as Olivia's waiting-gentlewoman.
In Posner's 2001 RSC production,
Guy Henry's Malvolio pointed to
the ground, demanding that Alison
Fiske's Maria come across stage to
him: she obeyed.

119–20 **give . . . rule** provide the drink
that encourages this unruly behaviour (*OED* rule *n.* 13a, giving this
example)

121 **by this hand** In Gielgud's 1955
Stratford production Laurence Olivier
raised his hand on this line, causing
his pants to fall down from under his
nightshirt (Brown, 237).

122 **Go . . . ears** i.e. like an ass (proverbial: Dent, E16)

123 **as good . . . drink** proverbial
phrase (Dent, D183.1); cf. *1H4*
2.1.28, 2.2.21–2; 'Sir Andrew's foolish amplification makes nonsense of
it' (Ard²).

114 Saint] *(S.), Rowe*   116 SD] *Mahood*   121 SD] *Exit* MALVOLIO, *followed by the Clown, mocking
him. / Kemble*

man's a-hungry to challenge him the field and then to
break promise with him and make a fool of him.　　　125

SIR TOBY　Do't, knight. I'll write thee a challenge, or I'll
deliver thy indignation to him by word of mouth.

MARIA　Sweet Sir Toby, be patient for tonight. Since
the youth of the count's was today with my lady, she
is much out of quiet. For Monsieur Malvolio, let me　130
alone with him. If I do not gull him into a nayword and
make him a common recreation, do not think I have wit
enough to lie straight in my bed. I know I can do it.

SIR TOBY　Possess us, possess us. Tell us something of
him.　　　135

MARIA　Marry, sir, sometimes he is a kind of Puritan.

SIR ANDREW　O, if I thought that, I'd beat him like a dog.

---

124 **a-hungry** 'the prefix [a-]. . . was
probably taken as emphatic' (*OED*,
giving this example)
　the field to a duel. Sir Andrew considers it the height of wit to break the
pledge of a challenge, thus confirming
his quarrelsome nature (see note to
66–7) and anticipating his cowardly
terror of duelling (in 3.4).

129 **of the count's** double genitive; cf.
Blake, *Grammar*, 3.3.2.2; Hope, 1.1.4d

130 **out of quiet** agitated
　Monsieur This aping of 'the French
custom of prefixing the title to designations of office' (*OED* 1c) mocks
Malvolio's self-importance, and
especially his pompous sense of *his*
office. Cf. 'Monsieur the Nice', *LLL*
5.2.325; 'Mounsieur Cobweb', *MND*
4.1.10.
　let leave (*OED v.*[1] 18b, giving this
example)

131 ***gull . . . nayword** trick him into
making his name a byword for stupidity; cf. 'have a nay-word', *MW*
2.2.118–19, 5.2.5. Rowe's emendation

is surely correct, even if some editions, such as Riverside, defend F's
'an ayword'.

132 **a common recreation** an object of
sport or entertainment

132–3 **wit . . . bed** This sounds like
a proverb (cf. 1.3.72–3) but is not
present in Tilley or Dent.

134 **Possess us** let us in on your plan

136 **Puritan** a somewhat ambiguous
term of abuse: 'Puritans', as their
opponents dubbed them, were
reformist Protestants who wished
to complete the Reformation with
further 'purification' of the church,
but the word came to be applied
more generally to self-righteous moralists. How literally we are to take
Malvolio's supposed 'Puritanism' is a
moot point: Maria's gibe at 142 places
its seriousness in doubt, but at the
same time there are other negative
allusions to Puritan ideology in the
play, notably Sir Andrew's reference
at 3.2.30 to the fanatical Brownists
(see pp. 22–3).

---

131 a nayword] *Rowe;* an ayword *F*　　134 SP] *Sir And / Dyce*[2]

SIR TOBY What, for being a Puritan? Thy exquisite
reason, dear knight?

SIR ANDREW I have no exquisite reason for't, but I have   140
reason good enough.

MARIA The devil a Puritan that he is, or anything constantly
but a time-pleaser; an affectioned ass that cons state
without book and utters it by great swathes; the best
persuaded of himself, so crammed, as he thinks, with   145
excellencies that it is his grounds of faith that all that
look on him love him, and on that vice in him will my
revenge find notable cause to work.

SIR TOBY What wilt thou do?

MARIA I will drop in his way some obscure epistles of   150
love, wherein by the colour of his beard, the shape of

---

138 **exquisite** far-fetched, abstruse (*OED
a.* 1a, giving this example). Mahood
notes that this word, particularly difficult to pronounce when drunk, is
given to the equally drunken Cassio in
Oth 2.3.18.

140–1 Sir Andrew clearly does not
understand Sir Toby's *exquisite*, but
in any case finds it self-evident that a
Puritan should be beaten like a dog.

142 **The devil . . . is** Maria casts doubt
on the seriousness or sincerity of
Malvolio's supposed Puritanism,
despite the fact that she herself calls
him a *Puritan* at 138: his pious severity is just one pose among others, and
will be opportunistically abandoned.
In doing so, Maria unleashes an appropriately anti-puritanical oath.
*devil F's 'diu'll' may imply a mono-
syllabic pronunciation of the word.
constantly consistently (*OED adv.*
3b, giving this example)

143 **time-pleaser** time-server or oppor-
tunist; cf. *Cor* 3.1.45.
affectioned affected (*OED* affection
n. 13)

143–4 **cons . . . book** learns haughty
behaviour by heart (*OED* state *n.*
19b); *without book* is a proverbial idiom (Dent, B532): cf. 1.3.25.
Malvolio, like Cesario at 1.5.169,
is compared to an actor 'conning'
his part.

144 **utters . . . swathes** speaks it (his
haughty part) in great quantities.
Swathes, swaths or 'swarths' (F) are
literally rows of grass cut down by the
mower's scythe (*OED* swath 3a); cf.
TC 5.5.25, 'Fall down before him, like
the mower's swath'.

144–5 **the best . . . himself** thinking
very highly of himself

146 **excellencies** excellent qualities
(*OED* 2a, first occurrence)
his . . . faith his utter conviction

147 **vice** moral defect. The vice was the
representative of evil in the medieval
morality play; cf. 4.2.123n.

150, 159 **epistles, letters** The fact that
both Maria and Sir Toby refer to letters in the plural suggests that more
than one may have been originally
intended.

142 devil] *(diu'll)*   144 swathes] *(swarths), Mahood;* swaths *Collier*

his leg, the manner of his gait, the expressure of his
eye, forehead and complexion he shall find himself
most feelingly personated. I can write very like my lady
your niece. On a forgotten matter we can hardly make   155
distinction of our hands.

SIR TOBY   Excellent, I smell a device.

SIR ANDREW   I have't in my nose too.

SIR TOBY   He shall think by the letters that thou wilt drop
that they come from my niece, and that she's in love   160
with him.

MARIA   My purpose is indeed a horse of that colour.

SIR ANDREW   And your horse now would make him an
ass.

MARIA   As I doubt not.   165

SIR ANDREW   O, 'twill be admirable.

MARIA   Sport royal, I warrant you. I know my physic will
work with him. I will plant you two – and let the fool
make a third – where he shall find the letter. Observe
his construction of it. For this night, to bed and dream   170
on the event. Farewell.   *Exit.*

---

152 **expressure** expression (*OED* b, first
occurrence)
154 **feelingly** appropriately, accurately
(*OED* 2, giving this example)
personated acted (*OED* v. 4a); like
'cons' (143), a theatrical term
155–6 **On . . . hands** when we no longer
remember what it refers to, we can
barely tell our handwriting apart
157 **smell a device** suspect a trick (*OED*
device 6, giving this example); cf.
AYL 1.1.144–5, 'entrap thee by some
treacherous device'.
162 **a horse . . . colour** one of that
nature: a proverbial phrase (Dent,
H665)

165 Maria puns on as/ass, thereby slyly
insulting Sir Andrew ([you] ass, I
doubt not). Cf. *Ham* 5.2.43, 'And many
such like "as", sir, of great charge'.
167 **Sport royal** a sport worthy of kings,
with reference to hunting
physic medicine
168–9 **let . . . third** Cf. *we three* (15–16
and n.). On this line said in Feste's
presence, cf. 115n. There may be a pun
here on third/turd; cf. Dr Caius in
MW 3.3.220, 'I shall make-a the turd';
cf. Kökeritz, 150; Partridge, 207.
170 **construction** interpretation (*OED*
7); from 'construe'
171 **event** outcome (*OED* 3a)

152 gait] *(gate), Johnson*   165 As] *this edn;* Asse *F*

SIR TOBY   Good night, Penthesilea.

SIR ANDREW   Before me, she's a good wench.

SIR TOBY   She's a beagle true bred, and one that adores
me. What o'that?   175

SIR ANDREW   I was adored once too.

SIR TOBY   Let's to bed, knight. Thou hadst need send for
more money.

SIR ANDREW   If I cannot recover your niece, I am a foul
way out.   180

SIR TOBY   Send for money, knight. If thou hast her not
i'th' end, call me cut.

SIR ANDREW   If I do not, never trust me, take it how you
will.

SIR TOBY   Come, come, I'll go burn some sack; 'tis too   185
late to go to bed now. Come, knight, come, knight.   *Exeunt.*

---

172 **Penthesilea** Queen of the
Amazons, adversary of Achilles in
the Trojan wars (Ovid, *Met.*, 12.677,
fol. 157ʳ): both an admiring reference to Maria's combative spirit
and a probable ironical allusion to
the boy actor's diminutive size (cf.
1.5.199n.).

173 **Before me** a mild oath in substitution of 'before God'

174 **beagle** small hunting dog: a further
allusion to Maria's size and to her
spirit in 'pursuing' Malvolio; one of
several hunting and blood sports metaphors for the gulling plot (cf. 2.5.6–7,
8–9, 19–20; 3.1.116–17; 3.4.133–4,
and notes).

175 **What o'that?** so what of it? – a piece
of bravado implying that he is quite
used to being adored by women

176 This poignant glimpse into Sir
Andrew's sentimental life is rapidly
dismissed by Sir Toby, anxious to get
back to business (i.e. *money*, 178).

177–8 **Thou . . . money** For Sir Toby
'milking' of Sir Andrew as a source

of income, cf. 1.2.21n., 3.2.52–3n. and
3.4.282n.

179 **recover** obtain (*OED v.*[1] 6a)

179–80 **I . . . out** I am in trouble, because
out of pocket (literally, I am lost in the
mire; cf. *LLL* 5.2.907, 'ways be foul').
Sir Andrew needs to *recover* the money
he has invested in his courtship of
Olivia: this suggests the nature of his
continuing interest in the countess.

182 **cut** short-tailed or gelded horse
(*OED n.*[2] 30); an idiomatic term of
abuse (Dent, C940). Sir Toby's invitation reintroduces the theme of castration (cf. 1.2.59n.), perhaps with
implied reference to Sir Andrew, who
will be *cut* or deprived of his money.
Malvolio unwittingly spells out the
word at 2.5.86.

183–4 **If . . . will** Sir Andrew promises to
call Sir Toby a *cut*; 'never trust me' and
'take it how you will' are both proverbial idioms (Dent, T558.1, T27).

185 **burn some sack** warm and spice
some white Spanish wine (equivalent
to modern sherry)

2.4   *Enter* ORSINO, VIOLA [*as Cesario*], CURIO *and others.*

ORSINO

    Give me some music. Now good morrow, friends.
    Now good Cesario, but that piece of song,
    That old and antic song we heard last night:
    Methought it did relieve my passion much,
    More than light airs and recollected terms   5
    Of these most brisk and giddy-paced times.
    Come, but one verse.

CURIO   He is not here, so please your lordship, that should
    sing it.

ORSINO   Who was it?   10

CURIO   Feste the jester, my lord, a fool that the Lady

2.4 This scene is dedicated principally to the long exchange between Orsino and Cesario on the theme of love, and contains the comedy's most extended play on Viola-as-Cesario's androgyny, together with her veiled confession of love to the duke, which he fails to understand. The scene opens with a musical prelude that is also a thematic and stylistic *echo* (21) of 1.1. Rowe locates it in '*The Palace*'.

1–20 Cf. 1.1.1–15.

2 **but** just (i.e. precisely that song)

3 **antic** àntic; strange, fantastic (cf. Hamlet's 'antic disposition', *Ham* 1.5.170), with a possible play on 'antique', synonym for *old* (see t.n.)

4 **passion** suffering, due to unrequited love; cf. 94.

5 **light airs** i.e. sprightly (modern) tunes, in contrast to *old and antic* songs (3); cf. 'these and all other kinds of light music . . . are by a generall name called ayres' (T. Morley, 180). 'Air' was a fashionable term in this period: cf. Dowland (1597) and Jones (1600).

    recollected terms affected phrases;

for *recollected*, *OED* (recollected *ppl. a.*[1] 1) – giving this as sole occurrence – glosses 'Meaning uncertain', and records hypotheses such as 'refined' and 'studied'. Orsino disdains the artificial lyrics as well as the lively music of the new *airs*.

6 **brisk** quickly passing (*OED a.* 2e, first occurrence)

    giddy-paced pacèd: so rapidly changeable as to cause dizziness

11–12 **Feste . . . delight in** the only reference in the play to the name of Feste, perhaps coined to form a rhyming jingle with *jester*. He is described here as an 'old' clown who has been part of Olivia's household for more than a generation, having survived her father (and brother). A dead man's delight in his jester is something of a Shakespearean topos: cf. the countess on the clown in *AW* 4.5.63–6, 'My lord that's gone made himself much sport out of him'; the theme is varied in Hamlet's recollections of Yorick, the dead King's dead jester (*Ham* 5.1.174–84).

2.4] *(Scena Quarta.)*   0.1 ORSINO] *Mahood; Duke F*   as Cesario] *Munro subst.*   3 antic] *(Anticke),* *Cam*[1]; antique *Pope*

Olivia's father took much delight in. He is about the
house.

ORSINO

Seek him out, and play the tune the while.

Music plays. [Exit Curio.]

[*to Viola*] Come hither, boy. If ever thou shalt love,   15
In the sweet pangs of it remember me;
For such as I am all true lovers are,
Unstaid and skittish in all motions else
Save in the constant image of the creature
That is beloved. How dost thou like this tune?   20

VIOLA

It gives a very echo to the seat
Where love is throned.

ORSINO   Thou dost speak masterly.
My life upon't, young though thou art, thine eye
Hath stayed upon some favour that it loves.
Hath it not, boy?

VIOLA   A little, by your favour.   25

ORSINO

What kind of woman is't?

VIOLA   Of your complexion.

ORSINO

She is not worth thee then. What years, i'faith?

---

17 **such . . . are** all true lovers are like me
18 **Unstaid and skittish** changeable and fickle: virtually synonyms, by way of emphasis
   motions else other emotions
19 **constant** stable (of *image*); faithful (of the lover; *OED a.* 2): in this second, attributive, sense, cf. *MA* 2.3.62–4, 'Men were deceivers ever . . .To one thing constant never.'
21–2 It is a perfect expression of the

sentiments of the heart, seat of love.
22 **masterly** with expertise
24 **stayed upon** lingered over
   favour face (*OED n.* 9b)
25 **by . . . favour** by your leave; with a pun on *favour* (= face) at 24. Viola's eye has indeed *stayed upon* a face, Orsino's.
26 **complexion** colouring and appearance of the face (as a reflection of temperament; *OED n.* 4a)

14 Seek] Go, seek *Capell* SD *Exit Curio*] *Pope* 15, 67 SDs] *Collier³* 18 motions] notions *Warburton*

227

VIOLA

    About your years, my lord.

ORSINO

    Too old, by heaven. Let still the woman take
    An elder than herself; so wears she to him,   30
    So sways she level in her husband's heart.
    For, boy, however we do praise ourselves,
    Our fancies are more giddy and unfirm,
    More longing wavering, sooner lost and worn
    Than women's are.

VIOLA   I think it well, my lord.   35

ORSINO

    Then let thy love be younger than thyself,
    Or thy affection cannot hold the bent;
    For women are as roses, whose fair flower
    Being once displayed doth fall that very hour.

---

29 **still** always

30 **An . . . herself** Coleridge (1.96n.)
detects an ironic autobiographical
reference here to Shakespeare's own
supposedly unhappy marriage to 'an
elder', Anne Hathaway; Orsino advises
Cesario to do the opposite.
    so . . . him so she adapts herself to
him, like clothes to the wearer

31 **So . . . level** thus she exerts a consistent influence; with a pun on *sways*:
holds sway (cf. 2.5.106), but also
swings, like a pendulum, whereby *level*
comes to mean 'in perfect balance',
implying that a man's heart is *giddy
and unfirm* (33) until stabilized by a
woman's influence. *Sway* is a recurrent thematic word, suggesting the
comedy's concern with interpersonal,
and especially inter-gender, 'power
relations'; cf. 4.1.51 and 4.3.17.

33 **fancies** inclinations, desires
    giddy dizzy: cf. 6.
    unfirm unsteady (*OED* 2, sole occur-
rence)

34 **longing wavering** yearningly inde-
cisive; the phrase is best understood
as an intensifier (*longing*) qualifying
an adjective (*wavering*); cf. *headstrong
potent*, 3.4.199.
    worn worn out. Hanmer's emendation
'won' – which presupposes a misreading ('worne' for 'wonne') – has the
merit of forming a more obvious couple with *lost*, but the result is a cliché
('lost and won'). F's *worn*, moreover,
continues the series of epithets denot-
ing man's fickleness; cf. 'my wonted
loue is worne' (Peele, F1ʳ).

35 **think** believe

37 **Or** otherwise
    hold the bent remain strong; literally,
stay taut like a drawn bow: a metaphor
from archery (*OED* bent *n.²* 9).

38–9 **women . . . hour** women's rose-like
beauty and its flower-like brevity are
poetic commonplaces; cf. *Son* 1.2, 'that
beauty's rose might never die'.

39 **displayed** unfolded, and so put on
show

---

34 longing] *this edn;* longing, *F*   worn] won *Hanmer*

VIOLA

And so they are. Alas that they are so,   40
To die even when they to perfection grow.

Enter CURIO *and* FESTE.

ORSINO [*to Feste*]

O fellow, come, the song we had last night.
Mark it, Cesario, it is old and plain.
The spinsters, and the knitters in the sun
And the free maids that weave their thread with bones   45
Do use to chant it. It is silly sooth
And dallies with the innocence of love
Like the old age.

FESTE

Are you ready, sir?

ORSINO

I prithee sing.   50

---

41 This is Viola's potentially tragic destiny (to die of unrequited love), adumbrated in Cesario's story of his 'sister' at 110–14.

43 Orsino's further description of the song sung *last night* (2, 42) is superfluous if Cesario *heard* it with him (3) and incongruous if he actually sang it, and may thus represent one of the comedy's 'loose ends': see pp. 11–14.

44 **spinsters** women spinning wool or flax (*OED* 1a; cf. 1.3.98–100); unmarried women, the modern meaning given by Minsheu: 'Spinster, *a terme . . . unto* Maids *unmarried*' (Minsheu, 683). Minsheu glosses an established use, and the reference at 45 to *maids* suggests that this derived meaning may already be present here.
knitters women who worked up yarn for clothing (*OED* 2, giving this example)

45 **free** nubile; carefree
bones See Johnson, *Dictionary*, bone

n. 5: 'A sort of bobbins, made of trotter bones, for weaving bonelace'.

46 **Do use** are accustomed
It . . . sooth The song tells a simple truth (about love); *silly* derives from ME 'seely', i.e. innocent, simple; cf. *R2* 5.5.25, 'like silly beggars'.

47 **dallies with** dwells amorously on

48 **the old age** i.e. the golden age, in which, according to classical pastoral myth, mankind lived in a state of innocence and freedom; cf. *golden time*, 5.1.375 and n. The most authoritative source for this is Ovid, *Met.*, 1.103–5, fol. 2ʳ: 'Then sprang up first the golden age . . . There was no feare of punishment, there was no threatning lawe'; cf. *AYL* 1.1.114–15: '[they] fleet the time carelessly, as they did in the golden world.'

50 **I prithee** I pray thee; please. Theobald reads F's 'I' as an adverb ('Ay' = 'yes'), but this does not change the overall meaning of the phrase.

41.1 FESTE] *Munro; Clowne* F   42 SD] *Oxf*   50 I] Ay, *Theobald*   sing.] *this edn;* sing. *Musicke.* F

229

FESTE (*Sings.*)

> Come away, come away death,
> And in sad cypress let me be laid.
> Fie away, fie away breath,
> I am slain by a fair cruel maid.
> My shroud of white, stuck all with yew,   55
> O prepare it.
> My part of death no one so true
> Did share it.
>
> Not a flower, not a flower sweet
> On my black coffin let there be strewn.   60
> Not a friend, not a friend greet
> My poor corpse, where my bones shall be thrown.
> A thousand thousand sighs to save,
> Lay me, O where

51–66 No contemporary musical setting survives for this song, whose words may or may not be Shakespeare's, although the 'death-wish' it expresses is in keeping with Orsino's general attitude.

51 **Come away** hurry here (to me)

52 **in sad cypress** in a coffin of black cypress wood; or, in a bier strewn with branches of cypress. It probably alludes to the material of the coffin itself: thus its *sad* funereal colour, characteristic of cypress wood; cf. *my black coffin* (60). The phrase 'sad cypress', however, occurs in *FQ*, 2.1.60, with reference to a branch-strewn grave (see *stuck . . . yew*, 55): 'The great earths wombe they open to the sky, / And with sad Cypresse seemely it embraue' (*FQ*, 65). To complicate matters further, Olivia at 3.1.119 refers to *cypress* in the sense of crepe material, which, since she wears it as a sign of mourning, is again presumably black; cf. *WT*

4.4.221, 'Cypress black as e'er was crow'.

53 **Fie away** be gone (from me). An Early Modern English idiom, in antithesis to 'come away' (51); cf. Florio's gloss for 'O': 'an interiection of . . . reproouing, as . . . figh, away' (Florio, *World*, 242; Oxf¹). Rowe's emendation 'Fly away' is unnecessary.

55 **stuck . . . yew** strewn with branches of yew. Like the cypress, the yew tree is traditionally associated with graveyards and mourning; cf. 'under that *Eu*, / As I sat sadly leaning on a graue' (Webster, *Devil*, 1.2, sig. C1ʳ).

57–8 No one as faithful as I ever accepted his lot, namely death.

60 **strewn** pronounced to rhyme with *thrown* (62)

61 **greet** salute; bewail (*OED* v.² 2: cf. *sighs*, 63). As Mahood notes, the transitive use of the verb in this second sense was obsolete in Early Modern English, giving Feste's song 'its antique flavour'.

51 SP] *Munro; not in F; Clo. / Capell*   SD] *(The Song.)*   53 Fie . . . fie] Fly . . . fly *Rowe*
55–8] *Pope; F lines* it. / it. /   56, 64 O] *om. Pope*   63–6] *Pope; F lines* where / there. /

Sad true love never find my grave,   65
  To weep there.

ORSINO

  There's for thy pains.   [*Gives money.*]

FESTE   No pains, sir. I take pleasure in singing, sir.

ORSINO

  I'll pay thy pleasure then.

FESTE   Truly, sir, and pleasure will be paid, one time or
  another.   70

ORSINO

  Give me now leave to leave thee.

FESTE   Now the melancholy god protect thee, and the
  tailor make thy doublet of changeable taffeta, for thy
  mind is a very opal. I would have men of such constancy   75
  put to sea, that their business might be everything and

---

65 ***true love** Capell's emendation elimi-
nates the jingle between F's 'louer'
and *never*. This would have been an
easy error, given the prevalence of *-er*
suspensions (RP).

68 **No . . . pleasure** It is unlikely that
Feste resents 'Orsino's offhand payment' (Mahood); on the contrary,
his *pleasure* at 70 may playfully suggest how content he is to receive the
reward.

70 **pleasure . . . paid** Feste is toying
with the proverb 'There is no pleasure without pain' (Dent, P420; cf.
Tilley, P408, 412, 413, 419), punning
on 'pain' and *pains* (67, 68).

72 **Give . . . thee** Orsino dismisses Feste
and his wordplay, but in so doing produces his own pun on *leave*: as noun =
permission; as verb = depart from.

73 **melancholy god** Saturn, the Roman
god of agriculture, identified in astrol-
ogy with the planet ruling over the
melancholy humour, and in alchemy
with lead. Feste is making fun of
Orsino's habitual 'dark' pose and his

current bad mood.

74 **changeable taffeta** shot silk; see
pp. 24–25. In Lyly's *Euphues* it is
associated with mood changes under
the influence of love: 'you haue giuen
vnto me a true loues knotte wrought
of chaungeable silke' (Lyly, *Euphues*,
fol. 24ʳ).

75 **opal** See p. 24; cf. Pliny, 'for in
the Opall, you shall see the burn-
ing fire of the Carbuncle or Rubie,
the glorious purple of the Amethyst,
the greene sea of the Emeraud, and
all glittering together mixed after an
incredible maner' (Pliny, 614). Feste
allows himself the fool's licence of
strongly satirizing the duke's incon-
stancy, while appearing to pay the
compliment of comparing him first
with valuable cloth (74) and then with
a prized gem.
men . . . constancy i.e. mood-
changing lovers: ironic

76 **sea** another traditional symbol of
mutability; cf. Ariel's 'suffer a sea-
change', *Tem* 1.2.401.

65 true love] *Capell (*true-love*); true louer* F

their intent everywhere, for that's it that always makes
a good voyage of nothing. Farewell.   *Exit.*

ORSINO

Let all the rest give place.   [*Exeunt all but Orsino and Viola.*]
                            Once more, Cesario,

Get thee to yon same sovereign cruelty.   80

Tell her my love, more noble than the world,

Prizes not quantity of dirty lands.

The parts that fortune hath bestowed upon her

Tell her I hold as giddily as fortune;

But 'tis that miracle and queen of gems   85

That nature pranks her in attracts my soul.

VIOLA

But if she cannot love you, sir?

ORSINO

I cannot be so answered.

VIOLA   Sooth, but you must.

76–8 **their business . . . nothing** i.e. the changeable sea would carry them to and fro on a profitless journey; a sardonic allusion to the proverb 'he is not any where who is every where' (Dent, E194)

77 **that's it** that's the thing; *it* is sometimes used by Shakespeare as a full noun before a relative clause (Hope, 1.3.2c, giving this example)

78 **of** out of; or, consisting of

79 **give place** leave

80 **sovereign cruelty** cruel sovereign (of my heart); supremely cruel lady

81 **the world** society at large, with its materialistic values

82 **dirty** corrupting, because lands and other possessions encourage greed; soiled, because made of earth. Cf. Hamlet's 'spacious in the possession of dirt' (*Ham* 5.2.74–5).

83 **parts** endowments, possessions (*OED n.* 7b)

84 **I . . . fortune** I regard as lightly as

fickle fortune does. Orsino plays on two related meanings of *fortune* here and at 83: the capricious goddess personifying chance (84), and the actual riches the goddess has bestowed upon Olivia as heiress (83). The wealthy duke can boast his indifference to the latter.

85 **that . . . gems** Olivia's precious innate qualities, especially her beauty; *miracle and queen* = 'miraculous queen' (rhetorical figure: hendiadys)

86 **pranks her in** adorns her with (*OED v.*[4] 1c). Contrast Coriolanus on the tribunes: 'they do prank them in authority' (*Cor* 3.1.23).
    attracts draws forth (*OED v.* 4a, first occurrence)

88 *****I** F's 'It' (= the question) is plausible in itself, but is belied by Cesario's reply, 'you must', which justifies Hanmer's emendation.
    Sooth in truth

---

79 SD] *Capell subst.*   80 yon] (*yond*)   88 I] *Hanmer;* It *F*

232

Say that some lady, as perhaps there is,
Hath for your love as great a pang of heart   90
As you have for Olivia. You cannot love her;
You tell her so. Must she not then be answered?

ORSINO

There is no woman's sides
Can bide the beating of so strong a passion
As love doth give my heart; no woman's heart   95
So big to hold so much – they lack retention.
Alas, their love may be called appetite,
No motion of the liver but the palate,
That suffer surfeit, cloyment and revolt.
But mine is all as hungry as the sea,   100
And can digest as much. Make no compare

90 **pang** sudden sharp pain (*OED n.*[1] 1b,
giving this example)
93–103 Orsino's misogynistic speech,
in part provoked by his anger at
Olivia's indifference, rehearses some
of the commonplaces of Renaissance
attitudes to women. In particular,
it recalls Gasparre Pallavicino's
thesis in Castiglione, 'that women
are unperfect creatures, and consequently of less woorthinesse then
men' (Castiglione, sig. Cc2ᵛ), and
that 'through the weakenes of their
kinde, [they] are much more enclined
to appetites', as opposed to true
passion (sig. Gg1ʳ). This contrasts
with Orsino's praise of the superior
constancy of women at 31–5. It is
of course ironical that he should
pronounce such a demeaning view
of the woman he claims to adore,
especially in the presence of Viola,
who has already demonstrated – to
the audience – her true *passion* for
him (94).
94 **bide** bear
96 **retention** the capacity to retain (love):

a medical term, referring literally to
the body's ability to retain liquid, especially urine; cf. 'Retention of vryne, &
costyfnes' (Vigo, fol. cixʳ). Early modern scientific discourse often classified
women as incontinent 'leaky vessels'
(Paster, 30–4). The incontinence of
which women were accused was above
all sexual, however: 'I beleave not that
men are so incontinent, as women
be', affirms Castiglione's Pallavicino
(Castiglione, sig. Ff4ʳ).
97 **appetite** bodily craving
98 **motion** emotion; inclination (*OED n.*
12a, giving both meanings). Cf. 18.
liver the seat of the passions; cf.
1.1.36–7n.
palate the seat of taste, which is rapidly satisfied
99 **surfeit . . . revolt** i.e. excess (of food
or sex) leading to satiety and revulsion;
cf. 1.1.2–3n. *OED* gives *cloyment*, satiety, as sole occurrence.
100 **as hungry . . . sea** unlimited in
capacity. Ironically, Orsino claims at
1.1.9–13 that the sea causes loss of
value.

99 suffer] suffers *Rowe*

233

Between that love a woman can bear me
And that I owe Olivia.

VIOLA　　　　　　　　　　　Ay, but I know –

ORSINO

What dost thou know?

VIOLA

Too well what love women to men may owe.　　　　　105
In faith, they are as true of heart as we.
My father had a daughter loved a man,
As it might be, perhaps, were I a woman,
I should your lordship.

ORSINO　　　　　　　　　　And what's her history?

VIOLA

A blank, my lord. She never told her love,　　　　　110
But let concealment like a worm i'th' bud

102 **bear** have towards; perhaps pun on 'bearing' sexually and on childbirth; cf. *AYL*, 5.4.207–8, 'O women, for the love you bear to men'.

103, 105 **owe** feel towards

107–15 This *history* of a girl pining stoically from unexpressed love – a barely veiled allusion to Viola's own predicament – recalls the story told by Cesare Gonzaga in Castiglione: significantly, as a reply to Pallavicino's tirade against female incontinency (see 93–103n. and 96n.), just as Cesario is responding to Orsino's misogyny. In Gonzaga's narrative, a young girl, like Viola, refrains from expressing her love for a man she cannot have: 'She thus ferventlye louinge, as a most louing minde coulde loue, continued two yeeres in suche contynencie, that she neuer made anye token to this yonge man of the love that she bore him' (Castiglione, sig. Gg3ʳ). The story ends tragically, since the girl dies from unrequited love: a fate that could await Viola herself.

107 **My . . . daughter** a 'hidden' clue to Viola's gender and her love for Orsino,

who, as elsewhere, fails to decipher the conundrum

109 **history** story; written historical narrative

110 **blank** plays on both senses of *history* (109): the story is blank (i.e. 'void': *OED n.* 7, first occurrence) because the young woman pined away and thus disappeared; and the page of Cesario's 'historical' narrative is blank because it is yet to be written and acted out: it may end well or tragically, depending on Orsino himself. Cf. 3.1.102.

told revealed (*OED v.* 5a, giving this example). In Bensley's 1785 production, according to Charles Lamb, Dorothy Jordan's Viola paused at the end of this line, 'as if the story had ended – and then the "worm in the bud" came up as a new suggestion – and the heightened image of "Patience" still followed after that . . . thought springing up after thought, I would almost say as they were watered by her tears' (C. Lamb, 185–6).

111 **concealment** the act of hiding (her love)

103 know –] *Rowe;* know. *F*

Feed on her damask cheek. She pined in thought,
And with a green and yellow melancholy
She sat like Patience on a monument,
Smiling at grief. Was not this love indeed?   115
We men may say more, swear more, but indeed
Our shows are more than will, for still we prove
Much in our vows, but little in our love.

ORSINO

But died thy sister of her love, my boy?

VIOLA

I am all the daughters of my father's house,   120
And all the brothers too; and yet I know not.
Sir, shall I to this lady?

ORSINO   Ay, that's the theme:

---

112 **damask** pink, like the damask rose (cf. *AYL*, 3.5.123); smooth, like damask silk
thought sadness

113 **green and yellow** pale and sickly, in contrast to pink *damask* (112); an allusion to the green sickness, an anaemic disease (chlorosis) mainly affecting young women, which made the complexion pallid and was often thought to be caused by unrequited desire. Cf. 'His daughter beeing at the age of twentie yeeres, would . . . fall into the greene sicknes for want of a husband' (Greene, *Mamillia*, fol. 8ʳ); cf. also *RJ* 3.5.156 (of Juliet), 'Out, you green-sickness carrion!'

114–15 **She sat . . . grief** Cesario's simile evokes an allegorical figure on a memorial or funerary monument, presumably similar to the emblem in Cesare Ripa's *Iconologia* (1593) that represents Patience as a woman sitting on a stone, bearing a yoke on her shoulders, with her feet placed on thorns (see Fig. 6). Chaucer's *Parliament of Fowls*, 242–3,

has 'Dame Pacience sitting there . . . / With face pale, upon an hil of sond' (Chaucer, *Works*, 313). Cf. *Per* 5.1.139–40, 'Like Patience gazing on kings' graves, and smiling / Extremity out of act.'

117 **Our . . . will** our outward displays of passion are greater than our actual sentiments
still always

120–1 another of Viola's riddling clues identifying her as the subject of her own *history*; again Orsino fails to take the point (cf. 107). Cf. the conundrum of the cross-dressed Phillida in Lyly's *Gallathea*: 'My Father had but one daughter, and therefore I could haue no sister' (Lyly, *Gallathea*, 3.2, sig. D4ᵛ). Viola's afterthought *and . . . not* (121) is evidently prompted by her melancholy reflection on Sebastian and his uncertain fate.

122 **theme** idea; literally, the subject of a school exercise (*OED* 3): wooing Olivia is Cesario's homework for the day. Orsino reminds Cesario, and himself, of the main business after their long digression.

To her in haste. Give her this jewel; say
My love can give no place, bide no denay.   *Exeunt.*

2.5   *Enter* SIR TOBY, SIR ANDREW *and* FABIAN.

SIR TOBY   Come thy ways, Signor Fabian.

FABIAN   Nay, I'll come. If I lose a scruple of this sport let
me be boiled to death with melancholy.

SIR TOBY   Wouldst thou not be glad to have the niggardly,
rascally sheep-biter come by some notable shame?   5

FABIAN   I would exult, man. You know he brought me out

---

123 **jewel** an ornament or piece of jewel-
lery, such as a ring. Cf. 3.4.203.

124 **can . . . denay** can neither yield nor
tolerate refusal; *denay* is an alternative
spelling for 'deny' (refusal: *OED* deny
n.[1] 2, giving this example), and is kept
here for the sake of the rhyme with
say (123).

2.5 The gulling of Malvolio through
Maria's forged letter – judged by
John Manningham in 1602 to be a
'good practise' (see pp. 3–4) – is the
play's most celebrated episode, giving
actors unrivalled opportunities for
both farcical comedy and potential
pathos. Pope gives the location as
'*Olivia's Garden*'.

1 **Come thy ways** come along (*OED*
way *n.*[1] 23b), an exclamation or discourse marker, in which the somewhat
archaic adverbial form *thy ways* has
fossilized (Blake, *Grammar*, 5.1.2.2ii,
giving this example); cf. *othergates*,
5.1.189.
Signor Fabian On Fabian and his
sudden appearance in the play, see
List of Roles, 15. *Signor* may be one
of Sir Toby's jovial terms of address,
or may be meant to indicate that
Fabian is an Italian visitor to Olivia's
house. He is often played, however,
as a servant or member of Olivia's
household.

2 **Nay** certainly (intensifier)
lose a scruple miss the tiniest part; a
scruple is a small unit of measurement
or weight: cf. 3.4.76n.

3 **boiled . . . melancholy** paradoxical, since melancholy was the cold
humour *par excellence*. Kökeritz, 95,
suggests a pun on 'boil' and 'bile' (i.e.
the cause of *melancholy*).

4 **niggardly** mean

5 **rascally** worthless, wretched
sheep-biter literally, a dog that har-
asses sheep, thus 'a shifty, sneaking,
or thievish fellow' (*OED* 2b, giving
this example); colloquially, a whore-
monger, from 'sheep' or 'mutton'
in the sense of 'prostitute' (*OED*
4). Intriguingly, since the subject is
Malvolio, Nashe associates the term
with lewd and hypocritical Puritans:
'he must . . . lier like a sheepbiter.
If he be halfe a puritan, and haue
scripture continually in his mouth, he
speeds the better' (Nashe, *Traveller*,
sigs G2[v]–G3[r]).
come by suffer

6 **exult** rejoice (*OED* 2, giving this
example)

6–7 Fabian's motive for participating in
this scene – setting it up in terms
of blood sports (cf. 8, 19–20; 2.3.174;
3.1.116–17; 3.4.133–4, and notes) –
may confirm Malvolio's supposed

2.5] *(Scena Quinta.)*   2 SP] *(Fab.), Cam*[1]   10.1 *with a letter*] *Oxf*

o'favour with my lady about a bear-baiting here.

SIR TOBY   To anger him we'll have the bear again, and we
will fool him black and blue, shall we not, Sir Andrew?

SIR ANDREW   An we do not, it is pity of our lives.   10

Enter MARIA [*with a letter*].

SIR TOBY   Here comes the little villain. How now, my
metal of India?

MARIA   Get ye all three into the box-tree. Malvolio's
coming down this walk. He has been yonder i'the sun
practising behaviour to his own shadow this half-hour.   15
Observe him for the love of mockery, for I know this
letter will make a contemplative idiot of him. Close, in
the name of jesting! [*The men hide. Maria drops letter.*]

'Puritanism', since, like theatre, *bear-baiting* was the object of reformist Protestant attacks. The *here* at 7 is almost literal, with reference to the Globe playhouse, since bear-baiting took place in arenas close to the theatres.

8   **To . . . again** In this scene it is Malvolio who will play the part of the *bear*, the others that of the dogs baiting him.

9   **fool . . . blue** make a complete fool of him: a variation on the proverbial idiom 'to beat one black and blue' (Dent, B160)

10   **An** if
      it . . . lives it is a shame that we should live; proverbial (Dent, P368.1). Cf. *MND* 3.1.40.

12   **metal of India** i.e. gold from India, legendary land of abundance, with a probable pun on 'mettle' (spirit); cf. 3.4.266, 5.1.316. For *of* = 'from', cf. Blake, *Grammar*, 5.4.2.

13   **box-tree** tree or hedge of box (*Buxus sempervirens*), an evergreen that can

be clipped into topiary forms. This is one of the few indispensable stage properties required in this play, although the 'tree' need not be literally such: mazes, plants in tubs, and walls (or sliding panels, as in Posner's 2001 RSC production) have been used in production, as well as multiple bushes (one for each eavesdropper).

14   **walk** i.e. a broad garden path, perhaps flanked by trees (*OED n.*[1] 9c, giving this example), an indication developed in some productions (e.g. Tree in 1901) into a full garden set, complete with mazes and the rest

14–15   **He . . . half-hour** another indication of Malvolio's *self-love* (1.5.86)

15   **behaviour** elegant deportment (*OED* 1e)

16   **for . . . mockery** for goodness' sake: discourse marker

17   **contemplative idiot** imbecile staring out vacantly
      Close keep close, hide

12 metal] *Malone;* Mettle *F;* Nettle *F2*   18 SD] *Capell subst.; Throws down a Letter / Theobald*

Lie thou there, for here comes the trout that must be   19
caught with tickling.   *Exit.*

Enter MALVOLIO.

MALVOLIO   'Tis but fortune, all is fortune. Maria once
told me she did affect me, and I have heard herself
come thus near, that should she fancy it should be one
of my complexion. Besides, she uses me with a more
exalted respect than anyone else that follows her. What   25
should I think on't?

SIR TOBY   Here's an overweening rogue.

FABIAN   O peace. Contemplation makes a rare turkey-cock
of him. How he jets under his advanced plumes.

SIR ANDREW   'Slight, I could so beat the rogue!   30

19–20 **the trout . . . tickling** Catching trout by stroking their gills in shallow water is proverbially easy, although Dent (T537) dates the figurative use of the proverb from this scene. Maria changes the animal metaphor from bears to fish.

20 SD Maria's exit at this point means that she does not witness the success of her plot (although she does see its effects in 3.4). Her unexplained absence turns the episode into an all-male affair.

21 **fortune** chance, i.e. it is mere chance that Olivia is an heiress and Malvolio an underling, and this state of affairs may change. Cf. Orsino's reflections on fickle *fortune* (= chance/riches) at 2.4.83–4; here too the secondary meaning of *fortune* as 'riches' is pertinent to Malvolio's ambitions.

22 **she** Olivia
  did affect me was attracted to me (*OED v.*[1] 2, giving this example). Malvolio already imagines himself as object of Olivia's desire before he reads the letter, thanks partly to Maria's skilful preparation of the trap.

22–3 **I . . . near** I have heard her as good as say

23 **fancy** fall in love (*OED v.* 8a, giving this example)

24 **complexion** colouring; temperament. Cf. 2.3.153, 2.4.26.

25 **exalted** high (*OED ppl. a.* 4b, first occurrence)
  follows her is in her service

26 **on't** of it

28 **Contemplation** thinking continuously about himself
  turkey-cock proverbial symbol of male self-importance, because it puffs itself up and, like the peacock, displays its tail-feathers (Dent, T612); cf. *H5* 5.1.14–15. Another animal metaphor for Malvolio: cf. 5, 6–7, 8, 19–20, 82, 102 and notes.

29 **jets** struts; cf. the description of the vain steward in *Faversham*, '[he] brauely iets it in his silken gowne' (*Faversham*, sig. A2[r]). Rubinstein, 137, detects a pun on 'jet' in the Elizabethan slang sense of 'come sexually', in association with *turkey-cock*.
  advanced plumes uplifted feathers. Onstage Malvolio sometimes sported a tall hat with a large feather in this scene.

30 **'Slight** by God's light: a mild oath

SIR TOBY   Peace, I say.

MALVOLIO   To be count Malvolio.

SIR TOBY   Ah, rogue!

SIR ANDREW   Pistol him, pistol him!

SIR TOBY   Peace, peace.   35

MALVOLIO   There is example for't: the Lady of the
    Strachy married the yeoman of the wardrobe.

SIR ANDREW   Fie on him, Jezebel!

FABIAN   O peace, now he's deeply in. Look how imagination
    blows him.   40

MALVOLIO   Having been three months married to her,

---

31 **Peace, I say** Cam[1] reattributes this line and *Peace, peace* at 35 to Fabian, who has already cried out *O peace!* at 28 (so that *I say* becomes an emphatic underlining), as he will do so again at 48, 54 and 62. It may be more comical, however, for the men to change roles, restraining each other in turn. Throughout the scene the eavesdroppers run the risk of being found out.

32 **count Malvolio** Malvolio's fantasy of social promotion is not limited by the law: he would not become count even if he were to marry Olivia.

34 **Pistol him** shoot him, or cudgel him with the butt of a pistol; *OED v.*[1] cites as first occurrence *The Famous History of Sir Thomas Wyatt* (1607) by Thomas Dekker and John Webster.

35 **Peace, peace** attributed by Cam[1] to Fabian; see 31n.

36 **example** precedent (*OED n.* 5)

36–7 **the Lady . . . wardrobe** This episode of marriage between a noblewoman and a servant, keeper of her clothes, may be invented, or it may be a theatrical in-joke. Sisson learned of one William Strachey, shareholder in the Children's company at the Blackfriars theatre in 1606, and one David Yeomans, the wardrobe master or 'tireman' of the company. A

more probable candidate as *yeoman* is Edward Kirkham, one of Strachey's partners in the Blackfriars company, who was granted a royal patent as 'yeoman or keeper' of 'our Great Wardrobe' in 1586 (Halliwell).

38 **Jezebel** a loose or 'painted' woman: originally, the biblical widow of King Ahab, who decked herself out in order to seduce Jehu and was condemned by the latter to be killed and eaten by dogs (2 Kings, 9.30–7). Sir Andrew is probably unaware of her story and gender, although Malvolio is compared to a loose woman at 2.3.75 and 77–8 (see notes). Malvolio, moreover, like Jezebel, is set upon by 'dogs' in this scene; cf. 8n.

39 **he's . . . in** i.e. he is quite lost in his own reveries
   imagination fancy (*OED* 4a, giving this example)

40 **blows him** swells him up. The metaphor probably alludes to flies depositing eggs in rotten flesh (*OED* blow *v.*[1] 28); cf. *LLL* 5.2.408–9, 'these summer flies / Have blown me full of maggot ostentation.'

41–78 Malvolio is *practising behaviour* (15); many actors here 'try out' the grand poses and gestures of Malvolio's future life as 'count'.

31, 35 SPs] *Fabian Cam*[1]   37 Strachy] *(Strachy)*; Stracci *Douai MS, Cam (Lloyd)*; Stratarch *(Hanmer)*; *Trachy / Warburton*; strachy *Steevens*[2]; Strozzi *(Collier)*; Strachey *Oxf*

sitting in my state –

SIR TOBY   O for a stone-bow to hit him in the eye!

MALVOLIO   Calling my officers about me, in my branched
velvet gown, having come from a day-bed where I have   45
left Olivia sleeping –

SIR TOBY   Fire and brimstone!

FABIAN   O peace, peace.

MALVOLIO   And then to have the humour of state, and
after a demure travail of regard – telling them I know   50
my place, as I would they should do theirs – to ask for
my kinsman Toby.

SIR TOBY   Bolts and shackles!

FABIAN   O peace, peace, peace! Now, now!

MALVOLIO   Seven of my people, with an obedient start,   55
make out for him. I frown the while and perchance
wind up my watch, or play with my [*touching his chain*]
– some rich jewel. Toby approaches, curtsies there to
me.

---

42 **state** canopied chair of state or throne
43 **stone-bow** crossbow used for shooting stones
44 **branched** ornamented with embroi-
dered branches
45 **day-bed** couch for resting in the day-
time; contrast *R3* 3.7.72 (Qq), 'He
is not lolling on a lewd day bed.' In
Posner's 2001 RSC production, Guy
Henry's Malvolio acted out his dream
by lying on a garden bench.
47 **Fire and brimstone!** Hell!: an oath
of biblical origin (Revelations, 19.20)
49 **humour of state** temperament and
behaviour of a great authority
50 **demure . . . regard** grave effort of
looking at them
travail F's 'trauaile' – as also at 1.2.21
and 5.1.159) – is usually modernized
to 'travel', in the sense of moving or
casting (eyes); the F spelling, retained

here, expresses Malvolio's ineffable
reluctance to look at his inferiors.
52 **my kinsman Toby** imagining Belch
as his relative and equal, Malvolio
familiarly drops the 'Sir' from Toby,
who underlines the offence at 65.
53 **Bolts and shackles** fetters (for
Malvolio in prison): an imprecation
55 **with . . . start** jumping obediently to
attention; *start* = sudden movement
56 **make out** set out (to fetch him) (*OED*
make *v.*[1] 93n, giving this example)
57 **watch** pocket watch. Originally a clock,
the *watch* in its modern sense was a
relatively recent term (*OED n.* 21a gives
LLL 3.1.187 as first occurrence) and
still a luxury item. *OED* (wind *v.*[1] 24e
(a)) also gives *wind up* as first occurrence
with reference to a watch or clock.
57–8 ***play . . . jewel** Collier's emendation
suggests that Malvolio suddenly inter-

42 state –] *Pope;* state. *F*   46 sleeping –] *Collier;* sleeping. *F*   50 travail] Travel *Rowe*   57 my] *om.*
F3   SD] *Cam*[1] *subst.*   58 – some] *Collier;* some *F*

240

SIR TOBY   Shall this fellow live?   60

FABIAN   Though our silence be drawn from us with cars,
    yet peace!

MALVOLIO   I extend my hand to him thus, quenching my
    familiar smile with an austere regard of control –

SIR TOBY   And does not Toby take you a blow o'the lips   65
    then?

MALVOLIO   Saying 'Cousin Toby, my fortunes, having
    cast me on your niece, give me this prerogative of
    speech' –

SIR TOBY   What, what?   70

MALVOLIO   'You must amend your drunkenness.'

SIR TOBY   Out, scab!

FABIAN   Nay, patience, or we break the sinews of our
    plot.

MALVOLIO   'Besides, you waste the treasure of your time   75
    with a foolish knight' –

SIR ANDREW   That's me, I warrant you.

MALVOLIO   'One Sir Andrew.'

SIR ANDREW   I knew 'twas I, for many do call me fool.

rupts his own train of thought, perhaps because he is about to refer to his steward's chain of office when he realizes that as 'count' he will no longer be wearing it, or because he cannot find a word grand enough to describe the *rich jewel* he imagines playing with. Onstage the actor at this point often toys with his chain; in Posner's 2001 RSC production Guy Henry's hand dangled uncertainly in front of his pelvis, as if he were about to *play with* himself.

61 **with cars** with carts or chariots: an allusion to a method of extorting information (rather than *silence*, as here) from prisoners by tying them to carts pulling in different directions; cf.

TGV 3.1.264–5, 'a team of horse shall not pluck that from me.'

63 **extend** hold out (*OED* 8, first occurrence)
   quenching suppressing

64 **familiar** intimate, friendly
   regard of control authoritarian gaze

65 **take . . . lips** give you a punch in the mouth

72 **scab** scoundrel: a common insult in Early Modern English

73 **break the sinews** disable, ruin: the risk of giving the game away

77 **That's me** In performance Sir Andrew usually sticks his head out at this point, running the risk of being discovered as well as named.

61 with cars] with cares *F2;* by th'ears *Hanmer;* with cables *(Tyrwhitt);* with cords *White*   64 control
–] *Cam¹;* controll. *F*   69 speech' –] *Rowe;* speech. *F*   76 knight' –] *Rowe;* knight. *F*

MALVOLIO [*Sees letter.*] What employment have we   80
    here?

FABIAN Now is the woodcock near the gin.

SIR TOBY O peace, and the spirit of humours intimate
    reading aloud to him.

MALVOLIO [*Takes up letter.*] By my life, this is my   85
    lady's hand. These be her very c's, her u's and her t's,
    and thus makes she her great P's. It is in contempt of
    question her hand.

SIR ANDREW Her c's, her u's and her t's. Why that?

MALVOLIO [*Reads.*]   *To the unknown beloved, this, and my*   90
    good wishes. Her very phrases! By your leave, wax. Soft –
    and the impressure her Lucrece, with which she uses
    to seal. 'Tis my lady. To whom should this be? [*Opens*
    letter.]

80 **employment** business (with reference to the letter)

82 **woodcock** a proverbially stupid bird, easy to snare in a net (cf. 'A springe to catch a woodcock', Dent, S788): a variation on the hunting metaphors used throughout this scene
gin snare

83 **the spirit . . . intimate** may the guiding genius of eccentricity suggest

86–7 **her very . . . P's** Malvolio unwittingly spells out a double innuendo. The first (c-u-t) is a sexual allusion, 'slang for the female genitals', according to Oxf[1], which quotes Webster's Induction to Marston's *The Malcontent*, 'the longest cut stil to draw an Apricoke' (Marston, 25–6, sig. A3ʳ). The second is an allusion to urination ('*P's* = piss', Partridge, 161; *great P's* = abundant urination), perhaps implying social ambition rather than an erotic suggestion, since witnessing the countess's *P's* might symbolize equality and intimacy, reserved for her husband. Steevens noted, disapprovingly, that in the inscription to the letter (90–1) 'there is neither a C, nor a P, to be found', but the absence of literal c's and p's only goes to emphasize Malvolio's state of self-deluding excitement.

87 **great** capital (*OED a.* 6b, giving this example)

87–8 **in . . . question** beyond all doubt (so much so as to make doubt itself absurd)

91 **Soft** gently (cf. 1.5.285), with a probable pun on *wax*; in some productions Malvolio touches the seal and discovers that the *wax* is indeed still *soft*.

92 **impressure** image (of the seal)
Lucrece seal-ring bearing the image of Lucretia, the model of chastity in Roman myth, probably in the act of stabbing herself after being raped by Tarquin. This is the subject of Shakespeare's poem *The Rape of Lucrece*.

92–3 **uses to seal** habitually seals

80 SD] *Collier; after 78 Cam*[1]   85 SD] *Collier; after 81 Rowe*   86, 89 c's . . . u's . . . t's] *(C's . . . V's . . . T's), Cam*[1] *subst.*   90 SD] *Capell; reads the superscription Cam*[1]   93, 95, 103, 140 SDs] *Capell*

FABIAN   This wins him, liver and all.

MALVOLIO [*Reads.*]

> *Jove knows I love,*   95
> > *But who?*
> *Lips, do not move,*
> > *No man must know.*

'No man must know.' What follows? The numbers altered. 'No man must know.' If this should be thee,   100
Malvolio?

SIR TOBY   Marry, hang thee, brock!

MALVOLIO [*Reads.*]

> *I may command where I adore,*
> > *But silence, like a Lucrece knife,*
> *With bloodless stroke my heart doth gore.*   105
> > *M.O.A.I. doth sway my life.*

FABIAN   A fustian riddle.

SIR TOBY   Excellent wench, say I.

MALVOLIO [*Reads.*]   *M.O.A.I. doth sway my life.* Nay, but first let me see, let me see, let me see.   110

FABIAN   What dish o'poison has she dressed him!

---

94 **liver and all** passionately. The liver is the seat of passion; cf. 1.1.36 and 2.4.98.

99–100 **The numbers altered** the metre has been changed

102 **brock** badger, proverbially malodorous (Dent, B679), with the further colloquial sense of 'rogue' (*OED n.*[1] 2, giving this example): another animal metaphor (cf. 5, 6–7, 8, 18–19, 28, 82)

104 *Lucrece knife* the 'harmful knife' with which Lucretia killed herself (*Luc* 1724); cf. 92n. *Lucrece* is a proper name used as a modifier (Hope, 1.2.6).

105 [silence] stabs my heart without loss of blood; unlike Lucretia's self-stabbing, after which 'the crimson blood / Circles her body in on every side' (*Luc*, 1738–39); *OED* bloodless 2, first occurrence

106, 109 *M.O.A.I* This *fustian riddle* (107) has proved over the decades to be as much a trap for critics as for Malvolio, giving rise to countless 'solutions': see pp. 15–16, for some of the many interpretations.

106 *sway* govern

107 **fustian** bombastic, inflated (*OED a.* 2)

111 **dressed him** prepared for him

95–8] *Capell; prose F*   99–101 The . . . Malvolio?] *Theobald; F lines* know, / *Maluolio?* / 103–6] *Capell; F lines* knife: / *life.* /   109–36 SDs] *this edn*   109 *doth . . . life*] *Capell;* doth sway my life *F*   111 dish o'] *(*dish a*), Cam;* dish of *F3;* a dish of *Rowe*

SIR TOBY   And with what wing the staniel checks at it!

MALVOLIO [*Reads.*]   *I may command where I adore.* Why, she may command me. I serve her, she is my lady. Why, this is evident to any formal capacity. There is   115 no obstruction in this. And the end – what should that alphabetical position portend? If I could make that resemble something in me! Softly – [*reading*] *M.O.A.I.*

SIR TOBY   O ay, make up that! He is now at a cold scent.   120

FABIAN   Sowter will cry upon't for all this, though it be as rank as a fox.

MALVOLIO   'M.' Malvolio. 'M' – why, that begins my name!

FABIAN   Did not I say he would work it out? The cur is   125 excellent at faults.

---

112 *staniel kestrel. F's 'stallion' may be, as *OED* (staniel) hypothesizes, a corrupt or dialectal variant of *staniel*. In any case, *wing* indicates a species of bird (cf. *woodcock*, 82), although in this case Malvolio is compared not to a hunted animal but to a bird of prey hovering over its victim.

checks at it turns to fly at it: a term from falconry (*OED* check *v.*[1] 6b, giving this example); cf. 'Checke, is when . . . birds comming in the view of the Hawke, shee forsaketh her natural flight to flie at them' (Latham, paras 1^r–1^v). Cf. 3.1.62.

115 **formal capacity** ordinary intelligence

116 **obstruction** obstacle

117 **alphabetical position** arrangement of letters

portend signify

120 **O ay** oh yes, with a pun on 'O, I', as the spelling in F underlines here and at 131 and 133 (see t.n.)

cold scent the point where the scent of the quarry becomes imperceptible to the hound

121–2 The hound will nevertheless sniff out the *cold scent* and bay at it, as if it stank like a fox's: i.e. Malvolio appears to have missed the clue, but will decipher it eventually and will cry out triumphantly (as indeed he does immediately at 123–4). This passage is often interpreted as meaning that Sowter-Malvolio, an incompetent hound, can only smell the obvious, whereas Fabian's comment in 125–6 suggests the opposite. 'As rank as a fox' was proverbial (Dent, F628). Malvolio becomes a dog again, as at 5.

121 **Sowter** a typical name for a hound (meaning literally 'cobbler'), often used of people as a term of abuse (*OED* souter 1b)

cry upon't yelp at the scent (*OED* cry *v.* 11b, giving this example)

for all this for all that, nevertheless

125–6 **The cur . . . faults** the hound is good at finding lost trails; *fault* is synonymous with *cold scent* (120; *OED* fault *n.* 8a). Cf. *VA* 694, 'The hot scent-snuffing hounds . . . have singled . . . the cold fault cleanly out.'

---

112 staniel] *Hanmer (*stanyel*); stallion F   116 this. And] *Collier;* this, and *F;* this – and *Rowe*   120 ay] *(I)*   123 Malvolio. 'M' –] *Oxf[1]; Maluolio, M. F*

MALVOLIO 'M.' But then there is no consonancy in
the sequel. That suffers under probation: 'A' should
follow, but 'O' does.

FABIAN And 'O' shall end, I hope.   130

SIR TOBY Ay, or I'll cudgel him and make him cry 'O!'

MALVOLIO And then 'I' comes behind.

FABIAN Ay, an you had any eye behind you, you might
see more detraction at your heels than fortunes before
you.   135

MALVOLIO [*Reads.*]   *M.O.A.I.* This simulation is not as
the former. And yet to crush this a little it would bow to
me, for every one of these letters are in my name. Soft,
here follows prose.

[*Reads.*] *If this fall into thy hand, revolve. In my stars*   140

127–8 **there . . . probation** there is no
logical consistency in what follows; that
(i.e. what follows) breaks down when
put to the test. Both *consonancy* and
probation are pseudo-logical or pseudo-
legal terms, which help to maintain
the self-important tone of Malvolio's
monologue. The absence of punctuation
in F – possibly due to lack of space, since
'sequel' ends a line – makes *that* govern
consonancy: i.e. there is no consistency
that stands up to investigation; this
renders *under* superfluous, while Rowe's
emendation restores its meaning.

130 **And . . . end** Johnson is surely right
in taking *O* to be the hangman's noose,
the *end* Fabian wishes for Malvolio.

133 **Ay . . . behind you** a pun on the
expression 'He has an eye behind'
(Dent, E236)
an if

134–5 **more . . . you** more disparagement
following you than the riches you are
pursuing: alluding to the comments
being made behind Malvolio's back

136 *M.O.A.I.* Actors frequently create comic business out of trying to
pronounce the word: in Judge's 1994
RSC production Desmond Barritt's
Malvolio emitted a feline 'miaow'.
simulation puzzle

136–7 **as the former** like the previous
puzzle (i.e. '*I may command where I
adore*', 103 and 113)

137 **crush** force

137–8 **bow to me** bend to form my
name; and/or indicate me, yield up its
meaning to me

138 **every . . . are** As often in Shakespeare,
the verb agrees here with the noun
letters because it is closer than the
subject pronoun *every one* (Blake,
Grammar, 6.1.1.6b).
Soft gently; cf. 91.

140 *revolve* reflect (*OED v.* 10, first
occurrence). On the various bits of
stage business actors use to accompany
this word, see pp. 129–30.

140–55 Malvolio reads the letter without
interruption, allowing the audience

---

128 sequel. That] *Rowe (*Sequel; that*);* sequell that *F*   131, 133 Ay] *(I)*   136 *M.O.A.I.*] *F2;*
M,O,A,I. F   140 *revolve.*] revolve. *Revolves but doesn't find answer then sits L. / Tree*   140–55 *In . . .
Unhappy*] *F3;* In . . . vnhappy *F*

I am above thee, but be not afraid of greatness. Some are
born great, some achieve greatness and some have greatness
thrust upon them. Thy fates open their hands: let thy blood
and spirit embrace them, and, to inure thyself to what
thou art like to be, cast thy humble slough and appear   145
fresh. Be opposite with a kinsman, surly with servants.
Let thy tongue tang arguments of state; put thyself into
the trick of singularity. She thus advises thee that sighs for

to hear it all. *TN* – together with *Ham* – is unusual in having three letters read aloud: cf. 3.4.143–65 and 5.1.297–305.

stars fortune, and hence the social rank that derives from it

141–3 *Some . . . them* This passage echoes Christ's speech on chastity and marriage to his disciples in Matthew, 19.12, which distinguishes between three kinds of chastity or celibacy: 'For there are some chaste, which are so borne . . . And there are some chaste, which be made chaste of me: And there be chaste, which haue made themselues chaste' (Bishops' Bible, 1568). The implication may be that Malvolio is doomed to remain chaste or celibate rather than become *great* by marrying Olivia. There may also be a veiled allusion here to the 'eunuch' topos (see 1.2.53n.): as John Astington notes, the Geneva and King James versions of the passage adopt the term 'eunuch' instead of 'chaste' ('For there are some Eunuches, which were so borne . . .'). Malvolio's humiliation by means of the letter can thus be read as 'a displaced gelding' (Astington, 26). See p. 60.

142 **born* Rowe's emendation of F's 'become' – an easy misreading of a posited copy form 'borne' (RP) – is clearly right, since the phrase is

repeated with *born* at 3.4.39 and again at 5.1.364.

143 *fates* This echoes Olivia's actual phraseology: cf. 'Fate, show thy force', 1.5.303.
    open their hands make you a generous offer

143–4 *blood and spirit* body and soul

144 *inure* accustom

145 *cast . . . slough* throw off your lowly status like a snake its skin; *slough* (pronounced 'sluff') is the outer or scarf skin shed by snakes and other reptiles (*OED n.*[2] 1): cf. *2H6*, 3.1.228–9, 'as the snake . . . / With shining checkered slough'. In Gielgud's 1955 production Laurence Olivier hesitated over the pronunciation of the word, suggesting Malvolio's social insecurity (Pennington, 17).

146 *opposite with* hostile towards (*OED a.* 3a, giving this example)

147 *tang* ring out like a bell (*OED v.*[2] 2, giving this example)
    arguments of state important political topics (cf. Malvolio's response at 157)

147–8 *put . . . singularity* take on the affected mannerisms of eccentricity

148 *trick* peculiar habit (*OED n.* 7)
    singularity conspicuously unusual behaviour (*OED* 9a). Cf. 'it comes too neare singularitie, and a desire to be noted' (Cornwallis, sig. B4[r]).

142 *born*] Douai MS, Rowe; become F   *achieve*] F2 (atcheeve); atcheeues F   143 *them*] F4; em F

thee. Remember who commended thy yellow stockings and
wished to see thee ever cross-gartered – I say remember. Go   150
to, thou art made if thou desir'st to be so; if not, let me see
thee a steward still, the fellow of servants and not worthy
to touch Fortune's fingers. Farewell. She that would alter
services with thee,

                                    The Fortunate Unhappy.   155
Daylight and champaign discovers not more. This is
open. I will be proud, I will read politic authors, I will

149 *yellow stockings* These may have
been, as Oxf[1] suggests, 'a garish
fashion associated with bachelors' in
1602, but it is more probable that they
were hopelessly *out* of fashion: hence
the jest. Thomas Overbury in 1615
describes the behaviour of a presumably uncouth country gentleman: 'If
he goe to court, it is in yellow stockings' (Overbury, sig. D1ʳ). *Tarlton's
News*, sometimes attributed to Robert
Armin, in 1590 describes how a husband, wrongly persuaded of his wife's
adultery, 'resolues with the crue of
the yellow hosde companions, that
Mulier . . . is a word of unconstancie'
(*Tarlton's News*, 23).

150 *cross-gartered* i.e. wearing what
Junius in 1585 defines as '*Fasciae
crurales* . . . Hose garters going
acrosse, or overthwart, both aboue
and beneath the knee' (Junius, 168;
see Fig. 15); the early date of this
gloss makes it probable that they, like
yellow stockings (149), had become
old-fashioned by 1602 (see 149n.).
The description of a 'footman' as
'more upright then any gross gartered
gentleman-usher' (Overbury, sig. K3ʳ)
probably refers back to Malvolio, as
does the proverb 'To wear yellow
stockings and cross-garters' (Dent,
S868), which testifies to the success
of this scene and of 3.4 onstage.

150–1 *Go to* 'Come on!': a common
catchphrase of exhortation or encouragement (*OED* go v. 93)

151 *thou art made* your fortune is made;
cf. *MND* 4.2.17–18, 'we had all been
made men'.

152 *fellow* equal

153–4 *alter services* change places (i.e.
between mistress and servant)

155 *The Fortunate Unhappy* she who
is blessed by wealth but unfulfilled
in love

156 **champaign** chàmpaign: open
country (from Old French *cham-
paigne*). The *ch* is pronounced as in
'church'.
  discovers not more could not make
this more plain; the meaning of the
letter is as clear as daylight

157 **open** perfectly clear
  politic authors writers concerned
with political doctrine or *arguments
of state* (147). The adjective was particularly associated in early modern
England with Machiavelli, taken to
be an amoral apologist for the cul-
tivation of power and self-advance-
ment: e.g. 'Secretarie *Machiavell*, a
politick not much affected to any
Religion' (Nashe, *Pasquill*, sig. B1ʳ).
Malvolio appears willing to abandon
his 'Puritan' principles in the interests of self-promotion; cf. 1.3.74,
2.3.142 and note.

155–6 *The . . .* Daylight] *Capell;* tht fortunate vnhappy daylight *F; The fortunate and happy.* Daylight
/ *Hanmer*   156 champaign] *Dyce (* champain*);* champian *F;* champion *F3*

baffle Sir Toby, I will wash off gross acquaintance, I
will be point-device the very man. I do not now fool
myself to let imagination jade me; for every reason   160
excites to this, that my lady loves me. She did commend
my yellow stockings of late, she did praise my leg
being cross-gartered, and in this she manifests herself
to my love and with a kind of injunction drives me
to these habits of her liking. I thank my stars, I am   165
happy. I will be strange, stout, in yellow stockings and
cross-gartered even with the swiftness of putting on.
Jove and my stars be praised! Here is yet a postscript.
[*Reads.*] *Thou canst not choose but know who I am. If thou
entertain'st my love, let it appear in thy smiling – thy smiles*   170
become thee well. Therefore in my presence still smile, dear
my sweet, I prithee. Jove, I thank thee. I will smile, I will
do everything that thou wilt have me.   *Exit.*

158 **baffle** treat with contempt (*OED v.*
  2); literally, degrade a perjured knight
  (*OED v.* 1) Malvolio's verb is turned
  against him at 5.1.363.
  wash . . . acquaintance rid myself of
  vulgar company; *gross* also alludes to
  Sir Toby's obesity.
159 **point-device . . . man** in every
  detail the man described in the letter
160 **jade** deceive (like a *jade* or wily old
  horse that throws its rider)
161 **excites** leads
161–3 **She . . . cross-gartered** This is evidently invented or imagined by Malvolio
  – unless he is referring to the letter –
  since at 193–4 Maria notes that Olivia
  abhors yellow and *detests* cross-gartering.
165 **habits** clothes; modes of behaviour
  (*OED n.* 4)
166 **happy** fortunate in love; contrast *The
  Fortunate Unhappy* (155).
  strange distant, aloof (*OED a.* 6); cf.
  RJ 2.2.102, 'I should have been more
  strange, I must confess.'

stout proud (from Old French *estout*,
  fierce); cf. *2H6* 1.1.187, 'As stout and
  proud as he were Lord of all'.
167 **putting on** (i.e. of the clothes)
168 **Jove** Since Malvolio is determined
  to become a lover and an unprincipled
  'Machiavellian' (157n.), his invocation
  of the pagan god of erotic conquest is
  apt enough.
  postscript In Carroll's 2002 Middle
  Temple production Oliver Cotton's
  Malvolio exited after *praised!*, and then
  returned to read the *postscript*, by way
  of an afterthought.
170 *entertain'st* accept (*OED v.* 14)
171 *still* always
  **dear* F's 'deero' is almost certainly
  a misprint – presumably due to 'foul
  case' error – although Daniel, 43, and
  some editors have justified it as 'dear,
  O'.
172 **smile** The actor may actually try
  out his smile, as in Posner's 2001 RSC
  production.

169 SD] *Collier*   171 *well.*] well; *looking out to audience gives extravagant smirk / Tree   dear*] *F2;
deero F;* dear, O *Cam¹*

FABIAN   I will not give my part of this sport for a pension
    of thousands to be paid from the Sophy.   175
SIR TOBY   I could marry this wench for this device –
SIR ANDREW   So could I too.
SIR TOBY   And ask no other dowry with her but such
    another jest.

Enter MARIA.

SIR ANDREW   Nor I neither.   180
FABIAN   Here comes my noble gull-catcher.
SIR TOBY [*to Maria*]   Wilt thou set thy foot o'my neck?
SIR ANDREW   Or o'mine either?
SIR TOBY   Shall I play my freedom at tray-trip and become
    thy bondslave?   185
SIR ANDREW   I'faith, or I either?
SIR TOBY   Why, thou hast put him in such a dream that
    when the image of it leaves him he must run mad.
MARIA   Nay, but say true, does it work upon him?

---

175 **thousands** i.e. (presumably) of ducats
from by
Sophy the Shah of Persia: a probable
allusion to the claim by Sir Anthony
Shirley and his brothers to have
received rich gifts, including 16,000
pistolets (cf. 'a pension of thousands'),
during an embassy to Shah Abbas the
Great in 1599, an episode recounted in
two pamphlets, *A True Report of Sir
Anthony Shirley's Journey*, 1600, and *A
New and Large Discourse of the Travels
of Sir Anthony Shirley*, 1601. The
Sophy is mentioned again at 3.4.272.
176 This is virtually a declaration of
intent by Sir Toby, who will indeed
marry Maria at the end of the play
(cf. 5.1.358).
177 Sir Andrew's habit of slavishly echoing Sir Toby creates the interesting

prospect of a *ménage à trois* between
them and Maria.
181 **gull-catcher** trapper of fools. The
expression imitates the more familiar
'cony-catcher'.
182 i.e. I am yours, do what you will with
me. Onstage, Sir Toby at this point
may bow down (as in Carroll's 2002
Middle Temple production) or even
(as in Posner's 2001 RSC production,
together with Sir Andrew) throw himself prostrate on the ground.
183, 186 **either** likewise
184 **play** wager
tray-trip a dice game in which one
must throw a three (*tray*) to win
188 **when . . . him** when he wakes up
from his dream. The same alternative between dreaming and madness is
posed by Sebastian at 4.1.60.

176 device –] *Dyce;* deuice. *F*   182 SD] *Oxf*

SIR TOBY   Like aqua vitae with a midwife.   190

MARIA   If you will then see the fruits of the sport, mark
   his first approach before my lady. He will come to her
   in yellow stockings – and 'tis a colour she abhors – and
   cross-gartered – a fashion she detests – and he will
   smile upon her, which will now be so unsuitable to her   195
   disposition, being addicted to a melancholy as she is,
   that it cannot but turn him into a notable contempt. If
   you will see it, follow me.

SIR TOBY   To the gates of Tartar, thou most excellent
   devil of wit.   200

SIR ANDREW   I'll make one too.   *Exeunt.*

3.1   *Enter* VIOLA *[as Cesario] and* FESTE
                 [playing on pipe and tabor].

VIOLA   Save thee, friend, and thy music. Dost thou live by
   thy tabor?

190 **acqua . . . midwife** spirits, such as
brandy, used by midwives, in theory
to revive their patients but in practice
to console themselves; cf. *RJ* 3.2.88,
4.5.16.
193 **a . . . abhors** In Barton's 1969 RSC
production, everyone turned at this
point to look at David Warner's Sir
Andrew, dressed from head to toe in
yellow (M. Billington, xx).
197 **turn . . . contempt** make him the
notorious object of disgrace; *OED* contempt *n.* 3 gives as first occurrence in
this sense the 1611 Authorized Bible.
199 **Tartar** hell. In classical mythology
Tartarus is the deepest part of the
underworld; cf. *H5* 2.2.123, 'He might
return to vasty Tartar back.'
devil clever rogue (*OED n.* 4b, first
occurrence)
201 **I'll be one** of the spectators. The
joke here may be that Sir Andrew, lost
as usual in the repartee, unwittingly

undertakes to make a *notable contempt*
(197) of himself, a promise he triumphantly fulfils.
3.1 This scene, which sees the disguised
Viola continuously present onstage, is
structured primarily on her duologues
with Feste and Olivia. While the first
is devoted to verbal fooling and to the
question of the reliability of language,
the second is dominated by Olivia's
increasingly explicit declaration of
love for Cesario. Pope locates the scene
in '*Olivia's Garden*'.
0.2 *Collier[2] expanded F's '*Enter Viola
and Clowne*' to make sense of Viola's
opening reference to Feste's *tabor* (2), a
small drum hanging from neck or belt,
conventionally played by jesters. Viola's
thy music (1) may mean that Feste is also
playing his pipe, holding it in one hand
while beating the drum with the other.
1 **Save thee** God save thee
   live by make your living by (playing)

201 SD] *(Exeunt. Finis Actus secundus)*   **3.1**] *(Actus Tertius, Scaena prima.)*   0.1 as Cesario] *Munro
subst.*   FESTE] *Munro; Clowne F   0.2*] *Powell MS subst., Collier[2]; with a tabor / Malone*   2 thy] the *F2*

FESTE   No, sir, I live by the church.

VIOLA   Art thou a churchman?

FESTE   No such matter, sir. I do live by the church, for I   5
do live at my house, and my house doth stand by the
church.

VIOLA   So thou mayst say the king lies by a beggar if a
beggar dwell near him, or the church stands by thy
tabor if thy tabor stand by the church.   10

FESTE   You have said, sir. To see this age! A sentence is but
a cheverel glove to a good wit: how quickly the wrong
side may be turned outward.

VIOLA   Nay, that's certain. They that dally nicely with
words may quickly make them wanton.   15

FESTE   I would therefore my sister had had no name, sir.

VIOLA   Why, man?

---

3 **live by** live next to

4 **churchman** clergyman. Viola's question is ironically superfluous, since Feste is presumably wearing jester's motley.

5, 6 **do**, **doth** These are not emphatic forms but parts of normal sentence structure in Early Modern English.

8 **lies by** dwells near

9 **stands by** is maintained by

11 **You . . . sir** I take note (of your ability in punning): a proverbial phrase (Dent, S118.1)
To . . . age! What a time we live in!

11–13 **A sentence . . . outward** Playing on the proverb 'To turn the wrong side out' (Dent, S431.1), Feste introduces the topic, much debated in Shakespeare's day, of the relationship between linguistic sign and referent (or words and things), and thus the reliability of language as a representation of truth (cf. 12n., 14–15n., 18–19n., 19–20n., 23n.; see pp. 86–7).

12 **cheverel** made of kid leather (*OED n.*[1] 2, giving this example), 'noted for its pliancy and capability of being stretched' (*OED n.*[1] 1). Proverbially, this material was associated with lack of moral integrity (Dent, C608), whereas in Feste's version it is language that becomes malleable, being – as this comedy demonstrates – all too readily subverted.

12–13 **the wrong side** the inside (proverbial: Dent, S431.1; see 11–13n.)

14–15 **They . . . wanton** Those who toy daintily with words render their meanings equivocal. Feste's unstable sign–referent relationship (11–13) is turned against him: words may be directly contaminated by their users, especially by punning clowns. Viola equivocates in turn, however: *dally* means idiomatically to indulge in sexual games (as in *R3* 3.7.74: 'Not dallying with a brace of courtesans') and *wanton* = unchaste (*OED a.* 2).

---

5 sir.] *Munro;* sir, *F*   church, for] *Staunton;* Church: For *F*   8 king] *F2;* Kings *F*   lies] lives *Collier*[2] *(Capell)*   12 cheverel] *(*cheu'rill*)*

FESTE   Why, sir, her name's a word, and to dally with that
     word might make my sister wanton. But indeed words
     are very rascals, since bonds disgraced them.   20

VIOLA   Thy reason, man?

FESTE   Troth sir, I can yield you none without words, and
     words are grown so false I am loath to prove reason
     with them.

VIOLA   I warrant thou art a merry fellow, and car'st for   25
     nothing.

FESTE   Not so, sir, I do care for something; but in my
     conscience, sir, I do not care for you. If that be to care
     for nothing, sir, I would it would make you invisible.

VIOLA   Art not thou the Lady Olivia's fool?   30

FESTE   No indeed, sir, the Lady Olivia has no folly. She
     will keep no fool, sir, till she be married, and fools
     are as like husbands as pilchards are to herrings – the
     husband's the bigger. I am indeed not her fool, but her
     corrupter of words.   35

18–19 **her name's . . . wanton** Feste playfully suggests a direct link between word and thing: unchaste name, unchaste referent (his *sister*). There may be a pun on *wanton* and 'want one'.

19–20 **words . . . them** either, words have lost their honour since legally binding written contracts replaced oral agreements (cf. the proverb 'An honest man's word is as good as his bond': Dent, M458); or, words have been made disreputable by being too often broken (through unfulfilled bonds), with a probable pun on *bonds* in the sense of 'shackles', as if words had been imprisoned following their downfall.

23 **words . . . false** Linguistic scepticism was increasingly prominent in Shakespeare's time, and found its most authoritative expression in Montaigne: 'the name, is neither part of the thing nor of substance: it is a stranger-piece ioyned to the thing, and from it' (Montaigne, 350).

27–9 **I do . . . nothing** The *something* that Feste cares for is money; but he also implies that Cesario is *nothing*, that he is a cypher, a zero: a possible allusion to his ambiguous gender as well as his social status. There may be a degree of hostility in the clown's gibe, since Cesario is his successful 'rival' as go-between between Orsino and Olivia.

29 **make you invisible** an invitation to Cesario to disappear from the scene

31 **folly** foolishness, madness

32–3 **fools . . . herrings** i.e. fools and husbands are akin in their folly, but husbands are the bigger fools. Pilchards and herrings are of the same family, but herrings can grow larger.

35 **corrupter of words** As a sophisticated court fool, Feste's main professional role is precisely that of 'dallier' with language rather than exponent of simpler forms of jesting.

---

33 pilchards] *(*Pilchers*), Capell*

VIOLA   I saw thee late at the Count Orsino's.

FESTE   Foolery, sir, does walk about the orb like the sun,
it shines everywhere. I would be sorry, sir, but the fool
should be as oft with your master as with my mistress.
I think I saw your wisdom there.   40

VIOLA   Nay, an thou pass upon me, I'll no more with thee.
Hold, there's expenses for thee. [*Gives coin.*]

FESTE   Now Jove in his next commodity of hair send thee
a beard.

VIOLA   By my troth I'll tell thee, I am almost sick for one,   45
though I would not have it grow on my chin. Is thy lady
within?

FESTE   Would not a pair of these have bred, sir?

---

36 **late** lately

37–8 **Foolery . . . everywhere** proverbial: 'The sun shines upon all alike'
(Dent, S985). Feste is alluding to his
own coming and going (like Cesario)
between both houses, but is also implying that we are all fools, a thought he
expands on at 38–40.

37 **orb** earth (*OED n.*[1] 2a, giving this
example)
like the sun a reference to the
Ptolemaic theory, still current in the
early modern period, according to
which the sun revolved around the
earth

38–9 **I would . . . mistress** i.e. I ought to
apologize, were it not for the fact that
it is the duty of the fool (or folly) to
be as much with your master as with
my mistress, since Orsino is as much a
fool as Olivia.

38 **would** should
but were it not that

40 Feste ironically extends his 'all fools'
theme (37–8) to Cesario, who, like him,
is no more than a hired attendant (cf.
142 and n.), and whose *wisdom* is thus
mere foolishness.

41 **an** if
pass upon me make a thrust against

me (a fencing metaphor, anticipating
the 'duel' scene: cf. 3.4.268n.). In *Ham*
5.2.280–2, *pass* is similarly found in
association with *dally* (14, 18) and
wanton (15, 19): 'you do but dally. / I
pray you pass with your best violence.
/ I am sure you make a wanton of me.'
A secondary meaning is 'pass judgement on me'; cf. *MM* 2.1.23, 'thieves
do pass on thieves.'

42 **expenses** reimbursement, payment
(*OED* 3c, giving this example)

43 **commodity** supply; cf. *1H4*
1.2.82–3.

43–4 **send . . . beard** Feste seems to
come close to seeing through Viola's
disguise; he may be taunting Cesario
for his lack of virility, as well as for his
(and the boy actor's) youth.

46 **I would . . . chin** (1) with emphasis
on *my*: Viola would like to possess
Orsino's beard (and thus him), rather
than one of her own; (2) with emphasis
on *chin*: Partridge, 63, suggests an allusion to the *beard* of pubic hair.

48 i.e. why not a second coin, which,
together with the first, might produce yet another, their 'child'? Feste
tries out another line to get Orsino to
double his tip at 5.1.26–30.

42 SD] *Hanmer subst.*

VIOLA   Yes, being kept together and put to use.

FESTE   I would play Lord Pandarus of Phrygia, sir, to   50
bring a Cressida to this Troilus.

VIOLA   I understand you, sir, 'tis well begged. [*Gives another coin.*]

FESTE   The matter, I hope, is not great, sir, begging but a
beggar: Cressida was a beggar. My lady is within, sir.
I will conster to them whence you come. Who you are   55
and what you would are out of my welkin. I might say
'element', but the word is overworn.   *Exit.*

VIOLA

This fellow is wise enough to play the fool,

---

49 **put to use** invested in order to produce interest (a form of 'usury'); also, brought together to reproduce.

50–1 **Lord . . . Troilus** Pandarus, Cressida's uncle, acted as go-between in Troilus' wooing of her (see *TC*). Feste is using his learning merely to beg another coin.

50 **Phrygia** an ancient country of Asia Minor, to which Troy supposedly belonged. Cf. 2.2.41n.

53–4 **The . . . ¹beggar** The question/tip, I fear, is of no great importance/amount, since it was begged of a beggar. Feste seems to be implying that there is not much social difference between him and Cesario, since both have to 'beg' for service to their superiors. He may also be alluding to the definition of players – which in reality they both are – as 'beggars' by hostile authorities and by Puritan commentators such as Philip Stubbes: 'for go they never so brave, yet are they counted and taken but for beggars' (Stubbes, 92ᵛ).

54 **Cressida . . . ¹beggar** In Henryson and other versions of the story, including Dekker and Chettle's lost play *Troilus and Cressida* (1599), the heroine becomes a leper and beggar, a fate spared her in Shakespeare's version.

Perhaps another (unwitting?) allusion to Cesario's real gender (see 27–9, 43–4 and notes).

55 **conster to them** explain to those in the house (see *within*, 54); *conster* is a variant of construe (*OED* construe 9, sole occurrence).

56 **welkin** sky (from Old English *weolcen*). By Shakespeare's time the word had become an affected archaism, used only for a rhetorical flourish, as in 'makes the Welkin cracke' (Marlowe, *Tamburlaine*, part 1, 4.2.45, sig. D4ʳ). Shakespeare makes fun of it through the pedant Holofernes in *LLL*: '*caelo*, the sky, the welkin, the heaven' (*LLL* 4.2.5).

57 **'element'** sky or air (*OED n.* 10b); a modish literary term that had been over-abused in recent years, as Feste's comment suggests. Sidney uses it with this meaning: 'As soone as the morning had taken a full possession of the Element' (Sidney, *Arcadia*, 446). Dekker pokes fun at it: 'Let the element alone, 'tis out a thy reach' (Dekker, *Satiromastix*, sig. M1ᵛ). Malvolio uses the word pompously at 3.4.120.

58–66 Viola's praise for Feste's clowning skills unites her with Olivia (see 1.5.69–92): perhaps a compliment to

---

52 SD] *Collier²* subst.   55 conster] construe *Douai MS, Boswell–Malone*   come.] *Mahood;* come, *F*

And to do that well craves a kind of wit.
He must observe their mood on whom he jests,   60
The quality of persons and the time,
And, like the haggard, check at every feather
That comes before his eye. This is a practice
As full of labour as a wise man's art;
For folly that he wisely shows is fit,   65
But wise men, folly-fallen, quite taint their wit.

Enter SIR TOBY *and* [SIR] ANDREW.

SIR TOBY   Save you, gentleman.
VIOLA   And you, sir.
SIR ANDREW   *Dieu vous garde, monsieur.*

the actor Robert Armin (Cam[1]) that may echo his own pamphlet: 'A merry man is often thought unwise; / Yet mirth in modesty's loude [i.e. loved] of the wise' (Armin, *Quips*, sig. C1[r]; Mahood).

58 **wise . . . fool** The saying 'No man can play the fool so well as the wise man' (Dent, M321) is alluded to by Shakespeare only here.

59 **wit** intelligence

60 **their mood** the mood of those

61 **quality** character

62 **haggard** wild (female) hawk, caught as an adult and thus difficult to train; cf. Hero on Beatrice in *MA* 3.1.36–7, 'Her spirits are as coy and wild, / As haggards of the rock.'

62–3 **check . . . eye** react to (literally, start at) everything he perceives. Like *haggard* (62), *check* is a term from falconry; cf. 2.5.112n.

62 **feather** bird (*OED n.* 4, first occurrence); a rhetorical figure: synecdoche (part for the whole)

63 **practice** profession

64 **As . . . labour** requiring as much skill and effort

65 The foolery that he expresses with discretion is to the point; cf. Armin, *Quips*, quoted in 58–66n.

66 **wise . . . wit** i.e. supposedly sensible men who behave foolishly quite spoil their reputation for intelligence: Malvolio's fate in this play.

taint spoil; literally, contaminate (*OED v.*[1] 4a). This is a thematic word in the play, recurring with various meanings: cf. 3.4.13, 128, 353; 5.1.134, 351 and notes.

69–70 *F's French spelling, since it involves both speakers, is presumably an error of transcription and does not necessarily indicate bad pronunciation. Indeed, despite Sir Andrew's admission that he has not studied *the tongues* (1.3.90), F's '*vou gard*' may be taken as a phonetic rendering of fairly good French, although actors often provide him with an atrocious accent. The fact that Viola responds promptly in French is an indication of her 'gentle' status.

62 And] Not *Rann (Johnson)*   64 wise man's] *(Wise-mans)*, *Hanmer*   66 wise . . . taint] *Capell*; wisemens folly falne, quite taint *F*; wise men's folly shewn, quite taints *Hanmer*; wise men's folly, fall'n, quite taints *Malone*   66.1 SIR] *Rowe*   69 vous garde] *Rowe*; vou guard *F*

VIOLA *Et vous aussi; votre serviteur.*   70

SIR ANDREW I hope, sir, you are, and I am yours.

SIR TOBY Will you encounter the house? My niece is
desirous you should enter if your trade be to her.

VIOLA I am bound to your niece, sir – I mean, she is the
list of my voyage.   75

SIR TOBY Taste your legs, sir, put them to motion.

VIOLA My legs do better understand me, sir, than I
understand what you mean by bidding me taste my
legs.

SIR TOBY I mean to go, sir, to enter.   80

VIOLA I will answer you with gait and entrance.

Enter OLIVIA *and* MARIA.

But we are prevented. [*to Olivia*] Most excellent
accomplished lady, the heavens rain odours on you.

SIR ANDREW [*aside*] That youth's a rare courtier; 'rain
odours' – well!   85

---

72 **encounter** 'Bombastically used for:
To go to, approach (nonce-use)', *OED*
v. 6, sole occurrence

74 **bound to** bound for, with a possible
pun on 'obliged to', alluding to Olivia's
'kind' invitation to enter.

75 **list** destination: literally, boundary
(*OED n.*³ 8)

76 **Taste** try (from Middle English *tasten*,
to touch, *OED v.* 2). Cf. Hotspur in
1H4 4.1.119, 'Come, let me taste my
horse.'

77–8 **understand . . . understand** support (i.e. stand under), 77; compre-
hend, 78. The 'under-stand' pun is,
as it were, a standing Shakespearean
joke: cf. Launce in *TGV* 2.5.31, 'Why,
stand under and understand is all one.'
Cesario understands (or has learned)

the verb *taste* well enough to use it with
the same sense of 'try' at 3.4.238.

81 **with . . . entrance** by walking and
going in (*OED* entrance 1a, first
occurrence): a deliberately affected
paraphrase of Sir Toby's *go . . . to enter*
(80), with a pun on 'gate' (Kökeritz,
109), through which Viola says she
will enter; in the event, the immediate stage *entrance* of Olivia makes it
unnecessary for her to move.

82 **prevented** anticipated

83 **the heavens rain** may the heavens
rain (subjunctive)

84 **rare** fine, splendid (*OED a.*¹ 6a)
courtier habitué of Orsino's court
(*OED* courtier¹ 1b, giving this example); wooer (*OED* courtier¹ 2)

85 **well!** a good phrase

---

70 *vous aussi*] *Pope; vouz ousie F; vouz ausie F2   votre serviteur*] *Capell; vostre seruiture F; vostre serviteur
/ Rowe*³   81 *gait*] *(gate), Capell*   81.1] *Mahood; after* preuented *82 F*   MARIA] *Rowe; Gentlewoman F*
82 SD] *Mahood*   84 SD] *Capell subst.*

VIOLA   My matter hath no voice, lady, but to your own
  most pregnant and vouchsafed ear.
SIR ANDREW [*aside*]   'Odours', 'pregnant' and 'vouchsafed'
  – I'll get 'em all three all ready.
OLIVIA   Let the garden door be shut and leave me to my   90
  hearing.   [*Exeunt Sir Toby, Sir Andrew and Maria.*]
  Give me your hand, sir.
VIOLA
  My duty, madam, and most humble service.
OLIVIA
  What is your name?
VIOLA
  Cesario is your servant's name, fair princess.   95

86 **My . . . voice** what I have to say cannot
  be spoken
  but except
87 **pregnant** receptive, ready: an almost
  exclusively Shakespearean use (*OED
  a.*² 3d, first occurrence); cf. *Ham*
  3.2.57, 'And crook the pregnant hinges
  of the knee.'
  vouchsafed kindly granted, well
  disposed
89 **I'll . . . ready** I'll learn all three by
  heart, to use on a suitable occasion
90 **garden door** door in the garden wall.
  This suggests that Olivia's imminent
  conversation with Viola takes place
  in a *hortus conclusus* or walled garden.
  Originally conceived as a symbol of
  the soul – 'A garden well locked is my
  sister, my spouse' (Song of Solomon,
  4.12) – the *hortus* was fashionable in
  the Renaissance as a space for private
  exchange.
90–1 **leave . . . hearing** let me alone
  to listen (to Cesario); leave me to my

audience. The term *hearing* has legal
connotations, as in *MM* 2.1.133–4,
'I'll . . . leave you to the hearing of
the cause' – although it is not clear
whether it is Cesario or Olivia who is
on trial.
91 SD In Posner's 2001 RSC production, Christopher Good's Sir Andrew,
before exiting, lingered, looked wist-
fully at Olivia and tried several times
to say something, but failed.
92–5 Olivia's taking of Viola's hand is
ambiguous: it is both an act of courtesy and the boldest move so far in her
attempted seduction. Viola responds
with defensive formality, in some productions kneeling and kissing Olivia's
hand.
93 **service** respect (*OED* 9a, first occurrence)
95 **fair princess** Cesario flatteringly
exaggerates Olivia's rank, thereby
underlining the social gulf separating
them.

88 SD] *this edn; to Sir Toby Oxf*   89 three all ready] *Malone;* three already *F;* three ready *F3*   ready.]
ready. *writing in his table-book. / Collier*³   91 SD] *Rowe*

OLIVIA

My servant, sir? 'Twas never merry world
Since lowly feigning was called compliment.
You're servant to the Count Orsino, youth.

VIOLA

And he is yours, and his must needs be yours.
Your servant's servant is your servant, madam.　　　100

OLIVIA

For him, I think not on him. For his thoughts,
Would they were blanks rather than filled with me.

VIOLA

Madam, I come to whet your gentle thoughts
On his behalf.

OLIVIA　　　　　　　O by your leave, I pray you;
I bade you never speak again of him.　　　　　　105
But would you undertake another suit,
I had rather hear you to solicit that
Than music from the spheres.

VIOLA　　　　　　　　　　　　Dear lady –

OLIVIA

Give me leave, beseech you. I did send,

---

96 **'Twas . . . world** things have never
been the same; a proverbial expression
(Dent, W878.I). The proverb was put
to ideological use (pertinent to this
comedy) in Throckmorton's 'Martin
Marprelate' *Dialogue*, 'Papist It was
neuer merry worlde since there was
so many puritans' (Throckmorton,
sig. D2ʳ); and to 'class' use (likewise
appropriate) in *2H6* 4.2.7–9, 'It was
never merry world in England since
gentlemen came up.'
97 **lowly feigning** servile hypocrisy
99 **his** what is his
102 **blanks** empty sheets of paper; cf.

2.4.110n.
103 **whet** predispose (literally, sharpen)
104 **by . . . you** Olivia refuses, politely but
impatiently, to hear Orsino's suit.
106 **suit** supplication
107 **solicit** petition (*OED v.* 2); seduce
(*OED v.* 4b). Cf. *MA* 2.1.60–2, 'if the
Prince do solicit you in that kind, you
know your answer.'
108 **music . . . spheres** a Platonic concept (*Republic*, 617b–d; Plato, 2.495)
widely current in Shakespeare's day.
Cf. Cleopatra on Antonio, 'his voice
was propertied / As all the tuned
spheres' (*AC* 5.2.82–3).

---

97 compliment] *(complement)*　　98 You're] *(y'are)*　　108 lady –] *Theobald;* Lady. *F*　　109 beseech]
I beseech *F3*

After the last enchantment you did here,   110
A ring in chase of you. So did I abuse
Myself, my servant and, I fear me, you.
Under your hard construction must I sit,
To force that on you in a shameful cunning
Which you knew none of yours. What might you
    think?   115
Have you not set mine honour at the stake
And baited it with all th'unmuzzled thoughts
That tyrannous heart can think? To one of your
    receiving
Enough is shown: a cypress, not a bosom,
Hides my heart. So let me hear you speak.   120

VIOLA

    I pity you.

---

110 **enchantment** continues the 'Platonic' compliment to Cesario's eloquence: the music of the spheres supposedly exerted a magical influence. This is possibly an echo of Belleforest's version of the story ('tu *m'as enchantée*'; Ard[2], xlii).

111 **abuse** misuse, wrong

113 **hard construction** severe judgement

114 **To force** for having imposed

115 **none of yours** did not belong to you

116–17 This elaborate bear-baiting metaphor is part of the recurrent discourse on blood sports in the comedy; cf. 2.3.174; 2.5.6–7, 8–9, 19–20; 3.4.133–4 and notes. Here Olivia is the bear-victim, Cesario's cruel thoughts the persecuting hounds.

116 **set . . . stake** tied my honour to a post (like a bear); cf. *JC* 4.1.48–9, 'we are at the stake, / And bayed about with many enemies.'

117 **baited it** attacked it with dogs

unmuzzled unrestrained, free (to attack my heart)

118–20 **To . . . heart** i.e. to someone as perceptive as you, no more need be said, since my feelings are quite transparent

118 **receiving** perceptiveness

119 **cypress** piece of transparent Cyprus gauze – so called because traditionally imported from the island (*OED* cypress[3] 1a) – associated (when black, as presumably here) with mourning. Cf. 2.4.52n.
    bosom breast; the part of the dress that covers the breast (*OED n.* 3a). Cf. *MND* 2.2.104, 'That through thy bosom makes me see thy heart'; with a possible allusion to the male actor, who has literally *not a bosom*; cf. 1.3.68n., 71n.

121 **I pity . . . love** proverbial: 'Pity is akin to love' (Dent, P370)
    degree step (upwards, as in a staircase)

110 here] *(heare)*, *Warburton* 120 my] my poore *F2*

OLIVIA   That's a degree to love.

VIOLA

No, not a grize, for 'tis a vulgar proof
That very oft we pity enemies.

OLIVIA

Why then, methinks 'tis time to smile again.
O world, how apt the poor are to be proud!   125
If one should be a prey, how much the better
To fall before the lion than the wolf!   *Clock strikes.*
The clock upbraids me with the waste of time.
Be not afraid, good youth, I will not have you,
And yet when wit and youth is come to harvest,   130
Your wife is like to reap a proper man.
There lies your way, due west.

VIOLA   Then westward ho.
Grace and good disposition attend your ladyship.
You'll nothing, madam, to my lord by me?

122 **grize** step (from Old French *grez*,
'flight of steps, staircase'): a synonym for *degree* (121). The Duke of
Venice's gloss in *Oth* 1.3.201 – 'a grise
or step' – suggests that it may already
have become somewhat obsolete in
Early Modern English.
vulgar proof common experience
124 **'tis . . . again** since you reject me, I
must show the world a brave face
126–7 **how . . . wolf** It is generally
accepted that Olivia 'refers to herself rather than Viola' (Mahood), and
that she is proud at least to have
fallen for the *lion* Cesario, but she may
equally well be referring to his heart-
lessly patronizing attitude, despite
his lowly status: he has, after all, just
implied that she is an enemy to be
pitied (123). Cesario thereby becomes
vicious *wolf* rather than noble *lion*.
Olivia, in any case, is casting herself
in the role of defenceless lamb, alluding to the proverb 'The lamb is more

in dread of the wolf than of the lion'
(Dent, L36).
130 **when . . . harvest** when intelligence
and youthfulness ripen
131 **like** likely
reap obtain; enjoy sexually
proper good-looking (cf. 2.2.29);
real. The second sense is particularly
ironical in the circumstances.
132 **There . . . west** i.e. the encounter is over
(setting in the *west*). At the same time, she
may indicate the exit: in the Elizabethan
theatre, one of the stage doors.
westward ho a London expression,
namely the Thames watermen's call to
passengers from the City going west,
for example to the court at Westminster
(thus implying, perhaps, the greater
social importance of Orsino's house
compared to Olivia's). Less flatteringly, the phrase also alluded to imprisonment in Tyburn (*OED* westward *adv.*
2), as in the title of the comedy by
Webster and Dekker (1604).

122 grize] grice *F2*; grece *Oxf*

OLIVIA

    Stay –   135

    I prithee tell me what thou think'st of me.

VIOLA

    That you do think you are not what you are.

OLIVIA

    If I think so, I think the same of you.

VIOLA

    Then think you right: I am not what I am.

OLIVIA

    I would you were as I would have you be.   140

VIOLA

    Would it be better, madam, than I am?

    I wish it might, for now I am your fool.

OLIVIA [*aside*]

    O, what a deal of scorn looks beautiful

    In the contempt and anger of his lip.

    A murderous guilt shows not itself more soon   145

---

136 **thou** Olivia shifts from formal *you* to familiar *thou*, a pronominal change that ushers in a more intimate exchange, culminating in her declaration of love for Cesario (147–54). On 'thou' and 'you', see pp. 79–80.

137 i.e. you are forgetting yourself in loving one so far beneath your rank (and of the same gender?)

138 ²**I think . . . you** i.e. I suspect that you are of higher rank than you pretend (cf. her soliloquy on Cesario's *parentage*, 1.5.281–6).

139 **I am . . . am** I am not what I seem; cf. *Oth* 1.1.63. Viola confirms Olivia's insight regarding her gentle blood, and hints at her disguise; cf. 'I am not that I play' (1.5.179). It may echo Corinthians, 15.10, 'I am that I am.'

140 i.e. my husband

142 **might** might be better

    I am . . . fool you are making a fool of me; I am a mere attendant, subject to your whims (cf. 38–9n.).

143–4 Cesario's contempt intensifies Olivia's attraction: an Elizabethan commonplace ('disdaine increaseth desire', Lyly, *Met.*, 3.1, sig. C3ᵛ); cf. Phebe on the cross-dressed Rosalind, 'Sweet youth, I pray you chide a year together' (*AYL* 3.5.64). Cesario's *lip* is the object of fascinated attention from both sexes: cf. Orsino's *Diana's lip* (1.4.31).

143 **deal** quantity, lot

145–62 The final speeches are in rhyming couplets, used elsewhere more parsimoniously, especially as scene closers (1.1.39–40, 1.4.41–2, 2.2.40–1, 2.4.123–4, etc.).

135–6] *Capell; one line F*   143 SD] *Staunton*   beautiful] *Pope;* beautifull? *F*   144 lip.] *this edn;* lip, *F;* lip! *Rowe*   145 murderous] *(murdrous)*

Than love that would seem hid. Love's night is noon.
– Cesario, by the roses of the spring,
By maidhood, honour, truth and everything,
I love thee so that maugre all thy pride
Nor wit nor reason can my passion hide.   150
Do not extort thy reasons from this clause:
For that I woo, thou therefore hast no cause.
But rather reason thus with reason fetter:
Love sought is good, but given unsought is better.

VIOLA

By innocence I swear, and by my youth,   155
I have one heart, one bosom and one truth,
And that no woman has, nor never none
Shall mistress be of it save I alone.
And so adieu, good madam; never more

145–6 **A murderous . . . hid** doubly
    proverbial: 'Murder will out', 'Love
    cannot be hid' (Dent, M1315, L500).
    Rather than 'indulging in wishful
    thinking' regarding Cesario (Oxf[1]),
    Olivia is surely referring to her own
    love for him, which she cannot hide
    and which she is about to declare
    openly.
145 **more soon** Cf. 1.4.28n.
146 **Love's . . . noon** a further prover-
    bial variation on 'love cannot be hid'
    (145–6n.): love shows all the more
    visibly as we attempt to obscure it (cf.
    'Dark night is Cupid's day', Dent,
    N167)
149 **maugre** in spite of (from Old French
    maugré)
    pride haughtiness, arrogance
150 In Hall's 1958 Stratford production,
    on this line Geraldine McEwan's young
    Olivia, 'erotically stirred by Cesario,
    . . . threw herself on her knees in front
    of him' (M. Billington, xviii).
152–3 **do not force a false conclusion**
    from this premise, namely that my
    wooing you is a good reason for you
    not to woo me (*OED* extort *v.* 2, first

occurrence)
152 **For that** because
153 **reason . . . fetter** restrain that argu-
    ment with this argument
156 **bosom** the breast as seat of inward
    thoughts and emotions; cf. *Oth* 3.1.56,
    'speak your bosom freely.'
157 **that . . . has** three concurrent mean-
    ings: no woman is capable of such
    integrity; nobody will ever win my
    heart; I will never love a woman.
    The first recalls Orsino's misogynis-
    tic speech at 2.4.93–103, as if Viola
    were imitating male discourse. For the
    ambiguity involving the second mean-
    ing (intended for Olivia) and the third
    (directed towards the audience), cf. the
    cross-dressed Rosalind's 'And I for no
    woman' (*AYL* 5.2.86, 91).
    no . . . none Viola makes emphatic
    use of the multiple (here quadruple)
    negation that was common in Early
    Modern English (see Blake, *Grammar*,
    6.2.3.1, quoting this example).
158 **save I alone** except for me, with
    the implication that Cesario is *mis-*
    tress rather than master: another half-
    confession

Will I my master's tears to you deplore.   160

OLIVIA

Yet come again, for thou perhaps mayst move
That heart which now abhors to like his love.   *Exeunt.*

3.2   *Enter* SIR TOBY, SIR ANDREW *and* FABIAN.

SIR ANDREW   No, faith, I'll not stay a jot longer.

SIR TOBY   Thy reason, dear venom, give thy reason.

FABIAN   You must needs yield your reason, Sir Andrew.

SIR ANDREW   Marry, I saw your niece do more favours to
the count's servingman than ever she bestowed upon   5
me. I saw't i'th' orchard.

SIR TOBY   Did she see thee the while, old boy? Tell me
that.

SIR ANDREW   As plain as I see you now.

FABIAN   This was a great argument of love in her toward   10
you.

SIR ANDREW   'Slight! Will you make an ass o'me?

---

160 **deplore** narrate lamentfully (*OED*
    1b, sole occurrence)
161–2 **thou . . . love** i.e. you may per-
    suade my heart to like your master's
    love instead of loathing it
3.2 This brief scene advances the double
    scheming of Sir Toby and his com-
    panions: on the one hand he incites Sir
    Andrew to challenge Cesario, and on
    the other Maria reports on the progress
    of the gulling of Malvolio. Rowe
    locates this in '*Olivia's House*'; the
    actor and director Michael Pennington
    complains, however, that 'the rhythm
    of [Rowe's location] is feeble on the
    stage' (Pennington, 155).
1   In Posner's 2001 RSC production, Sir
    Andrew already had his cases packed.
2–4 **Thy . . . your** Sir Toby, as usual,
    adopts familiar *thou*, Sir Andrew and

Fabian formal *you*, suggesting different degrees of respect.
2   **dear venom** oxymoron, alluding sar-
    castically to Sir Andrew's supposedly
    fierce resolution to leave
4   **favours** gestures of goodwill: Sir
    Andrew saw Olivia take Cesario's hand
    in the previous scene (3.1.92).
6   **orchard** garden, with which it was
    originally a synonym (both equivalent
    to Latin *hortus*: cf. 3.1.90n.); it remains
    so in Shakespeare: cf. *RJ* 2.2.63, 'The
    orchard walls are high, and hard to
    climb.' Shakespeare's contemporaries,
    though, often made the modern dis-
    tinction between the two terms.
7   **the while** at the same time
10 **argument** proof
12 **'Slight** by God's light, one of Sir
    Andrew's preferred oaths (see 2.5.30)

3.2] *(Scoena Secunda.)*   7 thee the] *F3;* the *F*

FABIAN I will prove it legitimate, sir, upon the oaths of
     judgement and reason.

SIR TOBY And they have been grand-jurymen since   15
     before Noah was a sailor.

FABIAN She did show favour to the youth in your sight
     only to exasperate you, to awake your dormouse valour,
     to put fire in your heart and brimstone in your liver.
     You should then have accosted her and, with some   20
     excellent jests, fire-new from the mint, you should have
     banged the youth into dumbness. This was looked for
     at your hand and this was balked. The double gilt of
     this opportunity you let time wash off, and you are now
     sailed into the north of my lady's opinion, where you   25
     will hang like an icicle on a Dutchman's beard, unless
     you do redeem it by some laudable attempt either of
     valour or policy.

13 **prove it legitimate** make good my
    case (literally, show it to be authorized
    by law: *OED* legitimate *a.* 2a)
15 **grand-jurymen** true witnesses
    (namely *judgement and reason*, 14, with
    a pun on 'judgement' in the legal
    sense); literally, members of a grand
    jury, who decided whether the evi-
    dence before them was strong enough
    to warrant a full trial by judge and
    jury
15–16 **since . . . sailor** from time imme-
    morial: a deliberately overblown
    periphrasis.
18 **dormouse valour** sleepy courage: a
    sarcastic oxymoron. Cf. the proverb
    'As dull as a dormouse' (Dent, D568).
19 **brimstone** ardour; literally, sulphur,
    associated in the Bible with hell-fire
    (cf. 2.5.47n.)
20 **accosted** boarded; the second time
    that Sir Andrew fails to *accost*: cf.
    1.3.47 and n.
21 **fire-new . . . mint** brand-new, like a

freshly minted coin: proverbial (Dent,
M985)
22–3 **looked . . . hand** expected of you
23 **balked** missed
    double gilt double gilding, as in gold-
    plated metal; thus a golden opportu-
    nity (Mahood), with a pun on 'guilt',
    i.e. Sir Andrew's fault in missing his
    opportunity with Olivia
25–6 **into . . . beard** into the cold region
    of Olivia's disfavour: an allusion to the
    1596–7 expedition to the East Indies
    via the north-east passage by the Dutch
    explorer Willem Barentsz, who became
    stranded in icefields off the island of
    Nova Zembla. The map resulting from
    this ill-fated voyage is alluded to at
    74–6: see 74–6n. and Fig. 18.
28, 30 **policy** shrewd diplomacy (Fabian's
    positive meaning); 'Machiavellian'
    political cunning (the pejorative mean-
    ing understood by Sir Andrew; cf.
    'base and rotten policy', *1H4* 1.3.108).
    Cf. 2.3.74.

15 grand-jurymen] *(*grand Iurie men*)*, Dyce

SIR ANDREW   An't be any way, it must be with valour, for
   policy I hate. I had as lief be a Brownist as a politician.   30
SIR TOBY   Why then, build me thy fortunes upon the basis
   of valour. Challenge me the count's youth to fight with
   him. Hurt him in eleven places – my niece shall take
   note of it. And assure thyself there is no love-broker
   in the world can more prevail in man's commendation   35
   with woman than report of valour.
FABIAN   There is no way but this, Sir Andrew.
SIR ANDREW   Will either of you bear me a challenge to
   him?
SIR TOBY   Go write it in a martial hand, be curst and brief.   40
   It is no matter how witty, so it be eloquent and full of

---

29 **An't** if it
30 **I . . . lief** I would as willingly
   Brownist a follower of the separatist
   Robert Browne, who in 1581 founded
   an extremist Puritan sect that later
   became the Independentists, advocat-
   ing the separation of church and state.
   The fact that even the blissfully ignorant Sir Andrew, in reintroducing the
   topic of Puritanism (see 2.3.136 and
   142), appears well informed on non-
   conformist sects may be an indication
   of the degree of public interest in the
   issue.
   politician unscrupulous political
   schemer (as in *1H4* 1.3.238, 'this vile
   politician Bolingbroke'; cf. 2.3.74). Sir
   Andrew's association of nonconform-
   ism with Machiavellism is probably
   accidental and ingenuous, but in the
   context of the comedy may represent
   a further questioning of Puritan ideology.
31 **build me** This use of *me* is an instance
   of the 'ethic dative' (literally, 'for
   me': Blake, *Grammar*, 3.3.2.1a), usually employed primarily for rhetorical
   emphasis, but here ironical. See also
   Challenge me (32). Sir Andrew's *bear
   me* (38) may be an attempt at imita-
   tion.
   basis 'a thing immaterial; a principle'

(*OED* 9a, first occurrence)
32 **Challenge me** See 31n.
33 **eleven places** an arbitrary and absurdly exaggerated number, in contrast
   with Andrew's actual physical cowardice. Cf. Falstaff's boast of having killed
   'seven of the eleven' assailants in *1H4*
   2.4.234.
34 **love-broker** go-between in love affairs,
   pander: the role Viola is obliged to play
   to Olivia on Orsino's behalf
37 Fabian may be facetiously implying
   that Sir Andrew faces mortal danger, alluding to the proverb 'There
   is no way but one (i.e. death)' (Dent,
   W148).
40 **in . . . hand** in an aggressive military style; or, in scrawling soldier-like
   handwriting. Sir Toby is setting up
   Sir Andrew as the traditional cowardly
   braggart soldier of comedy, the *miles
   gloriosus* (cf. 3.4.175n.); with a possible
   pun on the Latin satirist Martial (i.e.
   the letter should be full of invective).
   curst bad-tempered
   brief curt; a radical version of Saviolo's
   precept that letters of challenge 'must
   be written with the greatest breuity
   that may be possible' (Saviolo, book 2,
   sig. X1ᵛ); see 44n.
41 **witty** clever
   so provided that

invention. Taunt him with the licence of ink. If thou
thou'st him some thrice, it shall not be amiss; and as
many lies as will lie in thy sheet of paper, although the
sheet were big enough for the bed of Ware in England,   45
set 'em down. Go, about it. Let there be gall enough
in thy ink – though thou write with a goose-pen, no
matter. About it.

SIR ANDREW   Where shall I find you?   49

SIR TOBY   We'll call thee at the cubiculo. Go.   *Exit Sir Andrew.*

FABIAN   This is a dear manikin to you, Sir Toby.

SIR TOBY   I have been dear to him, lad, some two thousand
strong or so.

---

42 **invention** matter; *eloquent* (41) and
invention allude to two of the five parts
of rhetoric, *elocutio* (style) and *inventio*
(subject matter). It is of course impossible for the letter to be stylish and full
of matter if it is not at the same time
witty or intelligent.
     with . . . ink with more freedom than
you would dare use in speech (i.e. to
his face)

42–3 **If . . . him** if you call him 'thou',
using a contemptuous sign of superiority, as in the master–servant
('you'/'thou') relationship: the play's
most explicit reference to pronouns
of 'power' (cf. Hope, 1.3.2b; Blake,
Grammar, 3.3.2.1.1; and see pp. 79–80).
Theobald compares the Attorney-
General Edward Cole's scathing
remark at the trial of Sir Walter Ralegh
(November 1603): 'for I thou thee,
thou traitor.' Sir Toby himself calls Sir
Andrew 'thou' here, as usual.

44 **lies** accusations of lying. The 'giving
of the lie' was the main cause of duels;
cf. Saviolo's discussion of 'the giuing
and receiuing of the Lie, whereupon
the Duello & the Combats in diuers
sortes doth insue' (Saviolo, book 2, sig.
R3ᵛ); cf. 3.4.151n. and Touchstone's

parodic discourse on 'a lie seven times
removed' (*AYL* 5.4.67–101).
     lie fit; tell lies (because the accusations
are false)

45 **bed of Ware** a famous Elizabethan
bedstead, measuring 3.35 metres (11
feet) square, now in the Victoria and
Albert Museum, London: see Fig. 12.

46 **gall** oak-gall, used as dye in the manu-
facture of ink; bitterness (proverbial:
'As bitter as gall', Dent, G11)

47 **goose-pen** goose-feather quill: an
implicit insult, since the goose is a
symbol of cowardice

50 **call** call on (*OED v.* 4d)
     cubiculo bedroom (Italian), prob-
ably borrowed from Florio, *World*, 93,
where it is glossed 'a chamber'. Sir
Toby uses it to mystify the linguisti-
cally innocent Sir Andrew; with a possible pun on Italian *culo*, 'arse' (Florio,
World, 93). Cf. 2.3.2n.

51 **dear** affectionate (of Sir Andrew)
     manikin puppet (literally, little man)

52–3 **I . . . strong** i.e. I have milked him
to the tune of two thousand ducats,
corresponding, according to Sir Toby's
calculations at 1.3.20, to two-thirds of
Sir Andrew's annual income.

52 **dear** costly (of Sir Toby)

---

46 down. Go,] *Capell subst.;* downe, go *F;* down, and go *Hanmer*

FABIAN We shall have a rare letter from him; but you'll
not deliver't?   55

SIR TOBY Never trust me then; and by all means stir on
the youth to an answer. I think oxen and wain-ropes
cannot hale them together. For Andrew, if he were
opened and you find so much blood in his liver as will
clog the foot of a flea, I'll eat the rest of th'anatomy.   60

FABIAN And his opposite, the youth, bears in his visage no
great presage of cruelty.

Enter MARIA.

SIR TOBY Look where the youngest wren of nine comes.

MARIA If you desire the spleen, and will laugh yourselves
into stitches, follow me. Yon gull Malvolio is turned   65

---

54 **rare** exceptional (ironical)
56 **Never . . . then** 'you bet I will': literally, never believe me again (if I fail to
deliver the letter). Sir Toby plans to
stage-manage an exchange of insults
leading to a duel (see *answer*, 57), but
changes his mind when he reads Sir
Andrew's masterpiece at 3.4.179.
stir on stir up, provoke
57 **oxen and wain-ropes** wagons drawn
by oxen; a rhetorical figure: metonymy
(*oxen* and *ropes* standing for the *wain* or
wagon)
58 **hale** drag
59 **opened** cut open surgically: a reference
to anatomy lessons conducted on
corpses to display the internal organs.
There is considerable violence in Sir
Toby's baroque image of dissection
and 'cannibalism'; cf. *I'll eat . . .* (60).
blood . . . liver The liver was
thought to be the organ that generated blood and was thus the seat of
courage; Sir Andrew is bloodless or
'lily-livered'.
60 **clog** weigh down (literally, encumber)

anatomy (dissected) corpse; *OED* 2b
cites Ben Jonson's *Every Man in his
Humour* (1598), 4.6, 'They must ha'
dissected, and made an *Anatomie* o'
me' (Jonson, *Works*, 52).
61 **opposite** adversary
62 **presage** promise (literally, omen)
63 *****the youngest . . . nine** i.e. the
smallest chick of the smallest bird: an
allusion to Maria's diminutive size.
Theobald's emendation of F's 'mine'
is justified in part by ornithology:
wrens do indeed lay a large number of
eggs. More to the point, broods of nine
are found elsewhere in Shakespeare,
as in the witches' '[the sow's] nine
farrow' (*Mac* 4.1.65) and Poor Tom's
'the nightmare and her nine foal' (*KL*
3.4.118).
64 **the spleen** a fit of laughter. In early
modern popular medicine the spleen
was synonymous with sudden passion
in general, and was thought to govern uncontrollable laughter as well as
anger and melancholy.
65 **gull** dupe

---

55 deliver't?] *Dyce;* deliuer't. F   60 th'] thy *Hanmer*   63 nine] *Theobald;* mine F   65 Yon] *(yond)*

heathen, a very renegado, for there is no Christian that
means to be saved by believing rightly can ever believe
such impossible passages of grossness. He's in yellow
stockings.

SIR TOBY   And cross-gartered?   70

MARIA   Most villainously, like a pedant that keeps a school
i'th' church. I have dogged him like his murderer.
He does obey every point of the letter that I dropped
to betray him. He does smile his face into more lines
than is in the new map with the augmentation of the   75
Indies. You have not seen such a thing as 'tis. I can
hardly forbear hurling things at him; I know my lady
will strike him. If she do, he'll smile and take't for a
great favour.   79

---

66 **renegado** renegade (Spanish): desert-
er of the Christian faith, especially a
convert to Islam. It was fashionable at
this time to give words a Spanish ending, and so Maria may be imitating her
'superiors'.

67 **to . . . believing** a reference to
the Protestant doctrine of salva-
tion through faith rather than (as in
Catholic doctrine) good works: ironic
in view of Malvolio's 'Puritanism'. Cf.
1.5.124–5n.
   rightly in an orthodox Christian (here
Protestant) manner
   can who can

68 **impossible . . . grossness** grossly
improbable discourses, i.e. the passages in the letter inviting Malvolio
to dress up, which he has credulously
obeyed

71 **villainously** abominably

71–2 **a pedant . . . church** a schoolteach-
er who teaches in church (presumably
because of the lack of a schoolhouse).
This suggests a rustic or old-fashioned
scene, confirming the suspicion that
Malvolio's 'fashionable' cross-garters
and yellow stockings are in fact hope-

lessly provincial and out of date: cf.
2.5.149, 150 and notes.

72 **his murderer** Maria's rather sinister
simile recalls the violent blood sports
metaphors against Malvolio in 2.5.

74 **smile his face** make his face smile.
The verb is transitive, suggesting
Malvolio's effort to practise expressions he is not used to making, in obedience to the letter (see 2.5.169–72).

74–6 **more . . . Indies** probable allusion to Edward Wright's 1600 map
showing the East Indies 'augmented'
because it includes the island of Nova
Zembla: cf. 25–6n. The wrinkles on
Malvolio's smiling face are compared
to the rhumb lines on the map: see
Fig. 18.

75 **is** The singular form of the verb *to
be* with plural subject is frequent in
Shakespeare (Blake, *Grammar*, 4.2.2.1,
giving this example).

78–9 **strike . . . favour** ironical; it is
of course highly unlikely that Olivia
would strike Malvolio, but the idea
allows Maria to play on three meanings
of *favour*: act of kindness; love token;
sexual concession.

66 renegado] *(*Renegatho*)*, *Rowe*

SIR TOBY   Come, bring us, bring us where he is.   *Exeunt.*

3.3   *Enter* SEBASTIAN *and* ANTONIO.

SEBASTIAN
    I would not by my will have troubled you,
    But since you make your pleasure of your pains
    I will no further chide you.
ANTONIO
    I could not stay behind you. My desire,
    More sharp than filed steel, did spur me forth,   5
    And not all love to see you – though so much
    As might have drawn me to a longer voyage –
    But jealousy what might befall your travel,
    Being skill-less in these parts, which to a stranger,
    Unguided and unfriended, often prove   10
    Rough and unhospitable. My willing love,

3.3 In this duologue – the 'continuation' of the somewhat distant 2.1 – Antonio discloses both his past conflicts with Orsino and, again, his passionate attachment to Sebastian, whom he sends off sightseeing in Illyria. Rowe locates it in '*The Street*'.

1   troubled you i.e. because Antonio has taken the trouble to follow him, as announced at 2.1.44; cf. 2.1.31.

2   since . . . pains since you have willingly gone to this trouble for me; with a pun on *pains* = effort or suffering (in antithesis to 'pleasure')

3   chide you i.e. reprimand you for going to such trouble for me

5   More sharp Cf. 1.4.28n.
   filed filèd: sharpened, like a sword. This is proverbial: 'As sharp as steel' (Dent, S839.1). On the possible homoerotic connotations of Antonio's sharp desire, see p. 50.

6   not all not only
   love desire
   so much so great

7   *me Rann's emendation of F's 'one' makes better sense and is in keeping with the other forms in the passage, such as *My* (4) and *me* (5); the mis-reading of *one/me* is among the easiest in secretary hand (RP).

8   jealousy anxiety (*OED* 3)

9   Being skill-less in since you are unfamiliar with
   stranger foreigner

11 Rough and unhospitable Illyria was traditionally associated with pirates; at 5.1.65 Orsino addresses Antonio himself as *Notable pirate* (see note).
   willing voluntary, hence spontaneous
   love desire (cf. 6): a personification, as subject of *Set forth* (13); i.e. his desire caused him to follow Sebastian

80 SD] *(Exeunt Omnes.)*   **3.3**] *(Scaena Tertia.)*   7 me] *Rann;* one *F*   8 travel] *(*rrauell*)*

The rather by these arguments of fear,
Set forth in your pursuit.

SEBASTIAN   My kind Antonio,
I can no other answer make but thanks,
And thanks, and ever thanks; and oft good turns   15
Are shuffled off with such uncurrent pay.
But were my worth as is my conscience firm,
You should find better dealing. What's to do?
Shall we go see the relics of this town?

ANTONIO
Tomorrow, sir; best first go see your lodging.   20

SEBASTIAN
I am not weary, and 'tis long to night.
I pray you, let us satisfy our eyes

---

12 **The rather** all the more readily (*OED adv.* 4a)
  by due to
  arguments persuasions (literally, reasons urged, *OED n.* 3a)
13 **Set . . . pursuit** set out to follow you
15–18 **good . . . dealing** This variation on the proverb 'one good turn deserves another' (Dent, T616) introduces, somewhat ironically, the theme of repaying one's debts, which becomes a real issue when Antonio actually lends Sebastian money (38) and Cesario later disclaims all knowledge thereof (3.4.338).
15 *****thanks . . . thanks** This line is two syllables short in F, and is omitted altogether in F2, perhaps because it was considered defective, although Oxf[1] defends it as indicating 'an embarrassed pause' by Sebastian, who cannot reciprocate Antonio's love. It is more likely that something is simply missing, and Theobald's emendation, which continues the emphatic but somewhat awkward reiteration of thanks, is still the best guess to date, since it was relatively easy for the scribe or compositor to miscount the number of repetitions.
16 **shuffled off** shirked, shrugged off. Cf. Hamlet's 'shuffled off this mortal coil' (*Ham* 3.1.66).
  uncurrent pay worthless payment, made in coin that is not of legal tender (*OED* uncurrent 1, first occurrence)
17 **worth** wealth
  conscience awareness of my debt
  firm substantial
18 **What's to do?** What must be done? This construction has lost its Shakespearean sense of obligation (Blake, *Grammar*, 4.4.4d, giving this example).
  relics antiquities. Sebastian wants to go sightseeing, to 'gaze upon the buildings' like Antipholus of Syracuse in *CE* 1.2.13.
  town The allusions to a supposed Illyrian *town* or *city* (24) are echoed at 5.1.250; in reality the 'urban' references in this scene are to London: cf. 39n.
21 **to** till

15–16] *om. F2*   15 and ever . . . good] *Theobald;* and euer oft good *F;* and ever oft-good *Pope;* and ever. Oft good *Steevens;* still thanks; and very oft good *Collier[2]*   20 lodging.] *F2;* Lodging? *F*

With the memorials and the things of fame
That do renown this city.

ANTONIO   Would you'd pardon me.
I do not without danger walk these streets.   25
Once in a sea-fight 'gainst the count his galleys
I did some service, of such note indeed
That were I ta'en here it would scarce be answered.

SEBASTIAN
Belike you slew great number of his people?

ANTONIO
Th'offence is not of such a bloody nature,   30
Albeit the quality of the time and quarrel
Might well have given us bloody argument.
It might have since been answered in repaying
What we took from them, which for traffic's sake
Most of our city did. Only myself stood out,   35

---

23 **memorials** monuments; cf. *relics* (19).
24 **renown** make famous
   city See 19n.
   Would you'd please
26 **count his** count's: a frequent form of
   the genitive in Early Modern English,
   in particular with proper names (Blake,
   Grammar, 3.2.1.2d; Hope, 1.1.4g, giving this example); the initial *h* of *his*
   was regularly dropped, producing here
   the pronunciation 'count iz'.
27 **service** military (naval) operation.
   The exact nature and occasion of
   Antonio's *service* against Orsino's fleet
   are not specified, although it was serious enough to put his life at risk (30–2)
   and involved the seizing of property
   (33–5), so much so that Orsino accuses
   him of piracy (5.1.65).
28 **ta'en** captured; pronounced as one
   syllable (cf. F's 'tane')
   scarce be answered be difficult to
   defend myself against (in court); or, be
   difficult to make amends for
29 **Belike** presumably

31 **quality** nature
   time occasion
32 **bloody argument** reason for bloodshed
33 **since** in the meantime
   answered settled (i.e. the dispute)
   in by
34 **for traffic's sake** in the interests
   of trade: i.e. the other members of
   Antonio's *city* returned the seized
   goods in order to restore commerce
   with Illyria.
35 **our city** members of our community
   or state. Antonio is presumably referring not to his home town but to the
   wider community or city-state (the
   polis or *civitas*) to which he belongs,
   and which is involved in trade wars
   with Illyria. Cf. *Cor* 3.1.199, 'What is
   the city, but the people?'
   stood out went against the general
   trend, isolating myself; stood firm. The
   reason for Antonio's refusal to restore
   Orsino's property, thereby exposing
   himself to danger, is again not specified.

---

26 count his] County's *(Malone)*   28 ta'en] *(tane)*   29 people?] *Dyce;* people. *F*

For which if I be lapsed in this place
I shall pay dear.

SEBASTIAN   Do not then walk too open.

ANTONIO

It doth not fit me. Hold, sir, here's my purse.
In the south suburbs, at the Elephant,
Is best to lodge. I will bespeak our diet   40
Whiles you beguile the time and feed your knowledge
With viewing of the town. There shall you have me.

SEBASTIAN

Why I your purse?

ANTONIO

Haply your eye shall light upon some toy
You have desire to purchase; and your store,   45
I think, is not for idle markets, sir.

36 **lapsed** lapsèd: apprehended. *OED* (lapse *v.* 8) gives this as sole occurrence of the verb in a transitive mode, possibly deriving from the expression 'to fall into the lap(s) of'. More plausibly the verb has its usual meaning in the intransitive mode, i.e. 'fall (into the hands of)', and thus 'be arrested'. Keightley's emendation 'latched', caught, is attractive but does not substantially change F's meaning.

37 **pay dear** pay a high price, i.e. my life
open i.e. to public view (adverb)

38 **fit** suit, behove (*OED v.*[1] 4). This is ambiguous: Antonio may mean either that it is not opportune for him to be seen, or that it does not suit him to go into hiding. In the event, he renders himself visible to all (3.4.307).

39 **south suburbs** an ironic reference to London, and in particular to the Liberties, an area outside the jurisdiction of the City of London, notorious as an area of brothels. Thomas Nashe asks, '*London*, what are thy Suburbes but licensed Stewes?' (Nashe, *Tears*,

fol. 77[r]): it is thus a dubious place to *lodge* (40). As it was also the area where the Globe theatre stood, Sebastian does not have to go very far. In the 2002 Middle Temple production Patrick Brennan's Antonio pointed south towards the Thames (and the Globe).

the Elephant a continuation of the *suburbs* joke: there was indeed an Elephant Inn on Bankside, which was in practice 'an inn-cum-brothel' (Ungerer, 103).

40 **Is best** it is best. The omission of the indefinite pronoun (*it*) is quite frequent in Shakespeare (Blake, *Grammar*, 6.3.1.4, giving this example).
bespeak our diet order our meal, 'perhaps in playful antithesis to "feed your knowledge" [41]' (Ard[2])

42 **have me** find me (Schmidt)

44 **Haply** perhaps
toy trifle

45–6 **your . . . markets** the money you possess is not enough to spend on luxuries

36 lapsed] latched *Keightley*

SEBASTIAN

    I'll be your purse-bearer, and leave you for an hour.

ANTONIO

    To th'Elephant.

SEBASTIAN   I do remember.   *Exeunt.*

3.4   *Enter* OLIVIA *and* MARIA.

OLIVIA [*aside*]

    I have sent after him; he says he'll come.

    How shall I feast him? What bestow of him?

    For youth is bought more oft than begged or borrowed.

    I speak too loud.

    [*to Maria*] Where's Malvolio? He is sad and civil,   5

    And suits well for a servant with my fortunes.

3.4 This hectic scene, the second longest in the play, is a *tour de force* of interwoven plots, bringing together nearly all the narrative threads of the comedy: the tormenting of the cross-gartered Malvolio; the farce of the failed duel between the supposed rivals for the hand of Olivia; the latter's continuing courtship of Cesario through the gift of her portrait; and the mistaken intervention and arrest of Antonio – all variations on 'fooling' or (self-)deception. Capell locates this in '*Olivia's Garden*': cf. 218, but see also 304.1n.

1 **he . . . come** This has worried commentators, since Olivia does not learn that Cesario will accept her invitation until 56. Audiences are less troubled by such inconsistencies, and in any case are likely to interpret the phrase as simply a statement of fact.

2 **of** on

3 **bought . . . borrowed** a variation on the proverb that Taverner translates from Erasmus as 'I had leuer [rather] bye, then begge' (Erasmus, *Proverbs*, fol.

13^v): as Taverner comments, something obtained by begging 'is i dede [indeed] derely bought' (Dent, B783). Olivia is determined not to debase herself by pleading with Cesario, but is willing to buy his love with a gift; in the event she both buys and begs (cf. 203–7).
more oft Cf. 1.4.28n.

4 *This short line is, as it were, an aside within the aside: Olivia comments on her own thinking out (too) loud. F makes this and the following line a single line, playing havoc with the metre. This is the first of a series of prosodic problems in this scene: 8–9, 19–21 and 23–4 are set as verse in F and have been emended by Pope, Capell and later editors to prose. The alternation of verse and prose evidently created difficulties for the compositor.

5 **sad and civil** orderly (*OED* sad *a.* 4a) and well behaved: virtual synonyms here

6 **fortunes** an allusion both to Olivia's bereavement and to her *mad* and *sad* love (14–15)

47] *Boswell–Malone; F lines* you / houre. /; *Theobald lines* for / hour.   48 SD] *they go off in different directions* Cam^1 **3.4**] *(Scoena Quarta.)*   1 SD] *Staunton*   4–5] *Pope; one line* F   5, 153 SDs] Cam^1

Where is Malvolio?

MARIA   He's coming, madam, but in very strange manner.
He is sure possessed, madam.

OLIVIA
Why, what's the matter? Does he rave?   10

MARIA   No, madam, he does nothing but smile. Your
ladyship were best to have some guard about you if he
come, for sure the man is tainted in's wits.

OLIVIA
Go call him hither.   [*Exit Maria.*]
                              I am as mad as he,
If sad and merry madness equal be.   15

Enter MALVOLIO[, *in yellow stockings and cross-gartered,
with* MARIA].

How now, Malvolio?

MALVOLIO   Sweet lady, ho, ho!

OLIVIA   Smil'st thou? I sent for thee upon a sad occasion.

MALVOLIO   Sad, lady? I could be sad. This does make

---

9   **possessed** i.e. by the devil, and thus
mad. Maria wants to influence Olivia's
interpretation of Malvolio's behaviour
in advance.

10 The two missing syllables in this
line give rise to a heavy caesura after
matter.

13 **tainted** diseased; cf. 128, 353; 3.1.66;
5.1.134, 351 and notes. Cf. also
Antonio's self-portrait in *MV* 4.1.114,
'I am a tainted wether of the flock.'

14–15 **I am . . . be** Olivia's madness
– a form of amorous 'furor' (see
1.1.14–15n.) – is melancholy because
unrequited, while Malvolio's is *merry*
because he smiles all the time.

15.1 *In F Malvolio enters after *hither*
at 14, as soon as Olivia tells Maria to

call him. This creates comic surprise,
but 'upstages' Olivia and makes her
comments on her own and Malvolio's
'madness' awkward in his presence.
Capell's postponing of the SD thus
makes good theatrical sense. In any
case, Malvolio's entry in yellow
stockings and cross-garters is one
of the play's most poignantly comical moments, and actors rarely fail
to make the most of it: 'Laurence
Olivier waved his fingers from a large
yew hedge, and disappeared again as
suddenly as he had appeared' (Brown,
257).

18 **Smil'st** Malvolio is smiling conspicuously at Olivia in obedience to the
letter.

8–9] *Pope; F lines* Madame: / Madam. /   14] *Capell; F lines* hither. / hee, /   SD] *Dyce*   15 merry]
F3; metry *F;* mercy *F2*   15.1 *Enter* MALVOLIO] *Capell; after* hither *14 F*   15.1–2 in . . . MARIA]
Kemble   17 ho, ho!] ha, ha. *Smile fantastically. / Rowe*

some obstruction in the blood, this cross–gartering, but   20
what of that? If it please the eye of one, it is with me as
the very true sonnet is: 'Please one, and please all.'

OLIVIA   Why, how dost thou, man? What is the matter
with thee?

MALVOLIO   Not black in my mind, though yellow in my   25
legs. It did come to his hands, and commands shall be
executed. I think we do know the sweet Roman hand.

OLIVIA   Wilt thou go to bed, Malvolio?

18,19 **sad, sad** serious (Olivia); melancholy (Malvolio). Malvolio attributes
his melancholy – denying his supposed
merry madness (15) – to the fact that
his garters cause an *obstruction* in the
flow of blood, slowing it down (19–20).
The adjective *sad* occurs five times
in fifteen lines here, with a range of
meanings: cf. 5n.
18 **occasion** matter
21 **of one** i.e. of Olivia
   with for
22 **sonnet** lyric poem, not necessarily of
fourteen lines (*OED n.* 2)
   'Please . . . all' A bawdy ballad of this
title – not a *sonnet*, as Malvolio claims
– was published in 1592, signed R.T.,
probably the clown Richard Tarlton.
Its theme is 'Let her doo what she
shall', i.e. let women have their way
sexually, which is presumably why
Malvolio quotes it to Olivia. It is ironic
that here, as at 25–6 and 29, the cultural references of the upright Malvolio,
designed to impress the countess,
should be so dubious. Some Malvolios
sing this line.
23 SP *F's attribution of this speech to
Malvolio ('*Mal.*') is clearly an error.
Collier's emendation '*Mar.*' (Maria)
suggests the most plausible compositor's misreading, but it seems

unlikely that Maria is speaking here,
first because, as Cam[1] puts it, 'Maria
nowhere else "thou's" Malvolio', and
above all because Malvolio's contemptuous response to her question at 32
indicates that it is Maria's first intervention in the dialogue. F2's attribution is therefore preferable.
25–6 **Not . . . legs** a probable allusion
to another popular ballad (cf. 22n.),
'Black and Yellow'. *Not black* also
refers to the theory of the humours,
and in particular to melancholy, caused
by black bile; cf. 2.5.3n. Malvolio contradicts himself (contrast *sad*, 19).
26 **It** the letter
27 **Roman hand** i.e. italic handwriting,
as opposed to the English 'secretary'
hand. Olivia uses the modish calligra-
phy imported from Italy, as evidently
does Maria.
28 **go to bed** i.e. in order to rest and
recover from his 'madness'. Malvolio
interprets the invitation as a sexual
advance: 'let's go to bed.' Another
moment of potential comedy:
Malvolios at this point have laughed,
cried, jumped, stumbled or simply
smiled triumphantly towards Olivia
or the audience; in Posner's 2001 RSC
production he chased her around the
stage, growling.

18] *Capell lines* thou? / occasion. /   19–21 Sad . . . that?] *Pope; F lines* be sad: / blood: / that? /
19 Sad, lady?] *Theobald;* Sad Lady, *F*   22 'Please . . . all.'] *Rowe;* Please . . . all. *F*   23 SP] *F2; Mal.*
F; Mar. (Collier)   23–4] *Pope; F lines* man? / thee? /

MALVOLIO   To bed? Ay, sweetheart, and I'll come to thee.

OLIVIA   God comfort thee. Why dost thou smile so and   30
kiss thy hand so oft?

MARIA   How do you, Malvolio?

MALVOLIO   At your request? Yes, nightingales answer
daws.

MARIA   Why appear you with this ridiculous boldness   35
before my lady?

MALVOLIO   'Be not afraid of greatness' – 'twas well writ.

OLIVIA   What mean'st thou by that, Malvolio?

MALVOLIO   'Some are born great' –

OLIVIA   Ha?   40

MALVOLIO   'Some achieve greatness' –

OLIVIA   What sayst thou?

MALVOLIO   'And some have greatness thrust upon them.'

OLIVIA   Heaven restore thee!

MALVOLIO   'Remember who commended thy yellow   45
stockings' –

OLIVIA   Thy yellow stockings?

---

29 This is yet another reference to a
bawdy popular ballad (cf. 22n.,
25–6n.), quoted in Brome's play *The
English Moor*, 1.3: 'Go to bed, sweet
heart, I'le come to thee, / Make thy
bed fine and soft I'le li[e] with thee'
(Brome, 13).

31 **kiss thy hand** Malvolio has been
blowing kisses to Olivia from his fingers, in a hopeful gesture of aristocratic courtly love.

33 **At your request?** i.e. How dare you
ask me? – with emphasis on *your*.
Malvolio questions Maria's right even
to address him, now that he is so
important.

34 **daws** jackdaws, which croak grace-
lessly; *daw* also meant 'fool' (*OED n.*

2a): cf. Warwick's 'I am no wiser than
a daw' (*1H6* 2.4.18). The contrast
with *nightingale* (= Malvolio) does not
necessarily imply that he 'has been
singing' (Mahood), but refers rather to
their supposed difference in class and
style.

37–52 Malvolio has learned the letter by heart, and is not put off by
Olivia's evident failure to recognize the
quotations.

47 Olivia repeats the phrases from the
letter in bewilderment. There is no
need to emend *Thy* to *My* as in some
editions (see t.n.), as if Olivia believed
Malvolio to be addressing her directly:
she can see that the yellow stockings
are his and not hers.

33–4] *Capell; F lines* request: / Dawes. /   33 request?] *Rowe³; request: F*   39 great' –] *Rowe;* great.
F   41 greatness' –] *Rowe;* greatnesse. *F*   46 stockings' –] *Rowe;* stockings. *F*   47 Thy] My *Dyce²*

MALVOLIO 'And wished to see thee cross-gartered.'

OLIVIA Cross-gartered?

MALVOLIO 'Go to, thou art made if thou desir'st to be so.'   50

OLIVIA Am I made?

MALVOLIO 'If not, let me see thee a servant still.'

OLIVIA Why, this is very midsummer madness.

Enter Servant.

SERVANT Madam, the young gentleman of the Count
Orsino's is returned. I could hardly entreat him back.   55
He attends your ladyship's pleasure.

OLIVIA I'll come to him.   [*Exit Servant.*]
Good Maria, let this fellow be looked to. Where's my
cousin Toby? Let some of my people have a special care
of him; I would not have him miscarry for the half of   60
my dowry.   *Exeunt* [*Olivia and Maria*].

MALVOLIO O ho, do you come near me now? No worse
man than Sir Toby to look to me! This concurs directly
with the letter. She sends him on purpose that I may
appear stubborn to him, for she incites me to that in the   65
letter. 'Cast thy humble slough,' says she, 'be opposite
with a kinsman, surly with servants. Let thy tongue

51 Olivia's change in pronoun (*thou* to
I) indicates that she interprets this as
direct address to her rather than quotation. She seems to hear either 'thou
art maid' or, more probably in the context, 'thou art mad' (and so responds
'Am *I* mad[e]?'). For the triple made/
maid/mad pun, cf. Kökeritz, 126.

53 **midsummer madness** proverbial
(Dent, M1117): the only occurrence
of the expression in Shakespeare,
although arguably the whole of *MND*
dramatizes it

55 **hardly** with difficulty (*OED* 6)

60 **miscarry** come to harm (*OED* 1)

62–80 This speech is a crescendo of self-
deception: Malvolio expresses no sense
of defeat at Olivia's failure to respond
to his allusions, but on the contrary
interprets her concern for his mental
health and her involving of Sir Toby as
confirmations of the letter's contents.

62 **come near me** begin to understand
me: idiomatic (Dent, N56.1); Blake,
Grammar, 5.4.2 (giving this example),
glosses *near* as 'close to what I mean'.

63 **look to** look after

65 **stubborn** fierce (*OED a.* 1a)

57, 295, 305, 316 SDs] *Capell*   61 SD] *Capell; exit F; Exeunt Olivia and Maria different ways /*
Mahood

tang with arguments of state; put thyself into the
trick of singularity', and consequently sets down the
manner how, as a sad face, a reverend carriage, a slow　　70
tongue, in the habit of some sir of note and so forth. I
have limed her, but it is Jove's doing and Jove make me
thankful! And when she went away now, 'Let this fellow
be looked to.' 'Fellow', not 'Malvolio', nor after my
degree, but 'fellow'! Why, everything adheres together　　75
that no dram of a scruple, no scruple of a scruple, no

68 *tang with The rare verb *tang* (= ring out) presents no problems to the compositor (or scribe) on its first appearance in the letter (2.5.147) but appears to baffle him here: F's 'langer' is a plausible misreading of secretary initial *t* (uncrossed, or looped) and final *e* (flourished so as to resemble -*er* suspension – as elsewhere in F, e.g. 'lover never' at 2.4.65) (RP). F2 corrects only the verb, while Capell and others go further, eliminating *with* in order to match the letter, and Turner argues that the particle is carried over from the two *with*s in the previous line. This is probably a piece of overcorrecting, since Malvolio, quoting from memory, does not always repeat the letter verbatim – cf. 48, which omits *ever* from the quoted passage (2.5.150) – and the verb phrase makes sense as it stands in F2.

69 consequently subsequently (*OED* 1)
sets down puts in writing

70 as such as
reverend carriage solemn bearing
slow deliberate

71 habit manner (literally, apparel). Cf. the cross-dressed Rosalind in *AYL* 3.2.291–2: 'I will speak to him like a saucy lackey and under that habit play the knave with him.'
sir of note important gentleman

72 limed caught; birdlime is sticky resin used to trap small birds, or, metaphori-

cally, the beloved's heart: cf. *TGV* 3.2.68–9, 'You must lay lime, to tangle her desires / By wailful sonnets.' It is, of course, Malvolio who has been *limed* by the letter.

72–3 it . . . thankful! probable echo of Psalm 118.23, 'This was the doyng of God: it is marueylous in our eyes' (Ard[1])

72 Jove Cf. 1.5.110n. and 2.5.168n.

73, 74, 75 fellow Malvolio interprets this optimistically as 'equal' or 'peer', as in *H5* 5.2.238–9, 'fellow with the best king'. Even more promisingly for Malvolio, the term could also signify 'spouse' or 'companion' (*OED n.* 4a), as in *Tem* 3.1.83–4, 'I am your wife, if you will marry me . . . To be your fellow'; but the word was mostly used, as at 58, to address a servant or social inferior.

74–5 after my degree according to my rank

75–7 Why . . . circumstance In Barton's 1969 RSC production Donald Sinden's Malvolio on these lines famously checked his watch against the garden sundial, and corrected the dial (Sinden, 'Malvolio', 62).

75–6 adheres together that coincides to prove that

76 no . . . ³scruple not the slightest impediment or doubt; *dram* and *scruple* are both small apothecaries' weights (respectively 1/8 and 1/24 of an

68 tang with] *F2;* langer with *F;* tang *Capell Halliwell*　76 ²a scruple] an ounce *Keightley*　72 Jove's] God's *Halliwell*　72, 79 Jove] God

obstacle, no incredulous or unsafe circumstance – what
can be said? – nothing that can be can come between me
and the full prospect of my hopes. Well, Jove, not I, is
the doer of this, and he is to be thanked.   80

Enter [SIR] TOBY, FABIAN *and* MARIA.

SIR TOBY   Which way is he, in the name of sanctity? If all
the devils of hell be drawn in little, and Legion himself
possessed him, yet I'll speak to him.

FABIAN   Here he is, here he is. [*to Malvolio*] How is't with
you, sir? How is't with you, man?   85

MALVOLIO   Go off, I discard you. Let me enjoy my
private. Go off.

MARIA   Lo, how hollow the fiend speaks within him. Did

ounce) so that 'scruple of a scruple'
is the smallest amount imaginable.
Metaphorically, *scruple* also signifies
uncertainty: Malvolio has no doubts at
all regarding his success. Cf. 2.5.2n.
77 **incredulous** incredible
   unsafe unreliable (*OED* 3, giving this
   example)
79 **prospect** view
   hopes i.e. their fulfilment
81 **in . . . sanctity** Sir Toby calls on holy
   powers as he is about to confront the
   possessed Malvolio.
82 **drawn in little** contracted into a small
   space (namely that of one body); with
   a pun on 'painted in miniature' (as in
   Ham 2.2.303, 'his picture in little')
   Legion himself i.e. the devil, with
   confused reference to the episode of
   possession by a multitude of devils
   in Mark, 5.9, where the 'foule spirite'
   tells Jesus 'my name is legion [i.e.
   innumerable], for we are many'; Sir
   Toby takes this to mean that *Legion*
   is literally another name for Satan.
   There is no evidence to suggest that

this was a standing joke, so it is probably a drunken blunder. This is also
the first of many possible echoes of
the notorious *True Narration* by the
Puritan exorcist John Darrell, who
affirms that through faith, 'Though
Belzabub the prince of Diuelles, and
with him Legions had bene in him,
yet had you cast them out' (Darrell,
41–2); cf. 4.2.25n., 31n., 32n. and
97n.
86, 87 **Go off** go away
86 **discard** reject: a recent import into
   English (from Italian *scartare*); *OED*
   v. 1 gives as first occurrence Florio's
   gloss, '*o via scartate . . .* goe to, dis-
   carde' (Florio, *Second Fruits*, 68–9).
   Since one of its meanings was 'dismiss
   from employment' (*OED* 3), Malvolio
   may be looking forward to when he is
   in a position to fire Fabian.
87 **private** privacy (*OED* *n.* 6a, first
   occurrence)
88 **hollow** with a hollow and echoing
   voice (adverb). *OED adv.* 1 (first occurrence) suggests 'insincerely'.

80 he] He *Halliwell*   80.1, 212.1, 266.1 SIR] *Rowe*   84, 328, 337, 382 SDs] *Oxf*   84 How] *Sir Toby*
How *Cam¹*

not I tell you? Sir Toby, my lady prays you to have a
care of him. 90

MALVOLIO Aha! Does she so?

SIR TOBY Go to, go to. Peace, peace, we must deal gently
with him. Let me alone. How do you, Malvolio? How
is't with you? What, man, defy the devil! Consider, he's
an enemy to mankind. 95

MALVOLIO Do you know what you say?

MARIA La you, an you speak ill of the devil, how he takes
it at heart. Pray God he be not bewitched.

FABIAN Carry his water to th' wise woman.

MARIA Marry, and it shall be done tomorrow morning, if 100
I live. My lady would not lose him for more than I'll
say.

MALVOLIO How now, mistress?

MARIA O Lord!

SIR TOBY Prithee hold thy peace, this is not the way. Do 105
you not see you move him? Let me alone with him.

FABIAN No way but gentleness, gently, gently. The fiend
is rough, and will not be roughly used.

---

91 **Aha . . . so** possibly an aside by
Malvolio, who takes Maria's statement
as confirming Olivia's love for him. In
Carroll's 2002 Middle Temple production, Oliver Cotton's steward started
towards Paul Chahidi's Maria on this
line, causing him/her to scream.
93 **Let me alone** let me deal with him
94 **defy the devil** Sir Toby pretends to
take Malvolio's 'madness' as a sign of
possession by the devil; cf. 82n.
96 **Do . . . say?** Do you realize the gravity
of what you are saying (i.e. that I of
all people should be possessed by the
devil)?; or, are you in your right mind
(or merely drunk)?
97 **La you** look you

an if
98 **at heart** to heart
bewitched Maria introduces a third
possible cause of Malvolio's behaviour,
in addition to madness and possession.
99 **water** urine (for diagnosis of disease)
wise woman a benevolent 'witch' or
herbalist, expert in charms and rem-
edies against disease and bewitchment
(*OED* 1). In *MW* Falstaff is made
to cross-dress as 'the wise woman of
Brainford' (*MW* 4.5.24–5).
100 **tomorrow morning** i.e. using
the urine from Malvolio's overnight
chamber-pot
106 **move** excite, upset

93 me] him *Rowe*   106 Let . . . him] *om. F3*

SIR TOBY   Why how now, my bawcock? How dost thou,
   chuck?   110

MALVOLIO   Sir!

SIR TOBY   Ay, biddy, come with me. What, man, 'tis not
   for gravity to play at cherry-pit with Satan. Hang him,
   foul collier!

MARIA   Get him to say his prayers, good Sir Toby, get him   115
   to pray.

MALVOLIO   My prayers, minx?

MARIA   No, I warrant you, he will not hear of godliness.

MALVOLIO   Go hang yourselves, all. You are idle shallow
   things; I am not of your element. You shall know more   120
   hereafter.   *Exit.*

SIR TOBY   Is't possible?

FABIAN   If this were played upon a stage now, I could
   condemn it as an improbable fiction.

109–12 **bawcock . . . biddy** childish
terms of endearment, patronizing
the 'mad' Malvolio. A *bawcock* (from
French *beau coq*) is literally a 'fine
cock' or good fellow (cf. *H5* 4.1.44,
'The king's a bawcock, and a heart
of gold'); *chuck*, 'chicken', was often
used with children, as was *biddy*,
likewise 'chicken' (*OED* biddy², first
occurrence).

113 **gravity** dignity, reverence. The noun
was sometimes used as a title of honour ('your gravity': first use cited in
OED 1618), and may imply an allegorical personification, as in a morality
play, both here and in *1H4* 2.4.285–6:
'What doth Gravity out of his bed at
midnight?'
   cherry-pit child's game of rolling cherry stones into a small hole:
Malvolio is thus on familiar terms with
the devil. Ungerer, 99, and Rubinstein,
48, suspect a sexual allusion.

114 **foul collier** dirty coalman, with reference to the devil's blackness. The
association is proverbial: 'Like will
to like, quoth the devil to the collier'
(Dent, L287), which is also the title
of a 1568 play by Ulpian Fulwell. In
Posner's 2001 RSC production, Sir
Toby used his walking stick to make
the sign of the cross as he uttered
this line.

117 **minx** hussy, impudent girl

119 **idle** foolish, frivolous

120 **of your element** on your low level.
At 3.1.56–7 Feste avoids the term
because it is *overworn*; Malvolio,
however, employs it with pompous
solemnity.

123–4 Fabian's ironic metatheatrical comment underlines the almost
too perfect success of their plot,
but also authenticates the *improbable* scene as *non*-fiction. Fabian's *now*
conflates dramatic or fictional time
with the 'real' time of the performance; cf. Cassius' and Brutus' reflections on 'this our lofty scene' in *JC*
3.1.111–16.

SIR TOBY   His very genius hath taken the infection of the   125
    device, man.

MARIA   Nay, pursue him now, lest the device take air and
    taint.

FABIAN   Why, we shall make him mad indeed.

MARIA   The house will be the quieter.   130

SIR TOBY   Come, we'll have him in a dark room and bound.
    My niece is already in the belief that he's mad. We may
    carry it thus for our pleasure and his penance till our
    very pastime, tired out of breath, prompt us to have
    mercy on him; at which time we will bring the device to   135
    the bar and crown thee for a finder of madmen.

Enter SIR ANDREW [*with a letter*].

But see, but see.

FABIAN   More matter for a May morning.

125 **genius** soul (literally, guardian
    spirit)
    hath . . . infection of has been con-
    taminated by: one of numerous refer-
    ences in the play to contagion (e.g.
    2.3.53–5)
127 **device** plot, dramatic representation
    (continuing Fabian's theatrical allu-
    sions). Cf. *MND* 5.1.48–50, '*The riot
    of the tipsy bacchanals . . . That is an
    old device.*'
127–8 **take . . . taint** be exposed and
    spoiled (*OED* taint, *v.*[1] C 4b): an allu-
    sion either to food going bad by being
    left in the open, or to the danger of
    catching a disease through exposure
    to the air; cf. 13, 353; 3.1.66; 5.1.134,
    351 and notes. Maria is afraid the plot
    might be ruined by becoming public
    knowledge.
130 **the quieter** i.e. because the 'mad'
    Malvolio will be put away (see next line)
131 **in . . . bound** the customary treat-
    ment at the time for madness (see

Reed, 11). Cf. Dr Pinch's proposed
cure for Antipholus and Dromio of
Ephesus in *CE* 4.4.96, 'They must be
bound and laid in some dark room.'
133 **carry it** bring it off (*OED v.* 15b).
    Cf. *AW* 4.1.26, 'It must be a very plau-
    sive invention that carries it.'
133–4 **till . . . breath** until we grow tired
    from an excess of enjoyment. As in
    2.5, the harsh treatment of Malvolio is
    planned as a form of spectator sport.
135–6 **bring . . . bar** bring our plot into
    the open (literally, to the prisoner's
    stand, and thus into open court)
136 **finder of madmen** i.e. member of
    a jury appointed to decide whether the
    accused is insane
138 **More . . . morning** more holiday
    entertainment (i.e. Sir Andrew's chal-
    lenge). The allusion is to the May
    games, namely the array of sports
    and performances associated with May
    Day festivities, and does not imply
    temporal setting of the play.

136.1] *this edn; after 137 F   with a letter*] *Cam*[1] *subst.*

SIR ANDREW Here's the challenge, read it. I warrant
    there's vinegar and pepper in't.   140

FABIAN Is't so saucy?

SIR ANDREW Ay, is't, I warrant him. Do but read.

SIR TOBY Give me. [*Reads.*] *Youth, whatsoever thou art,*
    thou art but a scurvy fellow.

FABIAN Good, and valiant.   145

SIR TOBY [*Reads.*] *Wonder not nor admire not in thy mind*
    why I do call thee so, for I will show thee no reason for't.

FABIAN A good note, that keeps you from the blow of the
    law.

SIR TOBY [*Reads.*] *Thou com'st to the Lady Olivia, and in*   150
    my sight she uses thee kindly. But thou liest in thy throat;
    that is not the matter I challenge thee for.

FABIAN Very brief, and to exceeding good sense [*aside*]
    -less.

SIR TOBY [*Reads.*] *I will waylay thee going home, where*   155
    if it be thy chance to kill me —

141 **saucy** spicy, insolent
142 **I warrant him** truly. A discourse marker: literally, I stand guarantor for it (the letter); *him* was the dative form of 'it' as well as 'he' (*OED* him 2a).
144 *thou* Sir Andrew has accepted Sir Toby's advice to *thou* Cesario (cf. 3.2.42–3).
    scurvy worthless
146 *admire* marvel (synonymous with *wonder*, and so – typically with Sir Andrew – tautological)
147 *I will . . . reason* I am not obliged to explain; I have no motive to produce
148 **A good note** well said
148–9 **keeps . . . law** protects you from the risk of legal action (for breach of the peace)
151 *thou . . . throat* you are a complete liar: idiomatic (Dent, T268). Sir Andrew is again following Sir Toby's advice at 3.2.43–4, and closely echoing Saviolo's example of a foolish and low-class challenge: 'euerye daye there riseth from the common sorte new and strange foolishnesses, as he who will giue the lye ere the other speake, saying: if they saye that I am not an honest man, thou lyest in thy throate' (Saviolo, book 2, sig. T2ʳ). See 3.2.40n. and 44n. Here the 'lie' is the very idea – never mentioned by Cesario – that Sir Andrew is jealous of him: hence there is no motive, as Fabian points out at 153–4.

142 is't,] *Collier;* ist? *F*   143, 313, 317 SDs] *Rowe*   146, 150, 155, 158, 161 SDs] *Mahood*   156 *me –*] *Rowe; me. F*

FABIAN   Good.

SIR TOBY [*Reads.*]   *Thou kill'st me like a rogue and a villain.*

FABIAN   Still you keep o'th' windy side of the law –
good.   160

SIR TOBY [*Reads.*]   *Fare thee well, and God have mercy*
upon one of our souls. He may have mercy upon mine, but
my hope is better, and so look to thyself. Thy friend as thou
usest him, and thy sworn enemy,

          Andrew Aguecheek.   165

If this letter move him not, his legs cannot. I'll give't
him.

MARIA   You may have very fit occasion for't. He is now
in some commerce with my lady, and will by and by
depart.   170

SIR TOBY   Go, Sir Andrew. Scout me for him at the corner
of the orchard like a bumbaily. So soon as ever thou
seest him, draw and, as thou draw'st, swear horrible,

---

157 **Good** a good line of argument; a
good thing if Sir Andrew were to be
killed
158 *like . . . villain* This phrase, apart
from the tautology, is ambiguous: it
could refer back to either *thou* or *me.*
159 **o'th'** . . . **law** at a safe distance
from legal punishment. Mahood takes
this to be a hunting metaphor, but it
is more probably derived from the
nautical expression 'on the windward
side', i.e. the law would have to sail
against the wind to reach you; cf. *MA*
2.1.296.
163 *my . . . better* i.e. I have a better
chance of surviving; Sir Andrew also
seems unwittingly to suggest that his
soul may not be saved.
163–4 *as . . . him* to the extent that you
treat him like one (i.e. not at all).
With this self-deconstructing phrase,
and the absurd contradiction between

Thy friend and *thy sworn enemy*, Sir
Andrew manages to cancel any residue
of meaning from his challenge.
166–7 **I'll give't him** Sir Toby confirms
his promise at 3.2.56; in reality, he
has no intention of giving Cesario the
letter, as he admits at 179 after Sir
Andrew exits.
169 **commerce** dealings, exchange (*OED*
n. 2a, giving this example)
171 **Scout . . . him** keep an eye open for
me (*OED v.* 1a, giving this example);
me is an 'ethic dative' (= for me: Blake,
Grammar, 3.3.2.1a); cf. 3.2.31–2n.
172 **bumbaily** bumbailiff, contemptuous term for bailiff, i.e. sheriff's
officer, who catches debtors from the
rear (hence *bum*; the expression is the
equivalent to French *pousse-cul*: *OED*,
giving this example)
173 **horrible** horribly (adverb): cf. *KL*
4.6.3, 'Horrible steep'.

166 If] *Hanmer; To.* If *F* 168 You] *F2;* Yon *F* 173 horrible] horribly *F2*

for it comes to pass oft that a terrible oath, with a
swaggering accent sharply twanged off, gives manhood   175
more approbation than ever proof itself would have
earned him. Away!

SIR ANDREW Nay, let me alone for swearing.   *Exit.*

SIR TOBY Now will not I deliver his letter, for the
behaviour of the young gentleman gives him out to   180
be of good capacity and breeding. His employment
between his lord and my niece confirms no less.
Therefore this letter, being so excellently ignorant,
will breed no terror in the youth. He will find it comes
from a clod-pole. But, sir, I will deliver his challenge by   185
word of mouth, set upon Aguecheek a notable report of
valour and drive the gentleman – as I know his youth
will aptly receive it – into a most hideous opinion of
his rage, skill, fury and impetuosity. This will so fright

174 *for it** the most likely reading for
F's 'for t' (with its wide space between
'for' and 't'); a less probable alternative
is 'for't'.

175 **swaggering** insolent, hectoring:
another possible allusion to the *miles
gloriosus* or cowardly braggart soldier
(see 3.2.40n.)
twanged off *OED* glosses *twang* (*v.*
5a) as 'utter with a sharp ringing tone',
quoting this example and giving the
verb as a variant of 'tang' (cf. 2.5.147).
Most early uses of the word, however,
suggest the sound of plucking a stringed
instrument (*OED* 1–2), which may be
closer to the sound being evoked here.
Alternatively, the term may already have
the more modern meaning, 'spoken with
a nasal intonation' (*OED v.* 6, first occurrence 1615). In Jonson's *Poetaster* (1601),
1.2, 'twang' means simply 'speak': 'The
tongue of the *oracle* neuer twang'd truer'
(Jonson, *Works*, 280).

176 **approbation** credit
proof trial

178 **let . . . swearing** I don't need any
help in swearing; cf. 93n. Saying oaths
is indeed one of Sir Andrew's few
gifts: see, for example, 387; 2.5.30;
3.2.12.

179 **Now . . . letter** Sir Toby changes his
mind about delivering the challenge,
presumably because of its dubious literary quality: cf. 166–7 and 3.2.56. In
Mendes's 2002 Donmar production,
Paul Jesson's Toby tore up the letter
contemptuously.

181 **of . . . breeding** intelligent and
well bred: a further underlining of
Cesario's 'gentle' status, despite his
servant role; cf. *the gentleman*, 187.

185 **clod-pole** blockhead: literally, having
a head (poll) made of a clod of earth
(*OED* clod-pate, first occurrence)

186 **set upon** attribute to

187–8 **his . . . receive it** his lack of
experience will lead him to react to
the challenge

188 **aptly** readily (*OED* 3, giving this
example)

174 for it] *Cam¹*; for't *F*

them both that they will kill one another by the look,   190
like cockatrices.

Enter OLIVIA *and* VIOLA [*as Cesario*].

FABIAN   Here he comes with your niece. Give them way
till he take leave, and presently after him.

SIR TOBY   I will meditate the while upon some horrid
message for a challenge.   195

[*Exeunt Sir Toby, Fabian and Maria.*]

OLIVIA
I have said too much unto a heart of stone
And laid mine honour too unchary on't.
There's something in me that reproves my fault,
But such a headstrong potent fault it is
That it but mocks reproof.   200

---

191 **cockatrices** basilisks, mythical monsters able to kill with a glance. Cf. *RJ* 3.2.47, 'the death-darting eye of cockatrice'. 'To kill like a cockatrice' was proverbial (Dent, C496.2), but Sir Toby's ironical conceit of a duel of deadly glances is grotesquely original.

192–3 **Give . . . leave** step aside until he leaves

193 **presently** immediately

194 **horrid** frightening

196 **heart of stone** proverbial (Dent, H311)

197 **laid . . . on't** placed my honour too rashly upon it (i.e. the stone). Most editors have adopted Theobald's emendation 'laid . . . out', in the sense of 'exposed', partly on the grounds that the same 'error' is supposedly made in *WT* 4.4.160 ('look on't' for 'look out') and may be a recurrent

vice on the part of compositor B. F's line, however, is surely stronger in developing the 'heart of stone' commonplace. Olivia is probably alluding to the Elizabethan custom of placing money on a stone in church by way of payment of a debt (Sisson, 1.193), with the further 'monetary' implication that she has recklessly wagered her honour on the stone-cold Cesario.

unchary rashly (adverb, from 'chary', cautious: *OED*, first occurrence)

198 **fault** misdeed

199 **headstrong potent** obstinately powerful; *headstrong* is best understood as an intensifier qualifying the adjective *potent*: cf. *longing wavering*, 2.4.34.

fault vice

200 **but** merely

mocks reproof ignores my attempts to correct it

191.1 *as Cesario*] *Munro subst.*   195 SD] *Capell; Exeunt. F2; Exit Maria. Sir Toby and Fabian stand aside / Mahood*   197 on't] *out Theobald*

VIOLA

With the same haviour that your passion bears
Goes on my master's griefs.

OLIVIA

Here, wear this jewel for me: 'tis my picture.
Refuse it not, it hath no tongue to vex you;
And I beseech you come again tomorrow.　　　　205
What shall you ask of me that I'll deny
That honour saved may upon asking give?

VIOLA

Nothing but this: your true love for my master.

OLIVIA

How with mine honour may I give him that
Which I have given to you?

VIOLA　　　　　　　　　　I will acquit you.　　　　210

OLIVIA

Well, come again tomorrow. Fare thee well.
A fiend like thee might bear my soul to hell.　　　　[*Exit.*]

Enter [SIR] TOBY *and* FABIAN.

SIR TOBY　　Gentleman, God save thee.

201–2 My master's pains of unrequited love continue without end. The *–es* plural ending (*Goes*) is quite frequent in Early Modern English (Hope, 2.1.8).

201 **same . . . bears** same behaviour that your desire provokes in you
haviour behaviour (*OED* 2): not an abbreviation, so no apostrophe required

203 **jewel** miniature set in jewels. The word *jewel* in Shakespeare 'does not properly signify a single gem, but any precious ornament or superfluity' (Johnson).
picture portrait

206–7 *F's punctuation of this somewhat contorted construction does not help to clarify its sense, which is roughly 'How can I deny you anything that I may give you without losing my honour (i.e. my virginity)?'

210 **acquit you** release you from your vows of love for me; take my leave of you (with a pun on 'quit')

211, 212 **thee** Olivia switches, as at 3.1.136, from formal *you* (204–10) to familiar *thou*, which she will continue to adopt with Sebastian at 4.1.50–63. Viola maintains a respectful *you* throughout.

202 Goes] Go *Malone*　griefs] Grief *Rowe*　207 honour saved] *Pope;* honour (sau'd) *F;* (honour sav'd) *F3*　212, 381 SDs] *F2*

287

VIOLA   And you, sir.

SIR TOBY   That defence thou hast, betake thee to't. Of   215
what nature the wrongs are thou hast done him, I know
not, but thy intercepter, full of despite, bloody as the
hunter, attends thee at the orchard end. Dismount thy
tuck, be yare in thy preparation, for thy assailant is
quick, skilful and deadly.   220

VIOLA   You mistake, sir. I am sure no man hath any quarrel
to me. My remembrance is very free and clear from any
image of offence done to any man.

SIR TOBY   You'll find it otherwise, I assure you. Therefore,
if you hold your life at any price, betake you to your   225
guard, for your opposite hath in him what youth,
strength, skill and wrath can furnish man withal.

VIOLA   I pray you, sir, what is he?

---

215 **That . . . to't** make use of whatever defence you possess; *betake thee
to* was commonly followed by 'thy
heels' (*OED* betake 4), so that Sir
Toby may be implying that Cesario's
only hope of survival is to run away.

217 **intercepter** stalker, persecutor:
probably borrowed – like *discard* at
86 – from Florio, *World*, 187, where
it appears for the first time in English
(*OED* 1a). It is glossed in Florio's
New World, 262, as '*Intercettore*, a
preuenter, a forestaller, an encrocher,
an interceptor'; there may be a hint
that this 'preventer' is a personification
of death awaiting his next victim (see
attends thee, 218).

despite contempt, defiance

217–18 **bloody . . . hunter** a reference to
the ritual of smearing the successful
huntsman with the blood of his prey
(Capell)

218 **attends** awaits

at . . . end outside the garden
(cf. 3.2.6); *at the end* here probably

means 'just beyond the limit', since
it is improbable that Sir Andrew,
who enters at 266, is to be imagined
as already present in Olivia's estate.

218–19 **Dismount thy tuck** draw thy
sword. A *tuck* (*OED* n.³) was a small
rapier (from Old French *etoc*, Italian *stocco*); cf. *stuck*, 269n. In *Hamlet* Osric calls
the straps attaching the sword to the belt
'carriages' (*Ham* 5.2.133), and *dismount*
seems to play on the same metaphor.

219 **yare** ready, quick

222 **to me** with me

remembrance recollection

225 **if . . . price** if you value your life
at all

225–6 **betake . . . guard** take up a defensive position: a fencing expression. Sir
Toby repeats his use of intimidating
'technical' terms with Sir Andrew at
268–70.

226 **opposite** opponent; cf. 3.2.61.

227 **withal** with: an emphatic form
(Blake, *Grammar*, 5.4.2)

228 **what** what rank; cf. 1.2.32n.

---

221 sir . . . no] *Theobald subst.;* sir I am sure, no *F;* sir, I am sure, no *F3*

SIR TOBY He is knight, dubbed with unhatched rapier
and on carpet consideration, but he is a devil in private   230
brawl. Souls and bodies hath he divorced three, and
his incensement at this moment is so implacable that
satisfaction can be none but by pangs of death and
sepulchre. 'Hob-nob' is his word: give't or take't.

VIOLA I will return again into the house and desire some   235
conduct of the lady. I am no fighter. I have heard of
some kind of men that put quarrels purposely on
others to taste their valour. Belike this is a man of that
quirk.

SIR TOBY Sir, no. His indignation derives itself out of a   240
very competent injury, therefore get you on and give
him his desire. Back you shall not to the house, unless
you undertake that with me which with as much safety
you might answer him. Therefore on, or strip your

229–30 dubbed . . . consideration
knighted at court rather than on the
battlefield. Sir Andrew is a 'coward
carpet knyght' (said of Paris in Ovid,
Met., 12.673, fol. 157ʳ; 13.123, fol.
159ʳ): i.e. he purchased his title, since
he was probably of low social origins.
Francis Markham affirms disapprovingly, 'these of the vulgar or common
sort, are called *Carpet-knights*, because
. . . they receiue their honour from the
Kings hand, in the Court, and upon
Carpets' (Markham, 71; Furness).
There is a likely pun on *consideration*
meaning sum of money.
unhatched unhacked, i.e. used not for
combat but for ceremonial purposes
(*OED ppl. a.*²)
232 **incensement** anger
234 **sepulchre** burial
'Hob-nob' *OED* glosses 'have or have
not', but Sir Toby's own gloss (*give't
or take't*) suggests a more specific and

sinister meaning, i.e. kill or be killed
('it' = death). In Carroll's 2002 Middle
Temple production, Sir Andrew emitted the war-cry 'Hob-nob!' offstage.
word motto
236 **conduct** escort (modern 'safe-
conduct')
238 **taste** test. Viola claims not to understand the verb when used in this sense
by Sir Toby at 3.1.76–8; either she was
pretending or she has learned.
Belike probably
239 **quirk** peculiar disposition (*OED n.*¹
4, first occurrence)
241 ***competent** legally sufficient (to
justify the duel) (*OED a.* 6b). F's
'computent' is a variant spelling.
injury offence
243 **undertake** engage in
that i.e. a duel. Sir Toby threatens to
fight Cesario himself if he refuses the
duel with Sir Andrew.
244 **on** go forward

---

229 unhatched] unhack'd *Pope;* an hatch'd *Keightley (Malone)*   234 'Hob-nob'] *this edn;* Hob, nob
F; 'Hob nob' *Oxf*¹   241 competent] *(computent), F4*   244 on, or] on, and *Rann*

sword stark naked, for meddle you must, that's certain,   245
or forswear to wear iron about you.

VIOLA   This is as uncivil as strange. I beseech you do me
this courteous office as to know of the knight what my
offence to him is. It is something of my negligence,
nothing of my purpose.   250

SIR TOBY   I will do so. Signor Fabian, stay you by this
gentleman till my return.   *Exit.*

VIOLA   Pray you, sir, do you know of this matter?

FABIAN   I know the knight is incensed against you even to
a mortal arbitrament, but nothing of the circumstance   255
more.

VIOLA   I beseech you, what manner of man is he?

FABIAN   Nothing of that wonderful promise to read him
by his form as you are like to find him in the proof of
his valour. He is indeed, sir, the most skilful, bloody and   260
fatal opposite that you could possibly have found in any
part of Illyria. Will you walk towards him, I will make
your peace with him – if I can.

VIOLA   I shall be much bound to you for't. I am one that
had rather go with Sir Priest than Sir Knight. I care not   265

244–6 **or . . . or** either . . . or. It is just possible, however, that the first *or* (244) is an error: F's 'on, or' might be a dittography (unintentional repetition) on the part of a scribe faced with a deletion (RP).

245 **meddle** fight (*OED v.* 6)

246 **forswear . . . you** give up wearing a sword, and thereby admit to cowardice

247–8 **do . . . of** be so kind as to find out from. This complex construction seems to conflate two idioms: 'be so courteous as to' and 'do me the office to'.

249, 250 **of** due to

255 **mortal arbitrament** trial by combat to the death

258–9 **Nothing . . . form** not as threatening, to judge from his external appearance, as you are likely to find him in the practical demonstration of his courage (i.e. in combat). In Barton's 1969 RSC production Fabian alarmingly rolled bandages during this speech, in preparation for the bloodshed.

261 **fatal opposite** deadly opponent

262 **Will . . . him** F's comma after *him* implies an elided conditional ('If you will . . .'), although actors often turn it into a direct and threatening question to Cesario.

265 **Sir Priest** *Sir*, the English equivalent of Latin *dominus*, was the title given to a graduate in theology, and hence to a clergyman (Johnson). The

248 as to] to *Capell*   252 SD] *(Exit Toby.)*

who knows so much of my mettle.   *Exeunt.*

Enter [SIR] TOBY *and* [SIR] ANDREW.

SIR TOBY   Why, man, he's a very devil. I have not seen
such a firago. I had a pass with him, rapier, scabbard
and all, and he gives me the stuck in with such a mortal
motion that it is inevitable; and on the answer, he pays   270

antithesis here with Sir Andrew's 'carpet' knighthood (*Sir Knight*) is ironical, since in reality neither title promises great martial prowess (see 229–30n.).

266 **mettle** temperament: in Early Modern English, a variant spelling of 'metal', used metaphorically; cf. 2.5.12, 5.1.316.

268 **firago** virago; literally, a man-like woman. Sir Toby implicitly questions Cesario's gender. In the Vulgate version of Genesis, 2.23, 'Virago' is Adam's name for Eve, and thus for woman as such. The term was also applicable, however, to a ferocious *male* warrior (*OED* 2b). On these gender ambiguities, cf. John Taylor the Water Poet's *Superbiae Flagellum, or The Whip of Pride* (1621): 'Like shamelesse double sex'd *Hermaphrodites*, / *Virago* Roaring Girles' (J. Taylor, 33). F's spelling probably indicates a colourfully expressive 'error' on Sir Toby's part, suggesting '*fire, fury, fiend, ferociousness*, all combined' (Furness), especially if the first syllable is pronounced as in 'fire'.

pass bout of fencing; literally, a move involving a thrust forward with the sword (from Italian *passata*). Cf. *MW* 2.3.23, 'your passes, stoccadoes, and I know not what'.

scabbard sheath protecting the sword. This implies ironically that Cesario's rapier remained unsheathed

during their *pass*. There is a crescendo of phallic references in the scene, leading up to Viola's confession that she has (metaphorically) no sword (295–6).

269 **stuck in** winning thrust: another fencing term (like *tuck*, 219, from Italian *stocco*), consisting in the fencer's 'putting the point of his Rapier under his [opponent's] Rapier, and so giuing him a thrust in the belly' (Saviolo, book 1, fol. 8ʳ). Cf. *Ham* 4.7.159, 'If he by chance escape your venomed stuck'. The particle *in* here has the sense of 'home', i.e. hitting the target, as in the SD in *RJ* 3.1.89, '*Tybalt under Romeo's arm thrusts Mercutio in.*'

269–70 **mortal motion** deadly movement; *motion* is a further fencing term indicating a highly disciplined and regulated stepping movement (*OED* n. 3c).

270 **it is inevitable** ambiguous: either the fencing *motion* cannot be avoided; or death (cf. *mortal*, 269) is the unavoidable consequence of the *stuck*.

270–1 **on . . . you** when you attempt to return his thrust, he puts paid to you. Sir Toby contradicts Saviolo, according to whom the fencer must 'breake the stoccata with his lefte hande, and aunswere againe with an other' (Saviolo, book 1, fol. 17ʳ): this becomes instead a supposedly fatal error against Cesario. For *pay* in the sense of 'kill', cf. *1H4* 2.4.189, 'Two I am sure I have paid.'

268 firago] virago *Rowe*

you as surely as your feet hits the ground they step on.
They say he has been fencer to the Sophy.

SIR ANDREW   Pox on't, I'll not meddle with him.

SIR TOBY   Ay, but he will not now be pacified. Fabian can
scarce hold him yonder.   275

SIR ANDREW   Plague on't, an I thought he had been
valiant, and so cunning in fence, I'd have seen him
damned ere I'd have challenged him. Let him let the
matter slip and I'll give him my horse, grey Capulet.

SIR TOBY   I'll make the motion. Stand here, make a good   280
show on't. This shall end without the perdition of
souls. [*aside*] Marry, I'll ride your horse as well as I ride
you.

Enter FABIAN *and* VIOLA [*as Cesario*].

[*aside to Fabian*] I have his horse to take up the quarrel.
I have persuaded him the youth's a devil.   285

FABIAN [*aside to Sir Toby*]   He is as horribly conceited of
him, and pants and looks pale as if a bear were at his
heels.

---

271 **as . . . on** as certainly as you touch
the ground when you walk (but evoking also the image of Sir Andrew's
dead body hitting the ground)
hits plural (an example of the
'Northern Personal Pronoun Rule'
in Early Modern English: Hope,
2.1.8a)
272 **Sophy** Shah of Persia: cf. 2.5.175.
276 **Plague on't** Cf. 1.3.1n.
an if
277 **cunning** skilful
279 ***Capulet** 'Capul' or 'caple' was a
Middle English and dialect word for
'horse' (*OED*), so that the name of Sir
Andrew's grey steed may mean simply

'little horse'; also presumably a pre-
tentious reference to the noble Italian
name Capulet, Juliet's surname in *RJ*:
hence Dyce's emendation.
280 **motion** proposal, offer
281–2 **perdition of souls** loss of life;
damnation (due to murder): a pun
282 **ride** have complete control of (*OED*
v. 17b). Sir Toby sees another opportunity to 'milk' Sir Andrew, and has
no intention of mentioning his offer to
Cesario (see 293n.).
284 **take . . . quarrel** settle the dispute;
cf. *AYL* 5.4.96–7.
286 **He . . . conceited** he has as terrify-
ing an idea

---

271 hits] hit *Rowe*   274–5] *Capell; F lines* Pacified, / yonder. /   279 Capulet] *(Capilet), Dyce*
282, 390 SDs] *Theobald*   283.1 *as Cesario*] *Munro subst.*   284 SD] *Oxf; to Fab: Douai MS,
Rowe*   286 SD] *Oxf; To Sir Toby / Collier*

SIR TOBY [*aside to Viola*]   There's no remedy, sir, he will
fight with you for's oath' sake. Marry, he hath better   290
bethought him of his quarrel and he finds that now
scarce to be worth talking of. Therefore draw for the
supportance of his vow. He protests he will not hurt
you.

VIOLA [*aside*]   Pray God defend me! A little thing would   295
make me tell them how much I lack of a man.

FABIAN [*aside to Sir Andrew*]   Give ground if you see him
furious.

SIR TOBY [*aside to Sir Andrew*]   Come, Sir Andrew, there's
no remedy. The gentleman will for his honour's sake   300
have one bout with you; he cannot by the duello avoid
it. But he has promised me, as he is a gentleman and a
soldier, he will not hurt you. Come on, to't.

SIR ANDREW [*aside*]   Pray God he keep his oath!

Enter ANTONIO.

290 **for's oath' sake** for his oath's sake
291 **bethought him** reconsidered
   quarrel the grounds for his complaint
   (against you)
293 **supportance** honouring: Cesario is
   obliged to fight, according to the code
   of honour, simply because Sir Andrew
   has (supposedly) vowed to do so (see
   301n.).
295–6 **A little . . . man** It would take little to make me reveal how much I am
   not a man, i.e. how fearful I am, with
   a probable innuendo on what Viola
   lacks in order to be a man: a *thing*,
   Elizabethan slang for penis (*OED n.*[1]
   11c; Partridge, 199). Cf. Portia on her
   disguise in *MV* 3.4.61–2, 'in such a
   habit / That they shall think we are

accomplished / With that we lack'.
298 **furious** mad with anger
301 **by the duello** by the formal rules
   governing the code of duelling. In
   LLL Don Armado complains, 'The
   passado he respects not; the *duello* he
   regards not' (*LLL* 1.2.174–5); by contrast, Mercutio has contempt for his
   opponent Tybalt as one 'that fights
   by the book of arithmetic', i.e. by the
   fencing manual (*RJ* 3.1.103).
304.1 There is some inconsistency
   regarding the location of this scene,
   apparently set in Olivia's *orchard* (218).
   After Antonio's arrest, the officers tell
   Orsino of a *private brabble* that took
   place 'Here in the streets' (5.1.60–1).
   Audiences do not notice such details.

289 SD] *this edn; to Viola. Douai MS, Capell*   290 oath'] *Oxf;* oath *F;* oaths *Douai MS;* oath's
Capell   297 SD] *this edn;* To Sir Andrew *Ard*[2]   299 SD] *this edn; crossing to Sir Andrew / Mahood*
304, 322 SDs] *this edn*   304 oath!] oath! *draws. / Capell*

VIOLA [*to Sir Andrew*]   I do assure you 'tis against my   305
    will. [*Sir Andrew and Viola draw swords.*]
ANTONIO [*Draws sword.*]
    [*to Sir Andrew*] Put up your sword. If this young
        gentleman
    Have done offence, I take the fault on me.
    If you offend him, I for him defy you.
SIR TOBY   You, sir? Why, what are you?   310
ANTONIO
    One, sir, that for his love dares yet do more
    Than you have heard him brag to you he will.
SIR TOBY [*Draws sword.*]   Nay, if you be an undertaker, I
    am for you.

Enter Officers.

FABIAN   O good Sir Toby, hold. Here come the officers.   315
SIR TOBY [*to Antonio*]   I'll be with you anon.
VIOLA [*to Sir Andrew*]   Pray, sir, put your sword up, if you
    please.
SIR ANDREW   Marry, will I, sir. And for that I promised

305–6 **against my will** Viola's resistance
    to a motiveless duel could be benevo-
    lently interpreted as a sign of gentil-
    ity (James Spedding, in Furness). At
    the same time, like Sir Andrew, she
    is admittedly terrified (295–6), and
    in performance Sir Toby and Fabian
    usually have to force them together.
307 **Put up** put away
310 **what** who; cf. 1.2.32n.
313 **undertaker** one who takes up a chal-
    lenge (*OED* 3c, sole occurrence); one
    who takes on someone else's business,
    especially a contractor or tax collector
    (*OED* 5)

314 **for you** i.e. the right person for you
315 **the officers** i.e. officers of justice
    or of the peace: an early form of
    police, usually under the command of
    the sheriff, here directly answerable
    to Orsino (see 324–5). One of their
    peace-keeping functions was the sup-
    pression of duels and brawls, hence
    Fabian's concern.
319 **that** i.e. his steed Capulet (see 279).
    Since Sir Toby has failed to men-
    tion Sir Andrew's offer, this adds to
    Viola's bewilderment. Aguecheek is so
    relieved not to have to fight that he is
    prepared to give her his horse anyway.

---

306 SD] *Ard²; after 303 Rowe; draws / Capell; Sir Toby and Fabian force them to make a few passes
in great fear. / Powell MS; they fight; VIOLA very timid, and* SIR ANDREW *tremulously parrying her
blows.* SIR TOBY *and* FABIAN *urging them on each other. / Lacy*   307 SD1] *Ard¹; after 309 Rowe*   SD2]
Inchbald   316 anon.] *anon. he hides from the officers behind a tree Cam¹; anon. Steps aside to avoid the
Officers Riv*

you I'll be as good as my word. He will bear you easily,   320
and reins well.

1 OFFICER [*Indicates Antonio.*]   This is the man; do thy
office.

2 OFFICER
Antonio, I arrest thee at the suit
Of Count Orsino.

ANTONIO   You do mistake me, sir.   325

1 OFFICER
No, sir, no jot. I know your favour well,
Though now you have no sea-cap on your head.
[*to Second Officer*] Take him away; he knows I know
    him well.

ANTONIO
I must obey. [*to Viola*] This comes with seeking you.
But there's no remedy; I shall answer it.   330
What will you do now my necessity
Makes me to ask you for my purse? It grieves me
Much more for what I cannot do for you
Than what befalls myself. You stand amazed,
But be of comfort.   335

2 OFFICER
Come, sir, away.

ANTONIO [*to Viola*]
I must entreat of you some of that money.

VIOLA
What money, sir?

---

321 **reins well** responds readily to the
rein
326 **favour** face; cf. 378 and 2.4.24–5.
The fact that the First Officer knows
Antonio suggests that he may have
taken part as one of Orsino's sailors in
the somewhat mysterious sea battle (cf.
sea-cap, 327); he is thus also an *officer*

in the naval sense (*OED n.* 4a).
327 **sea-cap** sailor's cap
329 **with** as a result of (Blake, *Grammar*,
5.4.2)
330 **answer** pay for; cf. 3.3.28.
334 **amazed** lost in wonder (*OED ppl.
a.* 4): more emphatic than in modern
English

324–5 Antonio . . . Orsino] *Capell; one line F*   329 SD] *Collier*   331 do now] *Oxf;* do: now *F;* doe?
now *F2;* do, now *Dyce*   332 purse?] *Dyce;* purse. *F*

For the fair kindness you have showed me here,
And part being prompted by your present trouble,   340
Out of my lean and low ability
I'll lend you something. My having is not much.
I'll make division of my present with you.
Hold, [*offering money*] there's half my coffer.
ANTONIO [*Refuses money.*]   Will you deny me now?
Is't possible that my deserts to you   345
Can lack persuasion? Do not tempt my misery,
Lest that it make me so unsound a man
As to upbraid you with those kindnesses
That I have done for you.
VIOLA   I know of none,
Nor know I you by voice or any feature.   350
I hate ingratitude more in a man
Than lying vainness, babbling drunkenness
Or any taint of vice whose strong corruption
Inhabits our frail blood.

---

339 **fair** pleasing, flattering
340 **part** in part. Cf. *Oth* 5.2.295, 'This wretch hath part confessed his villainy.'
341 **ability** financial means (*OED* 4, giving this example)
342 **My having** what I possess. Cf. *AYL* 3.2.368, 'your having in beard is a younger brother's revenue.'
343 **my present** such money as I have at present
344 **coffer** money (literally chest): an ironic hyperbole, given Viola's limited means
345 **deserts** gestures deserving recompense (*OED n.*[1] 1)
346 **persuasion** the force to move (you)
tempt put to the test
347 **unsound** morally deficient (since *kindnesses*, 348, should not be made in hope of a reward)
349–54 **I know ... blood** Cesario's list of vices is effectively an expansion of the

proverb 'Ingratitude comprehends all faults' (Dent, I66).
352 *lying . . . drunkenness* F's punctuation has *lying* as a noun, on a par with *vainness*; this, however, creates an asymmetrical relationship with *babbling drunkenness* (adjective + noun), whereas Rowe[3]'s emendation produces two symmetrical phrases.
vainness boastfulness (vainglory). The word is used and glossed by the Chorus in *H5* 5.0.20, 'Being free from vainness, and self-glorious pride'.
babbling incoherent
drunkenness In Posner's 2001 RSC production, Zoë Waites's Viola looked towards Sir Toby.
353 **taint** stain (*OED v.* C 2a, first occurrence); cf. 13, 128; 3.1.66; 5.1.134, 351 and notes.
corruption power of contagion: primarily a medical metaphor, but

---

344 SDs] *Cam*[1] *subst.*   352 lying vainness, babbling] *Rowe*[3]*;* lying, vainnesse, babling *F*

ANTONIO   O heavens themselves!

2 OFFICER

    Come, sir, I pray you go.   355

ANTONIO

    Let me speak a little. This youth that you see here

    I snatched one half out of the jaws of death,

    Relieved him with such sanctity of love,

    And to his image, which methought did promise

    Most venerable worth, did I devotion.   360

1 OFFICER

    What's that to us? The time goes by. Away!

ANTONIO

    But O, how vile an idol proves this god!

    Thou hast, Sebastian, done good feature shame.

    In nature there's no blemish but the mind:

    None can be called deformed but the unkind.   365

    Virtue is beauty, but the beauteous evil

    Are empty trunks o'erflourished by the devil.

1 OFFICER

    The man grows mad, away with him. Come, come, sir.

'corruption of blood' was also a legal concept, i.e. the effect of an attainder whereby the blood of the culprit was tainted by his crime, causing him and his descendants to lose all rights of rank and title (*OED* 2b). Here the 'crime' is vice in general, which deprives the guilty party of his right to the title of *man* (351) and in particular to that of gentleman.

357 **one . . . death** out of the jaws of death which had half swallowed him

358 **Relieved** aided (*OED v.* 1a, giving this example)

    sanctity of love holy love. This and the following passage are couched in the language of religious devotion (cf. 2.1.43), applied to profane love as in the Sonnets, where it is likewise directed towards another man.

359 **image** appearance; religious icon

360 **venerable** worthy of veneration

363 **Sebastian** the first explicit evidence for Viola that her brother is alive: cf. her 'delayed' reaction, 370–3.
    feature looks

364 **the mind** in the mind

365 **unkind** hard-hearted; unnatural. Cf. Lear's 'unkind daughters'(*KL* 3.4.73).

366 **beauteous evil** oxymoron. Cf. *proper false*, 2.2.29.

367 **trunks o'er flourished** In prosperous Elizabethan households, trunks, often elaborately ornamented with emblematic and other devices, were an important part of the furniture (Steevens). The trunk plays a conspicuous role in the stage history of this comedy, in part because of this reference: cf. 1.2.01n.

362 vile] *(vilde)*, *Pope*

ANTONIO

    Lead me on.   *Exit [with Officers].*

VIOLA [*aside*]

    Methinks his words do from such passion fly   370
    That he believes himself. So do not I.
    Prove true, imagination, O prove true,
    That I, dear brother, be now ta'en for you!

SIR TOBY   Come hither, knight; come hither, Fabian. We'll
    whisper o'er a couplet or two of most sage saws. [*They*   375
    stand aside.]

VIOLA

    He named Sebastian. I my brother know
    Yet living in my glass. Even such and so
    In favour was my brother, and he went
    Still in this fashion, colour, ornament,
    For him I imitate. O, if it prove,   380
    Tempests are kind, and salt waves fresh in love!   [*Exit.*]

SIR TOBY [*to Sir Andrew*]   A very dishonest, paltry boy,
    and more a coward than a hare. His dishonesty appears
    in leaving his friend here in necessity and denying him;

---

370 **passion** overpowering emotion; with a possible allusion to the *passion* of Christ. On the passions in the comedy, see pp. 54–5.

371 **So . . . I** I do not share his belief; or 'I do not yet believe myself, when . . . I gather hope of my brother's life' (Johnson).

372 **imagination** mental image or representation: the earliest sense of the word (*OED* 1)

375 **saws** wise maxims; Sir Toby may wish to mock Antonio's moralizing (Deighton).

376–7 **I . . . glass** I see my brother's living image when I look at myself in the mirror. Viola cross-dressed is Sebastian's perfect double (hence the vicissitudes of the plot).

378 **favour** appearance; cf. 326.
    went appeared

379 **Still** always
    fashion way of dressing

380 **For . . . imitate** an interesting insight into one of Viola's motives for cross-dressing, in order as it were to 'reincarnate' her brother (cf. *Yet living*, 377)
    prove should prove to be so; for the omitted 'so', cf. Blake, *Grammar*, 5.1.3.5(xxii).

381 **fresh** made of fresh water (in contrast to *salt*). Viola's paradoxes suggest that Sebastian's survival would be a miracle of nature.

383 **a coward** cowardly: proverbial ('As fearful as a hare', Dent, H147)

368] *Dyce; F lines* him: / sir. /   369 SD *with Officers*] *Theobald*   370 SD] *Oxf (Furness)*   371 I.] I? *Cam¹*   373 ta'en] *(tane)*   375 SD] *Capell subst.*

and, for his cowardship, ask Fabian.   385

FABIAN   A coward, a most devout coward, religious in it.

SIR ANDREW   'Slid, I'll after him again and beat him.

SIR TOBY   Do, cuff him soundly, but never draw thy
    sword.   389

SIR ANDREW   An I do not –   [*Exit.*]

FABIAN   Come, let's see the event.

SIR TOBY   I dare lay any money 'twill be nothing yet.   *Exeunt.*

4.1   *Enter* SEBASTIAN *and* FESTE.

FESTE   Will you make me believe that I am not sent for
    you?

SEBASTIAN

    Go to, go to, thou art a foolish fellow.

    Let me be clear of thee.

FESTE   Well held out, i'faith! No, I do not know you, nor   5
    I am not sent to you by my lady to bid you come speak
    with her, nor your name is not Master Cesario, nor this

---

386 **religious in it** i.e. he practises
    cowardice religiously
387 **'Slid** by God's eyelid (oath)
388 **cuff** beat
390 i.e. if I do not cuff him
391 **event** outcome (*OED n.* 3a)
392 **yet** after all
4.1 This scene involves the unwitting
    Sebastian in three brief encoun-
    ters – with Feste, with Sir Toby
    and Sir Andrew and, finally, with
    Olivia – all of whom mistake him
    for Cesario, provoking in him a cre-
    scendo of bewilderment. Rowe gives
    '*The Street*' as location. Sir Toby's
    threat to throw Sebastian's dagger
    'o'er the house' (27–8) suggests such
    an outdoor setting; an alternative
    possibility is the 'orchard' or gar-

den mentioned at 3.4.172 and 218
(AT).
1 The scene opens *in medias res*: Feste
    and Sebastian have apparently been
    discussing the question of the latter's
    identity. The clown has evidently been
    sent by Olivia to fetch Cesario: cf. *come
    again tomorrow*, 3.4.211.
    Will you do you want to
3 **Go to** come, come (expression of dis-
    approbation)
4 **clear** rid (*OED v.* 18b, giving this
    example)
5 **held out** kept up, insisted: Sebastian
    continues to deny that he is Cesario.
5–8 **No . . . neither** Feste is playfully
    exaggerating the use of multiple nega-
    tives (Hope, 2.1.9; Blake, *Grammar*,
    6.2.3.3): cf. 3.1.157–8n.

---

390 not –] *Theobald;* not. F   392 SD] *Rowe; Exit.* F   **4.1**] *(Actus Quartus, Scaena prima.)*
0.1 FESTE] *Munro; Clowne* F

is not my nose neither. Nothing that is so is so.

SEBASTIAN

I prithee vent thy folly somewhere else,
Thou knowst not me.   10

FESTE   Vent my folly! He has heard that word of some
great man and now applies it to a fool. Vent my folly!
I am afraid this great lubber the world will prove a
cockney. I prithee now ungird thy strangeness, and tell
me what I shall vent to my lady. Shall I vent to her that   15
thou art coming?

SEBASTIAN

I prithee, foolish Greek, depart from me.

---

8 **Nothing . . . ²so** This is the general
principle of deception or 'fooling' in
the play, which Feste adopts as his
philosophy. Whether the clown – who
may already have seen through Viola's
disguise (see 3.1.43–4n.) – recognizes
that Sebastian is indeed not *Cesario*
is an open question. Contrast Feste's
'That that is' (4.2.14–15).

9 **vent** give vent to, express (literally
blow, from Latin *ventus*, wind); cf. *TS*
1.2.176, ''tis now no time to vent our
love.' The verb is taken up by Feste in
a more vulgar sense: cf. 15n.

9–10, 17–19 *These lines appear as prose
in F; Capell converted them into
(incomplete) verse comprising one or
two more or less regular pentameter
lines followed by one half-line, as here.
There is a precedent for this solution at 2–3, given as verse in F. Feste,
however, speaks in prose throughout
the exchange.

11–12 **He . . . fool** Feste's deriding of
Sebastian's phrase, supposedly bor-
rowed from his betters, recalls Moth in
LLL: 'They have been at a great feast
of languages and stolen the scraps'
(*LLL* 5.1.35–6).

12 **great** eminent

13–14 **this . . . cockney** this clumsy
fool, the world, will turn out to be a
milksop: another sarcastic comment on
Sebastian's 'affected' language

13 **lubber** clumsy person, lout (ety-
mologically related to Danish *lubbe*,
clown: *OED n.* 1a)

14 **cockney** milksop (literally, chicken's
egg). *OED* glosses 'effeminate fellow'
(*n.* 2a, giving this example): this is
ironical in view of Sebastian's – as
opposed to Cesario's – virility.
ungird thy strangeness drop your
formality: i.e. stop pretending not to
know me
ungird release, free (literally by undo-
ing your belt: *OED v.* 2, giving this
example)
strangeness aloofness, formality
(*OED* 2a)

15 **vent** probably a pun on the colloquial
meaning 'excrete' (*OED v.²* 2b), perhaps developing the unbelting metaphor in *ungird*: cf. *Tem* 2.2.105–6, 'Can
he vent Trinculos?'

17 **Greek** buffoon. The noun was usually qualified by *merry* (Dent, M901).
Matthew Merrygreek is an unruly
character in Udall's comedy *Roister
Doister*.

9–10, 17–19] *Capell; prose F*   13 lubber the world] lubberly world *Hudson*

There's money for thee. If you tarry longer
I shall give worse payment.

FESTE   By my troth thou hast an open hand. These wise   20
men that give fools money get themselves a good
report, after fourteen years' purchase.

Enter [SIR] ANDREW, [SIR] TOBY *and* FABIAN.

SIR ANDREW [*to Sebastian*]   Now, sir, have I met you
again. [*Strikes him.*] There's for you.

SEBASTIAN
Why, [*striking Sir Andrew*] there's for thee,   25

---

19 **worse payment** Sebastian, while
giving Feste a tip (presumably using
Antonio's money), adopts a more
'manly' mode that distinguishes him
from the gentler Cesario at 3.1.1–66;
this contrast in manners is expressed
physically at 25 in his reaction to Sir
Andrew, who receives the *worse payment* threatened here.

20 **thou . . . hand** you are generous
(perhaps he hopes to receive a second
tip, as he did from Viola at 3.1.52); you
are ready to give me a beating (implying that Sebastian may have raised his
hand in a threatening manner)

21–2 **get . . . purchase** acquire a good
reputation at a high price: a reference to the economic laws of the
Elizabethan land market in which the
purchase value of land was equivalent
to twelve years' rent. Sebastian and
the others (Viola, Orsino, Sir Toby, Sir
Andrew) who have given Feste money
have paid more than the market rate
for his gratitude.

22 **report** reputation
after at the rate of
purchase payment

23–5 **you . . . thee** Sir Andrew returns
incongruously to formal *you* at the
very moment he hits Sebastian;
Sebastian contemptuously calls him
thee: cf. 3.2.42–3n.

24 SD Sir Andrew, who did all he could to
avoid coming to blows with Cesario in
3.4, ironically finds the courage to hit
out only when he meets a 'real' man.
In Carroll's 2002 Middle Temple production Angus Wright's Sir Andrew
derisively knocked off the hat of Rhys
Meredith's Sebastian, who responded
likewise.

25 SD *Mahood and Oxf have Sebastian
beat Sir Andrew with his dagger, by
way of explanation for Sir Toby's
threat to throw it away (27–8), but
this is surely an exaggerated response
to Sir Andrew's (presumably fee-
ble) attack; Sir Toby is belittling
Sebastian's prowess rather than referring literally to what he is holding at that moment. In performance,
Sebastian usually limits himself to a
slap, while in Mendes' 2002 Donmar
production he stamped on his opponent's feet.

20–1 wise men] *(*Wise-men*)*, *Rowe*   22.1 SIR] *Rowe*   23 SD] *Oxf*   24 SD] *Rowe subst.*   25–6] *this
edn; F lines* there, and there, / mad? /   25 SD] *Douai MS, Rowe subst.; he knocks him down Cam¹; He
beats Sir Andrew with the handle of his dagger / Mahood*

And there, and there. Are all the people mad?

SIR TOBY [*Restrains Sebastian.*]   Hold, sir, or I'll throw
     your dagger o'er the house.

FESTE   This will I tell my lady straight. I would not be in   29
     some of your coats for twopence.   [*Exit.*]

SIR TOBY   Come on, sir, hold!

SIR ANDREW   Nay, let him alone, I'll go another way to
     work with him. I'll have an action of battery against
     him if there be any law in Illyria. Though I struck him
     first, yet it's no matter for that.   35

SEBASTIAN [*to Sir Toby*]
     Let go thy hand.

SIR TOBY   Come, sir, I will not let you go. Come, my young

---

26 **Are... mad** Sebastian's bewilderment recalls that of the twin Antipholus of Syracuse in *CE*, mistaken for his brother: 'Am I . . . / Mad or well advised?' (*CE* 2.2.211–12).

28 **dagger** Since Sir Toby later refers to Sebastian's *iron* (i.e. sword, 38), he may be making fun of Sebastian's weapon here (Oxf[1]).

     o'er the house Hotson, 140–1, suggests that this refers to an actual roofed structure onstage. It is, however, one of several references to Olivia's *house* (see 2.3.97, 3.1.72, 3.4.235, etc.) and probably does not imply a precise physical space, although it does suggest that the scene takes place outdoors. In performance Sir Toby sometimes gestures backstage or towards the audience.

29 **This . . . straight** Feste is careful to dissociate himself from his erstwhile fellow revellers by acting as 'spy', now that the fooling is degenerating. Yet he remains loyal to the plot against Malvolio, as the following scene demonstrates.

     straight straightaway

29–30 **in . . . coats** in some of their shoes (proverbial: Dent, C473; *OED v.* 13, giving this example); with an implied allusion to Feste's own motley 'coat', which gets him out of trouble, since as a fool he – unlike Toby and Andrew – is licensed to be unruly.

30 **twopence** a proverbially modest sum: in Shakespeare's day, a small silver coin. Feste is used to receiving tips of sixpence (see 2.3.30–2). On currency in the play, cf. 1.3.20n. and 2.3.19n.

32–3 **I'll . . . work** I'll deal with him in another fashion: proverbial (Dent, W150)

33 **action of battery** lawsuit claiming an unlawful attack by beating or wounding (*OED* battery 1a, giving this example). As Sir Andrew notes, it is in fact he who committed the offence against Sebastian at 23: 'another joke for the law students' (Mahood).

34 **any . . . Illyria** Sir Andrew is referring to English common law: *Illyria* is as usual a thin disguise.

34–5 **struck him first** Aguecheek continues to disregard the law, as in his challenge at 3.4.143–65.

---

26 there.] there, and there: *Capell*   27 SD] *Dyce subst.; after 31 Rowe*   30 SD] *Rowe*   34 struck] *F4;* stroke *F;* strook *F3*   36, 49 SDs] *this edn*

soldier, put up your iron. You are well fleshed. Come
on.

SEBASTIAN

I will be free from thee.   [*Frees himself.*]
                            What wouldst thou now?   40
If thou dar'st tempt me further, draw thy sword.
    [*Draws sword.*]

SIR TOBY   What, what? Nay then, I must have an ounce
    or two of this malapert blood from you. [*Draws sword.*]

                    Enter OLIVIA.

OLIVIA

Hold, Toby! On thy life I charge thee hold.

SIR TOBY   Madam.   45

OLIVIA

Will it be ever thus? Ungracious wretch,
Fit for the mountains and the barbarous caves,
Where manners ne'er were preached. Out of my sight!
[*to Sebastian*] Be not offended, dear Cesario.
[*to Sir Toby*] Rudesby, be gone!
                    [*Exeunt Sir Toby, Sir Andrew and Fabian.*]

---

38 **iron** sword (metonymy): cf. 3.4.246.
   well fleshed hardened, inured to
   bloodshed (*OED* 2). Since the phrase
   can also mean 'well furnished with
   flesh', it is somewhat ironical coming
   from Sir Toby.
42–3 **ounce . . . blood** Cf. *Cor*
   3.1.298–300, 'the blood he hath lost
   . . . is more than he hath / By many
   an ounce.'
43 **malapert** impudent (*OED a.*, giving
   this example)
44 **charge** command (*OED v.* 14a, giving
   this example)
46 **Will . . . thus** must you always behave
   in this way

Ungracious rude (*OED* 3a, giving
this example)
47 i.e. who should live in distant uncivilized regions
   mountains i.e. territory remote
   from civilization (*OED* 1d, giving this
   example)
   barbarous uncultured, savage (*OED*
   3, giving this example)
48 **preached** taught
49 **dear Cesario** Olivia's use of the name
   underlines the irony of her error. In
   performance Sebastians often react
   with surprise at the misnaming, for
   example by giving the audience a per-
   plexed look.

40, 41 SDs] *Capell subst.*   43 SD] *Capell subst.; They draw and fight. / Rowe*

> I prithee, gentle friend,   50
> Let thy fair wisdom, not thy passion, sway
> In this uncivil and unjust extent
> Against thy peace. Go with me to my house
> And hear thou there how many fruitless pranks
> This ruffian hath botched up, that thou thereby   55
> Mayst smile at this. Thou shalt not choose but go.
> Do not deny. Beshrew his soul for me,
> He started one poor heart of mine in thee.

SEBASTIAN

> What relish is in this? How runs the stream?
> Or I am mad or else this is a dream.   60
> Let fancy still my sense in Lethe steep:

50 **Rudesby** insolent fellow; cf. Guazzo on the lack of manners: 'he which is not [ceremonious] may be taken to be a clowne, a rudesby, or a contemner of others' (Guazzo, fols 77ʳ–77ᵛ; *OED*). Shakespeare uses the term only here and in *TS* 3.2.10, 'a mad-brain rudesby full of spleen'.

gentle courteous (a polite term of address, as in the expression 'gentle reader'); gentlemanly: cf. Olivia's meditations on Cesario's social rank at 1.5.283.

friend acquaintance; lover (*OED n.* 4). The latter meaning is optimistic on Olivia's part but will soon be justified.

51 **wisdom . . . passion** Contrary to her advice here, Olivia admits at 3.1.150 that reason cannot hide her own passion.

sway prevail; cf. 2.4.31, 2.5.106, 4.3.17 and notes.

52 **uncivil and unjust** barbarous and lawless

extent attack (*OED n.* 2c, giving this example)

53 **peace** tranquillity

54 **fruitless** idle

pranks mischievous tricks. Cf. Polonius' advice to Gertrude regarding Hamlet: 'Tell him his pranks have been

too broad to bear with' (*Ham* 3.4.2).

55 **botched up** stitched clumsily together (*OED v.*[1] 3)

thereby thanks to that

56 **choose but go** choose otherwise than to go

57 **Beshrew** the devil take (mild imprecation)

58 By attacking you, he [Sir Toby] frightened me, since my heart is now yours. Olivia, playing on the heart/ hart homophone adopted by Orsino at 1.1.16–22, compares herself to a startled deer during the hunt. Technically, harts are 'roused' from cover rather than *started* (used of hares), 'but "start" is used because of its associations with human demonstrations of fear' (Ard[2]). In Carroll's 2002 Middle Temple production Mark Rylance's *started* Olivia fainted on this line.

59 **relish** sense (literally, taste or flavour) **How . . . stream?** what is going on? (proverbial: Dent, S925.1). Sebastian's metaphor anticipates his reference to the Lethe river at 61.

60 **Or . . . or** either . . . or

61 i.e. may my imagination/desire continue to make me forgetful of my senses.

50 SD1] *Oxf*   SD2] *Capell; Exeunt Sir Toby and Sir Andrew. / Rowe*

> If it be thus to dream, still let me sleep.

OLIVIA

> Nay, come, I prithee, would thou'dst be ruled by me.

SEBASTIAN

> Madam, I will.

OLIVIA   O say so, and so be.   *Exeunt.*

4.2   *Enter* MARIA[, *carrying a gown and false beard,*]
                        and FESTE.

MARIA   Nay, I prithee put on this gown and this beard;

fancy imagination; sexual desire (*OED* 8b; cf. *MV* 3.2.63–4)

sense senses: the noun is probably plural.

Lethe in Greek mythology, the river in Hades whose water caused those who drank it to forget the past; cf. *2H4* 5.2.72, 'May this be wash'd in Lethe and forgotten?'

steep soak

62 **still . . . sleep** let me go on sleeping

63 **would . . . me** if only you would do what I would have you do; cf. Olivia's earlier 'I would you were as I would have you be' (3.1.140).

64 **Madam, I will** Sebastian's readiness to accept Olivia's invitation, despite not knowing her, usually raises a laugh in performance, especially if he gives the impression of taking advantage; but his willingness to go with her can also be seen as part of his surprised surrendering to the *dream* (60).

O . . . be Some Olivias deliver this line as an expression of delight (Brown, 269).

4.2 This is the notorious 'dark room' scene, in which the imprisoned Malvolio is tormented by the disguised Feste, who has the chance here to show off his acting skills. As the opening lines indicate, it is still Maria who directs the practical joke. In per-

formance the 'dark room' has been represented in many different ways: it may be an 'inner stage' or hidden space behind the doors or curtains (see 18 t.n.); or a more claustrophobic space, often – as in Posner's 2001 RSC production – under a stage trapdoor with a grating through which Malvolio speaks and puts his hands. In the 2002 Middle Temple production it was a trunk, which Feste dragged across the stage. Alternatively, the room and its darkness may be shown directly on stage, as in 1884, when Henry Irving was 'seen actually visible, chained as a madman, and recumbent on his pallet' (*Illustrated London News*, quoted by Brown, 76). In Bill Alexander's 1987 RSC production Anthony Sher's Malvolio was likewise visible on stage, tethered to a post like a bear – taking up the 'baiting' metaphors in 2.5 – while the darkness was paradoxically figured by bright light. In Mendes' 2002 Donmar production Simon Russell Beale's Malvolio was simply blindfolded.

1 Feste's dressing up on stage underlines his self-consciously stagy acting of a part, but, as Maria points out at 63–4, his disguise is superfluous: a change of voice would have been sufficient for the 'blind' Malvolio.

4.2] *(Scoena Secunda.)*   0.1 *carrying . . . beard*] *Cam¹ subst.*   0.2 FESTE] *Munro; Clowne F*

make him believe thou art Sir Topas the curate. Do it
quickly. I'll call Sir Toby the whilst. [*Exit.*]

FESTE   Well, I'll put it on, and I will dissemble myself in't,
and I would I were the first that ever dissembled in such   5
a gown. I am not tall enough to become the function
well, nor lean enough to be thought a good student, but
to be said an honest man and a good housekeeper goes
as fairly as to say a careful man and a great scholar.

Enter [SIR] TOBY [*and* MARIA].

The competitors enter.   10

2   **Sir Topas** On the significance of Feste's
     adopted name, see List of Roles, 14n.
     Sir Cf. 3.4.265n.
     curate parish priest (rather than his
     assistant, as in modern English)
3   **the whilst** in the meantime
4   **dissemble** disguise (*OED v.*[1] 2, giving
     this example); cf. 5n.
5–6 **I would . . . gown** The hypocrisy
     and corruption of the clergy are tradi-
     tional targets of satire, as in the case of
     Chaucer's Pardoner. There may be an
     allusion to Puritan clergymen's 'hypo-
     critical' wearing of the Calvinist black
     gown under their obligatory – but hated
     – white surplice (Ard[2]), with a glance
     towards the 'Puritan' Malvolio perhaps.
5   **dissembled** deceived; cf. 4n.
6–9 **I am . . . scholar** i.e. to be a sin-
     cere and companionable fellow is as
     honourable as being a learned man
     (probably continuing the reference to
     dissembling priests). Feste's paradoxi-
     cal 'nonsense' implies the levelling of
     social differences between men.
6   **not tall enough** i.e. 'to overlook a
     pulpit' (Steevens). Since there is no
     evident reason why a priest should be
     tall, this has been interpreted as mean-
     ing 'portly', in contrast with *lean* at 7.
     Other commentators suspect a com-

positor's error for 'fat' (Farmer) or for
'pale' (Tyrwhitt). It may instead be an
allusion to the height of the actor, since
Robert Armin was notorious for his
dwarfishness (Wiles, 148). The phrase
may imply comic stage business involving a gown too long for the clown.
     become . . . function fulfil the office
     (of priest)
7   **lean . . . student** Scholars were tra-
     ditionally thin, because poor. Feste's
     supposed plumpness may be con-
     firmed by *good housekeeper* at 8.
     student scholar (of divinity)
8   **said** called, reputed
     honest honourable (*OED a.* 1a); sin-
     cere (*OED a.* 3c). Cf. 'he, which plain-
     ly telleth the truth, sheweth himselfe
     to be an honest man, and of noble
     condition' (Guazzo, 42).
     good housekeeper generous host
     (literally, one who keeps a good or
     hospitable house); *OED* 2 cites
     Holinshed, 2.137, 'a great housekeeper,
     and of great hospitalitie'.
8–9 **goes as fairly** is as becoming
9   **careful** careworn from study (Onions;
     cf. *OED* 2)
10   **The competitors** my associates in the
     gulling of Malvolio. Cf. *R3* 4.4.504–5,
     'And every hour more competitors /

3 SD] *Theobald*   5 in] *F2;* in in *F*   6 tall] pale *(Tyrwhitt);* fat *(Farmer)*   7 student] *(Student)*
9 careful] graceful *Hanmer*   9.1] *this edn; after 10 F*   SIR] *Rowe   and* MARIA] *Theobald*

SIR TOBY   Jove bless thee, Master Parson.

FESTE [*as Sir Topas*]   *Bonos dies*, Sir Toby. For as the old
hermit of Prague, that never saw pen and ink, very
wittily said to a niece of King Gorboduc, 'That that
is is'; so I being Master Parson am Master Parson, for   15
what is 'that' but 'that' and 'is' but 'is'?

SIR TOBY   To him, Sir Topas.

FESTE   What ho, I say, peace in this prison.

SIR TOBY   The knave counterfeits well – a good knave.

Flock to the rebels.' The plural noun
indicates that Maria returns onstage
with her fellow *competitor* at 9.1, even
if she does not speak until 63 and even
if F has only '*Enter Toby*.'

11 **Jove** As Feste is not a real *Parson*, the
invocation of a pagan deity is comically apt. Cf. 1.5.110n.

12 SD Feste's ventriloquism in this scene
reflects the ability of the original actor,
since 'the projection of multiple identities is the staple of Armin's clowning' (Wiles, 139; see also Preiss).

12 *Bonos dies* Good-day. This may
be bad Latin (for *bonus dies*, itself
a dubious construction), or bad
Spanish (for *buenas días*). In any case,
Sir Topas begins with a display of
false learning, in keeping with Feste's
satirical comment on dissembling
priests at 5–6.

12–14 **old . . . Gorboduc** false literary
authorities: cf. *Quinapalus*, 1.5.33. The
fact that the old hermit of Prague
is supposedly illiterate (*never . . .
ink*) suggests that he is an extempore
(non-literary) invention. Gorboduc, a
legendary British king, is the eponymous protagonist of the first English
tragedy in blank verse, by Thomas
Norton and Thomas Sackville (1565);
there is no record, however, of a niece.

14–16 'That . . .' . . . but 'is' Feste paro-

dies logical analysis, in particular the
self-consistent and self-evident 'axiom
of affirming', 'whereby a thing is saide
to bee or not to be' (Fenner, *Arts*, C1ʳ).
This is in direct contrast to Feste's
'Nothing that is so is so' (an 'axiom of
denying') at 4.1.8: both are true in this
comedy, in which nothing is what it
appears to be, but in which 'true' identities are (more or less) re-established
at the end.

15 **so . . . ²Parson** This may be an echo
of a celebrated jest in which the clown
Richard Tarlton, for the benefit of the
Queen, 'got on a Parsons gowne, and
. . . repeated these words: a Parson or
no Parson?' (*Tarlton's Jests*, A3ʳ).

18 **peace . . . prison** This parodies the
order for the Visitation of the Sick
in the Elizabethan *Book of Common
Prayer* (1559, still in use in 1602),
which begins: '*The Priest entringe into
the sicke persones house, shal saye*, Peace
be in this house, and to all that dwel
in it' (sig. O3ᵛ; Ard²). The 'priest' Sir
Topas is indeed visiting a sick (i.e.
'mad') man, but the house in question
is a *prison*.

19 **knave** rogue (said 'jocularly', *OED n.*
3c); cf. King Lear to his Fool: 'How
now, my pretty knave, how dost thou?'
(*KL* 1.4.95).

counterfeits acts his part

11 Jove] God *Halliwell*   11, 15, 27, 84 Master] *(M.), Steevens;* Mr. *Rowe*   12 SD] *Cam¹ subst.*
14 Gorboduc] *(Gorbodacke), Capell*   14–15 'That . . . is'] *this edn;* that that is, is *F*   15–16 for . . .
'is'?] *Mahood subst.;* for what is that, but that? and is, but is? *F*   18 What] *Opens the door of an inner
room.* What *Cumberland*

MALVOLIO (*within*)　Who calls there?　　　　　　　　　　　　20

FESTE　Sir Topas the curate, who comes to visit Malvolio
the lunatic.

MALVOLIO　Sir Topas, Sir Topas, good Sir Topas, go to
my lady.

FESTE　Out, hyperbolical fiend, how vexest thou this man!　　25
Talkest thou nothing but of ladies?

SIR TOBY　Well said, Master Parson.

MALVOLIO　Sir Topas, never was man thus wronged.
Good Sir Topas, do not think I am mad. They have laid
me here in hideous darkness.　　　　　　　　　　　　　　30

20 SD *within* i.e. from inside the 'dark room'. F's stage direction leaves no doubt that in early performances Malvolio was heard but not seen onstage: see 4.2n.

22 **lunatic** This generic term for 'mad-man' (literally, someone moonstruck: cf. 1.5.195) often occurs in Shakespeare in the context of feigned or imagined madness, as in *CE* 4.3.91, *TS* Induction 1.62 and 2.1.281, *MW* 3.5.97, etc; cf. also 'Hamlet's lunacy' (*Ham* 2.2.49).

25 **Out** 'to hell with you': a common interjection expressing reproach (Blake, *Grammar*, 5.2.2.4, giving this example); cf. *TG* 2.7.54, 'Out, out, Lucetta. That will be ill-favour'd.' At the same time, however, Feste is literally bidding the devil to leave Malvolio's body.
hyperbolical excessive, mendacious. Malvolio's supposedly exaggerated behaviour and language (in his one line so far) betrays the presence of the devil. Hyperbole was condemned by moralists as dishonest, because it strategically departs from truthful description: Guazzo condemns as 'lyers' those who 'craue the Poets priviledge, to use the figure *Hyperbole* at their pleasure' (Guazzo, 43; cf. 8n.). Puttenham, 159, rebaptizes it as the 'loud lyer'. On hyperbole in the comedy, see p. 83.
fiend the devil supposedly possessing Malvolio

vexest thou you torment. The treatment reserved for Malvolio may parody the methods of the Puritan exorcist John Darrell, imprisoned in 1598 and publicly exposed by Harsnett, *Discovery*, which claimed that the 'possessed' were dissemblers and – perhaps significantly, given Feste's performance – that the devils' voices within them were the result of ventriloquism. Darrell describes the 'horrible passions and torments' of the supposed victims, manifested in the 'strong and violente casting up and downe of their bodyes . . . scriking or crying' (Darrell, 34–5); cf. 31n., 32n., 97n. and 3.4.82n. It is ironically appropriate for Malvolio to be cured by 'Puritan' methods of exorcism (on Darrell and this scene, see Schleiner; Hamilton, 86–110; Gibson).

26 **Talkest . . . ladies** Feste pretends to interpret Malvolio's anxiety to see his mistress as a sign of uncontrollable sexual passion, another symptom of diabolical possession. At the same time, he recalls Malvolio's 'mad' ambition to win Olivia.

29 **laid** placed

30 **hideous darkness** Malvolio perceives the dark room as a Dante-like hell (cf. 35), while Sir Topas claims (31–44) that the darkness is caused by Malvolio's possession.

20 SD] *Capell; Maluolio within. F after 19*

FESTE   Fie, thou dishonest Satan! I call thee by the most
modest terms, for I am one of those gentle ones that
will use the devil himself with courtesy. Sayst thou that
house is dark?

MALVOLIO   As hell, Sir Topas.   35

FESTE   Why, it hath bay-windows transparent as
barricadoes, and the clerestories toward the south-
north are as lustrous as ebony, and yet complainest thou

---

31 **Fie** shame on you
dishonest mendacious; lewd (*OED* 2),
perhaps still alluding to Malvolio's talk
of *ladies* (26)
Satan Darrell, 77, recommends the
use of 'proper names of devils' during
exorcisms.
I call thee Sir Topas addresses the
'devil' in familiar terms (as 'thou'),
suggesting a lack of fear or of undue
respect.

32 **modest** moderate; demure (cf. *gentle* and *courtesy*, 32–3). The adjective
dishonest at 31 is mild compared to the
abuse hurled at devils by exorcists, who
'mocke them with reuilinges, Iniuries,
and the remembrance of thire salua-
tion' (Darrell, 78).
gentle ones refined people

33 **use . . . courtesy** Feste makes fun of the
politeness and gentility that are so central to the play's concerns; see pp. 81–2.

34 **house** room. The two terms are synonymous; cf. Sir Toby's *dark room*,
3.4.131; cf. also Rosalind's claim that
love, being 'a madness', 'deserves . . .
a dark house' (*AYL* 3.2.389–90). In
'Of Two Brethren and their Wives',
the fifth story in Riche – which also
contains the prose version of the
Twelfth Night story – a man ties his
wife 'in a darke house' and pretends
that she is a lunatic; she obligingly
'shewed her self . . . to be a right
Bedlem, she used no other wordes but

Cursynges and Bannynges' (Riche,
sig. T2ᵛ).

36–9 **Why . . . obstruction** Feste's self-
contradictory description plays on the
theme 'as clear as mud' and the fact that
the two actors perceive different spaces:
Feste sees the playhouse, Malvolio a
darkened 'inner stage', under-stage or
box.

36 **bay-windows** 'These were the rage
of the period' (Mahood). They were
particularly valued in great houses and
halls precisely because they captured
light.

37 **barricadoes** barricades, originally
made of casks filled with earth and
stones (from Spanish *barrica*, cask):
thus decidedly untransparent
clerestories rows of windows high up
in a wall, letting in daylight (*OED* 1b,
giving this example). Sir Topas is probably referring to the windows above the
roofs of church aisles, making a spir-
itual as well as physical contrast with
the dark room. High windows are also
found in the Middle Temple hall, so
that the detail was architecturally accurate, at least in the 1602 performance.

37–8 **south-north** i.e. everywhere or
nowhere

38 **lustrous as ebony** luminous as dark
wood: another paradox. Ebony was
proverbial for its blackness (Dent,
E56a): cf. *LLL* 4.3.243, 'thy love is
black as ebony.'

---

31 Satan] *(*sathan*)*   33 that] this *Rann;* that this *Halliwell*   37 clerestories] *Craig;* cleere stores *F;*
cleare stones *F2*   37–8 south-north] *(*South north*)*

of obstruction?

MALVOLIO I am not mad, Sir Topas. I say to you this   40
house is dark.

FESTE Madman, thou errest. I say there is no darkness
but ignorance, in which thou art more puzzled than the
Egyptians in their fog.

MALVOLIO I say this house is as dark as ignorance, though   45
ignorance were as dark as hell; and I say there was never
man thus abused. I am no more mad than you are.
Make the trial of it in any constant question.

FESTE What is the opinion of Pythagoras concerning
wildfowl?   50

MALVOLIO That the soul of our grandam might haply
inhabit a bird.

FESTE What think'st thou of his opinion?

---

39 **obstruction** shutting out of light
(*OED* 2a, first occurrence). Feste may
be using one of Malvolio's own more
affected terms against him: cf. 2.5.116
and 3.4.20 (Oxf¹).

42–3 **no . . . ignorance** proverbial (Dent,
I16.1)

43 **puzzled** bewildered, lost (*OED v.* 1a,
giving this example)

43–4 **the . . . fog** an allusion to the biblical plague of darkness described in
Exodus, 10.21: 'and there was a thicke
darkenesse upon all the lande of Egypt
three dayes long.' It is presumably
due to the 'thickness' of the Egyptian
darkness that Sir Topas calls it a *fog*.
fog darkness (*OED n.²* 3a, first occurrence)

47 **I . . . are** Malvolio repeats this claim
to Feste (rather than Sir Topas) at 88,
allowing the clown to reply in his own
voice, as he cannot here, 'Then you are
mad indeed' (89).
more mad Cf. *more grave*, 1.4.28n.

48 **Make . . . question** Test me through
any logically consistent question and
answer.

constant consistent (*OED a.* 8)

49–50 **Pythagoras . . . wildfowl** The
Greek philosopher Pythagoras was
renowned for his doctrine of metempsychosis – cf. Dr Faustus' doleful
'Ah Pythagoras *metem su cossis* were
that true' (Marlowe, *Faustus*, sig. F2ᵛ)
– which propounded the migration of
the soul from one body to another, and
especially its reincarnation after death
into a new human or animal form
(Ovid, *Met.*, 15.183–7, fol. 189ʳ). Cf.
Rosalind's irreverent 'I was never so
berhymed since Pythagoras' time that
I was an Irish rat' (*AYL* 3.2.173–4).

51–2 Malvolio gives the correct answer,
showing that he can respond aptly to
constant question (48); what he does not
realize is that the question regarding
wildfowl is a trap, setting up the 'woodcock' joke at 58.

51 **grandam** grandmother (literally,
'grand dame', from French). This
was already a somewhat outmoded form:
'grandame words' were precisely obsolete terms (*OED* 5).
haply by chance

51 haply] *Capell;* happily *F*

MALVOLIO   I think nobly of the soul, and no way approve
    his opinion.   55

FESTE   Fare thee well. Remain thou still in darkness. Thou
    shalt hold th'opinion of Pythagoras ere I will allow of
    thy wits, and fear to kill a woodcock lest thou dispossess
    the soul of thy grandam. Fare thee well.

MALVOLIO   Sir Topas, Sir Topas!   60

SIR TOBY   My most exquisite Sir Topas.

FESTE   Nay, I am for all waters.

MARIA   Thou mightst have done this without thy beard
    and gown. He sees thee not.

SIR TOBY [*to Feste*]   To him in thine own voice, and bring   65
    me word how thou find'st him. I would we were well
    rid of this knavery. If he may be conveniently delivered,

---

54–5 **no . . . opinion** The pagan doctrine of metempsychosis was attacked
by early modern Christian writers,
including John Donne in *The Progress
of the Soul* (1612).
56 **darkness** ignorance; the dark room
56–7 **Thou . . . th'opinion** It is of
course absurd that a priest should wish
to convert even a 'Puritan' to pagan
beliefs: this is an arbitrary pretext for
leaving Malvolio in the dark, although
it does again raise the question of his
religious opinions.
57–8 **allow . . . wits** admit your sanity
58 **woodcock** proverbially stupid bird:
cf. Fabian's comparison of Malvolio
himself to a 'woodcock near the gin'
(2.5.82); Malvolio is now decidedly in
the gin.
    dispossess drive out (*OED* 3). There
is a further allusion here to Malvolio's
'possession' and the (failed) attempt to
dispossess him.
61 **exquisite** perfect (i.e. in acting his
part) (*OED* 4); the third occurrence of
the adjective: cf. 1.5.165 and 2.3.140.

62 **Nay** indeed
    I . . . waters I can turn my hand
to anything (Malone): a variation on
the proverb 'to have a cloak for all
waters' (Dent, C421). Feste's motley
garb – apart from his present disguise
– authorizes him to play any role, as
does his skill as an actor and ventriloquist in this scene: he is satisfied with
his performance. There may also be a
play on the topaz-like lustre of *waters*.
63–4 Maria's comment on Feste's superfluous disguise takes up the clothing
metaphor implied at 62. It was she
who got Feste to dress up in the
first place; Mahood suggests that this
is an 'afterthought' indicating 'rapid
composition', but Maria may simply
be trying to put Feste down after his
boast. In any case, if the disguise is
unnecessary for Malvolio, it certainly
helps the audience, who *can* see: cf. the
paradoxical SD in *Tem* 3.2.40.1, '*Enter
Ariel, invisible.*'
67 **conveniently delivered** set free without too much trouble (Ard[2])

---

59 soul] house *F2*   62 waters.] waters. *he puts off the disguise Cam¹*   65 SD] *Oxf*   66 well] all *F2*

I would he were, for I am now so far in offence with my
niece that I cannot pursue with any safety this sport to
the upshot. Come by and by to my chamber.   70

Exit [with Maria].

FESTE [*As himself; sings.*]

Hey Robin, jolly Robin,
Tell me how thy lady does.

MALVOLIO   Fool!

FESTE [*Sings.*]

My lady is unkind, pardie.

MALVOLIO   Fool!   75

FESTE [*Sings.*]

Alas, why is she so?

MALVOLIO   Fool, I say!

FESTE [*Sings.*]

She loves another –

Who calls, ha?

MALVOLIO   Good fool, as ever thou wilt deserve well at   80
my hand, help me to a candle, and pen, ink and paper.

68–9 **I . . . niece** I have gone so far
in provoking my niece's displeasure.
Sir Toby attributes great authority to
Olivia, fearing her anger.

68 **offence** 'the condition of being
regarded with displeasure' (*OED n.*
4a, giving this example)

69 **pursue** proceed with (*OED* 9, giving
this example)

70 **upshot** outcome (literally, the final
shoot-off to decide the winner of an
archery match): cf. *Ham* 5.2.368.

Come . . . chamber Some directors
– most influentially, John Barton in
his 1969 RSC production – have Sir
Toby address this line only to Maria,
following Cam[1], who takes it to be an
indication 'that the couple are already
married'. It is surely more plausible for

Sir Toby to tell Feste himself to bring
him word how he finds Malvolio, after
which he goes off with Maria (whose
exit is not marked in F but who fails to
speak again), leaving the clown to go
about his task.

71–9 Feste signals his presence to
Malvolio by singing an old dialogue
song which perhaps allows him to
alternate two voices (*My lady . . .* and
She loves . . . being the replies) as he
will do later at 94–128. For words and
music, see Appendix 3. Feste probably
chooses this song as a further means of
provoking Malvolio, whose lady likewise *loves another*, namely Cesario.

74 **pardie** by God (from French *par Dieu*)

80–1 **thou ... hand** Malvolio, who so far
has treated Feste meanly (see especially

69–70 to the] *Rowe;* the *F;* t'the *Riv*   70 SD *with Maria*] *Theobald*   71 SD *as himself*] *this edn   sings*]
Rowe   71–2] *Capell; prose F*   74, 76, 78 SDs] *Cam[1]*   74 pardie] *(perdie)*

As I am a gentleman, I will live to be thankful to thee
for't.

FESTE   Master Malvolio?

MALVOLIO   Ay, good fool.   85

FESTE   Alas, sir, how fell you besides your five wits?

MALVOLIO   Fool, there was never man so notoriously
abused. I am as well in my wits, fool, as thou art.

FESTE   But as well? Then you are mad indeed, if you be
no better in your wits than a fool.   90

MALVOLIO   They have here propertied me: keep me in
darkness, send ministers to me, asses, and do all they
can to face me out of my wits.

FESTE   Advise you what you say, the minister is here. [*as*

1.5.71–85), promises him a reward for
bringing him writing materials: he will
repeat the offer at 112–13. Having
got into trouble by reading an epistle,
he hopes to get himself out of it by
writing one, namely the letter read
aloud at 5.1.297–305.

82 **gentleman** Malvolio considers himself a gentleman already (as steward),
but he may still be alluding to his ever
more improbable promotion as Olivia's
husband.

84 **Master Malvolio** F's *M*. is probably
an abbreviation for *Master*, although it
might stand for *Monsieur*: cf. *Monsieur
Malvolio* at 2.3.130.

86 **how . . . wits?** how did you come to
lose your senses? In the poem *Pastime*
Stephen Hawes lists the five wits or
mental faculties as common wit, imagination, fantasy, estimation and memory. Five Wits is a personified character
in the morality play *Everyman* (*c*. 1495;
Ard[2]).

87–8 **notoriously abused** disgracefully
mistreated. Olivia repeats the phrase,
as if quoting Malvolio, at 5.1.372:
these are the only uses of the adverb

in Shakespeare. *Notorious* is one of
Malvolio's theme words, expressing
his 'sense of wounded dignity' (Cam[2]):
cf. 5.1.323 and 372.

89 **But** only

89–90 **Then . . . fool** Feste plays on two
meanings of *fool*: jester; idiot.

91 **propertied me** used me like an object
(*OED v*. 1). Cf. the equally proud
Louis the Dauphin in *KJ*: 'I am too
high-born to be propertied' (*KJ*
5.2.79).

92 **ministers** priests (i.e. Sir Topas).
Malvolio employs the term adopt-
ed by Protestants after the example
of Calvinists (*OED n*. 2c): another
hint at his 'Puritan' sympathies? Cf.
the Puritan Phillip Stubbes: 'Such
[names] as at anie hande a Minister of
the Gospell ought not to bee called by'
(Stubbes, 106[r]).
asses Malvolio appears to allude
unwittingly to Feste, an *ass* (fool) who
played the part of a *minister*.

93 **face . . . wits** bully me out of my senses
(*OED* face *v*. 3c, giving this example)

94 **Advise you** consider (*OED* 5, giving
this example)

78–9] *Mahood; one line* F 78 another –] *Rowe;* another. *F* 86 besides] beside *Steevens
(Capell)* 94–5, 99, 100, 101 SDs] *Hanmer subst.*

Sir Topas] Malvolio, Malvolio, thy wits the heavens　　95
restore. Endeavour thyself to sleep and leave thy vain
bibble babble.

MALVOLIO　Sir Topas!

FESTE [*as Sir Topas*]　Maintain no words with him, good
fellow. [*as himself*] Who, I, sir? Not I, sir! God b'wi' you,　100
good Sir Topas. [*as Sir Topas*] Marry, amen. [*as himself*]
I will, sir, I will.

MALVOLIO　Fool, fool, fool, I say!

FESTE　Alas, sir, be patient. What say you, sir? I am shent
for speaking to you.　　105

MALVOLIO　Good fool, help me to some light and some
paper. I tell thee I am as well in my wits as any man in
Illyria.

FESTE　Welladay that you were, sir.

MALVOLIO　By this hand, I am. Good fool, some ink,　110

94–102 The clown's performance as ventriloquist reaches its climax in this
direct exchange between his two voices,
in which Sir Topas reproaches Feste
for having dealings with Malvolio.
95–6 **thy . . . restore** may you come to
your senses
96 **Endeavour thyself** try (to get).
Shakespeare, here as elsewhere, creates
a reflexive verb by adding a reflexive
pronoun as object of an intransitive
verb (Blake, *Grammar*, 4.4.2).
97 **bibble babble** empty talk. This is the
closest of the comedy's possible echoes
of Darrell, who recounts that '3. or 4.
of [the possessed] gaue themselues to
Scoffing and Blasphemy, calling the
holy Bible being brought up *bible bable,
bible bable*' (Darrell, 9); cf. 25n., 31n.,
32n., 3.4.82n. *OED*, however, quoting this example, describes the expression as 'very common in 16th c.'; cf.
Fluellen's 'pibble-pabble' in *H5* 4.1.72.
99–100 **good fellow** Feste has Sir Topas
address him with respect, not as a 'fool'.

100 **God . . . you** a corruption of 'God
be with you', equivalent to modern
'goodbye'
101 **Marry** a mild oath, literally invoking
the Virgin Mary (*OED int.* 2a, giving
this example)
102 **I will** Since Feste has already responded to *Maintain no words*, 99, he seems
to be replying either to something we
have not heard 'as if, in the meantime,
Sir Topas had whispered' (Johnson),
or alternatively to *Marry*, 101, perhaps
interpreting it wilfully as 'Get married.'
104 **shent** blamed (past participle of the
archaic verb *shend*). Cf. Hamlet of his
mother, 'How in my words somever
she be shent' (*Ham* 3.2.388).
109 **Welladay** alas. Cf. the Nurse in *RJ*,
speaking of Tybalt, 'Ah weraday, he's
dead, he's dead, he's dead!' (*RJ* 3.2.37).
Feste plays on Malvolio's *well*, 107.
110 **By this hand** truly (mild oath), alluding
to giving the (right) hand when making a
pledge. Malvolio might offer his hand
through the grating or other opening.

100 b'wi'] *Pope;* buy *F*

paper and light, and convey what I will set down to my
lady. It shall advantage thee more than ever the bearing
of letter did.

FESTE   I will help you to't. But tell me true, are you not
mad indeed, or do you but counterfeit?   115

MALVOLIO   Believe me, I am not, I tell thee true.

FESTE   Nay, I'll ne'er believe a madman till I see his brains.
I will fetch you light, and paper, and ink.

MALVOLIO   Fool, I'll requite it in the highest degree. I
prithee be gone.   120

FESTE [*Sings.*]

> I am gone, sir, and anon, sir,
>   I'll be with you again,
>   In a trice, like to the old Vice,

---

111 **convey** deliver. Feste does indeed
deliver the letter to Olivia, at
5.1.281–2.

112 **advantage** benefit (*OED v.* 4b)

114–15 **are . . . counterfeit?** a trick question: neither possibility (mad or acting
mad) places Malvolio in a good light.
He responds to *mad* at 116, implying
that he *counterfeits*. The question is,
of course, the one posed (in earnest)
by and of Hamlet: cf. his 'I essentially
am not in madness, / But mad in craft'
(*Ham* 3.4.185–6).

    counterfeit act, pretend (*OED v.* 6,
giving this example): cf. 19.

117 **I'll . . . madman** Malvolio is in the
'All Cretans are liars' (or catch-22)
trap: as he is 'mad', even his denials
confirm his madness.

    till . . . brains till I can check whether
he has any brains at all (i.e. when he is
dead): a variation on the proverb 'you
will not believe he is dead till you see
his brain' (Dent, B597)

119 **requite** repay

121–8 It is not known whether the words

of this song are Shakespeare's. No
contemporary music has survived, but
Robert Armin as Feste almost certainly sang rather than spoke it. It is an
apt conclusion to the scene in so far as
it describes both comic acting and the
maltreatment of the devil.

121 **anon, sir** at once, sir; the same
catchphrase is used repeatedly in *1H4*
2.4.37–95.

123 **In a trice** immediately; synonymous
with *anon* (121)

    Vice the comic representative of evil
in the medieval morality play: appo-
site, first because the Vice was in some
ways the forerunner of the clown/fool,
and more specifically because Feste
in this scene adopts various Vice-like
lazzi or comic stage business: changes
in costume and voice (cf. the disguises
of the Vice Infidelity in *Magdalene*),
wordplay (cf. Richard in *R3*, 'Thus
like the formal Vice, Iniquity, / I mor-
alize two meanings in one word', *R3*
3.1.82–3), the display of false Latin,
dubious learning, etc.

119–20] *Mahood; F lines* degree: / gone. /   121 SD] *Rowe subst.*

> Your need to sustain,
> Who with dagger of lath, in his rage and his wrath,   125
>   Cries 'Aha!' to the devil,
> Like a mad lad, 'Pare thy nails, dad.
>   Adieu, goodman devil.'   *Exit.*

124 ironical: the Vice pretended to befriend his victims, just as Feste and Sir Topas pretend to be concerned for Malvolio's health.

125 **dagger of lath** the wooden weapon worn by the Vice in morality plays and interludes. This prop survived until quite late in the sixteenth century, for example in the moral interlude *Trial of Treasure* (sig. B1ᵛ). It became synonymous with stagy behaviour: cf. *1H4*, where Falstaff promises Prince Hal to 'beat thee out of thy kingdom with a dagger of lath' (*1H4* 2.4.134–5). There is no extant play in which the Vice beats the devil, but Feste's allusion suggests a specific episode that the audience might recall. This is confirmed by Samuel Harsnett's *Declaration*, which reminisces: 'It was a prety part in the old Church-playes, when the nimble Vice would skip up nimbly like a Iacke an Apes into the deuils necke, and ride the deuil a course, and belabour him with his wooden dagger, til he made him roare' (Harsnett, *Declaration*, 114–15; on Harsnett, cf. 3.4.25n.).

wrath This may be pronounced comically to rhyme with *lath*.

126 **Cries 'Aha!'** i.e. in defiance: cf. Sir Topas' challenging of the devil at 25 and 31.

127 **mad lad** The Vice is *mad* in his colourful and exuberant behaviour; there may also be a further allusion to Malvolio.

Pare thy nails The devil was sup-

posed to keep his nails long and uncut, so that paring them was an affront (Malone). The phrase was proverbial (Dent, N12). Feste seems to allude again to a specific and recognizable piece of stage business: this is confirmed in *H5* 4.4.68–9, where Pistol is described as 'this roaring devil i'th' old play, that everyone may pare his nails with a wooden dagger.'

dad In some morality plays, such as *Lusty Juventus* (sig. B2ᵛ), the Vice is the devil's son.

128 **goodman   devil**   probably addressed to Malvolio rather than to the *devil* supposedly possessing him. Feste's farewell would have been appropriate if Malvolio was under the trapdoor, i.e. in the under-stage space known as 'hell'. Morality play devils often appeared from under the trap, accompanied by smoke and thunder. In some productions, Feste, before exiting, dances triumphantly on the trapdoor (Brown, 273); in Barton's 1969 RSC production he first stamped on Malvolio's hands and then slammed down the trap, causing the screaming steward to fall back into his prison (Sinden, 'Malvolio', 65).

goodman a somewhat condescending title, usually prefixed either to designations of occupation (*OED* 3a), as in 'Goodman Delver' (*Ham* 5.1.14), or to the name of a low-ranking person (*OED* 3b), as in 'goodman Dull' (*LLL* 4.2.37–8). This may be a gibe at Malvolio's servant status.

126 'Aha!'] *this edn;* ah ha, *F;* 'Ah ha!' *Mahood*   127–8 'Pare . . . devil.'] *Mahood;* paire . . . diuell. *F*
128 goodman devil] *Capell;* good man diuell *F;* good Man Drivel *Rowe³*

4.3   *Enter* SEBASTIAN.

SEBASTIAN

This is the air, that is the glorious sun;
This pearl she gave me, I do feel't and see't,
And though 'tis wonder that enwraps me thus,
Yet 'tis not madness. Where's Antonio, then?
I could not find him at the Elephant;   5
Yet there he was, and there I found this credit,
That he did range the town to seek me out.
His counsel now might do me golden service,
For though my soul disputes well with my sense

4.3 In this, the play's briefest scene, Olivia prepares to become betrothed as quickly as possible to the finally co-operative Cesario, while Sebastian accepts his unexpected good fortune with happy disbelief. As in all the comedy's more solemn or romantic episodes, the entire scene is in verse. Sebastian's opening lines indicate that the scene is set outdoors, while Olivia's reference to her *chantry* at 24 suggests a space separate from the main house (the latter was represented on the Elizabethan stage by the door through which they exit).

1–21 Sebastian's sense of bewilderment produces a semantically dense and self-contradictory speech expressing his disbelief at his good luck in the language of logical disputation, as if engaged in an inner debate or psychodrama.

1–2 Sebastian is both celebrating the world, which he now perceives with new enthusiasm, and reassuring himself that his senses are still functioning. His three deictics (*This, that, This*) take us progressively from the widest and most general (*air*) to the smallest and most particular (*pearl*); on deictics, see p. 89.

2 **pearl** Olivia has given Cesario another jewel: the third, after the ring (1.5, 2.2)

and her *picture* (3.4.203).

3 **wonder** amazement
enwraps me absorbs me in contemplation; *OED* 2b, giving this example, suggests that the verb is sometimes confused with the participle 'enrapt' (i.e. carried away).

4 **madness** Sebastian – as at 4.1.60 – fears for his own sanity. This takes on particular piquancy after the 'dark room' episode: in Barton's 1969 RSC production, Malvolio uttered at this point 'a faint sound of nonsensical gibberish' from his prison under the stage (Sinden, 'Malvolio', 65), while in Mendes' 2002 Donmar production Simon Russell Beale's Malvolio, still visible on stage, wept.

5 **Elephant** See 3.3.39n.
6 **was** had been
credit report (literally, something believed; *OED n.* 3, sole occurrence)
7 **range** wander through (*OED v.*[1] 7)
8 His advice would be of inestimable help to me now
golden precious (*OED a.* 4a); cf. 5.1.375n.
9 **disputes . . . sense** argues thoroughly with what I perceive; alluding to formal logical disputations in universities and inns of court. There is a problem

---

4.3] *(Scaena Tertia.)*   1 SP] *not in F; Rowe subst.*   6 credit] current *Hanmer*

That this may be some error but no madness,   10
Yet doth this accident and flood of fortune
So far exceed all instance, all discourse,
That I am ready to distrust mine eyes
And wrangle with my reason that persuades me
To any other trust but that I am mad,   15
Or else the lady's mad. Yet if 'twere so
She could not sway her house, command her followers,
Take and give back affairs and their dispatch
With such a smooth, discreet and stable bearing
As I perceive she does. There's something in't   20
That is deceivable.

here precisely of logical consistency: Sebastian's *soul* seems to dispute in favour of *error* and his *sense* in favour of *madness*, while at 13–15 he appears to argue with both faculties in favour of someone's being *mad*. But it is probably wrong to look for overall coherence, since at 16–21 he contradicts himself again. He is engaged in a dialectical process: i.e. he changes his mind.

10 **some . . . madness** i.e. a mistake (of identity?) rather than mere folly. This is the main issue in *CE*, which the term *error* seems to recall. Sebastian comes close to realizing that there may be a comedy of errors at work in Illyria but does not take the insight any further.

11 **accident . . . fortune** an overwhelming series of unexpected and fortunate events
accident and flood accidental flood (rhetorical figure: hendiadys)

12 **So far exceed** goes so far beyond
instance precedent: continuing the metaphor of logical and perhaps legal debate
discourse reasoning, understanding; cf. *Ham* 1.2.150, 'a beast that wants discourse of reason'.

14–16 **wrangle . . . mad** i.e. resist any rational argument against the conclusion that one of the two of us is mad. This somewhat baroque construction suggests the convoluted nature of Sebastian's internal dialectic: cf. 9n.

14 **wrangle** argue; synonym of *dispute* (9), likewise signifying a formal public debate at a university or law school (*OED v.* 2)

15 **trust** belief

16–20 **Yet . . . does** Sebastian's testimony to Olivia's skill in governing her household confirms other evidence of her increased authoritativeness, e.g. Sir Toby's fear at 4.2.68–70.

17 **sway** rule; a recurrent thematic word in the comedy: cf. 2.5.106, 4.1.51 and notes.

18 i.e. undertake business and bring it to completion
affairs commercial or professional business (*OED* 2b)
dispatch execution, settlement (*OED n.* 5a)

19 **stable** steadfast (*OED a.* 6a; not found elsewhere in Shakespeare as an adjective)
bearing demeanour, behaviour

21 **deceivable** deceptive (*OED* 1a; Hope, 1.2.2a)

21 SD] *this edn; after 21 F*   the lady] she *Pope*

Enter OLIVIA *and* Priest.

But here the lady comes.

OLIVIA

Blame not this haste of mine. If you mean well,
Now go with me and with this holy man
Into the chantry by. There before him,
And underneath that consecrated roof,   25
Plight me the full assurance of your faith,
That my most jealous and too doubtful soul
May live at peace. He shall conceal it
Whiles you are willing it shall come to note,
What time we will our celebration keep   30

---

22 **Blame . . . mine** This is one of the
play's ironical perspective games (see
pp. 24–32). From Olivia's point of
view, her *haste* is due to the fact that
Cesario is at last responding to her
advances (and may change his mind
again); from Sebastian's perspective,
her rapidity is so precipitate as to be
mad (16), but this does not stop him
going along. In Mendes' 2002 Donmar
production Helen McCrory's Olivia
entered draped only in a sheet, giving
her *haste* decidedly erotic overtones.

24 **chantry** chapel, dedicated to the singing of daily mass for the souls of the
dead (*OED* 3): cf. *H5* 4.1.296–7, 'Two
chantries, where the sad and solemn
priests / Sing still for Richard's soul'.
Olivia's chantry is presumably where
the *holy man* (23) sings for the soul of
her dead brother (see 1.1.29–30), but
it is now transformed into the venue
for their marriage vows: a sign of how
far Olivia has come from her pledge
to shun the world for seven years
(1.1.25–7).
by nearby

26 i.e. make a solemn pledge of your
true intention to marry me. Olivia
proposes a *contract*, as the priest terms
it at 5.1.152 (or 'pre-contract' as it

is called in *MM* 4.1.72), consisting
of an exchange of pre-marital vows.
Such a declaration of future intent
(*Sponsalia per verba de futuro*) was not
absolutely binding but was nevertheless recognized within English common law: hence Olivia's insistence that
Cesario is to all intents and purposes
her *husband* at 5.1.139–40. The priest
describes the betrothal ceremony in
detail at 5.1.152–9.

27 **jealous** fearful, apprehensive (*OED* 5)

28–9 **He . . . note** On the priest's concealing of the ceremony he has conducted,
cf. Friar Laurence's pledge of silence
'till we can find a time / To blaze
your marriage' in *RJ* 3.3.150–1. In
the event, Olivia's chaplain is obliged
to reveal the pre-marriage on his next
appearance at 5.1.152–9.

29 **Whiles** until (*OED* 5, giving this
example)
you . . . note you want to make it
public

30 **What time** at which time (Blake,
Grammar, 5.3.2.4e)
celebration wedding, i.e. the full public ceremony which will take place later
to ratify their preliminary exchange of
vows
keep hold

---

27 jealous] *(*iealious*)*   28 live] henceforth live *Hanmer*   it] it still, *Keightley*

According to my birth. What do you say?

SEBASTIAN

    I'll follow this good man and go with you,

    And, having sworn truth, ever will be true.

OLIVIA

    Then lead the way, good father, and heavens so shine   34

    That they may fairly note this act of mine.   *Exeunt.*

5.1   *Enter* FESTE[, *with a letter,*] *and* FABIAN.

FABIAN   Now, as thou lov'st me, let me see his letter.

FESTE   Good Master Fabian, grant me another request.

FABIAN   Anything.

FESTE   Do not desire to see this letter.

31 **According . . . birth** in keeping with
my rank. Olivia's status as countess
makes a secret wedding – as opposed
to a 'pre-contract' – unthinkable. This
is the only moment in the play in
which she explicitly asserts her *birth*:
another sign, perhaps, of her increasing authoritativeness (see 16–20n.).
    What . . . say? Do you agree? This
often raises a laugh: Sebastian is
dumbfounded, and in any case seems
to have little *say*, since Olivia has
already arranged everything.
34–5 **heavens . . . mine** probable allusion to the proverb 'Happy is the bride
the sun shines on' (Dent, B663, sole
occurrence in Shakespeare)
35 **fairly note** look favourably upon.
Olivia's wish may be extended to
the audience as a plea for indulgence
towards her *haste* (22).
5.1 This, the last and longest scene in the
play, is also the most hectic, bringing
onstage nearly all the characters and at
the same time pulling together – but

not altogether resolving – the separate
strands of the various plots. The great
number of entrances and exits and the
sheer amount of information given
make this finale notoriously difficult
to stage, so much so that Granville
Barker calls it 'a scandalously ill-
arranged and ill-written last scene,
the despair of any stage manager'
(Barker, 'Preface', 28). Particular theatrical problems are created by the
'optical illusion' of the denouement
with both twins on stage, although
when successful this is one of the
play's more memorable episodes. The
language of the scene, moreover, is at
times extraordinarily dense. Capell's
location '*Before Olivia's House*' is suggested by Olivia's offer of hospitality
at 310–13.
1 **his** i.e. Malvolio's
4 Feste's request not to request is, as
Fabian observes, another of his paradoxical logical games: cf. 4.1.8 and
4.2.14–16 and notes.

35 SD] *(Exeunt. Finis Actus Quartus.)*   **5.1**] *(Actus Quintus. Scena Prima.)*   0.1, 184.1, 276.1 FESTE]
Munro; Clowne F   0.1, 320.1 *with a letter*] *this edn*   1 his] *this* F2   2 Master] *(M.), Steevens; Mr.
Rowe*

FABIAN This is to give a dog and, in recompense, desire   5
my dog again.

Enter ORSINO, VIOLA [*as Cesario*], CURIO *and Lords.*

ORSINO
Belong you to the Lady Olivia, friends?
FESTE Ay, sir, we are some of her trappings.
ORSINO
I know thee well. How dost thou, my good fellow?
FESTE Truly, sir, the better for my foes, and the worse for   10
my friends.
ORSINO
Just the contrary: the better for thy friends.
FESTE No, sir, the worse.
ORSINO How can that be?
FESTE Marry, sir, they praise me and make an ass of me.   15
Now my foes tell me plainly I am an ass, so that by my
foes, sir, I profit in the knowledge of myself, and by my

5–6 **This . . . again** a probable topical allusion. In his diary entry for 26 March 1602 (= 1603, two days after the death of Queen Elizabeth and a year or so after his description of the Middle Temple performance of *TN*: see pp. 3–4) Manningham records an anecdote about the Queen and her kinsman Dr Boleyn, who 'had a dog which he doted one, soe much that the Q[ueene], understanding of it, requested he would graunt hir one desyre, and he should have whatsoever he would aske. Shee demaunded his dogge; he gave it, and "Nowe, Madame," q[uoth] he, "you promised to give me my desyre." "I will," q[uothe] she. "Then I pray you give me my dog againe"' (Manningham, 210).

6.1 *Lords* Cf. 1.1.0.2n.
7, 9, 25 In this exchange Orsino appears to be speaking verse, while Feste is unambiguously prosaic; cf. 168–84.
7 **Belong you to** are you dependants of; Feste interprets this at 8 as 'are you appendages of' (*OED v.* 4a, giving this example).
8 **trappings** ornaments (literally, the ceremonial harness of a horse)
10–11 **the better . . . friends** Feste's paradox makes fun of Orsino's somewhat patronizing *friends* at 7.
15–18 **Marry . . . abused** The clown's pseudo-logical defence of sincerity plays on the favourite Renaissance moral dictum *nosce teipsum*, 'know thyself': cf. 145n.

5 This] That *Steevens²*   6.1 ORSINO] *Mahood; Duke F   as Cesario*] *Munro subst.*   9] *Oxf; prose F*

friends I am abused. So that, conclusions to be as kisses,
if your four negatives make your two affirmatives, why
then, the worse for my friends and the better for my   20
foes.

ORSINO   Why, this is excellent.

FESTE   By my troth, sir, no, though it please you to be one
of my friends.

ORSINO

Thou shalt not be the worse for me: there's gold.   25
    [*Gives coin.*]

FESTE   But that it would be double-dealing, sir, I would
you could make it another.

ORSINO   O, you give me ill counsel.

FESTE   Put your grace in your pocket, sir, for this once,
and let your flesh and blood obey it.   30

ORSINO   Well, I will be so much a sinner to be a double-
dealer. There's another. [*Gives coin.*]

---

18 **abused** deceived (by flattery)

18–19 **conclusions . . . affirmatives**
i.e. since in grammar (especially
Latin grammar) two negatives make
an affirmative (and four make two),
a woman who says 'no, no, no, no' to
a kiss is really saying 'yes, yes'. This
probably alludes to Sidney, *Astrophel*,
sonnet 63, in which Astrophel asks
Stella for a kiss and 'Least one should
not be heard [she] twice, said no no.'
Astrophel interprets this 'grammati-
cally' as a yes: 'For Grammer says (to
Grammer who sayes nay) / That in one
speech two negatiues affirme' (Sidney,
Astrophel, 540; Farmer, in Steevens).

19 **your** an indication not of possession
but of being 'one of a group' (Wales;
Blake, *Grammar*, 3.3.4.5c), and used
by Feste for playful emphasis; cf.
Lepidus' abuse of the form in *AC*
2.7.26–7: 'Your serpent of Egypt is
bred, now, of your mud by the opera-

tion of your sun; so is your crocodile';
cf. also *Ham* 4.3.21–4.

22 **this is excellent** Orsino joins Olivia
and Viola as one of the admir-
ers of Feste's wit: cf. 1.5.69–92 and
3.1.58–66.

23–4 **though . . . friends** i.e. even if you
are so kind as to say so (and possibly
reward me)

26 **double-dealing** Feste's usual request
to double the tip: cf. 3.1.48–51,
4.1.20.

29 **Put . . . pocket** put away your sense
of propriety; put your hand in your
pocket (to find money). Feste plays on
the expression *your grace* as the proper
term of address towards a duke (*OED*
grace *n.* 16b); cf. *MM* 4.3.135–6, 'And
you shall have . . . / Grace of the
Duke.'

30 **let . . . it** i.e. let your instincts follow
my *ill counsel* rather than your *grace*

31 **to** as to

---

18 that . . . kisses] that, Conclusion to be asked, is, *Theobald;* the conclusion to be asked is
Hanmer   25 SD] *Collier² subst.*

FESTE *Primo*, *secundo*, *tertio* is a good play, and the old
    saying is 'The third pays for all.' The triplex, sir, is a
    good tripping measure, as the bells of Saint Bennet, sir,   35
    may put you in mind – one, two, three.

ORSINO You can fool no more money out of me at
    this throw. If you will let your lady know I am here to
    speak with her, and bring her along with you, it may
    awake my bounty further.   40

FESTE Marry, sir, lullaby to your bounty till I come
    again. I go, sir, but I would not have you to think that

---

33 *Primo, secundo, tertio* first, second,
third (Latin). This probably alludes
to an elaborate form of mathemati-
cal chess, supposedly invented by
Pythagoras and known as the philosophers' game or table (*Rythmomachia*).
Odd numbers were opposed to even
numbers on a double chessboard, and
the object was to capture opposing
numbers through arithmetical opera-
tions such as addition: for example,
one and two together could capture
three. Lever & Fulwood defend it in
their manual of 1563, while Scot refers
dismissively to 'a childish and ridiculous toie . . . like unto childrens plaie
at *Primus secundus*, or the game called
The Philosophers table' (Scot, 198).
    play game (cf. Lever & Fulwood's
    title, '*The Most Noble . . . Play*')
34 '**The third . . . all**' This is, as Feste
notes, an *old saying* (Dent, T319), the
equivalent of the modern 'third time
lucky'. The clown now wants Orsino
to triple his tip.
    triplex triple time in music (*OED n.*
    1a, first occurrence)
35 **tripping** dancing (cf. 'Each one tripping on his toe', *Tem* 4.1.46), with a
pun on *triplex*
    measure rhythm; *OED* 17a, giv-
    ing this example, quotes T. Morley,

annotation to 29, '*Tripla*. This is the
common hackney horse of all the
Composers, which is of so manie
kindes as there be maners of pricking
. . . and yet all one measure.'
    Saint Bennet St Benedict. There
    were several churches in London
    dedicated to this saint, but Feste
    could be alluding in particular to
    St Bennet Hithe across the Thames
    from the Globe in Paul's Wharf, since
    its bells may have been audible at the
    theatre.
36 **one, two, three** i.e. three chimes of
the *bells*. Feste varies his earlier *Primo,
secundo, tertio* (33) to underline his
request for a third coin.
38 **throw** occasion; literally, cast of the
dice in gambling (perhaps taking up
Feste's *good play*, 33)
40, 41, 44 **bounty** generosity, especially
on the part of the wealthy (*OED* 4a)
41 **lullaby** *OED* (*n.* 1b) glosses this as
'farewell'; cf. *PP* 15.15–16. According
to Ard[2], the meaning is closer to 'good
repose': cf. *take a nap*, 44. It is more
probable, however, that the word is
used here as a verb (functionally shifted from the noun) meaning 'sing a
lullaby (and so send to sleep)': cf.
Copley, 59: 'Sweet Sound that all mens
sences lullabieth' (Dyce).

---

32 SD] *Cam* subst.   34 triplex] triplet *Johnson*   35 as] *Hanmer;* or *F*   Saint] *(S.), Capell*

  my desire of having is the sin of covetousness. But as
  you say, sir, let your bounty take a nap, I will awake it   44
  anon.   *Exit.*

              Enter ANTONIO *and* Officers.

VIOLA
  Here comes the man, sir, that did rescue me.
ORSINO
  That face of his I do remember well,
  Yet when I saw it last it was besmeared
  As black as Vulcan in the smoke of war.
  A baubling vessel was he captain of,   50
  For shallow draught and bulk unprizable,
  With which such scatheful grapple did he make
  With the most noble bottom of our fleet

43 **of having** to possess
   covetousness excessive desire for
   money or property, considered the
   deadliest of the seven sins and often
   personified in morality plays as the
   principal vice (cf. 4.2.123n.)
44 **take a nap** rest
45 **anon** at once: cf. 4.2.121n.
46 **rescue** Cesario's choice of verb adds
   to the confusion of identity between
   the twins: he is referring to Antonio's
   intervention to stop the duel at 3.4.307,
   but it is Sebastian that Antonio literally rescues following the shipwreck
   (see 2.1).
47–55 Orsino's retrospective eulogy of
   his military enemy is something of a
   Shakespearean topos (although it is
   usually reserved for the dead): cf. e.g.
   Prince Hal's praise for Hotspur in *1H4*
   5.4.86–100, or Octavius' for Antony in
   AC 5.1.35–48.
48 **besmeared** dirtied, blackened
49 **Vulcan** the Roman god of fire and
   metal-working
   smoke of war i.e. smoke produced by

   Vulcan preparing weapons in his foun-
   dry, and by the naval battle between
   Orsino and Antonio
50 **baubling** contemptibly small (literally,
   like a bauble or child's plaything; *OED*,
   first occurrence); cf. 'How many shallow bauble boats dare sail' (*TC* 1.3.35).
51 i.e. of little importance in terms of size
   and depth (and so not worth captur-
   ing)
   draught depth (literally the amount
   of water displaced)
   unprizable of little worth (*OED* 1,
   sole occurrence); a 'passivized' adjective (Hope, 1.2.2c)
52 **such . . . make** he engaged in such
   destructive combat
   scatheful harmful, injurious (sole
   occurrence in Shakespeare)
   grapple combat (literally with grap-
   pling irons). In Shakespeare the term
   often retains its nautical connotations: cf.
   Hamlet on the pirates, 'and in the grapple I boarded them' (*Ham* 4.6.17–18).
53 **bottom** ship; literally, hull (rhetorical
   figure: synecdoche (part for whole))

45.1] *after* 46 Dyce

That very envy and the tongue of loss
Cried fame and honour on him. – What's the matter?   55

1 OFFICER

Orsino, this is that Antonio
That took the Phoenix and her fraught from Candy,
And this is he that did the Tiger board,
When your young nephew Titus lost his leg.
Here in the streets, desperate of shame and state,   60
In private brabble did we apprehend him.

VIOLA

He did me kindness, sir, drew on my side,
But in conclusion put strange speech upon me.
I know not what 'twas but distraction.

ORSINO [*to Antonio*]

Notable pirate, thou salt-water thief,   65

54–5 That . . . him that even envy itself
and the voices of those he defeated
called for him to be honoured; *envy* is a
personification here, as at 2.1.27.
Cried . . . on invoked by outcry (*OED
v.* 17, giving this example)
56–61 The officer 'seems to be spurring
Orsino to revenge' (Oxf[1]) by giving
more information than appears to be
called for – e.g. regarding Orsino's
nephew – and by characterizing
Antonio as a mere street-brawler.
56 Orsino It is odd that the officer should
omit Orsino's title, as if addressing an
equal.
57, 58 Phoenix, Tiger ships of Orsino's
navy; *Tiger* is also the name of a ship
in *Mac* 1.3.7.
57 fraught cargo (variant of 'freight')
Candy Crete (from Candia, a town on
the island)
59 Titus . . . leg The name of Orsino's
nephew, together with his loss of limb,
evokes *TA*, in which Titus' daughter
Lavinia loses her hands and tongue.
60 desperate . . . state regardless of

personal disgrace and of public order.
Some commentators interpret *state* as
'danger to himself', but the context
of the conflict between Antonio and
the Illyrian authorities suggests public
(versus *private*, 61) decorum.
61 private brabble personal skirmish;
cf. 'this petty brabble' (*TA* 1.1.561).
apprehend arrest
62 drew . . . side drew his sword in my
defence: cf. 3.4.307.
63 in conclusion i.e. in his final speech
before his arrest: cf. 3.4.362–7.
put . . . me spoke to me in a strange
manner
64 but distraction if not madness
65 Notable notorious
pirate Illyria was renowned for its
dangerous pirates: cf. Suffolk's reference to 'Bargulus, the strong Illyrian
pirate' (*2H6* 4.1.108), a paraphrase of
'Bargulus, the Illyrian robber' (Cicero,
De officiis, fol. 88ᵛ).
salt-water thief pirate; cf. Shylock's
'water rats, water thieves . . . (I mean
pirates)', *MV* 1.3.22–3.

57 fraught] freight *Oxf*   65, 125, 160, 179, 190, 205, 260, 363 SD] *Oxf*

What foolish boldness brought thee to their mercies
Whom thou in terms so bloody and so dear
Hast made thine enemies?

ANTONIO   Orsino, noble sir,
Be pleased that I shake off these names you give me.
Antonio never yet was thief or pirate,   70
Though I confess on base and ground enough
Orsino's enemy. A witchcraft drew me hither:
That most ingrateful boy there by your side
From the rude sea's enraged and foamy mouth
Did I redeem. A wreck past hope he was.   75
His life I gave him and did thereto add
My love, without retention or restraint,
All his in dedication. For his sake
Did I expose myself – pure for his love –
Into the danger of this adverse town,   80
Drew to defend him when he was beset,
Where, being apprehended, his false cunning,
Not meaning to partake with me in danger,
Taught him to face me out of his acquaintance,

66 **brought . . . mercies** led you to put
   yourself at the mercy of those
67 **dear** dire, grievous (*OED a.*² 2); cf.
   'our dear peril' (*TA* 5.1.228).
69 **Be . . . I** please let me
   shake off repudiate; cf. 'these offers
   . . . he shakes off' (*AC* 3.7.32–3).
70 **thief or pirate** The deletion of the
   indefinite article (*a*) is common in
   Shakespeare after *never* (Hope, 1.1.3c,
   giving this example).
71 **base . . . enough** sufficient grounds:
   the two nouns are synonyms.
72 **A witchcraft** a spell. Cf. Olivia's 'the
   last enchantment you [Cesario] did
   here', 3.1.110.
73 **ingrateful** ungrateful, the first in a
   crescendo of accusations against the
   bewildered Cesario in this scene; cf.

99, 142–3 and 175–81.
74 **rude** rough
75 **wreck** ruined person; Sebastian
   was both literally and morally shipwrecked.
77 **retention** reserve; *OED* 3a, giving this
   example, glosses as 'keeping to oneself
   or in one's own hands'. Cf. 2.4.96
   and n. for a different use of the same
   term.
78 **All . . . dedication** devoted entirely to
   him
79 **pure** purely, only
80 **adverse** hostile
81 **Drew** drew my sword; cf. 62.
   beset attacked from all sides
83 **Not . . . partake** not intending to share
84 **face . . . acquaintance** brazenly deny
   that he knew me

75, 262 wreck] *(*wracke*)*

And grew a twenty years' removed thing   85
While one would wink, denied me mine own purse,
Which I had recommended to his use
Not half an hour before.

VIOLA   How can this be?

ORSINO
When came he to this town?

ANTONIO
Today, my lord, and for three months before,   90
No interim, not a minute's vacancy,
Both day and night did we keep company.

Enter OLIVIA *and Attendants.*

ORSINO
Here comes the countess; now heaven walks on earth.

---

85 **grew . . . thing** became as distant as if
he had not seen me for twenty years
86 **While . . . wink** in a wink (referring to
the rapidity of Cesario's transformation)
87 **recommended** committed (*OED v.*[1]
1c, giving this example)
88 **half an hour** This corresponds more
or less to real time in performance: i.e.
the brief time-lag between Antonio's
giving his purse to Sebastian at 3.3.38
and Cesario's denial of having received
it at 3.4.338. Contrast the slow fictional time of *three months* at 90 and
95.
88–9 In performance the first two of these
three half-lines (spoken by Antonio
and Viola) are usually delivered as
making up a metrical and rhetorical
unit (statement/rapid response), while
Orsino pauses before asking his half-
line question.
90, 95 **three months** The length of
time that has supposedly passed
since the shipwreck – and thus the
comedy's opening scene – is more

symbolic than descriptive: contrast
the *three days* that have elapsed at
1.4.3. Antonio's temporal reference
here emphasizes the intensity and
intimacy of his bond with Sebastian,
while Orsino's repetition of the
phrase underlines the fact that his
relationship with Cesario has had
time to mature. Both point to the
quite different temporal patterns
of the Sebastian and Cesario plots
respectively. On the play's multiple
time scheme, cf. pp. 77–8.
91 **interim, vacancy** synonyms for
'interval'
92 **day and night** implying that Antonio
and Sebastian slept together. This is
not unusual in Shakespeare: cf. e.g.
Iago and Cassio (*Oth* 3.3.416).
93 **heaven . . . earth** Orsino returns
briefly to the adulatory style of 1.1,
in stark contrast with his rough manner towards Olivia at 108–11, thus
confirming the rapid changes of mood
and attitude suggested in the opening
scene (see 1.1.7–8).

91 interim] *(intrim)*   92.1] *after 96 Dyce*

But for thee, fellow – fellow, thy words are madness.
Three months this youth hath tended upon me.   95
But more of that anon. – Take him aside.

OLIVIA

What would my lord, but that he may not have,
Wherein Olivia may seem serviceable?
Cesario, you do not keep promise with me.

VIOLA

Madam –   100

ORSINO

Gracious Olivia –

OLIVIA

What do you say, Cesario? Good my lord –

VIOLA

My lord would speak, my duty hushes me.

OLIVIA

If it be aught to the old tune, my lord,

---

97 **but . . . have** except what I cannot give
him (my love)

98 **Olivia** Olivia's self-naming gives her
an air of importance just as she is supposedly offering her humble services
to the duke (on this rhetorical device,
see Viswanathan).

serviceable willing to serve. Olivia
defers verbally to Orsino's rank, but
– in addition to refusing him – she
happily ignores him at 102 (as Cesario
points out).

99 Olivia is evidently referring to an
appointment made with Sebastian
after their exchange of marriage vows,
which, the priest tells us at 152–9,
took place two hours earlier. Even
after the marriage vows, she continues
to address her 'husband' as Cesario:
Sebastian is named as such in her

presence only at 217. Her ignorance of
his name serves to keep the mistaken-
identity plot alive.

100–1 Viola and Orsino speak simultaneously, the former anxious to defend
herself from another 'false' accusation,
the latter keen to seize the opportunity to woo Olivia directly: a comic
moment in performance.

102–3 Olivia gives precedence to
Cesario over his master: indeed,
Good my lord, while acknowledging
Orsino's desire to speak, effectively
invites him to shut up. Viola not only
re-establishes decorum but implicitly criticizes Olivia for her disregard
of hierarchy.

104 **aught** anything
to . . . tune in your usual (amorous)
style

---

94 fellow – fellow] *Dyce subst.;* fellow, fellow *F*   100 Madam –] *Riv;* Madam: *F;* Madam? *Capell*
101 Olivia –] *Theobald subst.; Oliuia. F*   102 lord –] *Rowe subst.;* Lord. *F*   104 aught] *(ought)*

It is as fat and fulsome to mine ear   105
  As howling after music.

ORSINO   Still so cruel?

OLIVIA

  Still so constant, lord.

ORSINO

  What, to perverseness? You uncivil lady,
  To whose ingrate and unauspicious altars
  My soul the faithfull'st offerings hath breathed out   110
  That e'er devotion tendered – what shall I do?

OLIVIA

  Even what it please my lord that shall become him.

ORSINO

  Why should I not, had I the heart to do it,

---

105 **fat** gross
   fulsome cloying, nauseating (from
   excessive repetition; *OED* 3c, giving
   this example). Olivia expresses outright revulsion at Orsino's courtship:
   these are strong words, provoking a
   violent reaction in the duke at 108–27.
106 **howling** i.e. like a dog: another insult;
   possibly looking back to Orsino's craving for a nauseating excess of music
   in 1.1.1–3
107 **constant** consistent (in my refusal)
108 **perverseness** obstinacy, wayward-
   ness (implying that her rejection of
   Orsino is altogether unreasonable); cf.
   the Duke of Milan on his daughter Silvia's refusal of Sir Thurio,
   'perversely she persevers so' (*TGV*
   3.2.28).
   uncivil ill-mannered, barbarous; a
   recurrent charge in the play, underlining its concern with civility.
   Malvolio uses it of Sir Toby's festivities (2.3.120), Cesario of Sir Andrew's
   challenge (3.4.247), and Olivia of Sir
   Toby's attack on Sebastian (4.1.52).
109 **ingrate** ungrateful

unauspicious inauspicious, unpro-
   pitious (*OED*, first occurrence; sole
   Shakespearean use)
110 **faithfull'st offerings** pledges of
   absolute fidelity (*OED* faithful 3b,
   giving this example)
   ***hath** F's plural 'haue' is probably due
   to the vicinity of *offerings*.
   breathed out expressed
111 **tendered** offered
112 Whatever suits you (a variation on
   'What you will'): Olivia patronizes him
   again. In response, Orsino points out
   that (as duke) he has indeed the power
   to do whatever he pleases (113).
113–27 The unexpected violence of
   this speech – in which Orsino first
   raises the possibility of killing
   Olivia, before changing strategy and
   threatening revenge on Cesario – is
   often underplayed in performance
   as one of the duke's passing moods,
   especially since there are no consequences and Orsino seems rapidly to
   forget the whole idea. It is none the
   less a potentially disquieting moment
   if played straight. The speech also

---

105 fat] flat *Warburton*   107 lord] my Lord *F3*   110 offerings] *(offrings)*   hath] *Capell;* haue *F;*
has *Pope*

Like to th'Egyptian thief at point of death,
Kill what I love – a savage jealousy　　　　　　　　　　115
That sometime savours nobly? But hear me this:
Since you to non-regardance cast my faith,
And that I partly know the instrument
That screws me from my true place in your favour,
Live you the marble-breasted tyrant still.　　　　　　　120
But this your minion, whom I know you love,
And whom, by heaven I swear, I tender dearly,
Him will I tear out of that cruel eye

marks a shift in the object of Orsino's affections, from *what I love* (presumably Olivia) at 115, to whom *I tender dearly* (Cesario) at 122. In some productions, though, Orsino indicates that Cesario may be *what I love* from the beginning of the speech, for example by immediately taking him 'hostage', as in Carroll's 2002 Middle Temple performance.

114 **Egyptian thief** This alludes to Thyamis, an Egyptian robber chief in the Greek romance *Ethiopica* by Heliodorus, who tries but fails to kill his beloved captive Chariclea when his own life is threatened by a rival band. Heliodorus comments, 'And if the barbarous people be once in despaire of their owne safetie, they haue a custome to kill all those by whome they set much, and whose companie they desire after death' (Heliodorus, fols 18ʳ–18ᵛ). In response to Olivia's *uncivil* behaviour, Orsino likens himself to the 'barbarous people' (see *savage*, 115), while characterizing his own predicament as that of a desperado ready to defend himself at all costs; the story suggests, however, that Olivia's (or Viola's) life is not really at risk.

116 **savours nobly** exudes or tastes of nobility
　　hear me ethic dative (i.e. listen to what I say: Blake, *Grammar*, 3.3.2.1a, giving this example); cf. 120 and 3.2.31–2, 3.4.171.

117 **non-regardance** disregard, oblivion (*OED*, sole occurrence)
　　cast my faith throw my fidelity into oblivion (by disregarding it)
118 **that** since
118–9 **instrument . . . screws** instrument of torture that wrenches
119 **my true place** i.e. Cesario has violently usurped Orsino's rightful position in Olivia's heart: a political metaphor to justify the duke's threatened abuse of power; cf. *tyrant* (120) and *crowned* (124).
120 **Live you** continue to live (ethic dative; cf. *hear me*, 116n.)
　　marble-breasted a conventional trope of Elizabethan love poetry; cf. Sidney's 'My mistresse Marble-heart' (in 'Ring out your bells', line 28, Sidney, *Arcadia*, 489; Ard²).
　　tyrant Orsino again justifies his threatened use of absolute power by accusing Olivia of tyranny over him; cf. Olivia's 'tyrannous heart' (of Cesario) at 3.1.118.
121 **minion** sexual favourite (from French *mignon*, pet); cf. the equally derisive 'O thou minion of her pleasure', addressed to the Fair Youth in *Son* 126.9. The term often bore homoerotic connotations: see B. Smith, 189–223.
122 **tender** care for (*OED v.*² 3a); rate: cf. *Ham* 1.3.106, 'Tender yourself more dearly.'
123 i.e. by definitively removing him from your view (through murder)

Where he sits crowned in his master's spite.

[*to Viola*] Come, boy, with me. My thoughts are ripe in

    mischief. 125

I'll sacrifice the lamb that I do love

To spite a raven's heart within a dove.   [*Goes to door.*]

VIOLA

And I most jocund, apt and willingly

To do you rest a thousand deaths would die.

    [*Follows Orsino.*]

OLIVIA

Where goes Cesario?

VIOLA   After him I love 130

More than I love these eyes, more than my life,

More by all mores than e'er I shall love wife.

If I do feign, you witnesses above

---

124 **crowned** crownèd; cf. Orsino's own fantasy of becoming the *one self king* occupying Olivia's *sovereign thrones*, 1.1.37–8.

   in . . . spite to the vexation of his master

125 **ripe in mischief** ready to do harm; cf. *H8* 1.1.160–1, 'as prone to mischief / As able to perform't'.

126 This may have biblical overtones, recalling both Abraham's near-sacrifice of Isaac (Genesis, 22) and Christ as the (sacrificial) lamb of God (John, 1.29).

127 **a raven's . . . dove** ambiguous. It may mean simply 'the cruel heart within Olivia's beautiful form' (Ard²; cf. 'Dove-feather'd raven', *RJ* 3.2.76), or it may involve a more complex conceit: a cruel heart (Olivia's) by means of a gentle one (Cesario's). The supposed cruelty of the raven was due mainly to its blackness; in some performances, such as Carroll's 2002 Middle Temple production, Olivia is still dressed in black, lending force to the second interpretation.

128–34 The forthrightness and intensity of Cesario's declaration of love, far

beyond the limits of a servant's dedication, is almost as surprising as Orsino's verbal violence at 113–27, and in some performances arouses equal surprise or alarm, especially from Olivia (see 137).

128–9 Cesario's readiness to die for his master recalls his 'Patience on a monument' story (2.4.110–21), in which his 'sister' possibly sacrifices her life for love.

128 **jocund, apt** cheerfully, readily (adjectives used as adverbs)

129 **To . . . rest** to put your mind at rest

   die with a possible innuendo on 'come sexually'; cf. 1.1.3n.

130 **After** This suggests that Orsino may already have begun to make his exit; his order to Cesario at 138 may be called from one of the doors, although both actually remain onstage until the end of the scene (see 139n.).

132 **by all mores** by all such comparisons

133 **feign** speak falsely; in another sense, of course, Viola feigns all the time.

   above i.e. in heaven, with a possible glance at the privileged spectators in the balcony above the Globe and Middle Temple stages

127, 129 SDs] *Collier³ subst.*

331

Punish my life for tainting of my love.

OLIVIA

Ay me detested, how am I beguiled! 135

VIOLA

Who does beguile you? Who does do you wrong?

OLIVIA

Hast thou forgot thyself? Is it so long?

[*to Attendant*] Call forth the holy father. [*Exit Attendant.*]

ORSINO [*to Viola*] Come, away.

OLIVIA

Whither, my lord? Cesario, husband, stay!

ORSINO

Husband?

OLIVIA Ay, husband. Can he that deny? 140

ORSINO

Her husband, sirrah?

VIOLA No, my lord, not I.

OLIVIA

Alas, it is the baseness of thy fear

That makes thee strangle thy propriety.

Fear not, Cesario, take thy fortunes up,

---

134 **tainting of** contaminating (by lying); cf. 351; 3.1.66; 3.4.13, 128, 353 and notes.

135 **Ay me** alas
detested hateful (to Cesario and so, perhaps, to herself)
beguiled deceived, cheated

136 Although it was possible in Early Modern English to use 'semantically empty auxiliary *do* . . . without any implication of contrastive emphasis' (Hope, 2.1.1b), the double use of *does* here is probably emphatic, expressing Viola's incomprehension at Olivia's reaction.

137 **Hast . . . thyself** have you lost all sense of propriety; have you forgotten your own identity

138 **Come, away** Cf. 130n.

139 **husband** In Carroll's 2002 Middle Temple production (Globe revival), Orsino and Viola, exiting at separate doors, stopped dead in their tracks on this word and stared at each other for several seconds in silent disbelief.

142 **baseness** meanness; moral turpitude

143 **strangle thy propriety** deny your true identity (as my husband) (*OED* propriety 3)

144 **take . . . up** accept your good luck/ your new prosperity (as husband of a countess)

138 SD1] *Cam¹* SD2] *Capell* SD3] *Theobald*

Be that thou knowst thou art, and then thou art   145
As great as that thou fear'st.

Enter Priest [*and Attendant*].

O welcome, father.
Father, I charge thee by thy reverence
Here to unfold – though lately we intended
To keep in darkness what occasion now
Reveals before 'tis ripe – what thou dost know   150
Hath newly passed between this youth and me.

PRIEST

A contract of eternal bond of love,
Confirmed by mutual joinder of your hands,
Attested by the holy close of lips,
Strengthened by interchangement of your rings,   155
And all the ceremony of this compact

145 **Be . . . ¹art** become that which you are, i.e. your true self; this alludes to the proverbial tag *nosce teipsum* ('know thyself'); cf. 15–18n.

145, 146 **that thou** that which you (145); **him whom** you (146). In both cases *that* represents both the demonstrative and relative pronoun, as commonly at this time (Blake, *Grammar*, 3.3.2.6–7, giving both these examples); cf. *that that* (180n.).

146 of the same rank as him whom you fear (Orsino). This is not actually true: Cesario would not become a count, still less a duke, by marrying a countess; cf. 2.5.32n.

147 **charge** order

148 **unfold** disclose
lately until now

149 **keep in darkness** conceal: as Olivia announced at 4.3.28. She unwittingly reminds us of Malvolio, still kept in the dark room.

occasion the course of events (*OED n.*¹ 6b)

150 **'tis ripe** it is time to disclose it

151 **newly passed** recently taken place

152 **contract** Cf. 4.3.26n. On the morally (as opposed to legally) binding status of the pre-marital contract, cf. *MM* 4.2.72–3, 'He is your husband on a pre-contract: / To bring you thus together 'tis no sin.'

153 An allusion to the ceremony known as handfasting, whereby couples clasped hands and exchanged vows before witnesses; this, like the *contract*, was popularly regarded as a non-canonical form of marriage. See Fig. 19.
joinder joining (from French *joindre*; *OED*, first occurrence)

154 **close** union (*OED* 3, giving this example)

155 **interchangement** exchange (*OED*, first of two occurrences; second 1796)

156 **compact** compàct: agreement

146 SD] *after 146 Capell   and Attendant*] *Capell subst.*   151, 346, 362 passed] *(past)*

333

Sealed in my function, by my testimony.
Since when, my watch hath told me, toward my grave
I have travelled but two hours.

ORSINO [*to Viola*]

O thou dissembling cub! What wilt thou be   160
When time hath sowed a grizzle on thy case?
Or will not else thy craft so quickly grow
That thine own trip shall be thine overthrow?
Farewell, and take her, but direct thy feet
Where thou and I henceforth may never meet.   165

VIOLA

My lord, I do protest –

OLIVIA   O do not swear!
Hold little faith, though thou hast too much fear.

---

157 **Sealed . . . function** ratified by my
priestly authority
158 **watch** Cf. 2.5.57n.
   toward my grave The priest's measuring of time in terms of movement
   towards death is a solemn, but also
   potentially comic, variation on the
   temporal awareness distinguishing this
   scene.
159 **but** only
   two hours This is the interval of time
   between the end of the previous scene
   and the current scene, during which
   Sebastian has managed not only to
   stipulate the marriage contract but also
   to inflict damage on Sir Toby and Sir
   Andrew (171–2). On time schemes in
   the play, cf. 88n., 90, 95n. and 1.4.3n.;
   and see pp. 77–8.
160 **dissembling cub** This may allude to
   the fox cub, and so to the proverb 'as wily
   as a fox' (Dent, F629; Oxf[1]), or perhaps
   to the bear cub, which was supposed to
   be formless (*OED* cub *n.*[1] 3a), and so able
   to assume a false appearance. On dissembling, cf. Feste at 4.2.4–6.
161 **sowed** sown

grizzle grey hair (*OED n.*[1] 3, first
occurrence)
case skin: literally, animal hide, especially fox-skin (cf. *cub*, 160); cf. 'And
if the Lyons skinne doe faile, / Then
with the Foxes case assaile' (Florio,
Second Fruits, 105). Orsino is alluding
to Cesario's lack of beard: cf. 3.1.43–4
(AT). There may also be a pun unwittingly alluding to Viola's real sexual
identity: Partridge, 76–7, glosses *case* as
'[female] pudend . . . because it sheathes
a sword'; cf. the play on 'genitive case/
Jenny's case' in *MW* 4.1.50–3.
162–3 Or, on the contrary (*else*), won't your
craftiness increase so rapidly that you
will bring about your own downfall?
163 **trip** a leg movement in wrestling
causing the opponent to fall (*OED n.*[1]
6b, giving this example)
167 **Hold little faith** keep at least a little faith
168–81 While Sir Andrew unmistakably
speaks prose in this exchange, the others appear to speak verse, culminating
in Viola's unequivocal lines of verse at
182–4.

---

159 travelled] *(*trauail'd*)*   166 protest –] *Rowe;* protest. *F*   167.1 ANDREW] *Andrew with his Head
broke. / Rowe*

Enter SIR ANDREW.

SIR ANDREW   For the love of God, a surgeon! Send one
    presently to Sir Toby.

OLIVIA

    What's the matter?   170

SIR ANDREW   Has broke my head across, and has given Sir
    Toby a bloody coxcomb too. For the love of God, your
    help! I had rather than forty pound I were at home.

OLIVIA

    Who has done this, Sir Andrew?

SIR ANDREW   The count's gentleman, one Cesario.   175
    We took him for a coward, but he's the very devil
    incardinate.

ORSINO

    My gentleman Cesario?

SIR ANDREW   'Od's lifelings, here he is! [*to Viola*] You
    broke my head for nothing, and that that I did I was   180
    set on to do't by Sir Toby.

169 **presently** immediately

171–2 **Has . . . too** Sebastian's beating
of Sir Andrew and Sir Toby has taken
place offstage at some point between
4.1 and the present scene; cf. 159n.

171 **Has** he has; cf. 1.5.143n.
broke a common form of the past
participle in Shakespeare (Blake,
Grammar, 4.2.5, giving this example)
across from one side to the other,
thoroughly

172, 185, 186 **coxcomb** head; the term
derives (appropriately) from the cap of
a professional fool, shaped like a cock's
comb; cf. 202n.

173 **forty pound** Cf. Sir Andrew's earlier
'I had rather than forty shillings I had
such a leg' (2.3.19): he is willing to pay
twenty times as much for his safety as
for his accomplishments (G. Wright).
Or does the increased amount suggest
that he is running out of money?

177 **incardinate** malapropism for
'incarnate' (i.e. made flesh); as a verb,
incardinate means raise to the rank
of cardinal or principal priest: an
incongruous (or unwittingly satirical)
association with *devil*. The blunder
confirms Sir Andrew's ignorance: cf.
the uneducated Launcelot Gobbo's
'the Jew is the very devil incarnation'
(*MV* 2.2.25).

179 **'Od's lifelings** by God's little lives:
one of Sir Andrew's many mild oaths.
Cam[1] notes that he swears like Slender
in *MW*: cf. ''Od's heartlings' (*MW*
3.4.56). Possibly both parts were
played by the same actor, John Sincler
(or Sincklo).

180 **nothing** no reason
and . . . did Sir Andrew immediately
contradicts his claim that he did *nothing*.
that that that which; cf. 145, 146n.

171 Has] *(H'as), Dyce;* He has *Malone;* 'Has *Dyce*[2]   177 incardinate] incarnate *Rowe*

VIOLA

Why do you speak to me? I never hurt you.
You drew your sword upon me without cause,
But I bespake you fair and hurt you not.

Enter [SIR] TOBY *and* FESTE.

SIR ANDREW   If a bloody coxcomb be a hurt, you have   185
hurt me. I think you set nothing by a bloody coxcomb.
Here comes Sir Toby halting. You shall hear more; but
if he had not been in drink he would have tickled you
othergates than he did.

ORSINO [*to Sir Toby*]   How now, gentleman? How is't   190
with you?

SIR TOBY   That's all one, has hurt me, and there's th'end
on't. [*to Feste*] Sot, didst see Dick Surgeon, sot?

FESTE   O he's drunk, Sir Toby, an hour agone. His eyes
were set at eight i'th' morning.   195

---

184 **bespake you fair** addressed you
kindly; cf. 'My gentle lord, bespeake
these nobles faire' (Marlowe, *Edward
II*, sig. C4ʳ).
186 **set nothing by** have no regard for
187 **halting** limping (because of his injuries); this is not always confirmed in
performance.
188 **in drink** drunk; the idea of a sober
Sir Toby is somewhat improbable.
tickled beaten (euphemism: *OED v.*
6b, giving this example)
189 **othergates** in another way, i.e. more
seriously (*gate* = way, road: *OED n.*²
1). This is an archaic adverbial form
(Blake, *Grammar*, 5.1.2.2.ii, giving this
example).
192 **That's all one** no matter; the phrase
recurs in Feste's song at 366–7 and 400.
192–3 **has . . . on't** Sir Toby's clipped
style suggests manly indifference, but

his elisions may be due to his drunken
slur; cf. 171.
192 **has hurt** he has injured
193 **on't** to it
Sot drunkard, fool; cf. 1.5.117n. The
drunken Sir Toby asks the supposedly drunken Feste about the drunken
doctor.
Surgeon i.e. the surgeon: his profession rather than his surname
194 **agone** ago: the earlier, unabbrevi-
ated form of the word, originally past
participle of the verb 'to ago', i.e. to
pass (of time)
195 **set** fixed (from drunkenness); cf.
the clown Stefano on the drunken
Caliban, 'Thy eyes are almost set in
thy head' (*Tem* 3.2.9).
eight . . . morning i.e. in a squint,
and thus pointing, like the hands of a
clock, in different directions

184.1 SIR] *Rowe*   189 othergates] *(other gates)*, *Capell*   192 has] he has *Douai MS, Pope;* 'has
*Dyce*²   th'end] an end *F3*   193, 279 SDs] *Mahood*   194 Sir Toby] sir above *F2;* sir, above *F4;* Sir
Toby, above *Theobald*

SIR TOBY   Then he's a rogue, and a passy-measures
     pavan. I hate a drunken rogue.

OLIVIA   Away with him! Who hath made this havoc with
     them?

SIR ANDREW   I'll help you, Sir Toby, because we'll be   200
     dressed together.

SIR TOBY   Will you help? An ass-head and a coxcomb and
     a knave, a thin-faced knave, a gull?

OLIVIA   Get him to bed, and let his hurt be looked to.

         [*Exeunt Sir Toby, Sir Andrew, Fabian and Feste.*]

Enter SEBASTIAN.

196–7 **passy-measures pavan** Sir
Toby's attempt at 'passing-measure
pavan', from Italian *passemezzo pavana*,
a slow and stately dance in double
time: he is presumably alluding to the
surgeon's drunken sluggishness. Florio
defines '*Passo mezzo*', as 'a cinquepace, a pace-measure' (Florio, *New
World*, 360), making it synonymous
with Sir Toby's earlier 'sink-apace'
(1.3.125), although in reality it was a
decidedly more leisurely dance than
the triple-time *galliard*, which Sir
Toby mentions approvingly at 1.3.115
and 123. He is an apparent connoisseur
of dance, with a preference for lively
pace; cf. his references to the *coranto*,
jig and *caper* (1.3.124–36).

200–1 **be dressed** have our wounds
dressed

202 **Will you help** The emphasis is on
you.

202–3 **An . . . gull** Sir Toby, having
milked Sir Andrew dry, can now
reveal all his contempt for him. This
is a chilling moment in performance,
to which Sir Andrews have reacted
with a range of responses from open-
mouthed shock to feigned indifference.

A similar series of scathing epithets is
delivered by Fluellen to Gower in *H5*
4.1.79–80, 'an ass and a fool and a
prating coxcomb'.

202 **ass-head** blockhead, fool; cf.
2.3.15–16n.

     coxcomb fool; cf. 172n.: Sir Andrew
both is a *coxcomb* and has a broken
one.

203 **thin-faced** an allusion to the physical trait indicated by Sir Andrew's
surname; cf. List of Roles, 12n.

     gull dupe (i.e. of Sir Toby himself)

204 SD This is the final exit of the two
knights, together to the end despite Sir
Toby's insults. They (and in some productions Maria) are the only characters
not present in the play's denouement.

204.1 This is the first time the twins are
onstage together, to the astonishment
(first silent, then vocal) of those present.
For the audience, the illusionist magic
of the episode depends partly on a convincing degree of likeness between the
actors. Ben Jonson abandoned the idea
of a play about twins 'for that he could
never find two so like others that he
could persuade the spectators they were
one' (reported in Drummond, 37).

196–7 and . . . pavan] *Malone subst.;* and a passy measures panyn *F;* after a passy measures Pavin
F2; and a past-measure *Painim / Pope*   202 help? An] *Malone subst.;* helpe an *F*   204 SD] *Capell
subst.; after 203 Rowe*

SEBASTIAN [*to Olivia*]

    I am sorry, madam, I have hurt your kinsman,   205
    But had it been the brother of my blood
    I must have done no less with wit and safety.
    You throw a strange regard upon me, and by that
    I do perceive it hath offended you.
    Pardon me, sweet one, even for the vows   210
    We made each other but so late ago.

ORSINO

    One face, one voice, one habit and two persons:
    A natural perspective, that is and is not.

SEBASTIAN

    Antonio! O my dear Antonio,
    How have the hours racked and tortured me   215
    Since I have lost thee!

---

206 **the . . . blood** my own brother. This anticipates Sebastian's rediscovery of his cross-dressed sister; cf. 'I never had a brother' (222).

207 **with . . . safety** with sensible concern for my own safety

208 **strange regard** distant look: Sebastian misinterprets Olivia's astonishment as anger. Cf. Antonio's similar complaint at 84–5.

210 **even for** precisely in consideration of

211 **so late ago** so recently

212–54 The denouement, with its revelation of the twins' identities, bears a striking similarity to the equivalent episode in *CE* 5.1.330–89.

212 **One** the same
habit costume. The twins are dressed identically: cf. Viola's 'in this fashion . . . him I imitate' (3.4.379–80).

213 **A natural perspective** an optical illusion produced by nature, rather than by a perspective glass, i.e. an instrument for creating fantastic or distorted images. Cf. Bertram on contempt's 'scornful perspective . . . Which warped the line of every other favour' (*AW* 5.3.48–99). Reginald Scot, making high claims for the illusionist powers of such instruments – 'But the woonderous deuises, and miraculous sights and conceipts made and contened in glasse, doo farre exceed all other; whereto the art perspective is verie necessarie' – lists sixteen different kinds of perspective, including the variety that produces double or multiple images: 'There be glasses also, wherein one man may see another mans image, and not his owne; others, to make manie similitudes' (Scot, 316).
perspective pèrspective
that . . . not Cf. Feste's 'Nothing that is so is so' (4.1.8).

215 **racked** synonym for *tortured* (*OED v.*[3] 1c, first occurrence)

207 safety.] safety. *All stand in amaze. / Theobald*

ANTONIO

    Sebastian are you?

SEBASTIAN   Fear'st thou that, Antonio?

ANTONIO

    How have you made division of yourself?

    An apple cleft in two is not more twin

    Than these two creatures. Which is Sebastian?   220

OLIVIA

    Most wonderful!

SEBASTIAN [*Sees Viola.*]

    Do I stand there? I never had a brother,

    Nor can there be that deity in my nature

    Of here and everywhere. I had a sister,

    Whom the blind waves and surges have devoured.   225

    [*to Viola*] Of charity, what kin are you to me?

---

217 **Fear'st thou that** do you doubt that

218 **made . . . yourself** split yourself in two

219 **apple . . . two** This recalls Plato's *Symposium*, and in particular Aristophanes' discourse on love, according to which each human being is the male or female half of an original androgynous whole. The primeval human being was a circular-shaped hermaphrodite, until Zeus decided to 'cut men in two, like a sorb-apple which is halved for pickling' (190d–e; Plato, 1.479–555, 522); as a result, each of us is destined to search for his or her lost half. Aristophanes' 'apple' parable also accounts for homoerotic (or 'platonic') love, since some individuals search for their similars and 'embrace that which is like them' (192a; Plato, 1.523). This theory is pertinent to the predicament of the twins in the comedy: not only does each look for the 'lost' other but, in so doing, each finds her or his 'other half' in love, while both attract 'that which is like them' on the way.

twin alike (*OED a.* 4a, giving this example)

221 Olivia's enthusiasm on discovering two Cesarios invariably raises a laugh in performance. Her predicament (but not her enthusiasm) is shared by Adriana in the final scene of *CE*: 'I see two husbands, or mine eyes deceive me' (*CE* 5.1.332).

223–4 **deity . . . everywhere** divine quality of being everywhere. Cf. Hamlet's '*Hic et ubique?*' ('Here and everywhere?') addressed to the ghost (*Ham* 1.5.156). Sebastian suspects a supernatural phenomenon or *witchcraft* (72).

225 **blind** undiscerning (because indifferent to Viola's beauty): possibly an allusion to the recurrent Shakespearean notion of being blind with weeping; cf. *TG* 2.3.13 ('wept herself blind') and *TA* 3.1.270 ('blind with tributary tears') (AT).

surges large waves

226 **Of charity** out of kindness (please tell me)

kin relation

222 SD] *Kemble*   226, 255, 263, 296, 315, 371, 401 SDs] *Rowe*

What countryman? What name? What parentage?

VIOLA

Of Messaline. Sebastian was my father.
Such a Sebastian was my brother too;
So went he suited to his watery tomb.   230
If spirits can assume both form and suit,
You come to fright us.

SEBASTIAN   A spirit I am indeed,
But am in that dimension grossly clad
Which from the womb I did participate.
Were you a woman, as the rest goes even,   235
I should my tears let fall upon your cheek
And say, 'Thrice welcome, drowned Viola.'

227 **What countryman** from which country
What parentage the question posed by Olivia at 1.5.269
229 **Messaline** Cf. 2.1.16n. In the 1950 Old Vic production, Peggy Ashcroft's Viola produced a long and emotionally charged pause before replying to Sebastian's questions (M. Billington, xvii).
228, 229 **Sebastian** Cf. 2.1.15–16.
229 **Such a** another
230 **So . . . suited** he was dressed in that way, i.e. like you (and me)
231 if ghosts can take on the physical appearance and dress of the living. This is one of Hamlet's dilemmas: 'If it assume my noble father's person' (*Ham* 1.2.242). Cf. also the duke's reaction to the Dromio twins in *CE* 5.1.334–5: 'which is the natural man, / And which the spirit?'
232 **fright us** i.e. being a ghost; cf. Horatio's 'It harrows me with fear and wonder' (*Ham* 1.1.43).
spirit soul; cf. 'My spirit is thine, the better part of me' (*Son* 74.8).
233 **am . . . clad** i.e. I (as soul) am dressed in a corporeal form (*dimension*). There may be a further Platonic

echo here (see 219n.): in Plato's *Phaedo* (80e–81e; Plato, 1.388–9), Socrates argues that the soul – which he identifies with the self (cf. 'A spirit I am') – is distinct from the impure body in which it is 'imprisoned'.
grossly materially (*OED* 5, giving this example)
234 **participate** have in common with others (i.e. the human body)
235–7 The logic of these lines (if you were a woman, *I* would cry) appears at first sight somewhat contorted; the point is, of course, that Sebastian would weep for joy (although in most productions he does not) if Cesario turned out to be his lost sister.
235 **as . . . even** as every other circumstance seems to suggest (literally, agrees: *OED* even *adv.* 2, giving this example)
237 **Thrice welcome** a conventional expression of courtesy that also occurs in *1H6* 1.2.47
drowned drownèd
Viola This is the first time that her name is pronounced in the play: it was thus as much a revelation for Shakespeare's audience as it is for the other characters.

228 Messaline] *Metelin / Hanmer*

VIOLA

My father had a mole upon his brow.

SEBASTIAN

And so had mine.

VIOLA

And died that day when Viola from her birth   240

Had numbered thirteen years.

SEBASTIAN

O, that record is lively in my soul!

He finished indeed his mortal act

That day that made my sister thirteen years.

VIOLA

If nothing lets to make us happy both   245

But this my masculine usurped attire,

Do not embrace me till each circumstance

238–44 The gradual and indirect mode of the twins' mutual revelation of identity, in addition to maintaining a degree of suspense, underlines their continuing doubt that all may be an optical illusion.

240–4 **when . . . years** Sebastian's *my sister* (244) might seem to imply that it was only Viola's birthday and not his. Since, however, Viola has just volunteered this fact about her father's death as proof of her identity, her brother is merely validating her evidence by repeating it as information applying also to his sister. Without external confirmation, there is still doubt about their identity as brother and sister.

240 **died** As with Olivia's father and brother at 1.2.33–6, the only thing we learn of their father – apart from his mole, his name and his place of residence – is that he is dead; on male mortality in the play, see pp. 56–7.

242 **record** reco̍rd: memory (*OED n.* 7, giving this example); cf. *AC* 5.2.117, 'The record of what injuries you did us'.

lively vivid

243 **finished** finishèd

mortal act act of dying; life, in the sense that *mortal* means 'pertaining to man as living creature' (cf. Hamlet's 'mortal coil', *Ham* 3.1.66) while *act* signifies a performance or perhaps division of a dramatic work (as in 'Act 5'): cf. Jaques' 'his acts being seven ages' (*AYL* 2.7.143).

244 **made . . . years** i.e. my sister reached her thirteenth birthday

245 **lets** hinders (*OED v.*[2] 1b, giving this example)

246 **But** except

masculine usurped attire false male disguise (*OED masculine* 6, first occurrence with meaning 'relating to the male sex')

247 **Do . . . me** Viola postpones the celebration of their reunion until she can resume her female attire and thus her full feminine identity, i.e. after the end of the play. On the 'inconclusive' aspects of the comedy's finale, see p. 68.

Of place, time, fortune do cohere and jump
That I am Viola – which to confirm
I'll bring you to a captain in this town, 250
Where lie my maiden weeds, by whose gentle help
I was preserved to serve this noble count.
All the occurrence of my fortune since
Hath been between this lady and this lord.

SEBASTIAN [*to Olivia*]

So comes it, lady, you have been mistook; 255
But nature to her bias drew in that.
You would have been contracted to a maid,
Nor are you therein, by my life, deceived.

248 **cohere and jump** agree and accord: synonyms (*OED* cohere 4b, first occurrence; jump *v.* 5a); cf. 'Both our inventions meet and jump in one' (*TS* 1.1.189).

249 **That** to prove that

250 **captain** This is the first mention of the captain since his brief appearance in 1.2. In most productions – and probably those of the Lord Chamberlain's Men – the actor playing the part later doubles in another role; see Appendix 2.
this town Cf. 3.3.19n. and 24n.

251 **Where** at whose house
maiden weeds clothes fit for a virgin (cf. 1.2.0.1n.); 'maidenweed' was a popular name for the camomile plant. *Weeds* occurs frequently in Shakespeare: cf. 'Weeds of Athens he doth wear' (*MND* 2.2.70). Such is the importance of the cross-dressed disguise in the play that only Viola's clothes can fully re-establish her 'true' identity. Since she does not change back, however, she remains in a sense Cesario to the end; cf. 259 and 263 and notes.
whose i.e. the captain's

252 **preserved to serve** saved so that

I could serve. Theobald emends to 'preferr'd to serve', i.e. helped into the service of (cf. 1.2.52–3). Despite the awkward assonance that this emendation avoids, however, F's reading (with its pun on pre*served*) makes sense as it stands.

253 **the occurrence of** that has happened to (*OED* 1, giving this example). Latin *occurrere* means literally 'run to meet', and in effect Viola's *fortune since* her arrival in Illyria has consisted in running between Orsino and Olivia.

255 **comes it** it turns out
mistook mistaken, misled: a common form of the participle in Early Modern English

256 **to . . . drew** inclined in the right direction: i.e. attracted you indirectly – through Viola's disguise – towards an appropriate (male) object of desire, namely myself. He is 'absolving' Olivia of the (well-founded) suspicion of homoerotic desire. *Bias* is a metaphor from the game of bowls, referring to the lead weight giving the bowl a curving movement, and to this movement itself.

257 **contracted** betrothed; cf. 152.

251 maiden] maids *Theobald*   252 preserved] preferr'd *Theobald*   253–4 occurrence . . . Hath] occurrents . . . Have *Hanmer*

You are betrothed both to a maid and man.

ORSINO [*to Olivia*]

Be not amazed, right noble is his blood.   260

If this be so, as yet the glass seems true,

I shall have share in this most happy wreck.

[*to Viola*] Boy, thou hast said to me a thousand times

Thou never shouldst love woman like to me.

VIOLA

And all those sayings will I overswear,   265

And all those swearings keep as true in soul

As doth that orbed continent the fire

---

259 **maid and man** This brings together three different but interconnected meanings expressing the gender confusions at play: a young woman (Viola) and a man (Sebastian); a man who turns out to be a woman (Viola); a man who is still a virgin (Sebastian). Viola's disguise as Cesario represents all three of these possibilities.

260 **right** most (intensifier)
noble Orsino promotes Sebastian (and so Viola) from the rank of *gentleman* claimed by Cesario at 1.5.271. The grounds for the duke's confident affirmation are not revealed, although both the twins are indeed to become *noble* through marriage.

261 **as . . . true** i.e. since the *natural perspective* glass still appears to provide real and not illusory images; cf. 213n.

262 **share** a part. A financial metaphor: Orsino has part of the investment in – and thus of the dividend deriving (paradoxically) from – the shipwreck (i.e. he has Viola).
happy wreck fortunate shipwreck: oxymoron. Orsino is presumably referring back to Sebastian's brief narrative at 224–5, since he seems to know

nothing of Viola's means of arrival in Illyria.

263 **Boy** Orsino continues to address Viola according to the gender he has known her by, often raising an uneasy laugh in performance. He avoids feminine appellatives to the end, while Viola maintains her male disguise.

264 Viola never actually says this onstage: Orsino may be alluding to Cesario's statement that 'perhaps, were I a woman, I should [love] your lordship' (2.4.108–9); Viola's affirmation that 'no woman has [my heart]' is made to Olivia at 3.1.157.
like to as much as

265 **overswear** swear over again: there may be an implication of greater emphasis (Ard[2]).

267 **As doth** i.e. as (the sun) keeps (its fire)

267–8 **orbed . . . night** i.e. the sun (rhetorical figure: periphrasis), or possibly the sphere in which, according to Ptolemaic astronomy, the sun was fixed. Cf. 'my good stars . . . / Have empty left their orbs' (*AC* 3.13.150–1). For *orbed* (pronounced orbèd) as 'spherical', cf. 'th'orbed earth' (*LC* 25). *Continent* has the customary Shakespearean meaning 'container'; cf. *AC* 4.14.41–2.

---

267 continent the fire] *Rowe;* Continent, the fire, *F*

That severs day from night.

ORSINO   Give me thy hand,
And let me see thee in thy woman's weeds.

VIOLA

The captain that did bring me first on shore   270
Hath my maid's garments. He upon some action
Is now in durance, at Malvolio's suit,
A gentleman and follower of my lady's.

OLIVIA

He shall enlarge him – fetch Malvolio hither.
And yet, alas, now I remember me,   275
They say, poor gentleman, he's much distract.

Enter FESTE, *with a letter, and* FABIAN.

A most extracting frenzy of mine own

268 **severs** divides: a probable echo of Genesis, 1.14, 'And God sayde: Let there be lyghtes in the firmament of the heauen, that they may deuide the day and the nyght.'
Give . . . hand the first explicit indication of their touching in the play; in most productions Viola is only too eager to oblige. There is further significant touching between them at 319.

269 **thy woman's weeds** your womanly clothes; cf. 251n.

270–1 **The captain . . . garments** Viola repeats the information she gave Sebastian at 250–1.

271–2 **He . . . suit** a curious piece of news, probably introduced to explain the captain's long absence: he has been imprisoned following a lawsuit brought by Malvolio. In addition to underlining the steward's litigious nature, it sets up a parallel with Malvolio himself, still imprisoned in the dark room. We are not informed of the motives for his *action*, but the allusion does suggest that the captain reached Olivia's house

as well as (presumably) Orsino's, in order to present Viola.

271 **action** legal charge

272 **in durance** imprisoned
suit lawsuit

273 This description is given for the benefit of Orsino, who does not know Malvolio, mainly because Olivia has always refused the duke entrance to her household. It serves as a pretext for introducing the steward first into the dialogue and then onstage.

274 **He . . . him** It is not altogether clear who is to *enlarge* (= free) whom: in the context of the preceding speech, it ought to be Malvolio who frees the captain, but in the event it is Malvolio who is freed by Fabian at 309, while we learn nothing more of the captain's fate.

275 **remember me** remember (reflexive; *OED v.*[1] 5a)

276 **distract** deranged; cf. 64.

277–8 A distracting madness of my own made me quite forget about his.

277 **extracting** distracting (*OED ppl. a.* 2, sole occurrence); with a punning echo of *distract* (276)

277 extracting] exacting *F2;* distracting *Hanmer*

From my remembrance clearly banished his.

[*to Feste*] How does he, sirrah?

FESTE   Truly, madam, he holds Beelzebub at the   280
stave's end as well as a man in his case may do. Has
here writ a letter to you. I should have given't you today
morning, but, as a madman's epistles are no gospels, so
it skills not much when they are delivered.

OLIVIA   Open't and read it.   285

FESTE   Look then to be well edified, when the fool delivers
the madman. [*Reads madly.*] By the Lord, madam –

OLIVIA   How now, art thou mad?

FESTE   No, madam, I do but read madness. An your

frenzy madness (i.e. her passion for Cesario); cf. 1.1.14–15n. and *MND* 5.1.12.

278 **remembrance** memory
clearly completely (*OED* 8)
his ambiguous: either my memory of him, or his madness

279 **he** As Feste has only just entered, he cannot in theory know who Olivia is referring to, although on entering he may have overheard her mention Malvolio. Since he is carrying the steward's letter, he might naturally interpret *he* as meaning Malvolio. Why Olivia should expect him to know how Malvolio *does* is another matter. Audiences do not have time to pose such problems.

280–1 **holds . . . end** keeps the devil at a distance. The metaphor, from the sport of quarterstaff fighting, is proverbial (Dent, S807). Feste, as if still playing the part of Sir Topas, is again suggesting that Malvolio is, or is about to be, possessed; cf. 4.2.31–3.

281 **case** condition
Has he has; cf. 1.5.143n.

282–3 **today morning** this morning

283 **epistles . . . gospels** multiple wordplay: *epistles* alludes both to Malvolio's

letter and to the New Testament Epistles; *gospels* refers both to the first four books of the New Testament and to the proverb 'All is not gospel that cometh out of his mouth' (Dent, A147).

284 **it . . . much** it is of no significance (*OED* skill v[1]. 2b): a now obsolete impersonal form (Blake, *Grammar*, 4.4.1a, giving this example)

284, 286 **delivered, delivers** Feste plays on four meanings of the verb: consign to their destination; report (284); set free; perform (286). This last meaning probably alludes to delivery or *actio*, the fifth and last part of rhetoric concerned with the performance of a speech, especially gesture and voice (cf. *vox*, 291).

286 **edified** instructed (*OED* v. 3b, giving this example)

287 SD *Alexander's SD is justified by Olivia's reaction at 288, as well as by performance tradition, in which Feste invariably *delivers* or acts out Malvolio by raving like a madman.

289 **read madness** i.e. in a style appropriate to the author of the letter
An if

281 Has] he has *Douai MS, Malone;* H'as *Rowe;* 'has *Dyce*[2]   287 SD] *Alexander;* reads. – *Douai MS, Rowe; Reads, very loud. / Collier*[1]*; he shrieks Cam*[1]*; He reads frantically / Mahood   madam –*] *Mahood; Madam. F*

ladyship will have it as it ought to be, you must allow   290
vox.

OLIVIA   Prithee read i'thy right wits.

FESTE   So I do, madonna, but to read his right wits is to
read thus. Therefore, perpend, my princess, and give
ear.   295

OLIVIA [*to Fabian*]   Read it you, sirrah.

FABIAN (*Reads.*)   *By the Lord, madam, you wrong me, and*
the world shall know it. Though you have put me into
darkness and given your drunken cousin rule over me, yet
have I the benefit of my senses as well as your ladyship. I   300
have your own letter that induced me to the semblance I put
on, with the which I doubt not but to do myself much right
or you much shame. Think of me as you please. I leave my
duty a little unthought of, and speak out of my injury.

The madly used Malvolio.   305

OLIVIA
Did he write this?

FESTE   Ay, madam.

ORSINO
This savours not much of distraction.

---

290 **allow** permit me to use
291 *vox* (an appropriate) voice or delivery
292 **i'thy . . . wits** according to your true
faculties
293 **read . . . wits** perform his true (i.e.
mad) state of mind; Johnson detects
a playful inversion of 'read his wits
right'.
294 **perpend** consider (*OED v.* 1b,
giving this example); a knowingly
affected term that probably echoes
Preston's tragedy *Cambises*: 'My
Queen parpend what I pronounce I
wil not violate' (*Cambises*, sig. E4^r). It
may have been a standing theatrical
joke: cf. Pistol's pompous 'Perpend

my words, O Signieur Dew, and mark'
(*H5* 4.4.8).
300 *have . . . well as* I am as sane as
301 *semblance* outward appearance (with
reference to the hose and garters) and
behaviour
302 *the which* i.e. the letter
but . . . right that I will fully vindicate
myself
304 *unthought of* neglected; Malvolio
fails to show Olivia his usual respect in
speaking out.
injury sense of wrong
305 *madly used* treated like a madman;
abused by madmen
308 **savours not** does not give the
impression; cf. 116n.

309 SD] *Capell*

OLIVIA

    See him delivered, Fabian; bring him hither.   [*Exit Fabian.*]

    My lord, so please you, these things further thought on,   310

    To think me as well a sister as a wife,

    One day shall crown th'alliance on't, so please you,

    Here at my house and at my proper cost.

ORSINO

    Madam, I am most apt t'embrace your offer.

    [*to Viola*] Your master quits you, and for your service

        done him –   315

    So much against the mettle of your sex,

    So far beneath your soft and tender breeding –

    And, since you called me master for so long,

    Here is my hand; you shall from this time be

    Your master's mistress.

OLIVIA   A sister – you are she.   320

Enter MALVOLIO[, *with a letter, and* FABIAN].

309 **delivered** set free; cf. 284, 286n.

310–11 **so . . . wife** if you please, when you have considered all that has happened, to think as well of me as a sister-in-law as you would have thought of me as a wife: an allusion to her marriage to Sebastian, but also, perhaps, an encouragement to Orsino to marry Viola. Here *thought on* – a 'past participle [forming] a non-finite clause resembling the Latin ablative absolute' (Blake, *Grammar*, 4.3.5, citing this line) – indicates time past.

312 **One . . . on't** this relationship will be sealed on the same (wedding) day **One** the same; cf. 212.

313 **at . . . cost** at my own expense

314 **apt** ready (*OED a.* 2b)

315 **quits** acquits, releases from service **your . . . him** the service you have done him

316 **mettle** nature, disposition; cf. 2.5.12 (*metal*), 3.4.266.

317 **beneath** unworthy of

320 **master's mistress** Orsino's paradox plays on two meanings of *mistress*: woman with power over him; object of amorous devotion (as in 'O mistress mine', 2.3.38). For the sexual and gender ambiguities of the phrase, cf. *Son* 20.2, 'the Master-Mistress of my passion' (addressed to the Fair Youth).

sister sister-in-law. Olivia's affirmation seems odd, since she is already Viola's *sister* through her marriage to Sebastian, and will not be more so if Viola marries Orsino, who is notoriously unrelated to her. She may simply be expressing wonder at the fact that her own 'master-mistress' Cesario has turned from lover into sister.

312 alliance on't, so] alliance, an't so *Rann;* alliance on's, so *Dyce²*   320.1 *and* FABIAN] *Capell subst.*

ORSINO

    Is this the madman?

OLIVIA   Ay, my lord, this same.

    How now, Malvolio?

MALVOLIO   Madam, you have done me wrong,

    Notorious wrong.

OLIVIA   Have I, Malvolio? No.

MALVOLIO

    Lady, you have. Pray you peruse that letter.

    You must not now deny it is your hand.   325

    Write from it, if you can, in hand or phrase,

    Or say 'tis not your seal, not your invention.

    You can say none of this. Well, grant it then,

    And tell me in the modesty of honour

    Why you have given me such clear lights of favour,   330

    Bade me come smiling and cross-gartered to you,

    To put on yellow stockings, and to frown

    Upon Sir Toby and the lighter people;

    And acting this in an obedient hope,

    Why have you suffered me to be imprisoned,   335

    Kept in a dark house, visited by the priest,

    And made the most notorious geck and gull

    That e'er invention played on! Tell me why!

---

323 **Notorious** disgraceful; cf. 372n. and 4.2.87–8n.

325 **must not** cannot

326 **from it** differently
hand or phrase handwriting or phraseology

327 **invention** composition (*OED* 7, giving this example)

329 **in . . . honour** in the name of decency and propriety (Ard²)

330 **clear lights** evident signs; this is probably a nautical metaphor, alluding to lighthouse signals (*OED* light *n.* 5d).

333 **lighter** lesser

334 **acting . . . hope** when I carried this out obediently in the hope of my reward

335 **suffered** allowed

337 **geck** dupe, synonym of *gull*; the only other occurrence in Shakespeare is in *Cym* 5.4.67–8: 'to become the geck and scorn / O'th' other's villainy'.

338 **That . . . on** that ever deception toyed with

321–2 Ay . . . Malvolio?] *Capell; one line F*   353 Toby] Sir Toby *Theobald*

OLIVIA

    Alas, Malvolio, this is not my writing –

    Though I confess much like the character –   340

    But out of question 'tis Maria's hand.

    And now I do bethink me, it was she

    First told me thou wast mad; then cam'st in smiling

    And in such forms which here were presupposed

    Upon thee in the letter. Prithee be content;   345

    This practice hath most shrewdly passed upon thee,

    But when we know the grounds and authors of it,

    Thou shalt be both the plaintiff and the judge

    Of thine own cause.

FABIAN   Good madam, hear me speak,

    And let no quarrel nor no brawl to come   350

    Taint the condition of this present hour,

    Which I have wondered at. In hope it shall not,

    Most freely I confess myself and Toby

    Set this device against Malvolio here,

339, 340, 341 **writing, character, hand** synonyms for 'handwriting'

343 **First . . . mad** Cf. Maria's 'for sure the man is tainted in's wits' at 3.4.13. **cam'st** you came; on the omission of the subject pronoun (*thou*), cf. Blake, *Grammar*, 6.3.1.2 (giving this example), and 2.3.112n.

344 **forms** ways (with reference to his dress and behaviour)

344–5 **presupposed / Upon** suggested beforehand (sole occurrence in Shakespeare)

345 **content** satisfied, calm

346 **practice** trick. Manningham echoes the term in his praise of the play: 'A good practise in it to make the steward beleeve his Lady widowe was in Love with him' (Manningham, 48); see pp. 3–4.

shrewdly mischievously

passed been played

347 **grounds** motives

348–9 an allusion to the proverb 'No man ought to be judge in his own cause' (Dent, M341). In the event, the perpetrators of the *practice* against Malvolio remain unpunished.

350 **quarrel, brawl** synonyms

nor no For the use of multiple negatives, cf. 3.1.157–8n.

to come in future

351 **Taint the condition** spoil the mood; cf. 134; 3.1.66; 3.4.13, 128, 353 and notes. Fabian's plea is of course biased, since he is one of the potential targets of Malvolio's *cause*.

352 **wondered** marvelled

354 **device** plot; cf. 3.4.127n.

356 against] in *Rann (Tyrwhitt)*

Upon some stubborn and uncourteous parts   355
We had conceived against him. Maria writ
The letter, at Sir Toby's great importance,
In recompense whereof he hath married her.
How with a sportful malice it was followed
May rather pluck on laughter than revenge,   360
If that the injuries be justly weighed
That have on both sides passed.

OLIVIA [*to Malvolio*]
    Alas, poor fool, how have they baffled thee!

FESTE   Why, 'Some are born great, some achieve greatness
    and some have greatness thrown upon them.' I was one,   365
    sir, in this interlude, one Sir Topas, sir, but that's all
    one. 'By the Lord, fool, I am not mad.' But do you

355–6 **Upon . . . him** on account of some
obstinate and uncivil qualities that we
had discerned and held against him

355 **parts** characteristics (Onions 3); acts
(Onions 4), with a possible allusion to
the dramatic roles that Malvolio performs (e.g. that of the misanthrope);
cf. 1.4.34 and 1.5.174 and notes.

356 **writ** wrote: a common form of the
past tense in Early Modern English;
cf. *AYL* 5.2.76.

357 **importance** importunity, insistence;
cf. *KJ* 2.1.7, 'At our importance hither
is he come.' In reality, it is Maria herself who proposes the *device* against
Malvolio at 2.3.150–6. Fabian may be
endeavouring to protect her from the
potential anger of her mistress.

358 **married her** This news is prepared
for by Sir Toby at 2.5.176, and Feste
also hints at the possibility at 1.5.24–6.
Onstage the announcement often provokes surprise among the other characters; it is usually made in the absence
of the interested parties, although in
some performances, such as Carroll's
2002 Middle Temple production,
Maria is present.

359 **sportful** playful (*OED* 1b, first
occurrence); *sportful malice* is an oxymoron (Cam²).
followed carried out

360 **pluck on** induce

361 **injuries** wrongs; cf. 304 and 3.4.241.
Fabian's equating of the *injuries* done
on both sides may strike audiences as
special pleading in view of the 'dark
room' scene.

362 **passed** occurred (*OED v.* 13)

363 **poor fool** This phrase recurs frequently in Shakespeare as an expression of pity or compassion, with the
sense of 'poor fellow' (Ard²); cf., for
example, *MA* 2.1.295. Malvolio, however, is more literally a *fool* or gull.
baffled gulled. Ironically, Malvolio
vows to *baffle Sir Toby* at 2.5.158.

366 **interlude** play, especially a comedy; cf. Prologue to *Roister Doister*,
'Our Comedie or Enterlude which
we intende to play' (*Roister Doister*,
sig. A2ᵛ).

366–7 **that's all one** it makes no difference; cf. 192n. Feste uses the same
expression at the end of his final song
(400).

364–5 'Some . . . them.'] *Theobald;* some . . . them. *F*   365 thrown] thrust *Douai MS, Theobald*
367 'By . . . mad.'] *Theobald;* By . . . mad: *F*

remember, 'Madam, why laugh you at such a barren
rascal, an you smile not, he's gagged'? And thus the
whirligig of time brings in his revenges.   370

MALVOLIO

I'll be revenged on the whole pack of you!   [*Exit.*]

OLIVIA

He hath been most notoriously abused.

ORSINO [*to Fabian*]

Pursue him, and entreat him to a peace.   [*Exit Fabian.*]
He hath not told us of the captain yet;
When that is known, and golden time convents,   375

368–9 'Madam . . . gagged' Feste para-
phrases, rather than quoting verbatim,
Malvolio's venomous gibe at 1.5.79–83,
although he recalls precisely the more
cutting phrases. The clown's confession of a personal grudge may cast
doubt on the apparently detached role
he has played until now.

369 an if

369–70 And . . . revenges Feste is
probably parodying the late medieval
doctrine of the wheel of fortune leading to the downfall of the great: in
Malvolio's case it is a mere spinning
top that undoes him. The clown's
attribution of events to fate may be
designed to lessen the importance of
his and his companions' own *revenges*
against the steward. The theme of the
circular or cyclical movement of time
also anticipates the clown's final song
(382–401).

370 **whirligig** spinning top or similar
whirling toy, hence circular movement
(*OED* 3e, giving this example); cf. *parish top*, 1.3.40.

371 **pack** gang. The expression *whole
pack* – recalling the hound metaphor
at 2.5.8–9 – invariably expressed con-
demnation or contempt; *OED* (pack
n.[1] 4a) quotes an anti-Semitic remark

in a translation of Erasmus: 'the
whole packe of the Jewes' (Erasmus,
Paraphrase, fol. 40[r]).

372 **notoriously** disgracefully; Olivia
echoes exactly Malvolio's complaint at
4.2.87–8; cf. also 323 and n.

373 SDs *Since F gives no indication of
anyone exiting, it is not clear whom
Orsino is addressing. Fabian is the
likeliest candidate, especially in view
of his plea for peace at 350–1, although
as a confessed conspirator against
Malvolio he has little chance of paci-
fying him.

375 **that** i.e. the outcome of Malvolio's
lawsuit against the captain; cf. 271–3.
The fate of the captain, so long forgotten in the play, now appears so
important as to delay the concluding
double wedding.

golden time This generalized personification of time as propitious agency
(*OED* golden *a.* 4b, first occurrence)
recalls Ovid's 'golden age' of pastoral
innocence (Ovid, *Met.*, 1.103, fol. 2[r]);
cf. *the old age*, 2.4.48 and n.; cf. also
'thy golden time' (*Son* 3.12, referring
to the Fair Youth's age).

convents convènts; is fitting (variant
of 'convene': *OED v.* 5, sole occurrence)

368–9 'Madam . . . gagged'] *Theobald;* Madam . . . gag'd *F*   373 SD1] *this edn*   SD2] *this edn; after
374 Ard*[2]

351

A solemn combination shall be made
Of our dear souls. Meantime, sweet sister,
We will not part from hence. Cesario, come –
For so you shall be while you are a man;
But when in other habits you are seen,   380
Orsino's mistress and his fancy's queen.

Exeunt [all but Feste].

FESTE (*Sings.*)
        When that I was and a little tiny boy,
            With hey, ho, the wind and the rain,
        A foolish thing was but a toy,
            For the rain it raineth every day.   385

---

376 **combination** alliance, union (*OED* 4c, first occurrence)

377 **dear** loving; precious

378 **We . . . hence** Since Orsino – in most productions and editions, as in this one – is about to exit, his *hence* presumably refers to Olivia's house, into which all except Feste repair: he is accepting her offer of hospitality at 312–13.

378–80 **Cesario . . . seen** Orsino, as at 263–4, seems to go out of his way to underline and even prolong the assumed male identity of the cross-dressed Viola, taking her *habits* (clothes) as a literal impediment to an immediate wedding.

381 **mistress** Cf. 320n..
his fancy's queen ruler of his desire; cf. 1.1.14n.

381 SD *It is not altogether clear whether F's *Exeunt* means that Feste leaves with the others and then returns to sing his song or – as is more likely and as occurs in nearly all productions – remains alone onstage. In *MND* and *AYL* a single character – Puck and Rosalind respectively – remains behind to speak the epilogue, to which the clown's song (especially

the closing distich) is in some ways an equivalent.

382–401 On the song (varied in *KL* 3.2.73–7) and its critical reception, see Appendix 3.

382 **and a** probably a metrical make-weight to fit the words to the tune, as in *Oth* 2.3.83, 'King Stephen was and-a worthy peer.'
little tiny catchphrase used twice by Shallow in *2H4* (at 5.1.28 and 5.3.56). Ard[2] considers this to be evidence of 'the (Shakespearean) authenticity of the song'; the expression, however, was relatively common in Early Modern English.

383 This refrain (repeated at 387, 391, 395 and 399) seems to evoke the adversities of life in general: hence *hey, ho,* expressing weariness or disappointment (*OED* heigh-ho *int.*). When adopted by the Fool in *KL* 3.2, the same line comes to evoke more literally the storm in progress.

384 a childish prank was considered merely trivial; with a possible pun on *thing* as phallus (cf. 3.4.295–6n.)

385 **the rain . . . day** i.e. (perhaps) troubles never end

---

381 SD *all but Feste*] Dyce subst.   382 SP] *Munro; not in F; Clo. / Capell*   SD] *(Clowne sings.)*   tiny] *(tine)*

But when I came to man's estate,
　　With hey, ho, the wind and the rain,
'Gainst knaves and thieves men shut their gate,
　　For the rain it raineth every day.

But when I came, alas, to wive,   390
　　With hey, ho, the wind and the rain,
By swaggering could I never thrive,
　　For the rain it raineth every day.

But when I came unto my beds,
　　With hey, ho, the wind and the rain,   395
With tosspots still had drunken heads,
　　For the rain it raineth every day.

386 **when . . . estate** when I grew up to be a man
　　estate condition, standing
388 implying that the 'I' of the song is a thief or knave, or perhaps, like Feste, an itinerant performer (considered a beggar and knave by the Elizabethan authorities) who failed to find hospitality in a house such as Olivia's; *shut* is in the past tense.
390 **alas** an ironic comment on matrimony
　　to wive to get married; cf. Petruchio's 'I come to wive it wealthily in Padua' (*TS* 1.2.74).
392 **swaggering** bragging, blustering; cf. Doll Tearsheet on Pistol, 'Hang him, swaggering rascal' (*2H4* 2.4.69). The implication is that the 'I' could not get away with bullying or making empty boasts to his wife, presumably because she saw through the bluster.
394 **when . . . beds** i.e. when I grew

old. Hotson, followed by Oxf[1], suggests that *beds* refers to 'the various spots where he happened to fall' (Hotson, 171). The song, however, narrates the different ages of man, rather like Jaques' 'All the world's a stage' speech, which ends with senile 'second childishness' (*AYL* 2.7.165). Cf. Overbury, 'it is beddetime with a man at threescore and ten' (Overbury, sig. G1[v]; Halliwell).
396 *With* may be repeated from the opening of the previous line, and makes no sense; A.W. Pollard's suggested emendation *We* (Cam[1]) is attractive, but identifies the speaking 'I' too directly with the *tosspots* and has not found favour among editors.
　　tosspots drunkards. There is no necessary connection between the drunkenness and taking *unto my beds*: the sense may simply be that drunkards were still drunkards, no matter how much time had passed.

387, 391, 395, 399 the . . . rain] *Boswell–Malone; &c.* F　389, 393, 397 it . . . day] *Boswell–Malone; &c.* F　390 alas] *at last* F3　394 beds] bed *Hanmer*　396 heads] head *Hanmer*

A great while ago the world begun,
　　With hey, ho, the wind and the rain,
But that's all one, our play is done,　　　　　　400
　　And we'll strive to please you every day.　　　[*Exit.*]

FINIS

---

398 At the end of its rapid journey through
life, the song seems about to make an
important statement about the world,
but immediately drops the idea.
begun began
400 **that's all one** it makes no difference;
cf. 366–7n..
our Feste is now speaking (or singing)

for the company; cf. *we* (401).
401 **strive . . . day** a conventional request
for applause, with a possible allusion to
the daily performances (in the theatre
season) by the Lord Chamberlain's
Men; cf. *AW*, 'we will pay / With
strife to please you, day exceeding day'
(*AW* Epilogue 3–4).

398 begun] *(begon), Rowe*　　399 With] *F2; not in F*

APPENDIX 1

THE TEXT AND EDITORIAL PROCEDURES

THE TEXT

Where lies your text?: the publishing of the play

The script of a play is never definitive. It is a metamorphic creature, destined to undergo continuous change. Throughout the history of the theatre, scripts have always been subject to the restless processes of cutting, addition and revision. What appears in print, in the case of published plays, may differ greatly from the playwright's initial manuscript, bearing the signs of the intervention of actors, scribes, printers and others. The printing of Shakespeare's plays, especially in the form of the collected First Folio volume, was the result of a chain of transmission – from author to company, sometimes perhaps via the company's 'bookkeeper', to the publishers to the printers to the booksellers – which did not leave the text unscathed. To begin with, printing entailed a choice of text (by the publishers or by the company): depending partly on availability, the copy-text adopted might be an authorial draft, a transcript of such a draft, a 'prompt' copy marked up for use by the company or a transcript thereof, possibly the transcript of an oral or written version by an actor or actors, or, in the case of republication, an existing printed text; or it might

355

be the result of an 'editorial' mediation between two or more of these. None of these forms of source text – even Shakespeare's manuscript – was pure or unproblematic: to which period of the play's life might an authorial manuscript correspond, for example, and what relationship might it have borne with what the actors performed at the Globe or Blackfriars? Moreover, every mode of mediation had its textual fallout: scribes would have corrected and 'tidied up' the text, normalizing forms, spellings and stage directions, and perhaps misinterpreting the authorial hand. The printers – and especially the workmen who actually set up the text – in turn interpreted, 'corrected' and at times misread or misprinted the copy they had received.

In the pages that follow an account will be given of the publishing of the text of *Twelfth Night*, at least to the extent that we are able to reconstruct it, and the questions that will be addressed are what kind of manuscript the printers used in carrying out their work and how that manuscript fared at their hands. Discussion will then turn to the question of possible revision of the text and of its various inconsistencies and idiosyncrasies.

The only authoritative text that we have of *Twelfth Night* is the one published in the 1623 Folio edition of *Mr William Shakespeare's Comedies, Histories and Tragedies* (see Fig. 28). That this was the first version of the play to appear in print is suggested not only by the lack of known copies or mentions of an earlier quarto edition, but also by the fact that *Twelfth Night* was entered, together with fifteen other hitherto unpublished Shakespeare plays, in the Stationers' Register on 8 November 1623 on behalf of the principal publishers of the Folio, Isaac Jaggard and Edward Blount. Such an optional 'entry of record' served to show that the publishers owned the rights to the work in question (not the same thing as modern 'copyright'). Entering *Twelfth Night* cost the publishers sixpence. They probably paid the Stationers' Company a further fee for a search to establish that no one had previously entered it or the other unpublished plays.

255

TwelfeNight, Or what you will.

Actus Primus, Scæna Prima.

Enter Orsino Duke of Illyria, Curio, and other Lords.

Duke.

IF Musicke be the food of Loue, play on,
Giue me excesse of it : that surfetting,
The appetite may sicken, and so dye.
That straine agen, it had a dying fall :
O, it came ore my eare, like the sweet sound
That breathes vpon a banke of Violets ;
Stealing, and giuing Odour. Enough, no more,
Tis not so sweet now, as it was before.
O spirit of Loue, how quicke and fresh art thou,
That notwithstanding thy capacitie,
Receiueth as the Sea. Nought enters there,
Of what validity, and pitch so ere,
But falles into abatement, and low price
Euen in a minute ; so full of shapes is fancie,
That it alone, is high fantasticall.
Cu. Will you go hunt my Lord ?
Du. What *Curio?*
Cu. The Hart.
Du. Why so I do, the Noblest that I haue :
O when mine eyes did see *Oliuia* first,
Me thought she purg'd the ayre of pestilence ;
That instant was I turn'd into a Hart,
And my desires like fell and cruell hounds,
Ere since pursue me. How now what newes from her ?

Enter Valentine.

Val. So please my Lord, I might not be admitted,
But from her handmaid do returne this answer:
The Element it selfe, till seuen yeares heate,
Shall not behold her face at ample view :
But like a Cloystresse she wil vailed walke,
And water once a day her Chamber round
With eye-offending brine : all this to season
A brothers dead loue, which she would keepe fresh
And lasting, in her sad remembrance.
Du. O she that hath a heart of that fine frame
To pay this debt of loue but to a brother,
How wil she loue, when the rich golden shaft
Hath kill'd the flocke of all affections else
That liue in her. When Liuer, Braine, and Heart,
These soueraigne thrones, are all supply'd and fill'd
Her sweete perfections with one selfe king :
Away before me, to sweet beds of Flowres,
Loue-thoughts lye rich, when canopy'd with bowres.
Exeunt.

Scena Secunda.

Enter Viola, a Captaine, and Saylors.

Vio. What Country (Friends) is this ?
Cap. This is Illyria Ladie.
Vio. And what should I do in Illyria?
My brother he is in Elizium,
Perchance he is not drown'd : What thinke you saylers ?
Cap. It is perchance that you your selfe were saued.
Vio. O my poore brother, and so perchance may he be.
Cap. True Madam, and to comfort you with chance,
Assure your selfe, after our ship did split,
When you, and those poore number saued with you,
Hung on our driuing boate : I saw your brother
Most prouident in perill, binde himselfe,
(Courage and hope both teaching him the practise)
To a strong Maste, that liu'd vpon the sea :
Where like *Orion* on the Dolphines backe,
I saw him hold acquaintance with the waues,
So long as I could see.
Vio. For saying so, there's Gold :
Mine owne escape vnfoldeth to my hope,
Whereto thy speech serues for authoritie
The like of him. Know'st thou this Countrey ?
Cap. I Madam well, for I was bred and borne
Not three houres trauaile from this very place :
Vio. Who gouernes heere?
Cap. A noble Duke in nature, as in name.
Vio. What is his name?
Cap. Orsino.
Vio. Orsino : I haue heard my father name him,
He was a Batchellor then.
Cap. And so is now, or was so very late :
For but a month ago I went from hence,
And then 'twas fresh in murmure (as you know
What great ones do, the lesse will prattle of,)
That he did seeke the loue of faire *Oliuia.*
Vio. What's shee ?
Cap. A vertuous maid, the daughter of a Count
That dide some twelue month since, then leauing her
In the protection of his sonne, her brother,
Who shortly also dide : for whose deere loue
(They say) she hath abiur'd the sight
And company of men.
Vio. O that I seru'd that Lady,
And might not be deliuered to the world
Y 2   Till

---

28 The opening scene in the First Folio text

357

In order to proceed with publication, Jaggard and Blount had probably already paid other fees and already sought other, obligatory, forms of permission. In order to be printed legally, a playtext required what was known as authority and licence. Authority, or allowance, was granted by a representative of the church or state. *Twelfth Night* would already have been allowed for performance by the Master of the Revels at the time of its first performance in or around 1601 (at a cost of about 7 shillings), but now required further allowance for publication – either from the Master or from the ecclesiastical authorities – for which the publishers paid another considerable fee (perhaps 10 shillings: Blayney, 'Publication', 2n.). They paid a further, smaller fee (sixpence again) for licence, i.e. permission to publish granted by the Stationers' Company, as opposed to the church or state authorities.

By the time Jaggard and Blount had paid for and obtained their various permissions and had entered their unpublished plays, towards the end of 1623, the actual printing of the Folio was almost complete. The printer, Isaac Jaggard's father William, took nearly two years to set the volume, having begun early in 1622. This was not an unusual length of time for such a substantial volume, and was due in part to the fact that printing was interrupted by problems of publishing rights or the temporary unavailability of manuscripts (as in the case of *Twelfth Night*, as we shall see), but more significantly to the fact that the printer worked concurrently on other texts, in particular Thomas Wilson's *Christian Dictionary*, William Burton's *Description of Leicestershire*, Augustine Vincent's *Discovery of Errors* and a translation from the French of André Favyn's *Theatre of Honour*.

Thanks to Charlton Hinman's full and detailed study, *The Printing and Proof-Reading of the First Folio of Shakespeare* (1963), and further research inspired by it, we know quite a lot about the typesetting of the volume in general and of *Twelfth Night* in particular. Hinman's meticulous comparison of fifty-five copies of the Folio in the Folger Library, in addition to identifying a wide range of variants between different individual copies, enabled him to determine the number of compositors employed by William Jaggard – at least five – and, more importantly, by establishing the spelling habits of each workman, to demonstrate which compositor or compositors worked on a given play. By examining the patterns in the use of type, ornaments and other typographic material in the setting of the Folio and the other volumes prepared in 1622–3, Hinman was able to reconstruct the sequence in which the playtexts and their component pages were set and printed.

Thanks to the relative lack of standardized spelling in Early Modern English, each compositor had his own orthographical idiosyncrasies, which allow us to know who was responsible for the typesetting of each play. It was usual for two compositors to work on a given text, but Hinman shows that *Twelfth Night* was set entirely by the so-called Compositor B, whose preferred spellings of frequently used common words – in particular, 'do', 'go', 'heere' and 'deere', rather than the 'doe', 'goe', 'here' and 'deare' characteristic of Compositor A, the other main workman – appear throughout (see Fig. 29).

B is generally considered to be the less accurate of the two main compositors: 'Both A and B made mistakes, but B made more than A and was especially given to particular kinds of aberration' (Hinman, 1.10). More recently, however, Paul Werstine ('Cases') has shown that, although B sometimes performed poorly, this was not invariable, and indeed, despite the compositor's reputation, the text of *Twelfth Night* is, in W.W. Greg's words, 'unusually clean' (Greg, Folio, 296), i.e. relatively free from major errors such as the wrong attribution of speeches or the mislining of verse, although it is not lacking in misprints, some of them probably due to the compositor's misreading of his copy manuscript (see Appendix 1 p. 364–365; on Compositor B see also Howard-Hill, 'Compositors' and 'Comedies').

In the production of a folio volume, the sheet was folded only once so as to create two large leaves (approximately 8½ × 13⅜ inches), or four printed pages. These were then sewn in sections or quires,

Twelfe Night, or

You ſhould finde better dealing : what's to do?
Shall we go ſee the reliques of this Towne?
   Ant. To morrow ſir, beſt firſt go ſee your ¡Lodging?
   Seb. I am not weary, and 'tis long to night
I pray you let vs ſatisfie our eyes
With the memorials, and the things of fame
That do renowne this City.
   Ant. Would you'l'd pardon me :
I do not without danger walke theſe ſtreetes.
Once in a ſea-fight 'gainſt the Count his gallies,
I did ſome ſeruice, of ſuch note indeede,
That were I tane heere, it would ſcarſe be anſwer'd.
   Seb. Belike you ſlew great number of his people.
   Ant. Th offence is not of ſuch a bloody nature,
Albeit the quality of the time, and quarrell
Might well haue giuen vs bloody argument :
It might haue ſince bene anſwer'd in repaying
What we tooke from them, which for Traffiques ſake
Moſt of our City did. Onely my ſelfe ſtood out,
For which if I be lapſed in this place
I ſhall pay deere.
   Seb. Do not then walke too open.

29 A passage from page 267 (Sig. Z2ʳ) of the First Folio (3.3.18–37), showing
the preferred spellings of Compositor B: 'do', 'go', 'heere' and 'deere'

normally consisting, with some exceptions, of six leaves (twelve
pages). In setting the quires, the master printer or compositors
would normally begin by 'casting off' the copy, namely estimating
exactly which portion of the text to be printed would fit each of
the quire's twelve pages. They then began setting at the middle of
the quire with pages 6 and 7 (the first 'forme'), working outwards;
pages 5 and 8 came next, followed by 4 and 9, 3 and 10, 2 and
11 and, finally, 1 and 12. If the cast-off had been miscalculated,
the affected pages might be too long or too short for the formes,
requiring space-saving cuts or increased spacing, for example after

scene divisions. In the case of *Twelfth Night* Compositor B seems to have cast off the copy accurately, and the spacing is quite regular. Hinman notes that evidence of proof-reading at press survives for only three pages of the text of *Twelfth Night*, and this proof correction applied only to minor typographical errors and left the text virtually unscathed.

Problems did arise, however, in the printing sequence of the Comedies, and in the composition of *Twelfth Night* in particular. *Twelfth Night* is printed as the penultimate play in the first section of the Folio – the section dedicated to the Comedies – where it follows *All's Well That Ends Well* and precedes *The Winter's Tale*. The text of *Twelfth Night* occupies twenty-one pages, numbered 255–75 and signed Y2 to Z6 (page 265 is misnumbered 273). Sig. Z6ᵛ, following the end of the play, is blank and was originally the end of the Comedies section, *The Winter's Tale* being interpolated after it only at a later stage of the printing of the Folio. In Hinman's reconstruction, the first twenty-one quires of the Folio were printed unproblematically in alphabetical sequence, from the beginning of *The Tempest* (page 1, the start of quire A) to the twenty-third page of *All's Well* (page 252, the end of quire X). At this point, however, the sequence was interrupted for reasons unknown. Instead of proceeding to quires Y and Z (pages 253–75), containing the end of *All's Well* and the whole of *Twelfth Night*, the printers jumped ahead to quires a and b, containing the first twenty-four pages of the Histories section (i.e. the whole of *King John* and the first two pages of *Richard II*). Only then was work resumed on the Comedies.

The probable reason for this interruption was delay in securing the copy of *Twelfth Night* for the compositors. As Hinman puts it, 'From these facts we can only conclude that for some reason the copy for *Twelfth Night* was not readily available when quire X was finished (though it evidently became so soon afterward)' (Hinman, 2.521). Since *Twelfth Night* had never been published, the delay cannot have been due to 'copyright' problems (of the kind that arose, for example, in reprinting *Troilus and Cressida*) but may have concerned physical access to the manuscript, or the need to have a transcript made for the use of the printer.

In addition to this interruption, work on the play was slowed by other, more urgent tasks, since the compositors did not work uninterruptedly on the Folio but moved between this and the other volumes simultaneously in press. There are signs that while working on quire Z of *Twelfth Night* the printers were also completing the typesetting of Vincent's *Discovery of Errors* in particular: the printer William Jaggard prefaced Vincent's text with an angry open letter of his own to the York Herald, Ralph Brooke, responsible for the 'Errors' in question. The final paragraph of this letter, perhaps added or changed at the last minute, contains several types distributed from *Twelfth Night*, suggesting that the two works were set contemporaneously (see Fig. 30).

What is your text?: the question of copy

Much of the debate concerning the printing of *Twelfth Night* – as of other plays in the Folio – has centred on the nature and source of the manuscript used as printer's copy. The copy, namely the manuscript or printed text from which the compositor sets his text, is the starting point for every edition.

Discussion of copy for the Folio plays has been greatly conditioned by W.W. Greg's seminal distinction between the author's so-called 'foul papers' (i.e. 'the text substantially in the form the author intended it to assume though in a shape too untidy to be used by the prompter': Greg, *Editorial*, 31), and the promptbook, namely the authorized manuscript of the text owned by the theatre company and marked up for performance. Each of these manuscripts might in turn have been transcribed, so that, according to Greg's categories, the compositors might have had as their copy-text one of four kinds of manuscript: Shakespeare's foul papers or a scribal transcript of them (a 'fair copy'), or the company's promptbook or a transcript thereof. They might alternatively have used a quarto edition of the play where this existed (as it did for four other comedies, *Love's Labour's Lost*, *The Merchant of Venice*, *A Midsummer Night's Dream* and *Much Ado About Nothing*). In the absence of a quarto edition of *Twelfth Night*, the copy manuscript must have been – in Greg's terms – authorial foul papers or a promptbook (or a transcript of one or other of these). In recent years the terms, and above all the absoluteness, of Greg's distinctions have come under considerable fire (see Werstine, 'Narratives' and 'Plays'). None

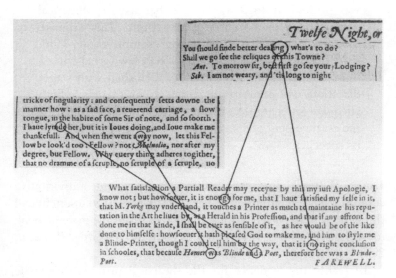

30 A comparison between the First Folio text of *Twelfth Night* and the open letter to the York Herald, Ralph Brooke, which the printer William Jaggard added to Vincent's *Discovery of Errors*. The two works were set contemporaneously, and the final paragraph of the letter contains several types distributed from *Twelfth Night*. Shown here are two passages from page 267 (sig. Z2ʳ) of the Folio (3.3.18–21, 3.4.69–76) – each containing two of the types in question – and the final paragraph of Jaggard's letter in which all four types reappear. From Peter W.M. Blayney, *The First Folio of Shakespeare* (1991)

the less, the debate about the provenance of the text of *Twelfth Night* has focused almost exclusively on whether the copy-text was Shakespeare's foul papers or a promptbook.

The relative 'cleanness' of the Folio text of *Twelfth Night*, together with the presence of supposedly 'theatrical' stage directions, led John Dover Wilson to argue that the copy for the play was either a theatrical promptbook or the transcript of a promptbook:

> Stage-directions like 'Enter Viola and Maluolio, at seuer-all doores' [2.2.0.1–2] and 'Maluolio within' [4.2.20 SD] suggest that the manuscript from which *Twelfth Night* was printed in 1623 was . . . either itself a theatrical prompt-book or a transcript therefrom. This original, moreover, must have been a fine example of its kind, since the transmitted text contains very few verbal cruxes, most of them long ago solved, is furnished with stage-directions and punctuation which are on the whole both adequate and competent, and gives no serious trouble in the arrangement of its verse or . . . in the distribution of its speeches.
>
> (Cam[1], 89)

Dover Wilson's argument gained cautious but authoritative support from Greg himself: 'There is little here to go upon, but all things considered it seems most likely that it was the prompt-book (or a transcript of it) that served as copy for F' (Greg, *Editorial*, 296).

In reality the evidence for the theatrical provenance of the text is decidedly scant ('There is little here to go upon,' Greg admits). Indeed, the text as printed does not seem to conform to Greg's own specifications regarding the distinctive features of prompt copy: 'characteristic of prompt-copy are the appearance of actors' names duplicating those of (usually minor) characters, possibly the general appearance of directions a few lines too early, and warnings for actors or properties to be in readiness' (Greg,

Editorial, 42). In *Twelfth Night* no actors' names duplicate those of characters. There is no certain instance of an early entrance stage direction. As R.K. Turner notes,

> Maria may be one line ahead of herself at TLN[1] 1188 [2.5.179.1], although the speech which intervenes between the entrance and the cue is so brief as to make the matter inconsequential. Malvolio seems to be brought on two lines early at 1535 [3.4.15.1]. Apart from these trivial instances, however, no entrances are indicated before they are required.

(Turner, 132)

Most of the stage directions are essential and not written in 'technical' theatrical language; Wilson's example of Viola and Malvolio '*at severall doores*' is the only instance of a direct reference to the physical character of the stage. Greg adds examples of directions indicating sound effects ('*Clocke strikes*': TLN 1344, 3.1.127) or music and song ('*Clowne sings*': TLN 2559, 5.1.382; 'Musicke playes': TLN 898, 2.4.14), etc. Cumulatively, these scarcely constitute compelling evidence of theatricality and hardly demonstrate the addition by the company bookkeeper of stage business to the authorial manuscript; in Turner's words, there is 'nothing that an experienced dramatist could not or perhaps would not have provided' (Turner, 132).

On these and other grounds, the promptbook hypothesis was rejected by Turner, who argued that the copy was indeed a scribal transcript – not of a promptbook, however, but of Shakespeare's foul papers. Signs of a 'literary' as opposed to 'theatrical' manuscript include the Latin notations at the end of acts: *Finis Actus Primus*, *Finis Actus secundus*, *Finis Actus Quartus* (the notation is omitted after the third act, presumably through

---

1   The first line references (TLN) in this section are to the Through Line Numbers of the Norton Facsimile of *The First Folio of Shakespeare*, prepared by Charlton Hinman (New York, 1968; 2nd edn, 1996); the act, scene and line references are to this edition.

oversight by the scribe or compositor); the only other instances in the Folio of such notations are at the end of Act 1 of *Love's Labour's Lost* and of *The Two Gentlemen of Verona*. Since these are, in Turner's words, 'more decorative than functional', they are probably, in his view, to be attributed to a scribe preparing a fair copy. Turner was followed in this opinion by editors such as J.M. Lothian and T.W. Craik: 'The probability is that the printer's copy was a transcript of Shakespeare's foul papers, that these gave the text of the play as it was originally written, and that nothing was added with the exception of what may be called editorial decoration' (Ard², xxxv). E.S. Donno asserts even more peremptorily of the Folio text that 'it derives from a transcript, and specifically . . . a transcript of Shakespeare's foul papers' (Cam², 156).

These editors' confidence in the origin of the text in Shakespeare's working papers is no less questionable, however, than Dover Wilson's faith in his promptbook theory. Turner arrives at his conclusion primarily through a rejection of Wilson's argument, on the grounds that *Twelfth Night* does not behave as a promptbook-based text should. As Stanley Wells and Gary Taylor point out, however, this presupposes the same kind of confidence regarding what a promptbook should be as Wilson's rejected hypothesis:

> [Turner's] conclusion is based almost entirely upon questionable assumptions about the comprehensive regularity of early prompt-books, combined with an unreasonable expectation that someone preparing a 'literary' transcript of the prompt-book would preserve theatrical annotations such as the names of particular actors, marginal notes about props, or added early 'warning' directions. In the circumstances it seems to us impossible to be confident about the scribe's own copy.

> (*TxC*, 421)

The problem with both arguments – the competing promptbook-transcript and foul-papers-transcript hypotheses – is that they depend equally on a rigid binary opposition that has been seriously questioned in recent years, on the grounds that it has more of an ideological than a historical basis (Werstine, 'Plays'). On the one hand, actual existing prompt copies do not behave in quite the way that Greg prescribes, and on the other hand the very term 'foul papers' as the designation of a specific genre of manuscript may be more of an ideal construction by twentieth-century bibliographical scholars than a hard-and-fast, early modern historical category. As a result, Greg's distinction no longer has the ontological clout it once seemed to wield. More generally, it has to be remembered that the copy is a purely virtual object, hypothetically reconstructed by working backwards from the printed play, and we should be cautious in reifying it as an autonomous textual entity that not only preceded and determined the printed play but was indeed more authentic than the latter (because closer to Shakespeare's 'intentions').

Even if we had definite parameters for distinguishing between different kinds or qualities of manuscript, the very 'tidiness' of the text of *Twelfth Night* would in any case render the enterprise problematic. The attempt to establish an absolute difference between a clean 'theatrical' transcript – what Wilson terms a 'fine specimen of good playhouse copy' (Cam[1], 90) – and an accurate 'literary' manuscript seems doomed to failure when the only evidence available is negative evidence (the lack of powerful signs in the printed text of extra-authorial intervention). 'A tidy text', as Wilson himself admits, 'tells us little about its history' (90). Perhaps the most we can say about the manuscript used by the printers is that it was probably a transcript rather than an unmediated authorial draft. Whether it was the transcript of such a draft, originally designed for private use or specially prepared for the printers, or whether it was the transcript of a copy belonging to the theatre company, we cannot know.

Out of your text: misprints, misreadings and other 'mistakes'

Despite the 'cleanness' of the text and the competence of Compositor B, errors inevitably occurred in the printing of the play. These range from banal 'typos' – such as 'tht' for 'the' at TLN 1163, 2.5.155, or 'metry' for 'merry' at 1538, 3.4.15 – to more debatable mistakes, some of which indeed may not be such. The following are the main categories of errors or probable departures from the copy-text (or, through it, from its original).

1 *Misreadings*: substitutions presumably due to the compositor's difficulties in deciphering the scribe's hand. These include 'coole my', probably for 'curle by' (TLN 211, 1.3.95); 'sit' for 'set' (243, 1.3.130); 'made, if' for 'made of' (688, 2.2.32); 'become' for 'borne' (1150, 2.5.142). Some errors may have been caused by the misreading of a final secretary *e* flourished so as to resemble –*er* suspension (RP): 'louer' for 'loue' (952, 2.4.65) and 'langer' for 'tange' (1593, 3.4.68); the latter may also involve a misreading of secretary initial *t* (uncrossed, or looped (RP)). As Turner points out (Turner, 130, n. 7), five Folio readings suggest that a final secretary flourish sometimes appeared to be an 's', or vice versa: 'That' for 'That's' (246, 1.3.134), 'suffer' for 'suffers' (986, 2.4.99), 'atcheeues' for 'atcheeve' (1150, 2.5.142), 'Kings' for 'King' (1221, 3.1.8), 'wisemens' for 'wise men' (1279, 3.1.66). 'Orion' for 'Arion' (65, 1.2.14) may have been a misreading or alternatively an authorial error. Other possible misreadings have given rise to editorial debate and speculation: 'south', possibly for 'sound' (9, 1.1.5); 'dam'd', perhaps for 'flame-' (243, 1.3.130); and 'mine', probably for 'nine' (1446, 3.2.63). For these more dubious cases, see the respective notes in the commentary.

2 *Foul case errors*: errors introduced when the compositor set a piece of type that had been misfiled in a case (i.e. the compositor went to the right box but found the wrong type there). The likeliest instance in *Twelfth Night* is 'deero', presumably for 'deere' (TLN 1179, 2.5.171), although Wilson chooses to read 'dear, O' (Cam[1]).

3 *Homophones*: the substitution of words or phrases with different meanings but identical pronunciation. A probable example is 'an ayword' for 'a nayword' (TLN 829, 2.3.131), although G. Blakemore Evans and Harry Levin (Riv) defend the F reading.

4 *Omissions*: due, for example, to the skipping of a grammatical word, as in '[to] the vppeshot' (TLN 2055, 4.2.69–70); or to the missing of a repeated word or phrase, as in 'And thankes: and euer [thankes: and?] oft' (1482, 3.3.15), or of a near–repetition, '[thee] the' (1389, 3.2.7); or to the jumping of an entire line, as in 'if one knight giue a' (733, 2.3.32–3), where in F the suspended indefinite article ends a justified line of type, so that the compositor may have unwittingly omitted the rest of the sentence in the following line.

5 *Misattribution*: the attribution of a speech to the wrong character. There is one almost certain instance at TLN 1546, 3.4.23, where F has the speech prefix '*Mal.*' (Malvolio, who has just finished speaking), most likely a misreading for '*Ol.*' (Olivia) but just possibly for '*Mar.*' (Maria, who is also present): see the commentary note.

5 *Intertextual contamination*: a compositor's error that has probably been influenced by his recent work on another text. At TLN 461, 1.5.162.1, F has the SD '*Enter Violenta*'; R.K. Turner (130) suggests that Compositor B, who had recently set the page in *All's Well* which has the name Violenta (Shakespeare's original choice of name for 'Diana'), may have expanded 'Vio.' accordingly here.

6 *Compositor B idiosyncrasies*: these are not errors but recurrent orthographic eccentricities of the compositor that may sometimes alter meaning or rhetorical effect. An example is Compositor B's preference for the form 'prethee' for 'prithee' or 'pray thee' – see TLN 939, 2.4.50; 1179, 2.5.172; 1353, 3.1.136; 1631, 3.4.105; 1927, 4.1.9; 1932, 4.1.14; 1935, 4.1.17; 1968, 4.1.50; 1981, 4.1.63; 1986, 4.2.1; 2104, 4.2.120; 2463, 5.1.292; 2521, 5.1.345. At 104, 1.2.49, this produces 'I prethee (and Ile pay thee bounteously)', described by Wells and Taylor as 'a sophistication that would obscure the symmetry of "pray thee"/"pay thee"' (*TxC*, 421; this edition reads 'I pray thee – and I'll pay thee

bounteously –'). The compositor (or his copy) also has a liking for superfluous apostrophes, which may create grammatical ambiguity. In *Twelfth Night* problems arise in particular with B's predilection for the forms 'ha's' or 'h'as' for 'has' in prose passages. These may simply be idiosyncratic spellings of the verb form, especially when preceded by a subject noun or pronoun: 'he ha's' (139, 1.3.20) or 'an ordinary man ha's' (198, 1.3.82). Difficulties arise when there is no subject: 'Ha's beene told so' (441, 1.5.143); 'H'as broke my head a–crosse' (2339, 5.1.171). Editors have usually emended these to 'He has', ''Has' or 'He's', interpreting B's apostrophe, as it were, as the sign of a missing pronoun; in Early Modern English, however, 'has' could stand alone as an elliptical form (= 'he/she has') and in this edition does so ('Has been told so', etc.), thereby interpreting B's apostrophes as mere eccentricities of spelling.

Another orthographic trick is B's use of space–saving abbreviations; in addition to the common *&* and *&c.* (the latter in Feste's closing song, for example), he frequently adopts in prose passages an abbreviated form consisting in *y*, standing for *th* (Old English *þ*), coupled with another character in superscript: y^u, for example, stands for 'thou' (rather than 'you'). The following are the occurrences in *Twelfth Night* : 'where y^t [that] saying was born' (TLN 304, 1.5.8–9); 'how dost y^u [thou] chuck?' (1635, 3.4.109–10); 'blow of y^e [the] Law' (1674, 3.4.148–9); 'What wouldst y^u [thou] now?' (1957, 4.1.40).

The numbers altered: questions of metre and prosody

Twelfth Night alternates frequently between verse and prose, sometimes within the same dialogical exchange (see pp. 78–9). This caused the compositor understandable problems with the layout of the text, due especially to the occasional indeterminacy of prosodic form; editors have to deal with the same problems of prosody, together with others probably created by the errors of the compositor or scribe.

The question of prosodic indeterminacy arises in the opening exchange of dialogue in 4.1, in which Feste, as usual, speaks prose, while his interlocutor Sebastian speaks what sounds like verse but is metrically defective, so much so that F alternates between verse ('Go too, go too, thou art a foolish fellow, / Let me be cleere of thee': TLN 1921–2, 4.1.3–4) and prose ('I prethee vent thy folly some-where else, thou know'st not me': 1927–8, 4.1.9–10). Modern editors, following Capell, often transform Sebastian's lines to imperfect verse made up of full lines and half-lines. This choice of verse for Sebastian is in part justified by the fact that metrically incomplete lines appear elsewhere in passages printed by F as verse, as at 547, 1.5.247, where the four-foot 'With adorations, fertill tears', among others, is left suspended; at 676, 2.2.20, where 'That me thought her eyes had lost her tongue' is missing a beat; at 2244–6, 5.1.88–9, with its three consecutive half-lines, etc. (see also 132–3, 3.1.104). Editors have sometimes been inspired to perform prodigious feats of prosodic surgery, on the assumption that the scribe or compositor mixed them up, in order to save the metre: a notable case in point is Hanmer's inversion of F's 'the sight / And company' at 90–1, 1.2.37–8.

Such are the vicissitudes of the dramatic text, subject as it is to scribal mediation, to compositorial error and substitution, to editorial inspiration and interpolation. Even in the case of a well-printed Folio play, the answer to Olivia's question 'what is your text?' is not always straightforward.

EDITORIAL PROCEDURES

No consonancy in the sequel: orthographic and lexical forms

This edition is based on the 1623 Folio text. Any substantive departure from the copy-text – i.e. any emendation adopted from later Folios or from subsequent editions, or introduced for the first time in this edition – is indicated in the textual notes and discussed in the commentary. All stage directions in F are

retained, sometimes with slightly different wording. Other SDs
are borrowed or adapted from later editions, particularly from
acting editions, or occasionally from promptbooks, if they provide
useful suggestions regarding movement or stage business; a case
in point is Kemble's '[*Takes his hand.*]' at 1.3.67. Occasional
SDs are introduced for the first time in this edition, particularly
with regard to possible stage business that clarifies the sense of
the dialogue: examples include '[*Brings his hand to her breast.*]'
at 1.3.68 and '[*Shows ring.*]' at 2.2.5. The textual notes record
the sources for all these as well as other interesting SDs present
especially in acting editions but not adopted in this text (see, for
instance, the textual notes to 2.3.104 and 105).

In keeping with Arden's third series practice, speech prefixes
are given in full. This is a relatively late editorial phenomenon:
in the case of *Twelfth Night* the first editor to give full names or
titles – rather than abbreviated forms such as '*Vio.*' or '*Du.*' –
was Elizabeth Inchbald in her 1808 acting edition. This edition
adopts names rather than titles or roles: thus 'Orsino' rather than
'Duke' (an option first taken up in 1968 by Mahood), and 'Feste'
as opposed to 'Clown' (a choice first made in 1958 by Munro).
'Feste' may need some justifying: the name occurs only once in
the Folio text and never in SPs or SDs; on the other hand, the
clown's name is habitually used by actors and critics alike, and
is familiar to audiences and readers, so much so that the speech
prefix 'Clown' looks today like a form of strategic distancing or
alienation.

As in other Arden Shakespeare editions, the text presented in
this edition modernizes the spelling and punctuation of the Folio
text, bringing them into line with current English usage. Some of
the characteristics of F's spelling are illustrated in the following
piece of clowning by Feste:

> *Clo.* Two faults Madona, that drinke & good counsell
>   wil amend: for giue the dry foole drink, then is the
>   foole not dry: bid the dishonest man mend himself, if

he mend, he is no longer dishonest; if hee cannot, let
the Botcher mend him: any thing that's mended, is
but patch'd: vertu that transgresses, is but patcht with
sinne, and sin that amends, is but patcht with vertue.

(TLN 335–41, 1.5.39–45)

In addition to Elizabethan orthographic conventions such as
medial *u* for *v* (see 'giue', 336; *i* was likewise used medially and
initially for *j*), the quoted passage illustrates the relative non-
standardization of Early Modern English orthography, whereby
the same lexical form may appear in different spellings not only
within the same text, but within the same speech or sentence: see
'he' (337) and 'hee' (338); 'patch'd' (339) and 'patcht' (340, 341);
'sinne' (340) and 'sin' (in the same line); 'vertu' (339) and 'vertue'
(341). Such variants are standardized and modernized in this
edition. This practice is justified by the need to make the play as
accessible as possible to contemporary readers. Since, moreover,
we do not know precisely whose spelling and punctuation the Folio
text represents at a given point – Shakespeare's, the scribe's, the
compositor's, a mixture of all three? – modernization, rather than
constituting a loss of the authorial 'authenticity' of the copy-text,
represents a further stage in the series of mediations to which the
script of *Twelfth Night* has been subjected. It may be that certain
idiosyncratic orthographic forms, such as 'Olyffe' (503, 1.5.204),
reflect Shakespeare's own spelling, but we cannot be sure, and
in any case the attempt to retain 'original' Shakespearean forms
while modernizing the rest (a practice adopted, for example, by
the Riverside edition) would be arbitrary.

A distinction, not always easy to uphold, has been made in this
edition between old spellings, which have been modernized, and
distinct Early Modern English lexical forms (according to the
OED), which have been retained. Examples of words retained as
autonomous forms include 'crowner' for modern 'coroner' (*OED*
crowner[2] 1; TLN 427, 1.5.130), 'comptible' for '(ac)countable'
(*OED* countable 1c; 469, 1.5.170), 'conster' for 'construe' (*OED* 9;

1268, 3.1.55) and 'convents' for 'convenes' (*OED* 5; 2552, 5.1.375). Likewise the noun 'grize' (*OED* 1; 133, 3.1.122), sometimes emended to 'grece', has been retained as a recurrent Early Modern (and Shakespearean) lexical rather than orthographic variant. On the other hand, 'computent' is considered an orthographic variant of 'competent' (*OED* 6b; 1765, 3.4.241), 'swarths' a variant spelling of 'swathes' (*OED* 3a; 841, 2.3.144), 'stroke' a variant of 'struck' (*OED* strike 2; 1951, 4.1.34) and 'wrack(e)' a variant of 'wreck' (*OED* 2; 2231, 5.1.75), to give selected examples: all have been modernized. No attempt is made, in general, to retain phonetic variations that may reflect Elizabethan pronunciation – for example 'Countrey' (71, 1.2.19) or 'huswife' (214, 1.3.99). An exception is Sir Toby's 'firago' for 'virago' (1792, 3.4.268), which, in addition to indicating the original pronunciation, may be an attempt to express the fiery ferocity of the referent Sebastian (see commentary note).

Particular problems arise in the relationship between spelling and pronunciation in the case of foreign words. It is often assumed that, when Sir Andrew greets Cesario in French in 3.1, the Folio text's spelling – '*And. Dieu vou guard Monsieur*' (TLN 1283, 3.1.69) – reflects his bad pronunciation, especially since Andrew himself admits his lack of 'the tongues' (1.3.90). Actors often give him a correspondingly atrocious French accent. F's spelling might instead represent a phonetic rendering of contemporary French, in particular because Cesario's reply, even more eccentric according to modern orthographical conventions – '*Vio. Et vouz ousie vostre seruiture*' (1284, 3.1.70) – is unlikely to indicate Viola's linguistic ignorance. In fact it probably consists mainly of an English phonetic version of spoken French, possibly one example of early seventeenth–century French orthography (the old spelling 'vostre') and at least one spelling error ('seruiture') by the author, scribe or compositor. In this edition the exchange has been modernized in correct French, and it is left to the actors to deform the pronunciation if they so choose. Elsewhere editorial problems are created by the difficulty of knowing precisely which language is being attempted. Sir Toby's '*Castiliano vulgo*' (TLN 158, 1.3.41) has been deciphered as Latin, Italian (*volto* or *voglio*) or Spanish. Similarly, Feste's '*Bonos dies*' (1998, 4.2.12) may be bad Latin (standing for the ungrammatical *bonus dies*) or bad Spanish (*buenas días*). In these cases emendation becomes arbitrary, limiting the range of possible interpretations.

Twelfth Night is replete with nonsense words, nonce words and drunken lexical deformations; the editorial task is to decide whether the monstrosities in question are produced by the speaker or by the compositor or scribe. Toby Belch is a particularly rich source of (usually inebriated) solecisms, such as 'substractors' for 'subtractors' (TLN 150–1, 1.3.32), sometimes emended but presumably to be taken as a sort of linguistic alcoholometer. Toby gets into particular trouble with dance terms. 'Sinke–a–pace' for 'cinquepace' (238, 1.3.125) seems to be a deliberate pun on 'sink' and has been left unemended (see commentary). The terpsichorean phrase 'passy measures panyn' (2363, 5.1.196–7) is more problematic and has been the object of much editorial guesswork; here Toby and the compositor may have combined forces to deform something like 'passing-measure pavan' and it is hard to know what degree of emendation, if any, is called for: in this edition a compromise is reached with 'passy-measures pavan'.

Analogous questions arise with Feste's fooling in its more nonsensical moments. The twin neologisms in his 'I did impeticos thy gratility' (TLN 726, 2.3.25) are clearly his own inventions (from the equally invented 'impetticoat' – i.e. to pocket – and from 'gratuity' respectively). Less certain is the much-commented passage at 723–4, 2.3.22–3, with its 'Pigrogromitus' and its 'equinoctial of Queubus'. The problem here is that Feste's clowning is being reported by Sir Andrew, who gives his own possibly garbled version, with or without the help of the compositor. The only reasonable option is to leave the speech gloriously unemended.

On the question of emendation, certain verbal cruces in *Twelfth Night* have a long textual and editorial history, giving the editor a range of options, in addition to the option of leaving the Folio text as it stands. The most notorious of these is Sir Andrew's enigmatic 'dam'd colour'd stocke' (TLN 243, 1.3.130), which has given rise over the centuries to an impressive array of often ingenious alternatives on the plausible assumption that 'dam'd' is a compositor's error (see textual notes and commentary); this edition opts for the 'flame-coloured stock' proposed by the play's first editor Rowe. Similar hermeneutic energy has been exercised on Feste's 'cleere stores' (2022, 4.2.37), variously interpreted by past editors as 'clear stones', 'clear stories', 'clearstores', etc.; the consensus today, followed in this edition, is for the architectonic 'clerestories'. There is less of a general consensus for other emendations adopted here, such as 'youngest wren of nine' for F's '. . . mine' (1446, 3.2.63), an emendation first introduced by Theobald but rejected by many later editors. More controversial still, and indeed decidedly unfashionable, is the emendation – first adopted by Pope and followed here – of 'the sweet south' for 'the sweet sound' (9, 1.1.5). Such editorial interventions will be seen by some as at best unnecessary and at worst arbitrarily invasive; my motives are expounded in the commentary.

Certain orthographical conventions in this edition differ from those adopted in F: 'and' in the sense of 'if' (for example 'and they be not' at TLN 130, 1.3.11) is given as 'an', in the interests of grammatical clarity and in keeping with common Early Modern English practice; 'yond' is given as 'yon', etc. An interesting case is F's 'I' as a space-saving orthographic variant of 'ay' (yes); in most cases 'ay' is an unproblematic substitution, but there is occasional ambiguity: Orsino's 'I prethee sing' (939, 2.4.50), for example, can be interpreted either as 'I prithee sing' (as in this edition) or as 'Ay, prithee sing' (Theobald). The I/ay (and indeed I/eye) homophone is also an easy target for puns, as in the letter scene:

'I, or Ile cudgel him, and make him cry *O*' (1140, 2.5.131); 'I, and you had any eye behinde you' (1142, 2.5.133). Since, however, these are aural rather than visual puns, 'ay' remains the preferred spelling here.

Every point of the letter: punctuation as interpretation

Norman Blake complains that 'It is common for modern editors of Shakespeare to harbour a dismissive attitude to punctuation in early Shakespearean prints', and adds, 'It needs to be taken more seriously than it usually is' (Blake, *Grammar*, 22). One of the problems for the editor is that F's punctuation, like Elizabethan punctuation in general, often has more of a rhetorical than a syntactic function, signalling pauses and emphases for declamation or reading out loud (see Sir Toby's wish in the letter scene: 'the spirit of humours intimate reading aloud to him': TLN 1108–9, 2.5.83–4). Such signs no longer correspond to the principles of modern punctuation, which instead are based primarily on private reading; as a result, certain marks have different values today. The colon, omnipresent in F as a versatile stop – marking a pause, signalling an interruption, adding emphasis to what follows, separating two contrasting clauses, etc. – is less widely used today and its expressive range has been restricted. F's colon may correspond to the modern full stop, comma, semicolon or dash. Other marks, such as inverted commas or exclamation marks, are virtually absent from F, but are often abundantly supplied (especially exclamations) in later editions.

It is not an exaggeration to say that the interpretation and modernization of F's punctuation is one of the more delicate tasks awaiting the editor. Among other things, the choice of punctuation has an important hermeneutic role, privileging one interpretation rather than another and thereby reducing potential ambiguity: as Blake notes (approvingly), 'Punctuation is one of the means used to ensure that, as far as possible, alternative interpretations are reduced to a minimum' (Blake, *Grammar*, 22).

An idea of the problems involved and of the kinds of choices to be made is provided by the false love letter to Malvolio:

> Remember who commended thy yellow stockings, and wish'd to see thee euer crosse garter'd: I say remember, goe too, thou art made if thou desir'st to be so: If not, let me see thee a steward still, the fellow of seruants, and not woorthie to touch Fortunes fingers Farewell, Shee that would alter seruices with thee, tht fortunate vnhappy daylight and champian discouers not more: This is open, I will bee

> (1158–64, 2.5.149–57)

The three colons here, for example, have three rather different functions: the first introduces the emphatic 'I say'; the second signals a mild stop after 'so', with the disjunctive 'If not' continuing the argument; the third indicates a more decisive stop after 'not more'. In this edition they are represented by colon, semicolon and full stop respectively. Likewise the commas after 'I say remember' and 'Farewell' – as the capitalized 'Shee' suggests – have a stronger value than the contemporary comma, and are in effect equivalent to the modern full stop. The punctuation is rendered more problematic by the compositor's omission of marks breaking 'tht . . . more' into clauses or sentences, or indeed signalling the end of the letter itself on 'vnhappy' (the lack of italics – in the institutional absence of inverted commas – does not help).

A question that is rarely posed by editors regards the punctuating of discourse markers, namely non–referential idiomatic expressions that indicate the speaker's attitude, adding colour to his or her speech (see p. 79; and Blake, *Grammar*, 290). These markers include single words such as 'why' ('Why so I do, the Noblest that I haue': TLN 23, 1.1.17) or 'fie' ('Fie, that you'l say so': 142, 1.3.23), but also longer idiomatic phrases like 'I warrant' ('I warrant thou art a merry fellow': 1238, 3.1.25), 'by my troth' ('By my troth I would not undertake her': 175, 1.3.56) or 'by this hand' ('By this hand they are scoundrels':

150, 1.3.32). Since such expressions are semantically empty, the question arises how they should be punctuated; in F they are frequently unaccompanied by punctuation marks, whereas in modern editions they are almost invariably separated from what precedes or follows by commas, which often lend them excessive weight, inviting the reader to take them literally. Sir Andrew's 'By my troth I would not undertake her' is not a solemn pledge of loyalty or truthfulness, as a comma after 'troth' might suggest, but a mere idiomatic expansion of 'I would not undertake her'. In this edition discourse markers are not usually set apart by commas, but are signalled in the commentary notes. The question of the choice of punctuation, which might appear the most dryly philological of issues, underlines the fact that every aspect of the editor's task has to do with interpretation.

APPENDIX 2

CASTING

Twelfth Night could be played – so David Bradley estimates – by fourteen actors on the Elizabethan stage (Bradley, 52). (T.J. King's hypothesis of eighteen is probably excessive, partly because it includes walk-on parts (King, 204–5).) Bradley's total is two less than the average number of sixteen required by plays performed between 1580 and 1642 (Bradley, 47). Of the eighteen speaking parts in the play, four minor roles could have been doubled without undue difficulty. The main keys to doubling are the long and crowded scenes 3.4 and 5.1, in which most of the characters are present onstage (eleven and twelve respectively). In 3.4 three minor parts, the servant and the first and second officers, appear for the first and only time; in 5.1 another minor figure, the priest, otherwise present in 4.3 alone, speaks his only lines. Such roles were almost certainly doubled. Two of the likeliest candidates for the doubling are the actors playing Valentine and the captain, missing in both the long scenes: the captain could have doubled, for example, as the servant, while the priest and one officer might have been played by Valentine, and the other officer by his fellow courtier Curio, who is likewise absent from 3.4.

Other combinations are possible. The captain, who appears only in 1.2, might have been played by the actor representing either Fabian – unemployed for the first nine scenes – or Antonio. The Antonio–captain doubling, although potentially confusing, makes some dramatic sense, since it underlines the parallel between the twins and their helpers (Viola–captain/Sebastian–Antonio), and it is a solution adopted in some modern productions (for example, by Branagh in 1987). Alternatively, the actor playing Fabian could have doubled as Valentine. And so on. Whichever combination is adopted, however, the overall number of speaking players remains fourteen.

The following table illustrates the distribution of parts in the play's eighteen scenes, indicating possible doubling solutions. The table also illustrates *Twelfth Night*'s somewhat asymmetrical scene and line economy, whereby some of the characters present in the greatest number of scenes are not those who speak the most or who are generally considered to be the most 'important' roles. It might come as a surprise to find Sir Toby at the head of the list with his presence in nine scenes, although his pre-eminence is confirmed by his 333 lines, compared to the 284 of Viola, who appears in seven scenes. In other cases, the number of scenes in which a character appears does not correspond to speaking time or centrality to the action. For example, Sir Andrew, also present in seven scenes, speaks only 152 lines, whereas Olivia, present in six, has 257. The low number of appearances (four scenes) by Orsino, the comedy's supposed romantic hero, is counterbalanced by his prolixity, which produces 219 lines. Malvolio, who appears in seven scenes, confirms his historically well-founded candidacy as protagonist with a total of seven scenes and 257 lines, six fewer than another central role, Feste, who has 263 lines distributed over the same number of scenes (the totals refer to the number of speaking lines, not including stage directions, etc.).

Roles and scenes	Total	1.1	1.2	1.3	1.4	1.5	2.1	2.2	2.3	2.4	2.5	3.1	3.2	3.3	3.4	4.1	4.2	4.3	5.1	Players	Line nos.
Sir Toby	9			x		x			x		x	x	x		x	x			x	1	333
Viola	8		x		x	x		x		x		x			x				x	2	284
Feste	7					x			x	x		x				x	x		x	3	263
Malvolio	7					x		x	x		x				x		x		x	4	257
Sir Andrew	7			x					x		x	x	x		x				x	5	152
Maria	7			x		x			x		x		x		x		x			6	147
Olivia	6					x						x			x	x		x	x	7	257
Sebastian	5						x							x		x		x	x	8	123
Orsino	4	x			x					x									x	9	219
Fabian	4										x		x		x				x	10	113
Antonio	4						x							x	x				x	11	106
Curio	4	x			x					x									x	12	7
1 Officer	1														x					12	18
Valentine	2	x			x															13	13
2 Officer	1														x					13	3
Priest	2																	x	x	14	8
Captain	1		x																	14	32
Servant	1														x					14	3
Lords, attendants																				misc.	
Sailors																				misc.	
Total		1.1	1.2	1.3	1.4	1.5	2.1	2.2	2.3	2.4	2.5	3.1	3.2	3.3	3.4	4.1	4.2	4.3	5.1		2,286

APPENDIX 3

MUSIC

Many sorts of music

Music is not a decorative addition to *Twelfth Night* but an essential part of the play's dramatic economy. *Twelfth Night* is the only Shakespeare play to begin and end with music. It is also the only play whose opening noun is, precisely, 'music', suggesting immediately the thematic as well as theatrical importance of the topic. This importance is confirmed by the play's later metaphorical or emblematic allusions to music and musicians: for example, the captain's comparison of the shipwrecked Sebastian to the legendary musician Arion, Orpheus-like tamer of animals and nature (1.2.14), introduces music as a magical and benevolent – indeed, literally life-saving – force in the comedy. In the same scene Viola entrusts her own fortunes, if not her life, to her boasted musical skills: 'I can sing / And speak . . . in many sorts of music' (1.2.54–5).

Viola's claim to musical prowess sets up a dialogue or dialectic between music and language ('sing / And speak'): she may intend literally to sing for her supper, or alternatively to achieve Arion-like magical effects through her music-like speech. That she succeeds only too well in this verbal–musical mission is amply confirmed by her unwitting conquest of Olivia, who exclaims hyperbolically: 'But would you undertake another suit, / I had rather hear you to solicit that / Than music from the spheres' (3.1.106–8). The comedy's principal artistic paradigm – perhaps influenced by the presence of the highly musical clown Robert Armin – thus becomes the interaction or co-operation between words and music, best exemplified in the song or ballad.

Part I.　　　　　*The Division-Viol.*　　　　3

Extento sidenter brachio, Fides haud procul à ponticulo sigillatim liquidéque vibrentur, genibus ne forté offendiculo sint, cauté reducis.

Holding the Bow in this posture, stretch out your arm, and draw it first over one String and then another ; crossing them in right angle, at the distance of two or three Inches from the Bridge. Make each several String yeild a full and clear sound ; and order your knees so, that they be no impediment to the motion of your Bow.

31 'Viol-de-gamboys' (1.3.23–4), from Christopher Simpson, *The Division-Viol,
or The Art of Playing Extempore upon a Ground* (1667)

Seven songs are sung in *Twelfth Night*, more than in any other Shakespeare play. Other ballads are begun and then dropped ('O'the twelfth day of December', 2.3.83) or quoted in passing ('Peg-o'-Ramsey', 2.3.75). Singing, moreover, contributes directly to the dramatic action, as in Malvolio's outrage at the revellers' noisy catches in 2.3, which sets off their revenge plot. The play also offers a veritable typology of songs and their singers: weavers' psalms (2.3.58), coziers' catches (2.3.88), the 'old and antic song' sung by Feste (2.4.3) as opposed to modern 'light airs' (2.4.5), which presumably he does not sing, Orsino's imaginary 'lullaby' (5.1.41), and so on.

Twelfth Night is also uniquely preoccupied with another aspect of music, namely tempo, and especially what Feste calls the 'tripping measure' or dance rhythm (5.1.35). The clown himself favours a rapid 'triplex' or triple time (5.1.34), as does Sir Toby, who praises such lively triple-time dances as the galliard (1.3.115), the jig (1.3.124) and the 'sink-apace' (cinquepace, 1.3.125), while scorning statelier rhythms like the 'passy-measures pavan' (5.1.196–7). The play's discourse of music and dance thus sets up an explicit opposition between slow time and fast time. Sir Toby's predilection for rapid rhythms is part of his campaign in favour of the good life, and against the encroachment of death. More in general, the question of musical tempo is closely related to the play's concerns with the passage of time, and the fast–slow opposition reflects the comedy's own double time scheme (see p. 77–8).

Sing both high and low: the songs

1 'O mistress mine' (2.3.38–51)

There is no surviving Elizabethan setting to this song, but two instrumental pieces exist with this title, both based on the same melody, respectively by Thomas Morley (in *The First Book of Consort Lessons*, 1599) and by William Byrd (in the Fitzwilliam Virginal Book, *c.* 1619). (Transcriptions of Morley's setting and of melodies for the other six songs in the play, taken from Ard², appear on pp. 339–44.) The tune probably existed prior to Morley's setting, and it is not certain that the words were actually sung to it, although they can be made to fit it. It is likewise unknown whether they are Shakespeare's or are traditional. Opting for Shakespeare, W.H. Auden observes: 'Taken seriously, these lines are the voice of elderly lust, afraid of its own death. Shakespeare forces this awareness on our consciousness by making the audience to the song a couple of seedy old drunks' (Auden, 521–2). The line 'That can sing both high and low', boasting of the lover's musical prowess, recalls Viola's claim to be able to 'sing . . . many sorts of music' at 1.2.54–5.

2 'Hold thy peace' (2.3.70 SD)

The catch 'Hold thy peace', referred to in the SD, was printed in Thomas Ravenscroft's *Deuteromelia* (1609). Another version appeared in a manuscript collection of Elizabethan rounds gathered by Thomas Lant (1580). Ravenscroft's version has been preferred on account of its livelier rhythm. The entire song is a joke where each singer in turn invites the others to keep quiet: a paradox underlined by Feste at 2.3.69.

3 'Three merry men be we' (2.3.75–6)

This is William Lawes's version of the catch, printed in John Hilton's *Catch that Catch Can* (1652). It is given here in the transcription edited by T.W. Craik (Ard²) in 3/4 (6/8) tempo (see p. 341). Another version appears in W. Chappell's *Popular Music of the Olden Time* (1855–9), where it is attributed to John Playford (1623–86). The song, a variation on the 'we three' theme, is appropriate to this scene, but it is not known whether the words are Shakespeare's.

4 'There dwelt a man in Babylon' (2.3.77–8)

The music for this song derives from the early sixteenth-century Mulliner Book, a manuscript collection of English keyboard music compiled by the organist Thomas Mulliner (BM MS Add. 30513). Claude M. Simpson claims that a number of ballads sharing the 'Lady, lady' refrain, including this one, were sung to it (Simpson, 410–12). The opening line of the ballad, popularly known as 'Constant Susan', is a biblical quotation: the story of Susanna in the Apocrypha begins, 'There dwelt a man in Babylon, called Joacim, that toke a wife whose name was Susanna, the daughter of Helcia, a very faire woman, and such one as feared God' (Apocrypha, 1–2).

5 'Farewell, dear heart' (2.3.100–10)

This is an adaptation of a song by Robert Jones, published in his *First Book of Songs and Airs* (1600), with the following words:

> Farewell dear love, since thou must needs be gone,
> Mine eyes do show my life is almost done.
> Nay, I will never die,
> So long as I can spy,
> There may be many mo
> Though that she do go.
> There be many mo, I fear not,
> Why then let her go, I care not.
>
> Farewell, farewell, since this I find is true,
> I will not spend more time in wooing you,
> But I will seek elsewhere,
> If I may find her there.
> Shall I bid her go?
> What and if I do?
> Shall I bid her go and spare not?
> Oh no, no, no, no, I dare not.

Shakespeare transforms the song into a comic duet between the two men: see commentary note.

6 'Hey Robin, jolly Robin' (4.2.71–8)

This song has been attributed to Sir Thomas Wyatt (BM MS Egerton 2711, fol. 37ᵛ), although it may rework a traditional lyric. The opening stanzas are: 'A Robin, / Joly Robin, / Tell me how thy leman doeth, / And thou shalt know of myn. / My lady is unkynd, perde! / Alack, whi is she so? / She loveth an othre better than me, / And yet she will say no' (for the third line, cf. Sir Andrew's 'thy leman' at 2.3.24). The music, by William Cornish, Wyatt's contemporary at the court of Henry VIII, was originally set as a round for three voices; Feste turns it into a one-man ventriloquist dialogue song.

7 'When that I was and a little tiny boy' (5.1.382–401)

The words of this song may be Shakespeare's or may be traditional – perhaps adapted by Shakespeare, with the addition of the final stanza – or, alternatively, the work of another author, such as Robert Armin. Lines adapted from this song are sung by the Fool in *King Lear*, also played by Armin: 'He that has and a little tiny wit, / With heigh-ho, the wind and the rain, / Must make content with his fortunes fit, / Though the rain it raineth every day' (*KL* 3.2.73–7).

The earliest known setting is Joseph Vernon's, published in *The New Songs in the Pantomime of the Witch . . . composed by J. Vernon* (1772); this is probably an arrangement of a traditional tune, however, that may go back to the Elizabethan era. The version of Vernon's setting given here in E minor (see p.344) first appeared in F.W. Sternfeld's *Music in Shakespearean Tragedy* (1963).

Interpretations of the song and of its relationship to the rest of the play have ranged from its dismissal by early editors as completely irrelevant to the comedy ('to the play it has no relation', Capell), to Knight's defence of it as an appropriate and philosophical reflection on 'the history of a life', to Hotson's reading of it as a bawdy warning against adopting Twelfth Night saturnalia 'as a way of life' (Hotson, 167–72).

Music transcriptions

These transcriptions are taken from Ard[2].

1 'O mistress mine' (2.3.38—51)

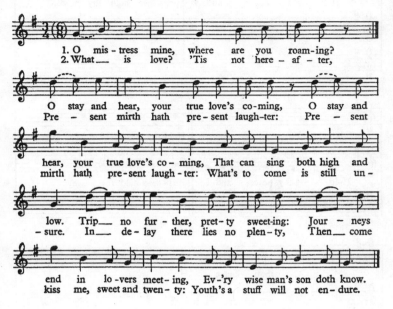

1. O mis - tress mine, where are you roam-ing?
2. What is love? 'Tis not here - af - ter,

O stay and hear, your true love's co-ming, O stay and
Pre - sent mirth hath pre - sent laugh-ter: Pre - sent

hear, your true love's co-ming, That can sing both high and
mirth hath pre - sent laugh - ter: What's to come is still un-

low. Trip no fur - ther, pret-ty sweet-ing: Jour - neys
- sure. In de - lay there lies no plen-ty, Then come

end in lo-vers meet-ing, Ev-'ry wise man's son doth know.
kiss me, sweet and twen-ty: Youth's a stuff will not en-dure.

2 'Hold thy peace' (2.3.70 SD)

3 'Three merry men be we' (2.3.75—6)

4 'There dwelt a man in Babylon' (2.3.77—8)

(Solomon) Was not good King So — lo — mon___
(Babylon) There dwelt a man in Ba — by — lon Of

Ra — vi–shed in___ sun – dry wise, With ev – ery live – ly
re — pu–ta — tion___ great by fame; He took to wife a

pa — ra–gon, That glis – ter–ed be — fore his eyes? If
(Twelfth Night) There
fair wo–man, Su — san – na she was___ call'd by name: A

this be true, as true it was, La — dy, La–dy, Why
dwelt a man in Ba· — by – lon, La — dy, La–dy.
wo — man fair and vir — tu — ous, La — dy, La–dy: Why

should not I serve you, a — las, My dear la — dy?
should we not of her learn thus To live god – ly?

5 'Farewell, dear heart' (2.3.100—10)

6 'Hey Robin, jolly Robin' (4.2.71—8)

Hey, Ro - bin, jol - ly Ro - bin, Tell me how thy

la - dy does... My la - dy is un - kind, per-die. A -

- las, why is she so? She loves a - no - ther...

7 'When that I was and a little tiny boy' (5.1.382—401)

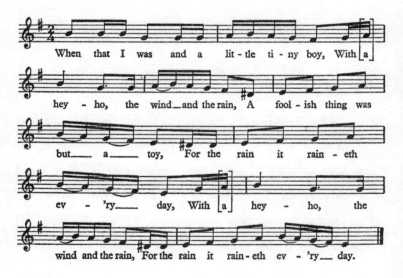

When that I was and a lit - tle ti - ny boy, With a

hey - ho, the wind and the rain, A fool - ish thing was

but a toy, For the rain it rain - eth

ev - 'ry day, With a hey - ho, the

wind and the rain, For the rain it rain - eth ev - 'ry day.

ABBREVIATIONS AND REFERENCES

Place of publication in references is London unless otherwise stated. Quotations and references to Shakespeare plays other than *Twelfth Night* are from *The Arden Shakespeare Complete Works*, ed. Richard Proudfoot, Ann Thompson and David Scott Kastan, rev. edn (2001). Biblical quotations are from the Geneva Bible unless otherwise indicated.

ABBREVIATIONS

ABBREVIATIONS USED IN NOTES

ed.	edited, editor
edn	edition
fol., fols	folio, folios
n.	(in cross-references) commentary note
n.d.	no date
om.	omitted in
Q	Quarto
RSC	Royal Shakespeare Company
sig., sigs	signature, signatures
SD	stage direction
SP	speech prefix
subst.	substantially
this edn	a reading adopted for the first time in this edition
TLN	through line numbering in *The Norton Facsimile: The First Folio of Shakespeare*, prepared by Charlton Hinman (New York, 1968)
t.n.	textual note
*	precedes commentary notes involving readings altered from the Folio edition on which this edition is based
( )	enclosing a reading in the textual notes, indicates original spelling; enclosing an editor's or scholar's name, indicates a conjectural reading

WORKS BY AND PARTLY BY SHAKESPEARE

AC	*Antony and Cleopatra*
AW	*All's Well That Ends Well*
AYL	*As You Like It*
CE	*Comedy of Errors*
Car	*The History of Cardenio*
Cor	*Coriolanus*
Cym	*Cymbeline*
DF	*Double Falsehood*
E3	*King Edward III*
Ham	*Hamlet*
1H4	*King Henry IV, Part 1*
2H4	*King Henry IV, Part 2*
H5	*King Henry V*
1H6	*King Henry VI, Part 1*
2H6	*King Henry VI, Part 2*
3H6	*King Henry VI, Part 3*
H8	*King Henry VIII*
JC	*Julius Caesar*
KJ	*King John*
KL	*King Lear*
LC	*A Lover's Complaint*
LLL	*Love's Labour's Lost*
Luc	*The Rape of Lucrece*
MA	*Much Ado about Nothing*
Mac	*Macbeth*
MM	*Measure for Measure*
MND	*A Midsummer Night's Dream*
MV	*The Merchant of Venice*
MW	*The Merry Wives of Windsor*
Oth	*Othello*
Per	*Pericles*
PP	*The Passionate Pilgrim*
PT	*The Phoenix and the Turtle*
R2	*King Richard II*
R3	*King Richard III*
RJ	*Romeo and Juliet*
Son	*Sonnets*
STM	*The Book of Sir Thomas More*
TC	*Troilus and Cressida*

Tem	*The Tempest*
TGV	*The Two Gentlemen of Verona*
Tim	*Timon of Athens*
Tit	*Titus Andronicus*
TN	*Twelfth Night*
TNK	*The Two Noble Kinsmen*
TS	*The Taming of the Shrew*
VA	*Venus and Adonis*
WT	*The Winter's Tale*

REFERENCES

EDITIONS OF SHAKESPEARE COLLATED

Alexander	*William Shakespeare: The Complete Works*, ed. Peter Alexander (1951)
Ard[1]	*Twelfth Night: or, What You Will*, ed. Morton Luce, Arden Shakespeare (1906)
Ard[2]	*Twelfth Night: or, What You Will*, ed. J.M. Lothian and T.W. Craik, Arden Shakespeare (1975)
Bantam	*Twelfth Night: or, What You Will*, ed. David Scott Kastan, Robert K. Turner, Jr, and David Bevington, Bantam Shakespeare (New York, 1988)
Barker	*Shakespeare's Comedy of Twelfth Night: An Acting Edition, with a Producer's Preface by Granville-Barker* (1912)
Bell	*Bell's Edition of Shakespeare's Plays, as they are performed at the Theatres Royal*, 9 vols, vol. 5 (1774)
Boswell–Malone	*Plays and Poems*, ed. James Boswell, 21 vols (1821)
Cam	*Works*, ed. W.G. Clark and W.A. Wright, 9 vols (Cambridge, 1863)
Cam[1]	*Twelfth Night or What You Will*, ed. Arthur Quiller-Couch and John Dover Wilson (Cambridge, 1930)
Cam[2]	*Twelfth Night or What You Will*, ed. Elizabeth Story Donno (Cambridge, 1985)
Capell	*Comedies, Histories, and Tragedies*, ed. Edward Capell, 10 vols (1767–8)
Collier	*Works*, ed. John Payne Collier, 8 vols (1842)
Collier[2]	*Plays*, ed. John Payne Collier (1853)
Collier[3]	*Comedies, Histories, Tragedies, and Poems*, ed. John Payne Collier, 6 vols (1858)
Collier[4]	*Plays and Poems*, ed. John Payne Collier, 8 vols (1878)
Craig	*Complete Works*, ed. William James Craig (Oxford, 1892)

Cumberland   *Twelfth Night; or, What You Will . . . as now performed at the Theatres Royal, etc.*, Cumberland's British Theatre, vol. 11 (1830)

Deighton   *Twelfth Night; or, What You will*, ed. K. Deighton (1890)

Douai MS   MS 7.87 in the Douai Public Library (seventeenth-century transcript of *Twelfth Night* and of five other plays by Shakespeare: see G.B. Evans)

Dyce   *Works*, ed. Alexander Dyce, 9 vols (1857)

Dyce[2]   *Works*, ed. Alexander Dyce, 8 vols (1864)

Everyman   *Twelfth Night*, ed. John F. Andrews, Everyman Shakespeare (1994)

F   *Comedies, Histories, and Tragedies*, The First Folio (1623)

F2   *Comedies, Histories, and Tragedies*, The Second Folio (1632)

F3   *Comedies, Histories, and Tragedies*, The Third Folio (1663)

F4   *Comedies, Histories, and Tragedies*, The Fourth Folio (1685)

Folg   *Twelfth Night, or What You Will*, ed. Barbara A. Mowat and Paul Werstine (New York, 1991)

Furness   *Twelfth Night, or What You Will*, ed. Horace Howard Furness (Philadelphia, 1901)

Halliwell   *Works*, ed. James O. Halliwell, 16 vols, vol. 7 (1856)

Hanmer   *Works*, ed. Thomas Hanmer, 6 vols (Hanmer, 1743– 4)

Harrison   *Twelfth Night; or What You Will. A Comedy. As it is Acted in the Theatres-Royal in Drury-Lane and Covent-Garden.* Printed for J. Harrison (1779)

Hudson   *Complete Works*, ed. Henry N. Hudson, 20 vols (Boston, Mass., 1881)

Inchbald   *Twelfth Night, or, What you will . . . as performed at the Theatres Royal . . . with remarks by Mrs Inchbald (1808)*

Johnson   *Plays*, ed. Samuel Johnson, 8 vols (1765)

Keightley   *Plays*, ed. Thomas Keightley, 6 vols (1864)

Kemble   *Twelfth night; or, What you will. A comedy. Revised by J. P. Kemble* (1810)

Kittredge   *Twelfth Night, or What You Will*, ed. George Lyman Kittredge (Boston, Mass., 1941)

Knight   *The Pictorial Edition of the Works of Shakespere*, ed. Charles Knight, 8 vols (1839–42)

Lacy   *Twelfth Night, or What You Will*, Lacy's Acting Edition (1858)

Mahood	*Twelfth Night, or What You Will*, ed. M.M. Mahood, New Penguin Shakespeare (Harmondsworth, England, 1968)
Malone	*Plays and Poems*, ed. Edmond Malone, 10 vols (1790)
Mercury	*The Mercury Shakespeare. Edited for Reading and Arranged for staging by Orson Welles and Roger Hill*, 3 vols (New York, 1939)
Munro	*The London Shakespeare*, ed. John Munro, 2 vols (1958)
Norton	*The Norton Shakespeare: Based on the Oxford Edition*, ed. Stephen Greenblatt, Jean E. Howard and Katharine Eisaman Maus (New York, 1997)
Nunn	Trevor Nunn, *Twelfth Night: A Screenplay* (1996)
Oxberry	*Twelfth Night, or What You Will, . . . Marked with the stage business, and stage directions, as it is performed at the Theatres Royal, by W*[*illiam Henry*] *Oxberry* (1821)
Oxf	*Complete Works*, ed. Stanley Wells and Gary Taylor (Oxford, 1986)
Oxf[1]	*Twelfth Night, or What You Will*, ed. Roger Warren and Stanley Wells (Oxford, 1994)
Pope	*Works*, ed. Alexander Pope, 6 vols (1723–5)
Powell MS	Manuscript notes by William Powell added in 1798 to the British Library copy (shelf mark C.136.bb.10) of *Twelfth Night, or What You Will . . . printed conformable to the representation at the Theatre Royal, Drury Lane under the inspection of James Wrighten, prompter* (1792); the MS hand is represented in the textual notes in italic to differentiate it from the printed text, represented in roman, where appropriate
Quiller-Couch	See Cam[1]
Rann	*The Dramatic Works of Shakespeare*, ed. Joseph Rann, 6 vols (Oxford, 1786–94)
Riv	*The Riverside Shakespeare*, ed. G. Blakemore Evans and Harry Levin (Boston, Mass., 1974; rev. edn 1997)
Rowe	*Works*, ed. Nicholas Rowe, 6 vols (1709)
Rowe[3]	*Works*, ed. Nicholas Rowe, 8 vols (1714)
Sisson	*Complete Works*, ed. C.J. Sisson (1954)
Smith	*Twelfth Night or What You Will: Texts and Contexts*, ed. Bruce R. Smith (Boston, Mass., 2001)
Smock Alley	*Twelfth Night, or What You Will*, Smock Alley prompt-book (*c.* 1685), in *Shakespearean Prompt-books of the Seventeenth Century*, 8 vols, ed. G. Blakemore Evans, vol. 8 (Charlottesville, Va., 1996)

Staunton	*Plays*, ed. Howard Staunton, 3 vols (1858–60)
Steevens	*Plays*, ed. Samuel Johnson and George Steevens, 10 vols (1773)
Steevens[2]	*Plays*, ed. Samuel Johnson and George Steevens, 10 vols, 2nd edn (1778)
Theobald	*Works*, ed. Lewis Theobald, 7 vols (1733)
Theobald[2]	*Works*, ed. Lewis Theobald, 7 vols (Dublin, 1740)
Tree	Herbert Beerbohm Tree, promptbook of *Twelfth Night, or What You Will*, Her Majesty's Theatre, 1901, Enthoven Collection, Theatre Museum, London
Warburton	*Works*, ed. William Warburton, 8 vols (1747)
White	*Works*, ed. Richard Grant White, 12 vols (Boston, Mass., 1857)
Wilson	See Cam[1]

OTHER WORKS CITED

Adams	Barry B. Adams, 'Orsino and the spirit of love', *SQ*, 29 (1978), 52–9
Ariosto	Ludovico Ariosto, *Orlando furioso*, trans. John Harington (1591)
Archer	William Archer, '"Twelfth Night" at the Lyceum', *Macmillan's Magazine*, 50 (1884), 271–9
Arlidge	Anthony Arlidge, *Shakespeare and the Prince of Love: The Feast of Misrule in the Middle Temple* (2000)
Armin, *Fool*	Robert Armin, *Fool upon Fool or, Six Sorts of Sots* (1600)
Armin, *Quips*	Robert Armin, *Quips upon Questions, or, A Clown's Conceit on Occasion Offered* (1600)
Astington	John Astington, 'Malvolio and the eunuchs: texts and revels in *Twelfth Night*', *SS 46* (1993), 23–34
AT	Ann Thompson, private communication
Auden	W.H. Auden, 'Music in Shakespeare', in *The Dyer's Hand and Other Essays* (1963), 500–27
Aveling	Edward Aveling, '"Twelfth Night" at the Lyceum', *Our Corner*, 4 (1884), 115–18
Barber	C.L. Barber, *Shakespeare's Festive Comedy* (Princeton, 1959)
Barker, *Observer*	Harley Granville-Barker, *Observer* review of *Twelfth Night* directed by Jacques Copeau at the Vieux-Colombier, Paris, in Wells, 187–94
Barker, 'Preface'	Harley Granville-Barker, '*Twelfth Night*', *Prefaces to Shakespeare* (1993)

Barton	Anne Barton, '*As You Like It* and *Twelfth Night*: Shakespeare's sense of an ending', in Malcolm Bradbury and David Palmer (eds), *Shakespearian Comedy*, Stratford-upon-Avon Studies 14 (1972), 160–80
Bate	Jonathan Bate, *Shakespeare and Ovid* (Oxford, 1993)
Beckerman	Bernard Beckerman, *Shakespeare at the Globe, 1599–1609* (New York, 1962)
Belleforest	François de Belleforest, *Le Quatrième Tome des histoires tragiques* (1571)
Belsey	Catherine Belsey, 'Disrupting sexual difference: meaning and gender in the comedies', in John Drakakis (ed.), *Alternative Shakespeares* (1985), 166–90
Berg & Erskine	Chuck Berg and Tom Erskine (eds), *The Encyclopedia of Orson Welles* (New York, 2003)
Berry	Ralph Berry, '*Twelfth Night*: the experience of the audience', *SS 34* (1981), 111–19
Billings	Timothy Billings, 'Caterwauling Cataians: the genealogy of a gloss', *SQ*, 54 (2003), 1–28
Billington, M.	Michael Billington (ed.), *Approaches to Twelfth Night* (1990)
Billington, S.	Sandra Billington, *Mock Kings in Medieval Society and Renaissance Drama* (Oxford, 1991)
Biographical Dictionary	*A Biographical Dictionary of Actors, Actresses . . . 1660–1800*, ed. Philip H. Highfill, Jr, Kalman A. Burnim and Edward A. Longhans (Carbondale and Edwardsville, Ill., 1973–91)
Bishops' Bible	*The Holie Bible Conteynyng the Olde Testament and the Newe* (1568)
Blake, 'Editing'	Norman Blake, 'Editing Shakespeare: the role of language studies', *European Journal of English Studies*, 1 (1999), 329–53
Blake, *Grammar*	Norman Blake, *A Grammar of Shakespeare's Language* (Houndmills, England, 2002)
Blake, *Language*	Norman Blake, *Shakespeare's Language: An Introduction* (Basingstoke, 1983)
Blayney, *Folio*	Peter W.M. Blayney, *The First Folio of Shakespeare* (Washington, DC, 1991)
Blayney, 'Publication'	Peter W.M. Blayney, 'The publication of playbooks', in Cox & Kastan, 383–422
Boaden	James Boaden, *Life of Mrs Jordan* (1831)
Boiardo	Matteo Maria Boiardo, *Orlando innamorato*, trans. Robert Tofte (1598)
Boorde, *Dietary*	Andrew Boorde, *Regiment or Dietary of Health* (1542)

Booth, *Nonsense*   Stephen Booth, *Precious Nonsense: The Gettysburg Address, Ben Jonson's Epitaphs on his Children, and 'Twelfth Night'* (Berkeley, Calif., 1998)

Booth, *'Twelfth'*   Stephen Booth, *'Twelfth Night*: 1.1.: The audience as Malvolio', in Peter Erickson and Coppélia Kahn (eds), *Shakespeare's 'Rough Magic'* (Newark, Del., 1985), 149–67

Boswell   John Boswell, *Same-Sex Unions in Premodern Europe* (New York, 1994)

Bradley   David Bradley, *From Text to Performance in the Elizabethan Theatre: Preparing the Play for the Stage* (Cambridge, 1991)

Brewer   Thomas Brewer, *The Life and Death of the Merry Devil of Edmonton* (*c.* 1608; 1631)

Britannica   *Encyclopaedia Britannica*, 15th edn (1998)

Brome   Richard Brome, *The English Moor* (1658)

Brown   John Russell Brown (ed.), *Shakespeare in Performance: An Introduction through Six Major Plays* (New York, 1976)

Brown & Gilman   Roger Brown and Albert Gilman, 'Politeness theory and Shakespeare's four major tragedies,' *Language in Society*, 18 (1989), 159–212

Browner   Jessica A. Browner, 'Wrong side of the river: London's disreputable south bank in the sixteenth and seventeenth century', *Essays in History*, 36 (1994), 35–72

Bullough   Geoffrey Bullough (ed.), *Narrative and Dramatic Sources of Shakespeare*, 8 vols (1957–75)

Burns   Elizabeth Burns, *Theatricality: A Study of Convention in the Theatre and in Social Life* (1972)

Burton   Robert Burton, *The Anatomy of Melancholy* (1652)

Burwick   Frederick Burwick, *Illusion and the Drama: Critical Theory of the Enlightenment and Romantic Era* (University Park, Pa., 1991)

Callaghan, *'All'*   Dympna Callaghan, '"And all is semblative a woman's part": body politics and *Twelfth Night*', *Textual Practice*, 7 (1993), 428–52

Callaghan, 'Castrator's'   Dympna Callaghan, 'The castrator's song: female impersonation on the early modern stage', *Journal of Medieval and Renaissance Studies*, 26 (1996), 32–53

Cambises   Thomas Preston, *The Life of Cambises King of Persia* (*c.* 1570)

Carr   Virginia M. Carr, 'The Shakespeare plays on TV: Season One', *Shakespeare on Film Newsletter*, 4.1 (1979), 4–5

Carroll, *Met.*	William C. Carroll, *The Metamorphoses of Shakespearean Comedy* (Princeton, 1985)
Carroll, 'Virgin'	William C. Carroll, 'The virgin not: language and sexuality in Shakespeare', *SS 46* (1994), 107–19
Castiglione	Baldassare Castiglione, *The Courtier*, trans. Thomas Hoby (1561)
Chaucer, *Works*	*The Works of Geoffrey Chaucer*, ed. F.N. Robinson, 2nd edn (Oxford, 1974)
Child	Francis J. Child, *The English and Scottish Popular Ballads*, 3 vols (New York, 1965)
Chillington Rutter	Carol Chillington Rutter, 'Looking at Shakespeare's women on film', in Jackson, 241–60
Cicero, *De officiis*	*Marcus Tullius Cicero's Three Books of Duties to Marcus his Son, (De officiis)*, trans. Nicolas Grimald (1558)
Coleridge	Samuel Taylor Coleridge, *Shakespearean Criticism*, ed. T.M. Raysor, 2nd edn, 2 vols (1960)
Common Prayer	*The Book of Common Prayer* (1559)
Copley	Anthony Copley, *A Fig for Fortune* (1596)
Cornwallis	William Cornwallis, *Essays* (1601)
Coote	C.H. Coote, *On Shakspere's New Map in 'Twelfth Night'* (1878)
Cotgrave	Randle Cotgrave, *A Dictionary of the French and English Tongues* (1611)
Cox	L.S. Cox, 'The riddle in *Twelfth Night*', *SQ*, 13 (1962), 360
Cox & Kastan	John D. Cox and David Scott Kastan (eds), *New History of Early English Drama* (New York, 1997)
D'Amico	Jack D'Amico, 'The treatment of space in Italian and English Renaissance theater: the example of *Gl'Ingannati* and *Twelfth Night*', *Comparative Drama* 23 (1989), 265–83
Daniel	P.A. Daniel, *Notes and Conjectural Emendations of Certain Doubtful Passages in Shakespeare's Plays* (1870)
Darrell	John Darrell, *A True Narration of the Strange and Grievous Vexation by the Devil, of Seven Persons in Lancashire* (1600)
Davis & Frankforter	J. Madison Davis and A. Daniel Frankforter (eds), *The Shakespeare Name and Place Dictionary* (1995)
Dekker, *Blurt*	Thomas Dekker, *Blurt, Master Constable* (1602)
Dekker, *Satiromastix*	Thomas Dekker, *Satiromastix* (1601)
Dent	R.W. Dent, *Shakespeare's Proverbial Language: An Index* (Berkeley, Calif., 1981)

Dodd	William Dodd, '"So full of shapes is fancy": gender and point of view in *Twelfth Night*', in Robert Clark and Piero Boitani (eds), *English Studies in Transition* (1993), 147–66
DNB	*Dictionary of National Biography* (Oxford, 1997)
Dowland	John Dowland, *The First Book of Songs or Airs* (1597)
Downes	John Downes, *Roscius Anglicanus* (1708)
Draper	John Draper, *The Twelfth Night of Shakespeare's Audience* (Stanford, Calif., 1950)
Drummond	*Ben Jonson's Conversations with William Drummond of Hawthornden*, ed. R.F. Patterson (1923)
Duncan-Jones	Katherine Duncan-Jones, *Ungentle Shakespeare: Scenes from His Life* (2001)
Eggert	Katherine Eggert, 'Sure can sing and dance: minstrelsy, the star system, and the post-coloniality of Kenneth Branagh's *Love's Labour's Lost* and Trevor Nunn's *Twelfth Night*', in Richard Burt and Lynda E. Boose (eds), *Shakespeare, the Movie II: Popularizing the Plays on Film, TV, Video and DVD* (2003), 72–88
Elam, 'Fertile'	Keir Elam, 'The fertile eunuch: *Twelfth Night*, early modern intercourse, and the fruits of castration', *SQ*, 47 (1996), 1–36
Elam, *Shakespeare's*	Keir Elam, *Shakespeare's Universe of Discourse: Language-Games in the Comedies* (Cambridge, 1984)
ELH	*English Literary History*
ELN	*English Language Notes*
Elze	Karl Elze, *Essays on Shakespeare* (1874)
Erasmus, *Paraphrase*	Desiderius Erasmus, *The First Tome or Volume of the Paraphrase of Erasmus upon the New Testament*, trans. Nicholas Udall, Thomas Caius and Mary Tudor (1548)
Erasmus, *Proverbs*	Desiderius Erasmus, *Proverbs or Adages*, trans. Richard Taverner (1539)
Evans, B.	Bertrand Evans, *Shakespeare's Comedies* (Oxford, 1960)
Evans, G.B.	G. Blakemore Evans, 'The Douai Manuscripts: six Shakespearean transcripts (1694–95)', *Philological Quarterly*, 41 (1962), 158–72
Everett	Barbara Everett, 'Or What You Will', *Essays in Criticism*, 35 (1985), 294–314
Farmer	Richard Farmer, contributions to Steevens
Faversham	Anon., *The Lamentable and True Tragedy of Master Arden of Faversham in Kent* (1599)
Fenner, *Arts*	Dudley Fenner, *The Arts of Logic and Rhetoric* (1584)
Fenner, *Song*	Dudley Fenner, *The Song of Songs* (Middleburgh, Netherlands, 1587)

Fletcher	John Fletcher, *The Elder Brother: A Comedy* (*c.* 1625; publ. 1637)
Florio, *World*	John Florio, *A World of Words, or Most Copious and Exact Dictionary in Italian and English* (1598)
Florio, *New World*	John Florio, *Queen Anna's New World of Words, or Dictionary of the Italian and English Tongues* (1611)
Florio, *Second Fruits*	John Florio, *Second Fruits* (1591)
Forde	Emanuel Forde, *Parismus, the Renowned Prince of Bohemia* (1598)
FQ	Edmund Spenser, *Fairie Queene*, 2nd edn (1611)
France	Richard France, *The Theatre of Orson Welles* (Lewisburg, Pa., 1977)
Freund	Elizabeth Freund, '*Twelfth Night* and the tyranny of interpretation', *ELH*, 53 (1986), 471–89
Frye	Northrop Frye, *A Natural Perspective: The Development of Shakespearean Comedy and Romance* (New York, 1965)
Garber	Marjorie Garber, *Vested Interests: Cross-dressing and Cultural Anxiety* (New York, 1992)
Gay	Penny Gay, *As She Likes It: Shakespeare's Unruly Women* (1994)
Genest	John Genest, *Some Account of the English Stage from the Restoration in 1660 to 1830*, 10 vols (Bath, 1832)
Gerard	John Gerard, *The Herbal or General History of Plants* (London, 1597)
Gibson	Marion Gibson, *Possession, Puritanism and Print: Darrell, Harsnett, Shakespeare and the Elizabethan Exorcism Controversy* (2006)
Gillies	John Gillies, *Shakespeare and the Geography of Difference* (Cambridge, 1994)
Gilman	Ernest B. Gilman, *The Curious Perspective: Literary and Pictorial Wit in the Seventeenth Century* (1978)
Girard	René Girard, '"Tis not so sweet now as it was before": Orsino and Olivia in *Twelfth Night*', *Stanford Literature Review*, 7 (1990), 123–32
Goar	Jacques Goar, *Euchologion* (Paris, 1647)
Goldberg	Jonathan Goldberg, 'Textual properties', *SQ*, 37 (1986), 213–17.
Golding	See Ovid, *Met.*
Gonzaga	Curzio Gonzaga, *Gli inganni* (Venice, 1592)
Goorney	Howard Goorney, *The Theatre Workshop Story* (1981)
Greene, *Friar*	Robert Greene, *The Honorable History of Friar Bacon and Friar Bungay* (1594)

Greene, *Mamillia*   Robert Greene, *Mamillia* (1583)

Greenblatt   Stephen Greenblatt, 'Fiction and friction', in *Shakespearean Negotiations: The Circulation of Social Energy in Renaissance England* (Oxford, 1988), 66–91

Greg, *Editorial*   W.W. Greg, *The Editorial Problem in Shakespeare* (Oxford, 1942)

Greg, *Folio*   W.W. Greg, *The Shakespeare First Folio: Its Bibliographical and Textual History* (Oxford, 1955)

Greif   Karen Greif, 'A star is born: Feste on the modern stage', *SQ*, 39 (1988), 61–78

Guazzo   Stefano Guazzo, *The Civil Conversation of M. Steeven Guazzo*, trans. George Pettie (1586)

Halstead   William P. Halstead, *Shakespeare as Spoken* (Ann Arbor, Mich., 1979)

Hamilton   Donna B. Hamilton, *Shakespeare and the Politics of Protestant England* (Lexington, Ky., 1992)

Harrison   William Harrison, *The Description of England*, in Holinshed, 1.131–250

Harsnett, *Discovery*   Samuel Harsnett, *Discovery of the Fraudulent Practices of John Darrel* (1599)

Harsnett, *Declaration*   Samuel Harsnett, *Declaration of Egregious Popish Impostures* (1603)

Hassel   R. Chris Hassel, Jr, *Faith and Folly in Shakespeare's Romantic Comedies* (Athens, Ga., 1980)

Hattaway   Michael Hattaway, 'The comedies on film', in Jackson, 85–98

Hazlitt   William Hazlitt, *Characters of Shakespear's Plays* (1817), in *The Selected Writings of William Hazlitt*, ed. Duncan Wu, 9 vols (1998), 1.83–270

Heliodorus   Heliodorus, *Ethiopica*; trans. *An Ethiopian History*, Thomas Underdown (1587)

Henryson   Robert Henryson, *Testament of Cresseid*, ed. Denton Fox (1968)

Henslowe   Philip Henslowe, *Henslowe's Diary*, ed. R.A. Foakes, 2nd edn (Cambridge, 2002)

Hilman & Mazzio   David Hilman and Carla Mazzio (eds), *The Body in Parts: Fantasies of Corporeality in Early Modern Europe* (1997)

Hinman   Charlton Hinman, *The Printing and Proof-Reading of the First Folio of Shakespeare*, 2 vols (Oxford, 1963)

Hodgdon   Barbara Hodgdon, 'Sexual disguise and the theatre of gender', in Leggatt, 179–97

Hogan   C.B. Hogan, *Shakespeare in the Theatre: A Record of Performances in 1701–1800* (Oxford, 1952)

Holinshed	Raphael Holinshed, *The First and Second Volumes of Chronicles* (1587)
Holland	Peter Holland, *English Shakespeares: Shakespeare on the English Stage in the 1990s* (Cambridge, 1997)
Hope	Jonathan Hope, *Shakespeare's Grammar* (2003)
Hopwood	C.H. Hopwood (ed.), *A Calendar of the Middle Temple Records*, 4 vols (1903)
Horace, *Odes*	*Horace, the Odes*, ed. J.D. McClatchy (Princeton, 2002)
Horner	Olga Horner, 'Christmas at the Inns of Court', in Meg Twycross (ed.), *Festive Drama* (Woodbridge, England, 1996), 41–53
Hotson	Leslie Hotson, *The First Night of Twelfth Night* (1954)
Howard	Jean Howard, 'Crossdressing, the theatre, and gender struggle in early modern England', *SQ*, 39 (1988), 418–40
Howard-Hill, 'Comedies'	T.H. Howard-Hill, 'The compositors of Shakespeare's Folio Comedies', *SB*, 26 (1973), 61–106
Howard-Hill, 'Compositors'	T.H. Howard-Hill, *Compositors B and E in the Shakespeare First Folio, and Some Recent Studies* (Columbia, SC, 1976)
Hunt, *Autobiography*	Leigh Hunt, *The Autobiography of Leigh Hunt: With Reminiscences of Friends and Contemporaries* (1850; repr. New York, 1965)
Hunt, *Criticism*	*Leigh Hunt's Dramatic Criticism, 1808–31*, ed. L.H. and C.W. Houtchens (New York, 1949)
Hunter	Joseph Hunter, *New Illustrations of the Life, Studies and Writings of Shakespeare* (1845)
Hutson	Lorna Hutson, 'On not being deceived: rhetoric and the body in *Twelfth Night*', *Texas Studies in Literature and Language*, 38 (1996), 140–74
Hutton, *Rise*	Ronald Hutton, *The Rise and Fall of Merry England: The Ritual Year, 1400–1700* (Oxford, 1994)
Hutton, *Stations*	Ronald Hutton, *The Stations of the Sun: A History of the Ritual Year in Britain* (Oxford, 1996)
Intronati	Accademia degli Intronati, *Gl'ingannati*, in Guido Davico Bonino (ed.), *Il teatro italiano, II: La commedia del Cinquecento* (Turin, 1977)
Jackson	Russell Jackson (ed.), *The Cambridge Companion to Shakespeare on Film* (Cambridge, 2000)
Jardine, *Daughters*	Lisa Jardine, *Still Harping on Daughters: Women and Drama in the Age of Shakespeare* (Brighton, 1983)
Jardine, 'Twins'	Lisa Jardine, 'Twins and travesties: gender, dependency, and sexual availability in *Twelfth Night*', in Susan Zimmerman (ed.), *Erotic Politics* (1992), 27–38

Johnson, *Dictionary*	Samuel Johnson, *A Dictionary of the English Language*, 2 vols (1755)
Jones	Robert Jones, *The First Book of Songs and Airs* (1600)
Jones & Stallybrass	Ann Rosalind Jones and Peter Stallybrass, *Renaissance Clothing and the Materials of Memory* (Cambridge, 2000)
Jonson, *Works*	Ben Jonson, *Works* (1616)
Junius	Adrianus Junius, *The Nomenclator*, trans. John Higgins (1585)
Kennedy	Dennis Kennedy, *Looking at Shakespeare: A Visual History of Twentieth-Century Performance*, 2nd edn (Cambridge, 2001)
Kerrigan	John Kerrigan, 'Secrecy and gossip in *Twelfth Night*', *SS 50* (1997), 65–80; repr. in John Kerrigan, *On Shakespeare and Early Modern Literature: Essays* (Oxford, 2001), 89–112
King, T.	T.J. King, *Casting Shakespeare's Plays* (Cambridge, 1992)
Kökeritz	Helge Kökeritz, *Shakespeare's Pronunciation* (New Haven, Conn., 1960)
Koller	A.M. Koller, *The Theater Duke: Georg II of Saxe-Meiningen and the German Stage* (Stanford, Calif., 1984)
Lamb, C.	Charles Lamb, 'On some of the old actors' (1822), in *Essays of Elia*, ed. N.L. Hallward and S.C. Hill (1959), 184–97
Lamb, M.	Mary Ellen Lamb, 'Tracing a heterosexual erotics of service in '*Twelfth Night* and the autobiographical writings of Thomas Hythorne and Anne Clifford', *Criticism*, 40 (1998), 1–25
Laneham	Robert Laneham, *A Letter* (1575)
Latham	Simon Latham, *Latham's Falconry* (1615)
Laqueur	Thomas Laqueur, *Making Sex: Body and Gender from the Greeks to Freud* (Cambridge Mass., 1990)
Leggatt	Alexander Leggatt (ed.), *The Cambridge Companion to Shakespearean Comedy* (Cambridge, 2002)
Lever & Fulwood	Ralph Lever and William Fulwood, *The Most Noble, Ancient and Learned Play, called The Philosophers' Game* (1563)
Levine	Laura Levine, *Men in Women's Clothes: Anti-Theatricality and Effeminization 1579–1652* (Cambridge, 1994)
Lewalski	Barbara Lewalski, 'Thematic patterns in *Twelfth Night*', *SSt*, 1 (1965), 168–81

Lewis   Cynthia Lewis, 'A fustian riddle? anagrammatic names in *Twelfth Night*', *ELN*, 22 (1985), 32–7

Lily   William Lily, *A Short Introduction of Grammar*, 2nd edn (1577)

Linthicum   Marie Channing Linthicum, *Costume in the Drama of Shakespeare and his Contemporaries* (Oxford, 1936)

Lloyd   W.W. Lloyd, *The Life of the Poet and Critical Essays on the Plays*, in Singer

Lodge   Thomas Lodge, *Treatise of the Plague* (1603)

London Stage   *The London Stage, 1660–1800* (Carbondale, Ill., 1960–8)

Long   John H. Long, *Shakespeare's Use Of Music: The Study of the Music and its Performance in the Original Production of Seven Comedies*, 3 vols (Gainesville, Fla., 1961–71)

Lusty Juventus   Robert Weaver, *An Interlude Called Lusty Juventus* (1550)

Lydgate   John Lydgate, *The Minor Poems*, ed. H.N. MacCracken (1911)

Lyly, *Endimion*   John Lyly, *Endimion* (1591)

Lyly, *England*   John Lyly, *Euphues and his England* (1580)

Lyly, *Euphues*   John Lyly, *Euphues: The Anatomy of Wit* (1578)

Lyly, *Gallathea*   John Lyly, *Gallathea* (1592)

Lyly, *Met.*   John Lyly, *Love's Metamorphosis* (1601)

Magdalene   Lewis Wager, *A New Interlude . . . Entreating of the Life and Repentance of Mary Magdalene* (1566)

Magnusson, *Dialogue*   Lynne Magnusson, *Shakespeare and Social Dialogue: Dramatic Language and Elizabethan Letters* (Cambridge, 1999)

Magnusson, 'Language'   Lynne Magnusson, 'Language and comedy', in Leggatt, 156–78

Malcolmson   Cristina Malcolmson, '"What You Will": social mobility and gender in *Twelfth Night*', in Valerie Wayne (ed.), *The Matter of Difference: Materialist Feminist Criticism of Shakespeare* (Ithaca, NY, 1991), 29–57

Manningham   John Manningham, *The Diary of John Manningham of the Middle Temple 1602–1603*, ed. Robert Parker Sorlien (Hanover, NH, 1976)

Marcus   Leah Marcus, *The Politics of Mirth* (Chicago, 1978)

Markham   Francis Markham, *The Book of Honour* (1625)

Marlowe, *Edward II*   *The Troublesome Reign and Lamentable Death of Edward the Second, King of England* (1594)

Marlowe, *Faustus*   Christopher Marlowe, *The Tragical History of Dr Faustus* (1604)

Marlowe, *Jew*   Christopher Marlowe, *The Tragedy of the Rich Jew of Malta* (1633)

Marlowe, *Tamburlaine*	Christopher Marlowe, *Tamburlaine the Great* (1590)
Marston	John Marston, *The Malcontent . . . With the Additions . . . by John Webster* (1604)
Meres	Francis Meres, *Palladis Tamia* (1598)
Minsheu	John Minsheu, *Ductoris in Linguas, The Guide into Tongues* (1625)
Montaigne	Michel de Montaigne, *Essays*, trans. John Florio (1613)
Morley, H.	Henry Morley, *The Journal of a London Playgoer, 1851–1866* (1891)
Morley, T.	Thomas Morley, *A Plain and Easy Introduction to Practical Music* (1597)
Mullaney	Steven Mullaney, *The Place of the Stage: Licence, Play and Power in Renaissance England* (Chicago, 1988)
Näcke	Paul Näcke, 'Über Homosexualität in Albanien', *Jahrbuch für sexuelle Zwischenstufen unter besonderer berücksichtigender Homosexualität*, 10 (1908), 313–37
Nashe, *Pasquill*	Thomas Nashe, *The Return of the Renowned Cavaliero Pasquill and his Meeting with Marforius* (1589)
Nashe, *Prognostication*	Thomas Nashe, *A Wonderful, Strange and Miraculous Astrological Prognostication* (1591)
Nashe, *Tears*	Thomas Nashe, *Christ's Tears over Jerusalem* (1593)
Nashe, *Traveller*	Thomas Nashe, *The Unfortunate Traveller* (1594)
NB	Norman Blake, private communication
Norbrook	David Norbrook, *Poetry and Politics in the English Renaissance*, rev. edn (Oxford, 2002)
OED	*Oxford English Dictionary*, 2nd edn (Oxford, 1989)
Odell	G.C.D. Odell, *Shakespeare from Betterton to Irving* (1921)
Onions	C.T. Onions, *A Shakespeare Glossary* (1911), rev. Robert Eagleson (Oxford, 1986)
Orgel	Stephen Orgel, *Impersonations: The Performance of Gender in Shakespeare's England* (Cambridge, 1996)
Osborne	Laurie E. Osborne, *The Trick of Singularity: Twelfth Night and the Performance Editions* (Iowa City, 1996)
Overbury	Sir Thomas Overbury, *New and Choice Characters* (1615)
Ovid, *Fasti*	Ovid, *Fasti*, ed. A.J. Boyle and R.D. Woodard (Harmondsworth, England, 2000)
Ovid, *Met.*	Ovid, *Metamorphoses*, trans. Arthur Golding (1567)
Oxberry, *Dramatic*	*Oxberry's Dramatic Biography and Histrionic Anecdotes*, ed. Catherine E. Oxberry, 5 vols (1825)

Palmer, *Shakespeare*	D.J. Palmer (ed.), *Shakespeare: 'Twelfth Night'; A Casebook* (1972)
Palmer, 'Echo'	D.J. Palmer, '*Twelfth Night* and the myth of Echo and Narcissus', *SS 32* (1979), 73–8
Partridge	Eric Partridge, *Shakespeare's Bawdy* (1968)
Paster	Gail Kern Paster, *The Body Embarrassed: Drama and the Disciplines of Shame in Early Modern England* (Ithaca, NY, 1993)
Pastime	Stephen Hawes, *The Pastime of Pleasure* (1509), ed. W.E. Mead (1928)
Peele	George Peele, *The Love of King David and his Fair Bethsabe* (1623)
Pennington	Michael Pennington, *Twelfth Night: A User's Guide* (2000)
Pepys	Samuel Pepys, *The Diary of Samuel Pepys*, ed. Robert Latham and William Matthews, 11 vols (1985)
Pequigney	Joseph Pequigney, 'The two Antonios and same-sex love in *Twelfth Night* and *The Merchant of Venice*', *English Literary Renaissance*, 22 (1992), 201–21
Petrarch	Francesco Petrarca, *Canzoniere*, ed. Rosanna Bettarini (Turin, 2005)
Plato	*The Dialogues of Plato*, trans. Benjamin Jowett, ed. D.J. Allan and H.E. Dale, 4 vols (Oxford, 1953)
Plautus	Titus Maccius Plautus, *A Pleasant and Fine Conceited Comedy, called Menechmus*, trans. William Warner (1595)
Playford	Henry Playford, *Wit and Mirth, or Pills to Purge Melancholy*, 4th edn, 6 vols (1719–20)
Pliny	Pliny the Elder, *The History of the World*, trans. Philemon Holland (1601)
PMLA	*Publications of the Modern Language Association*
Potter	Lois Potter, *Twelfth Night: Text and Performance* (Basingstoke, 1985)
Preiss	Richard Preiss, 'Robert Armin do the police in different voices', in Peter Holland and Stephen Orgel (eds), *From Performance to Print in Shakespeare's England* (Houndmills, England, 2006), 208–27
Primaudaye	Pierre de la Primaudaye, *The French Academy* (1586)
Proclamation	Elizabeth I, [*Proclamation*] *By the Queen . . . [against] Inordinate Excess in Apparel* (1597)
Puttenham	George Puttenham, *The Art of English Poesy* (1589)
Rackin	Phyllis Rackin, 'Androgyny, mimesis and the marriage of the boy heroine on the English Renaissance stage', *PMLA*, 102 (1987), 29–41

Ralegh	Walter Ralegh, *The Discovery of the Large, Rich and Beautiful Empire of Guiana* (1596)
Reed	Robert Reed, *Bedlam on the Jacobean Stage* (Cambridge, Mass., 1952)
Relihan	Constance C. Relihan, 'Erasing the east from *Twelfth Night*', in Joyce Green MacDonald (ed.), *Race, Ethnicity, and Power in the Renaissance* (Madison, NJ, 1997), 89–94
Riche	*Barnabe Riche his Farewell to Military Profession* (1583)
Robinson	Henry Crabb Robinson, *Diary, Reminiscences, and Correspondence*, ed. Thomas Sadler, 2 vols (1872)
Roister Doister	Nicholas Udall, *Roister Doister* (1566)
Rothwell & Melzer	Kenneth S. Rothwell and Annabelle Henkin Melzer (eds), *Shakespeare on Screen: An International Filmography and Videography* (1990)
RP	Richard Proudfoot, private communication
R.T.	Richard Tarlton [?], *A Pretty New Ballad, Entitled: The Crow Sits upon the Wall / Please One and Please All* (1592)
Rubinstein	Frankie Rubinstein, *A Dictionary of Shakespeare's Sexual Puns and their Significance*, 2nd edn (Basingstoke, 1984)
Salgādo	Gāmini Salgādo (ed.), *Eyewitnesses of Shakespeare: First Hand Accounts of Performances 1590–1890* (1975)
Saintsbury & Palmer	H.A. Saintsbury and Cecil Palmer (eds), *We Saw Him Act: A Symposium on the Art of Sir Henry Irving* (1939)
Saslow	James Saslow, *The Medici Wedding of 1589* (New Haven, Conn., and London, 1996)
Saviolo	Vincenzo Saviolo, *Vincentio Saviolo's Practice in Two Books* (1595)
Sawday	Jonathan Sawday, *The Body Emblazoned: Dissection and the Human Body in Renaissance Culture* (1995)
SB	*Studies in Bibliography*
SC	*Shakespearean Criticism* (Detroit, 1984–)
Schafer	Elizabeth Schafer, *Ms-Directing Shakespeare: Women Direct Shakespeare* (1998)
Schalkwyk	David Schalkwyk, 'Love and service in *Twelfth Night* and the Sonnets', *SQ*, 56 (2005), 76–100
Schlegel	August Wilhelm von Schlegel, *A Course of Lectures on Dramatic Art and Literature*, trans. John Black, 2 vols (1815)
Schleiner	Winfried Schleiner, 'The Feste–Malvolio scene in *Twelfth Night* against the background of Renaissance ideas about madness and possession', *Deutsche Shakespeare Gesellschaft West: Jahrbuch* (1990), 48–57

Schmidt   Alexander Schmidt, *Shakespeare Lexicon* (New York, 1968)

Scot   Reginald Scot, *Discovery of Witchcraft* (1584)

Scragg   Leah Scragg, '"Her C's, her U's, and her T's: why that?" A new reply for Sir Andrew Aguecheek', *Review of English Studies*, 42 (1991), 1–16

SEL   *Studies in English Literature*

Shattuck, *Shakespeare*   Charles H. Shattuck, *The Shakespeare Promptbooks: A Descriptive Catalogue* (Urbana, Ill., and London, 1965)

Shattuck, *Kemble*   *John Philip Kemble Promptbooks*, ed. Charles H. Shattuck (Charlottesville, Va., 1974)

Shaw   George Bernard Shaw, 'The point of view of a playwright', in Max Beerbohm (ed.), *Herbert Beerbohm Tree: Some Memories of Him and of his Art* (1920), 240–52

Shelley   Mary Shelley, 'Review of Prosper Merimée, *Le Guzla, ou Choix de poésies illyriques*', *Westminster Review*, 10 (1829), 71–81

Shirley   Anthony Shirley, *A True Report of Sir Anthony Shirley's Journey . . . to Casbine in Persia: His Entertainment there by the Great Sophy* (1600)

Sidney, *Arcadia*   Philip Sidney, *The Countess of Pembroke's Arcadia* (1598)

Sidney, *Astrophel*   Philip Sidney, *Astrophel and Stella*, in Sidney, *Arcadia*, 519–69

Simmons   J.L. Simmons, 'A source for Shakespeare's Malvolio: the Elizabethan controversy with the Puritans', *Huntington Library Quarterly*, 36 (1973), 181–201

Simpson   Claude M. Simpson, *The British Broadside Ballad and its Music* (New Brunswick, NJ, 1966)

Sinden, *Laughter*   Donald Sinden, *Laughter in the Second Act* (1985)

Sinden, 'Malvolio'   Donald Sinden, 'Malvolio in *Twelfth Night*', in *Players of Shakespeare*, ed. Philip Brockbank (Cambridge, 1985), 41–66

Sisson   C.J. Sisson, *New Readings in Shakespeare* (Cambridge, 1956)

Smith, B.   Bruce R. Smith, *Homosexual Desire in Shakespeare's England* (Chicago, 1991)

Smith, P.   Peter J. Smith, 'M.O.A.I.: "What should that alphabetical position 'portend?" An answer to the metamorphic Malvolio', *Renaissance Quarterly*, 51 (1998), 1199–224

Sohmer   Steve Sohmer, *Shakespeare's Mystery Play: The Opening of the Globe Theatre 1599* (Manchester, 1999)

Speaight, *Poel*   Robert Speaight, *William Poel and the Elizabethan Revival* (1954)

Speaight, *Shakespeare*   Robert Speaight, *Shakespeare on the Stage: An Illustrated History of Shakespearian Performance* (1973)

Sprague   A.C. Sprague, *Shakespeare and the Actors: The Stage Business in his Plays (1660–1905)* (Cambridge, Mass., 1945)

Sprague & Trewin   A.C Sprague and J.C. Trewin, *Shakespare's Plays Today: Some Customs and Conventions of the Stage* (1970)

SQ   *Shakespeare Quarterly*

SS   *Shakespeare Survey*

SSt   *Shakespeare Studies*

Sternfeld   F.W. Sternfeld, *Music in Shakespearean Tragedy* (1963)

Stubbes   Philip Stubbes, *Anatomy of Abuses* (1583)

Styan   J.L. Styan, *The Shakespeare Revolution: Criticism and Performance in the Twentieth Century* (Cambridge, 1977)

Tarlton's Jests   Richard Tarlton, *Tarlton's Jests* (1613)

Tarlton's News   Richard Tarlton, *Tarlton's News out of Purgatory* (1590)

Taylor, J.   John Taylor, *Works* (1630)

Taylor, G.   Gary Taylor, *Castration: An Abbreviated History of Western Manhood* (New York, 2000)

Thomas   Sir H. Thomas, Letter, *TLS*, 4 June 1933

Throckmorton   Job Throckmorton, *A Dialogue* (1589)

Tilley   Morris P. Tilley, *A Dictionary of the Proverbs in England in the Sixteenth and Seventeenth Centuries* (Ann Arbor, Mich., 1950)

Tree   Herbert Beerbohm-Tree, Promptbook for Her Majesty's Theatre production of *Twelfth Night*, 1901 (Bristol University Drama Library, Tree Collection, Box 138)

Trewin   J.C. Trewin, *Shakespeare on the English Stage, 1900–64* (1964)

Trial of Treasure   *A New and Merry Interlude, Called the Trial of Treasure* (1567)

Turner   Robert K. Turner, Jr, 'The text of *Twelfth Night*', *SQ*, 26 (1975), 128–38

TxC   Stanley Wells and Gary Taylor, with John Jowett and William Montgomery, *William Shakespeare: A Textual Companion* (Oxford, 1987)

Tyrwhitt   Thomas Tyrwhitt, *Observations and Conjectures upon Some Passages of Shakespeare* (Oxford, 1766)

Ungerer   Gustav Ungerer, 'My Lady's a Cathayan', *SS 32* (1979), 85–104

Van Doren	Mark Van Doren, *Shakespeare* (New York, 1939)
Vigo	Giovanni da Vigo, *The Most Excellent Works of Chirurgery*, trans. Bartholomew Traheron (1543)
Viswanathan	S. Viswanathan, '"Illeism with a difference" in certain middle plays of Shakespeare', *SQ*, 20 (1969), 407–15
Wales	Kathleen M. Wales, 'Generic "your" and Jacobean drama: the rise and fall of a pronominal usage', *English Studies*, 66 (1985), 7–24
Walker	W.S. Walker, *A Critical Examination of the Text of Shakespeare*, ed. W.N. Lettsom (1860)
Webster, *Devil*	John Webster *The White Devil* (1612)
Webster, *Malfi*	John Webster, *The Tragedy of the Duchess of Malfi* (1623)
Wells	Stanley Wells (ed.), *Shakespeare in the Theatre: An Anthology of Criticism* (Oxford, 1997)
Welsford	Enid Welsford, *The Fool: His Social and Literary History* (1935)
Werstine, 'Cases'	Paul Werstine, 'Cases and compositors in the Shakespeare First Folio comedies', *SB*, 35 (1982), 206–34
Werstine, 'Narratives'	Paul Werstine, 'Narratives about printed Shakespeare texts: "foulpapers" and "bad" quartos', *SQ*, 41 (1990), 65–86
Werstine, 'Plays'	Paul Werstine, 'Plays in manuscript', in Cox & Kastan, 481–97
Wilde	Oscar Wilde, 'The truth of masks: a note on illusion', in *Intentions* (1891)
Wiles	David Wiles, *Shakespeare's Clown: Actor and Text in the Elizabethan Playhouse* (Cambridge, 1987)
Williams	Gordon Williams, *A Dictionary of Sexual Language and Imagery in Shakespearean and Stuart Literature* (1994)
Wilson, *Happy*	John Dover Wilson, *Shakespeare's Happy Comedies* (1962)
Wilson, R.	Richard Wilson, *Secret Shakespeare: Studies in Theatre, Religion and Resistance* (Manchester, 2004)
Winter	William Winter, *Shakespeare on the Stage* (New York, 1915)
Witch of Edmonton	Thomas Dekker, John Ford and William Rowley, *The Witch of Edmonton* (1658)
Woodbridge	Linda Woodbridge, '"Fire in your heart and brimstone in your liver": towards an unsaturnalian *Twelfth Night*', *Southern Review* (Australia), 17 (1994), 270–91
Woolf	Virginia Woolf, '*Twelfth Night* at the Old Vic' (1933), in Wells, 206–10

Wright, E.   [Edward Wright], *The Map of the World, A.D. 1600, Called
                    by Shakespeare 'The New Map, with the Augmentation of
                    the Indies': To Illustrate the Voyages of John Davis* (1880)
Wright, G.   George T. Wright, *Shakespeare's Metrical Art* (Berkeley,
                    1988)
Wright, T.   Thomas Wright, *The Passions of the Mind* (1601)

INDEX

Abington, Frances (actor) 139–40, 146
Accademia degli Intronati *Gl'ingannati* 62–3
Accoramboni, Vittoria 157
Actaeon 30, 33
Adams, Barry B. 162
Adamson, Ames (actor) 100, 153
Adaptations 1, 5, 7, 96–7, 99–100, 105
Adree, Ingrid (actor) 123, 151
Adrian, Max (actor) 136, 150
Agate, James 133
Aguecheek, Sir Andrew (character) 10, 14, 17, 22, 23, 27, 34, 40, 41, 43, 45–6, 53, 55, 56, 60, 64–6, 68, 69, 80, 84, 85, 86, 88, 91, 95, 98, 158
    actors in role of 2, 103, 122, 123, 124, 132–4, 146–153
Ainley, Henry (actor) 148
Alciato, Andrea *Emblemata 33*
Alexander, Bill (director) 108, 109, 152
Anagrams 16, 25
Andersson, Bibi (actor) 151
Androgyny, theme of 27, 112, 117, 119, 144
Anglin, Margaret (director) 102, 148
Antonio (character) 23, 41, 46, 50, 55, 68, 70, 71, 75, 78, 79, 83, 84, 98, 99, 112, 117, 118, 119, 157
Apolinair, Danny 100, 151
Apuleius 14
Arbeau, Thoinot 65
Archer, William 22, 102
    Arden of Faversham 238
Arion 33, 34, 36
Ariosto, Ludovico *Orlando Furioso* 217
Arlidge, Anthony 20, 95
Armfield Neil (director) 123, 152
Armin, Robert 134–5, 137
    Fool upon Fool 135
    Quips upon Questions 135
    Two Maids of More-clacke 135
Armstrong, Archie 12
Armstrong, Derry 12
Arne, Thomas (composer) 139
Ashcroft, Peggy (actor) 145, 149, 150
Astington, John 60
Atkins, Robert (actor–director) 103, 123,148, 149

Auden, W. H. 56
Audience, role of 3–11
Audley, Maxine (actor) 150
Aveling, Edward 125, 143

'B., J.G.' 105
Barber, C.L. 18–20, 118
Barber, John 127, 138
Barentsz, Willem 73
Barker, Harley Granville (director) 2, 90, 91, 92,102–3, 104, 136, 145, 148
Barrit, Desmond (actor) 127, 126, 129, 152
Barton, Anne 401
Barton, John (director) 2, 107, 136, 151
Bate, Jonathan 30, 32
Beckerman, Bernard 90
Bedford, Brian (actor) 151
Belch, Sir Toby (character) 8, 10, 11, 19, 20, 22, 26, 34, 40, 55, 56, 57, 60, 64–5, 66, 70, 72, 75, 77, 79–80, 81, 84, 85, 89, 90, 91, 92, 96, 100, 106, 135, 158
    actors in role of 2, 120, 121, 122, 124, 130–2, 133, 146–53
Belleforest, François de 259
Belsey, Catherine 27
Benassi, Memo (actor) 150
Bensley, Robert (actor) 122, 124, 127, 128, 146
Benson, Constance (actor) 148
Benson, Frank (actor–manager) 125, 148
Beresford, Stephen (director) 111, 153
Berg, Chuck 105
Berry, Ralph 8, 9, 10
Betterton, Thomas (actor) 122, 130. 132, 146
Bhattacharjee, Paul (actor) 127, 153
Bible, 158, 169, 179, 185, 198, 210, 246, 257, 261, 278, 279, 291, 331, 344, 345
Billings, Timothy 217
Billington, Michael 92, 112, 126, 137, 141, 145
Billington, Sandra 19, 20
Bing, Suzanne (actor) 122, 145, 148
Black, Dorothy (actor) 149

417

Blake, Norman 79
Blakewell, Michael (director) 151
Bland, George (actor) 123, 147
Blayney, Peter W.M. 313
Blood sports, theme of 8, 242
Bloom, Claire (actor) 150
Body, theme of 38, 50-55, 57-66, 89
Boiardo,Matteo Maria *Orlando innamorato* 217
Bonham-Carter, Helena (actor) 152
Book of Common Prayer 307
Boorde, Andrew *Dietary of Health* 176
Booth, Stephen 10, 11, 16
Boswell, John 73
Bourke, Meyer (actor) 123, 143, 147
Boxer, Stephen (actor) 114, 152
Bradley, David 380
Bradley, David (actor) 134, 152
Branagh, Kenneth (director) 98, 108, 121, 152
Brandauer, Klaus Maria (actor) 151
Brayton, Lily (actor) 122, 145, 148
Brennan, Patrick (actor) 272
Brewer, Thomas 215
Briers, Richard (actor) 152
Brome, Richard *The English Moor* 276
Brook, Lesley (actor) 139, 149
Brooke, Ralph 362, 363
Brougham, John (actor) 147
Brown, John Russell 128, 129, 133
Brown, Michael (actor) 144
Brown, Roger 402
Browne, Robert 265
Browner, Jessica A. 75
Brownists 23
Bryden, Ronald 138
Bulos, Yusef (actor) 111, 152
Buontalenti, Bernardo 34, 36
Burbage, Richard 105
Burnaby, William 96, 145
Burns, Elizabeth 88
Burton, Richard (actor) 150
Burton, Robert *Anatomy of Melancholy* 402
Burton, William Evans (actor) 147
Burwick, Frederick 27
Byron, Lord George 75

Caesar, Julius 158
Caird, John (director) 108, 152
Callaghan, Dympna 17
Calendar 3, 21-3
Capell, Edward (editor) 161

Captain (character) 15, 34, 56, 62, 70, 72, 78, 84, 85, 119, 157
actors in role of 113
Carey, Denis (director) 150
Carnival 18-19, 23, 95
Carr, V. 121
Carradine, John (actor) 150
Carroll, Tim (director) 113-5, 116, 153
Carroll, William C. 30
Castration, theme of 14, 17, 57-63, 169, 170, 183, 194, 246
Castellani, Renato (director) 150
Castiglione, Baldassare *Book of the Courtier* 58-9, 64, 68
Catholicism 23, 73
Chahidi, Paul (actor) 122, 141, 142, 153
Chandos, Lord 134
Charles I, King of England 5
Charles II, King of England 6
Chaucer, Geoffrey, *Canterbury Tales* 60, 159
Chettle, Henry *Troilus and Cressida* 254
Chillington Rutter, Carol 119
Christina of Lorraine 34, 36
Christy, Bunnie (designer) 108, 152
Cicero, Marcus Tullius *De officiis* 325
Civility, theme of 58-9, 63-4
Class, theme of 9, 45-6, 51, 79-80, 111, 127, 157
Clayton, Harold (director) 120, 150
Clive, Kitty (actor) 139, 146,
Cloth, theme of 24, 40-5
Clunes, Alec (actor) 149, 150
Coates, Wells (designer) 103, 149
Coe, Fred (director) 150
Coffin, Hayden (actor) 136, 148
Cole, Edward 266
Coleridge, Samuel Taylor 14
Collier, John Payne (editor) 162,176, 179, 180, 202, 208, 223, 227, 239, 240, 242, 244, 248, 250, 251, 257, 270, 275, 283, 292, 295, 322, 331, 397
Commedia dell'arte 97, 110
Compositor B 169, 195, 286, 359, 360-1, 368-9
Cook, Edward Dutton 139
Copeau, Jacques (actor-director) 103, 145, 148
Copley, Anthony 323
Corbett, Harry H. (actor) 150
Cornwallis, William 212, 246
Costa, Orazio (director) 150

Costume 45-6, 91, 101, 103, 105, 106, 107, 110, 113, 127, 132, 144
Cotton, Oliver (actor) 130
Courtesy, theme of 64, 82-3
Cox, L.S. 16
Crane, William H. (actor) 147
Craven, Hawes (designer) 100, 103, 148
Cross-dressing 2, 26-8, 49-50, 58-63, 66-8, 113, 119, 136, 142
Crowley, Bob (designer) 153
Cumberland, John (editor) 307
Curio (character) 158
Curio, Gaius Scribonius 158
Cushman, Charlotte (actor) 119, 123, 147
Cushman, Susan (actor) 119, 123, 147

Dahlin, Hans (director) 151
Daly, Augustin (director) 98, 99, 139, 145, 147, 148
Dance 34, 64, 65, 94, 124
Daneman, Paul (actor) 150
Daniel, P. A. 48
Dante Alighieri 308
Darlington, W.A. 132, 133
Darrell, John 279, 308-9, 314
Davenant, William 6, 132
Davenport, Mrs (actor) 142
Death, theme of 3, 4, 21, 34, 56-7
de Bruyn 48
de Nobili, Lila (designer) 107, 150
Deighton, K. (editor) 298
Deictics 89
Dekker, Thomas, 161, 162, 163, 169, 171, 172, 173, 175, 176, 178, 184, 186, 187, 189, 190, 191
    Blurt, Master Constable 177
    Satiromastix 254
    Sir Thomas Wyatt 239
    Troilus and Cressida 254
    Westward Ho 260
    Witch of Edmonton 194
Dench, Judi (actor) 119, 123, 144, 145, 151
Dent, R. W. 194, 197, 200, 203, 204, 215, 216, 221, 222, 223, 224, 225, 231, 232, 237, 238, 242, 243, 244, 245, 247, 251, 252, 253, 255, 258, 259, 260, 262, 264, 265, 266, 269, 270, 273, 277, 281
Devine, George (actor–director) 130, 149, 151
Dexter, John (director) 121, 151
Digges, Leonard 6
Dignam, Mark (actor) 150

Diocletian 23
Discourse markers 79
Disease, theme of 55-7
Dodd, James (actor) 122, 124, 132, 133, 146
Dodd, William 11-12, 13
Donne, John *Progress of the Soul* 311
Donnellan, Declan (director) 112, 117, 152, 153
Doors, stage, use of 34, 89-90, 115
Douai manuscript 157
Double, theme of 25-9, 84-5
Doubling of roles 103, 123, 135
Dowland, John (composer) 226
Downes, John (prompter) 6
Doyle, Pat (composer) 152
Draper, John 9, 93
Driver, Donald 151
Drummond, William 337
Dubey, Neha (actor) 141, 153
Dudley, William (designer) 31, 112, 151
Duke George II of Saxe-Meiningen (director) 101, 147
Duncan-Jones, Katherine 95
Dunlap, William 131, 132
Dunn, Geoffrey (actor) 120, 150
Dunstall, John (actor) 146
Duologue 97-8
Dyce, Alexander (editor) 208, 292, 323

Eggert, Katherine 136, 137
Elam, Keir 16, 62
Elizabeth I, Queen of England 2, 60, 119, 141, 157
Ellington, Duke (composer) 100, 153
Elze, Karl 171
Emblems 32-4
Enigmas 11, 14, 16
English, Early Modern 29, 158
Epiphany, theme of 21-2, 23, 24
Erasmus, Desiderius
    Paraphrase 351
    Proverbs 273
Erskine, Thomas L. 105
Eunuch: *see* castration
Evans Burton, William (actor) 147
Evans, Edith (actor) 142, 149
Evans, Bertrand 91
Evans, G. Blakemore (editor) 369
Evans, Maurice (actor) 120, 121, 126, 149
Everett, Barbara 180, 404

Fabian (character) 8, 14, 15, 21, 23, 26, 30, 53, 69, 72, 73, 81, 87, 88, 95, 159
  actors in role of 122, 133
Farmer, Richard 322
Farren, William (actor) 147
Fencing 64–6, 67
Fenner, Dudley *Song of Songs* 162
Fensom, Jonathan 111
Feste (character) 3, 10, 11, 14, 19, 23, 24, 25, 26, 29, 32, 34, 45, 46, 53, 55, 56, 69, 76, 79, 80, 81, 83, 84, 85, 86, 87, 89, 91, 100, 107, 112, 158-9
  disguised as Sir Topas 23, 26, 46, 75, 83, 87, 91, 135, 137, 159
  actors in role of 2, 113, 114 118, 121, 122, 123, 126, 134–7
Fiennes, Joseph (actor) 119
Film, *Twelfth Night* on 117–21
Findlay, Deborah (actor) 109
Finney, Albert (actor) 151
Fiske, Alison (actor) 221
Fitton, Mary 179
Fletcher, John *Elder Brother* 178
  Faithful Shepherdess 22
Florio, John 24, 65
  World of Words 66–7, 158
  New World of Words 405
  Second Fruits 279
Forbes-Robertson, family 123
Forbes-Robertson Jean (actor) 149
Forbes-Robertson Johnson (actor) 149
Forbes-Robertson Maxine (actor) 149
Ford, John *Witch of Edmonton* 194
Forde, Emanuel *Parismus* 157
Frame, Colin 144
France, Richard 105
Fraser, Bill (actor) 130, 151
Freeman, Cheryl (actor) 153
Freund, Elizabeth 11
Fried, Yakow (director) 123, 150
Frohman, Charles (director) 148
Frye, Northrop 2, 21, 27, 56, 108
Fuller, Rosalinde (actor) 149
Fulwell, Ulpian *Like Will to Like* 281
Fulwood, William *Philosopher's Game* 323
Furness, Horace Howard (editor) 162
Furor, amorous 126
Füssli, Johann Heinrich 38, 39

Galen 53
Garber, Marjorie 28
Garfield, Leon 152

Garson, Greer (actor) 120, 148
Gender, question of 2, 27–8, 45, 49–50, 51, 58–61, 63, 67–8, 72, 88, 111-3, 116, 118, 119, 143–4, 157, 183
Genest, John 99
Gentile, Nikki (actor) 118, 151
George IV, King 142
Gerard, John *Herbal 221*
Gesture 34, 35, 89, 113, 127, 132
Ghir, Kulvinder (actor) 111, 153
Gibbs, Ann (actor) 139, 146
Gibson, Marion 305, 405
Gielgud, John (actor-director) 149, 150
Giles, David (director) 151
Gill, Peter (director) 30, 31, 33, 112, 137, 138, 144, 151
Gilman, Albert 402
Girard, René 32
Globe theatre 8, 89, 96, 102, 115, 134, 141, 144, 153
Goar, Jacques 75
Goldberg, Jonathan 17
Golding, Arthur 194
Gonzaga, Cesare 58
Gonzaga, Curzio *Gli inganni* 61, 62, 157
Gonzaga, Elisabetta 58
Good, Christopher (actor) 257
Goorney, Howard 106
Gorrie, John (director) 121, 152
Gould, Jack 120
Graham, Morland (actor) 136, 149
Grant, Duncan (costume designer) 148
Gray, Charles (actor) 151
Greenblatt, Stephen 10
Greene, David (director) 120, 150
Greene, Robert *Friar Bacon and Friar Bungay 405*
  Mamillia 235
Greene, Thomas 95
Greet, Ben (director) 102, 148
Greg, W.W. 359, 362-7
Greif, Karen 98, 136
Grim, the Collier of Croydon 173
Guazzo, Stefano, *Civil Conversation* 64, 68
Guidobaldo, Duke of Urbino 58
Guinness, Alec (actor-director) 121, 123, 132, 149, 150, 151
Gunter, John (actor) 110, 152
Guthrie, Tyrone (director) 103, 105, 131, 136, 139, 149

Hadfield, Mark (actor) 122, 129, 137, 153
Hall, Peter (director) 107, 150
Halliwell, James O. (editor) 7, 239
Halvorson, Gary (director) 153
Hamilton, Donna B. 406
Hamlett, Dilys (actor) 120, 150
Hands, Terry (director) 108, 151
Hanmer, Thomas (editor) 168, 197, 232, 371
Hardwicke, Cedric (actor) 122, 132, 150
Hardy, Robert (actor) 150
Harington Sir John *Metamorphosis of Ajax* 16
Harker, Joseph (designer) 100, 148
Harris, Henry (actor) 132, 146
Harris, Rosemary (actor) 150
Harrison, William *Description of England* 210
Harsnett, Samuel 316
Hassel, R. Chris 21, 22
Hathaway, Ann 228
Hattaway, Michael 118
Hawes, Stephen *Pastime of Pleasure* 313
Hawthorne, Nigel (actor) 152
Hayes, Helen (actor) 149
Hazlitt, William 7, 9, 144
Heliodorus *Ethiopica* 330
Heminge, John (actor) 130
Henderson, John (actor) 146
Hendiadys 85
Henry, Guy (actor) 128, 153
Henryson, Robert *Testament of Cresseid* 254
Henslowe, Philip 45
Hentschel, Irene (director) 105, 106, 113, 139, 149
Herbert, Sir Henry 4, 5
Hester, Hal (composer) 100, 151
Hillyer, Terence (actor) 110, 152
Hilman, David 406
Hinman, Charlton 90 n.2
Holinshed, Raphael 306
Holland, Peter 110
Holm, Ian (actor) 127, 151
Homer *Iliad* 214
Homoeroticism, theme of 49-50, 83, 111-2, 157
Hopwood, C.H. 20
Hoppner, John 144
Horace *Odes* 187
Horden, Michael (actor) 150
Horner, Olga 19
Hotson, Leslie 14, 16, 18, 93-4, 137
Howard, Alan (actor) 122, 138, 151

Howard, Andrée (choreographer) 99, 149
Howard, Jean 49
Howard-Hill, T.H. 359
Hoyle, Martin 108, 126, 137
Hudd, Walter (actor) 149
Humours, role of 24, 53-55
Hudson, Henry N. (editor) 398
Hunsdon, Lord 93
Hunt, Helen (actor) 153
Hunt, Hugh (director) 110, 145, 150
Hunt, Leigh 99, 139, 144
Hunt, Marsha (actor) 150
Hunter, Joseph 22
Hutchings, Geoffrey (actor) 136, 151
Hutton, Ronald 19, 20, 21
Hylton, Jack (director) 149
Hyperbole 83
Hytner, Nicholas (director) 153

Identity, question of 26-8, 46-7, 49, 56, 59, 61, 80, 82, 97
Illyria 2, 18, 23, 64, 68-77, 100, 106-11, 118, 119, 121, 132
Inchbald, Elizabeth (editor) 97
Ingham, Barrie (actor) 133, 151
Interpretation, theme of 2, 10-24, 25, 32-4, 37, 50-2
Intertextuality 57-68, 72, 119-20, 127
Irving, Henry (actor-manager) 99, 100, 125, 148
Italian culture, influence of 3-4, 61-7, 68, 71, 93-4, 100

Jaggard, William 313
James I, King of England 5
James, Emrys (actor) 122, 123, 126, 129, 136, 151, 152
Jardine, Lisa 49
Jeffries, Maud (actor) 148
Jesson, Paul (actor) 285
Jhutti, Ronny (actor) 121
Johnson, Richard (actor) 133, 150
Johnson, Samuel (editor)
    Dictionary 7
Jones, Ann Rosalind 47
Jones, David (director) 151
Jones, Freddie (actor) 152
Jones, Gillian (actor) 123, 152
Jones, Robert (composer) 387, 405
Jonson, Ben *Every Man in his Humour* 130, 267
    Poetaster 285
    Volpone 189

Jordan, Dorothy (actor) 122, 123, 124, 144, 146, 147
Jouvet, Louis (actor–designer) 103, 148
Judge, Ian (director) 110, 152
Junius, Adrianus *Nomenclator* 247

Kafno, Paul (director) 121, 152
Kahn, Michael (director) 111, 152
Kean, Charles (actor–manager) 147
Keeley, Robert (actor) 133, 147
Keightley, Thomas (editor) 162, 254, 272, 278, 289, 319
Kemble, John Philip (actor–manager) 97, 98, 128, 146, 147
Kemble, Mrs Charles (actor) 139, 147
Kendall, Felicity (actor) 152
Kennedy, Dennis 103, 111
Kent, Charles (director) 117, 129, 148
Keown, Eric 126
Kerrigan, John 15
King, T. J. 300
King, Thomas (actor) 146
Kingsley, Ben (actor) 136, 137, 152
Kirkham, Edward 239
Kittredge, George Lyman 163, 218
Kluick, Brian (director) 153
Kneale, Patricia (actor) 150
Knight, Charles (editor) 388
Knight, Joseph 133, 142
Koenig, Rhoda 142
Kohler, Estelle (actor) 141, 151
Kökeritz, Helge 161, 167, 177, 184, 194, 202, 213, 224, 236, 256, 277

Lamb, Charles 124, 128, 132
Lambert, J.W. 147
Laneham, Robert *Letter* 167
Lange, Bernd (actor) 152
Langrishe, Caroline (actor) 141, 152
Language 16, 50–1, 66–7, 78–87
    Foreign 66
    French 66, 88
    Italian 3, 66–7, 71, 75, 158
    Latin 14
Lapotaire, Jane (actor) 144, 145, 151
Larionova, Anna (actor) 150
Latham, Simon *Falconry* 244
Laurie, John (actor) 122, 149
Law, theme of 20, 95–6, 159
Leach, Joseph 143 n.1
Lehmann, Beatrix (actor) 140, 144, 149
Leigh, Andrew (actor–director) 122, 148, 149

Leigh, Vivien (actor) 143, 150
Leighton, Edmund Blair (painter) 38
Lesser, Anton (actor) 152
Lever, Ralph *Philosopher's Game* 323
Levin, Harry (editor) 369
Levine, Laura 49
Lewalski, Barbara 21
Lewes, G.H. 210
Lily, William *Grammar* 211
Linthicum, Marie Channing 47
Liston, John (actor) 124, 147
Littlewood, Joan (director) 106, 150
Lloyd, W. W. 409
London, allusions to 25, 75–7
Lodge, Thomas *Treatise of Plague* 163
Logic 15, 84, 87
Long, John H. 409
Loose ends (in the plot) 11–14, 68
Lopokova, Lydia (actor) 139, 149
Lord Chamberlain's Men, company of 3, 93, 115, 134, 146
Lott, Barbara (actor) 150
Love, James (actor) 132, 133
Lovell, Thomas (actor) 146
Luchko, Klara (actor) 117, 118, 123, 150
Lunghi, Cherie (actor) 151
Lydgate, John 162
Lyly, John
    Campaspe 21
    Endimion 159
    Euphues 231
    Gallathea 235
    Love's Metamorphosis 261

Macaulay, Alistair 137
Machiavelli, Niccolò 217, 247, 248, 264, 265
Macklin, Charles (actor) 146
McLane, Derek 111
Madden, John 119
Magnusson, Lynne 82
Mahood, Molly M. (editor) 135
Maloney, Michael (actor) 153
Malvolio (character) 4–6, 7, 8–10, 15–17, 19–21, 22, 25, 27, 28, 29–30, 32, 40, 43, 45, 46, 47, 49, 51, 53, 55, 60, 68, 70, 77, 78, 79, 80, 81, 88, 90, 96, 97, 99, 158
    actors in role of 2, 90, 91, 98, 100, 101, 102, 103, 105, 106, 107, 108, 109, 114, 113, 117, 120, 121, 122, 123–30, 145, 146–53, 207, 208, 209, 238, 240, 241, 242, 245, 275, 280, 305, 308, 317

Manningham, John *Diary* 3-4, 5, 7, 20, 22. 93, 95, 96, 101, 102, 123, 130
Maps 32, 73, 74
Marcus, Leah 71
Markham, Francis 289
Maria (character) 19, 22, 80, 81, 92, 158
    actors in role of 2, 112, 113, 122, 123, 141-2
Marlowe, Christopher
    Dr Faustus 164, 310
    Edward II 336
    Jew of Malta 173
    Tamburlaine 254
Marlowe, Julia (actor) 145, 148
Marston, John *Malcontent* 242
    What You Will 161
Martial 265
Martin, John G. (actor) 147
Martin, Richard 20
Materiality 24, 39-46
Matthison, Edith Wynne (actor) 148
Mauri, Glauco (actor) 150
McCarthy, Lillah (actor) 148
McCartney, Paul (composer) 152
McCowen, Alec (actor) 121, 152
McCrory, Helen (actor) 319
McEwan, Geraldine (actor) 122, 140, 150
McGillis, Kelly (actor) 111, 152
McKluskie, Kathleen 49
McLane, Derek (deigner) 111, 152
Maynard, Terence (actor) 138, 153
Medici, Ferdinando de' 34, 36, 157
    Isabella de' 157
Melancholy, theme of 21, 27, 53-4, 107, 120, 121, 130, 136, 144
Mellish, Fuller (actor) 129, 148
Melzer, Annabelle Henkin 120, 121
Mendes, Sam (director) 2, 115, 116, 128, 153
Meredith, Rhys (actor) 113, 116
Meres, Francis *Palladis Tamia* 192, 215
Mesdach, Saolomon 37
Messina, Cedric (producer) 151, 152
Middle Temple 3, 20, 22, 89, 94, 95, 96, 101, 102, 112, 113, 116, 128, 141, 146, 148, 150, 153, 159
Mills, Peter (composer) 100, 153
Minsheu, John *Ductoris in Linguas* 229
Mnouchkine, Ariane (director) 110, 152
Moffatt, John (actor) 150
Montaigne, Michel de *Essays* 24, 86
Morley, Christopher (designer) 107
Morley, Henry 125

Morley, Sheridan 126
Morley, Thomas (composer) 215, 226, 323, 385-6
Motley (designer) 106, 149
Muat, Mariya (director) 152
Mullaney, Steven 75
Mullin, Eugene (designer) 148
Munro, John (editor) 399
Murray, William (actor) 123, 147
Music 14, 19, 34, 60, 94, 99-100, 134, 139, 144-5

Näcke, Paul 73
Names of characters 23, 25, 71, 157-9
Narcissism, theme of 15, 25, 29, 32, 33
Narcissus 30, 32, 33, 112
Neilson, Adelaide (actor) 143, 147
Neville, John (actor) 150
Nicholls, Kate (actor) 141, 151
Nightingale, Benedict 127, 141
Noble, Adrian (director) 112, 113, 114, 152
Norbrook, David 203
Norman, Marc 119
Norton, Thomas *Gorboduc* 203
Nunn, Trevor (director) 71, 98, 99, 105, 117, 118, 119, 121, 136, 137, 138, 152

Odell, G.C.D. 99
O'Donnell, Anthony 153
Olivia (character) 7, 15, 16, 17, 19, 21, 25, 26, 27, 28, 29, 30, 32, 34, 35, 37, 38, 40, 44, 46, 47, 49, 50, 51, 52, 53, 54, 55, 56, 57, 58, 60, 62, 68, 69, 70, 75, 77, 78, 79, 81, 83, 84, 85, 87, 88, 89, 90, 91, 92, 96, 98, 100, 103, 134, 158
    actors in role of 4, 108, 109, 112, 113, 115, 117, 122, 123, 138-42, 143, 146-53
Olivier, Laurence (actor) 120, 122, 126, 128, 129, 130, 131, 149, 150
Onions, C.T. 350
Orgel, Stephen 58
Orientalism 72-3, 111, 119
Ormerod, Nick (designer) 152, 153
Orsini of Bracciano, Duke 60, 71, 93, 94, 157
Orsino (character) 11, 15, 21, 24, 25, 27, 28, 29, 30, 32, 39, 45, 50, 51, 52, 53, 54, 55, 56, 57, 58, 59, 67, 68, 69, 71, 75, 78, 81, 83, 84, 87, 89, 90, 93-4, 119, 157, 158
    actors in role of 99, 103, 106, 108, 110, 111, 112, 113, 114, 115, 118, 112, 137-8, 150-3

Osborne, Laurie E. 97, 98, 117, 121
Ostermayer, Christine (actor) 90
Overbury, Sir Thomas *Characters* 247, 353
Ovid 16, 30, 33, 34
  Fasti 166
  Metamorphoses 30, 72
Oxberry, William (editor) 98, 136, 143

Paintings, *see* visual images
Pallavicino, Gaspare 59
Palmer, D.J. 30
Palmer, Cecil 125
Palmer, John (actor) 122, 124, 146
Paltrow, Gwyneth (actor) 119
Parminder, Nagra (actor) 121, 153
Parsons, Robert 23
Partridge, Eric 183, 224, 242, 253, 293, 354
Paryla, Katja (director) 152
Passions, theme of 24, 30, 50, 53-5, 85, 98, 141
Paster, Gail Kern 17
Peacock, Trevor (actor) 152
Peele, George *David and Bethsabe* 228
Peg of Ramsay 217
Pember, Ron (actor) 137, 151
Pembroke, Earl of 179
Pennington, Michael 129
Pepys, Samuel *Diary* 6, 18, 96, 130
Pequigney, Joseph 157
Peretti, Francesco 157
Perception, theme of 28-9, 77, 107, 118
Performance, first (see also prroductions) 93-6
Peri, Iacopo, *Euridice* 59
Petrarch 138
  Canzoniere 164
Phelps, Samuel (actor) 125, 147
Pictures, see visual images
Pinkins, Tonya (actor) 153
Place 2, 18, 23, 25, 64, 68-77, 100, 106-11, 118, 119, 121, 132
Plague, theme of 56-7
Plato 14, 87
Plautus, Titus Maccius *Menechmus* 3, 4, 72
Playfair, Nigel (actor) 149
Playford, Henry 411
Pliny the Elder *History of the World* 231
Plowright, Joan (actor) 121, 123, 151
Plym, Miss (actor) 146

Poel, William (director) 101-2, 115, 148
Pollard, A.W. 353
Pope, Alexander (editor) 376, 399
Politeness 64, 81, 82, 83, 84
Pope, Thomas (actor) 130
Porter, Eric (actor) 150
Posner, Lindsay (director) 112, 128, 137, 153
Potter, Lois 77, 89, 95, 128
Pounds, Courtice (actor) 136, 148
Powell, Snelling (actor) 147
Powell, William 399
Preiss, Richard 307
Preston, Thomas *Cambises* 346
Primaudaye, Pierre de la *French Academy* 179
Pritchard, Hannah (actor) 142, 144, 146
Pritt Harley, John (actor) 147
Proclemer, Anna (actor) 150
Productions of *Twelfth Night* 1, 6, 30, 45, 50, 90, 92, 93-153
Pronunciation 120, 126, 129, 157, 158, 159
Properties, stage 89, 91, 127
Prose, use of 78-9, 95
Protestantism 19, 22, 23, 45
Proudfoot, Richard xviii, 395, 412
Proverbs 49, 186, 273
Punctuation 79
Puritanism 8, 19, 21, 22, 23, 45, 47, 53, 75, 107, 127, 137
Puttenham, George 83, 84, 85, 86
Pythagoras 310-11, 323

Quartermaine, Leon (actor) 148, 149
Quick, John (actor) 146
Quiller-Couch, (editor) 2
Quintilian 14

Rabelais, François 186
Rackin, Phyllis 50
Raffles, Gerry (actor) 150
Rainolds, John 49
Ralegh, Walter 166, 266
  Discovery of Guiana 412
Randone, Salvo (actor) 150
Rann, Joseph (editor) 201, 269
Reception, critical, of *Twelfth Night* 1, 2, 3, 6-24
Redgrave, Lynn (actor) 151
Redgrave, Michael (actor) 133, 149
Redgrave, Vanessa (actor) 145, 151

Redmayne, Eddie (actor) 113, 116, 153
Reed, Robert 282
Rehan, Ada (actor) 145, 148
Reichel, Cara (director) 100, 153
Relihan, Constance C. 72, 73
Reynolds, Frederick (director) 99, 147
Reynolds, Joshua 144
Rhetoric 30, 80-2, 82-6
Rhetorical figures 82-5
Rhys Jones, Griff (director) 110, 152
Richardson, Ralph (actor) 121, 130, 132, 149, 151
Riche, Barnabe 'Of Apollonius and Silla' 4, 61, 62, 63, 72
Rigg, Diana (actor) 151
Ripa, Cesare *Iconologia* 34, 35
Robinson, Henry Crabb 124, 143
Robinson, Mary (actor) 142, 146
Robson, Stuart (actor) 147
Rothwell, Kenneth S. 120, 121
Rowe, Nicholas (editor) 157
Rubinstein, Frankie 175, 217, 238, 281
Rush, Geoffrey (actor) 152
Rusport, Charlotte 139
Russell Beale, Simon (actor) 126, 153
Russell, Thomas 95
Rylance, Mark (actor) 113, 141, 153

Sackville, Thomas *Gorboduc* 307
Saint-Denis, Michel (director) 149
Saints, names of 23-4, 157-9
Saintsbury, H.A. 125
Salgãdo, Gãmini 125
Santuccio, Gianni (actor) 150
Sarrazin, Gregor 93
Savary, Jérôme (director) 152
Saviolo, Vincenzo *Practise* 64-65, 66
Sawday, Jonathan 51
Scenes, order of 97-9, 121
Schafer, Elizabeth 106, 140
Schalkwyk, David 81, 82
Schanke, John 124
Schenk, Otto (director) 151
Schlegel, August Wilhelm von 27
Schleiner, Winfried 308
Schmidt, Alexander 272
Scot, Reginald *Discovery of Witchcraft* 159, 323, 338
Scragg, Leah 17
Seasons, theme of 2, 18, 21-3, 77, 106-10
Sebastian (character) 21, 22, 23, 25, 26-7, 29, 46, 50, 55, 66, 69, 75, 77, 78, 79, 80, 83, 85, 87, 89, 90, 97, 98, 100, 157

actors in role of 112, 113, 114, 115, 117, 119, 121, 122, 123, 143
Secrecy, theme of 11, 15-17, 24, 72
Service, theme of 81-82
Shakespeare, William
  Antony and Cleopatra 258, 396, 524
  All's Well That Ends Well 2, 18
  As You Like It 2, 67, 90, 134
  Comedy of Errors 4, 26, 81
  Coriolanus 232, 396
  Cymbeline 396
  Hamlet 68, 119, 130
  King Henry IV, Part 1 396
  King Henry IV, Part 2 396
  King Henry V xvi, 396
  King Henry VI, Part 1 396
  King Henry VI, Part 2 396
  King Henry VIII 396
  Julius Caesar 158
  King John 361, 396
  King Lear 134-5, 307, 388, 396
  A Lover's Complaint 396
  Love's Labour's Lost 363, 366, 369, 404
  The Rape of Lucrece 242, 396
  Much Ado about Nothing 363, 396
  Macbeth 130
  Measure for Measure 2, 18
  A Midsummer Night's Dream 4, 18, 90
  The Merchant of Venice 2, 18, 67
  The Merry Wives of Windsor 396
  Othello xv, 205, 396
  Pericles 396
  The Passionate Pilgrim 396
  King Richard II 396
  King Richard III 396
  Romeo and Juliet 119, 396
  Sonnets 29, 99
  Troilus and Cressida 362, 396
  The Tempest 99, 118
  The Two Gentlemen of Verona 2, 18, 81
  Timon of Athens 397
  Titus Andronicus 397
  Twelfth Night productions of, 106-7, 124, 146
  The Taming of the Shrew 18
  Venus and Adonis 397
  The Winter's Tale 361, 397
Shattuck, Charles H. 413
Shaw, George Bernard 125, 129, 145
Shelley, Mary 73, 75

Sher, Anthony (actor) 109, 126, 129, 130, 152
Shirley, Anthony *True Report* 72, 95
Sichel, John (director) 121, 151
Siddons, Mrs Henry (actor) 123, 147
Sidney, Philip *Arcadia* 162, 254, 330
  Astrophel and Stella 322
Sign, theme of 46, 51, 86–7
Sikora, Cornelia (actor) 152
Simpson, Christopher 334
Sincler, John (actor) 335
Sinden, Donald (actor) 122, 125, 128, 129, 150
Sisson, C.J. 239, 286
Sisto V, Pope 157
Slater, Daphne (actor) 140, 149
Smith, Bruce R. 330
Smith, Peter J. 16
Smock Alley promptbook 344
Sohmer, Steve 23
Sothern, E.H. (actor-director) 148
Sources 4, 57–68, 72
Space 2, 40, 68–70, 72
Speaight, Robert (actor-critic) 101, 102, 107, 125, 145, 149
Spedding, James 168, 294
Spencer, Charles 108, 127
Spenser, Edmund *Fairie Queene*
Sprague, A.C. 128, 132
Spranger, Mrs Barry (actor) 146
St. Andrew 23
St. Anne 23
St. Fabianus 23
St. Valentine 23
Saint-Denis, Michel 149
Stallybrass, Peter 47
Stanton, Barry (actor) 131, 153
Staunton, Howard (editor) 147, 251, 261, 273, 400
Steele, Tommy (actor) 151
Stephens, Toby (actor) 138
Steevens, George (editor) 3, 217, 239, 242, 247, 306, 307, 313, 320–21, 322
Stiles, Julia (actor) 153
Stoppard, Tom 119
Stone, John 189
Stow, John 19
Strachey, Willian 239
Strehler, Giorgio (director) 150
Strong, Mark (actor) 138, 153
Stubbes, Philip *Anatomy of Abuses* 19, 20
Styan, J. L. 102, 103
Suett, Richard (actor) 136, 146

Sumptuary laws 44–5
Supple, Tim (director) 121, 153
Surrey, Kit (designer) 108, 152
Suzman, Janet (actor) 151

Tandy, Jessica (actor) 123, 149
Tarlton, Richard 247, 275, 307
Taverner, Richard 273
Taylor, Gary xix, 366
Taylor, John 219, 291
Taylor, Joseph 124
Taylor, Paul 126
Teller, Herr (actor) 147
Terence 60
Terry, Ellen (actor) 122, 143, 148
Terry, Kate (actor) 123, 147
Text, theme of 15, 51–2, 55
  of *Twelfth Night* 2, 14, 102, 121, 130, 161, 162, 168, 169, 180, 188, 191, 197, 201, 214, 222, 231, 232, 236, 244, 245, 246, 248, 255, 267, 269, 273, 274, 275, 278, 286, 287, 289, 296, 300, 329, 351, 352, 355
Theatre, language of 28, 195, 196, 281, 282
Theobald, Lewis (editor) xviii, xx, 177, 192, 198, 213, 218, 220, 224, 237, 247, 258, 266–7, 270, 273, 275, 286, 288, 292, 295–99, 306, 312, 322, 328, 332, 336, 338, 342, 348, 350–51, 376, 395
Thomas, H. 64
Thorndike, Sybil (actor) 149
Throckmorton, Job *Dialogue* 258
Tilley, Morris P. 176, 185, 222, 231
Time, theme of 2, 37–8, 57, 77–8, 89
  scheme 77–8
Tree, Ellen (actor) 143, 145, 147
Tree, Herbert Beerbohm (actor-manager) 2, 99, 100, 108, 117, 125, 128–9, 136, 145, 148
Tree, Maria (actor) 142, 147
Trewin, J.C. 103, 107, 125, 128, 130, 132, 141, 145
Trial of Treasure 316
Troughton, David (actor) 153
Turner, Florence (actor) 117, 148
Turner, Robert K. 195, 278, 365–6, 368–9
Tutin, Dorothy (actor) 159
Tyrwhitt, Thomas 306, 414

Udall, Nicholas *Roister Doister* 300
Ultz (designer) 110, 152
Underhill, Cave (actor) 135, 146
Ungerer, Gustav 76

Valentine (character) 23, 53, 56, 78, 157
Valentine and Orson 158
Van Doren, Mark 8
Vanbrugh, Violet (actor) 139, 148
van Nesse, Adriana 37
Ventriloquism, use of 26, 134, 135, 137, 143
Verse, use of 78-8, 83
Viola (character) 13-14, 15, 21, 26, 77,
    78, 79, 80, 81, 82, 97, 98-9, 100, 108,
    113, 135, 157
  disguised as Cesario 7, 14, 19, 21,
    25-8, 30, 32, 45, 46, 49-50, 51, 55,
    57-60, 66-8, 71-2, 75, 81, 82, 88, 91,
    119, 157, 165, 168, 181, 196
  actors in role of 2, 111, 113, 117, 118,
    120, 121, 122, 123, 124, 132, 133,
    139, 140, 141, 142-5, 146-53, 165,
    195, 210, 234, 294, 296
Visconti, Luchino 107
Visual Images 10-22, 32-8, 118
Viswanathan 328
Voice 46, 55, 59, 60, 113, 118, 126, 135,
    137, 142, 143, 144, 145
Voss, Philip (actor) 114, 129, 152

Waites, Zoë (actor) 153
Waldron, Francis 133
Walker, W.S. 218
Wallack Henry (actor) 147
Wallack, James (director) 147
Wanamaker, Zoë (actor) 152
Warburton, William (editor)
Ward, Anthony (designer) 152
Wardle, Irving 112, 126, 129, 144
Warner, David (actor) 250
Waring, Herbert (actor) 149
Watson, Emily (actor) 153
Webb, Charles (adapter) 147
  Sir Thomas Wyatt 239
  White Devil 157
Webster, Margaret (director) 126, 149
Webster, Peter (actor) 111, 152

Welles, Orson (actor–director) 105, 106,
    149
Wells, Stanley (editor) 366
Werner, Fräulein (actor) 34
Werstine, Paul 367
Wertheim, Ron (director) 151
West, Cheryl L. (composer) 153
Wheatley, Francis 133
White, Richard Grant (editor) 367
Widdoes, Kathleen (actor) 151
Wilde, Oscar 43
Wiles, David 134
Wilkinson, Norman (designer) 103, 104,
    148
Wilkinson, Tate 142
Williams, Clifford (director) 110, 151
Williams, Harcourt (director) 105, 107,
    149
Williams, Stephen 105, 130,
Williamson, Nicol (actor) 127, 129,
    151
Wilson, John Dover (editor) 2, 95,
Wilson, Richard 23
Winter, William 5, 6, 124, 128, 131, 132,
    136, 143, 144, 145
Wirth, Franz Peter (director) 151
Wither, George *Emblems* 76
Woffington, Peg (actor) 122, 139, 142,
    146
Wolfit, Donald (actor) 149, 150
Wood, John (actor) 152
Woodvine, John (actor) 125, 130, 151
Woodward, Henry (actor) 146
Woolf, Virginia 139
Wrede, Caspar (director) 150
Wright, Edward *Map of World* 73, 74
Wright, Thomas *Passions of the Mind* 54

Yanshin, M. (actor) 150
Yates, Richard (actor) 122, 146
Yeomans, David 239
Younge, Elizabeth (actor) 132, 133, 146